www.wadsworth.com

www.wadsworth.com is the World Wide Web site for
Wadsworth and is your direct source to dozens of online
resources.

At www.*wadsworth.com* you can find out about
supplements, demonstration software, and
student resources. You can also send e-mail to many of
our authors and preview new publications and exciting new
technologies.

www.wadsworth.com
Changing the way the world learns®

American Passages

Free study resources for your American History course—*available online!*

Primary source documents, video and audio clips, activities, and self-quizzing—all FREE to you when you purchase this text!

American Passages Book Companion Web Site

http://history.wadsworth.com/ayerscompact2/

Filled with exclusive resources designed specifically to accompany this text!

This Web site adds interest and interactivity through a rich collection of maps, audio clips, photographs, cartoons, and documents. Every chapter in the textbook includes elements that are linked to material found exclusively on the Web site. Carefully coordinated with the text and following the book's chronology, 400 items are available to enhance the student's learning experience, including documents with accompanying introductions, images, links, and animated maps with exercises that encourage student interactivity. This site also offers, for each chapter, "Opposing Voices" features, which present a series of documents that are related around key points relevant to the chapter. These features stimulate discussion and allow students to compare and contrast sets of relevant documents.

The Wadsworth American History Resource Center

http://history.wadsworth.com

At this Web site, you'll find: interactive "You Are There" simulations, which give you the opportunity to "virtually" experience life in another place and time; an *At the Movies* feature, which provides descriptions, critical thinking questions, and Web links for major films throughout American history; the Wadsworth U.S. Image Bank, which contains hundreds of images and maps that can be incorporated into multimedia presentations; *American Journey Online* activities; a link to the "Today in U.S. History" Web site, which shares the events that occurred on a specific date in the nation's development; a link to the *American Passages Book Companion Web Site;* and more!

American Journey Online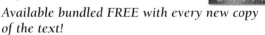

http://ajaccess.wadsworth.com

Available bundled FREE with every new copy of the text!

American Journey Online comprises 16 primary source collections that capture the landmark events and major themes of the American experience—through images and the words of those who lived it. Discover hundreds of rare documents, pictures, and archival audio and video, along with essays, headnotes, and captions that set the sources in context.

Also Available:
American Journey Online User's Guide with Activities
Available on the home page of http://ajaccess.wadsworth.com, at the *Book Companion Web Site* (http://history.wadsworth.com/ayerscompact2/), or as a print resource (ISBN 0-534-17433-7).
Documenting America's Past
Choose from over 900 primary source documents and build a reader for your course. http://www.textchoice2.com

American Passages

A HISTORY OF THE UNITED STATES

VOLUME I: TO 1877
COMPACT SECOND EDITION

Advantage Series

Edward L. Ayers
UNIVERSITY OF VIRGINIA

Lewis L. Gould
UNIVERSITY OF TEXAS AT AUSTIN

David M. Oshinsky
UNIVERSITY OF TEXAS AT AUSTIN

Jean R. Soderlund
LEHIGH UNIVERSITY

THOMSON
WADSWORTH

Australia • Canada • Mexico • Singapore • Spain
United Kingdom • United States

THOMSON

™

WADSWORTH

Publisher: Clark Baxter
Senior Development Editor: Margaret McAndrew Beasley
Senior Assistant Editor: Julie Yardley
Editorial Assistant: Anne Gittinger
Senior Technology Project Manager: Melinda Newfarmer
Marketing Manager: Lori Grebe Cook
Marketing Assistant: Mary Ho
Advertising Project Manager: Stacey Purviance
Project Manager, Editorial Production: Kimberly Adams

Print/Media Buyer: Rebecca Cross
Permissions Editor: Joohee Lee
Production Service and Compositor: Graphic World
Photo Researcher: Lili Weiner
Cover Image: The Eerie Canal. The Granger
    Collection, New York.
Printer: Webcom

Printed in Canada
2   3   4   5   6   7   08   07   06   05   04

For more information about our products,
contact us at:
Thomson Learning Academic Resource Center
1-800-423-0563

For permission to use material from this text
or product, submit a request online at
http://www.thomsonrights.com
Any additional questions about permissions
can be submitted by email to
thomsonrights@thomson.com

Library of Congress Control Number:
2004102704

Student Edition: ISBN 0-495-00361-1

Thomson Wadsworth
10 Davis Drive
Belmont, CA 94002-3098
USA

Asia
Thomson Learning
5 Shenton Way #01-01
UIC Building
Singapore 068808

Australia/New Zealand
Thomson Learning
102 Dodds Street
Southbank, Victoria 3006
Australia

Canada
Nelson
1120 Birchmount Road
Toronto, Ontario M1K 5G4
Canada

Europe/Middle East/Africa
Thomson Learning
High Holborn House
50/51 Bedford Row
London WC1R 4LR
United Kingdom

Latin America
Thomson Learning
Seneca, 53
Colonia Polanco
11560 Mexico D.F.
Mexico

Spain/Portugal
Paraninfo
Calle Magallanes, 25
28015 Madrid, Spain

About the Authors

EDWARD L. AYERS Edward Ayers is the Hugh P. Kelly Professor of History at the University of Virginia. He was educated at the University of Tennessee and Yale University, where he received his Ph.D. in American Studies. He has written and edited several books. His most recent book, *In the Presence of Mine Enemies: War in the Heart of America, 1859–1863,* was published in September, 2003. *The Promise of the New South: Life After Reconstruction* (1992) won prizes for the best book on the history of American race relations and on the history of the American South. It was a finalist for both the National Book Award and the Pulitzer Prize. He is the co-editor of *The Oxford Book of the American South* (1997) and *All Over the Map: Rethinking American Regions* (1996). Ayers has won a number of teaching awards, including the Outstanding Faculty Award from the State Council of Higher Education and the Distinguished Young Teacher Award from the Alumni Board of Trustees.

The World Wide Web version of Ayers's work, "The Valley of the Shadow: Two Communities in the American Civil War," has been ranked as one of the top four education sites in the world by the *Encyclopedia Britannica* and named as the best Civil War site by Yahoo!. Ayers is Executive Director of the Center for Digital History, an institute at the University of Virginia dedicated to crafting and teaching history in new media, and is currently serving as Dean of the College and Graduate School of Arts and Sciences. Ayers is the author of Chapters 9–15.

LEWIS L. GOULD   Lewis Gould is the Eugene C. Barker Centennial Professor Emeritus at the University of Texas at Austin. After receiving his Ph.D. from Yale University, he began a teaching career in which he had more than ten thousand students. He was recognized for outstanding undergraduate teaching in large lecture sections of the American History survey and for his excellent graduate teaching.

Gould is a nationally recognized authority on first ladies and the presidency. His comments have appeared in numerous press accounts about presidential wives, including The *New York Times,* the *Washington Post,* and the *Los Angeles Times.* He has appeared on C-Span, *The CBS Morning News, Nightline, The ABC Evening News,* and a large number of nationally syndicated radio programs. He also participated in the PBS program on Lyndon Johnson and the A&E biography of Lady Bird Johnson. Among his important publications are *American First Ladies: Their Lives and Their Legacy* (2001); *1968: The Election That Changed America* (1993); *The Presidency of Theodore Roosevelt* (1991); *Lady Bird Johnson: Our Environmental First Lady* (1999); *The Modern American Presidency* (2003), and *Grand Old Party: A History of the Republicans* (2003). Gould is the author of Chapters 16–24, 31, and 32.

DAVID M. OSHINSKY   David Oshinsky received his undergraduate degree from Cornell University and his doctorate from Brandeis. He is currently Littlefield Professor of History at the University of Texas at Austin. Prior to that he taught for twenty-six years at Rutgers University, where he held the Board of Governors Chair as well as chairman of the History Department. Oshinsky is the author of four books, including *A Conspiracy So Immense: The World of Joe McCarthy* (1983), which was voted one of the year's "best books" by the *New York Sunday Times Book Review,* and won the Hardeman Prize

for the best work about the U.S. Congress. His latest book, *Worse than Slavery: Parchman Farm and the Ordeal of Jim Crow Justice* (1996), won both the Robert Kennedy Book Award for the year's most distinguished contribution to the field of human rights and the American Bar Association's Scribes Award for distinguished legal writing.

Oshinsky is a regular contributor to scholarly journals, the *Washington Post Book World, New York Sunday Times Book Review, New York Times* Op-Ed page, and *New York Times Sunday Magazine.* He was awarded a senior fellowship by the National Endowment for the Humanities and spent 1999–2000 as a Phi Beta Kappa Visiting Scholar. Oshinsky is the author of Chapters 25–30.

JEAN R. SODERLUND   Jean Soderlund is Professor and Chair of the Department of History at Lehigh University and Co-Director of the Lawrence Henry Gipson Institute for Eighteenth-Century Studies. She received her Ph.D. from Temple University and was a post-doctoral fellow at the McNeil Center for Early American Studies at the University of Pennsylvania. Her book *Quakers and Slavery: A Divided Spirit* won the Alfred E. Driscoll Publication Prize of the New Jersey Historical Commission. Soderlund was an editor of three volumes of the *Papers of William Penn* (1981–1983) and co-authored
Freedom by Degrees: Emancipation in Pennsylvania and Its Aftermath (1991). She has written articles and chapters in books on the history of women, African Americans, Native Americans, Quakers, and the deveopment of abolition in the British North American colonies and early United States. She is currently working on a study of the Lenape people within colonial New Jersey society. She is a council member of the McNeil Center for Early American Studies, and she served as a committee chair for the American Historical Association. Soderlund is the author of Chapters 1–8.

Brief Table of Contents

Table of Contents

Passages • 1764–1814 • 128

5 • Wars for Independence, 1764–1783 • 131

6 • Toward a More Perfect Union, 1783–1788 • 165

List of Maps

For animated versions of selected *American Passages* maps, please visit the companion Web site at http://history.wadsworth.com/ayerscompact2/.

Preface

A "Novel" Approach: Telling the Story of the American Past

In the first edition of *American Passages* we introduced a tight narrative organization that places readers directly into the story of the past, experiencing events as they unfolded for the people of that era—whether simultaneously or in a sequential chain. Judging by the responses from instructors and students who are using the text and web resources, this approach has proven both engaging and valuable in making history make sense.

Why Story Is at the Center of Our History

History textbooks often focus on one topic at a time—politics, culture, reform, or the economy, for example. That kind of presentation, logical as it may seem, comes with a cost: it turns textbooks simply into gathered information rather than compelling stories.

People do not live one topic at a time. We experience many facets of history every day, all in the flow of time. Things happen simultaneously and in connection. We are used to the idea that our lives combine a mixture of major and minor events, of fads and movies and TV shows as well as elections, wars, and laws. The past was like that as well.

People confront surprise every day, for history seldom follows a straight line. No one could have predicted Bacon's Rebellion, John Brown's Raid, the Haymarket Riot, or the Watergate break-in. Nor could Americans have foreseen the emergence of Thomas Paine, Harriet Beecher Stowe, Henry Ford, or Martin Luther King, Jr. And who could have known on the morning of September 11, 2001, how different life would seem just that afternoon and in the days, weeks, and months that followed?

Features of *American Passages*

American Passages is written to convey the excitement and uncertainty of this nation's past—to see it whole. Eight "Passages" sections, appearing regularly throughout the text, provide broad overviews that connect ideas and themes across chapters. "Passages" timelines, available on the companion Web site, help students place smaller stories into context and to understand interrelationships of people, ideas, movements, and events.

This edition of *American Passages* includes the Picturing the Past feature, which uses extended captions to link illustrations in each chapter to the larger themes explored in the

"Passages" sections. Since photos, cartoons, maps, and other visual materials are so important in our understanding of the past, we have paused a little longer over three images in each chapter to call students' attention to the detail and meaning those images convey. These extended captions are labeled corresponding to three major organizing principles—Politics and Diplomacy, Social and Cultural Events, and Economics and Technology. This visual and thematic association will help students understand how people and events connected across time. And the exercise of looking at images through a historian's eye will also help them learn to evaluate images on their own.

Map captions explain the significance of specific features and relationships. By high-lighting the important information in various types of maps, these captions will help students develop their own map-reading and critical-thinking skills. Web icons throughout the text alert students to the remarkable resources available on the Web site custom-built for *American Passages.* Far more than any traditional ancillary or generic Web site, the site for this book amplifies and deepens the specific topics students are reading about, offering hundreds of documents, maps, illustrations, and multimedia selections—all organized to match up with the text's table of contents. Its dynamic maps and expanded entries make the *American Passages* site the most helpful and engaging resource of its kind. Visit the companion site at http://history.wadsworth.com/ayerscompact2/.

American Passages

A HISTORY OF THE UNITED STATES

COMPACT SECOND EDITION

Passages
Prehistory to 1763

*And so we journeyed for seventeen days, at the end
of which we crossed the river [Rio Grande] and traveled for seventeen more. At
sunset, on plains between some very tall mountains, we found some people who
eat nothing but powdered straw for a third of the year. Since it was that season of
the year, we had to eat it too. At the end of our journey we found a permanent
settlement where there was abundant corn. The people gave us a large quantity of
it and of cornmeal, squash, beans and cotton blankets. . . . From here we traveled
[to where people] gave me five emeralds made into arrowheads. . . . Since they
seemed very fine to me, I asked them where they had gotten them. They told me
that they brought them from some very high mountains to the North.*

—Cabeza de Vaca, 1542*

From 1534 to 1536, the Spanish explorer Álvar Núñez Cabeza de Vaca and three others traveled through Texas and northern Mexico, trying to reach Mexico City. They had been part of an expedition to Florida that ran afoul of Apalachee Indians, escaped across the Gulf of Mexico in makeshift boats, then were enslaved in Texas by Karankawa

*Martin A. Farata and José B. Fernandez, *The Account: Álvar Núñez Cabeza de Vaca's Relación* (1993), p. 103.

Population Growth of the Thirteen British Mainland Colonies, 1630–1760

1630	1640	1650	1660	1670	1680	1690
4,646	26,634	50,368	75,058	111,935	151,507	210,37:

Indians. In his *Relación,* Cabeza de Vaca described their adventures, including the harrowing passage across the gulf, long journeys without food, and sojourns among Texas Indians.

Warpaths, ocean voyages, hunting trails, trade routes, death, communication and exchange among people—creating societies in America embodied passages of every kind. Asians migrated across the Bering land bridge and along the Pacific coast more than 10,000 years ago, settling throughout North and

Indians in Florida transporting crops in a dugout canoe for storage in a large granary. Engraving by Theodor de Bry.

South America. Over time, they created distinct cultures in every part of the hemisphere, from the Aztecs of Mexico to the Algonquians of eastern North America. Over thousands of years, American civilizations rose and fell, as empires built pyramids and temple mounds, developed cities and cultures, and competed for territory and trade.

In the fifteenth century A.D., Western Europeans came to America to fish, trade, and establish colonies, bringing new technology, lust for wealth, and destructive microbes that spelled death for millions of Native Americans. The Europeans adapted their traditions and goals to exploit the abundant, yet often unfamiliar, resources of the New World. The Spanish struck it rich with the Potosí and Zacatecas silver mines that financed their religious wars in Europe and became the envy of other nations. Privateers from France, England, and the Netherlands attacked the Spanish silver fleets, while explorers searched unsuccessfully for mines in North America. Instead, they found treasures in furs, sugar, tobacco, and rice.

To reap fortunes from the earth, the colonizers first exploited Native Americans, who died in such numbers from disease and harsh treatment that Europeans turned to another continent, Africa, for laborers. Portugal developed the Atlantic slave trade during the fifteenth century, initially buying slaves to toil on sugar islands near Africa. With the development of sugar, and later tobacco, rice, and indigo in America, the Portuguese and other Europeans purchased millions of people from African merchants for transport across the Atlantic. For more than 350 years, the cultures, sweat, and blood of enslaved Africans enriched the New World societies.

1700	1710	1720	1730	1740	1750	1760
250,888	331,711	466,185	629,445	905,563	1,170,760	1,593,625

From the sixteenth century on, Europeans battled for North America with Native Americans and among themselves. The French settled Canada and the Mississippi Valley, primarily for furs. Spain held Florida, Texas, and New Mexico as outposts to protect its silver mines and fleets. The English founded colonies in New England, the Chesapeake, and Carolinas for economic opportunity and religious freedom. In 1664, they pushed the Dutch out of New Netherland, thus connecting their chain of colonies along the Atlantic. Throughout America, Europeans hoped for a new chance in the New World.

The thirteen mainland British colonies had various beginnings, charters, provincial governments, economic bases, peoples, and religions. Yet they all had ties with England, in language, imperial government and laws, culture, and commerce. During the eighteenth century, the colonies forged closer bonds with the English—with greater participation in imperial wars, increased trade, and better communication. At the same time, the British provinces also became more distinctly American, as people from Africa, Ireland, and the European continent diversified the population and its culture. With natural population growth and swelling immigration, the British colonies expanded across the continent.

Native Americans responded to depopulation, defeat, and white expansion by creating new worlds of their own. Despite some military successes, they ultimately reshaped their communities and cultures, as disease worked its tragic course and European-American societies grew. The surviving members of Indian nations often merged to forge new ethnic identities, or lived together in multi-ethnic communities, often with whites and escaped slaves. Some retained remnants of their land within white settlements, while the majority moved to the frontier for political autonomy.

Three centuries passed from the time Western European fishermen first camped on North American shores until Great Britain and its colonies expelled France from the continent with the Seven Years' War. By 1763, the land and people of America had permanently changed.

North America in the Early Seventeenth Century

This map shows the location of some of the Native American groups in North America, indicating the areas in which Indians of the eastern woodlands and American Southwest grew Indian corn, beans, squash, and other crops. The map also includes the earliest European settlements, from St. Augustine in 1565 to New Netherland in 1624.

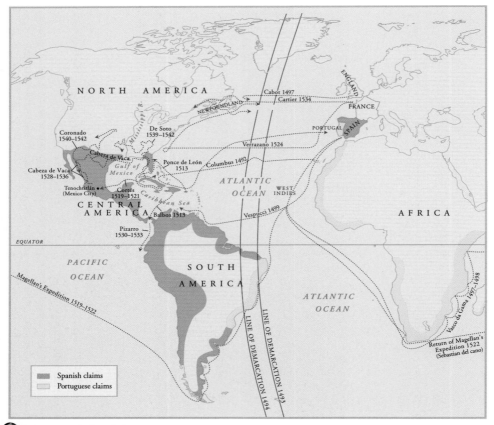

European Explorations, 1492–1542

Before 1542, Spain and Portugal dominated European exploration. Generally conforming to the 1494 Line of Demarcation, Portugal's "sphere of influence" included Brazil (in eastern South America), Africa, and South Asia. Spain claimed the rest of South and Central America. France and England sent out explorers but did not establish permanent colonies in North America until the early seventeenth century.

View an animated version of this map or related maps at http://history.wadsworth.com/ayerscompact2/.

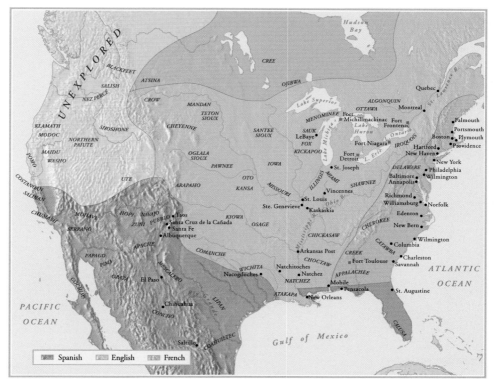

North America in 1750

Great Britain, France, and Spain claimed the indicated areas just before the Seven Years' War. While waves of immigrants from Germany and the British Isles had expanded settlement in the British provinces since 1700 (see Map 3.3), the French colonies still consisted primarily of trading posts, forts, and relatively small agricultural areas. Native Americans controlled much of the territory claimed by France.

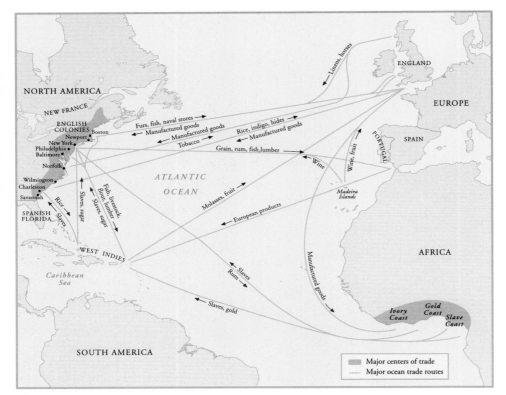

Map labels:
- NORTH AMERICA
- NEW FRANCE
- ENGLISH COLONIES
- Boston
- Newport
- New York
- Philadelphia
- Baltimore
- Norfolk
- Wilmington
- Charleston
- Savannah
- SPANISH FLORIDA
- WEST INDIES
- Caribbean Sea
- SOUTH AMERICA
- ATLANTIC OCEAN
- ENGLAND
- EUROPE
- SPAIN
- PORTUGAL
- Madeira Islands
- AFRICA
- Ivory Coast
- Gold Coast
- Slave Coast

Trade route labels:
- Linens, horses
- Furs, fish, naval stores
- Manufactured goods
- Manufactured goods
- Rice, indigo, hides
- Manufactured goods
- Tobacco
- Grain, rum, fish, lumber
- Wine
- Wine, fruit
- Fish, livestock, flour, lumber
- Slaves, sugar
- Slaves, sugar
- Rice
- Slaves
- Molasses, fruit
- European products
- Manufactured goods
- Slaves
- Rum
- Slaves, gold

Legend:
- Major centers of trade
- Major ocean trade routes

Colonial Overseas Trade

By 1750, the Atlantic economy had matured, as each of the British mainland colonies developed products for sale in Great Britain, Europe, Africa, and the West Indies. Patterns of trade were much more complicated than the notion of a "triangular trade route" in which England sold manufactured goods in Africa in exchange for slaves who were sent to America where they produced sugar, tobacco, and rice destined for Europe. While this exchange was important, other trade patterns sustained colonial economies as well: shipment of fish and lumber from New England to the West Indies; and mid-Atlantic flour and meat to southern Europe and the West Indies. The fur trade linked Native Americans to the Atlantic economy. West Indies sugar—and the rum New England and Philadelphia distillers manufactured from it—found markets everywhere. Because the Navigation Acts allowed American ships to carry goods, the shipping trade itself became a significant source of income.

Contact, Conflict, and Exchange in the Atlantic World to 1590

When the Italian navigator Christopher Columbus sighted San Salvador on October 12, 1492, Native Americans lived in cities and towns throughout North and South America. Their numbers had already begun to decline from disease as a result of contact with Europeans who fished off the North American coast in the late fifteenth century. Columbus called the Native Americans *Indios,* or Indians, because he thought he had reached islands in the Far East. Though not the first European to arrive, his landfall initiated the conquest and settlement of two continents, whose vast extent and wealth were previously unknown to Europeans.

For Native Americans, white men and sailing ships spelled demographic catastrophe. Within 150 years, the Indian population was reduced by 90 percent, their cities defeated and destroyed, and, for many, their lands appropriated for farming and grazing livestock. For Europeans, Columbus's unexpected "discovery" represented new challenges and opportunities. For sub-Saharan Africans, European colonization of America would stimulate the slave trade, which over the next four centuries transported at least 10 million Africans across the Atlantic. To exploit the riches of America, Europeans used the labor of both Native Americans and Africans.

Yet contact among Native Americans, Europeans, and Africans involved more than conquest, enslavement, and death. Together the three major cultural groups created new traditions and societies in the New World. Although the Europeans must be declared winners in the contest for power, the American colonies were shaped by exchange of knowledge, culture, and work among all participants. Three major cultural traditions came together in the Western Hemisphere. This chapter explores Native American, European, and African societies at the time of contact; European exploration; and Spanish colonization in Central and South America. The Spanish empire subsequently extended into New Mexico and California, serving as an important model for English settlement in North America.

The First Americans

Estimates of the number of Native Americans in 1492 vary widely, from 8 million to more than 100 million. They possessed widely divergent cultures, ranging from the Inuit who hunted seal and walrus along the shores of the Arctic Ocean, to the Aztecs of central Mex-

CHRONOLOGY

38,000–12,000 B.C.	Migration of ancient hunters to the Americas
300–900 A.D.	Height of Mayan civilization in Yucatan
300–1600 A.D.	Succession of empires, Ghana, Mali, and Songhay, in West Africa
700–1450 A.D.	Mississippian people build Cahokia and other urban centers in North America
c. 1000 A.D.	Leif Eriksson establishes Viking colony on Newfoundland
c. 1300 A.D.	Aztecs settle in Valley of Mexico
1420	Prince Henry of Portugal initiates search for ocean route to Asia
1440s	Portuguese mariners take Africans as slaves
c. 1452	Portugal begins sugar production on Madeira
c. 1460–1500	European improvements in navigation and ships
1487	Bartholomeu Dias of Portugal rounds Cape of Good Hope
1492	Christopher Columbus crosses Atlantic Ocean
1494	Treaty of Tordesillas establishes Line of Demarcation
1497–1498	Vasco da Gama reaches India for Portugal
1517	Martin Luther challenges the Church of Rome
1519–1521	Hernán Cortés conquers the Aztecs
1519–1522	Magellan's expedition circumnavigates the world
1528–1536	Cabeza de Vaca's adventures in Florida and Texas
1534	Act of Supremacy separates England from the Church of Rome
1539–1542	Hernando de Soto explores the region from Florida to the Mississippi River
1540–1542	Coronado explores the American Southwest
1541	Cartier establishes Charlesbourg-Royal in Canada
1556	Philip II of Spain takes the throne
1558	Elizabeth I becomes queen of England
1564	French Huguenots build Fort Caroline in northern Florida
1577–1580	Francis Drake circumnavigates the globe
1585	English attempt colonization at Roanoke Island
1588	English defeat the Spanish Armada

ico and Incas of the Peruvian Andes who lived in state-level agricultural societies. In the geographic area that now encompasses the United States, they included mound-building farmers of the Mississippi valley, the pueblo-dwelling Hopi and Zuñi Indians and nomadic Apaches of the southwest, and the Iroquois and Algonquians of the eastern woodlands.

Native American Societies Before Contact

Archeological evidence from various sites in North and South America suggests these diverse peoples were descendants of Asians who migrated by boat along the Pacific coast or who crossed the Bering land bridge from Siberia to Alaska more than 10,000 years ago. As glaciers from the last Ice Age receded, groups migrated throughout the hemisphere. Their cultures and languages diverged as they adapted to their environments. Initially, they hunted game, fished, and collected berries, seeds, and nuts.

When ancient Americans began cultivating crops, they laid the foundation for more densely populated societies. Of greatest importance to Indians of North America was the development of maize, or Indian corn, probably from the grass *teosinte,* which grew in dry areas of Mexico and Guatemala. In addition to maize, early Mexicans domesticated beans, squash, chili peppers, and avocado. Agriculture proved revolutionary for some ancient American societies, as higher yields spurred population growth and a greater division of labor.

Between 1500 B.C. and Columbus's arrival, civilizations rose and declined throughout the Americas. Ancient Americans built empires, much like their counterparts in Egypt, Greece, and Rome, with cities, extensive trade networks, systems of religion and knowledge, art, architecture, and hierarchical social classes. Two of the best-known civilizations of pre-contact America were the Mayan, located on the Yucatán peninsula, and the Mexican. The Maya, at their height from 300 to 900 A.D., built cities of stone pyramids, temples, and palaces, with populations ranging to more than 60,000. Mayan kings, considered divine, extended their empire to over fifty different states and maintained trade with distant peoples. The Maya had a numeral system based on units of twenty, hieroglyphics, knowledge of astronomy, and several calendars.

The Mexicans, who lived in the Valley of Mexico, built the city of Teotihuacán east of Lake Texcoco. Its population of about 200,000 depended on intensive farming of nearby irrigated lands. The grid-patterned Teotihuacán held at its core the Pyramid of the Sun and the Pyramid of the Moon. Even after the city's decline it retained religious significance for later Mexicans.

The Aztecs settled in the Valley of Mexico in the fourteenth century, building their capital, Tenochtitlán, on an island in Lake Texcoco, which they connected to the shore by causeways. They cultivated intensively the marshlands surrounding their island and built a militaristic state. By the time the Spanish *conquistadores* arrived in 1519, the Aztecs controlled territory from the Pacific to the Gulf Coast. The Aztecs required tribute from the people they conquered—gold, feathers, turquoise, food, cotton, and human beings for sacrifice. They believed that every day they had to feed human hearts to the sun god, Huitzilpochtli, to prevent the world from coming to an end.

To the north of the Valley of Mexico, the Hohokam occupied desert lands in Arizona and northern Sonora, where, with irrigation, they cultivated Indian corn, cotton, squash, and beans. Their canals, up to ten miles long, diverted water from nearby rivers. When Athabaskan raiders from the north attacked Hohokam towns, they tried to protect them-

Map 1.1 America Before Columbus The first inhabitants of North America probably migrated from Asia by boat and across the Bering land bridge (Beringia), which was created when sea levels dropped during the last Ice Age. Archaeological evidence along the Pacific coast and from sites such as Cahokia and Mesa Verde provide important information about Native American societies before 1492.

selves by building high adobe walls, then after 1400 A.D. simply abandoned many of their villages.

Enemy attacks and crop failures from lack of rain forced other Indians of the southwest to leave their towns. The Anasazi farmers of northern Arizona and New Mexico, Colorado, and Utah relied on rain and floods to water their crops. One of their settlements was Pueblo Bonito in Chaco Canyon, which housed perhaps 1,000 people in 800 rooms surrounded by high walls; another was the complex of rock dwellings built high in the canyon cliffs at Mesa Verde. Descendants of the Anasazi—the Hopi and Zuñi Indians— were called "Pueblo" Indians by the Spanish for the adobe villages with large apartment dwellings in which they lived.

Farther east, in a large area drained by the Mississippi River, by 1000 B.C. early Americans developed civilizations characterized by large earthen burial mounds, some sixty feet high. These mounds entombed corpses and such grave goods as copper spoons and beads made from seashells. The Adena-Hopewell people, who built the Great Serpent Mound located in southern Ohio, lived in small villages along rivers, hunted game, fished, and raised squash, Indian corn, sunflowers, and gourds. As evidenced by the grave goods, their trading network extended from the Gulf Coast (shells) to Lake Superior (copper). By 800 A.D., people in the Mississippi Valley constructed large towns, including Cahokia, which was located near present-day St. Louis. At the center of these towns stood large rectangular mounds topped by temples and mortuaries in which members of the upper class were buried. By 1450, the region's population declined, perhaps as a result of illness spread by urban crowding.

People of the Eastern Woodlands

Along the Atlantic seaboard extending inland to the Appalachian Mountains lived Native Americans of two major language groups, the Algonquian and the Iroquois. The eastern woodlands incorporated a wide variety of habitats. In most parts, decent soil and moderate rainfall and temperatures supported agriculture and many kinds of game, fish, and wild plants. Algonquian-speaking people dominated the Atlantic coast from Canada to Florida; they included the Pokanokets, Narragansetts, and Pequots in New England; the Lenapes of the middle Atlantic region; and members of the Powhatan confederacy in what became Virginia. Many of the Iroquois lived in the Finger Lakes area of central New York. They belonged to five tribes: the Mohawks, Oneidas, Onondagas, Cayugas, and Senecas, from east to west, who banded together in the Iroquois confederacy.

Although important cultural differences existed between the two language groups and even among bands within each group, Indians of the eastern woodlands had much in common. They held land cooperatively: the tribe as a whole claimed ownership rights, not individual members or families. Except in far northern New England, Indians had a mixed economy of agriculture, gathering, fishing, and hunting. Women were responsible for raising corn, squash, beans, and (where possible) tobacco. They also gathered nuts and fruit, built houses, made clothing, took care of the children, and prepared meals, while men cleared land, hunted, fished, and protected the village from enemies. The combination of corn, squash, and beans enriched the soil, providing high yields from small plots of land; eaten together these foods were high in protein. The Native Americans cleared land by girdling the large trees (removing a strip of bark around the trees about three feet from the ground). When the trees died, the Indians removed them, burned the underbrush, and sowed crops among the stumps. Eastern woodlands people used nets and weirs to catch fish and, to assure good hunting, they periodically burned underbrush from sections of forest. The burning stimulated the growth of lush grass, providing fodder for deer and other game. The fires allowed some sunlight to penetrate the forest, promoting the growth of strawberries, raspberries, and blackberries.

Indian religions, though widely diverse in many ways, incorporated a common worldview. The people of the eastern woodlands believed that the earth and sky formed a spiritual realm of which they were a part, not the masters. Spirits inhabited the earth and could be found in plants, animals, rocks, or clouds. Each spirit, or *manitou,* could become the guardian of a young Indian man (less often a young woman), who, in search of a manitou, went into the woods alone, without eating or sleeping perhaps for days. If the spirit made itself known, it would provide help and counsel to the individual for the rest of his or her life. These Native Americans also believed in a Master Spirit or Creator, who was all-powerful and all-knowing, but whose

Secotan Village, 1585, by the Englishman John White, who journeyed to North America with the Roanoke expedition. His watercolor drawings depict Algonquians of the North Carolina coast.

presence was rarely felt. Religious leaders were *shamans* who performed rituals to influence weather conditions or ward off danger. They were usually men, but in some communities were women. Indians believed that shamans could cure illness, interpret dreams, bring good weather, and predict the future.

The kinship group, or extended family, formed the basis of Native American society. The heads of kinship groups chose the band's chief leaders, called *sachems,* who with advice assigned fields for planting, decided where and when to hunt, managed trade and diplomacy with other Indians and Europeans, and judged whether or not to go to war. Among Algonquian-speaking natives, the heads of extended families were men, as were the sachems they chose. But in Iroquois culture, women served as clan leaders, taking a share of political power. Iroquois society was matrilineal, with family membership passing from mother to children; and matrilocal, as the husband left his family to live with his wife's. Women elders could not speak publicly at tribal councils or serve as sachems, but they chose these political leaders and advised them on such matters as waging war.

Thus, in 1492, highly complex and differentiated societies existed in North and South America. Dense populations inhabited parts of South, Central, and North America.

Throughout the hemisphere, Indian people had distinctive cultures tied to the resources of their environment. Despite this wide variety of languages and cultures, most Europeans adopted the single name that Columbus mistakenly employed—Indians. An alternative the colonists used was "savages." The view of many Europeans—that Native Americans had undifferentiated, uncivilized societies—justified conquest and expropriation of their lands.

Beginning of European Overseas Expansion

Europeans had more in common with Native Americans than they liked to admit; nevertheless, in important ways, their cultures were distinct. Like the people of America, Europeans spent most of their energy producing or gathering food. They farmed, raised livestock, and gathered nuts and berries. In the south and west of England, for example, farmers engaged in intensive cultivation of wheat, rye, and other crops. In most of England and Wales, however, farmers planted just an acre or two and spent more time gathering. In contrast to Native Americans, Europeans believed that individuals could own land and thus had the right to sell, fence, plant, erect buildings, hunt, cut lumber, and exclude others from use.

The societies from which most colonizers came were patriarchal, meaning that descent followed the father's line and political power was nearly always in the hands of men. Though women occasionally took the throne, for instance, Isabella of Spain and Elizabeth I of England, men controlled government, the church, and the military. Married women were considered subordinate to their husbands. Under English common law, a married woman was a *feme covert,* or covered woman, who could not own or manage property, make a contract, write a will, take custody of her children, own a business, or sue in court, without her husband's permission. An unmarried woman or widow, in legal terms a *feme sole,* was not subject to these restrictions.

In the fifteenth century, the pope headed a united Christian church in western and central Europe. At the same time, monarchs consolidated power in Portugal, Spain, France, and England, providing financial support and a greater sense of national identity to fuel European expansion. In turn, wealth from distant empires and trade funded wars among these emerging nations.

Trade with the East

When Columbus sailed out into the Atlantic Ocean in 1492, he expected to establish a new trade route with Asia. In the fifteenth century, eastern trade was a chief source of riches, for affluent Europeans wanted spices that would not grow in Europe such as black pepper, cinnamon, and cloves for preserving and flavoring their food. Merchants commanded high prices for transporting spices, silk, cotton cloth, and jewels from India, the East Indies, and other parts of East Asia.

Before 1500, Arab and Italian merchants dominated the eastern trade. Arabs controlled eastern trading centers and carried goods to the Red Sea and Persian Gulf. From there, caravans took cargoes to Mediterranean ports for purchase by Italian merchants. The Italians

Woman and Girl of Pomeioc

A cheife Herowans wyf. of Pomeoc. and her daughter of the age of. 8. or. 10. yeares.

© British Museum

The Englishman John White painted this watercolor in 1585, during his stay in the Roanoke colony on the coast of what is now North Carolina. It is one of a series of illustrations, also including *Secotan Village,* that provide some of the best evidence about the Algonquians of eastern North America in the late sixteenth century.

The label at the top states that this is the wife of a chief of Pomeioc and her daughter aged 8 or 10 years. White tried to present the Indians' appearance faithfully, including their hairstyles, jewelry, and clothing. The chief's wife is dressed like other women of the Eastern Woodlands during the summer and is carrying a container for liquids. The girl has an English doll that Thomas Harriot, another colonist, said Indian children enjoyed. Algonquian women in North Carolina and Virginia cared for children and raised crops including corn and tobacco.

then distributed the spices and other goods throughout Europe by way of pack train and coastal shipping. European cities developed to handle the exchange of valued eastern products in return for silver, gold, woolen and linen cloth, furs, and leather. Centers of trade and banking included Paris, Lyons, Amsterdam, London, Hamburg, Danzig, Barcelona, Cadiz, Lisbon, Venice, and Genoa. The rise of great cities accompanied the growth of unified political states. Merchants provided funding for kings to consolidate small feudal states into nations. In Portugal, Spain, France, and England, commercial interests supported unification to obtain social order, monopolistic privileges, and standardized codes of law.

Portugal Explores the West African Coast

Early in the fifteenth century, Prince Henry of Portugal, called "the Navigator," decided to challenge the Arab and Italian hold on eastern commerce. Henry brought together men interested in overseas trade and exploration. Beginning in 1420, he sent ships down the

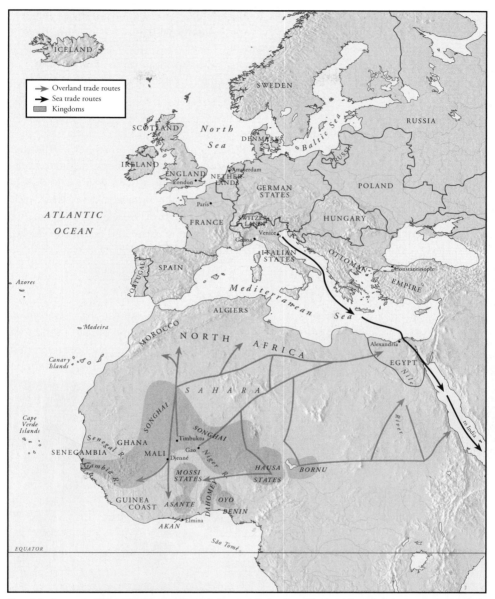

Map 1.2 Europe and West Africa in the Fifteenth Century Exploration of North and South America was an outgrowth of trade in the Eastern Hemisphere. Europeans delivered cloth and other manufactures to northern Africa; then camels carried the cargoes across the Sahara to cities such as Timbuktu, Gao, and Djenné. There they loaded gold, ivory, and kola nuts for return to the Mediterranean. Africans also traded with Asia to obtain cloth, porcelain, and spices.

western coast of Africa. He had four goals: to increase the power of Portugal by adding territorial possessions; to benefit economically from commerce with the African coast; to reach Asia and take a share of that trade; and to spread Christianity.

Headway down the African coast was slow because European sailors knew nothing of the ocean beyond Cape Bojador. In 1420, cartographers knew a great deal about the Mediterranean Sea and constructed highly accurate charts, called *portolano,* of its shorelines and harbors. Such maps did not exist for the West African coast, so one task of Prince Henry's explorers was to chart their progress. Seamen had heard that monsters and perhaps even Satan swelled in the waters beyond Cape Bojador, while other stories told that the ocean boiled at the equator. In fact, strong southward ocean currents facilitated outbound progress, but made return to the Mediterranean difficult. From ancient mathematicians and geographers, most notably Ptolemy, mapmakers knew that the world was round, but they also adopted Ptolemy's belief that a southern continent joined Africa to China, thus eliminating the possibility of a sea route from the Atlantic to the Indian Ocean. Prince Henry challenged current wisdom by sending ships down Africa's coast to find a route to the east.

New Technology

In the early and mid-fifteenth century, the lack of adequate instruments hampered navigation. Compasses had been in use since at least the thirteenth century, but not until about 1460 did Europeans develop the means of determining latitude (distance north or south

National Maritime Museum

Engraving of an early sixteenth-century cosmographer working in his study with contemporary instruments, including dividers, rule, compass, quadrant, and sand glass.

from the equator). In the Northern Hemisphere, sea captains calculated the height of the Pole Star from the horizon to determine their latitude. The Pole Star cannot be seen south of the equator, however, so navigators there measured the altitude of the sun at midday. In making these calculations, they used the astrolabe or the quadrant to determine the angle of the sun from the horizon, then consulted astronomical tables that Abraham Zacuto, a Jewish astronomer, compiled in 1478. A method for determining longitude remained unknown until the eighteenth century.

Improvements in ships and gunnery during the fifteenth century also aided exploration and conquest. By 1400 it had become clear that Mediterranean galleys, powered by oarsmen, were impractical in the high waves of the Atlantic. The first European oceangoing ships were square-rigged. Their broad sails could power large vessels, but they required a favorable tailwind to proceed from one point to another. To increase maneuverability along jagged coastlines, Portuguese seafarers designed the caravel with lateen (triangular) sails. The most successful Portuguese ship for long voyages was the *caravela redondo,* the square-rigged caravel, developed late in the fifteenth century, and adopted by other European nations. This ship combined the speed of square rigging with the agility of lateen sails. For protection from privateers and in time of war, the Portuguese mounted artillery on the caravels and by 1500 introduced the practice of broadside fire. They changed nautical warfare by sinking enemy vessels with gunfire instead of boarding them with foot soldiers.

Despite these improvements in the design of ships, they remained uncomfortable places in which to live on voyages of months and years. Except for senior officers, none of the seamen had regular sleeping quarters—they slept on deck, or below in bad weather. Their shipmates included rats and cockroaches. When it rained, everything got wet, including the cooking fire built in a sandbox on deck. The mariners ate ship's hardtack, beans, salt pork, and beef, and drank mostly wine, since their casked water quickly became foul.

Africa and the Atlantic Slave Trade

Despite their limited technology, the Portuguese explorers ventured farther and farther down the West African coast. In 1434, Gil Eannes sailed past Cape Bojador. Subsequent voyages established a lucrative coastal trade in slaves, gold, and malaguetta pepper in the Senegal region and farther south and east to the Gold Coast and Benin. Merchants now began investing in expeditions. Between the 1440s and 1505, Portuguese traders transported 40,000 Africans to perform domestic labor in Portugal and Spain and to work on the sugar plantations of the Azores, Madeira, and Canary Islands.

West African Cultures

From before 300 A.D. to 1600, a succession of empires—Ghana, Mali, and Songhay—dominated western Africa. They had large armies, collected tribute over vast distances, and traded with Europeans and Arabs. West Africans were predominantly agricultural people.

Ghana declined by 1100 as a result of droughts that dried up several rivers. Mali then took control, as its monarchs regulated the gold trade. The Mali kings were followers of Islam: one of the most famous, Gonga-Mussa, made a pilgrimage to Mecca in 1324 to fulfill his religious duty as a Muslim. His caravan is said to have included 60,000 people and 80 camels carrying over 24,000 pounds of gold.

Mali provided stable government over a wide area until the fifteenth century, when Songhay successfully challenged its dominance. Songhay was centered at Gao. Under Sonni Ali, who ruled from 1468 to 1492, Songhay captured Timbuktu, an important trading and cultural center of Mali. Askia Mohammed, who ruled from 1493 to 1528, expanded the empire even farther. He strengthened ties with other Muslims and reformed government, banking, and education. He adopted Islamic law and encouraged intellectual growth at Timbuktu and Gao. After his reign, Songhay declined; Moroccans conquered Timbuktu in 1593.

Beyond these empires, along the West African coast lay smaller states with highly developed cultures. Although influenced by Islam, they retained much of their traditional religions. Divine kings governed many of the coastal states. Like Native Americans and Europeans, the people of Africa kept religion central to their lives and endowed their leaders with both political and religious authority.

Most important in traditional African religions was a single all-powerful God, the Creator. The Creator provided lesser gods, including gods of rain, thunder, and lightning; of rivers and lakes; of animals, trees, and hills. These gods could be benevolent or harmful, so people had to seek positive relationships through rituals, sacrifice, and prayer. Africans also believed that their ancestors watched over the extended family, with power over fertility, health, and even life. When the eldest father, or patriarch, of a kinship group died, his spirit became a god. Elaborate funeral rites demonstrated the importance of the dead to the living. All family members paid respect to the deceased, whose internment was delayed until distant relatives could arrive. Before his death, the patriarch had been the extended family's priest; he communicated with its ancestors through prayer and the sacrifice of animals such as chickens and sheep. The patriarch also served as political leader. Thus in many African societies, the state, religion, and family united under a single hierarchical structure.

Kinship in West Africa varied from one culture to another, as extended families could be either patrilineal or matrilineal. In all cases, however, a child belonged to only one kin group. If the system was patrilineal, then descent flowed from father to child. If it was matrilineal, descent proceeded from mother to child, but the mother's brother, not the mother, assumed responsibility. When a woman married, she usually went to live with her husband's family. The husband compensated her family for the loss of her services with a payment called bridewealth. *Polygyny,* or having more than one wife, was generally reserved to men of high status. When men had more than one wife, each woman lived with her children in a separate house.

The extended family held land in common and assigned plots to individual families. Women and men worked in fields growing crops such as rice, cassava, wheat, millet, cotton, fruits, and vegetables. They had livestock, including cattle, sheep, goats, and chickens. Families produced food for their own use and for the market, where women were the primary traders. Artisans were skilled in textile weaving, pottery, basketry, and woodwork. They also made tools and art objects of copper, bronze, iron, silver, and gold. As in the case of Native Americans, West Africans had experienced the rise and fall of empires and possessed diverse, complex cultures at the time Europeans arrived on their shores in the mid-fifteenth century.

The Atlantic Slave Trade Begins

Over the course of four centuries, Africa lost more than 10 million people to the Atlantic slave trade. Slavery had existed in Africa and throughout the Mediterranean for centuries before the Portuguese arrived on the West African coast. African slavery was different, however, from the institution that developed in America. Most African slaves were prisoners of war; others had committed some offense that caused their kinfolk to banish them. All were considered "outsiders." The primary function of slavery in West Africa was social rather than economic—to provide a place in society for people cut off from their families. Trans-Saharan traders transported some African slaves for sale to wealthy European households. Because this trade was limited, most slaves remained in West Africa, where they achieved status as a member of a household, married, and had children. Enslaved Africans could be transferred from one owner to another at will, but their children could not be sold and were frequently emancipated.

The plantation slave system that became dominant in America began near Africa. Portugal began growing sugar as early as 1452 on the island of Madeira, off West Africa. Sugar cane required large amounts of menial, unpleasant labor in a hot climate. To supply Madeira, Portuguese merchants purchased black slaves from Muslim trans-Saharan traders and from Africans along the coast. When sugar production could expand no further in Madeira, the Portuguese colonized the small islands in the Gulf of Guinea: São Tomé, Príncipe, and Fernando Po. Sugar production was successful, but mortality was high and the demand for laborers great, spurring growth of the slave trade on the Gold Coast. By the end of the fifteenth century, before European settlement in America, Portugal developed both the plantation system and the commercial mechanism for purchasing human beings from African traders. The growth of slavery and the slave trade in America after 1500 represented an expansion of these earlier developments.

Spain and Portugal Divide the Globe

Once Portugal had established trade on the West African coast, Spanish merchants tried to participate. Prince Henry appealed to the pope, who in 1455 gave Portugal sole possession of lands to the south and east toward India. The pope's decision gave Portugal a monopoly on the Atlantic slave trade. Spain and Portugal affirmed the decision with the Treaty of Alcaçovas (1479), in which Spain recognized Portugal's sphere of interest in Africa, and Portugal acknowledged Spain's claim to the Canary Islands.

As the Portuguese sailed south, they came to recognize the vastness of the African continent. They made rapid progress only after 1482, when King John II of Portugal stepped-up the program of discovery. In 1483, Diogo Cão reached the Congo River and in 1487 Bartholomeu Dias rounded the Cape of Good Hope. The Portuguese now knew that a sea route to India existed.

Columbus Sails West

The Spanish had to find another course if they were going to trade with the Far East. Thus, Isabella funded Christopher Columbus, despite skepticism of his calculation of the distance to Asia. In August 1492, Columbus sailed west from the Canaries, taking advantage of the favorable current and trade winds. The ships reached San Salvador in October, but Columbus thought they had located the East Indies. Hoping to establish trade, Columbus sailed southward to Cuba, then touched Hispaniola, where Native Americans offered gold in return for the trade goods he brought. When the Spanish lost their flagship *Santa Maria* on a coral reef, they built a small fort with its timbers.

Leaving a small contingent of men, Columbus set out for home in January 1493, again found favorable winds, but encountered a violent storm and sought shelter in Portugal. King John II, whose explorers had not yet reached India by sailing around Africa, refused to believe that Columbus had located Asia. The lands he had found, the king claimed, lay within Portugal's sphere.

Reproduced from the Collections of the Library of Congress

A Fula town in West Africa, drawn by a European. West Africans, like Europeans but not Native Americans, kept domestic livestock. The village raised Indian corn, which had been brought from America.

Spanish and Portuguese "Spheres"

The Spanish monarchs Isabella and Ferdinand rejected Portugal's argument, petitioning Pope Alexander VI, who was Spanish, to grant them dominion over the newly discovered lands. After negotiations with John II, the pope established a Line of Demarcation, giving all lands "discovered or to be discovered" west of the line to Spain and all lands east of the line to Portugal. The Treaty of Tordesillas (1494) located the line 370 leagues (about 1,000 miles) west of the Azores and expanded the principle of "spheres of influence" by which European nations sought to dominate most of the world. Portugal retained its rights to the Atlantic slave trade and the sea route around Africa to India. Spain received permission to explore, conquer, and Christianize all lands and people to the west. The question of where Portuguese and Spanish spheres should be divided in the Far East was left unresolved until 1529, when the Treaty of Saragossa established a line seventeen degrees to the east of the Moluccas (Spice Islands), thus placing most of Asia within Portugal's sphere.

Between 1494 and 1529, Portugal and Spain sent out expeditions to explore their spheres. Columbus made three more voyages to the west: in November 1493 he sailed with seventeen ships to the Lesser Antilles, Puerto Rico, and Hispaniola. Later he explored the shores of South and Central America. Meanwhile, Columbus's claim that he had found a passage to the East by sailing west prodded the Portuguese to complete their efforts to reach India. In 1497–1498, Vasco da Gama rounded the Cape of Good Hope and sailed across the Indian Ocean, returning to Portugal with a cargo of pepper and cinnamon. The voyage to India was much more difficult than Columbus's Atlantic crossing. During the two-year journey that took at least 300 days at sea, more than one-third of the crew died. In 1500, Portugal instructed Pedro Álvares Cabral to find the Cape of Good Hope by sailing west. Instead, he touched the coast of Brazil, further convincing the Portuguese that this was not Asia. On the basis of Cabral's expedition and because a section of Brazil lay east of the Line of Demarcation, Portugal claimed that part of South America. Amerigo Vespucci made two separate voyages, in 1499 and 1501, for Spain and Portugal respectively. He explored much of the Atlantic coast of South America, demonstrating that it was a huge land mass that had to be circumnavigated to reach Asia. In reward for his insights, many Europeans associated his name—not that of Columbus—with the newly "discovered" continents.

An Expanding World

Europeans continued to search for a western sea route to Asia. Ferdinand Magellan convinced King Charles I of Spain that he could sail around the cape of South America and claim the Molucca Islands. Magellan was Portuguese, but his country gave him no support since it already had a profitable sea route to the East. With five ships, in 1519 Magellan set out on an expedition that would take three years. The voyagers faced shipwreck, a harrowing passage through the straits subsequently named for Magellan, and starvation. The Pacific was so much wider than anticipated that the mariners had to eat ship rats and leather. When inhabitants of the Philippines killed Magellan, Sebastian del Cano took command, returning to Spain with one surviving ship, laden with cloves. Together, Magellan and del Cano commanded the first

Map 1.3 European Explorations, 1492–1542 Before 1542, Spain and Portugal dominated European exploration. Generally conforming to the 1494 Line of Demarcation, Portugal's "sphere of influence" included Brazil (in eastern South America), Africa, and South Asia. Spain claimed the rest of South and Central America. France and England sent out explorers but did not establish permanent colonies in North America until the early seventeenth century.
View an animated version of this map or related maps at http://history.wadsworth.com/passages2e.

circumnavigation of the globe. In doing so, however, they demonstrated that the southwest passage through the Straits of Magellan was much more difficult than envisioned.

England and France ignored the pope's division of the world between Spain and Portugal. With their more northerly location and some knowledge of the coast of North America, they sought a northwest passage to the East. During the fifteenth century (before Columbus's landfall), seafarers from England and France had caught fish in the Newfoundland Banks. Some sailors had camped ashore, where they traded with Native Americans. When King Henry VII of England sent John Cabot, an Italian whose name was really Giovanni Caboto, in search of a northwest passage in 1497, the expedition reached Newfoundland. Cabot sailed again the next year, but most of his ships were lost and he died at sea. Although the

English were discouraged by Cabot's failure to find a passage, his efforts supported England's later claim to land in North America.

A generation after Cabot, the French entered the search for a route to Asia. In 1524, King Francis I sent another Italian sea captain, Giovanni da Verrazano, to look for the elusive passage. Landing at Cape Fear (now North Carolina), Verrazano sailed north along the Atlantic seaboard to Newfoundland, finding no evidence of a waterway through the continent. In expeditions dating 1534 and 1535, Jacques Cartier hoped to find the route by way of the gulf and river of St. Lawrence. Although neither Verrazano nor Cartier found a northwest passage, they supported France's claim to part of the continent.

The Spanish Empire in America

Because England and France showed only occasional interest in America before 1560, and Portugal focused on the eastern trade and Brazil, the Spanish had little interference from other Europeans in exploring and settling the rest of the New World. By 1543, their colonies extended south to Chile and north through Mexico; they had explored from Florida to California in what is now the United States. Spanish conquistadores advanced from island to island in the West Indies, then moved through Mexico and Central America. The conquistadores expected to make their fortune in America and retire to Spain. In contrast, the Spanish Crown had a more complicated set of goals in colonizing America: to enhance its power among European nations; to exploit the wealth of the New World; and to convert the Native Americans to Christianity. While in many ways the goals of the Spanish monarchy and its settlers overlapped, sometimes their interests diverged, especially when it came to the welfare of Native Americans.

Spanish Invasion

When the Spanish found little gold on Hispaniola, they enslaved its inhabitants and expropriated the land. The natives died when forced to work on plantations and tend livestock. European diseases and cruel treatment took their toll. As a result, the colonists sent slave-raiding parties to other islands and to the mainland. The conquistadores who explored Cuba and Puerto Rico were seeking slaves and gold. Juan Ponce de León, known for his search in 1513 for the legendary "fountain of youth" in Florida and Yucatan, sought Indian slaves. The same year Vasco Núñez de Balboa led explorers across the Isthmus of Panama, becoming the first Europeans to see the Pacific Ocean. Alonso Álvarez de Pineda, in 1519–1520, sailed the coastline of the Gulf of Mexico from Florida to Mexico.

As Spanish explorers became aware of the vastness of the Americas, they organized militarily to subdue the Americans. Despite the small size of their armies, the Spanish prevailed over large empires, aided significantly by diseases such as smallpox. They also made alliances with the enemies of the Indian emperors and took advantage of metal weaponry and horses. The most famous of the conquerors is Hernán Cortés who, in 1519, launched an expedition against the Aztecs of Mexico. With an army of only 500 troops, Cortés persuaded the Totonacs of Cempoala, who were dominated by the Aztecs, to join him. Then defeating the Tlaxcalans and gaining their support as well, he marched to Tenochtitlán, the Aztec capital. He entered the city without opposition and seized Moctezuma, the emperor. When Cortés outlawed human sacrifice and made incessant demands for gold, the Aztecs rebelled. In the heat of battle, they killed Moctezuma and forced the Spanish and their allies to retreat, slaying many as they tried to escape across the causeways linking Tenochtitlán with the shore of Lake Texcoco.

Cortés returned in 1521, however, after smallpox ravaged the Aztec capital. With thousands of Indian allies, the Spanish built small ships to cross Lake Texcoco, took control of the causeways, and after a long siege and bitter fighting destroyed Tenochtitlán building by building. They rebuilt the city as Mexico City, the capital of New Spain. Cortés then sent troops to take Guatemala; rival conquistadores seized Honduras. Francisco Pizarro advanced to the south, preceded by smallpox, defeating the Incas of Peru after a difficult struggle. Others expanded into Argentina and Chile.

Exploration of Florida and the American Southwest

In 1528, Pánfilo de Narváez led an expedition to Florida. His venture led to later exploration of territories that became the southern United States. Narváez and his men landed at Tampa Bay where they met Native Americans who warned them to return to the sea. When the Europeans refused, and spoke of their search for silver and gold, the Indians directed them to "Apalachen," near the present site of Tallahassee. The Spanish marched northward through insect- and snake-infested terrain. Soon discouraged, they made the mistake of kidnapping a chief of the Apalachees. The Indians attacked, convincing the Spanish to return to New Spain immediately. The soldiers constructed barges to carry them across the Gulf of Mexico. When storms separated the craft, most of the explorers, including Narváez, were lost at sea.

Two barges crossed the gulf intact, beaching their occupants on the Texas coast. The native Karankawas captured the survivors. After several years, one of the Spaniards, Álvar Núñez Cabeza de Vaca, who had become an Indian priest and healer, escaped with three others, including Alonso del Castillo, Andrés Dorantes, and a slave Esteban. They hoped to reach New Spain, but lacked maps or instruments to find their way. For several years they sojourned with a series of Native American peoples, learning their languages and customs. The Spanish earned the Indians' friendship and respect with seemingly miraculous cures. When they finally reached Mexico City in 1536, Cabeza de Vaca told the Spanish viceroy about their journey.

Cabeza de Vaca's report excited interest in exploring lands north of Mexico. When Cabeza de Vaca refused to head an expedition, the viceroy sent Esteban with a Franciscan missionary, Fray Marcos de Niza, along with several Indians. When Esteban was killed by Zuñis, Fray Marcos returned to Mexico City with extravagant claims that the land flowed with riches.

In 1540, an army of 336 Spanish and about 1,000 Indians marched north under command of Francisco Vásquez de Coronado, with Fray Marcos as their guide. The explorers intended to conquer the cities of gold (the so-called "Seven Cities of Cibola") but were disappointed. The "golden" city that Fray Marcos had spotted was actually a Zuñi Indian pueblo, Hawikúh, made of adobe. The Zuñis unsuccessfully resisted the intruders, then informed the Spanish that the cities of gold lay to the west. Another Indian told stories about great wealth in the country to the east. Over the next year, Coronado's troops explored in both directions. They encountered the Hopi of northeastern Arizona and buffalo-hunting Indians of the Great Plains, saw the Grand Canyon, and traveled as far east as Kansas. They found no gold or silver but left descriptions of a substantial part of the American Southwest.

To reinforce Coronado's army, the viceroy in 1540 sent Hernando de Alarcón by ship up the western coast of Mexico. Though the two explorers failed to make contact, Alarcón sailed into the Colorado River. Two years later, Juan Rodríguez Cabrillo sailed with two ships up the coast of Baja California. They were the first Europeans to visit what is now California. After Cabrillo died in January 1543, his deputy Bartolomé Ferrelo sailed almost as far north as Oregon.

Unknown to Coronado, an expedition led by Hernando de Soto, governor of Cuba, came within a few hundred miles of his own company at about the same time. In 1539, De Soto and about 600 troops landed in Tampa Bay. Over the next three years they trekked through the southeast, exploring lands hitherto unknown to the Spanish. They plundered the towns of the Apalachees and other Florida Indians who were part of the Mississippian cultures, with temple mounds and long-range trading networks. Stealing food, taking Indians as slaves, and killing those who resisted, De Soto's men marched north from the Florida peninsula, through central Georgia to the Carolinas, then west across the Appalachians into the Tennessee River valley. They followed the river south into Alabama, then traveled west toward the Mississippi. Despite heavy losses when Chickasaws burned their camp and supplies, De Soto crossed into Arkansas. After he died of a fever in 1542, the 300 survivors of his expedition safely reached New Spain by boat.

In 1542, the initial period of Spanish expansion came to a close throughout America. Without discovery of precious metals, they had little immediate reason to push farther into North America. During the half century since Columbus sailed west, contact and exchange among Native Americans, Europeans, and Africans created new social and political systems. Although the Spanish expected to create a society much like the one at home, the results of colonization proved different than planned.

Demographic Catastrophe and Cultural Exchange

Contact among Europeans, Native Americans, and Africans after 1492 changed societies in both hemispheres. This process, called the *Columbian exchange,* included transmission of disease, knowledge about food and technology, and culture.

Disease was the chief ally of the Spanish in their drive through Central and South America. Smallpox was most lethal; other killers included measles, bubonic plague, chicken pox, influenza, whooping cough, and diphtheria. These diseases were particularly deadly because the microbes were new to America, and the Indians lacked immunity. Populations declined by an estimated 90 percent, as whole tribes were eliminated and others weakened severely. Illness spread from one native population to another, infecting the people of North America even before the English and French established colonies along the Atlantic coast. Some regions of the continent seemed uninhabited to European latecomers because of prior contact with disease.

Sixteenth-century drawings of Aztecs suffering from smallpox when the Spanish invaded. An Aztec description stated that "first an epidemic broke out, a sickness of pustules. . . . They spread everywhere, on the face, the head, the chest, etc. [and] brought great desolation" as people could neither "move nor stir" and many died.

The Columbian exchange also included livestock and crops that diversified cultures across continents. European settlers imported horses, sheep, cattle, pigs, and chickens for transportation, clothing, and food. While Europeans and Africans raised livestock as part of their agricultural economies, Native Americans depended on hunting and fishing to supplement crops. After European settlement, some Indians adopted horses and became skilled riders; others raised pigs and fowl. Problems resulted, however, because Europeans often allowed their animals to roam. Cattle and pigs trampled native fields, and helped spread disease and the seeds of aggressive European plants that changed the American landscape by forcing out native species.

Indians introduced the Europeans and Africans to crops that soon circled the globe and had a major impact on the growth of world populations: Indian corn (or maize), tomatoes, potatoes, peppers, beans, chocolate, pumpkins, and tobacco. The white potato of South America became a major staple in northern Europe; the sweet potato and Indian corn were important throughout the world. New crops also came to America from Europe and Africa, including cultivated rice, wheat, oats, sugarcane, bananas, onions, peaches, and watermelon. And while Europeans brought firearms and iron tools, Native Americans showed them how to build canoes and catch fish with weirs.

Native Americans generally resisted assimilation to Spanish culture. They retained their languages, clothing, housing, agricultural methods, and, to a considerable extent, religion. The degree to which they blocked acculturation depended largely on class. The Spanish focused much attention on the local Indian leaders (caciques) and their sons, with whom they interacted more frequently than with ordinary Indians. Many caciques learned to speak Spanish, converted to Christianity, and adopted Hispanic clothing. Their sons attended schools where they learned Latin and other advanced subjects. The common Indians avoided some Spanish ways of living and accepted others. They raised and ate chickens, but grew wheat primarily to pay as tribute. They abhorred cattle, but groups like the Apaches quickly accepted the horse. Natives favored their digging-sticks over the European plow, which would have required the use of draft animals and alteration in the assignment of fields.

Religion

The complexity of interaction between the Spanish and Native Americans can be seen most vividly in religion. The Europeans had a mandate from the pope to convert the "pagans" of America to Christianity. The missionaries believed that it was an act of humanity to introduce the Indians to Catholicism. The Spanish eliminated human sacrifice and destroyed temples and relics, but for the most part avoided forced conversion. At first, the missionaries expected most Native Americans to accept Spanish religious practice without change, as many Indians consented to baptism and voluntarily built churches in every town. But most Indians merged the European faith with rituals and beliefs of their traditional religions, resulting in *syncretism,* the blending of two faiths. For example, some natives added the Christian God to their polytheistic system; others focused on the saints or the Trinity rather than the supreme God. Indians organized *cofradías,* which were societies to raise money for church functions and festivals. The natives controlled the cofradías and at times asserted independence from the Spanish church authority.

The retention of native beliefs and practices disappointed many Spanish priests, who would accept nothing less than complete submission to their form of Catholicism. Nevertheless, missionaries worked for humane treatment of Indians. Colonists often justified enslaving Indians because they had "inferior" cultures and religion. A number of priests, of whom Bartolomé de Las Casas is best known, condemned the cruelty and enslavement. In his *Short Account of the Destruction of the Indies,* written in 1542, las Casas argued for more enlightened policies. Describing atrocities and slaughter in one colony after another, he informed the king of "the excesses which this New World has witnessed, all of them surpassing anything that men hitherto have imagined even in their wildest dreams."

Spanish Imperial Government

As conquest of the Americas progressed, Spain established a colonial government whose purposes were to convert Native Americans and bring them under control of the Spanish monarchy, and to exploit their labor and the wealth of the New World. The Spanish were only partly successful in imposing their rule over the Indians. The colonial government was most effective in central Mexico and the Andes, where the Europeans substituted their own imperial rule for that of the Aztecs and Incas. Native Americans in northern Mexico, Florida, Arizona, New Mexico, and central Chile, who had never been subject to empires, evaded Spanish rule. Many in the fringe areas, such as the Apaches, avoided Spanish domination altogether because their bands were highly mobile and autonomous.

The Spanish colonial administration was hierarchical and tied closely to Spain. Sovereignty, or supreme political power, rested in the monarch. The Spanish, like other Europeans at the time, believed that God vested such power in the Crown. Neither Spanish colonists nor Indians had much say in making and enforcing laws. The right of subjects to appeal official decisions to the king, however—along with delays caused by distance, corruption, and inefficiency—introduced flexibility into the governmental structure.

Directly below the monarch was the Council of the Indies, located in Spain and composed of men who knew little about the New World. The council regulated trade, appointed officials, made laws, and determined who should be allowed to emigrate. The highest officials residing in America were the viceroys. In the sixteenth and seventeenth centuries, the Spanish empire consisted of two viceroyalties: New Spain, with its capital in Mexico City, and Peru, with its capital in Lima. The viceroyalties were divided into provinces, ruled by governors and *audiencias,* which advised the governors and functioned as courts. The audiencias could appeal all decisions to the king, thus limiting the wide powers of the viceroys and governors. So did the *residencia,* which investigated these officials at the end of their terms and reported any corruption to Spain.

In central Mexico and Peru, the Spanish viceroys, governors, and audiencias took the place of the ruling native elite. At the local level, however, native leaders often retained their positions. Called caciques, they headed the Indian towns, collected tribute from households, and recruited forced laborers upon demand of the colonial authorities.

Spanish Mercantilism

The Crown regulated commerce through the *Casa de la Contratación,* a trading house founded in 1503 in Seville. Thus Spain elaborated its economic policy of mercantilism, which held that nations had monopolistic rights to trade with their colonies. With tight governmental control, the primary goal of economic activity under mercantilism was to achieve a favorable balance of trade. Colonies were expected to serve as markets for goods from the home country and provide raw materials, gold, and silver to increase its wealth. All merchants desiring to send ships to Spanish America needed permission from the Casa, as did anyone wishing to emigrate. The Casa denied leave to persons of Jewish ancestry, for example, though in fact many found passage to America without official permission. To the monarch, a crucial function of the Casa was registration of precious metals, because the king received one-fifth, called the "royal fifth," of all silver and gold. Colonists had to obtain permission to build plantations and mines. In return they paid taxes to the king and, if they found precious metals, the royal fifth.

When Columbus obtained gold from the inhabitants of Hispaniola, he raised expectations of great wealth. However, the explorers at first met disappointment. Even the Aztecs failed to satisfy the Spanish thirst for gold, so most colonists turned to agriculture to make their fortunes. Then, in the 1540s, the Europeans located two immensely rich silver mines, one at Potosí in present-day Bolivia and the other at Zacatecas in Mexico. Between 1500 and 1650 about 181 tons of gold and 16,000 tons of silver officially reached Europe from America. Production of silver expanded greatly in the 1570s with the introduction of mercury to the refining process.

The Spanish organized their silver trade to outwit privateers of other nations, especially France and England. In 1565, the Spanish founded St. Augustine in Florida as a base to fight the buccaneers and reinforce Spain's claim to North America. They devised a convoy system to protect their fleets. Two convoys left Seville each year, carrying goods such as wine, books, oil, grain, clothing, and other luxuries: one left in May headed for Mexico, and the other departed in August for the Isthmus of Panama, from which mules carried the goods to Peru. Both convoys stayed the winter with the intention of meeting in Cuba by early summer so they could return to Spain before the onset of hurricanes. The Panama fleet sometimes ran into trouble when the mule train carrying Potosí silver arrived late.

For the Spanish monarchy, the discovery of rich mines fulfilled their dreams in the New World. The king used the bullion to pay for his European wars. American silver and gold helped to create inflation throughout Europe, as the immense supply depressed their value and the prices of other goods increased. Merchants depended on the bullion to pay for luxuries from the East. Goods worth about one-half the value of the metals were returned to the colonies.

Forced Labor Systems

Because Spanish immigrants were few in number and had no intention of working in the mines or fields, they adopted ways to compel Native Americans to work. In the mid-sixteenth century, the white colonists remained a small percentage of New World inhabitants, with a population of about 100,000 in New Spain compared with an estimated 2.6 million Native Americans in central Mexico. But if some European settlers hoped to have millions of Christianized Indian workers do their bidding, they were disappointed. The catastrophic level of native deaths and resistance of Indians to conversion created New World societies unlike those the Spanish and Native Americans had previously known.

When the first explorers on Hispaniola tried to consign the native Arawaks to slavery, most of the Indians died. In 1500, the Spanish Crown ruled that only Indians captured in a "just war" could be forced into perpetual bondage. This judgment had little impact because conquistadores could define as hostile any natives who resisted capture. In 1513, the government drew up a document called the *Requerimiento* (or Requirement), which explorers read when they entered an Indian town for the first time. The requerimiento informed the natives that they must accept the sovereignty of the Catholic church and the Spanish monarchy. If they did, they would become Spanish subjects in peace; if they did not, the soldiers would "make war against you . . . take you and your wives and your children and . . . make slaves of them . . . and shall do to you all the harm and damage that we can." By the time the king outlawed most Native American slavery in 1542, the Arawaks of the West Indies had been destroyed. The Spanish had expropriated their lands for sugar plantations, replacing the Indians with enslaved Africans. On the mainland, the Spanish government established two forms of forced Indian labor. With the *encomienda,* Indians living on specified lands had to pay tribute to individual colonists and sometimes provide labor for which they received minimal wages. At first, the encomienda system included no transfer of land to the colonists, but as the numbers of Native Americans declined and Spanish increased, the colonists took Indian property for farms and ranches. By the seventeenth century, grazing livestock replaced Indian farms on vast stretches of Spanish America.

In 1600, about 1 million Indians survived in central Mexico, a significant decrease from a generation earlier, when the population was 2.6 million. This severe decline caused problems for the Spanish who depended upon the natives for food and labor. Thus, the government devised the *repartimiento* system. Indians could be forced to work in mines, agriculture, or public works for several weeks, months, or even a year. For example, natives labored for yearlong stints at the Potosí silver mines in Bolivia. At Potosí, workers assigned as carriers climbed some 600 feet through tunnels about as wide as a man's body with heavy loads of silver ore on their backs. Those who worked in refining were exposed to mercury poisoning because part of the process involved walking with bare legs through the slurry of mercury, water, and ore. As the Indian population declined, the Spanish had difficulty in finding enough workers. When they attempted to increase the length and frequency of work periods, Indians resisted the changes, sometimes successfully.

As early as 1502, on West Indies plantations, the Spanish turned to the people of Africa to meet their insatiable labor demands. They had already purchased Africans from Portuguese traders to work in Spain and on the sugar plantations of the Canary Islands. The government set up a system of licenses, or *asientos,* for merchants to supply certain numbers of slaves. During the sixteenth century, ships transported approximately 75,000 Africans to Spanish America, with perhaps an equal number dying en route, either in Africa or at sea. The Spanish imported Africans to work on sugar plantations in the West Indies and coastal areas of the mainland where most Native Americans had died. Severe work regimes and rampant disease also resulted in high death rates among imported blacks.

Protestant Northern Europeans Challenge Catholic Spain

Until 1560, French and English activity in America remained much more tentative and sporadic than Spain's. Although fishing expeditions regularly visited the North American coast, initiatives for permanent colonies gained little support. But religious and political change in Northern Europe provided the impetus to test Spain's domination of the New World. In the age of Reformation and religious wars, America became both a refuge for religious dissidents and a battlefield on which European nations fought for wealth, glory, and national sovereignty.

The Protestant Reformation

When the German priest Martin Luther in 1517 issued his ninety-five theses against the sale of indulgences, the Church of Rome was the sovereign faith of western and central Europe. Luther believed the church was corrupt. The sale of indulgences, which were supposed to reduce the amount of time a deceased person spent in purgatory, was an example of its decline. Luther believed that people received salvation as a gift from God in return for faith ("justification by faith") rather than for good works. They could not earn salvation by taking pilgrimages, giving money to the church, hearing masses, or going on crusades against the Muslims. Luther also challenged the authority of priests, arguing for a "priesthood of all believers." Christians should seek the word of God in the Bible, which he translated into German to make it more available to laypeople. Luther contended that the Bible recognized only two sacraments, baptism and communion, not the seven authorized by the Catholic church. He also opposed the requirement of celibacy for priests, marrying Katharina von Bora, a former nun.

Luther's teachings led to many divisions in western Christianity, as common people and princes alike adopted his beliefs. In Germany, which was composed of many individual states, some princes accepted Lutheranism and others remained Catholic, requiring their subjects to follow their example. Lutheranism spread through northern Germany and into Scandinavia. Luther inspired other critics of Catholicism to offer variant Protestant doctrines, including the Mennonites, Hutterites, and Swiss Brethren, all called Anabaptists because they required adult baptism.

The most influential of the systems of belief that Lutheranism spawned was that of John Calvin, a native of France, who attempted to create a model society at Geneva, Switzerland. Followers of Calvin established churches in the Reformed tradition: they were known variously as French Huguenots, English Puritans, Scottish Presbyterians, and Dutch and German Reformed. Calvin went further than Luther in arguing that humans could do nothing to save themselves. This concept of predestination meant that God alone determined who would be saved (the "elect"). Through communion with God, the elect learned that they were saved; they strove to live blamelessly to reflect their status.

Calvin and his followers convinced the city council and churches of Geneva to adopt many Reformed doctrines, stripping the churches of decoration, images, and colorful rituals. The Bible, as interpreted by Calvin, became the basis for law. The civil government punished moral offenders and nonbelievers identified by the church elders. The Calvinists disciplined individuals for dancing, wearing fancy clothes, and insubordination. They forced one man to walk through the city wearing only a shirt because he criticized Calvin, and burned another at the stake for heresy. Although Calvin failed to obtain all of his demands from the Geneva council, he came close to establishing a theocracy, in which the church fathers ruled in the name of God.

Protestant ideas spread to France and England quickly. In France, Calvin attracted many adherents, called Huguenots, among the nobles and prosperous commoners. The French monarchy considered Protestants a threat to its monopoly of power. Even after the Edict of Nantes of 1598, which offered freedom to worship, Huguenots faced serious discrimination.

In England, years before Luther, opposition had existed to the Catholic hierarchy, its taxes, monasteries, and the use of images in church. Thus Henry VIII found sympathy for his break with Rome when the pope refused to allow an annulment of his marriage to Catherine of Aragon. Henry wanted to marry Anne Boleyn, who he hoped would provide a male heir. Parliament passed the Act of Supremacy (1534), mandating that the king be "taken, accepted, and reputed the only supreme head on earth of the Church of England." The Crown dissolved the monasteries and confiscated their property. Henry was no Lutheran, however, for the Six Articles (1539) that formed the theological basis of Anglicanism confirmed Catholic beliefs on priestly celibacy, the mass, confession, and sacraments. But because the Six Articles were ambiguous on many points, the Church of England from its inception allowed a fairly wide range of doctrine. In 1552, the revised Anglican prayer book incorporated many Protestant beliefs. Soon after, Henry's daughter Mary I attempted to force England back to the Church of Rome. Her persecution of Protestants earned her the name "Bloody Mary"; her marriage to the staunch Catholic Philip II of Spain inspired an English nationalism that fused loyalty to church and state. When Mary died in 1558, her half-sister, Elizabeth I, became queen, ending the immediate threat that England would return to Catholicism. The new English monarch and a large proportion of her subjects identified Spain as a threat to their national church, now Protestant, and their independence as a nation.

Under Elizabeth, the English confronted Spain on a number of fronts, leading to a showdown in 1588. In the religious struggles of the late sixteenth century, England became a dominant Protestant power, supported the Dutch revolt against Philip II, and challenged Spain's monopolistic claims to the New World. Though pragmatic and more interested in power than theology, Elizabeth confirmed England's break with the pope and approved earlier moderate Protestant reforms. The Act of Uniformity (1559) required adherence to the Anglican Book of Prayer. The queen suppressed resistance from both Calvinists, who wanted further reforms, and the supporters of Rome. Some Catholics turned to Elizabeth's cousin, Mary, Queen of Scots, a Roman Catholic and heir to the English throne. In 1587, after several unsuccessful plots on Elizabeth's life, Mary was tried as a conspirator and beheaded.

One of Mary, Queen of Scots's most fervent supporters was Philip II of Spain. Throughout Europe he strove to wipe out the Protestant heresy. He considered Elizabeth a dangerous foe, not least for her support of the revolt in the Netherlands. When many Dutch adopted Calvinism, Philip retaliated with his Inquisition, executing thousands. The Dutch rebelled. In 1581, the northern part of the Netherlands, composed of seven provinces, including Holland, declared its independence as the United Provinces. The southern region, called the Spanish Netherlands (now Belgium), remained under Philip's control. When Elizabeth sent aid to the United Provinces in 1585, she in effect declared war on Spain. The most important battle occurred in 1588, when Philip sent his mighty Armada of 130 ships and 30,000 men to invade England. The English defeated the Armada, thus preserving their national sovereignty and religion.

French Huguenots and English Sea Dogs

In France, persecution led some Protestant Huguenots to look to America as a refuge. In 1555, a group of wealthy Frenchmen sent Huguenot settlers to Brazil. When disputes occurred among the colonists, some returned to France; the Portuguese, who claimed Brazil, killed or enslaved the majority who remained. In 1562, Huguenots tried again, establishing Charlesfort on the South Carolina coast, in part to attack the Spanish silver fleet as it headed home. When the Spanish moved against the small French colony in 1564, they found it already abandoned. But the Huguenots attempted another settlement that year, this one at Fort Caroline on the St. Johns River in northern Florida. The Spanish quickly destroyed it, murdering most of the settlers.

The English "sea dogs" learned a great deal about the New World from the Huguenots. With Elizabeth I's ascension to the throne in 1558, seafarers and colonizers like John Hawkins, Francis Drake, Humphrey Gilbert, and Walter Raleigh gained favor and support. Hawkins visited Fort Caroline in 1565; other Englishmen gained knowledge of the North American coast from the French. The English also acquired a taste for conquest in Ireland, where their brutal subjugation of the native Irish presaged later actions against the Indians.

The English took their time before attempting an American colony. The Spanish remained a serious threat. Thus for two decades, until the 1580s, English adventurers sought wealth by sea. In 1562, John Hawkins took 300 Africans to Hispaniola without a license. The local Spanish officials allowed him to exchange the slaves for sugar and hides because the colony needed labor. Hawkins made a second voyage, earning another handsome profit, this time mostly in silver. When the Spanish authorities protested, Elizabeth forbade further expeditions, but reversed her decision in 1567. On his third voyage, Hawkins was conducting business in the harbor of San Juan de Ulúa, Mexico, when the annual fleet arrived from Spain several weeks early, destroying three of his ships. Hawkins and his cousin Francis Drake escaped with two badly damaged vessels. Their crews nearly starved on the return to England.

Hawkins stopped interloping in Spanish trade, but other English privateers followed. The most famous was Francis Drake, who in 1572 intercepted the mule train carrying Potosí silver across Panama with the help of Native Americans and runaway African slaves. Five years later he set out to circumnavigate the globe. Following Magellan's route through the straits, he attacked Spanish towns along the Pacific coast, explored the North American coast for evidence of a northwest passage, and returned to England in 1580 by way of Asia and the Cape of Good Hope. Six years later, when England and Spain were formally at war, Drake attacked Spanish ports in America, including St. Augustine in Florida, which he looted and burned.

While Drake was making his fortune through piracy, other sea dogs hoped to make their mark by starting colonies. With experience in Ireland, they decided to ignore Spain's claim to North America. On the basis of Cabot's voyage of 1497, Elizabeth granted a charter to Humphrey Gilbert, who sailed to Newfoundland in 1583. He assumed ownership for the English Crown. Nothing came of Gilbert's colony, however, as he was lost at sea on his return to England.

Walter Raleigh then attempted a settlement farther south, in the land named for the "virgin" Queen Elizabeth. In 1585, the first group of settlers arrived at Roanoke Island, in what is now North Carolina. After their ships returned home leaving them with short supplies, the colonists tried to force neighboring Indians to provide food. Quickly a pattern of hostility emerged between the English and Native Americans. Francis Drake saved the Roanoke colonists from starvation, carrying them home in 1586. A year later, Raleigh sent out another expedition. This time the war with Spain prevented ships from returning to Roanoke until 1590, when all that was left of the colony was the word "Croatoan" carved on a tree. The colonists may have moved to nearby Croatoan Island, or farther inland to live with Native Americans, but the fate of the "Lost Colony" has never been determined. The English did not colonize successfully in North America until the founding of Jamestown in 1607.

Conclusion

By 1590, the Spanish had created an empire that extended from South America through the West Indies and Mexico. They funded their European wars to extinguish Protestantism with American silver and gold. The Portuguese, united under the Spanish Crown in 1580, had developed the Atlantic slave trading system that sent enslaved Africans to Brazil and New Spain.

The irony of colonization in America was that European nations at war in the Old World emulated one another in the New. The Spanish and Portuguese provided the model for later colonizers in expropriating land and labor from Indians and Africans. Europeans justified their behavior toward the people of America and Africa by emphasizing religious and cultural differences, ignoring much that they had in common. Although European nations organized colonization in various ways, all sought mercantilistic ends. In the early seventeenth century, when the English, French, and Dutch settled in North America, their goals were very similar to those of Spain. They hoped to locate precious metals, find the elusive northwest passage, exploit Indian labor, extend Christianity to America, and expand the power of the state.

RECOMMENDED READINGS

Bethell, Leslie, ed. *Colonial Spanish America* (1987). Essays provide useful syntheses on the development of the Spanish colonies.

Casas, Bartolomé de las. *A Short Account of the Destruction of the Indies.* Ed. and trans., Nigel Griffin (1992). A priest's sharp denunciation of Spanish colonization, written in 1542.

Davidson, Basil. *The Search for Africa: History, Culture, Politics* (1994). A readable history by a veteran historian of the continent.

Dixon, E. James. *Bones, Boats, and Bison: Archeology and the First Colonization of Western North America* (1999). Clear review of archeological evidence of first Americans.

Klein, Herbert S. *The Atlantic Slave Trade* (1999). Surveys the growing literature about the international slave trade.

Kupperman, Karen Ordahl. *Roanoke: The Abandoned Colony* (1984). A lively account of the early English attempt to settle in North America.

Lockhart, James. *The Nahuas After the Conquest: A Social and Cultural History of the Indians of Central Mexico, Sixteenth Through Eighteenth Centuries* (1992). Explores the development of Nahua society and culture, including chapters on households, social structure, land tenure, religion, language, and the arts.

Nash, Gary B. *Red, White, and Black: The Peoples of Early North America,* 4th ed. (2002). An excellent introduction to the meeting of cultures in the New World.

Schwartz, Stuart B. *Victors and Vanquished: Spanish and Nahua Views of the Conquest of Mexico* (2000). A very good collection of documentary sources on Mexican society and the Spanish invasion.

Weber, David J. *The Spanish Frontier in North America* (1992). The best synthesis on Spanish exploration and colonization north of Mexico.

Additional resources, exercises, and Internet links related to this chapter are available on the American Passages Web site: http://history.wadsworth.com/ayerscompact2/

Colonization of North America
1590–1675

In 1590, the only permanent European settlement in what is now the United States was St. Augustine, the struggling Spanish town in Florida that the English privateer Francis Drake had burned four years earlier. Spain was much more concerned with its silver mines and West Indies plantations than in colonizing along the Atlantic coast, yet wanted to prevent intrusion by other nations, for good reason. In the late sixteenth century, buccaneers from France and England thought the best way to get rich was by looting the Spanish silver fleet and ports.

Though Spain expanded in Florida and New Mexico in the 1600s, the English defeat of the Armada and Dutch surge in overseas trade eroded Spanish control of the New World. France, England, the Netherlands, and Sweden all established colonies in North America by 1638, hoping to duplicate Spain's success. While none found gold or an easy route to Asia—and the Swedes and Dutch soon lost their toeholds in the Delaware and Hudson valleys altogether—Europeans prospered from the West Indies sugar boom, Canadian fur trade, and Chesapeake tobacco. New England offered a haven for Puritan dissenters.

By 1675, the English held a string of settlements along the Atlantic coast. Unlike the Spanish, England's colonization proceeded with little regulation from the Crown, resulting in a variety of social, economic, and political structures. The English government helped to create the diversity by granting different kinds of charters to individuals and groups.

The expansion of European settlement in North America changed the countryside forever. Cheap, even free, land and developing commerce offered opportunity to men and women of all economic classes who were willing to risk their lives by crossing the Atlantic. Their farms eliminated Indian hunting lands, altering the ecological balance of plants and animals. Though many Native Americans resisted the European invasions, disease seriously undermined their power. The fur trade also changed the cultural values of many Indians, drawing them into Atlantic commerce and tempting them to overhunt. For Native Americans from New Mexico to Canada, European colonization was a disaster.

CHRONOLOGY

1598	Spanish expedition into New Mexico
1599	Destruction of Ácoma by the Spanish
1603	James I takes the English throne
1605	French establish Port Royal
1607	English found colony at Jamestown
1608	French establish Quebec
1609	Henry Hudson explores for the Dutch East India Company
1609–1614	Anglo-Powhatan War in Virginia
1616–1618	Plague epidemic decimates eastern New England natives
1619	Africans arrive in Virginia • Virginia Company establishes a representative assembly
1620	Separatists found the Plymouth colony
1622	Native Americans attack the Virginia colony
1624	Virginia Company loses charter • Virginia becomes a royal colony • Dutch West India Company establishes New Netherland
1625	Charles I becomes king of England
1630	Massachusetts Bay colony founded by Puritans
1634	The *Ark* and the *Dove* arrive in Maryland
1636	Founding of Connecticut and Rhode Island
1637	Massachusetts and Connecticut troops destroy the Pequots • Anne Hutchinson is tried for heresy
1642–1648	English Civil War
1649	Charles I of England is beheaded
1651	English Parliament passes first Navigation Act
1660	Charles II of England becomes king
1663	Carolina proprietors receive charter
1664	English forces conquer New Netherland • New York and New Jersey are founded
1673	Dutch recapture New York, then return the colony to England with the Treaty of Westminster (1674)

The Spanish in North America

After Coronado and de Soto failed to locate cities of gold, Spain abandoned further exploration in North America. Then, Francis Drake's voyage along the Pacific coast raised alarms of foreign interest in the region north of Mexico. In 1581, the viceroy of New Spain gave Franciscan priests permission to establish missions among the Pueblo Indians of the Rio Grande Valley. The friars named the area San Felipe del Nuevo México. The missionaries described the Pueblos as friendly and numerous: thousands could be converted to Christianity and forced to labor for Hispanic colonists. But by the time a party arrived in 1582 to escort the Franciscans back to Mexico, the missionaries had been killed by the Native Americans.

Settlement of New Mexico

Despite this setback, the Spanish remained interested in the region. Conquistadores needed permission from the Crown to invade new lands, however, for the king had issued Orders for New Discoveries (1573), which more strictly regulated colonization, in part to protect Native Americans from the atrocities Bartolomé de las Casas had described decades before. When one would-be conqueror led an illegal expedition into New Mexico in 1590, he was arrested and returned to Mexico City in chains.

The Spanish government delayed appointing a governor of New Mexico until 1595, when the viceroy authorized Juan de Oñate to undertake settlement with his own funds. Oñate, a native of Mexico, inherited great wealth and obtained even more by marrying Isabel Tolosa Cortés Moctezuma, a descendant of both Cortés and the Aztec emperor. The expedition proved expensive as delays increased costs. Finally, in 1598, 129 soldiers, their families, servants, and slaves, and 7,000 livestock headed north. Ten Franciscan missionaries accompanied the colonists. Oñate expected his investment to yield an empire. As he wrote King Philip II, "I shall give your majesty a new world, greater than New Spain." The governor envisioned mines of silver and gold and a water passage through the continent. He believed his province would extend from the Atlantic to the Pacific.

Upon arrival in New Mexico, Oñate declared Spanish sovereignty over Pueblo lands. In a ritual complete with trumpets and High Mass, he promised peace and prosperity to those who cooperated. According to the Spanish, the Pueblos acquiesced "of their own accord." The Franciscans founded missions in the largest pueblos and supervised construction of a church in the Tewa pueblo, Yungé, which the Spanish designated as their capital, San Gabriel.

For some months, the Spanish and the Indians coexisted without serious incident. The colonists moved into the Pueblos's apartments in San Gabriel, forcing the inhabitants to depart. Soon the Indians tired of providing food, which they had intended as gifts but the Spanish considered tribute. The soldiers resorted to murder and rape to obtain supplies. The crisis came in December 1598, when a Spanish troop demanded provisions from the people of Ácoma, a pueblo high atop a mesa west of the Rio Grande. One of Coronado's party had described Ácoma as "the greatest stronghold ever seen in the world." The Pueblos refused to give flour to the soldiers and killed eleven men when they attempted to take the food by force. Oñate moved swiftly, his small army laying siege to Ácoma with several cannons, as men and women defended the town with arrows and stones. The Spanish killed approximately 500 men and 300 women and children; they captured the survivors. The town was leveled. Everyone was sentenced to servitude, and each man over age twenty-five had one foot cut off. The Ácomas would not rebuild their town until the late 1640s.

With this harsh action, Oñate only temporarily prevented further opposition among the Pueblos, for another town resisted the following year. The colonists also complained of food shortages and the governor's mismanagement; many returned to Mexico. The Franciscans charged that Oñate's cruelty to the Indians made conversion difficult. Oñate was removed as governor, tried, and found guilty of mistreating the Native Americans and some of his settlers. He was banished from New Mexico, but sailed to Spain, where he received a knighthood and position as the Crown's chief inspector of mines.

After Oñate's departure, New Mexico became a royal province. Pedro de Peralta, the next governor, established a new capital at Santa Fe in 1610. As late as 1670 only 2,800 Spanish colonists inhabited the Rio Grande Valley. The Hispanics lived on farms and ranches along the river, exploiting the Pueblos's labor through the encomienda system to produce hides, blankets, sheep, wool, and pine nuts for sale in Mexico.

Spanish Missions in New Mexico and Florida

The Franciscan missionaries, who assumed a major role in colonizing the Spanish borderlands, were members of the Catholic religious order that Francis Bernardone of Assisi had founded (in Italy) in 1209. The friars vowed not to engage in sexual relations or acquire property, living on the gifts of others. Unlike other religious brotherhoods, which remained in seclusion, the Franciscans operated in the world among ordinary Christians. The Orders for New Discoveries of 1573 gave primary responsibility to the friars for "pacifying" the Indians of New Mexico and Florida.

During the first part of the seventeenth century, many Pueblos seemed to accept the Franciscans' message. The friars initially offered gifts of food, metal tools, beads, and clothing. Placing some confidence in the priests, the natives agreed to build convents and churches. Women built the walls, while men did carpentry. The priests decorated the sanctuaries with paintings, statues, and silver chalices. They created missions by imposing their influence over existing Indian towns, backed by threat of military force. In New Mexico, the Spanish started more than fifty churches by 1629; in Florida, missions extended west from St. Augustine to the Gulf Coast and north into Georgia (or Guale, as the region was called).

The Native Americans who came under Spanish control could, in theory, choose whether or not to accept Christian baptism, but recognized that soldiers supported the priests. The Franciscans expected the natives to learn the catechism and enough of the Castilian (Spanish) language to communicate, and to adopt European dress, food, and farming methods. Many Indians embraced Catholicism, but in doing so, modified the religion. Even in the twentieth century, the Pueblos preserved both native and Catholic religious practices. Christian Indians in Florida continued to play a ball game during the 1600s until the missionaries realized it had religious significance and abolished the game, calling the pole used as a target the "ballpost of the devil."

In merging Indian gods with the Christian Trinity and adding Catholic holidays to native celebrations, Native Americans altered Spanish Catholicism. With the "Lady in Blue," they created a religious tradition that both the Indians and Spanish accepted. In the 1620s, Plains Indians reported that a nun appeared to them, telling them in their language to become Christians. Though the woman remained invisible to the missionaries, they believed the stories. On a trip to Spain, one priest discovered that a Franciscan nun, María de Jesús de Agreda, claimed to have made flights to America with the help of angels. María de Agreda's claims and the Indians' visions together created the resilient legend of the Lady in Blue.

The English Invade Virginia

New Mexico and Florida remained marginal outposts in the Spanish empire. Spanish control was tenuous because their military forces were small and cultural influence weak. After the defeat of the Spanish Armada, Philip II's government could not keep other European nations out of North America. During the first decade of the seventeenth century, the English, French, and Dutch sent expeditions to fish, search for a northern passage to the East, trade for furs, and establish colonies.

English Context of Colonization

Seventeenth-century England was an intensely hierarchical society, in which the king claimed divine right, or God-given authority, and the nobility and gentry dominated Parliament. But it was a society undergoing turmoil and change. Elizabeth I's successor was her cousin, James I, who governed from 1603 until 1625, when he died and his son, Charles I, took the throne. Both James and Charles had strife-torn reigns marked by power struggles with Parliament, culminating in Charles's loss of the English Civil War and his beheading in 1649. Parliament was composed of two houses: the House of Lords, made up of nobles and high church officials; and the House of Commons, who were elected representatives from the counties and boroughs. The Commons normally comprised country gentry, government officials, and lawyers; the electorate included male landowners, or an estimated 15 to 30 percent of all Englishmen. By imposing levies without Parliament's consent, James I and Charles I challenged its prerogative to approve or reject new taxes. For their part, the legislators tried to whittle away at royal powers. The fundamental issue concerning the balance of power between the king and property holders, as represented in Parliament, remained unsettled until the Glorious Revolution of 1688.

Economic developments loosened English society, giving individuals greater opportunity to change from one social class or occupation to another. Many found it necessary to move geographically as the woolen industry expanded, causing landowners to raise more sheep. In what has been called the "enclosure movement," landlords ended leases for tenant farmers living on their lands, confiscating common fields that peasant communities had shared for grazing their livestock and raising crops. The landowners enclosed the commons with fences and hedges. In 1500, peasants had farmed 70 percent of arable land in England, but by 1650, they farmed only 50 percent. Thus many tenants were forced from the land. Some went to London, where the population expanded from 55,000 in 1520 to 475,000 in 1670. Others were among the colonists who signed for America.

A developing economy meant dislocation for poor tenants; it spelled opportunity for merchants. They found it first in the woolen trade with Antwerp, in what is now Belgium. When this trade declined after 1550, they looked for alternative investments, which they found as war with Spain brought demand for coal, lead, glass, ships, salt, iron, and steel. Investors formed joint-stock companies to explore trade routes and establish new markets. The companies obtained capital by selling stocks. These investments were risky, for shareholders were liable for all company debts. The stocks could also be immensely profitable, as in the case of Francis Drake's circumnavigation of the globe, which brought a 4,600 percent profit.

Joint-stock companies provided capital for the first permanent English colonies in America. Unlike the Spanish monarchy, the English Crown had little role in funding, or even governing, its first New World settlements. In 1606, James I granted a charter to the Virginia Company with rights to settle colonies in North America. The Virginia Company included two groups, one in London and the other in Plymouth, in the west of England. The groups received overlapping claims, with the Plymouth group obtaining lands from what is now Maine to Virginia and the London group receiving Connecticut to the Carolinas. Either could settle in the overlapping area, but initial colonies had to be at least one hundred miles apart.

Jamestown

In 1607, the Virginia Company of London funded the first permanent English colony at Jamestown. When the first 104 settlers arrived in May 1607, they had endured a long winter crossing. The native inhabitants watched them select a site on the James River, chosen for safety from Spanish attack, but next to malarial swamps. The Native Americans called their territory Tsenacommacah, or "densely inhabited land." They were Algonquian-speaking Indians; most belonged to a confederacy that Powhatan, head sachem of the Pamunkey tribe, had forged in eastern Virginia. Before the arrival of the English, the chief unifying force among the bands of the Powhatan confederacy was the threat from powerful enemies, the Manahoacs and the Monacans, who controlled lands to the west. The leaders of tribes subject to Powhatan were supposed to pay tribute and provide military assistance, but they sometimes refused.

One of Powhatan's brothers was Opechancanough, described as having "large Stature, noble Presence, and extraordinary Parts" and being "perfectly skill'd in the Art of Governing." Historical evidence suggests that he was born around 1544 and, at about age sixteen, was taken by a Spanish ship to Spain, where he received instruction in the Castilian language and adopted the name Don Luis de Velasco after the viceroy of New Spain. The new Don Luis stayed with the Spanish until 1570, when he accompanied several missionaries to his homeland on Chesapeake Bay. He broke with the priests when they criticized him for taking several wives and murdered the priests the next year. If Opechancanough and Don Luis were the same man, as seems likely, he was well prepared with knowledge of Europeans when the Jamestown settlers arrived.

The English colony's first decade was a struggle. The company ran Virginia as a business enterprise, keeping control of government, land, and trade. Settlers were company

Colonial Williamsburg Foundation

In this conjectural view of Jamestown c. 1614, the fortified wall shows concerns for defense against the Spanish and the Powhatan confederacy.

employees, not landholders. To satisfy investors, the company instructed the colonists to search for gold and silver mines, find a passage to Asia, and establish industries and trade that would offer handsome returns. The company had chosen individuals for these purposes, not people who were willing to grow crops. Among the first Jamestown settlers were many gentlemen, who by definition avoided manual labor. They were adventurers who expected to strike it rich and return to England. The rest of the first colonists, who were nearly all men, included the gentlemen's personal servants, a jeweler, goldsmith, perfumer, carpenters, blacksmiths, and some laborers. No one described himself as a farmer.

When the colonists failed to locate mines or a passage to the East, their lives became aimless. Rather than plant crops or even hunt and fish, they expected the company and neighboring Indians to provide food. When sufficient provisions failed to arrive, the settlers starved. One of the leaders, a young officer named John Smith, took control in 1608, stabilizing the colony briefly by making everyone work. When criticism of his strict discipline reached company officials the next year, they removed him from command. During the particularly bitter winter of 1609–1610, one man killed his pregnant wife and chopped her up, planning to eat her body. Some of the colonists dug up graves to eat the corpses. By spring 1610, only sixty colonists remained of at least 600 who had come to Jamestown in three years. Though some had returned to England or escaped to live with the Indians, the majority died of starvation and disease.

In 1609, without gold mines or a trade route to Asia, the Virginia Company hoped to salvage its investment by exploiting the land. To recruit farmers, the company offered each emigrant one share of stock and a parcel of land after seven years of service. The settlers remained employees of the company in the meantime, with assigned tasks and the obligation to buy all supplies and ship all products through the company store.

Still, the Jamestown settlers refused to work. When Sir Thomas Dale arrived as governor in May 1611, he found nothing but a few gardens planted and the inhabitants at "their daily and usual work, bowling in the streets." He established his *Laws Divine, Morall and Martiall,* which were mostly martial. The men received military ranks, were divided into work gangs, and proceeded from home to work—and to church twice daily—at the beat of a drum. Laws prescribed death for a variety of crimes, including rape, adultery, theft, lying, slander against the company, blasphemy, and stealing an ear of corn. For taking two or three pints of oatmeal, one man had a large needle thrust through his tongue, then was chained to a tree until he starved. For the first offense of failing to work regular hours, an idler was tied neck to heels all night. The punishment for a second offense was whipping and for a third offense, death. Though the required hours of work were reasonable—five to eight hours per day in the summer and three to six in the winter—the punishments specified in "Dale's Laws" became a scandal in England, discouraging prospective emigrants. In the words of John Smith, "no man will go from [England] to have less liberty there."

The Struggle for Virginia

The Jamestown adventurers had expected to put the Indians to work in silver mines and fields, as in New Spain, but the inhabitants proved too few in number for an adequate workforce, yet too powerful for the wretched gang of settlers to conquer. During the early years at Jamestown, the English seemed irrational in their dealings with the Native Americans. To many colonists, the natives were barbarians. While some settlers attempted to trade for food, others burned Indian villages and crops.

In 1608–1609, Captain John Smith tried to force the sachems to provide food. The Indians had spared his life several times; nevertheless, he kidnapped two men, obligating Opechancanough to beg for their release. Next, he entered the Pamunkey village with soldiers demanding food, which the Indians refused to give, and again humiliated the tall sachem: in Smith's words, he did "take this murdering Opechancanough . . . by the long lock of his head; and with my pistol at his breast, I led him [out of his house] amongst his greatest forces, and before we parted made him [agree to] fill our bark with twenty tuns of corn." Otherwise, Smith warned, he would load the ship with their "dead carkases." Opechancanough probably never forgot this scene. Between 1609 and 1614, full-scale war existed between the Virginia colonists and the Powhatan confederacy. The English, with reinforcements from the Virginia Company, defeated Powhatan, taking control of the James River.

In contrast to Spain, the English Crown failed to take responsibility for protecting any rights of Native Americans. When colonists had sufficient power, they enslaved Indians, sending them away from their homelands to prevent escape. The English justified expropriation of native lands with the belief that the king of England, as the Christian monarch, received sovereignty over North America from God. Thus, the Virginia Company obtained rights to land from the Crown, not the Indians. Another basis for taking native territory was the legal concept, *vacuum domicilium,* which meant that lands not occupied could be taken. To the English, "occupation" meant improving the land with buildings, fences, and crops; they did not recognize Indian sovereignty over the vast stretches of hunting lands that extended beyond small villages and fields. Even when the English purchased land from the Indians, their contrasting concepts of ownership caused grave misunderstanding. Whereas the colonists believed in private property, the natives thought they were selling the rights to use lands for hunting, fishing, and communal farming. They expected to continue using the territory they had "sold" for these purposes. Conflicts resulted when, for example, a settler's cattle trampled Indian crops, or when a native killed a colonist's cow, mistaking it for a deer.

© Bettmann/Corbis

Tobacco Boom

Demand for land became paramount in Virginia after 1617, when the colonists discovered tobacco as a staple crop. Though James I called smoking "a custom loathsome to the eye, hateful to the nose, harmful to the brain, dangerous to the lungs, and in the black stinking fumes thereof, nearest resembling the horrible stygian smoke of the pit that is bottomless," the habit consumed England. The mercantilist advantages were clear. With production in Virginia, the English could acquire tobacco from its own colony, rather than pay premium prices to foreign countries, and could generate an industry to process the leaves. For Virginians, the tobacco trade meant capital to purchase manufactures from home. Tobacco became the first

To cure tobacco for sale, workers hung leaves from rafters in a tobacco house until sufficiently dry. The laborers then cut the leaves from the plant stalks, removed the largest fibers from the leaves, and "prized" or packed the leaves into hogsheads.

staple crop in England's colonial mercantilist system, followed by sugar, after 1640, in the West Indies.

In 1619, the Virginia Company updated the land policy, granting "headrights" of one hundred acres of land to those who came before 1616 and fifty acres to those who came after. Settlers who paid their own way received land immediately; those who immigrated at the company's expense received land after seven years of service. Virginia settlers thus fell into two categories: freeholders who paid for their own transportation; and servants, whose way the Virginia Company or someone else financed. Recipients of headrights did not pay for the land, but owed quitrents, annual payments to the company, of one shilling per year for each fifty acres. Also in 1619, the Virginia Company relaxed its hold on the government of Virginia by establishing an assembly of elected delegates. The governor, who was appointed by the company, retained the right to veto all laws; the company's General Court in London could also disallow any decision. The Virginia Company also adopted English common law to replace the martial law under which the colony had operated.

While the revised land policy and the assembly gave settlers a greater stake in society, the adoption of tobacco assured Virginia's ultimate success. During the 1620s, tobacco drew high prices, as much as three shillings per pound. Virginia became the first North American "boom town," as settlers threw all of their energies into growing tobacco. Between 1617 and 1623, approximately 5,000 new immigrants arrived. Because the amount of the crop a planter could grow depended largely on the number of workers, those with capital eagerly paid to transport servants. The Virginia Company imported workers too, but still failed to show a profit, partly because company officials diverted many servants to their own plantations.

Africans in Early Virginia

English servants provided most of the labor in the colony until late in the seventeenth century. But Virginia planters needed as much labor as they could afford to strike it rich from tobacco, so they also purchased Africans, probably even before 1619 when a Dutch ship brought about twenty blacks. Though some Africans became servants with terms shorter than lifetime bondage, others probably were slaves. Little is known of their status during the early decades. In 1625, Africans numbered twenty-three of 1,200 Virginia colonists. Fifteen were the property of two men: Abraham Peirsey, the wealthiest man in the colony, and George Yeardley, who had served as governor. In 1660, about 900 blacks and 24,000 Europeans lived in the Chesapeake Bay area.

In contrast, by 1660, Africans outnumbered whites in Barbados, the richest of the English West Indies. Founded in 1627, Barbados quickly turned to sugar production, importing Africans to raise and process the crop. The white islanders created a harsh slave regime to prevent organized rebellion and to force the rapidly growing black population to perform hard, repetitive labor.

Until the 1660s, conditions for Africans remained less rigid in Virginia than in the West Indies. Some Virginia blacks achieved freedom, married, and a few acquired land.

For example, by the 1650s, free blacks Anthony and Mary Johnson owned a 250-acre plantation on Virginia's eastern shore and, like neighboring whites, protected their property by going to court. Even so, other Africans remained in bondage, as Virginians adopted the practice by example from the Portuguese, Spanish, and Dutch. In purchasing people from slave traders, the white colonists bought into the Atlantic slave system.

Early Virginia documents distinguished consistently between white servants and blacks, always with the suggestion that Africans were subordinate. In a 1627 will, Governor Yeardley bequeathed his "goode debts, chattels, servants, negars, cattle or any other thing" to his heirs. Censuses of the 1620s also point to the lower regard for Africans: English settlers were listed with full names while most Africans were enumerated simply with a first name or designated as "negar" or "Negro." For example, Anthony and Mary Johnson were called "Antonio a Negro" and "Mary a Negro Woman" in early records. The Virginia tax law of 1643 further demonstrated that the colonists viewed Africans as different from themselves. Everyone who worked in the field was to be taxed—all men and black women. White women apparently were not expected to tend tobacco. Virginia also excepted blacks, but not white servants, from the obligation to bear arms.

The Colony Expands

The colonists had found the way to success—by growing tobacco—but Virginia faced difficulty for many years. Because mortality remained high and settlers had few children, the population grew slowly despite immigration that averaged about 1,000 people per year. From 1619 to 1640, the population rose from 700 to about 8,000, though approximately 20,000 immigrants had arrived during that time. Young men and women who left England to become servants in Virginia gambled with their lives to obtain land, which they could not gain at home. Dysentery, typhoid fever, and malaria took their toll on new settlers who suffered a period of "seasoning" after their arrival in Virginia. Men were much more likely to migrate to the colonies than women. A 1625 census indicated that more than three-quarters of the Virginia colonists were male and less than one-fifth were children. Many people came as servants, which meant that they could not legally marry and have children for years, until their terms expired. The census also provided ample evidence of mortality and disrupted families, as many of the married couples were childless, in part because of high infant and childhood mortality. And with short life expectancy for adults, more than one-half of the colony's children had lost one parent, and one-fifth apparently had no relatives in Virginia at all.

By 1621, Opechancanough and a prophet named Nemattanew, whom the colonists called "Jack of the Feathers" because he wore clothes covered with plumes, recognized the threat of increased immigration. Now that the English had tobacco, they were not going to leave. Nemattanew inspired a nativist religious revival among the Powhatans, rejecting Christianity and European customs. Opechancanough organized a military offensive to push the English back into the sea. At the same time, he used diplomacy to convince the settlers to lower their guard. When several whites killed Nemattanew in 1622, Opechancanough rallied his troops, slaying one-fourth of the settlers before the colony could react. A ten-year war followed, in which each side tried to annihilate the other, but failed, and in 1632 agreed to peace.

Though the bankrupt Virginia Company lost its charter in 1624, immigration to the colony continued. Its economic promise helped convince the English Crown to claim it as a royal colony. Desire for new tobacco lands placed constant pressure on the Powhatans, so in 1644, Opechancanough launched another attack. After two years of war, the Powhatans submitted and Opechancanough was captured and murdered by a guard. The 1646 treaty required the Native Americans to live on lands north of the York River and, to symbolize their subordination, pay an annual tribute of twenty beaver skins. Colonists expanded rapidly north and south of the James River and to the eastern shore.

Map 2.1 Eastern North America By the mid-seventeenth century, northern European nations established colonies along the Atlantic coast from French Quebec and Montreal in the St. Lawrence Valley to the English settlements on Chesapeake Bay. Although at this date all of the colonies were relatively small, New England and the Chesapeake were expanding agricultural societies while the French, Dutch, and Swedes concentrated on trade.

Fishing, Furs, and Settlements in the North

While settlers and Native Americans struggled for Virginia, French, Dutch, and English adventurers explored and colonized the region to the north. French and English sailors had fished the Newfoundland Banks since the fifteenth century. By 1600, groups monopolized specific waters, such as the French who caught walrus in the Gulf of St. Lawrence. The beaver furs that Europeans obtained in petty trade with Native Americans became popular in Europe for making felt hats, exciting merchants in France, the Netherlands, and England to seek more permanent arrangements. All three nations claimed the northern territories as their own, ignoring of course the prior ownership of the Indians.

New France

In North America, French traders focused on furs. When a ship sent to North America in 1582 returned to France with a cargo of furs earning a 1,500 percent profit, merchants enthusiastically organized more voyages. Samuel de Champlain established the first successful French colony in the New World. Working for Pierre du Gua de Monts, who had received a charter from the king of France, in 1605 Champlain planted a temporary base at Port Royal on the Bay of Fundy in Canada. He sailed south to Cape Cod looking for a permanent site, but decided in 1608 to retain Port Royal and establish a main settlement on the St. Lawrence River. The French chose Quebec, which meant "the place where the river narrows" in Algonquian, an ideal location for controlling the Canadian interior.

For two decades, both Port Royal and Quebec remained little more than trading posts. The French had already traded with the Micmacs of the coastal region and Algonquins of the St. Lawrence Valley. Champlain strengthened these ties, and made new alliances with several groups: the Montagnais, who lived in the region north of the St. Lawrence River and like the Algonquins and Micmacs were Algonquian; and the Hurons, who were Iroquoian and lived north of Lake Ontario. This location enabled the Hurons to link French outposts with the interior, the source of the most valuable furs. In 1609, to demonstrate allegiance to his allies, Champlain helped them fight a group of Iroquois from what is now New York, thus making the Five Nations enemies of New France. He also explored the watershed of the St. Lawrence River and lands as far west as Lake Huron.

In 1627, Quebec was still essentially a trading post with about 100 French inhabitants, including a few women. Cardinal Richelieu, who for all practical purposes ruled France, organized the Company of One Hundred Associates to spur colonization. The company received a charter for territory from the Arctic Circle to Florida and from the Atlantic to the Pacific, with a monopoly on the fur trade. The company also pledged to send missionaries to the Indians and grant them the status of "natural French" when they were baptized. The priests established missions in Indian villages and learned their languages, looking for similarities between the two cultures in an effort to make the Indians part of French society.

Because the company focused on the fur trade and considered transporting settlers too expensive, in 1663 just 3,000 French settlers lived in the colony. The Crown revoked the company's charter, making New France a royal province. Nevertheless, population growth remained slow. From the beginning, the government refused to allow Protestants, who were the most likely immigrants, to settle there; it wanted to maintain control of the society through the Catholic church. Further, New France developed under feudal land tenure, in which wealthy lords received large manors, or *seigniories,* along the St. Lawrence River. Ordinary settlers on these manors became tenants rather than independent farmers. Lacking the opportunity to improve their status in the New World, French peasants were reluctant to make the dangerous transatlantic voyage.

The fur trade and small population made French relations with the Native Americans different from those of New Spain and Virginia where labor demands and white expansion put greater pressure on the Indians. The most efficient way to obtain furs was to offer desirable products from Europe, including textiles, guns, metal tools, pots, and alcohol, not to drive trading partners from the land or to exploit their labor. One French priest reported that, at least for a while, the Montagnais thought they were getting the better deal. "I heard my [Indian] host say one day, jokingly, *Missi picoutau amiscou,* 'The Beaver does everything perfectly well, it makes kettles, hatchets, swords, knives, bread; and in short, it makes everything.' He was making sport of us Europeans . . . [and said], showing me a beautiful knife, 'The English have no sense; they give us twenty knives like this for one Beaver skin.' "

Nevertheless, the French arrival had tragic effects for the Indians of Canada, who succumbed to disease in large numbers. The demand for furs altered cultural attitudes and intensified hostility among nations. In keeping with their religion, Indians had taken only what they needed from nature and little more; they generally used entire animals, the meat as well as the skins. With the fur trade, natives killed animals just for their furs and in numbers far greater than before. As a result, the balance of nature that the Native Americans had maintained was broken. They had to reach farther and farther back into the continent as they exterminated the deer, beaver, and other fur-bearing animals.

New Netherland

In the first decade of the seventeenth century, the Dutch, too, challenged the dominance of Spain in the New World. The seven northern United Provinces had declared independence from Spain in 1581 and remained at war until 1609, when they signed a twelve-year truce. With its expiration, the war resumed and continued as part of the Thirty Years' War, which ended in 1648 with the Treaty of Münster, recognizing Dutch independence.

Despite this ongoing struggle, Dutch commerce flourished. Because land was scarce and high-priced in the Netherlands, and agriculture insufficient, affluent individuals put their capital into trade. In 1602, merchants formed the United East India Company, which six years later had 160 ships around the globe. In 1609, the company sent out Henry Hudson, an Englishman, to search for the long-sought northwest passage through North America. He sailed up the river that later bore his name, trading for furs with the Native Americans. The pelts brought a good return in Holland, so the company dispatched traders who set up a post near the present site of Albany and explored Long Island Sound and the Connecticut River. In 1621, the Dutch government chartered another group, the West India Company, to establish commerce and colonies in America. Like the East India Company, it received broad powers, including the rights to make war and sign treaties. During the seventeenth century, the Dutch muscled their way to control a large part of international commerce, including the Atlantic slave trade and routes to Asia.

To provide a base for trade in the Hudson River region, in 1624 the Dutch West India Company appointed Cornelius Jacobsen May to found New Netherland; the first colonists were mostly Protestant refugees from the Spanish Netherlands. They established their primary settlement, called New Amsterdam, on Manhattan Island, and maintained trading posts at Fort Orange (near Albany), and on the Delaware and Connecticut Rivers. As in Jamestown, the first settlers were employees of the company who received no land of their own. The company paid for their transportation, tools, livestock, and two years' worth of supplies, assigning them company land on which to plant. The colonists were expected to trade only with the company. The government consisted of appointed company officers headed by a director-general, or governor, with wide powers. The colonists could not elect an assembly or any of their officials.

With good soil, the lucrative fur trade, and lumbering, the colony prospered economically, though its population grew slowly. Brewing became the second most important industry; in 1638, New Amsterdam residents complained that they were losing sleep from the singing of drunken sailors. People of many nationalities and religions arrived to take advantage of the Dutch policy of religious freedom, but few Dutch could be convinced to emigrate. In 1629, the company attempted to spur population growth by offering huge manors, called patroonships, to any member of the company who transported fifty persons to work his land. On the Hudson River, each patroonship extended for miles along one bank or both banks. Similar to New France, the settlers were tenants of the manor. This arrangement attracted few settlers: in fact it discouraged immigration because the manors tied up large tracts that might otherwise go to small farmers.

At first, New Netherland had good relations with the Indians because the colony grew slowly and depended on the fur trade. In the famous 1626 purchase, Director-general Peter Minuit exchanged goods worth about sixty guilders for Manhattan Island. Upriver, the Dutch bought furs from the Iroquois, the enemies of the Algonquians and Hurons who supplied the French, thus contributing to the devastating warfare among tribes. By the late 1640s, the Iroquois, with help from epidemics, destroyed the Hurons, a nation of about 20,000 people. At the same time, constant warfare and disease seriously debilitated the Iroquois as well.

In the region surrounding New Amsterdam, relations deteriorated between the whites and the Indians after 1638. As with the English, the Dutch and natives had different conceptions of land ownership. Although the Indians understood that they had sold rights to share the land and intended to continue using it themselves, the Dutch believed they had bought exclusive rights. Violence erupted as the settlers' cattle destroyed the Indians' corn, and dogs belonging to Native Americans attacked Dutch livestock. Beginning in 1640, the Dutch and Indians of the lower Hudson Valley fought a series of damaging wars that ended only in 1664, when the English took control of New Netherland and made peace with the Native Americans.

New England Before the Pilgrims

Along the coast of New England, relations between the Indians and English were rocky from the start. Before the Pilgrims established Plymouth in 1620, a number of expeditions explored the region, traded, and tried to colonize. In 1602, Bartholomew Gosnold and thirty-two men sailed the *Concord* to Maine and continued south to Martha's Vineyard, where they traded for furs. When they alienated the natives and one of their men was wounded, Gosnold and his crew returned to England. In 1607, the Plymouth group of the Virginia Company sent an expedition to the Kennebec River in Maine, but the colony lasted only one year. The company abandoned efforts to establish a permanent base, instead funding voyages for fish and furs. Like the Dutch and French, the English set up commercial networks with tribes who had contested land and resources before the Europeans arrived, thereby intensifying these rivalries.

Even before the founding of Plymouth, then, the natives of New England had considerable experience with the English. This contact had catastrophic effects on the Indian population. A plague epidemic brought by Europeans swept eastern New England during 1616–1618, killing thousands. Large areas along the coast were depopulated. The Massachusetts natives were initially friendly and interested in trade, but good relations proved elusive. The English shot some Native Americans and set dogs on others. A few they kidnapped, then expected them to serve as diplomats to their people. The English also made trade agreements, then failed to honor them. By the time the Pilgrims arrived in 1620, the surviving Indians along the coast had been severely weakened by disease and were understandably wary of the newcomers.

Religious Exiles from England

While the colonizers of Virginia, New France, and New Netherland had primarily economic motives, the English founders of Plymouth, Massachusetts Bay, and Maryland sought a place where they could practice their religion free from persecution and at the same time earn a decent living. Seventeenth-century England was rife with religious controversy. The government required attendance at Anglican worship and financial support of ministers. When dissenters refused to obey, holding separate services, they could be imprisoned and fined. Roman Catholics could also be stripped of their property and jailed for life if they refused to take the oath of supremacy to the king, which denied the authority of the pope. The search for freedom of worship became a major impetus for crossing the Atlantic.

English Calvinists

By 1603, when James I took the throne, two strains of English Calvinism, or Puritanism, had developed. One group included the Separatists, or Pilgrims, who founded Plymouth in 1620; the others, known as Puritans, established the Massachusetts Bay colony ten years later. Both groups charged that the Anglican church needed to be "purified" of its rituals, vestments, statues, and bishops. They rejected the church hierarchy, believing each congregation should govern itself. The Separatists started their own congregations, abandoning all hope that the church could be reformed. The Pilgrims' decision to begin a colony in America was the ultimate expression of this separatism. The Puritans, on the other hand, hoped to reform the Church of England from within. Their purpose in founding Massachusetts Bay was to develop a moral government that they hoped the people of England would someday make their own.

The Plymouth Colony

The Pilgrims were a small band who had originated in Scrooby, England, where they established a separate congregation. In 1607, when some were jailed as nonconformists, they decided to leave England for the Netherlands, which offered freedom of worship. The Pilgrims settled in Leyden, but were unhappy there, so made an agreement with a group of London merchants who obtained a patent for land from the Virginia Company. In exchange for funding to go to America, the Pilgrims promised to send back fish, furs, and lumber for seven years.

Thirty-five of the Leyden congregation chose to emigrate. Sailing first to England, they joined sixty-seven others, of whom many were not Separatists. In September 1620, the *Mayflower* departed Plymouth, England, crowded with 102 passengers, about twenty crew members, and assorted pigs, chickens, and goats. Headed for Virginia, the ship reached Cape Cod on November 9th. In shallow waters, fearing shipwreck, the exhausted travelers built their colony at Plymouth, even though they were outside the jurisdiction of the Virginia Company. They now lacked a legal basis for governing themselves or for claiming land. The first problem was most urgent because some of the colonists questioned the authority of the Pilgrim leaders. The group avoided a revolt by drafting and signing the "Mayflower Compact," a social compact by which they agreed to form a government and obey its laws. The London merchants eventually solved the second problem by obtaining title to the land.

Plymouth's first years were difficult, though the settlers found unused supplies of corn left by Indians struck recently by epidemic disease, and chose the site of a deserted Patuxet village with relatively clear fields. Over the first winter they built houses, but one-half of the colonists died of illness and exposure to the cold. In the spring of 1621, they planted corn with the help of Squanto, perhaps the lone surviving Patuxet, and other crops. Squanto and neighboring Pokanokets helped the Plymouth colony despite earlier problems with Englishmen. In 1614, Squanto and about twenty other Patuxets had been kidnapped by an English sea captain, who intended to sell them as slaves in Spain. Saved from bondage by Spanish priests, Squanto made his way to England, where he learned the language, then to Newfoundland, and finally back to Patuxet in 1619. There he found unburied bodies of many of his people who had perished in the epidemic. One Englishman described the scene: "[T]heir bones and skulls made such a spectacle . . . . it seemed to me a new found Golgotha."

At harvest in 1621, the Indians and colonists celebrated together for three days. Soon after their feast, the ship *Fortune* arrived with thirty-five new settlers, for whom no food was available until the next year's crop. When the colonists filled the *Fortune* with furs and lumber in hopes of starting to repay their debt to the London merchants, the French captured the ship.

By 1623, though, the Plymouth colony was well established and growing, as new immigrants arrived. The community solved the problem of food supply by assigning individual plots to families. Still, the hardworking colonists had trouble fulfilling their bargain with the merchants. During a trading voyage, the crew mutinied. On one fishing trip, the ship sank; when it was raised and sent out again, the Spanish captured it. The London merchants gave up and in 1626 agreed to sell the land to the colonists for a large sum, which they paid by 1645, receiving a patent of ownership. Although Plymouth's economic fortunes improved, the colony remained small and self-consciously separate from the larger group of English dissenters who streamed into New England.

Massachusetts Bay

The Puritan migration to Massachusetts Bay was much larger and more tightly organized than the Plymouth settlement. During 1630, the first year, 700 women, men, and children arrived in eleven ships. Though at least 200 died during the first winter, the colony grew quickly as about 12,000 people went to Massachusetts during the 1630s. From King Charles I, the Massachusetts Bay Company obtained a charter specifying its government and the colony's boundaries. When most of the company officials emigrated, taking the charter with them, they greatly enhanced the colony's independence from the Crown and the Anglican church.

Thus the Massachusetts Bay colonists did not answer to London merchants who expected handsome profits. The Puritans themselves financed colonization; they included wealthy investors as well as many middling families who could pay their own way. As a result, the founders devoted much of their energy to creating a model society. In the words of leader John Winthrop, the colony would be "as a Citty upon a Hill, the Eyes of all people are uppon us; soe that if wee shall deale falsely with our god in this worke wee have undertaken and soe cause him to withdrawe this present help from us, wee shall be made a story and a by-word through the world." The Puritans believed that in addition to their charter from the king they had a covenant with God that bound them to create a moral community. As Calvinists, they held that individuals were saved from eternal damnation by faith, rather than by good works. Men and women could seek to avoid sin and work hard throughout their lives, but unless they were among God's chosen, or the "elect," they would go to hell. Under the covenant, the elect were responsible for the behavior of unsaved members of their community. The Puritan leaders were responsible to God. They thought that if they maintained a moral society, the Lord would help it prosper.

In Massachusetts, the Puritans restructured the company government to create their version of a godly commonwealth. According to the Massachusetts Bay charter, the company officials included a governor, deputy governor, and executive board of eighteen "assistants," to be elected by "freemen" (stockholders) who would meet in a general assembly, called the General Court. These officers could make laws and regulations, appoint lower officials, grant lands, and punish lawbreakers. The colony's leaders changed the rules to allow all male church members (the male elect), not just stockholders in the company, to become freemen. In theory, every freeman would be a member of the General Court, or colonial legislature. But as the population grew and towns formed quickly, freemen voted in town meetings for representatives to the assembly.

With the governor and assistants, the General Court drew up a law code for the colony, which after several revisions was published as the *Laws and Liberties of Massachusetts* (1648). The code was a combination of biblical law, English common law, and statutes tailored specifically to colonial needs. It protected the liberties of individuals by upholding trial by jury and due process of law, including the rights of the accused to a prompt public trial and to call witnesses. It also prohibited feudal tenure of lands and outlawed slavery, "unlesse it be lawfull captives, taken in just warrs, and such strangers as willingly sell themselves or are solde to us." This provision limited the possibility that whites would be enslaved, but had little effect on black bondage. The *Laws and Liberties* prescribed the death penalty for fewer crimes than in England, but included as capital offenses blasphemy and adultery (in cases where the woman was married), which under the English common law were lesser crimes. Children could be put to death for failing to respect their parents, while fornicators were required to marry and be whipped or fined. The code enabled judges to extend the terms of negligent servants and send back to England any married persons who arrived in Massachusetts without their spouses. Although these terms may seem harsh, the colony did not actually impose the death penalty for blasphemy or abuse of parents by children, and executed only two people for adultery. The magistrates evidently wanted to instill fear in the hearts of potential offenders rather than to exact harsh punishments.

The Puritans attempted to create a theocracy, a government operated according to God's will, as determined by the colony's leaders. The Puritan government was composed of members of the elect; ministers advised the magistrates but could not serve officially. The government required all inhabitants to attend Puritan churches. Persons who disagreed with orthodox doctrines could be expelled, whipped, fined, and even executed. The church was the center of each town, with all property owners paying taxes for its support. Though the Puritans had suffered persecution for their beliefs in England, they refused to allow freedom of worship in Massachusetts. Instead, they replaced one established church for another.

New England Society

Unlike the Jamestown settlers, a large proportion of Puritan immigrants came in families. Many originated from Norfolk, Suffolk, and Essex (together called East Anglia). Located directly across the North Sea from the Netherlands, East Anglia was the center of both the wool trade and Puritanism. By 1630, its residents had kept contact with European Calvinists for almost a century; entire congregations, ostensibly part of the Church of England, adopted Puritan ways. For decades they had worshipped freely, protected by the local Puritan gentry. Then during the 1620s and 1630s, the Puritans faced a series of hardships, including a depressed market for woolen cloth, poor harvests, and bubonic plague. Charles I and the Anglican church hierarchy, notably Archbishop William Laud, enforced laws against nonconformists, removing Puritan ministers from their pulpits. Many families migrated to Massachusetts, where they could make a new start under a congenial government. Some entire communities accompanied their minister.

In Massachusetts, the migrants created towns that often resembled the ones they had left. When a group arrived, its leaders petitioned the General Court for a place to settle and permission to establish a church and town government. The town meeting elected a board of selectmen who administered town business, including road building, maintenance of schools, and law enforcement. The town meeting also divided the town lands. The amount of land a family received depended upon its wealth and social status. Typically, a town followed one of two patterns of land distribution according to the kind of land tenure its founders knew in England. Emigrants from East Anglia generally chose the *closed field* system, in which families received individual farms, with house lot and land for planting, grazing livestock, and cutting lumber. These settlers also created commercial towns. In contrast, emigrants from Yorkshire, in northern England, chose the *open field* system, designating town lands for different purposes—house lots lined up in compact rows, fields, meadows, and wood lots. In Rowley, Massachusetts, for example, families received strips in the fields, where they grew crops in cooperation with their neighbors. Together they made many decisions, including which fields to plant and which to leave fallow. Families also received "stinting rights," or permission to pasture animals on common lands. The number of cattle and sheep a family could pasture depended upon the size of their lands.

Worcester Art Museum, Worcester, Massachusetts, Gift of Mr. & Mrs. Albert W. Rice

Mrs. Elizabeth Freake and Baby Mary, painted c. 1674 by an unknown artist, illustrates one of the many roles of seventeenth-century women, that of mother. The wife and child of a successful merchant, their clothing depicts the family's wealth.

The Puritan notion of an ideal community defined the ways in which the Puritans acted toward one another and toward outsiders. If the model society were to succeed, everyone had to have a place in the family, church, and commonwealth. Like other English, the Puritans kept a hierarchical social order. In the family, the husband was superior to the wife, but together they ruled the children and servants. In the church, the minister and elders dominated the congregation. In the commonwealth, the officials led the people. Ideally, this hierarchy required little coercion, when people saw themselves as part of the community and worked for the common good, or "weal" (hence "commonwealth"), rather than for their own benefit. They understood that all humans were equal spiritually but accepted social inequality as the will of God.

Most Puritan women accepted a subordinate place in their society without complaint. They viewed themselves as part of a community and a family, with duties determined by their sex and age, not as individuals with equal rights. Women raised children; kept the house and garden; preserved fruits and vegetables; made beer, cider, cheese, and butter; tended livestock and poultry; spun and wove cloth; sewed clothing; cared for the sick; and supervised the training of daughters and servants. Women often specialized in certain trades, such as spinning, weaving, poultry raising, or medicine; they conducted trade among themselves, separate from the commercial networks of their husbands. Men had responsibility for raising grain such as wheat, Indian corn, and rye; cutting firewood; and maintaining the fences, buildings, and fields. In addition to farming, many followed a trade or profession such as fishing, carpentry, shopkeeping, overseas trade, medicine, or the ministry. Only men could vote in church and town meetings, serve as government officials, or become ministers. Only when a man became incapacitated, or was away from home, was his wife expected to take his place at work or to represent the family in legal matters or disputes. She temporarily assumed the role of "deputy husband," then yielded it when he became well or returned. Puritans recognized women's ability in public matters, but expected them normally to confine themselves to accepted women's tasks.

The role of Puritan women in the church was indicative of their place in society. On the one hand, women were the spiritual equals of men and held responsibility for the religious education of their children. On the other hand, the Puritans emphasized the inheritance of Eve, who they believed led Adam to sin in the Garden of Eden. Women were expected to keep quiet in the church. They could not preach or vote on church business, though they could exert informal influence on their husbands. The Puritans, like other Christians of the time, embraced Saint Paul's instruction to the Corinthians: "Let your women keep silence in the Churches. . . . And if they will learn anything, let them ask their husbands at home." The Puritans believed that by nature women were morally and intellectually weak. The pain of childbirth was God's punishment of all women for Eve's seduction of Adam. Although a few rebelled against the injunction to keep quiet, most Puritan women and girls accepted their subordination to men.

In this patriarchal society, children deferred to their fathers, assuming a subservient role until they were able to establish households of their own. Though some New England colonists held servants and a few owned enslaved Africans, sons and daughters comprised the majority of the workforce. Families on average had five children who reached adulthood. They worked for their parents until marriage—longer in the case of sons who inherited the family farm. Unlike seventeenth-century Virginia, living conditions in Massachusetts promoted patriarchy, for life expectancy was long. Persons who survived childhood diseases often lived past age sixty or even seventy. Thus, eldest sons could be middle-aged before their fathers died and willed them control of the family homestead. On the other hand, younger sons who had little hope of receiving the farm often moved away from their parents, settling in the new towns that developed throughout New England. Parents usually attempted to give all of their children a start in life, with a farm, apprenticeship, money, or college tuition to sons, and personal property or cash to daughters.

Connecticut and New Haven

An early destination for emigrants looking for good land was Connecticut. The first Puritans went there to trade with Native Americans, but when news of attractive land in the Connecticut Valley arrived in Massachusetts, many settlers decided to move. The Earl of Warwick owned the rights to the land at the mouth of the Connecticut River, which he ceded to a group of Puritan noblemen. To build a trading post and settlement they sent John Winthrop, Jr., who convinced Thomas Hooker, the minister of Newtown, Massa-

Pequot War Diagram

This engraving of the attack on the Pequots at Mystic River in 1637 by the English and Narragansetts was published in Captain John Underhill's *News from America* (1638). According to labels on the entrances to the palisade, Underhill's troops entered the Pequot town on one side while Captain John Mason's soldiers entered on the other. The engraver shows English warriors shooting inhabitants, some of them unarmed, between rows of houses. Outside the palisade are rings of soldiers with muskets and Narragansetts with bows and arrows.

The English killed the Pequots and burned the town to the ground. The Narragansetts, who had nearly ended their long-standing conflict with the Pequots before the attack, were shocked by the slaughter. According to Underhill, the Narragansetts were pleased with the conquest but cried "mach it, mach it; that is, it is naught, it is naught, because it is too furious, and slaies too many men."

The Granger Collection

chusetts, to lead some of his congregation there. With another group that left from Dorchester, they founded Connecticut in 1636. Lacking a charter from the king, the founders agreed upon the *Fundamental Orders of Connecticut,* which created a General Assembly of representatives from each town. In most respects, the Connecticut government resembled that of Massachusetts, with the exception that freemen, or voters, did not have to be church members. The assembly elected a governor, who could serve only one year at a time, and a group of magistrates who functioned as the upper house of the assembly. As in Massachusetts, Puritanism was the only recognized religion and received tax support.

As white settlement expanded, relations between the Puritans and Native Americans deteriorated. Like other English, the Puritans believed that the Indians worshipped the devil and had barbarous customs. The settlers justified expropriation of native lands on the basis of *vacuum domicilium*. Even more, the Puritans considered the Indians "strangers," who could have no role in building the model society. They were dispensable and dangerous, presenting a dual threat because their customs could corrupt the holy commonwealth and they resented their loss of lands.

The 1637 war against the Pequots of eastern Connecticut showed the lengths to which the New England settlers could go. The Pequots, a powerful tribe, attempted to unite New England Indians against the English. In May 1637, troops from Massachusetts and Connecticut, with their Indian allies, the Narragansetts, attacked a Pequot village on the Mystic River before dawn, killing hundreds of sleeping women, children, and old men. The Pequots who escaped this massacre, mostly young men absent from the town, were later executed or enslaved. The Treaty of Hartford (1638) declared their nation dissolved.

Shortly after the Pequot War, in 1638, a group of staunch Puritans established New Haven, on the Long Island Sound west of the Connecticut colony. Persecuted in England, Reverend John Davenport took his flock first to Boston, but decided to move on. They had no charter for New Haven, so the freemen made the Bible their law, eliminating trial by jury, for example, because it had no scriptural basis. Only male church members could vote. The colony grew as the settlers built towns farther west along the sound and on Long Island. Together, the towns agreed upon a government comprised of a governor, magistrates, and a representative assembly.

Exiles to Rhode Island

The founding of Rhode Island resulted from another kind of emigration from Massachusetts, that of people who refused to submit to the Puritan magistrates. The first was Roger Williams, a likeable but stubborn, independent-minded minister who challenged Massachusetts Bay's policy toward the Indians and its theocratic laws. Williams had studied divinity at Cambridge University, where he became a vocal Separatist. He immigrated to Massachusetts Bay in 1631, arousing the colony when he refused the pulpit in Boston's church because its members had not renounced the Church of England.

Williams then accused Massachusetts of holding fraudulent title to its territory because the king had no authority to give away Indian lands. The colony should send the charter back to the king for correction; the settlers should return to England if they could not obtain rights from the true owners of the land. Williams raised a troublesome issue that the Puritan officials refused to recognize, so they ordered him to be still. He would not be quiet, soon broaching the issues of religious freedom and separation of church and state. "Forced worship stinks in God's nostrils," he proclaimed. "There is no other prudent,

Christian way of preserving peace in the world, but by permission of differing consciences." He attacked the laws requiring church attendance and tax support of Puritan churches. Williams feared that government would pollute the church, not that giving legal preference to one religion was unfair. He opposed laws regulating religion to protect the church from state interference.

The General Court banished Williams from Massachusetts for challenging the government; in 1636 he went to Narragansett Bay. There he purchased land from the Narragansett Indians, establishing Providence Plantation at the Great Salt River. With the sympathizers who joined him, he created a society based on religious toleration, separation of church and state, and participation in government by all male property owners. Williams welcomed people of all religions to Providence Plantation, as long as they accepted the right of others to worship freely. Williams himself became wealthy through trade with the Native Americans and the Dutch. In 1638, he transferred ownership of Providence to a group of thirteen associates, of whom he was one.

Another exile from Massachusetts was Anne Hutchinson, a midwife and nurse, who in 1634 arrived in Boston with her husband, merchant William Hutchinson, and children. As Hutchinson assisted women in childbirth and sickness, she became convinced that Bostonians placed too much emphasis on good works and not enough on faith. She was a follower of one of Boston's ministers, the influential John Cotton, who stressed the importance of the individual's relationship with God over the obligation to obey laws. Hutchinson went further than Cotton, nearly saying that if a person were saved it did not matter how she or he behaved, a belief known as the Antinomian heresy.

To the orthodox Puritan faction led by Governor John Winthrop, Hutchinson was a threat for several reasons. She emphasized individual judgment over communal authority, thus questioning the rule of colonial leaders. She told the Puritan patriarchs that God spoke to her directly, that she did not need the assistance of magistrates and ministers in interpreting God's will. Further, Hutchinson went outside the accepted role of women by taking a public stand on religion. But most seriously, she became the standard bearer for a group who contested power with the Winthrop faction. In 1637, Winthrop's government put Hutchinson on trial for defaming ministers and exiled her from the colony. With her family and supporters she founded a colony at Portsmouth on Narragansett Bay.

Following the settlement of Williams and Hutchinson on Narragansett Bay, several other dissenters established colonies there. William Coddington, a supporter of Hutchinson, started the town of Newport; and Samuel Gorton founded Warwick. The four leaders had trouble cooperating, but knew they needed a charter from the English government to avoid annexation by Massachusetts. Roger Williams went to England for that purpose during the Civil War. The 1644 Rhode Island charter, which Parliament granted, united the four settlements under one representative assembly, which could pass statutes consistent with the laws of England. The Rhode Island colonists based their government on Williams's principles of freedom of worship, separation of church and state, and wide participation in government.

The Proprietary Colony of Maryland

In 1632, Charles I granted a charter for Maryland to George Calvert, the first Lord Baltimore, who had served in high office until he converted to Catholicism. Forced to resign, but still a royal favorite, Calvert requested a grant in America to build a haven for Catholics. He also expected to support his family by selling the land. He died before actually obtaining the charter, so his son, Cecilius Calvert, the second Lord Baltimore, became lord proprietor of Maryland. The colony was carved out of the northern part of Virginia. Calvert received ownership of the soil and was sovereign in government, subject only to the king.

Calvert spent £40,000 for two ships, the *Ark* and the *Dove,* with supplies to send the first settlers, who arrived in Maryland in 1634. The proprietor planned a feudal system in which manorial lords received large tracts depending on the number of tenants they transported. For example, a person who brought five laborers to Maryland at a total cost of £20 received a manor of 2,000 acres.

Though Maryland settlers suffered no "starving time" as in Virginia and had a cash crop in tobacco, the colony grew slowly. Mortality was high and immigration sluggish. By 1642, Calvert had granted rights for only sixteen manors, mostly to wealthy Catholic friends. To improve his income, Calvert distributed farms to more ordinary immigrants, who had to pay annual quitrents. Over the seventeenth century, rich investors acquired sixty manors but by far most settlers were small landowners.

The extension of land ownership beyond Calvert's circle of loyal supporters created problems for the lord proprietor. Under the charter, he was obligated to call together an assembly of freemen, or landowners, to enact laws. Calvert interpreted this to mean that they should approve legislation he prepared, while the freemen, meeting first in 1635, claimed the right to draft the code of laws. Calvert refused to accept their draft, so for three years the colony operated without a code. In 1638, they reached a compromise, with the proprietor and assembly each drafting some of the bills. The colony finally had a legal basis for governing and punishing crime.

But the struggle for power between the proprietor and freemen continued. The ordinary planters, who formed the majority of freemen and were mostly Protestant, resented the power of the Catholic elite and had little sympathy for Calvert's vision of a society in which all Christians could worship freely. Religious and political strife became most acute in Maryland during the English Civil War and the Puritan Commonwealth, from 1642 to 1660.

The Impact of the English Civil War

For two decades, the English Civil War altered the political situation in England. The war resulted from a contest for power between Parliament and Charles I. Charles imprisoned opponents without due process, and launched a crusade to force all his subjects, even those in Presbyterian Scotland and Catholic Ireland, to conform to the Anglican church. In 1642, war broke out between the "Cavaliers," or royalists, and the "Roundheads," or parliamentary forces, of whom many were Puritans. Oliver Cromwell led the Roundheads to victory in 1648; the following year they beheaded the king.

The revolutionaries attempted to rule through an elected Parliament, but conflicting factions of Puritans and radical sects undermined their plans. Some radical theorists wanted an entire restructuring of society—in the words of one contemporary, "a world turned upside down." They called for extension of the vote to all men and redistribution of land. The gentry and wealthy merchants who had led Parliament to victory utterly rejected these ideas. In 1653 they named Cromwell the Lord Protector of the Commonwealth of England, Scotland, and Ireland. He ruled alone, backed by the army, until his death in 1658. An attempt failed to make his son Richard the successor, and two years later, the monarchy was restored. The accession of Charles II did not mean a complete reversal to the time of his father. The king confirmed Parliament's right to approve taxes and abolished the royal courts that had punished opponents of the Crown. But the Restoration brought the Cavaliers back into power, making the Anglican church the state religion once again.

The struggle for power during the Civil War and its aftermath had repercussions in the colonies. Initially, the rebellion of English Puritans against the king raised hopes among New Englanders that English society would be reformed. Of more practical importance to the colonies was the lack of military protection from England. Plymouth, Massachusetts, Connecticut, and New Haven counted among their enemies the French, Dutch, Native Americans, and Rhode Island. In 1643, they formed the New England Confederation, agreeing to share the cost of war, provide soldiers in proportion to population, and make no treaties without each colony's consent. The New England Confederation was the first league of colonies in English North America and the only successful one before the Revolutionary War. In assuming power to conduct war and make treaties, it went beyond colonial rights. The English government, in the midst of Civil War, was too preoccupied to react.

In the Chesapeake colonies, the Civil War and its aftermath were more disruptive. In 1652, the English Commonwealth removed the royalist Virginia governor, William Berkeley, because he had proclaimed Charles II the king upon his father's execution. In Maryland, the parliamentary revolt weakened the position of Lord Baltimore, whose authority came directly from the king. Protestants, especially Puritans, constituted an antiproprietary force. Ironically, the proprietor had encouraged Puritans to migrate from Virginia, where they had suffered Governor Berkeley's persecution. Calvert had approved the "Act Concerning Religion" (1649), which guaranteed freedom of religion to all Christians. Nevertheless, in 1654, the Maryland Puritans established a commonwealth. Their assembly deposed the proprietor's government, restricted the right of Catholics to worship, and created a Puritan code of behavior, including laws against swearing, drunkenness, and breaking the Sabbath. Calvert appealed to Oliver Cromwell, who confirmed his proprietorship, but Lord Baltimore regained control of the colony only in 1657, after a period of local civil war.

English Colonization After 1660

The accession of Charles II in 1660 initiated a new phase of colonization, in which the English government paid more attention to its colonies than it had before the Civil War. In 1662, the Crown granted Connecticut a charter, and the following year confirmed the charter

Rhode Island had received from Parliament. To tighten colonial administration, the king and Parliament approved a series of navigation acts that formed the basis of a mercantilist colonial policy.

Navigation Acts

The English Commonwealth, recognizing the growing economic value of the colonies, had passed the Navigation Act of 1651. The law required that goods brought to England or its colonies from Asia, Africa, or America be carried on English ships (including those of English colonies). Goods from European nations had to be transported on either English ships or those of the country of origin. The chief purposes of the act were to encourage growth of England's merchant marine and to challenge Dutch ascendancy on the seas and in colonial ports. The Commonwealth went further in 1652–1654, with the first Anglo-Dutch War, by attacking Dutch vessels in the English Channel and North Sea.

The Navigation Acts of 1660, 1663, and 1673 confirmed the 1651 restrictions on transport and created a list of "enumerated articles"—major colonial products including tobacco, sugar, indigo, cotton, ginger, and dyewoods—that could be shipped only to England or another English colony. The colonists could not sell these goods directly to other nations. The "articles" first went to England, where they were taxed and reexported by English merchants, who benefited from the business. Conversely, with some exceptions, goods shipped from other nations to the English colonies had to go to England first. The colonists considered these laws detrimental because English middlemen added charges to products going in both directions. The English government created a colonial administration to enforce the acts, but the results were complicated and inefficient. Colonial governors lacked the resources (and in many cases the will) to eliminate smuggling.

Carolina

Charles II was penniless when he ascended the throne and owed substantial debts to his supporters. Expansion of the colonial empire permitted him to repay these creditors and at the same time advance England's commerce and national power. Carolina was the first post-Restoration colony on the North American mainland. In 1663, the area between Virginia and Spanish Florida was unoccupied by Europeans, but Spain had better title to the land than England had. With the Treaty of Madrid (1670), the English obtained Spain's concession of lands north of present-day Charleston. The chief promoters of Carolina were Anthony Ashley Cooper, Governor William Berkeley of Virginia, and John Colleton, a West Indies planter. They obtained help from five men who were close to the king; together the eight associates became proprietors of Carolina. They obtained a charter like Maryland's and received wide latitude in matters of religion. They drew up the "Fundamental Constitutions of Carolina," creating a complicated feudal society with nobles and lords, a scheme the ordinary settlers of Carolina refused to accept.

Two colonies developed in Carolina. Small planters from Virginia built the first, which later became North Carolina. As early as 1653, people had settled on the shores of Albemarle Sound, where they raised tobacco, corn, and livestock. In 1664, Berkeley sent William Drummond to organize a council and assembly. The Albemarle settlement remained poor, a haven for pirates, and difficult to govern. In 1691, the Carolina proprietors effectively established North Carolina by appointing a separate governor.

The second Carolina colony was located at Charles Town, in the future South Carolina. After two unsuccessful attempts, Anthony Ashley Cooper in 1670 organized a permanent settlement. Many of its early settlers came from the West Indies island of Barbados, which had run out of vacant land. The Barbadian planters had money to develop plantations in Carolina and owned African slaves to do the work. The proprietors offered generous acreages to household heads for each person brought to the colony. A planter, with his own family and several enslaved blacks, could qualify for hundreds of acres. From the colony's founding, a large proportion of South Carolinians were African slaves. They produced food, livestock, firewood, and barrel staves for Barbados.

New York and New Jersey

To control eastern North America, the English next had to seize New Netherland. With a series of outposts, the Dutch held the region between Connecticut and Maryland, including lands on the Delaware River that Sweden had settled in 1638 and the Dutch captured in 1655. The English justified their attack in 1664 against New Netherland on several grounds, including John Cabot's 1497 voyage to the region and Dutch illegal trade with English colonies. Settlers from New England living under Dutch jurisdiction reported that Dutch military defenses were weak. James, the duke of York, Lord High Admiral of the Navy, urged his brother, Charles II, to send a fleet. The king granted James a proprietary charter for lands between the Connecticut and Delaware Rivers, as well as Long Island, Nantucket, Martha's Vineyard, and part of present-day Maine. The charter gave the duke wide governmental powers, even dispensing with an assembly. The duke could write his own legal code as long as it conformed to the laws of England.

With charter in hand, James quickly forced out the Dutch. In 1664, his deputy governor, Richard Nicolls, took New Amsterdam without a fight. The second Anglo-Dutch War (1665–1667) in part resulted from this action. Assuming ownership, James called his colony New York, but granted the land between the Delaware and lower Hudson Rivers to John Lord Berkeley and Sir George Carteret, who named the area New Jersey.

Despite his extensive powers, James realized that he had to make New York attractive to inhabitants if his colony was to prosper. He gave residents the choice of keeping their Dutch citizenship or becoming naturalized as English subjects. In 1665, he issued a legal code, called the "Duke's Laws," which guaranteed freedom of religion, recognized preexisting titles to land, and allowed New Englanders living in towns on Long Island to choose selectmen. The New York government consisted of a governor and council appointed by the duke, but no legislature.

When England and the Netherlands continued their rivalry in the third Anglo-Dutch War (1672–1674), the Dutch easily recaptured New York. After sixteen months they

New Amsterdam in 1643

This view of New Amsterdam suggests a bustling trading port with two successful Dutch inhabitants. Note at the bottom, behind the woman, four African laborers. The illustration reflects both the economic focus and ethnic diversity of New Netherland. The colony welcomed immigrants from many European countries, including France, Germany, and Sweden. Despite official recognition of the established Dutch Reformed Church, people of other religions, including Jews, Quakers, Lutherans, and Puritans, could practice their beliefs.

The West India Company imported enslaved Africans into New Netherland to provide much needed labor. By the English takeover in 1664, about 500 slaves lived in the colony, the majority in New Amsterdam. The WIC, which owned many of the Africans, began a policy of offering land and freedom to some individuals. Some others received a status of "half-freedom" in which they owned independent farms but had to provide waged labor to the company when needed. In 1664, about seventy-five free blacks lived in the city.

Rare Books Division, The New York Public Library, Astor, Lenox and Tilden Foundations

returned the colony to England as part of the Treaty of Westminster (1674). Receiving a new charter, James resumed possession of New York and reconfirmed his grants to New Jersey. The territory had by then been divided into two colonies, West New Jersey and East New Jersey. Berkeley had sold West New Jersey to a Quaker, Edward Byllinge, who then transferred title to a group of coreligionists, including William Penn. The duke confirmed Carteret's right to East New Jersey immediately, but waited until 1680 to approve the Quaker proprietorship of West New Jersey.

Conclusion

During the first three-quarters of the seventeenth century, the English, French, and Dutch ended Spain's mastery of the New World. By 1675, the English held colonies along the Atlantic coast from New England to the Carolinas. The French controlled Canada and had explored the Great Lakes and the upper Mississippi Valley. The Dutch established, but lost, New Netherland. Spain retained its borderland outposts in New Mexico and Florida. Everywhere the Europeans colonized, the Indians died from epidemic disease. Their relations with the white invaders depended a great deal on the numbers of Europeans who arrived, their attitudes, and goals of settlement.

From the beginning, the English colonies were diverse—in their form of government, degree of stability, relations with Native Americans, and economic base. The Crown fostered this variety by granting charters to an assortment of companies and individuals, including Puritan and Catholic opponents of the established church. Virginia and Maryland prospered from tobacco, but battled persistent high mortality. Still, in the mid-seventeenth century, the Chesapeake was "the best poor man's country" for English people willing to take risks. Most New Englanders came primarily to start a model society based on their Calvinist beliefs. They enjoyed a healthier climate than the people of the Chesapeake, but inferior soil. They supported themselves modestly by fishing and mixed farming, developing trade with the West Indies to pay for English imports. In New Mexico, Hispanic colonists exploited the Pueblos' labor to support their trade with Mexico, while Catholic missionaries tried to claim the Indians's souls. In all three areas—New England, the Chesapeake, and New Mexico—pressures between Europeans and Native Americans, and within the colonial societies, would soon erupt in war.

RECOMMENDED READINGS

Anderson, Virginia D. *New England's Generation: The Great Migration and the Formation of Society and Culture in the Seventeenth Century.* (1991). Compares the motivations and experiences of Puritan settlers with succeeding generations.

Berlin, Ira. *Many Thousands Gone: The First Two Centuries of Slavery in North America* (1998). An important synthesis of stages in the rise of slavery in the British colonies and Louisiana.

Cronon, William. *Changes in the Land: Indians, Colonists, and the Ecology of New England* (1983). Contrasts Native American and settler use of the environment.

Dunn, Richard S. *Sugar and Slaves: The Rise of the Planter Class in the English West Indies, 1624–1713* (1972). An insightful history of the creation of slave regimes in the English Caribbean.

Greene, Jack P. *Pursuits of Happiness: The Social Development of Early Modern British Colonies and the Formation of American Culture* (1988). Provides a useful framework for understanding the various ways in which British settlements evolved.

Gutiérrez, Ramón A. *When Jesus Came, the Corn Mothers Went Away: Marriage, Sexuality, and Power in New Mexico, 1500–1846* (1991). Provocative evaluation of Spanish settlement, focusing particularly on women's status.

Kupperman, Karen Ordahl. *Indians and English: Facing Off in Early America* (2000). A perceptive analysis of the complexity of Native-European encounters during the early seventeenth century.

Mancall, Peter C. and Merrell, James H., eds. *American Encounters: Natives and Newcomers from European Contact to Indian Removal, 1500–1850* (2000). A collection of path-breaking articles.

Morgan, Edmund S. *American Slavery, American Freedom: The Ordeal of Colonial Virginia* (1975). A detailed, stimulating account of English settlement and the transition to slavery.

Ulrich, Laurel Thatcher. *Good Wives: Image and Reality in the Lives of Women in Northern New England, 1650–1750* (1982). A thoughtful study of the various roles of colonial women.

Additional resources, exercises, and Internet links related to this chapter are available on the American Passages Web site: http://history.wadsworth.com/ayerscompact2/

Crisis and Change
1675–1720

In February 1676, Narragansett Indians burned Lancaster, Massachusetts, killing many of the English settlers and taking others prisoner, including Mary White Rowlandson, a minister's wife, and her three children. The Narragansetts had joined the Wampanoags and other New England Algonquians to destroy the European settlements. Their leader was the Wampanoag sachem, Metacom, called King Philip by the colonists. In the Indians' words, according to Rowlandson, "they would knock all the Rogues in the head, or drive them into the Sea, or make them flie the Country."

Though Rowlandson began her captivity with hatred toward the Indians, whom she called "Barbarous Creatures," she came to respect some as individuals and to appreciate aspects of their culture. She was most impressed, she said, that while the Algonquians had little corn, "I did not see (all the time I was among them) one Man, or Woman, or Child, die with Hunger." They ate "Ground-nuts . . . also Nuts and Acorns, Hartychoaks, Lilly-roots, Ground-beans, and several other weeds and roots that I know not." Desperately hungry, Rowlandson ate unfamiliar foods too, surviving to rejoin her husband in Boston.

King Philip's War, as the English settlers called it, was just one of the crises that afflicted colonial America in the last quarter of the seventeenth century. In Virginia, a comparatively minor skirmish between Indians and whites escalated into Bacon's Rebellion, a civil war among the English settlers. In New Mexico, the Pueblos expelled the Spanish for thirteen years. Following closely upon King Philip's War and Bacon's Rebellion, William Penn intended to avoid conflict with the Indians in founding Pennsylvania. An unstable English government disrupted politics in the colonies when James II, a Roman Catholic, succeeded his brother King Charles II in 1685. James's attempt to make sweeping changes in both the home and colonial governments met strong resistance. The Glorious Revolution quickly ended his reign. In 1689, settlers in Massachusetts, New York, and Maryland overthrew his provincial governments, declaring allegiance to the new king and queen, William and Mary. In Massachusetts, the impact of years of political uncertainty helped spread witchcraft hysteria from Salem to other towns.

CHRONOLOGY

1675	Appointment of English Lords of Trade
1675–1676	King Philip's War • Bacon's Rebellion
1678	Charles II demands renegotiation of Massachusetts charter
1680	Popé's Rebellion
1681	William Penn receives Pennsylvania charter
1682	La Salle claims the Mississippi Valley for France
1683	Iroquois of New York defeat New France
1684	Revocation of Massachusetts charter
1685	James II becomes king of England • Dominion of New England created
1688–1689	Glorious Revolution in England • William and Mary ascend throne
1689	Revolutions in Massachusetts, New York, and Maryland
1689–1697	King William's War
1690	Spanish settlements in Texas
1691	Massachusetts receives its new charter
1691–1692	Salem witchcraft hysteria
1693	Spanish regain control of New Mexico
1696	Board of Trade and Plantations replaces Lords of Trade
1698	Royal African Company loses slave trade monopoly
1699	French establish Louisiana
1701	Iroquois treaty of neutrality
1702–1713	Queen Anne's War
1704	South Carolina defeats Spanish Florida
1712	Slave revolt in New York City
1715	Calverts regain Maryland government • Yamassee War in South Carolina

From 1689 to 1713, European wars spilled into North America, fueling hostilities in Florida and Canada among Native Americans, English, French, and Spanish. The French moved south through the Mississippi Valley and founded Louisiana, while the English pushed south into Florida, west across the Appalachian Mountains, and north into Maine. As the English colonies expanded and matured, their economies and labor systems diverged, particularly with the entrenchment of slavery. Despite revolutions and wars, planters built successful staple crop economies in the southern colonies, while northerners profited from networks of trade with England, Europe, and the West Indies.

Rebellions and War

The wars of 1675 to 1680 in New England, Virginia, and New Mexico resulted from pressures that had been building for decades. In Massachusetts, the spread of settlement forced Native Americans to defend their homes. In Virginia, demands of ex-servants for good land precipitated a civil war, while in New Mexico, severe droughts deepened opposition to forced labor, impelling the Pueblos to rid themselves of Spanish overlords. After the upheavals, elites in each settlement made changes that avoided further serious revolt.

Decline of New England Orthodoxy

In 1675, Massachusetts seemed to have lost sight of the goals of its first settlers. When the Indians attacked, Puritan ministers warned the sons and daughters of the founding generation that God was punishing them for their faithlessness and sin.

Courtesy American Antiquarian Society

Metacom, the Wampanoag leader, who in 1676 tried to drive the New England settlers back "into the Sea."

In fact, Puritan church membership had declined since 1650, especially among men. After mid-century, women became a large proportion of the "elect," comprising 60 percent, and in some congregations 75 percent, of newly admitted members. The ministers believed that men were becoming more worldly, thus undermining the church's social and political authority. A related problem was that the children of nonchurch members could not be baptized. In 1662, the clergy devised an alternative to full church membership, the Half-Way Covenant, which permitted adults who had been baptized but who were not yet saved to be "half-way" members. In congregations that accepted this innovation (not all churches did), people could assume partial status by showing that they understood Christian principles and would strive to obey God. As unconverted members, they were not entitled to take communion, but could have their children baptized.

The growth of competing religions in New England also proved to Puritan ministers that the model society had failed. Believing theirs to be the only true religion, Puritans rooted out dissent. After 1650, the Quakers and Baptists threatened religious unity. The Society of Friends, or Quakers, was a radical Protestant sect born in the turmoil of the English Civil War. Like the Puritans, they were reformers who believed that the Church of England was corrupt and should be purified of its rituals, decorations, and

A Quaker Woman Preaching

The Quakers were unique among English religions in the seventeenth century in recognizing women as ministers. Women were among the earliest followers of George Fox of England, considered the founder of Quakerism around 1650. Female missionaries then traveled through the British Isles, Europe, and America. They believed that God spoke through them, and they hoped to convince others of the "Light."

In New England, the women ministers challenged both the Puritan faith and expectations of female subordination. When Quaker missionaries interrupted church services and gained followers, Massachusetts leaders banished them and threatened to execute those who returned to the colony. Several were hanged, including Mary Dyer in 1660, who had determined to "look their bloody laws in the face." This illustration was published somewhat later, in J. F. Bernard, *The Ceremonies and Religious Customs of the Various Nations of the Known World . . .* (1733–1739), when Quakers had become less controversial and worshipped openly in Massachusetts.

Courtesy of Special Collections, University Research Library, University of California at Los Angeles

QUAQUERESSE qui preche.

hierarchy. But the Quakers went even further. They claimed that the Puritans also practiced false doctrine by paying ministers to preach, relying too much on the Bible as the word of God, and retaining the sacraments of baptism and communion. The Friends believed that God communicated directly with individuals through the "Spirit" or "Light." They worshipped by gathering in plain meetinghouses to "wait upon the Lord." In worship services, they had no Bible reading, prepared sermon, music, or ritual. Rather, they waited in silence for the Spirit to inspire one or several of the congregation to communicate God's message. Ministers, who included women as well as men, regularly received inspiration to speak. They required no advanced learning because their words were supposed to come straight from God, not from a prepared text.

Appalled by these Quaker teachings, Puritan leaders tried to prevent their spread by deporting the traveling missionaries. The Friends were stubborn, however, repeatedly returning to Massachusetts. They interrupted Puritan church services, preached in the streets, and made some converts among the people. The Puritan magistrates arrested and whipped them, even cropping their ears. In 1658, the General Court prescribed the death penalty for Quakers who returned after banishment.

The hangings of several Quaker missionaries caused consternation on both sides of the Atlantic. When Charles II demanded an explanation, the Puritans ended the executions. The magistrates continued to persecute nonconformers, but over the decades following 1660 realized that their policy of intolerance had failed. Rhode Island served as a base for Quaker missionaries to evangelize in the Puritan colonies, further supporting its reputation among Puritans as "the sewer of New England." The Baptists, whose objection to infant baptism was their chief disagreement with orthodox Puritans, increased in numbers after approval of the Half-Way Covenant, which they vehemently opposed. They believed that a church should include only the saved, indeed that only the saved should be baptized. Despite persecution, dissenters successfully formed congregations throughout New England.

King Philip's War

The unceasing expansion of white settlers into the frontier destroyed the relative peace between the Algonquians and the settlers of New England. By 1675, more than 50,000 whites inhabited the region. The colonists had large families of sons and daughters who desired farms of their own. These settlers occupied more and more of the hunting, fishing, and agricultural lands of the Indians.

Since the massacre of the Pequots in 1637, the Puritans and Native Americans of New England had managed an uneasy peace. The colonists traded for furs with local nations and with the Mohawks, the closest nation of Iroquois in New York. Some Puritan ministers, of whom John Eliot is best known, convinced several local tribes who were greatly diminished by disease and loss of lands to dwell in "praying towns." In these villages, adjacent to but separate from the towns of white settlers, the Indians were supposed to adopt English customs and learn the fundamentals of Puritan religion. By 1674, Eliot had organized fourteen praying towns of Native Americans who took the first steps toward giving up their traditional ways.

Many New England Indians, including Wampanoags and Narragansetts, did not form praying towns, but even so remained allies of the Puritan governments for many years. Trouble began in 1671, when the Plymouth government attempted to force the Wampanoags to surrender their firearms and obtain permission to sell land. Metacom (or King Philip) built a league with neighboring tribes. When John Sassamon, an Indian educated at Harvard College, informed the Plymouth government of impending attack and was murdered, the white authorities hanged three Wampanoags for the deed.

In 1675, Metacom mobilized Algonquians throughout New England, attacking fifty-two English towns. White refugees fled to Boston. But by the end of summer 1676, with the help of the Mohawks, the colonial governments turned back the attack, as disease, hunger, and a weapons shortage weakened Metacom's troops. The war took a heavy toll on both sides, for the Algonquians destroyed twelve towns and killed many colonists. White frontier settlement would not reach its 1675 limits for another forty years.

Map 3.1 New England at the Time of King Philip's War, 1675–1676 The Indians and English destroyed and damaged each other's towns throughout Plymouth, Rhode Island, and Massachusetts. The Narragansetts, who lived in Rhode Island and had assisted the Puritan governments against the Pequots in 1637, entered King Philip's War after an English army invaded their territory.

For the Indians of southern New England, the war was calamitous. Thousands died and many others were enslaved. Even bands who supported the English lost autonomy. At the outbreak of war, the colonists had forced residents of the praying towns to live on desolate Deer Island in Boston Harbor, where they suffered from lack of food and shelter. Some of the Indian men later fought in the colonial militia against Metacom, but when the war was over, all Native Americans in southern New England had to live in praying towns, where they worked as servants or tenant farmers for neighboring whites. Metacom was killed, his head paraded before the white settlements and kept on a pole in Plymouth for twenty years; his wife and son were sold as slaves.

War in the Chesapeake

Just as New England struggled over land in King Philip's War, Virginia faced a similar crisis in Bacon's Rebellion. The Chesapeake uprising involved civil war among the English as well as Indian-white conflict. But at its root, the chief issue was land: how could the competing interests of landless immigrants and dispossessed natives be resolved? Since the 1640s, the white population of Virginia and Maryland had grown quickly. By 1670, approximately 40,000 colonists lived in the Chesapeake, including native-born sons and daughters of early settlers as well as more recent arrivals. Among the new immigrants were servants who expected to obtain land upon completing their terms. In the 1670s, however, many Virginians discovered that the combination of low tobacco prices and high land prices blocked their dream of obtaining plantations. They received headrights, but could find no good vacant tobacco land to claim.

Part of the problem, these landless freemen believed, was that the Indians held too much territory. Specifically, the 1646 treaty between the Virginia government and the Powhatans designated the area north of the York River for Native Americans. This agreement had been acceptable to whites in the 1640s when space south of the York seemed ample, but was unsatisfactory thirty years later, when white settlement was pushing north. It was also true, many freemen recognized, that wealthy planters, powerful in government, speculated in large acreages that they left empty while others starved for land.

The first flames of war occurred in July 1675, when some Doeg Indians attempted to take hogs as payment for a settler's unpaid debt. After people on both sides were killed, the Susquehannocks got involved. When they attacked frontier settlements, a thousand-man army of Virginia and Maryland colonists marched against their village on the Potomac River. Vastly outnumbered, several Susquehannock sachems agreed to negotiate, but when they left their stockade, the colonists murdered them. During the winter of 1675–1676, the Susquehannocks retaliated, raising fears that King Philip's War had spread south. Discontented and vengeful colonists responded indiscriminately, killing friendly neighboring Indians rather than those who were actually attacking the frontier.

The landless freemen found a leader in Nathaniel Bacon. Only twenty-nine years old, Bacon had come to Virginia with enough money to purchase a large plantation. Governor Berkeley nominated him to the Virginia council, despite his youth. Nevertheless, Bacon evidently saw his opportunity to challenge Berkeley for leadership of the colony by mobilizing freemen and small planters against the Indians. While Berkeley wanted peace with the Susquehannocks, Bacon's forces intended to annihilate all of the natives. The settlers knew that the natives were weak, with just a fraction of their pre-1607 population. Bacon's supporters also demanded a greater voice in the Virginia government.

Governor Berkeley declared Bacon a traitor and sent troops to end his forays against the Indians. He also called new elections that brought many Bacon supporters into the House of Burgesses. The delegates passed measures that extended suffrage to landless freemen, taxed provincial councilors, and placed limits on the terms and fees of local officials. These efforts failed to end the rebellion, as Bacon's army burned Jamestown. For months, Virginians plundered the plantations of neighbors who took the other side. Few white fatalities occurred, however, as rebels vented most of their frustration by killing Indians. The rebellion finally ceased with Bacon's death, probably of dysentery, in October 1676. The war marked a serious defeat for the Indians of the Chesapeake, who lost the protection of the 1646 treaty and gradually surrendered their lands.

Bacon's Rebellion awakened the Virginia elites to the dangers of a large class of land-less freemen, but resulted in no substantive political change. A new assembly in 1677 reversed the reform acts of the 1676 House of Burgesses, including the law extending the vote to landless freemen. A commission appointed by the Crown to end the rebellion also opposed expanding popular power, stating that to grant suffrage to unpropertied men was "repugnant to the Lawes of England and to the Lawes and Peace of the Colony." The commission did call for taxing "the great Ingrossers of Lands" who caused "misery and mischiefs" by "occasioning the Planters to stragle to such remote distances when they can-not find land neerer to seat themselves but by being Tenants which in a Continent they think hard," but nothing was done. Rather than create a society in which power and wealth were distributed more evenly, in which Virginia once again would offer opportu-nity to poor Englishmen, the planter elite began importing more enslaved Africans. Bound for life and restricted by laws, black slaves could not demand farms or a voice in government. With settlement in New Jersey, Carolina, and Pennsylvania during the 1670s and 1680s, immigrants had better options than Virginia.

The Pueblo Revolt

Four years after Bacon's Rebellion, across the continent in New Mexico, the Pueblos drove out the Spanish—and kept them out for thirteen years. The Pueblos had the advantage of a much smaller white population in New Mexico—2,800—than in New England or the Chesapeake. The Spanish hold over the missions was tenuous, for native fighting men greatly outnumbered Spanish troops. Nevertheless, the Hispanic settlers and priests demanded forced labor and strict adherence to Christianity. A number of Indian towns had rebelled during the previous half century, but most failed to win autonomy.

The Pueblos became more desperate during the 1670s, when New Mexico endured severe drought. As famine persisted, they faced Apache and Navajo attacks. The Pueblos became convinced that the root of their troubles lay in their rejection of ancient gods, the *katsina*. To bring rain and renewed prosperity, some presented gifts to the katsina and per-formed dances that the Spanish had outlawed. When punished for abandoning Catholi-cism, the Indians felt even greater resentment, leading to revolt.

The leader of the 1680 rebellion was Popé, a medicine man of the village of San Juan, north of Santa Fe. When the katsina told him that the Spanish must be driven from the land, he organized a general insurrection, sending knotted ropes to allied villages, indi-cating when the uprising should start. On August 10, 1680, the Pueblos launched a full-scale attack, killing 400 colonists and twenty-one priests. Strategically, the Indians con-fiscated or destroyed the settlers' chief means of transportation, their horses and mules. When Santa Fe fell to the rebels on September 21, the whites escaped south, settling in the area of present-day Ciudad Juárez, Mexico. Some Spaniards explained the revolt as God's punishment for their sins, whereas others blamed the harsh labor and efforts to repress native religions. As Popé supervised, the Pueblos destroyed churches, broke up church bells, and burned images of Christ and the saints. According to one witness, "in

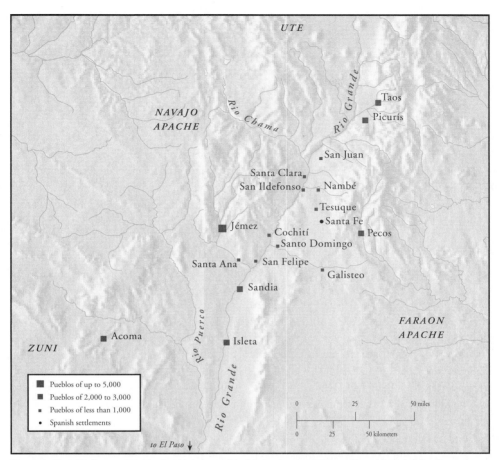

Map 3.2 New Mexico, c. 1680 The Spanish had established their colony in 1598 by sending soldiers, their families, and Franciscan missionaries north through the Rio Grande Valley. In 1680, the Spanish population remained small and centered in the capital, Santa Fe.

order to take away their baptismal names, the water, and the holy oils, [the Indians] were to plunge into the rivers and wash themselves."

Several times during the next few years, the Spanish attempted unsuccessfully to retake New Mexico. The rebellion spread south into northern Mexico, where Native Americans demolished settlements and missions. But by 1692, as famine continued, the Pueblo alliance fell into disarray. The new Spanish governor of New Mexico, Don Diego de Vargas, marched north to Santa Fe with 160 troops. Though many Indians resisted, the Spanish reestablished control over the province. In December 1693, after a three-day siege, Vargas's troops took Santa Fe, killing all of the Indian men and making slaves of the women and children. The Spanish subsequently retained a foothold in New Mexico, but not without further struggle. The Pueblos rejected the Franciscan missionaries, revolting once again in 1696. Some Pueblos fled from New Mexico while others submitted as Vargas systematically conquered the Indian towns once again. After 1696, the Spanish and Pueblos lived together in relative peace, but only because the Hispanics eased requirements for tribute, forced labor, and adherence to Christianity.

William Penn's "Holy Experiment"

In England, the Quaker leader William Penn approached Charles II with a petition to establish a new colony in America, one that would avoid bloodshed by dealing justly with the Indians. While the Pueblos had not yet driven out the Spanish, Penn knew of King Philip's War and Bacon's Rebellion. He was determined to do things differently in Pennsylvania.

Plans for Pennsylvania

Penn had inherited a £16,000 debt owed to his father by the king, but had little hope for repayment in cash, so he requested a colony on the west bank of the Delaware River. The king approved Penn's request in 1681, granting him a charter for Pennsylvania that was more restrictive than Lord Baltimore's, in part because the English government was attempting to assert greater control over its colonies, in part because Penn was a Quaker. The new proprietor received the right to enact laws and impose taxes with the consent of the freemen, but was required to submit all laws for approval to the home government within five years of passage. And to protect the status of the Church of England, the charter stipulated that twenty Anglican inhabitants could request a minister from the bishop of London.

In establishing Pennsylvania, Penn hoped to provide a haven for Quakers, who faced persecution in England because they would not pay tithes for church support or attend Anglican services. Friends also refused to give oaths, so they could not legally pledge allegiance to the king. A Quaker ideal was to live according to the doctrine that all were equal in the eyes of God; thus they rejected certain customs, such as removing one's hat in the presence of superiors. For practicing their faith, they were jailed and fined, and when they refused to pay, local English officials took their property.

William Penn conceived of his colony as a "holy experiment," a place where Quakers could exercise their beliefs without interference and the government would operate like a Quaker meeting, acting in unison as it followed God's will. Penn also intended to pay the Lenape Indians for tracts of land and to set up arbitration panels of Native Americans and colonists to resolve conflicts peacefully. He paid the Lenapes a much lower price than he in turn charged the settlers, however, and assumed the Indians would leave after they sold their land.

Like Lord Baltimore, Penn intended to make a fortune from Pennsylvania, summing up his goals: "the service of God first, the honor and advantage of the king, with our own profit." Despite Penn's strong Quaker convictions, which for some suggested a simple life, he appreciated fine food, drink, and accommodations. He possessed large landholdings in southern England and Ireland, retained many servants, and enjoyed such delicacies as salmon, partridges, saffron, and chocolate. Urgently needing money, he thought the sale of millions of acres in America would solve his financial problems.

Penn spent a great deal of time planning the colony. His scheme of government established an assembly with two houses, both elected by the freemen. Freemen included adult males who owned at least fifty acres of land or paid taxes on other property. During the early decades, when servants received fifty acres at the end of their terms, nearly every man in Pennsylvania could vote. Penn did not extend that right to women, nor did he alter the common law restrictions on married women. Though women Friends took an active role in their meetings as ministers, missionaries, and supervisors of discipline, their legal status in the Quaker commonwealth was similar to that in other colonies. Penn's laws stood out in another respect, however, requiring capital punishment for just two offenses, treason and murder.

The proprietor's planning went beyond politics, for he also drew up specifications for his capital city. In designing Philadelphia, in taking on the role of city planner, Penn was unique among early English colonizers. He conceived the city as a large "green country town," with wide streets in a grid pattern, public parks, ample lots, and brick houses. He failed to fulfill his plan completely because he could not obtain enough acreage to build Philadelphia as he wanted. Dutch and Swedish residents already owned the land along the Delaware River, so Penn decided to buy a site of just 1,200 acres between the Delaware and Schuylkill Rivers. His plan remained orderly, with the grid design and parks, but with lots of one-half to one acre instead of one hundred acres for those who purchased "proprietary shares" of 5,000 acres. To maintain a constant income from the colony, landowners would pay annual quitrents.

A Diverse Society

Penn sold land briskly, as 600 people bought 700,000 acres within four years. Most of the buyers were Quaker farmers, merchants, artisans, and shopkeepers from England, though many also originated from Scotland, Ireland, Wales, Europe, the West Indies, Maryland, and New York.

Penn's settlers moved into an area inhabited by the Lenapes, who welcomed the newcomers, and by Swedes, Finns, and Dutch, who served as intermediaries with the Indians. The Lenapes, or Delawares as the colonists later called them, had conducted trade with the Dutch as early as 1610 and yielded land to the whites. Because Dutch and Swedish settlements remained small, relatively few violent incidents occurred. By the time Penn arrived with thousands of colonists, the Lenapes had declined significantly from disease. As they sold their lands, some moved to northern or western Pennsylvania, while others remained on marginal tracts in the Delaware Valley.

Wampum belt, which, according to legend, the Lenape gave to William Penn in 1682. It has become a symbol of Penn's efforts to preserve peace with the Indians of Pennsylvania.

The European "old residents" integrated with the new arrivals, though not without friction. Some earned money by selling land and provisions, or serving as guides and interpreters. One local Swede, Captain Lasse Cock, in 1682 translated for the Indians and English, and traveled to the Susquehanna and Lehigh Rivers as Penn's emissary. The Swedes, Dutch, and Finns continued to worship in their own congregations, but became naturalized as English subjects and some served in the assembly and local government. The old residents made up a large part of the population in the Lower Counties (later Delaware), leading to conflict as the different interests of the Lower Counties and Pennsylvania became clear. In 1704, after two decades of wrangling, the three southern counties obtained their own separate Delaware assembly.

Pennsylvania got a boost from its late arrival on the colonial scene because its merchants could tap existing networks in the Atlantic economy. Substantial traders came from New York, the Chesapeake, and the West Indies, bringing their connections and capital to build breweries, tanneries, warehouses, wharves, and ships. Farmers found a market for wheat, livestock, and lumber in the West Indies. By 1700, Philadelphia became a thriving port town, with 700 houses and more than 3,000 people.

But for William Penn, his colony was deeply disappointing, as land sales reaped smaller profits than he had hoped and the costs of administering the colony soared. When purchasers refused to send him quitrents, he went more seriously into debt. Penn traveled to his colony twice, but stayed a total of only four years. Although the province became prosperous and quite successful as a tolerant, diverse society, he reckoned it a failure.

The Glorious Revolution and Its Aftermath

The founding of Pennsylvania coincided with the Crown's effort to tighten colonial government. Compared with the Spanish empire, English administration was a hodgepodge. The Privy Council at first appointed temporary committees to address colonial concerns, then in 1675 formed a permanent committee, the Lords of Trade, which met sporadically. Even after 1696, when the more formalized Board of Trade and Plantations was established, this body could gather information and give advice, but lacked authority to appoint colonial officials or enforce laws. These powers belonged to a host of governmental offices, including the secretary of state, the Treasury, and the War Office.

Dominion of New England

While experimenting with these committees, the Crown made other efforts to rein in the colonies. Most vulnerable was the Massachusetts Bay colony, both for its unrestrictive charter and the perceived intransigence of Puritan leaders. In 1678, Charles II required Massachusetts to send agents empowered to renegotiate the charter. He specifically wanted the New Englanders to comply with the Navigation Acts and apologize for having coined their own money. The colonists delayed action, though they sent regrets for having passed laws contrary to the laws of England. They offered to renounce any "except such as the repealing whereof will make us to renounce the professed cause of our first coming hither."

Impressed by neither the Puritans' arguments nor the speed of their response, the English government brought legal proceedings against the Massachusetts Bay Company for "usurping to be a body Politick," and revoked the charter in 1684. The colony's assembly, the General Court, was prohibited from meeting. In February 1685, before a royal governor could be appointed, Charles died and his brother James became king. James II quickly took advantage of events to move toward centralizing the colonies. With the Privy Council's consent, in 1685, he combined Massachusetts, New Hampshire, and Maine under the Dominion of New England, added Plymouth, Rhode Island, and Connecticut in 1686, and New York and New Jersey in 1688. Apparently, James's plan for the colonies was to create two large dominions, one north of the fortieth degree of latitude (the approximate location of Philadelphia) and one to the south. These dominions would supersede colonial charters, eliminating the confusing diversity of laws and political structures. Representative government would end.

For Massachusetts Puritans, the Dominion of New England was a disaster. James's governor-general, Sir Edmund Andros, made sweeping changes that undercut the Puritan notion of a covenanted community. He levied taxes without the approval of a representative assembly, restricted the power of town meetings, mandated religious toleration, and confiscated a Boston church for use by Anglicans. Andros enforced the Navigation Acts, favored his own cronies over the Puritan elite in distributing patronage, required landowners to obtain new land titles from the Crown, demanded payment of quitrents, and took control of common lands. A number of colonists rebelled, refusing to pay taxes without a voice in their passage, but were jailed and fined.

Revolutions of 1689

Governor Andros managed to avoid serious revolt until the spring of 1689, when news of James's removal from the throne reached Massachusetts. The king's rule had been as heavy-handed in England as in the colonies. A Roman Catholic, he installed his friends in office and defied Parliament. Protestants feared James would make England a Catholic nation under authoritarian rule. Thus, parliamentary leaders forced him into exile in France, inviting his Protestant daughter Mary and her husband William of Orange, the leader of the Dutch, to take the throne. The Glorious Revolution, though bloodless, had long-lasting results in England: it permanently limited the king's power by establishing parliamentary control of taxation, supremacy of law, and autonomy of the courts.

In the morning of April 18, 1689, many of Boston's populace formed companies with the militia. Numbering more than one thousand by afternoon, the insurgents, who included several Puritan ministers and some wealthy merchants, deposed the dominion government. They interpreted the revocation of the charter and James's illegal taxation and expropriation of lands as part of a "popish plot" that Protestant New England must help destroy.

With the dominion gone, Plymouth, Rhode Island, and Connecticut reactivated their charters, but Massachusetts, which had lost its charter under Charles II, had to negotiate a new one. The colonists' arguments for the charter were based less on the old covenant theory than on the fundamentals of the Glorious Revolution, especially the right of English people to representative government. The resulting 1691 Massachusetts charter, which annexed Plymouth to the Bay colony, established a royal province with an elected assembly and a governor appointed by the king. The charter required freedom of worship and forbade religious restrictions on voting.

Revolutions also took place in New York and Maryland in the wake of James II's loss of power. New York fell into turmoil with news of William and Mary's ascent to the throne in England and the revolt in Boston. The reports unleashed opposition to Lieutenant Governor Francis Nicholson, who headed the dominion's government in New York. Again the struggle was defined in religious terms, as a crusade to destroy the "papist" threat.

In the city of New York, insurgents included merchants and artisans who had been denied economic privileges to trade and mill flour under James's government. In 1689, led by Jacob Leisler, a German-born merchant and militia captain, they forced Nicholson back to England and elected a Committee of Safety to replace James's council. When Henry Sloughter, the new governor appointed by William and Mary, arrived in 1691, however, he reinstalled James's councilors and executed Leisler for treason. Despite Leisler's early proclamation of the new monarchs in 1689, his enemies had better connections in London.

In Maryland, simmering resentment of Protestants against the Roman Catholic proprietor, Charles, Lord Baltimore, erupted in the summer of 1689. Baltimore's troubles intensified when his nephew, George Talbot, president of the provincial council, murdered the king's customs collector "with a dagger newly prepared and sharpened" aboard a royal ship. This event rocked the colony, so Baltimore sent a man he thought would provide strong leadership as governor, William Joseph, a Roman Catholic and adherent of James II. Upon arrival in 1688, Joseph proceeded to alienate Maryland's assemblymen, calling them adulterers and drunks. When he required them to renew their oaths of fidelity to the proprietor, they refused.

In July 1689, a handful of Maryland leaders formed the Protestant Association. Aroused by rumors that Catholics were plotting with the Indians to destroy the

Protestants, the Association raised troops, defeating the proprietary government without a shot. The rebels obtained articles of surrender that banned Catholics from provincial offices; sent a message to William and Mary informing them of the takeover and requesting a Protestant government; and elected an assembly—the "Associators' Convention"—that ruled Maryland for the next two and one-half years.

The three provincial revolutions of 1689, in Massachusetts, New York, and Maryland, had similarities to England's Glorious Revolution in the relative absence of bloodshed and the recurring theme of "popish plots." They failed, however, to bring about permanent change in the constitutional relationship between England and its colonies. The provincials, lacking delegates in Parliament, continued to endure taxation and mercantilist regulation without their assent. The colonial revolts of 1689 resembled Bacon's Rebellion of 1676, as they mobilized out-of-power elites against those who controlled the colonial governments. In 1676, in Virginia, the insurgents had manipulated landless discontents by appealing to hatred against Native Americans as well as grievances against Berkeley's government. In 1689, the leading rebels employed the twin specters of authoritarianism and Catholicism, with rumors of impending French and Indian attack, to gain support from the populace.

Witchcraft in New England

In May 1692, Governor William Phips arrived in Boston Harbor with the new Massachusetts charter. He found the colony in disarray. Symptomatic of the Massachusetts state of affairs was the witchcraft hysteria that had erupted months earlier in Salem Village, a farming community north of Boston. Since 1675, the Bay colony had one crisis after another—King Philip's War, loss of the charter, Andros's dominion, the Revolution of 1689. Accompanying this turmoil were structural changes in the society, as traditional religious authority yielded to elites whose power rested on mercantile wealth. The Salem witch mania was a tragic holdover from a passing culture. Its fury was aggravated by the psychological reaction of traditionally minded folk to the new, more commercial, secular society of turn-of-century New England.

Belief in witchcraft was embedded in European and Anglo-American culture, though, ironically, it was losing force by the time of the Salem outbreak. The colonists, like their contemporaries in the Old World, believed that both God and Satan influenced everyday events. When something bad happened that they could not explain, people turned to supernatural explanations, including the possibility that an individual had compacted with the devil to do evil deeds. In England, witchcraft had been a capital offense since the time of Henry VIII in the early sixteenth century; colonial governments followed suit in condemning those who gave "entertainment to Satan." Over the seventeenth century, the Puritan governments charged many more men and women with witchcraft than did other English colonies: three hundred and fifty New Englanders were accused during the years 1620 to 1725. Of this number, the Salem episode accounted for almost 200. The southern and middle colonies tried few accused witches and executed none.

The witchcraft cases of Salem in 1691–1692 at first resembled those in other places and times. Several girls experimented with magic, aided by a slave woman Tituba and her husband John, who together baked a "witch cake" of rye meal and urine, feeding it to a dog. The girls, who included nine-year-old Betty Parris, the daughter of Salem Village's minister, started having fits, presumably caused by witches. According to one report, the girls began "getting into holes,

Courtesy, Peabody Essex Museum, Salem, Mass.

Hanging of witches in England c. 1650. No similar image exists of the Salem hangings.

and creeping under chairs and stools, and to use sundry odd postures and antic gestures, uttering foolish, ridiculous speeches." Possession spread to other village girls, leading to the arrest of three women as witches—Tituba; a poor beggar, Sarah Good; and an ailing elderly woman, Sarah Osborne.

These three alleged witches were the sort of people traditionally prosecuted for the crime. Generally, in witchcraft cases, the accused were women past menopause, who in various ways deviated from expected roles. They had fewer children than the average woman their age. Lacking sons, a significant percentage of accused witches were heirs or potential heirs of estates, with greater economic autonomy than most New England women. Some claimed the power of a "cunning woman" to heal and foretell the future; many had been convicted of assaultive speech; and they were often involved in conflict within their families and neighborhoods. Revealingly, men of the same age group and troublesome character were much less likely to be identified as witches. These assertive old women went beyond the accepted bounds of female behavior and, as a result, became vulnerable to prosecution as witches.

While the Salem craze commenced in the timeworn pattern, it soon engulfed people of all social levels. Accusations descended upon prosperous church members, a minister, a wealthy shipowner, and several town officials. Hysteria spread from Salem to adjacent towns. Over three-quarters of the alleged witches were women; half of the accused men were their relations. Of those executed, fourteen women and five men were hanged on "Witches Hill" and another man was crushed to death with stones. Only one of the dead was of high status—the Puritan minister George Burroughs. Governor Phips, supported by influential clergymen, had allowed the prosecutions to proceed after his arrival, but put a stop to them when the accusers pointed to people at the highest levels of society, most significantly, to his own wife, Mary Phips. It had become clear, to many besides the governor, that the situation was out of control, that the evidence presented by the possessed was unreliable and quite likely the work of the devil. After Salem, witchcraft no longer assumed its earlier importance in New England society.

Wars and Rivalry for North America

From 1680 to 1713, the Spanish, English, French, and many Indian nations battled for territory in North America. Despite the political and social turmoil of the 1680s and early 1690s, the English settlements were the largest and most dynamic European colonies on the continent. By the mid-1680s, New France had approximately 10,000 settlers, compared with more than 70,000 in New England alone. Spanish Florida was comprised chiefly of missions, run by forty Franciscan priests, and the fortified town of St. Augustine, which held about 1,400 Hispanic, African, and Indian residents. Despite declining populations, many Native American peoples remained powerful in eastern North America, in particular the Five Nations of the Iroquois in New York.

In the late seventeenth century, the three primary areas of dispute on the continent were Florida and Guale (later Georgia), Louisiana and Texas, and Canada. Conflict occurred against the backdrop of two long European wars, the War of the League of Augsburg,

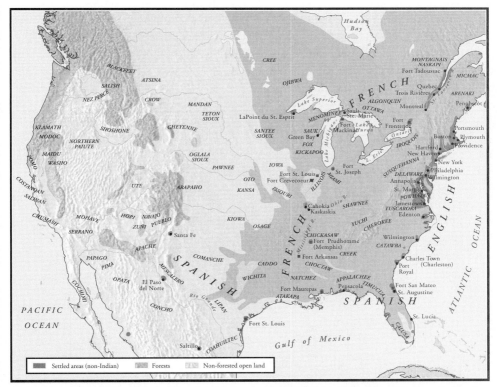

Map 3.3 North America in 1700 Significant change had occurred in North America since the early 1600s. Along the Atlantic coast, the English now had settlements from Maine (part of Massachusetts) to South Carolina. As the English population expanded, Native Americans declined, with many groups absorbed into other nations, such as the Catawbas of South Carolina.

1689–1697, and the War of the Spanish Succession, 1702–1713 (respectively known as King William's War and Queen Anne's War to the English colonists).

Florida and Guale

Beginning in 1680, the English colonists of South Carolina decided to take advantage of smoldering unrest among the mission Indians of Guale and Florida to attack the Spanish colony. The Native Americans had rebelled against forced labor and efforts to stamp out their traditional religions. They killed Spanish missionaries and destroyed property, but had not closed the missions altogether. The Carolinians raided Guale and Florida with no humanitarian motives to assist the Indians. In fact, a chief reason for attacking the Spanish missions was to capture Native Americans to sell as slaves in the West Indies. The English also wanted to control the deerskin trade in the southeast.

By 1686, the Carolinians thrust the missionaries out of Guale. Then in 1704, during Queen Anne's War, an army under former Carolina governor James Moore crushed the missions in Apalachee. The Carolinians obtained help from their trading partners, the Yamassees, and from many of the mission Indians, who resented Spanish oppression. Moore's troops inflicted brutal torture, burning people alive. The surviving Apalachees dispersed, losing their identity as a nation. The Spanish retained St. Augustine and a fort they built at Pensacola in 1698, but lost control of Guale and most of Florida.

Map 3.4 Southeastern North America in the Early 18th Century French colonies along the Mississippi River and Gulf Coast challenged Spanish dominance in the region. The Spanish settlements in Texas and Florida included missions and provided a defensive buffer for Mexican silver mines and shipping lanes off the Florida coast.

Louisiana and Texas

The Spanish erected their fort at Pensacola Bay in response to French efforts to establish a colony in Louisiana. At risk, the Spanish knew, were their silver mines in Mexico and domination of the Gulf of Mexico. In 1682, René Robert Cavelier, Sieur de La Salle, had explored the Mississippi River from New France to the gulf, naming the territory Louisiana in honor of King Louis XIV. La Salle sailed to France, then returned to set up a colony. However, he miscalculated the location of the Mississippi, instead building Fort St. Louis in Texas, near Matagorda Bay. The colony quickly dissolved from disease, loss of ships, and attacks by Karankawa Indians; in 1687, La Salle was murdered by his men.

The French incursion in the Gulf of Mexico inspired the Spanish to expand their settlements in the borderlands. In 1690, they founded missions among the Caddo people of eastern Texas and western Louisiana, from whom they took the Caddo word, Tejas or Texas, meaning "friends." Three years later, when the Caddos blamed the friars for bringing smallpox, they escaped. The Spanish abandoned Texas until the French once again entered the area.

In 1699, Pierre LeMoyne, Sieur d'Iberville, resumed the French search for an opening to the Mississippi River, which was difficult to locate in the muddy Mississippi Delta. Iberville found the river's mouth by accident, then built forts at Biloxi Bay and on the Mississippi to establish French possession. Spain might have forced the French out of Louisiana with quick action, but in 1700, the grandson of French King Louis XIV took the Spanish throne; the two nations became allies against the English, Dutch, and Austrians in the War of the Spanish Succession.

Although the French-Spanish alliance gave Louisiana a chance to develop without interference from New Spain, the colony grew slowly. In 1708, about one hundred white soldiers and settlers lived in Louisiana. They obtained food, deerskins, and the right to occupy the land from local Native Americans by exchanging firearms and other goods. Relations between the French and Indians were not trouble-free, however. In 1715, for example, after Natchez Indians killed four French traders, the colonists literally demanded the assassins' heads. When the Natchez failed to execute all of the perpetrators, the French murdered Indian hostages and required the Natchez to accept a fortified trading post on their land.

Canada

Conflict developed in the north when the Iroquois confederation attacked New France to stop French fur trading in the Ohio Valley and Illinois. The Iroquois defeated New France in 1683, but war continued as the English, French, and Native Americans struggled over trade routes and territory. The outbreak of King William's War in 1689 fueled the contest, as the Five Nations attacked settlements in Canada, while the French and their Indian allies destroyed English frontier outposts from New York to Maine. New England troops took Port Royal in Acadia, but failed to conquer Quebec. Though the European belligerents agreed in the Peace of Ryswick (1697) to return to prewar status in North America, the Canadians won an important victory over the Iroquois and their English allies. The Five Nations signed a neutrality treaty in 1701. Frustrated by New York's failure to provide reinforcements, they ended their alliance with the English. New France then developed trade, religious missions, and agricultural settlements in the Great Lakes and Illinois Territory.

The renewal of hostilities between the English and French in 1702, with Queen Anne's War, again brought raids on the New England frontier. In 1704, the Canadians and Native Americans attacked Deerfield, Massachusetts, burning houses and barns, killing inhabitants, and taking many captives. The English once again took Port Royal, but called off an attack on Quebec when they lost 900 men in storms on the St. Lawrence River. This time, however, the peace treaty gave the victory to England (which had joined with Scotland in 1707 to form Great Britain). In North America, the Treaty of Utrecht (1713) ceded Nova Scotia (formerly Acadia), Newfoundland, and control of the Hudson Bay territory to the British. Yet they had failed to oust France from North America.

The Entrenchment of Slavery in British America

Despite wars, rebellions, and witch hysteria, the most significant development in British North America during the late seventeenth and early eighteenth century was large-scale investment in enslaved Africans. The decisions of thousands of individual colonists to purchase men, women, and children who had been seized from their homelands in Africa left an indelible imprint on American society and culture. The slave buyers could not foretell the monumental effects of their actions. They responded to economic conditions: their need for workers, the declining availability of white servants, and the developing Atlantic slave trade.

Adopting Slavery

How could people who increasingly prized their own freedom—who had braved a treacherous ocean voyage to find opportunity in a new land—deprive other human beings of liberty, and often life itself? The answer lies in traditional English culture and the colonists' perceived economic needs.

The English, like other Europeans, believed that hierarchies existed in human society and, indeed, all of nature. Humans were superior to animals; Christians superior to "heathens." English language and culture also differentiated sharply between white and black, with whiteness suggesting purity and good, blackness imbued with filth and sin. The English compared their light skin with the Africans' darker brown color, judging the latter to be inferior. In African religion, social customs, dress, and political organization, the Europeans found serious deficiencies, just as they had found deficiencies among Native Americans. The people of sub-Saharan Africa, the English thought, were lower on the scale of humanity and could justifiably be enslaved. The example of the Portuguese, Spanish, and—most recently—the Dutch, who had fabricated the Atlantic slave trade over the previous two cen-

Theodor de Bry's illustration of a Dutch ship trading on the coast of West Africa. The people in the canoe, indicated with "B," represent African merchants who traded human beings to the Europeans for goods such as cloth, rum, and firearms.

turies, made the decision to buy Africans seem natural. The mainland English colonists could also look to their countrymen in the West Indies, where thousands of African slaves toiled in sugar fields, outnumbering whites.

Despite this cultural context, colonists viewed their investment in slaves as an economic decision. In Virginia and Maryland, planters purchased Africans because they needed large numbers of workers to grow tobacco. Chesapeake settlers had learned that Native Americans, who easily escaped enslavement and died in catastrophic numbers, would not fill their labor needs. White servants filled the gap until about 1675. Many young Englishmen, and fewer women, had willingly signed up to work for three or more years in return for passage and rights to fifty acres of land. In the last quarter of the century, however, the supply of English servants declined in Maryland and Virginia. Economic conditions improved in England, while good tobacco land became scarce. Bacon's Rebellion taught Chesapeake elites the danger of importing thousands of white servants under these circumstances. With the founding of the Carolinas, New Jersey, and Pennsylvania, where land was plentiful, servants had a wider range of options.

Chesapeake planters searching for an alternative labor supply turned to African slaves. Population figures for Virginia and Maryland demonstrate graphically the result of individual decisions. In 1660, only 900 blacks resided in the Chesapeake, some of whom had come as servants and were free. Two decades later, their number had grown to 4,300; by 1720, blacks comprised one-fifth of the population. A similar increase occurred in the Carolinas (primarily South Carolina), where 38 percent of the residents in 1720 were African slaves. The situation was different in New England, where only 2 percent of the population was enslaved, and in the Middle Colonies (New York, New Jersey, Pennsylvania, and Delaware), where about one resident in ten suffered perpetual bondage.

The Slave Trade

English entry into the Atlantic slave trade helped spur the transition to an African work-force. Though smugglers like John Hawkins had interloped earlier in the Spanish trade, England officially became involved in selling human beings in 1663. Charles II granted a monopoly to supply captives to the English colonies first to the Company of Royal Adventurers, then in 1672 to the Royal African Company. When the companies could not meet the demand of labor-hungry colonists, smugglers got involved, so in 1698, the Crown abandoned the monopoly, opening the slave trade to any English merchant who wanted to participate. As a result, the supply of Africans in the English colonies soared and slave prices declined, thus encouraging colonists to invest in even more black labor.

The experience of enslavement and transit across the Atlantic Ocean was dehumanizing and perilous. Probably one-half of the persons sold into slavery died while still in Africa before transport or during the Atlantic passage. Approximately three-quarters of those taken to English North America came from the area of West Africa between Senegambia and the Bight of Biafra, with the remainder coming mostly from Angola. As European sea captains made successive trips to the coast, African traders had to reach farther and farther into the continent to find enough people to enslave. Some captives marched 500 miles or more to the sea in "coffles," the term given to the files of shackled prisoners. On the coast, they were confined in enclosures called barracoons, often exposed to the sun for long periods without adequate food and drink. When a ship arrived, according to a Dutch trader, Willem Bosman, in 1700, the Africans were lined up on shore,

> where, by our surgeons . . . they are thoroughly examined, even to the smallest member, and that naked both men and women, without the least distinction or modesty. Those that are approved as good, are set on one side; and the lame or faulty are set by as invalids, which are here called *mackrons:* these are such as are above five and thirty years old, or are maimed in the arms, legs or feet; have lost a tooth, are grey-haired, or have films over their eyes; as well as all those which are affected with any venereal distemper, or several other diseases.

For the Africans chosen for transport, the horror had only begun. The Europeans branded them with the insignia of the company—for example, slaves of the Royal African Company had their skins burned with the letters "DY," for James, duke of York. Then followed the voyage across the Atlantic, called the "middle passage," which could take from three weeks to more than three months, depending upon the weather and destination. Ships normally carried rations for three months, so bad storms could mean starvation. Weather permitting, the captives spent their days on deck, the men in chains, the women and children unrestrained. At night, and around the clock if weather was bad, slaves occupied spaces about the size of coffins in the hold of the ship, where temperatures could reach extremely high levels. Disease was often rampant. Some slaves attempted suicide by jumping overboard or refusing to eat: the latter was so common that traders invested in a tool called the *speculum oris* to force open a person's mouth.

Africans also rebelled violently, attacking the white captain and crew, occasionally taking over the ship. Because they were unfamiliar with ocean navigation, mutineers had the best hope of success when the ship was still in African waters and large numbers could carry out the revolt, escaping to shore. When rebels failed, punishment was swift and brutal. The slave trader Bosman described an incident when a sea captain placed an extra anchor in the ship's hold. The enslaved Africans,

> unknown to any of the ship's crew, possessed themselves of a hammer, with which, in a short time they broke all their fetters in pieces upon the anchor: After this, they came above deck, and fell upon our men, some of whom they grievously wounded, and would certainly have mastered the ship, if a French and English ship had not very fortunately happened to lie by us; who perceiving by our firing a distressed-gun, that something was in disorder on board, immediately came to our assistance with shallops and men, and drove the slaves under deck: notwithstanding which, before all was appeased, about twenty of them were killed. The Portuguese have been more unlucky in this particular than we; for in four years they lost four ships in this manner.

Upon arrival in America, the Africans faced the ordeal of sale by auction or prearranged contract. They were stripped naked once again and examined for disease and physical defects. Because the greatest need was for strong field hands who would provide years of labor, plantation owners paid the highest prices for healthy young men in their prime. Buyers paid less for women, children, and older men. For both the Africans and their owners, the year following debarkation was most critical. During this period of seasoning, Africans endured serious illness and high mortality from the new disease environment.

Systems of Slavery in British North America

As more and more Africans arrived, colonial assemblies instituted black codes to define slavery and to control the black population. Before 1660, Maryland had officially sanctioned perpetual bondage, but Virginia moved more slowly. Enough flexibility existed in Virginia society to allow black servants to gain freedom, earn their livelihoods, and in some cases acquire land. In the 1660s, however, Virginia joined Maryland in enacting laws that recognized differences in the terms of white servants and African slaves. By law, slavery lasted a person's entire lifetime, descended from mother to child, and was the normal status of blacks, but never whites.

In the late seventeenth and early eighteenth century, both Virginia and Maryland created clearly articulated caste systems based on perceptions of race. A person's skin color denoted status: all Africans and their descendants encountered severe discrimination, whether enslaved or free. The Virginia assembly ruled that any master who killed a slave during punishment was not guilty of a felony. Conversely, no black person, slave or free, could strike a white, even in self-defense. Virginia lawmakers made emancipation difficult to obtain. Evolving black codes banned interracial marriage, forbade owners from releasing their slaves except in special cases, and restricted enslaved blacks from traveling without permission, marrying legally, holding property, testifying against whites, or congregating in groups. Over the course of the eighteenth century, other British colonies passed similar codes that ranged from fairly moderate New England laws to a harsh regime in Carolina, keyed in large part to the density of the black population.

In the life of an African slave, these laws had force, but more direct was the power of the master over work and family. To be a slave meant that someone else possessed your body and could command your daily activities. The

A 1730 depiction of the slave market in New York Harbor. In Northern port cities, slaveholding was common at this time among upper class and middling families.

owner chose your job; he or she decided whether your children would stay with you or be sold away. During off-hours, Africans generally maintained autonomy in religion, social customs, and family life.

The work Africans and native-born African Americans performed varied from one region to another. In the Chesapeake and the Carolinas, most slaves spent long hours planting, weeding, and harvesting tobacco, corn, and rice. A farm's production depended largely upon the number of workers tending the crop. Over time, as the southern black population increased naturally and importation continued, the supply of labor became more plentiful. Plantation owners assigned slaves to different tasks, though most still raised the staple crop. Some men became drivers and artisans; some women served as nurses, cooks, and spinners. Both women and men performed domestic service. At the same time, female slaves were responsible for the household needs of their own families, including food preparation, laundry, and sewing.

Agricultural production in the Middle Colonies and New England centered on grains and livestock, which demanded less labor than tobacco or rice, so most parts of the northern countryside had relatively few slaves. Exceptions included New York and neighboring eastern New Jersey, which had difficulty attracting European immigrants; thus, well-to-do farmers purchased large numbers of Africans to work their land. The largest slaveholder in New Jersey was probably Colonel Lewis Morris of Shrewsbury, who employed more than sixty slaves at his plantation and ironworks. In Rhode Island's Narragansett region, some plantation owners held as many as fifty blacks. Most northern slaves lived in the port towns, however, where women worked as cooks and household servants, and men labored at crafts, domestic service, and as shipbuilders and sailors. Boston, New York, and Philadelphia merchants imported Africans as part of the West Indies trade. In New York City, blacks were about one-fifth of the population; in Boston and Philadelphia they comprised about one-tenth.

A source of comfort to slaves who had lost their African homelands and kin was to establish new families in America. Slaves achieved some autonomy from their masters by creating families and kinship networks. All knew, however, that owners could destroy loving relationships by selling away spouses, children, brothers, and sisters. The ability of blacks to form families changed over time and varied from one region to another. High mortality and a skewed sex ratio prevented many African-born men from marrying and having children. In the disease-ridden West Indies and northern cities like Philadelphia, mortality was so high that colonists had to keep importing Africans to avoid population decline. In the Chesapeake colonies, however, natural population growth began with the first generation of native-born slaves. African American women had more children than their African mothers, creating communities of slaves on large plantations. Whereas most of the first Africans dwelled in white households with just a few blacks, their offspring, known as "country-born" slaves, lived with parents, brothers, and sisters. The third generation lived with grandparents and cousins as well.

Resistance and Rebellion

For many slaves, family and kin helped to reduce their feelings of despair; for others nothing relieved the pain of lifetime bondage. Many resisted their masters' power by staging slowdowns, pretending illness, destroying crops and tools, committing theft, arson, assault, and murder. Newly arrived Africans were especially likely to rebel against their new status, often running away. Slaves who were sold away from their families frequently escaped to join them again. Men ran away in greater numbers than women, who, as mothers, found it difficult to escape with children in tow.

Although slaves in the English West Indies often rebelled, blacks in the mainland colonies rarely took the ultimate step of armed insurgency, primarily because they were so outnumbered by whites. Before 1713, West Indian blacks staged seven full-scale revolts; their large population made success seem possible. In Barbados, in 1675, for example, conspirators planned to take over the island, installing an elderly slave Cuffee as king. When whites got wind of the plot, they burned alive or beheaded thirty-five blacks. On the mainland, just one slave revolt occurred by the early 1700s. In New York City, in 1712, about twenty slaves set fire to a building, attacking the white men who came to extinguish it. Nine whites were killed; terror spread up and down the Atlantic coast. As in the case of later slave revolts and conspiracies, the revenge wreaked upon the black community surpassed any violence the rebels had committed. In the wake of the New York revolt, thirteen slaves were hanged, three burned at the stake, one tortured on the wheel (an instrument used to stretch and disjoint its victims), and another starved to death in chains; six committed suicide to avoid such treatment.

Early Abolitionists

As slavery became entrenched in North America, a few white colonists questioned its morality. They feared slave rebellions and abhorred the violence needed to enslave Africans, transport them to the colonies, and keep them in bondage. Slavery was morally repugnant, they believed, because all humans are equal in the eyes of God. One of the American opponents of perpetual bondage was Samuel Sewall, a Boston judge, who wrote in 1700, "It is most certain that all Men, as they are the Sons of Adam . . . have equal Right unto Liberty, and all other outward Comforts of Life."

Quakers also spoke out publicly against the institution. Certainly not all Friends were abolitionists—in Pennsylvania and New Jersey before 1720 a large proportion of the Quaker elite owned slaves—but a few interpreted Quaker ideals to mean that human bondage reeked with sin. According to John Hepburn of New Jersey, for example, slavery violated the Golden Rule to do unto others as you wish others to do unto you. Whereas owners got rich without physical labor, wore fine-powdered wigs and greatcoats, and their wives and children similarly lived well, slaves endured beatings, wore rags, and slept in the ashes of the fire. In the context of rising importation throughout the colonies, however, the protests of Sewall, Hepburn, and a few other critics had little effect.

Economic Development in the British Colonies

Despite differences in agriculture, labor, and commerce from one region to another, the mainland colonies were all part of the Atlantic economy, dominated by the staple crops of sugar, tobacco, and rice. The developing mercantile economies of New England and the mid-Atlantic region depended heavily upon the slave system, because their chief market was providing food for the multitudes of blacks laboring on West Indies sugar plantations.

Northern Economies

Family farms and dependence on the sea characterized New England's economy. When its agriculture failed to provide a lucrative staple crop, traders turned to fishing and shipping. With rocky, generally poor soil and a cool climate, the region could not grow a profitable commercial crop like tobacco or sugar, so rural New England families raised livestock, wheat, rye, Indian corn, peas, other vegetables, and fruit. They ate most of what they produced—a fairly monotonous diet of brown bread, boiled or baked peas, boiled meat and vegetables, and dark beer or apple cider—within their families and communities.

Fishing and shipping developed as important industries during the seventeenth century. The New England fishers initially sold their catch, in return for manufactured goods such as shoes, textiles, glass, and metal products, to London merchants, who sent the fish to Spain, Portugal, and the Wine Islands, off the coast of Africa.

The fishing industry spurred the growth of maritime trade, as New England merchants recognized even greater profits to be made by trading directly with the Wine Islands and the West Indies. They formed partnerships among themselves and with English merchants, encouraging a local shipbuilding industry. The New Englanders exported fish, barrels, and other wood products. They imported wine, fruit, and salt from the Wine Islands, and rum, molasses, sugar, dyes, and other goods from the Caribbean. Soon, aided by the Navigation Acts, they were the chief carriers of goods along the North American coast, exchanging enslaved Africans and rum distilled from West Indies molasses for Pennsylvania wheat and livestock, Chesapeake tobacco, North Carolina tar and turpentine, and

South Carolina rice. The credits they earned in shipping were as significant as the value of New England products sold in the trade.

The economy of the Middle Colonies resembled New England's in a number of ways, but was much more prosperous agriculturally. With plenty of good land, farmers raised wheat and livestock commercially, purchasing servants and some slaves to supplement family labor. The region had two ports: one at New York City and the other at Philadelphia. Though neither city matched Boston in population or commercial importance before 1750, both quickly surpassed the Massachusetts seaport after that date. New York merchants maintained links with Amsterdam, the Dutch West Indies, and New Spain even after the English takeover in 1664. Philadelphia Quakers exploited their connections with Friends in other ports, especially in England and the West Indies.

Life in the Seaports

Maritime trade encouraged the development of port cities in the British provinces: Boston, New York, Philadelphia, and Charleston. Until 1750, merchants of Boston and other seaport towns in Massachusetts and Rhode Island dominated colonial trade. The ports thrived because they forged commercial links between farmers and external dealers, housing the markets through which imports and exports flowed. The maritime industry itself created demand for shipbuilders, suppliers of provisions, rope and sailmakers, carters, dockworkers, and sailors.

Commercial growth brought social change, distinguishing an urban lifestyle from the countryside. Some merchants became fabulously wealthy from transatlantic and coastal trade. They spent their income conspicuously, building costly mansions, purchasing enslaved Africans as household servants, and wearing expensive clothes. They lived comfortably, with servants and slaves to do their menial chores. Other city dwellers were much less fortunate because they earned minimal wages or lacked employment. Port cities stimulated both affluence and dire poverty. They attracted many people who hoped to make their fortunes, or at least a decent living, but died with little more than the clothes on their backs. Maritime commerce frequently suffered disruption from war, bad weather, and economic downturns. Seamen and artisans, dependent on overseas trade, could expect little work during the winter, when few ships sailed. City folk were also at greater risk of death than those who lived in the country, as some arriving ships spread smallpox and other diseases to the dense urban populations. The towns lacked adequate sanitation facilities, so garbage and waste cluttered streets, polluting the water supply.

As trade expanded, sailors became an important segment of the labor force. They were a varied lot. Some went to sea only part-time, to supplement the income of their farms. Others chose seafaring as a career, joining a fraternity and dividing their time between shipboard and the taverns and boardinghouses of port towns throughout the Atlantic world. Some had no choice in the matter at all, for they were enslaved Africans whose masters purchased them to man the ships. Sailors led a difficult and dangerous life. Crews on ordinary merchant ships were small, so seamen worked long hours loading and unloading the ship, maintaining the rigging and sails, and pumping water from the bilge, an especially backbreaking job. The organization of labor on board was hierarchical, with power descending from the captain to mate, to specialists like ship carpenter and surgeon, to seamen. Discipline could be harsh. The crewmen had little hope of moving up through the ranks, for captains were generally from affluent families, often merchants and part-owners of their ships. Instead, the more common fate of an ordinary "Jack Tar" was early death or disability from shipwreck, combat with enemies or pirates, and such occupational hazards as falling overboard, broken bones, scurvy, rheumatism, and hernias, or the "bursted belly" as they called it.

When conditions on ship became insufferable, the seamen rebelled, sometimes deserting the ship at the next port. Most radically, men mutinied and, if successful, sometimes became pirates. They plundered merchant vessels and port towns, sharing the proceeds evenly among themselves, electing officers, and recruiting much larger crews than could be found on merchant ships. With eighty or more men on a pirate ship of average size, compared with fifteen on a comparable merchant vessel, each had much less work to do. One pirate, Joseph Mansfield, admitted in 1722 that "the love of Drink and a Lazy Life" were "Stronger Motives with him than Gold."

Plantation Economies in the Chesapeake and South Carolina

From 1675 to 1720, tobacco remained king in Maryland and Virginia, as planters increasingly purchased enslaved Africans instead of white servants. The wealth of plantation owners grew with each child born to a slave mother. At the same time, the richest planters bought up the land of small farmers who found it difficult to compete with the slaveholders. The wealthiest man in early eighteenth-century Virginia was Robert Carter of Lancaster County, called "King" Carter. As a slave trader and land speculator, he parlayed his inheritance of £1,000 and 1,000 acres into an estate of £10,000 in cash, 300,000 acres of land, and over 700 slaves. Carter, with his relatives and friends, formed a tightly knit group of Chesapeake gentry.

In 1720, and throughout the eighteenth century, Chesapeake society was hierarchical. At the bottom of the social structure were African and country-born slaves, who owned no property and had little hope for freedom. Above them were the non-landholding whites, perhaps 40 to 50 percent of white families, who rented land, owned a horse or two, some cows, a few pigs, tools, and some household goods, but rarely held bound servants or slaves. They lived in shanties and ate from wooden dishes rather than from pottery. Their incomes from tobacco were so meager that they had trouble paying taxes and rent. Often they were in debt to the local merchant-planter for needed manufactured goods, such as ammunition, fabric, shoes, and tools. Next higher were small landholders whose incomes allowed them to live more comfortably, with pottery, more furniture, and nicer (though still quite small) homes. If they owned several slaves, which few did before 1720, they worked alongside them in the fields and house.

In the upper 5 percent were the gentry, who owned many slaves, large acreages, and usually acted as merchants as well. They served as intermediaries for smaller planters, selling tobacco abroad and importing manufactured goods. As such, they became creditors of their poorer neighbors, who often owed them substantial debts. In Maryland and Virginia, the merchant-planters conducted trade without the development of port cities. Ships docked at their plantations along the many tributaries of the Chesapeake Bay to load casks of tobacco and unload imported goods. Tobacco required relatively little processing: workers dried the leaves in sheds, removed large fibers, and packed the tobacco in casks made by local coopers. Merchant-planters and rural artisans, including slaves, provided goods and services for the community without centralizing their activities in towns. Even the two capitals, Williamsburg and Annapolis, remained small throughout the colonial period.

Situated in a semitropical climate, South Carolina developed a plantation economy that was linked to, and in many ways resembled, the West Indies. Most early settlers, both black and white, came from the English colony of Barbados, where land was in short supply and almost entirely devoted to sugar cultivation. White planters claimed Carolina headrights, then sold corn, salt beef, salt pork, barrel staves, firewood, and Native American slaves to the islands. South Carolinians enslaved the Indians they captured in raids throughout the American Southeast and obtained them from native traders in exchange for guns, ammunition, and cloth. Native Americans also supplied deerskins, which found a ready market in England, though they were not valued quite so highly as Canadian furs.

As with the northern fur trade between Europeans and Indians, the Carolinians used English trade goods to establish alliances with native groups. Such major trading partners as the Yamassees, however, quickly discovered that white merchants used theft, violence, rum, and false weights to gain unfair advantage. In 1715, in league with the Creeks, the Yamassees attacked white settlements, nearly destroying the colony. The whites saved themselves by getting help from the Cherokees. The Yamassees and Creeks were defeated, their people killed, enslaved, or forced to migrate from the coastal area. White South Carolinians then expropriated their lands.

The settlers wanted the new territory because they had found an export that became much more lucrative than provisions, enslaved Indians, or deerskins. Planters had experimented with a variety of crops—tobacco, cotton, sugar, silk, wine grapes, and ginger—but rice proved most successful in the wet lowlands of the Carolina coast. Also significant were the skills in rice production that many Africans brought to America. Rice exports expanded rapidly in South Carolina, reaching 1.5 million pounds per year by 1710 and nearly 20 million pounds by 1730. The chief markets for rice were Europe and the West Indies. Carolinians first sent their crop directly to Portugal, but in 1705 Parliament added rice to the list of enumerated products that had to be shipped to England first, taxes paid, and then reexported to Europe. The colonists argued that, in the case of southern Europe, this detour made their crop arrive too late for Lent, when much of it was consumed. In response, Parliament allowed South Carolina after 1731 to trade directly with Spain, Portugal, and Mediterranean Europe, but the larger share of the rice crop, which went to northern Europe, still required transit through Britain.

The conversion to rice transformed South Carolina society, affecting the black population with special force. Before planters adopted full-scale rice production, slaves had performed a variety of jobs in crafts, timber, livestock, and agriculture. Their workloads were moderate, especially in comparison with the West Indies. Rice monoculture changed this situation altogether, as planters imported thousands of Africans. In the coastal areas north and south of Charleston, blacks reached 70 percent of the population in the 1720s. With high importation and harsher working conditions, death rates surged. As in the Chesapeake, wealthy planters bought up neighboring farms while investing heavily in slaves. They created large rice plantations, worked by growing numbers of African slaves. Small planters moved to the periphery, where they raised grain and livestock for the rice district and the Caribbean. The rice planters found the Carolina lowlands isolated and unhealthy, so they left their plantations part of the year. However, the Carolinians supervised their plantations directly—unlike British West Indian sugar planters who fled to England, leaving management in the care of overseers.

Charleston, where the rice planters spent at least several weeks each year, was the fourth largest city in the British colonies. The port channeled the trade in provisions, deerskins, rice, slaves, and English manufactures. Charleston remained smaller than Boston, Philadelphia, and New York because British and New England shippers controlled its trade. Without a strong merchant community, the South Carolina seaport lacked the impetus for shipbuilding and associated crafts.

Conclusion

Between 1675 and 1720, the people of North America shed blood over territory, trade, and political autonomy. As English, French, and Spanish settlers expanded into new regions, they established commerce, but also spread smallpox and fostered conflict among the Indians. The Narragansetts and Wampanoags of New England waged a costly war in 1675–1676, while the Pueblos successfully, though temporarily, expelled the Spanish from New Mexico. Native Americans throughout the continent, weakened by disease and war, yielded to the Europeans. During Bacon's Rebellion and the Revolutions of 1689, governments in Virginia, Massachusetts, New York, and Maryland faced challenges from rival elites and their discontented, lower class allies.

By the turn of the eighteenth century, the Spanish reconquered New Mexico and infiltrated Texas, France moved into the Great Lakes region and Louisiana, and the English pushed out in many directions. To develop their economies, the British colonists imported Africans in large numbers. With the growth of plantation slave economies in the South and maritime commerce in the North, British North America developed distinctive regional characteristics. Yet in 1720, the Atlantic seaboard colonies had much in common: their settlement by enterprising men and women, regard for English rights of property and representation, and governance within the British imperial system. During the next half century, the importance of these commonalities would become clear.

RECOMMENDED READINGS

Demos, John. *The Unredeemed Captive: A Family Story from Early America* (1994). The evocative tale of a Puritan minister's daughter who was held captive by the Mohawks and refused to return home.

Hoffman, Ronald et al., eds., *Through a Glass Darkly: Reflections on Personal Identity in Early America* (1997). Interesting essays relating individual biography to colonial development.

Innes, Stephen, ed. *Work and Labor in Early America* (1988). Insightful essays that demonstrate the range of labor systems and working conditions in the British colonies.

Jordan, Winthrop D. *White Over Black: American Attitudes Toward the Negro 1550–1812* (1968). Basic source on the construction of ideas about race in Anglo-America.

Karlsen, Carol F. *The Devil in the Shape of a Woman: Witchcraft in Colonial New England* (1987). Convincing argument about the significance of gender in witchcraft trials.

Lovejoy, David S. *The Glorious Revolution in America* (1972). The best introduction to the colonial revolutions of 1689.

McCusker, John J., and Menard, Russell R. *The Economy of British America 1607–1789, with Supplementary Bibliography* (1991). An excellent survey of economic and demographic development.

Thornton, John. *Africa and Africans in the Making of the Atlantic World, 1400–1680* (1998). An influential work demonstrating the impact of Africa and Africans on the slave trade and the development of colonial American societies.

Tomlins, Christopher L., and Mann, Bruce H., eds. *The Many Legalities of Early America* (2001). Path-breaking essays that explore relationships among early Americans through the law.

Usner, Daniel H., Jr. *Indians, Settlers, and Slaves in a Frontier Exchange Economy: The Lower Mississippi Valley Before 1783* (1992). A history of colonial Louisiana and West Florida, focusing on relations between Europeans and Native Americans.

Additional resources, exercises, and Internet links related to this chapter are available on the American Passages Web site: http://history.wadsworth.com/ayerscompact2/

4

The Expansion of Colonial British America
1720–1763

In 1721, smallpox hit Boston viciously, infecting about 6,000 residents and killing 844. Business stopped for several months, as almost every family battled the contagion. In many respects, this epidemic was unremarkable in the British American colonies: settlers and Native Americans alike had previously experienced the ravages of disease. But this time, one Puritan minister took an unprecedented step. Cotton Mather, who thirty years earlier had helped aggravate the Salem witch hysteria, encouraged a Boston doctor, Zabdiel Boylston, to test inoculation. Mather had learned from Onesimus, his African slave, and from English scientific papers, that inoculation was used in Africa and Turkey to prevent smallpox epidemics. An experiment would be risky, for the procedure involved introducing the smallpox virus into the body, thereby giving the person what was usually (but not always) a mild case of the disease. Many doctors, as well as much of Boston's populace, condemned the proposal. Nevertheless, Dr. Boylston inoculated about 250 persons over the course of a year. Those who submitted to the procedure had a much lower death rate than Bostonians who contracted the disease naturally.

Mather was far ahead of his time in advancing the theory that disease was caused by an invasion of the body by viruses, which he called invisible "worms." Significantly, it was a minister, rather than a physician or scientist, who advanced this hypothesis. During the eighteenth century, science lacked the rigid boundaries of complexity and specialization that would later separate it from other fields of intellectual endeavor. American theologians and philosophers, as well as doctors, naturalists, and astronomers, read the latest scientific literature from England and Europe. The great divide between science and religion did not yet exist. Like many other theologians, Mather understood epidemics as God's punishment for sin. But he also believed inoculation was a divine gift, that people should use any means available to combat disease.

Mather's support for inoculation has been called the greatest contribution to medicine by an American during the colonial period. Certainly it represented change, as the Enlightenment, a new intellectual movement, spread from Britain to the colonies. During the years 1720 to 1763, the British provinces experienced intellectual, religious, and social ferment as they continued to expand through North America. As new knowledge, beliefs, and consumer goods arrived from Europe, colonists from Maine to Georgia (founded in 1732)

CHRONOLOGY

1720	Theodore Jacob Frelinghuysen begins revivals in New Jersey
1721–1722	Smallpox inoculation in Boston
1732	Founding of Georgia • Hat Act
1733	Molasses Act
1734	Jonathan Edwards starts revivals in Northampton, Massachusetts
1737	Walking Purchase in eastern Pennsylvania
1739	Stono Uprising in South Carolina
1739–1740	George Whitefield tours northern colonies
1739–1744	War of Jenkins' Ear
1740	James Oglethorpe leads invasion of Florida
1741	British attack on Cartagena
1744–1748	King George's War
1745	New Englanders conquer Louisbourg
1747	Boston riot against impressment
1750	Iron Act
1754	Defeat of Virginia militia at Fort Necessity • Albany Congress proposes plan for colonial unity
1754–1763	Seven Years' War
1755	Braddock's defeat near Fort Duquesne
1758	British capture Louisbourg
1760	British conquer Montreal, seizing control of Canada
1763	Pan-Indian war begins in Ohio Valley and Great Lakes region • Proclamation of 1763 outlaws white settlement west of the Appalachians • Paxton Boys revolt in Pennsylvania

increasingly lived within a common cultural framework. With rising wealth, colonial elites supported colleges and purchased books and luxury goods. This common culture had important ties to England, yet was not altogether English, for immigrants from Scotland, Ireland, and the continent of Europe, and slaves from Africa brought ideas and practices from their native lands. Immigration into the British colonies also promoted regional diversity, as the newcomers from Europe settled on the frontier from Pennsylvania to Georgia, and the numbers of enslaved Africans grew to 40 percent of the southern population. The Europeans came looking for land: when they set up farms in contested territory, they provoked conflicts with the Native Americans, French, and Spanish, resulting in a series of wars that lasted a quarter century. When the Seven Years' War ended in 1763, the British colonies took a great deal of pride in their contribution to the victory, offering it as evidence of their economic and political maturity within the empire.

Intellectual Trends in the Eighteenth Century

The willingness of Mather and Boylston to try inoculation showed important changes in the way people viewed their world. The Puritan clergyman's personal journey from witch hunter in 1692 to medical investigator in 1721 reflected the growing inclination to find natural rather than supernatural causes for unexplained events. The Enlightenment blossomed first in Europe and then in America, encompassing political theory and philosophy as well as science. Though primarily intellectual, the Enlightenment had far-reaching effects, inspiring new technology as well as concepts of human freedom. For Americans, its greatest significance lay in the acceptance of natural rights philosophy, which paved the way for independence and republican government.

Newton and Locke

In the late seventeenth century, two English theorists, Sir Isaac Newton and John Locke, had challenged traditional notions that humans had no role in determining their fate, that they could only trust in God to rule the universe. They confronted this older view without denying the existence of God. Newton discovered universal laws that predictably govern the motion of planets, moons, and comets, the motion of falling bodies on earth (gravity), and the ebb and flow of tides. His work demonstrated that the universe operated according to fixed principles, which humans are capable of detecting and understanding. Locke built upon Newton's breakthrough in his *Essay Concerning Human Understanding* (1690). Locke argued against the accepted belief in innate knowledge, that infants are born with ideas implanted by God in their minds. He contended that all knowledge is gained by experience, not preordained at birth. Humans are born with the ability to learn, to use their acquired knowledge to benefit society.

Locke, and the Enlightenment thinkers he inspired, believed in freedom and the possibility of human progress, in the right of people to improve the conditions in which they live. Science, of course, was an important means of such improvement. The English philosopher also had a major impact upon eighteenth-century politics, in particular providing a theoretical basis for the American Revolution and the Constitution. In *Two Treatises on Civil Government* (1690), he argued that humans, according to natural law, had rights to life, liberty, and property. By social contract, they formed governments to guarantee those rights. If a state failed in its obligation, the people had the duty to rebel and establish a new government.

Education in the British Colonies

Throughout British North America, formal education beyond basic reading, writing, and arithmetic was rare, so few read the works of Locke and Newton directly. After 1720, however, as newspapers became more available and reprinted articles from London, provincial readers gained greater familiarity with Enlightenment thought. Many colonists learned to read, though boys and girls spent much of their time learning the occupations they would pursue as adults. The availability of formal schooling varied widely by region, class, and gender. Nowhere did a system of universal, free, public education exist, though New England had some tax-supported schools. Everywhere, schools emphasized moral behavior and used religious texts.

New England made the greatest effort of the British colonies to educate its populace. In 1642, the Massachusetts legislature required parents and ministers to teach all children to read so they could obtain direct understanding of the Bible and the colony's laws. In 1647, the assemblymen ordered towns with at least fifty families to establish petty (elementary) schools, and those with one hundred families to maintain Latin grammar (secondary) schools. Connecticut and Plymouth passed similar legislation. Though some towns ignored the laws, most New England children learned to read, whether from their parents, at the town school, or at dame schools, where women in their homes taught young girls and boys for a fee. Writing was considered a separate skill, and was less crucial for girls to learn. The percentage of New England females who could write and do arithmetic was significantly lower than for males. Girls, on the other hand, commonly learned sewing and knitting. Boys who planned to enter college attended grammar school from about age seven to fourteen, studying Latin, elementary Greek, and sometimes Hebrew. Latin was necessary for the professions, including law, medicine, and the ministry.

South of New England, colonial governments did not require town schools. In the Middle Colonies, churches and private teachers offered instruction. Affluent Quaker and Anglican boys were most likely to obtain formal education, though after 1750 girls and poor boys, including African Americans, had better access to schools. As in Massachusetts, females were much less likely to learn to write than males. In the Chesapeake, with dispersed settlement, neither Maryland nor Virginia had many schools. Upper-class boys and girls had private tutors, while middling families in some localities pooled their resources to establish schools. Overall, sons received much more instruction than daughters, and large numbers of poor whites obtained no education at all. Very few slaves learned to read and write, for owners thought these skills would breed discontent and enable slaves to forge passes, facilitating escape.

New England also surpassed other regions in higher education, as the Puritans established Harvard College in Massachusetts in 1636 and Yale College in Connecticut in 1701. William and Mary, founded in Virginia in 1693, was the only other college in the British colonies before the 1740s. None of the colonial colleges admitted women. The Puritans intended Harvard to preserve classical learning and civilization, provide liberal education to the region's male elite, and ensure a supply of well-educated ministers. Harvard offered a curriculum of ethics, religion, logic, mathematics, Greek, Hebrew, rhetoric, and natural history (biology and geology). Most early graduates became clergymen, while others went into medicine, public service, teaching, commerce, and agriculture.

Harvard alumni in Connecticut established Yale to provide advanced education closer to home. Yale had a tentative beginning, but gained more stability by 1720, after receiving funds from Elihu Yale and about 800 volumes for its library, including the books of Locke, Newton, and other Enlightenment figures. The College of William and Mary also struggled at first. Chartered by the Crown to train Anglican clergy, educate young men in religion, and convert Native Americans, the school failed to offer college-level courses until the 1720s. Many elite families in the southern provinces continued to depend upon private tutors, trips to Britain, and northern colleges to educate their sons.

The Growth of Science

After 1720, influenced by Scottish universities that quickly absorbed Enlightenment thinking into their curricula, American colleges expanded their coursework to include French, English literature, philosophy, and science. They offered mathematics and what was then called natural philosophy—astronomy, physics, and chemistry. The colleges hired some of their faculty from Scotland and purchased scientific apparatus, including telescopes, sextants, clocks, and orreries, which demonstrate the motion of planets and moons within the solar system.

American professors of natural philosophy were part of a larger community of scholars centered in the prestigious Royal Society of London, which published a journal, *Philosophical Transactions,* of the latest scientific ideas and knowledge. This transatlantic community included academics like John Winthrop of Harvard College, as well as largely self-taught men like Benjamin Franklin and John Bartram. More than thirty colonists belonged to the Royal Society. Scientists took from the Enlightenment a commitment to experiment and observe natural phenomena to obtain information that would lead to human progress. John Winthrop was the most renowned professor of natural philosophy in British America, with research interests in such wide-ranging subjects as sunspots, mathematics, earthquakes, and the weather. In 1761, Winthrop participated in an important international scientific effort to calculate the distance between the Earth and sun, made possible by the transit of the planet Venus across the face of the sun. Venus had last crossed the sun in 1639, when no useful measurements had been made. Winthrop journeyed to Newfoundland to observe the transit. His data, combined with observations from the Cape of Good Hope, were inexact, but eight years later, scientists—including Winthrop—had another chance. This time, at least part of the transit could be viewed in the mainland British colonies. The stakes were high because another transit would not occur for 105 years. The data were again imprecise, but when combined with measurements from around the globe, yielded results very close to the accepted distance of 93 million miles between the Earth and sun.

Other colonists contributed to understanding the physical world. Perhaps best known for his diplomacy and political leadership during the Revolutionary era, Benjamin Franklin has become a symbol of the American Enlightenment for his efforts to improve society through science, inventions, and civic organizations. Franklin was born in Boston, ran away at age seventeen from an apprenticeship with his older brother, and arrived in Philadelphia nearly penniless. He built a highly successful printing business, publishing a newspaper, books, and *Poor Richard's Almanack,* which gained a wide readership. Throughout his life, Franklin put the Enlightenment ideal of human progress into action. He founded a debating club to discuss politics, morals, and natural philosophy, and helped establish the first American lending library, a hospital, and the College of Philadelphia. Franklin's experiments in electricity yielded information about its properties, including the basic concepts of "plus" and "minus." His inventions, which applied scientific principles to improving daily life, included bifocal eyeglasses, the lightning rod, and an iron stove that was more efficient than colonial fireplaces.

John Bartram, also of Pennsylvania, was the most energetic of American naturalists, whose chief contribution to science was collecting specimens of New World plant life. In return for a yearly pension from the king and payment for seeds he sent to wealthy collectors in England, Bartram traveled all over the eastern seaboard searching for new plants and animals. His efforts greatly expanded botanical knowledge of the Western Hemisphere, for he sent specimens to such scholars as Carl Linnaeus, the Swedish author of the modern classification system.

Another prominent American naturalist was Cadwallader Colden, a Scot who immigrated to the colonies after receiving his medical degree. Like many well-educated doctors, Colden had broad interests in science. While serving as surveyor-general and lieutenant-governor of New York, he collected and classified plants in the neighborhood of his estate. He corresponded with European botanists, sending them specimens and descriptions. As their demands became overwhelming, Colden taught his daughter, Jane, how to classify according to Linnaeus's scheme. Her accurate descriptions and drawings earned high praise from Linnaeus, Bartram, and other naturalists.

Changes in Medical Practice

Just as Colden and other university-trained doctors were interested in many scientific fields, the practice of medicine itself attracted people of widely different backgrounds. Medicine was beginning to develop as a profession. During the colonial period, men with formal medical education comprised a small proportion of the people who provided care for disease, physical injury, and childbirth. Having completed formal coursework abroad—the first medical school in the British colonies, located in Philadelphia, did not open until 1766—educated physicians were at the top of their profession and charged the highest fees. Consequently, they practiced primarily in the cities. Below them were men who learned their craft as apprentices; though they assumed the title of doctor in the colonies, they were actually akin to the surgeon-apothecaries of Great Britain. As surgeons, they performed emergency procedures such as setting bones, amputating limbs, and removing superficial tumors, but no major surgery. As apothecaries, they prepared and prescribed drugs for a variety of illnesses.

Female midwives traditionally attended childbirth, treated the ill, and prescribed herbal remedies. Having learned their skills through informal apprenticeships and from witnessing the childbirths of neighbors and relatives, they received payment for their services. During the colonial period, childbirth was the province of women. As an expectant mother's labor began, she called together a group of women, presided over by the midwife, who assisted in the birth. In the early stages of her labor, the woman provided special refreshments, called "groaning beer" and "groaning cakes." The attendants helped her walk around and offered herbal teas or liquor to relieve the pain. In normal deliveries, the mother squatted on a "midwife's stool" or remained standing while supported by several women. If complications occurred, the midwife manipulated the infant manually, but would not perform a Caesarean section. In the worst cases, the midwife had to kill the child; sometimes the mother died. Without modern antibiotics, women constantly faced the threat of infection during pregnancy and in the weeks following delivery.

In the last half of the eighteenth century, the practice of obstetrics changed. In 1762, Dr. William Shippen, Jr., returned from studying medicine in England and Scotland to give lectures in anatomy to Philadelphia midwives and doctors. Soon he accepted only male students. Shippen established an obstetrical practice of his own, quickly attracting well-to-do patients who expected a more elevated level of care than they received from midwives. Affluent urban women were convinced that the male physicians offered a better chance for a safe, less painful delivery. The doctors' obstetrical training, their use of opiates and instruments such as forceps, spelled progress to these women, inducing them to abandon the traditional woman-dominated rituals of childbirth. That the new obstetrics brought improvement is doubtful. The male doctors, faced with taboos against observing the private parts of ladies, attended their clients in darkened rooms, with the woman lying in bed under covers. The physicians also lacked the means to prevent infection; their use of blood-letting and opium could impede safe delivery. In any case, midwives continued to attend the great majority of women, those who lived in rural areas and the poor who could not afford the doctors' fees.

The Great Awakening

As Enlightenment ideas gained sway, many Protestant ministers embraced Christian rationalism, a theology that stressed moral, rational behavior and the free will of individuals to lead their lives and achieve salvation. Some rationalists spoke of an impersonal God who had long ago created the universe to operate according to natural laws, rather than a loving or angry God who controlled a person's daily life. For many, the rationalist religion was comforting, because it included in the church all who tried to live decent Christian lives, not just those who believed they were saved. To others, however, Christian rationalism was heretical, for it rejected the Calvinist belief that salvation came from grace, as the gift of God, and that people must be saved to be full members of the church.

From the 1720s to the 1760s, ministers from various denominations called for the renewal of these beliefs in a series of revivals, known as the Great Awakening. Several of the most important Awakeners brought the impetus for revival from Europe and Great Britain. Religious ferment convulsed British North America, spreading from the churches to threaten social and political authority.

Religious Diversity Before the Great Awakening

In 1720, the British provinces varied widely in religious and ethnic makeup. New England was the most homogeneous, for Massachusetts, New Hampshire, and Connecticut remained predominantly Puritan and of English descent. The established Puritan churches received tax support, but Anglicans, Baptists, and Quakers could also worship freely. Rhode Island, which still embraced the principles of religious liberty and separation of church and state, was home to various denominations, including Quakers, Baptists, and Separatists.

From their founding, the Middle Colonies offered an open door to people of various backgrounds. In the late seventeenth century, according to one report, residents of New York City spoke eighteen different languages. In eastern New Jersey, Scottish Presbyterians, Dutch Reformed, New England Puritans, Baptists, and Quakers settled towns and plantations, and farther south, on both sides of the Delaware River, Native Americans, Dutch, Swedes, and Finns met the Quakers who accompanied William Penn. Philadelphia and its environs in the 1720s boasted organized meetings of many denominations. Though disputes occasionally arose between churches, the Quaker government upheld liberty of conscience throughout the colonial period.

With few towns in the Chesapeake, the established Anglican church suffered from southern rural conditions, as ministers in Virginia faced serious obstacles in meeting the spiritual needs of their scattered congregations. Only half of the Anglican churches had regular preachers. Few planters were interested in converting their African slaves, who kept—and passed on to their children—many traditional African beliefs. The colony's laws against nonconformity prevented most dissent, so only a few Presbyterians and Quakers worshiped openly. In Maryland, many Quakers and Roman Catholics retained their faith, but suffered legal disabilities. The established Church of England in South Carolina was in better condition than in Virginia; some prosperous parishes could afford to pay their well-trained clergy adequately. Even so, Presbyterians, Baptists, Huguenots, and Quakers worshiped freely, for the proprietors had actively recruited dissenters to increase population and obtain their political support.

The Great Awakening shattered the existing church structure of the colonies, as congregations wakened to the teachings and vigorous preaching style of revivalist, or New Light, ministers. Religious diversity grew in provinces where established churches, with government support, dominated religious life—especially Puritan churches in Connecticut and Massachusetts, and the Anglican establishment in Virginia. As a result of the revivals, these colonies became more like Rhode Island, New York, and Pennsylvania.

Early Revivals in the Middle Colonies and New England

In 1720, New Jersey felt the first stirrings of the Great Awakening, when Theodore Jacob Frelinghuysen emigrated from Holland to serve four churches in the Raritan Valley. He had been educated in Dutch Reformed pietism, which emphasized the importance of conversion and personal religious experience (or piety). Using an emotional, revivalist preaching style, he led many people to experience salvation. But Frelinghuysen created a split in the Dutch Reformed churches of New Jersey between his followers, who believed a person must experience God's saving grace before participating in church sacraments, and his opponents, who thought that a commitment to living a godly life was sufficient.

Next, revivals engulfed Presbyterian churches in New Jersey, as they adopted doctrines preached by Gilbert and John Tennent, the sons of William Tennent, a Scots-Irish immigrant and Presbyterian minister. The younger Tennents took pulpits in New Brunswick and Freehold, close to Frelinghuysen's congregations. Impressed by the Dutch Reformed pastor's style of preaching, they inspired revivals of their own. Meanwhile, in Neshaminy, Pennsylvania, the elder Tennent established a seminary, called the "Log College" by his critics, where many New Light ministers received training.

In Massachusetts, revivals began in 1734, when minister Jonathan Edwards of Northampton preached a series of sermons on salvation, inclining many of his parishioners to believe they were saved. They went through the process of self-judgment—first feeling despair as sinners who were damned to hell, then rejoicing in the conviction that God rescued them from this fate. Edwards wrote to a colleague that "this town never was so full of Love, nor so full of Joy, nor so full of distress as it has lately been." Over the next few years, the revival spread to other towns along the Connecticut River.

Revivalism Takes Fire

Beginning in 1739, the Great Awakening spread throughout the British mainland colonies after a young Anglican minister, George Whitefield, arrived from England to tour the Middle Colonies. Called the Grand Itinerant, he had a magnificent voice, ranging from a whisper to a roar, that could be heard by large crowds in fields and city streets. Benjamin Franklin calculated that 25,000 people could easily hear the spectacular preacher at one time.

The Granger Collection, New York

Whitefield found adherents across denominational lines and among native-born Americans and immigrants alike. In 1740, Jonathan Edwards invited Whitefield to Northampton, prompting the itinerant to travel through New England, where he attracted crowds as large as 8,000 in Boston. Other New Light ministers followed, including Gilbert Tennent and James Davenport, a Puritan preacher of Southold, Long Island. Davenport took the Awakening to extremes, harshly attacking other pastors as "unconverted." In 1743, he instigated the burning of books written by well-known clergymen; a year later he repented this excess.

George Whitefield, the itinerant English evangelist, had a spellbinding effect on his listeners, as portrayed here by John Wollaston.

The full force of the Awakening hit the South later than New England and the Middle Atlantic. During the 1740s, Presbyterian missionaries—men who received their education at Tennent's Log College—set up churches on the southern frontier. The new settlements were a fertile field for the revivalists because few regular clergy had migrated west. The more explosive Baptist revivals began in the 1750s, when itinerants traveled through Virginia and North Carolina making converts and forming churches. The Baptists believed that individuals should be saved before they were baptized. With their emotional religious style and challenge to the Anglican establishment in Virginia, they appealed particularly to ordinary white farm families and enslaved African Americans. Followers called each other "Sister" and "Brother," whether slave or free, affluent or poor. They refused to attend their local parish services and condemned many aspects of gentry culture, including horseracing, cockfights, elegant dress, and entertaining on Sunday. Lacking formal churches, Baptists met in fields and homes. The ministry was open to all, even women and slaves, with no requirement for college training.

The Awakening's Impact

The revivals proved to be socially divisive, as many communities split into two groups, the "New Lights" and the "Old Lights." The style of most New Light preachers was to give impassioned, extemporaneous sermons that contrasted dramatically with the closely reasoned sermons of their opponents, the rationalist Old Light ministers. New Lights believed that salvation was more important than religious training; they required a "saved" ministry, with a dynamic preaching style. Congregations responded by fainting, shrieking, and shedding tears. Old Light clergymen, who defended their advanced education in theology, Greek, Hebrew, and ethics, resented accusations that they were unsaved. In turn, they charged the revivalists with being unlearned.

As congregations broke apart, bitter disputes ensued over church property and tax support, spilling what had begun as a religious controversy into the courts and politics. Where strong established churches existed—as in Massachusetts, Connecticut, and Virginia—the New Lights challenged political as well as religious authority. In response, the Connecticut Assembly, for example, passed an Anti-Itinerancy Act, which made it illegal for a clergyman to preach in another's parish without his permission and repealed the 1708 law permitting religious dissent.

Higher education in the British colonies also felt the flames of revivalistic fervor. Yale College was at the center of the intense religious and political battles in Connecticut. When the New Haven church separated, a large number of students, many of them studying for the ministry, followed the New Lights. They skipped classes to attend revivals, challenged Yale's curriculum, and questioned whether their teachers were saved. To suppress the student rebellion, Thomas Clap, head of the college, obtained permission from the Connecticut Assembly to expel any student who attended New Light services. Clap's opposition to the Awakening was not permanent, however, for by 1753 he himself had become a New Light. As in many congregations, people eventually found ways to heal the bitterness and division that the Great Awakening had caused.

A more lasting effect of the revivals was the founding of new colleges. Until the mid-1740s, only Harvard, William and Mary, and Yale—all with ties to established churches—existed in the British colonies. The revivals created a need for ministerial training. Between 1746 and 1769, the revivalists founded the College of New Jersey (now Princeton), the College of Rhode Island (Brown), Queen's College (Rutgers) in New Jersey, and Dartmouth College in New Hampshire. Anglicans established King's College (Columbia) in New York City, while a group of civic leaders, headed by Benjamin Franklin, started the College of Philadelphia (University of Pennsylvania) on a nonsectarian basis. Though each of these new schools except the College of Philadelphia was tied to a specific religious denomination, they all accepted young men of various faiths. These new colleges taught traditional subjects, but also adopted the new curricula in mathematics, science, and modern languages.

Cultural Diversity and Expansion

Between 1720 and 1760, the population of British North America grew from 472,000 to 1,600,000. Much of this growth came from natural increase, but new arrivals also spurred population growth, as thousands of Germans and Scots-Irish immigrated, and slave traders continued to import blacks.

The newcomers brought ideas, religious beliefs, skills, and ways of life that significantly altered the cultural mix of the British colonies. Some played important roles in spreading the Enlightenment, while others started the Great Awakening. The immigrants from the European continent and the British Isles sought a new beginning in "the best poor man's country": many disembarked in the Middle Colonies, traveling west to settle the backcountry from Pennsylvania south through the Shenandoah Valley to the Carolinas. Others went directly to Georgia, which reformers started in 1732 as a haven for the poor. The population explosion and demand for new lands brought the British colonists face to face with the Spanish in Florida, the French in Canada and the Ohio Valley, and Native Americans all along the frontier.

German and Scots-Irish Immigrants

More than 100,000 Germans left their homelands for America during the century after 1683; most of them immigrated between 1727 and 1756. Some were forced out by religious persecution, oppressive regulations, and war; others sought economic opportunity. Promoters called "newlanders" told Germans of cheap fertile land and mild government in the British colonies. Many immigrants paid their own passage. Those who could not signed on as "redemptioners," the equivalent of indentured servants, whose labor would be sold for a number of years upon arrival. Immigrants went to ports from New York to Georgia, with most entering the Delaware Valley. Some Germans remained in Philadelphia, but the majority headed for the Pennsylvania hinterland and south through the backcountry of Maryland, Virginia, and the Carolinas.

German-speaking immigrants found the freedom they sought in North America, congregating in distinct communities, building separate churches and schools, and maintaining German language and culture. Pennsylvania was the heart of German America, as the colony's religious freedom allowed a multitude of sects and churches to flourish—the Mennonites, Amish, Brethren, Moravians, Schwenkfelders, Lutheran, and Reformed.

Cultural exchange between the Germans and English enriched American society. German churches installed organs and introduced the sophisticated choral music of their homelands. The printer Christopher Saur reprinted German hymnals along with his German-language newspaper and almanac. Congregations founded schools in which children learned both German and English. Immigrants retained the old tongue in their churches and homes, but used English in business, the courts, and politics. German American decorative arts proliferated by the 1740s, in house ornaments, furniture, and elaborately illustrated documents, such as marriage certificates, with gothic *Fraktur* lettering.

Map 4.1 German and Scots-Irish Settlements in Colonial British America, c. 1760 Germans and Scots-Irish were relative latecomers in colonial British America, so they established farms outside the first English settlements. Many entered ports on the Delaware River, moved north and west in Pennsylvania, then south through western Maryland, the Shenandoah Valley of Virginia, and North and South Carolina.

German farm women did much heavier fieldwork than most English wives, but otherwise played a similar role in maintaining domestic culture. Germans favored the more efficient European stoves over English fireplaces, and pewter over tinware. In diet, they ate relatively little meat and preferred coffee to tea. But like their English neighbors, German women served as midwives and dispensed herbal remedies.

Though some German immigrants engaged in politics and law, most remained uninvolved in government during the colonial period. As non-British immigrants with little wealth, they needed time to become naturalized, learn the language and political culture, and establish themselves economically. As exiles from persecution, high taxes, and war, Germans were grateful for the high degree of freedom that they found in the new land.

Large numbers of Scots, Scots-Irish, and Irish Catholics also came during the eighteenth century, settling in New York, Pennsylvania, Delaware, western Maryland, and the southern backcountry. Most were Ulster Scots (or Scots-Irish as they were called in America), Presbyterians whose families had migrated during the 1600s from Scotland to northern Ireland in search of economic opportunity. There they had combined tenant farming and weaving until the early eighteenth century, when their leases expired. Because landlords raised rents exorbitantly, many Ulster Scots left with their families for the colonies. The first large wave of immigrants departed during 1717–1718; poor harvests and downturns in the linen industry impelled successive groups toward America.

In the colonies, the Scots-Irish achieved a reputation as tough defenders of the frontier. As relatively late arrivals, they had to stake out farms on the edges of existing white settlements. The combination of agriculture and linen manufacture was a distinctive contribution of the Ulster Scots to the colonial economy. As frontier inhabitants, the Scots-Irish came into frequent contact with Native Americans, often with tragic results. The new settlers often marked out their farms on Indian hunting lands without negotiating a sale. One Pennsylvania frontiersman, not recognizing the Indians' rights, echoed the early Puritans when he argued that it was contrary to "the laws of God and nature, that so much land should be idle, while so many Christians wanted it to labor on, and to raise their bread."

The Founding of Georgia

The last of the British mainland colonies, Georgia lured many German and Scots-Irish immigrants, as well as Scots and English. Animated by Enlightenment ideals of human progress and freedom, James Oglethorpe and John Viscount Percival, members of the Associates of the Late Doctor Bray, a philanthropic society, sought a charter for the colony. They were convinced that something had to be done to help the poor. They also argued that the settlement could serve as a buffer between Spanish Florida and South Carolina. The English had craved the region since the late seventeenth century when Carolinians destroyed the Spanish missions of Guale. George II granted the charter, placing control of the colony in the hands of trustees, or proprietors, who could neither receive financial benefits from the province nor own land within its bounds.

The double function of Georgia as a haven for the poor and a military outpost shaped the terms under which settlers immigrated. The trustees intended to create a peaceful, moral society of small farmers in which everyone, except indentured servants, worked for themselves. The proprietors wanted to avoid duplicating lowland South Carolina where large plantation owners lived off the toil of their slaves. The Georgia Trustees, led by Oglethorpe, set three significant policies: they prohibited importation of hard liquor, banned slaveholding, and limited land ownership to 500 acres or less. Each free male immigrant was granted land at no charge, but no one could buy or sell real estate, and only men could inherit land. The trustees hoped to keep Georgia as a refuge for small farmers who, coincidentally, would defend the southern frontier.

In February 1733, the ship *Anne* with approximately one hundred passengers arrived at a site on the Savannah River. Here they built the first town, Savannah, on a high bluff overlooking the river. Oglethorpe purchased land from the Native Americans and pledged to prevent price gouging in trade, a significant complaint of the Indians against South Carolina merchants. He established alliances with Lower Creeks, Cherokees, and Chickasaws against Spanish Florida, not least because English traders offered better merchandise than their rivals.

Many settlers in Georgia believed that the prohibitions on liquor, land sales, and slavery were unreasonable, but they could do little to change the colony's direction because they lacked a representative assembly. The embargo on rum, a major Caribbean commodity, prevented expansion of trade with the West Indies, a ready market for their abundant lumber. The bans on slavery and large landholdings were also unpopular with many settlers, who coveted the grander lifestyle of planters north of the Savannah River, in South Carolina.

In consequence, Georgia grew slowly, as some settlers left almost immediately. The trustees gradually recognized their failure, allowing the importation of rum in 1742, and land sales and slavery in 1750. Preparing to turn the colony over to the Crown, in 1751 they called together Georgia's first elected assembly, which obtained legislative powers three years later when the royal government took control. The Georgia population swelled as South Carolinians migrated across the Savannah River, transforming Georgia into a slave society. By 1773, the province had 33,000 inhabitants, of whom 45 percent were enslaved blacks.

Despite its halting start before 1750, Georgia attracted settlers of a variety of nationalities and religions. The colony tapped the eighteenth-century flow of European immigrants, including Spanish and German Jews and German-speaking Lutherans. One of the Lutheran ministers described their satisfaction with the new land: "Every year God gives them what they need. And since they have been able to earn something apart from agriculture, through the mills which have been built and in many other ways, they have managed rather well with God's blessing, and have led a calm and quiet life of blessedness and honesty." Another group of German Protestants, the Moravians, were less content in Georgia, where they hoped to convert the Native Americans. Led by Count Nikolaus Ludwig von Zinzendorf, they arrived in 1735 and were gone five years later, because as pacifists, Moravian men could not serve in the militia. When the threat of Spanish invasion intensified in the late 1730s, most of the Moravians departed for Pennsylvania, which required no military service.

The Growth of the African American Population

The failure of the trustees to create a free society in Georgia was symptomatic of the entrenchment of slavery in America. Like the Germans and Scots-Irish, Africans helped diversify the American population and shape its culture. Though the number of African Americans grew naturally in many places, slave traders imported over 200,000 people between 1720 and the Revolution, most from West and Central Africa. In 1750, blacks comprised one-fifth of the population of the mainland colonies, including about 40 percent in the Chesapeake and the Lower South.

As the number of African Americans increased and slave societies matured, blacks created patterns of community, work, and culture. Extended kinship networks structured community life on large plantations, and even in places where slaves lived in small households, such as in northern cities, family ties remained paramount. Blacks were most successful in perpetuating African language and customs in regions where they were most numerous, particularly the South Carolina low country and, later, Georgia. Because they came from hundreds of societies in Africa, with many different cultural attributes, they had difficulty keeping traditional ways intact. They melded African and European forms together, and in the process, influenced evolving mainstream cultures, especially in the South.

The opportunity of slaves to engage in independent activities varied with the amount of time they had to spend working for their master. In South Carolina, blacks labored by the task; each slave received a certain amount of work to perform each day—a field to hoe, thread to spin, a fence to build. Those who completed their assignments quickly had time to raise their own crops and livestock. Consequently, Carolina slaves participated in trade, selling

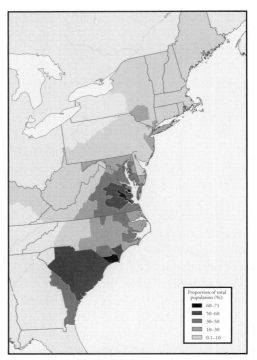

Proportion of total
population (%):

■ 60–71
■ 50–60
■ 30–50
□ 10–30
□ 0.1–10

Map 4.2 African American Population in Colonial British America, c. 1760 A much higher concentration of enslaved African Americans lived in colonies south of Pennsylvania. Notice, however, that the percentage of slaves in parts of New York and New Jersey was as high as in portions of the Chesapeake region and North Carolina. Uniform data for South Carolina mask the fact that the population of African Americans was much larger along the seacoast than in the upcountry.

their production at the "Negro market" in Charleston on Sundays. As in Africa, women were responsible for marketing the family's goods. In the Chesapeake, most slaves on plantations labored for a specified number of hours rather than by the task. They planted, weeded, or harvested in gangs until the overseer told them to stop. As a result, they had little time to work for themselves.

The persistence of African culture was conspicuous in language, food, music, dance, and religion. Some newly arrived Africans knew Dutch, Spanish, Portuguese, French, or English from former contacts in Africa or the West Indies, but to communicate with other slaves and with Europeans, most adopted Creole speech, a combination of English and African languages. In the Lower South, for instance, the Creole tongue known as Gullah evolved from English and various languages from southern Nigeria, the Gold Coast, Angola, and Senegambia. African Americans retained black dialect from Creole. For example, most blacks used the word *buckra,* from the African word meaning "he

Slave Advertisements

Colonial newspapers regularly published advertisements of enslaved Africans for sale and notices of escaped servants and slaves. These items often provide detailed information about the skills, health, and living conditions of African Americans. This excerpt includes, first, a notice for "A Parcel of likely young Negroes to be Sold." These slaves had probably been imported from Africa or the West Indies. Another advertisement is to sell "A Strong, healthy and handy Negro Woman, that has had the Small Pox and can do all sorts of Houshold Business, can speak English, and has been several years in the Country." This suggests qualities that were important to owners in cities such as Boston—ability to do all kinds of domestic work and familiarity with the language and region.

In the advertisement for the escaped slave Caesar, we learn about his age and appearance, and that he took some of his master's clothes. Like other owners who composed runaway advertisements, John Woods tried to guess the slave's motivation.

Courtesy, American Antiquarian Society

who governs," to refer to white men. Africans also influenced white speech patterns, when white children and immigrants sometimes adopted African American dialect. One British traveler complained that plantation owners allowed "their children . . . . to prowl amongst the young Negroes, which insensibly causes them to imbibe their manners and broken speech." Some African words became part of American vocabulary, including cola, yam, goober (peanut), and toting (carrying) a package.

Blacks contributed to the food and material culture of British America, popularizing new foods such as okra, melons, and bananas. They made clay pipes, pottery, and baskets with African designs, and carved eating utensils, chairs, and other useful objects from wood. They built houses on African models rather than European. In music, they introduced the use of percussion instruments—cymbals, tambourines, and drums—to British military bands. While masters discouraged Africans from drumming because of the potential to call others to revolt, whites enjoyed the music of black fiddlers. Slaves helped create the Virginia "jig," a fusion of African and European elements, accompanied by banjos and fiddles.

Along with whites, during the Great Awakening, Africans shaped the forms of worship in southern Baptist churches. Blacks retained traditional African concepts of the hereafter, where the deceased reunited with ancestors, combining these beliefs with European views of heaven. Funerals remained important to African Americans through-out the colonies, as mourners buried the dead facing Africa, with traditional rituals, music, and dance. In Philadelphia, for example, the blacks' burial ground was the focus of community activities where they gathered on Sundays and holidays, "dancing after the manner of their several nations in Africa, and speaking and singing in their native dialects." Blacks also passed down African medical practice, a combination of physical and psychological treatment including magic. More African American women than men were doctors, practicing midwifery as well as nursing and providing cures.

Despite cultural exchange and indications of human understanding, the antagonism and economic exploitation inherent in slavery poisoned relationships among whites and blacks. Whites believed that African Americans were an inferior race; masters used their power in the slave system to control their human property with harsh punishments. Nev-ertheless, blacks refused to accept their subordinate position, as increasing numbers ran away or were truant for weeks at a time.

Some enslaved Africans took more violent means, killing their masters or setting fire to fields and homes. In 1739, a group of more than fifty bondmen revolted near the Stono River in South Carolina. For most of a day, they marched with drums and banners from one plantation to another, killing about twenty whites. When armed planters defeated the rebels in battle, some of the slaves regrouped and headed for St. Augustine, Florida. But the South Carolina militia pursued the insurgents, putting to death everyone suspected of being involved. The Stono Uprising sent shock waves throughout the American colonies. The South Carolina legislature enacted a harsh slave code in an effort to prevent future revolts and limited slave importation for a decade. Most of the core group who planned the Stono Rebellion were African-born slaves, who hoped to escape to Florida, where Spanish authorities offered them religious sanctuary and freedom. By 1740, about one hundred former Carolina slaves had built the village of Gracia Real de Santa Teresa de Mose, called Mose, two miles north of St. Augustine.

During the eighteenth century, newly arrived Africans, often called "salt-water Negroes," were more likely to rebel or run away than Creole, or "country-born" slaves. With Native Americans and runaway white servants, escaped slaves created maroon soci-eties in frontier areas. They farmed, raised livestock, hunted, and fished. In the Great Dis-mal Swamp, on the North Carolina-Virginia border, communities numbering perhaps 2,000 people took refuge from colonial authorities. The Dismal Swamp settlements grew from small groups of Native Americans from Virginia to include Indians and whites from the Carolinas and increasing numbers of escaped Africans.

Native American Worlds in the Mid-Eighteenth Century

As the British colonies grew, Native Americans chose strategies to maintain their commu-nities and cultures. Those who remained within the British provinces were called by white Americans "Settlement Indians," "domestic Indians," or "little Tribes." Many lived among

Euro-Americans and worked as servants, slaves, day laborers, mariners, artisans, and tenant farmers, assimilating some parts of English culture, but rejecting others. Others lived on remnants of traditional lands, such as the Mashpees in Massachusetts, Lenapes (or Delawares) in New Jersey, and Catawbas in South Carolina. They continued to hunt, fish, gather berries and wood, and raise corn while also trading with neighboring whites. Indians peddled venison and turkeys to the colonists or crafted baskets and brooms for sale. The Lenapes of central New Jersey farmed parcels of land through the eighteenth century: they pursued their traditional seasonal economy by hunting in Pennsylvania, fishing at the Jersey shore, and gathering berries and wood for baskets in the Pine Barrens.

Dr. Alexander Hamilton, a recent immigrant from Scotland, recorded many encounters with Indians in 1744 as he traveled through the settlements from Maryland to Maine. The Native Americans he met varied greatly in status, from an Indian sachem who had established himself as a wealthy planter to those on the margins, who tried to hold on to native traditions within an alien culture. In Rhode Island, he approached the large plantation of

> an Indian King named George . . . upon which he has many tennants and has, of his own, a good stock of horses and other cattle. The King lives after the English mode. His subjects have lost their own government policy and laws and are servants or vassals to the English here. His queen goes in a high modish dress in her silks, hoops, stays, and dresses like an English woman. He educates his children to the belles letters and is himself a very complaisant mannerly man. We pay'd him a visit, and he treated us with a glass of good wine.

During worship in a Boston church, Hamilton sat near several Native Americans. He met an Indian at Princeton who saluted him with "How' s't ni tap" and, in New York, watched "about ten Indians fishing for oysters . . . stark naked" near his tavern. While most native people who stayed in white settled areas had given up political autonomy, they had not surrendered all of their traditions. Many spoke English in addition to their native language, but did not learn to read and write.

The Great Awakening made a significant impact on many Indians within colonial settlements who had long resisted Christianity. The dynamic preaching of New Light ministers, who welcomed enthusiastic response from their listeners, was attractive to Native Americans who had retained traditional rituals and dance. The Society in Scotland for Propagating Christian Knowledge, a group of Presbyterian ministers and laymen, supported missions in the Middle Colonies, particularly that of Reverend David Brainerd and, after his death in 1747, his brother Reverend John Brainerd. David Brainerd was expelled from Yale College because he had joined the New Lights and became a missionary to Indians in Pennsylvania and New Jersey. With crucial assistance from his Lenape interpreter, Moses (Tunda) Tatamy, he inspired a revival at Crossweeksung in central New Jersey. The community soon outgrew its limited space, so Brainerd encouraged the Lenapes to move to another site, where he attempted to create a New England-style praying town. While the Indians attended the Presbyterian church and school, they did not give up their seasonal economy of hunting, fishing, and gathering as the Brainerds hoped. Other New Jersey Lenapes joined the Moravian missions near Bethlehem, Pennsylvania, while many continued to resist Christianity altogether.

Native Americans who intended to preserve their political independence moved west, a strategy that worked temporarily. From 1660 to the 1740s, for example, Iroquois, Shawnees, and Lenapes relocated in the eastern part of the Ohio Valley, from the Allegheny River in western Pennsylvania to west-central Ohio. Wyandots inhabited the lands to the west, at Sandusky and near the French fort at Detroit. Some Iroquois migrated from western New York, while Lenapes and Shawnees moved from eastern Pennsylvania under pressure from white settlers. Some of the Lenapes left the east as a result of the "Walking Purchase" of 1737, when two of William Penn's sons, the proprietors, used an alleged 1686 deed to cheat the Indians out of their territory on the Pennsylvania side of the Delaware River. The deed, of which only a copy survived, ceded lands as far as a man could walk in one and a half days. Coerced by an alliance between the Penns and the Iroquois, the Lenapes agreed to comply. The Penns sent runners in relay to cover more than sixty miles of land in a day and a half, a deception the Lenapes could not fail to remember; in 1754, with the outbreak of war on the Pennsylvania frontier, many sought revenge.

By permission of Yale University Press

The Lenape leader Teedyuscung by William Sauts NetamuX'we Bock. In this drawing, Teedyuscung's combination of a Euro-American coat and vest and Indian hairstyle and jewelry reflects his attempt to bridge cultures.

The Ohio Valley became the focus of conflict in the 1740s as the British and French competed for trade. Following the Lenapes and Shawnees west, some Pennsylvania traders took up residence in the multi-ethnic towns such as Chiningue (or Logstown), where Iroquois, Lenapes, Shawnees, Ottawas, and other Indians lived. The Ohio Valley, as one Indian leader said, was "a country in between" the English and the French, unfortunately a country that the Europeans craved. From 1754 to 1814, the Native Americans fought the British and Americans to keep their lands and native religions, forging pan-Indian alliances to meet the Anglo threat.

Wars for Empire

For a quarter century beginning in 1739, the British colonies took part in conflicts between Great Britain and Spain, France, and Native Americans. The War of Jenkins' Ear (1739–1744) against Spain; King George's War (1744–1748) against France; the Seven

Years' War (1754–1763), also called the French and Indian War in the colonies; and the Indian war for autonomy in the Ohio Valley (1763–1765) all required British colonists to participate more actively in defending the empire.

The Southern Frontier

The colonies along the southern tier—British South Carolina and Georgia, Spanish Florida, French Louisiana, and Spanish Texas and New Mexico—competed for trade with Native Americans and control of territory. Except for war between Georgia and Florida in the early 1740s, the most important battles along the southern rim were commercial, a competition the British traders often won because they had more plentiful and cheaper goods. They exchanged tools, clothing, scissors, guns, ammunition, and rum, in return for slaves, deerskins, and furs from the Indians. In comparison with the English provinces, the Spanish and French colonies remained small and badly supplied by their parent nations. In 1760, Florida had approximately 3,000 Hispanic settlers, Texas had 1,200, and New Mexico about 9,000, while Louisiana counted 4,000 whites and 5,000 enslaved Africans. In contrast, in the same year, South Carolina and Georgia had a population of about 45,000 whites and 59,000 black slaves.

Governor James Oglethorpe of Georgia tried to use the outbreak of the War of Jenkins' Ear to eject the Spanish from Florida. As part of the 1713 Treaty of Utrecht, Britain had obtained the *asiento,* the right to sell a specified number of African slaves and commodities to the Spanish provinces. This opening led to British smuggling, which the Spanish countered with heavy-handed searches of British ships. Accounts of Spanish brutality inflamed the British public, especially when Captain Robert Jenkins displayed one of his ears, which he claimed the Spanish cut off when they caught him smuggling. In 1740, Oglethorpe attacked Florida with seven ships and 2,000 troops. They captured several Spanish forts and Mose, the village of escaped Carolina blacks, but failed to conquer Fort San Marcos, where the residents of St. Augustine and Mose took cover. A large percentage of Florida residents were soldiers to guard Atlantic shipping lanes. When Hispanic and black soldiers slipped out of the fort and recaptured Mose, and then the fort was resupplied by Cuba, Oglethorpe retreated.

In 1741, a force of 3,600 colonists participated in the British expedition against the Spanish fort at Cartagena, in what is now Colombia. The campaign ended bitterly, with heavy losses from battle and smallpox. The following year, the Spanish took revenge for the invasion of Florida by attacking St. Simon's Island, Georgia, but withdrew before conquering it. After some minor skirmishes, both sides gave up, bringing calm to the Georgia-Florida border.

King George's War

The British avoided further conflict with Florida because, in 1744, they began hostilities with France in the War of the Austrian Succession, known to the colonists as King George's War. The war began in Europe, but spilled into North America when, provoked by French attacks on Nova Scotia, Governor William Shirley of Massachusetts launched an attack on Louisbourg, which controlled access to the St. Lawrence River. In April 1745, 4,000 New England farmers and fishermen assaulted the French garrison, which held out against the badly organized offensive until June, then surrendered. New Englanders considered Louisbourg a great victory, even after many of their troops succumbed to disease. The war degenerated into a series of debilitating border raids. The Canadians and their Indian allies ravaged Saratoga, New York, and northern New England. In spring 1746, a fleet of seventy-six ships left France to retake Louisbourg, but after fighting disease and Atlantic storms for three months they returned to France empty-handed.

Despite this reprieve, New Englanders had little to celebrate, for they faced another threat—from their own imperial navy. During the war, Parliament permitted naval officers to impress sailors without the permission of colonial authorities. The Royal Navy used impressment, or involuntary recruitment, because many seamen fled the harsh conditions on naval vessels. In 1747, several thousand Bostonians protested when a British press gang from the fleet of Admiral Charles Knowles swept up men along the waterfront. The mob surrounded the governor's house and burned a British barge in his courtyard. When the governor called up the militia, the troops refused to move. Knowles threatened to shell the town, but after negotiations lasting several days, he released the impressed men instead.

As the colonists became more involved in imperial politics, they learned that their interests held little sway. To their shock, the British government restored Louisbourg to the French in the Treaty of Aix-la-Chapelle (1748), as the combatants agreed to return all North American territories seized during the war. Despite heavy human and financial costs, the war brought no change in the power balance between Great Britain and France in North America.

The Seven Years' War

During King George's War, the British and Iroquois had evicted French traders from the Ohio Valley. The Canadians returned, however, backed by a government that was determined to force out the British colonists who had stepped-up activity in the area. The Ohio Company of Virginia, which had received the rights to half a million acres from the British government, in 1749 made preparations to sell land in the region of present-day Pittsburgh, Pennsylvania, where the Monongahela and Allegheny rivers combine to form the Ohio River. Virginia's claim to the territory dated from its charter. In response, the French constructed forts to stop the incursion of Anglo-American traders and Virginia's land speculators. In 1754, the governor of Virginia sent a young militia officer, George Washington, with about 160 troops to erect a stronghold to defend the colony's interests. When hostilities resulted, the Virginians were defeated at the inadequate structure they had built, Fort Necessity, by a superior force of French and Indians.

Recognizing that war was imminent, seven colonies sent delegates to a congress at Albany, New York, where they negotiated unsuccessfully with the Iroquois for an alliance against the French. The Albany Congress also amended and adopted the Albany Plan devised by Benjamin Franklin to unite the colonies for common defense. The plan would have to be endorsed by each colony and the Crown. When the delegates returned home with the pro-

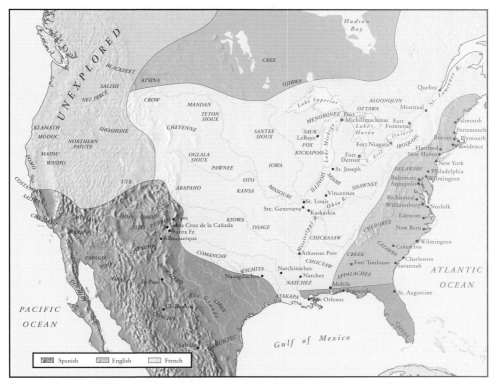

Map 4.3 North America in 1750 Great Britain, France, and Spain claimed the indicated areas just before the Seven Years' War. While waves of immigrants from Germany and the British Isles had expanded settlement in the British provinces since 1700 (see Map 3.3), the French colonies still consisted primarily of trading posts, forts, and relatively small agricultural areas. Native Americans controlled much of the territory claimed by France.

posal for an intercolonial government empowered to tax, pass laws, and supervise military defense, not one of the assemblies approved.

The British decided to destroy French forts in what they considered their territory even before a formal declaration of war. In early 1755, Major General Edward Braddock landed in the colonies with two British regiments. Joined by hundreds of provincial soldiers, the army marched through the Virginia backcountry to capture Fort Duquesne (now Pittsburgh). The British troops were unprepared for frontier fighting, but thought their mission was easy because the garrison had only 250 French troops. Ten miles short of Fort Duquesne, however, the French and allied Indians ambushed Braddock's army, killing or wounding two-thirds of the British force. The general himself was mortally wounded. George Washington, his uniform ripped by bullets, led the retreat.

The 650 Native Americans who fought with the French included their traditional allies and some Delawares and Iroquois of the Ohio Valley who had previously supported the British. By 1754, some Ohio Indians were convinced that Britain and its colonies posed the

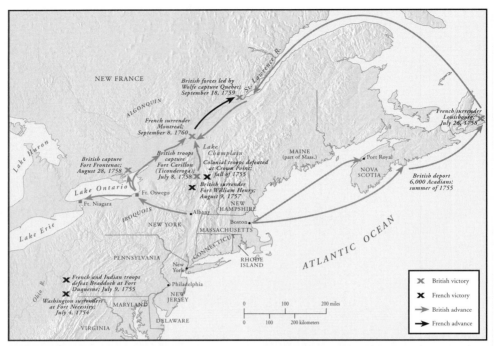

Map 4.4 Seven Years' War in North America The war began in the Ohio Valley, an area Virginians claimed and hoped to sell to settlers. To do so, they had to force out the French, who sent troops to establish ownership; defeat the Delawares and Shawnees, who had built towns along the Allegheny and Ohio Rivers; and prevail over Pennsylvania's competing charter claims.

greatest threat to their lands; with the defeat of Braddock, many more joined the French. Between 1755 and 1757, Delawares, Shawnees, Iroquois, and many others attacked the white frontier from Pennsylvania to Virginia, burning settlements and killing or capturing thousands of colonists.

Help for the westerners was slow in coming. In 1756, the struggle in North America became part of the larger European conflict known as the Seven Years' War, in which Great Britain supported Prussia against Austria, Russia, and France. The French penetrated into New York, seizing Fort William Henry and 2,000 soldiers at Lake George. The tide changed after the British statesman William Pitt took command of the war effort. He poured money and men into the American theater, expecting colonial legislatures to

Benjamin Franklin published his "Snake Device" just before the Albany Congress in 1754. Considered the first political cartoon in the colonies, it later became an important symbol of American resistance to Britain.

do the same. The new generals Jeffery Amherst and James Wolfe, with an army of almost 10,000 men, captured Louisbourg in July 1758. The French then pulled their troops out of the Ohio Valley to protect Quebec and Montreal, allowing the British to take control of the west. Without French supplies and devastated by smallpox, the Native Americans ended their war on the frontier.

In 1759, the British and provincial armies had even greater success, leading some of the Iroquois of New York to abandon neutrality to join their side. The British reestablished control of New York, while from Louisbourg, General Wolfe sailed up the St. Lawrence to Quebec, where after several months his forces pierced the defenses of the well-fortified city. The next year, Amherst's army seized Montreal, thus ending French control of Canada.

While the defeat of Canada marked the end of the war in North America, the Seven Years' War continued off the coast of France, in India, and in the West Indies. The British military took a number of French sugar islands, including the richest, Guadeloupe. When Spain entered the conflict as France's ally in 1762 in return for the promise of lands west of the Mississippi River, the British captured Manila in the Philippines and Havana, Cuba.

During the Seven Years' War, thousands of colonists joined the British army, and many more served in the provincial forces. The experience brought ordinary settlers into close contact with the imperial authorities—and many loathed the experience. The British army contained professional soldiers drilled rigorously in military tactics, cleanliness, and order. Women served in the field, generally soldiers' wives who cooked, washed, and nursed. British officers, from the upper classes, maintained discipline with punishments of death for major offenses such as desertion, and up to 1,000 lashes—which could also kill—for lesser crimes. The British officers disdained the colonial units, which submitted to much lighter discipline and sometimes elected their superiors. Because the provincials failed to keep their camps and clothing clean, many died from disease. For their part, some colonial soldiers thought the British regulars were immoral, profane men who needed to be controlled with brutal discipline.

The British colonists welcomed the Treaty of Paris in 1763, which finally ended the war. Under the treaty, France lost all of its territory in North America, but retrieved the valuable sugar islands of Guadeloupe and Martinique. Spain relinquished Florida to get back Cuba and the Philippines and, because the British lacked interest in the region, acquired French territory west of the Mississippi and New Orleans, located on the east side of the river. The Treaty of Paris gave the British colonists security from France and Spain, while the home government received two unprofitable colonies, Canada and Florida. The provincials celebrated the victory with patriotic fervor, as New York City raised a statue of George III, who had taken the throne in 1760 at age twenty-two. Many colonists, especially New England ministers, had interpreted the war as a fight against Catholicism and tyranny. They viewed the victory as a sign that God favored Britain and its colonies. One Massachusetts clergyman preached,

> Safe from the Enemy of the Wilderness, safe from the gripping Hand of arbitrary Sway and cruel Superstition; Here shall be the late founded Seat of Peace and Freedom. Here shall our indulgent Mother [Britain], who has most generously rescued and protected us, be served and honoured by growing Numbers, with all Duty, Love and Gratitude, till Time shall be no more.

The Indians Renew War in the Ohio Valley

The Treaty of Paris seriously undermined the position of Native Americans east of the Mississippi whether they had fought for the British or French, or had remained neutral. The defeat of France worsened the situation of native people in the Ohio Valley, for they could no longer play one European nation off the other. The British alone supplied European goods, so they could set prices and the terms of trade. They ended the custom of giving annual presents, charged high prices, stopped selling rum, and reduced the amount of ammunition sold. Further, with the end of the Seven Years' War, white settlers streamed west into Indian lands, as wealthy land speculators and poor squatters alike ignored treaties that colonial governments had made with the Native Americans.

The altered British trade policies and land grabbing drove many Delawares, Shawnees, Iroquois, and others to renew the fighting. They gained spiritual unity from the Delaware prophet Neolin, one of a line of spiritual leaders among the Delawares and Shawnees, who preached that Indians must reject Christianity and European goods, particularly rum, and revitalize their ancient culture. Neolin called on Native Americans to drive the Europeans out, demanding: "Whereupon do you suffer the whites to dwell upon your lands? Drive them away; wage war against them. I love them not." He warned his followers, "if you suffer the English among you, you are dead men. Sickness, smallpox, and their poison will destroy you entirely."

Many Indians throughout the Ohio Valley adopted Neolin's strategy, boycotting the fur trade by hunting only for their own food and personal needs. The Delaware councils called for a gradual return to military skills with bow and arrow and adopted a ritual tea, which caused vomiting, to cleanse themselves of the "White people's ways and Nature." In 1763, Native Americans from western Pennsylvania through the Great Lakes region launched a pan-Indian assault on British garrisons, often called Pontiac's War. A follower of Neolin and leader of the Ottawas, Pontiac laid siege unsuccessfully to the British fort at Detroit. Other Indians defeated thirteen British outposts, though not Forts Niagara or Pittsburgh. While the British army established military dominance in the Ohio Valley by the end of 1763, after the Native Americans ran short of ammunition and succumbed to smallpox, fighting continued for two more years.

In addition to armed force, the British government tried to end the war by keeping white settlers out of the Ohio Valley. The king issued the Proclamation of 1763, which drew a line along the crest of the Appalachian Mountains from Maine to Georgia, requiring colonists to stay east of the line. Colonial governors were instructed to prohibit surveys or land grants west of the Proclamation line; only authorized agents of the Crown could buy lands from the Indians for future settlement. The Proclamation failed in its purpose, however, as land speculators continued their operations and immigrants demanded farms. The British government, weighed down by debt from the Seven Years' War, failed to supply manpower to enforce the law. The government withdrew troops from the Ohio Valley and Great Lakes region, while provincial governments, dominated by speculators, ignored encroachment on Indian lands.

Treaty Negotiations

This engraving, *The Indians Giving a Talk to Colonel Bouquet . . . in Octr. 1764*, was based on a sketch by the artist Benjamin West. The illustration was first published in a 1766 account of Henry Bouquet's successful 1764 expedition against the Ohio Indians during Pontiac's War. Bouquet's troops left Fort Pitt on October 3rd, marching west toward the Muskingum River in what is now eastern Ohio. While en route they received a message that the Delaware and Shawnee leaders "were coming as soon as possible to treat of peace." After building fortifications, Bouquet and his aides met with the Indians October 17–20th. They struck a truce, and the Natives pledged to return white captives. When they delivered more than 200 captives by November 9th, the war ended east of the Muskingum but continued in the west. The engraving shows a typical treaty scene, with a Native leader using a wampum belt to speak, while a scribe took minutes.

The British Provinces in 1763

The end of the Seven Years' War brought pivotal changes in British North America. For over a century and a half, Europeans had crossed the ocean to trade with the Native Americans, build farms and businesses, and develop networks of Atlantic commerce. The colonies had dealt with crises, from economic slumps to rebellions, becoming ever more confident of their position as semi-independent societies. During the last quarter century, with greater involvement in imperial affairs and rising importation of consumer goods, the provincials felt more a part of the British empire—more English—even as they created a separate identity as Americans. Most importantly, they believed that they were equal to the residents of Great Britain, that they possessed the rights of English people.

The Economy

In 1763, the mainland provinces still operated within the system of British mercantilism, which consisted of regulations on colonial trade and manufactures. For mercantilism to work to Britain's benefit, the colonies had to produce raw materials and agricultural staples needed by the home economy and serve as a market for its manufactured goods. Such colonial products as sugar, molasses, tobacco, cotton, certain wood products, copper, and furs were "enumerated," meaning that they could be shipped only to Britain or British colonial ports, not to foreign countries such as France and Spain. The basic laws establishing the British mercantilist system were the seventeenth-century Navigation Acts, which Parliament supplemented from time to time. Though most colonial trade conformed to the law by the eighteenth century, smuggling occurred often enough to prompt demands within the British government for strict enforcement. In particular, colonial shippers bribed customs officials to ignore the Molasses Act (1733), which levied prohibitive duties on foreign sugar products, including a tax of sixpence per gallon on molasses. The British West Indies planters had pushed for the act to create a monopoly for themselves, lowering the cost of provisions and raising the price of their exports. If the Molasses Act had been enforced, it would have severely damaged the economies of New England and the Middle Colonies, which traded with the French, Spanish, and Dutch West Indies as well as the British islands.

Other laws passed by Parliament prior to 1763 had a significant but uneven impact on colonial economic growth. British legislation, combined with lack of investment capital, limited the development of most manufactures. The Woolen Act (1699) and the Hat Act (1732) banned the export of American-produced woolen products and hats from one colony to another. Other laws prohibited the export of machinery and the migration of skilled craftsmen from Britain to America. The Iron Act (1750) allowed duty-free import of colonial bar iron into Britain, but forbade fabrication of iron goods in the colonies. Nevertheless, crude iron production received substantial investment, as did shipbuilding and rum distilling. Unhampered by mercantilist regulation, North American shipbuilders produced nearly 40 percent of vessels in the British-owned merchant fleet.

Despite these laws, the wealth of the British colonies increased between the 1720s and 1760, as trade flourished with the West Indies and, after 1750, with southern Europe, where crop failures and population growth swelled demand for wheat and flour. The Middle Colonies, already expanding with German and Irish immigration, were well situated to supply new markets. Philadelphia became the largest city in the British colonies: its wealthy merchants invested in ships, built mansions, purchased coaches and other luxuries, and speculated in western lands from the profits of trade. Artisans, shopkeepers, and farmers prospered. To the south, large planters in the Chesapeake and Carolinas accumulated great estates, while ordinary farmers more modestly improved their standard of living. All along the eastern seaboard, after 1750, white families indulged in what has been called a "consumer revolution." Not only could they purchase cloth, clothing, carpets, paper, gloves, mirrors, clocks, silverware, china tea sets, pottery, and books, but they had more choices in the specific kind of cloth or paper or gloves they could buy. In New York City in the 1750s, for instance, merchants advertised gloves of various colors—purple, orange, white, and flowered—as well as different sizes and materials, including chamois, silk, "Maid's Lamb Gloves," and "Men's Dog Skin Gloves." This is just one example of the wide variety of consumer goods that became available in mid-century.

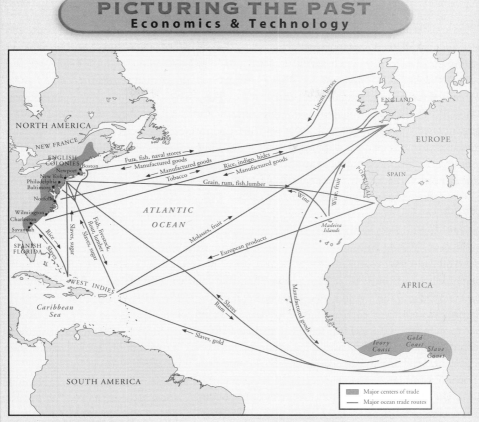

Map 4.5 Colonial Overseas Trade

By 1750, the Atlantic economy had matured, as each of the British mainland colonies developed products for sale in Great Britain, Europe, Africa, and the West Indies. Patterns of trade were much more complicated than the notion of a "triangular trade route" in which England sold manufactured goods in Africa in exchange for slaves who were sent to America where they produced sugar, tobacco, and rice destined for Europe. While this exchange was important, other trade patterns sustained

colonial economies as well: shipment of fish and lumber from New England to the West Indies; and mid-Atlantic flour and meat to southern Europe and the West Indies. The fur trade linked Native Americans to the Atlantic economy. West Indies sugar—and the rum New England and Philadelphia distillers manufactured from it—found markets everywhere. Because the Navigation Acts allowed American ships to carry goods, the shipping trade itself became a significant source of income.

The colonies became major markets for textiles, metalware, and other items, which under the Navigation Acts they could import only from Britain. The consumer revolution made the British more attentive to their North American provinces, while at the same time, the imports helped to create in America a more standardized English culture. Affluent colonists became aware of the latest fashions in England, and complained when they received out-of-date merchandise. The young George Washington groused in 1760, for example, "that instead of getting things good and fashionable in their several kinds we often have Articles sent Us that coud only have been usd by our Forefathers in the days of yore."

The economic upswing of the 1750s gave way to a depression after 1760, as the Seven Years' War moved to the Caribbean and military spending dropped. The seaport towns, having attracted workers during the wartime boom, faced deepening poverty and rising demands for relief. With depressed wages and long periods of unemployment, families found survival difficult. The resumption of immigration from Europe after the war intensified economic hardships and contributed to unrest on the frontier.

Politics

In late 1763, after months of Indian attacks in the Ohio country, a band of western Scots-Irish Pennsylvanians used violence to force the Quaker-dominated assembly to provide military protection. The "Paxton Boys" of Lancaster County murdered a number of Christian Indians at Conestoga, then marched on Philadelphia. By the time the rebels reached the capital, the legislature had passed a bill raising 1,000 troops to defend the frontier. The westerners returned home without attacking the city. At the heart of their revolt was the belief that they were poorly represented in the provincial government. As the backcountry population exploded, eastern politicians guarded their power by allotting fewer assembly seats to outlying counties than they deserved.

The Paxton Boys revolt signaled the end of an era of political stability that had prevailed since the late 1720s in the British mainland provinces. As part of Britain's empire, the eighteenth-century colonists believed themselves among the most fortunate people on earth. The Glorious Revolution of 1688–1689, which removed James II, had ended the long, bitter contest between king and Parliament. The monarch's power was subsequently limited by the national legislature, comprised of the House of Lords, which represented the aristocracy, and the House of Commons, which in theory represented everyone else. As a result of the 1689 settlement, Parliament's consent was necessary for taxes, new courts, raising an army in peacetime, and foreign invasions. It gained control over its own meetings and, after 1707, the Crown lost veto power over legislation.

The balance of powers, political theorists argued, prevented domination by a single segment of society, the monarch, aristocracy, or common people. Thus, the British avoided forms of government con-

The Library Company of Philadelphia

The Paxton Expedition, by Henry Dawkins, depicts the threat by western "Paxton Boys" against Philadelphia, demanding frontier defense during Pontiac's War.

sidered destructive of liberty: rule by a single despot (tyranny); corrupt and self-serving rule by a group of aristocrats (oligarchy); and uncontrolled rule by the mob (democracy). In their provincial governments, the British colonists expected to find a similar balance, one that would protect their rights. Indeed, the prevailing structure of governor, appointed council, and elected lower house of assembly reflected the English model.

The British provinces were the only European settlements in North America where ordinary people could vote for representative legislatures. An estimated 50 to 75 percent of white men were qualified to vote in the British colonies, the result of much broader property ownership than in England, where about 15 to 30 percent of adult males had the franchise. According to English political theory, a person needed a "stake in society," a certain amount of property, to vote or hold office. Servants, slaves, children, and unpropertied men were beholden to someone else, so they could not make independent decisions. Giving them suffrage would award their owner, father, or employer another vote, the theorists claimed, especially in many places where people voted orally, in public. By tradition, women also lacked the franchise, whether or not they owned property or were married. Denial of the vote to all females arose from the belief that they were intellectually and morally inferior to men and thus should have no formal role in government.

The colonists favored direct representation, requiring their legislators to live in the area from which they were elected and to advocate the interests of their constituents, unlike England, where members of the House of Commons did not have to reside in their electoral districts. The British believed that Parliament represented all of the people of the empire whether they elected delegates or not, a concept known as virtual representation.

Beyond suffrage, English political theory also recognized the right of common people to resort to crowd action to withstand tyranny and require authorities to protect them from harm. The people had this right, theoretically, as long as violence was limited—directed at property rather than at persons. At various times, colonial mobs protested to prevent grain from being exported when food was in short supply, to destroy houses of prostitution, and to stop the British navy from impressing men into the king's service, as with the 1747 Knowles riot in Boston.

The most important and sustained political development in British America during the first half of the eighteenth century was the rise of the elected lower houses of assembly. The legislatures acquired greater power and assumed more functions, most significantly, the right to initiate bills to raise taxes and disburse public funds—the "power of the purse." They also gained the authority to initiate other legislation, choose their own leadership, and settle disputed elections.

The political stability and rise of the assemblies that marked the mid-eighteenth century resulted from a number of factors, including the long period of economic growth that began in the 1720s. Prosperity supported the formation of cohesive elites—mostly second, third, and fourth generation Americans with inherited wealth and large estates, enslaved Africans or servants to meet their domestic needs, and (consequently) sufficient leisure time for politics. They formed a class of skilled politicians, men who learned from their fathers how to govern, then elaborated the art. Many studied the law: the growth of the colonial bar accompanied the professionalization of politics. Economic prosperity inclined ordinary whites to defer to the elites as long as opportunity was good and they had crops to tend or other work to do. Their deference to social and economic superiors became most visible after 1725, when participation at the polls declined among eligible voters, and incumbent assemblymen won reelection year after year.

The provincial elites also benefited after 1720 from the British decision to administer the colonies with a light touch, allowing royal governors to accommodate the assemblies. And while riots occurred during the 1740s and 1750s over land claims and impressment, none threatened social disorder on the level of the seventeenth-century rebellions. Indeed, most ordinary whites feared attacks by Native Americans and slave revolts more than misuse of governmental power by elites.

Conclusion

By the end of 1763, the British colonists of North America had reason to be optimistic about their future, despite the pan-Indian assaults in the Ohio Valley and postwar economic downturn. The British army had withstood the worst attacks in the west, and colonists could expect a return to prosperity. After a quarter century of war, they celebrated the withdrawal of Spain and France east of the Mississippi and looked forward to peace and semi-autonomy within the empire. Free colonists appreciated the benefits of being British—their liberties and right to participate in government as well as access to advanced learning and consumer goods. At the same time, the Americans were creating societies quite different from the English, with greater ethnic and religious diversity, dependence on enslaved labor, and wider opportunity to acquire land (even if it meant pushing out the Indians). After 1763, the London government shocked the American colonists with its effort to rein in the empire, to make them surrender some of their accumulated rights. In turn, the British were unprepared for the coordinated fury with which the thirteen mainland provinces greeted their "reforms."

RECOMMENDED READINGS

Anderson, Fred. *Crucible of War: The Seven Years' War and the Fate of Empire in British North America, 1754–1766* (2000). A convincing analysis of the significance of the Seven Years' War.

Bailyn, Bernard, and Morgan, Philip D., eds. *Strangers within the Realm: Cultural Margins of the First British Empire* (1991). Important essays on specific groups, including Native Americans, Scots-Irish, African Americans, Germans, and Dutch.

Carson, Cary, et al., eds. *Of Consuming Interests: The Style of Life in the Eighteenth Century* (1994). Excellent essays on topics ranging from housing and art to consumer behavior.

Daunton, Martin, and Halpern, Rick, eds. *Empire and Others: British Encounters with Indigenous Peoples, 1600–1850* (1999). Significant essays on relations between Natives and English in eastern North America and elsewhere.

Isaac, Rhys. *The Transformation of Virginia, 1740–1790* (1982). Uses anthropological methods to explore cultural and political change in eighteenth-century Virginia.

Merrell, James H. *Into the American Woods: Negotiators on the Pennsylvania Frontier* (1999). Focuses on Indian and Euro-American go-betweens and their ultimate failure to preserve peace in the Ohio Valley.

Morgan, Philip D. *Slave Counterpoint: Black Culture in the Eighteenth-Century Chesapeake and Lowcountry* (1998). A comprehensive study of African American work and culture in the South.

Richter, Daniel K. *Facing East from Indian Country: A Native History of Early America* (2001). Approaches significant events in relations between Indians and settlers from Native perspectives.

Steele, Ian K. *Warpaths: Invasions of North America* (1994). Examines the Seven Years' War as one of a series of European invasions of Indian territory during the colonial period.

Ulrich, Laurel Thatcher. *A Midwife's Tale: The Life of Martha Ballard, Based on Her Diary, 1785–1812* (1990). The prize-winning account of a Maine midwife within the context of eighteenth-century society.

 Additional resources, exercises, and Internet links related to this chapter are available on the American Passages Web site: http://history.wadsworth.com/ayerscompact2/

Passages
1764–1814

During the American Revolution, sixteen-year-old Dicey Langston of the South Carolina frontier left home in the middle of the night, by herself, to warn her brother's unit about Tory troop movements. As a historian later described Langston's journey,

> Many miles were to be traversed, and the road lay through woods, and crossed marshes and creeks where the conveniences of bridges and foot-logs were wanting. She walked rapidly on, heedless of slight difficulties; but her heart almost failed her when she came to the banks of the Tyger—a deep and rapid stream, rendered more dangerous by the rains that had lately fallen. . . . But the energy of a resolute will, under the care of Providence, sustained her.*

Dicey Langston's effort, like those of thousands of Americans, was emblematic of her country's passage from a collection of British provinces in 1764, to a stable republic with some international standing a half century later. The thirteen mainland colonies, proud of their contribution to victory in the Seven Years' War, were stunned by Britain's program to curtail their rights. Stretching from the mountains of northern New England to the rice fields of coastal Georgia, diverse in economics, religion, ethnicity, and politics, the colonies mustered enough unity to organize a revolutionary Congress, stop British imports, raise an army, obtain help from France, and win the war.

The Federal Pillars, from the Centinel (Boston, Massachusetts), August 2, 1788, illustrates ratification of the Constitution of 1787.

*Elizabeth F. Ellet, *Domestic History of the American Revolution* (1850), p. 234.

The states refused to create a unified nation, however, and instead established, under the Articles of Confederation, thirteen separate republics joined loosely by a representative Congress. Without power to tax or raise troops, the Congress faced severe postwar problems in demobilizing the army, paying the war debt, protecting the frontiers, and unifying a populace divided by war. In the wake of bankruptcy and insurrection, in 1787 nationalists called together a constitutional convention. Through a series of compromises, the framers drafted the new Constitution, which gave more authority to the central government, yet retained considerable power in the states. Americans ratified the document with the understanding that amendments to protect individual liberties and states' rights would be approved.

After the first national elections, the Constitution's proponents, the Federalists, controlled the new government, with George Washington as president. Having agreed upon the frame of government, they were unprepared for the bitter factionalism that forged political parties in the 1790s. Nor were they ready for the foreign entanglements that resulted from two decades of war between Great Britain and post-revolutionary France. Only after the United States declared war on the British in 1812 and held its own as the conflict ended in stalemate, did the nation finally demonstrate its independence. By 1814, most of the men who led the American Revolution had passed from power—though James Madison would remain president for several years—and a new generation was taking control.

Source of Data: Bureau of the Census, Historical Statistics of the United States Colonial Times to 1970 Part 2 (Washington, D.C., 1975), p. 1176.

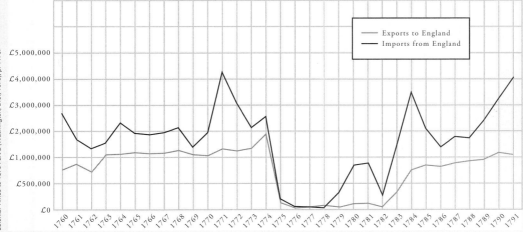

Trade Between Thirteen Colonies/United States and England, 1760–1791 (pounds sterling). Though trade with England was only part of American commerce, this chart suggests the Revolution's impact. British imports spiked between 1769 and 1771, after Parliament partially repealed the Townshend Act. Imports and exports then plummeted during the Revolution, rising unevenly after 1782. The trade imbalance led to political unrest such as Shays's Rebellion.

The heroic story of the young nation surmounting difficulties—two wars against Great Britain, a constitutional crisis, several internal rebellions, an undeclared conflict with France, and constant fighting on the frontier—masks other narratives, those of women, African Americans, and Native Americans, who failed to achieve autonomy. Though Dicey Langston was just one of thousands of sisters, mothers, and wives who risked their lives during the Revolution, after the war women still lacked basic legal and political rights to hold property after marriage, vote, and take part in government. And while revolutionary rhetoric against slavery resulted in abolition in the North and many private manumissions in the Chesapeake region, most African Americans remained enslaved, a condition perpetuated by the new Constitution and development of cotton. Even most free blacks had little opportunity to acquire property and were denied suffrage and participation in government.

For Native Americans, the success and growth of the new nation meant their decline. Despite revitalization movements to restore traditional cultures led by Neolin, Handsome Lake, Tenskwatawa, and others, and destructive wars to defend their homelands in Alabama, Tennessee, Kentucky, and Ohio, by 1814 the United States dominated most of the territory east of the Mississippi River. Native Americans tried various routes to survive and retain as much of their autonomy as possible—adoption of white culture, cession of some lands for the promise they could keep others, alliances with Great Britain and Spain, and pan-Indian war. In the face of unremitting westward settlement and continuing disease, the Indian peoples of eastern North America became remnants of formerly powerful nations.

5

Wars for Independence
1764–1783

The treaty of 1763 forced Spain and Great Britain to reassess their North American colonies. Both nations had new kings, as Charles III took Spain's throne in 1759 and George III became the British monarch in 1760. For the Spanish, the borderlands in North America were of secondary importance, serving as a buffer to protect the Mexican silver mines. For Britain, however, the mainland provinces had become increasingly significant as a source of revenue and market for consumer goods. The Seven Years' War marked Britain's ascendancy to world power, but resulted in a national debt of £130 million. Annual interest payments alone amounted to £4.5 million, equal to more than half of the government's yearly expenditures prior to the war.

When Parliament imposed levies on the American colonies to help pay expenses, the colonists protested vehemently that they should not be taxed without their consent. They complained that they had no representatives in Parliament, that only their elected provincial assemblies could constitutionally tax them. Beginning in 1764, the Americans petitioned, rioted, boycotted British goods, destroyed tea, and ultimately defied George III and parliamentary leaders when they sent troops. The colonists' belief that they possessed the same rights as the English was something for which many were willing to fight. Nevertheless, the consensus to declare independence did not come quickly, nor was the war to defend independence easily won. Americans who disagreed that the British actions warranted insurrection remained loyal to the king. These loyalists, also called Tories after the pro-monarchy faction in England, tried to subvert the revolutionary governments and formed loyalist militia units to fight alongside British troops. They found allies in many Indians and African Americans who conducted wars of independence of their own. Other colonists remained neutral, whether from principled opposition to violence or from sheer indifference. The Revolution touched everyone, Native Americans, women, and enslaved blacks, as well as the white men who served as military and civilian leaders and comprised most of the armed forces. The cause of the patriots—or Whigs, as the American revolutionaries called themselves after the English party that had led opposition to the Crown—depended upon the efforts of many people, those who supplied and supported the troops, as well as those who fought.

CHRONOLOGY

1764	Sugar and Currency Acts • St. Louis founded
1765	Stamp Act provokes widespread colonial protest • Stamp Act Congress
1766	Parliament repeals Stamp Act, passes Declaratory Act • Spanish governor arrives in Louisiana
1766–1771	North Carolina Regulator movement
1767	Passage of Townshend Act • John Dickinson publishes "Farmer" letters
1767–1769	South Carolina Regulator movement
1768	Massachusetts assembly sends "circular letter" • Non-importation movement against Townshend duties • British troops stationed in Boston • Louisianans expel Spanish governor
1769	Spanish reestablish control of Louisiana
1770	Boston Massacre • Partial repeal of Townshend Act
1772	Burning of *Gaspée*
1772–1773	Committees of Correspondence established
1773	Boston Tea Party
1774	Passage of Coercive Acts; port of Boston closed • Quebec Act • First Continental Congress • Congress organizes Continental Association
1775	Battles of Lexington and Concord • Second Continental Congress • Battle of Bunker Hill • Congress authorizes invasion of Canada • Lord Dunmore's proclamation to servants and slaves
1776	Thomas Paine publishes *Common Sense* • British evacuation of Boston • Declaration of Independence • Cherokee War on the southern frontier • Americans defeated on Long Island; British occupation of New York City • Battle of Trenton
1777	Battle of Princeton • British occupy Philadelphia after defeating Washington at Brandywine • Battle of Germantown • Burgoyne surrenders to Americans at Saratoga • Congress approves Articles of Confederation; sends document to states for ratification
1778	Alliance with France • Iroquois and loyalist attacks in New York and Pennsylvania • British withdraw from Philadelphia • Whig frontiersmen take settlements in the Illinois country • British invade Georgia
1780	Americans surrender at Charleston • Battle of Camden
1781	Battle of Cowpens • Articles of Confederation ratified • Battle of Guilford Courthouse • Southern army reconquers most of South Carolina and Georgia • Surrender of Cornwallis at Yorktown
1782	Massacre at Gnadenhutten
1783	Signing of Treaty of Paris

Realignments in the Spanish Borderlands

The peace of 1763 required Spain to withdraw from Florida, assume the government of Louisiana, and rethink its defenses in Texas and New Mexico. With Britain's enhanced power, safeguarding the Mexican silver mines took high priority. The Spanish also considered the soaring population of the British colonies a threat to their American empire.

Florida and Louisiana

Spain ordered all of its subjects to leave Florida when Britain took control. Though the British promised religious freedom to the Catholic Floridians, some 200 Christian Indians, 79 free African Americans, 350 slaves, and nearly all of the 3,000 Hispanics departed. They sold their property at a loss to British bargain hunters. The free blacks of Mose, near St. Augustine, could expect enslavement by the English, so took Spain's offer of homesteads in Cuba. They received some tools and money from the government, but faced hard times because they never received adequate compensation for their property in Florida.

Acquisition of Louisiana, including all French territory west of the Mississippi River and New Orleans, on the east bank, gave Spain an extensive region to administer. The Spanish needed to win the loyalties of French inhabitants and Native Americans and hoped to keep the British colonists out. The concern about British expansion became all too real as interlopers spanned the Mississippi River to trade with Indians on the Great Plains. Indeed, within a decade, 4,000 British colonists and their 1,500 African American slaves were living on the Gulf Coast and eastern shore of the Mississippi.

The more immediate challenge for Spanish authorities in Louisiana, however, was asserting political control of the province. For several years, French government remained; even after the first Spanish governor, Antonio de Ulloa, arrived in 1766, he tried to govern jointly with the last French governor. Adhering to Charles III's instructions, Ulloa left the French administration and legal system intact, even allowing the French flag to fly over the capital.

Ulloa did not extend this leniency to commerce, however. He tried to stop business with France and Great Britain and restricted the Native American trade to certain dealers. New Orleans merchants feared loss of markets and lower prices for their tobacco, indigo, sugar, deerskins, and lumber. Like the thirteen British provinces on the Atlantic coast, at about the same time, the merchants protested the new restrictions, then in October 1768 issued a declaration of loyalty to the king of France. With few Spanish troops at his disposal, Governor Ulloa left for Cuba. When the French refused to intervene, the colony became independent, but only for a year.

The Spanish regained Louisiana when General Alexander O'Reilly arrived in 1769 with more than 2,000 soldiers. An Irishman with a successful career in the Spanish army, O'Reilly arrested the rebels, put five of them to death, but pardoned most who had participated in the uprising. He raised the Spanish flag and within a year ended French government, changed the legal system, made Castilian the official language, and outlawed trade with other nations. Despite the merchants' fears, the economy flourished as smuggling continued with Britain, and Spanish markets welcomed their goods. St. Louis, established in 1764, became the thriving center of trade for beaver, buffalo, and deerskins with Native Americans of the Illinois and Missouri countries. Louisiana remained culturally French, as the numbers of French settlers far surpassed the Spanish.

Fortifying the Southwest

With ownership of Louisiana, the Spanish could alter their defenses along the frontier in Texas and New Mexico. They removed several forts from East Texas. By the 1760s, the most immediate danger in the southwest came from the Apaches and Comanches, who defended their freedom from Hispanic slave catchers and attempted to drive the Spanish back into Mexico. Skillfully adopting the European horse and gun, they refused to submit to Spanish rule or Christianity. Spain gave up trying to convert them through missions, emphasizing military defense instead. The Apaches and Comanches raided settlements and pack trains, stole horses, mules, cattle, and supplies, killing Pueblos and white settlers alike.

During the 1760s and 1770s, in the face of constant Indian assaults, Spain tried to reform administration and improve defense. From 1766 to 1768, the Marqués de Rubí, a high-level military official from Spain, inspected the fortifications and missions of the Southwest. He discovered badly located presidios (or forts) and soldiers suffering from lack of food and clothes because of their commanders' greed. At one Texas presidio, Rubí found sixty troops without shoes or uniforms and, among them, only two muskets that worked. He recommended building new presidios and relocating others to create an orderly cordon of military bases situated about a hundred miles apart. The presidios would extend from the Gulf of California to the Gulf of Mexico, along a line that was close to the present boundary between the United States and Mexico. Small numbers of Spanish troops would hold garrisons at Santa Fe and San Antonio, north of the cordon, to help defend Hispanics and allied Indians in New Mexico and Texas. The borderlands officials also received more autonomy to deal with local problems, but lacked sufficient troops to conquer the Apaches and Comanches.

The British Colonies Resist Imperial Reform

In Britain's colonies, which experienced few restrictions before 1763, trouble began when George III appointed George Grenville as first minister, with responsibility for solving the debt crisis. Grenville decided that Americans should pay more taxes because they benefited from the Seven Years' War and continued to drain the government's budget for administrative and military costs. Because the British at home were highly taxed, Grenville's plan to make the colonies pay their way seemed reasonable to many. The Americans saw it differently, however, and quickly moved to the brink of revolt.

The Sugar and Currency Acts

Grenville began his program in 1764 with the Sugar Act, which initiated a new policy of charging duties primarily to raise revenue rather than to regulate trade. It reduced the duty on foreign molasses from sixpence (under the Molasses Act of 1733) to threepence per gallon, which was further reduced to one penny in 1766. Grenville assumed merchants would pay the lower tariff rather than go to the risk of smuggling and bribery. The law also added timber, iron, and hides to the list of enumerated goods. To make smuggling more hazardous, the act gave increased powers to the vice-admiralty courts. Because these courts lacked juries, the government expected easy convictions for smuggling. In addition, the law expanded the use of writs of assistance (search warrants), empowered the Royal Navy to inspect ships, and required endless bureaucratic paperwork from colonial shippers. Parliament also passed the Currency Act (1764), which had the potential to cause further hardship by forbidding colonies from issuing paper money, thus creating a shortage of currency.

Coming in the midst of an economic depression, this legislation stirred up colonial protest. Provincial assemblies sent petitions to England requesting relief. Most urgently, merchants feared that if imports of foreign molasses were cut off, their provision trade to the Spanish and French West Indies would be lost. Without foreign credits, they could not pay for British manufactures. The Americans slowed down their orders from Britain and encouraged home industry, arousing opposition to Grenville's policies from English businessmen. One colonial merchant wrote to associates in England that if the government deprived Americans of paper currency, "we shall not be able to export Provisions &c. in the same Degree as formerly, and if we are not on any Terms allow'd a Trade to get Money from abroad, we shall have none to pay you for Goods, and then unless you will send them Gratis our Dealings must end."

The Stamp Act

Passed by Parliament in 1765, the Stamp Act provoked an even greater storm of protest. The law departed entirely from the confines of mercantilist policy, for its purpose was to raise an internal revenue, which would be used to pay troops in the colonies. The act required individuals to purchase stamps for official documents and published papers, including deeds, liquor licenses, bills of lading, court documents, wills, passports, playing cards, newspapers, and pamphlets. All publications and official transactions were to be subject to this special tax, which increased with the value of a land sale or the size of a pamphlet. The tax could be paid only in specie, an onerous requirement because colonists generally used paper money and credit instead of the scarce gold and silver. The vice-admiralty

A woman and African American man are prominently portrayed in this illustration of the Stamp Act riots in Boston, 1765.

courts would enforce the act, confiscating any land or property involved in transactions conducted without the stamps.

Colonists of all walks of life found the Stamp Act offensive. Everyone who engaged in public business, whether to buy a newspaper or sell property, would have to pay the tax. Because Parliament, not their provincial assemblies, passed the act, Americans considered it a violation of their rights as British subjects. As they understood the British constitution, the people must consent to taxes through their representatives. The provinces could not send delegates to Parliament, so that body should not tax them to raise revenue. As one Philadelphia merchant said succinctly, "the point in dispute is a very Important one, if the Americans are to be taxed by a Parliament where they are not nor can be Represented, they are no longer Englishmen but Slaves." Only tariffs to regulate trade such as the 1733 duty on molasses, many colonists believed, were constitutionally valid.

Recognizing Parliament's attack on their powers, provincial assemblies protested the Stamp Act. In the Virginia House of Burgesses, the newly elected Patrick Henry, only twenty-nine years old, introduced fourteen resolves against the tax. The Virginia assembly refused to accept all of Henry's proposals, but in June 1765, approved the more moderate resolutions that defended the colonists' right to tax themselves.

When newspapers spread word of Virginia's action, other provinces responded. Rhode Island instructed its officials to ignore the stamp tax; Massachusetts, Connecticut, New York, New Jersey, Pennsylvania, Maryland, and South Carolina passed resolves similar to Virginia's. In October 1765, representatives from nine colonies traveled to New York City to attend the Stamp Act Congress. In resolutions and petitions to Parliament, the congress upheld the power of representative assemblies, not Parliament, to tax the colonists. Further, the congress defended trial by jury, which the expanded authority of the vice-admiralty courts threatened. By issuing resolves and organizing the Stamp Act Congress, the colonial elite challenged British efforts to assert control.

Ordinary colonists joined the challenge. They drew upon the tradition of the mob to protest what they considered tyranny. The anti-Stamp Act riots began in Boston on August 14, 1765, when a group who called themselves the Loyal Nine organized a demonstration to hang in effigy the appointed stamp collector for Massachusetts, Andrew Oliver. The crowd destroyed a partially constructed building they thought he intended as his stamp office, then damaged his home. Oliver resigned his commission. Twelve days later, a Boston mob attacked the houses of several other officials, gutting the mansion of Lieutenant Governor Thomas Hutchinson.

Protesters all along the Atlantic seaboard mobilized to prevent stamp distribution, scheduled to begin November 1. News of Oliver's resignation prompted anti-Stamp Act mobs in other cities to demand the same from their appointed stampmen. In some colonies, rioters forced stamp officials to relinquish their commissions. In others, just the threat of disorder was effective. By the end of 1765, distributors in every colony except Georgia had resigned.

The men who led the crowds called themselves Sons of Liberty. They were mostly propertied men—small merchants, shopkeepers, and craftsmen. The activists were people who needed documents to conduct business, who would regularly feel the pinch of the stamp tax. The Sons of Liberty also established networks to organize boycotts of British goods. Merchants and retailers in New York City, Philadelphia, and Boston signed pacts to stop imports until Parliament repealed the act. By early 1766, the Sons of Liberty coerced customs officials and judges to open the ports and resume court business without stamps. To Thomas Hutchinson, it appeared "the authority of every colony is in the hands of the sons of liberty." In truth, the American resistance aimed to expunge the stamp tax, not end British authority. The movement achieved success in 1766, when Parliament repealed the Stamp Act, after British businessmen from more than twenty cities petitioned for relief. Suffering from postwar economic depression and unemployment, the British textile industry faced even worse times with an American boycott. British merchants clearly understood the growing significance of the colonial market.

Protest Widens in the Lower South

In the Carolinas, the Stamp Act resistance spawned revolts against colonial elites. To blacks, the radicals' oft-spoken argument that the English government intended to deprive white Americans of freedom—to make them slaves—seemed ironic. Yet such statements also gave hope, for the revolutionary movement spotlighted the institution of slavery and its immorality and injustice. In January 1766, in Charleston, 1,400 seamen and a group of black slaves threatened serious disorder. The sailors became restless because the customs agents refused to release ships from port without stamped documents. The people of Charleston were even more concerned, however, when a group of enslaved men marched through the town shouting "Liberty!" The city armed itself against a slave revolt, while the South Carolina assembly became so frightened that it restricted slave imports for three years.

The North Carolina Regulator movement also began in 1766, inspired by the uproar against the Stamp Act, but targeted the colonial elite, not Britain. Six thousand western farmers demanded confirmation of land titles and the end of speculators' monopoly of the best land. The Regulators also protested corrupt local officials, excessive court fees and taxes, and lack of adequate representation for ordinary backcountry farmers in the North Carolina legislature. They called for a secret ballot to reduce the influence of wealthy planters in assembly elections. The North Carolina Regulators refused to pay taxes and closed several courts. In 1771, when the government sent the eastern militia, 2,000 Regulators met them at Alamance Creek but were dispersed.

Most of the grievances of the South Carolina Regulators were different, except that they too lacked fair representation in the provincial government. They were planters who wanted to bring order, "to regulate" the backcountry. The South Carolina legislature had failed to create local government for the westerners, so they had no courts or jails. Everyone had to travel to Charleston to conduct legal business, but even worse, bandits roamed freely, stealing horses and cattle, destroying property, and sometimes torturing and killing their victims. The frontier robbers were mostly propertyless whites and some free blacks and escaped slaves; one report in the *South-Carolina Gazette* noted "a Gang of Banditti, consisting of Mulattoes—Free Negroes, and notorious Harbourers of run away Slaves." The Regulators resorted to vigilante "justice," capturing and whipping suspected felons, taking some to jail in Charleston, and evicting others from the colony. They finally ceased their activities in 1769 when the legislature established a circuit court system for the entire province.

The Townshend Revenue Act

In other British mainland colonies, attention focused on imperial tensions rather than on regional disputes. The British government and American radicals emerged from the Stamp Act crisis with conflicting views: while the Americans celebrated the Stamp Act's repeal, the British yielded no authority. In the Declaratory Act, passed with the repeal in March 1766, Parliament affirmed its power "to make laws and statutes of sufficient force and validity to bind the colonies and people of America, subjects of the crown of Great Britain, in all cases whatsoever." The act generated little response in the colonies, but should have, for it laid the basis for subsequent restrictions.

In June 1767, Parliament passed three more laws affecting the Americans: an act establishing the American Board of Customs Commissioners to enforce legislation against illegal trade, the New York Restraining Act, and the Townshend Revenue Act. The Restraining Act would have dissolved the New York Assembly for refusing adequate supplies to British soldiers stationed in the province. Instead, the New York legislators gave in, pledging additional funds for the troops. The Townshend Revenue Act was conceived by Charles Townshend, the British chancellor of the exchequer, who wanted the Americans to contribute, over time, an increasing percentage of imperial expenses in North America. The Townshend Act, which placed duties on tea, glass, paper, lead, and paint would be just the beginning, for they would raise less than one-tenth of the colonial administrative and military costs. The revenues would pay the salaries of governors and judges, thus removing their dependence upon the provincial legislatures. The act also required colonial courts to provide customs officials with writs of assistance to search houses and businesses for smuggled merchandise.

To American Whigs, the Townshend Act was dangerous for two reasons: It raised revenue without the approval of colonial assemblies and it removed royal officials from the lawmakers' control. If the king rather than the legislatures paid provincial governors, the colonies lost a powerful negotiating tool for obtaining consent to the laws they wanted. While the British saw the Townshend Act as an appropriate way to force the Americans to begin paying their share, the colonists believed it was a step toward tyranny.

At first, colonial reaction to the Townshend Act was restrained. Then, in December 1767, a few weeks after the Townshend Act went into effect, John Dickinson, a Philadelphia lawyer and owner of a Delaware plantation, began publishing a series of twelve letters signed "A Farmer." Soon reprinted by newspapers throughout the thirteen colonies and published in pamphlet form as *Letters from a Farmer in Pennsylvania* (1768), Dickinson's arguments galvanized opposition to the Townshend duties. He rejected the position that the colonists should accept external taxes (duties) but not internal taxes (like the stamp tax), stating that only elected representatives could legally impose *any* revenue tax. He believed that Parliament could collect duties in the colonies if the purpose was to regulate trade (as with the Molasses Act of 1733), but not to raise revenue. Further, the purpose of the funds collected under the Townshend Act was oppressive, for it eliminated the power of the colonial legislatures over Crown officials. Dickinson predicted: "If we can find no relief from this infamous situation . . . we may bow down our necks, with all the stupid serenity of servitude, to any drudgery which our lords and masters shall please to command." Dickinson urged the thirteen colonies to petition for repeal; if that failed, they should once again boycott British goods.

Massachusetts responded first. In early 1768, its assembly petitioned George III for redress, then dispatched a "circular letter" to the other twelve colonies suggesting they do the same. The new English secretary of state for the colonies, Lord Hillsborough, realized that the circular letter was a call to unified resistance. Denouncing Dickinson's pamphlet as "extremely wild," he ordered the Massachusetts assemblymen to rescind their circular letter. They refused. When he directed colonial governors to dissolve assemblies that responded to the letter, most legislatures sent petitions and were disbanded.

Simultaneously, Hillsborough reassigned military units from the Ohio Valley to Florida, Nova Scotia, Quebec, and the mid-Atlantic region where they could be called upon to control the defiant provinces. In June 1768, he sent British regiments to Boston when the customs commissioners demanded protection against rioters. As the troops disembarked in October, they heard cries of protest but met no armed resistance.

During 1768, Boston residents signed a non-importation agreement, using the same strategy against the Townshend Act that had proved successful against the Stamp Act. Most of the city's merchants pledged to stop importing goods from Great Britain after January 1, 1769, unless the Townshend duties were repealed. The non-importation movement soon spread to New York City, where artisans supported the merchants by agreeing to boycott any retailer who imported British goods. Traders in Philadelphia, New Haven, and other northern ports delayed action, however, because they would face economic loss. They waited until 1769 for the imperial government to respond to their petitions, then approved non-importation. In Virginia, George Washington kindled the boycott. He wrote, "At a time when our lordly masters in Great Britain will be satisfied with nothing less than the deprivation of American freedom, it seems highly necessary that some thing should be done to avert the stroke and maintain the liberty which we have derived from our Ancestors."

The boycotts, which were unofficial agreements without the force of law, met uneven success. Between 1768 and 1769, American imports from England declined by 38 percent. As the months passed, however, importers wavered as their incomes fell. In contrast, craftspeople—beyond their concern for liberty—often benefited from the boycott because it created a demand for their products. Some artisans organized into street groups to threaten merchants and customs officials who tried to undermine the non-importation pacts.

Women participated both as purchasers of goods and as producers. Many "Daughters of Liberty" gave up imported tea and clothing, signing agreements to avoid the banned goods. The *Boston News-Letter* reported that "a large circle of very agreeable ladies in this town . . . unanimously agreed" not to purchase ribbons and other imports. Instead, throughout New England, women organized spinning bees to produce woolen yarn. In Boston, some impoverished women profited from the temporary demand for American-made cloth, when William Molineaux, a merchant and radical Whig, contracted with local artisans to build 400 spinning wheels, which he distributed to women to spin yarn in their homes. With this "putting-out" system, Molineaux and the spinners responded to both their patriotism and economic needs.

Crisis in Boston

During the years 1769 to 1775, Boston became the powder keg of the Revolution. Violence broke out in the summer of 1769 between the Bostonians and British redcoats, whose chief responsibilities were to protect the despised customs commissioners and help them collect duties. The soldiers became even more unpopular when they took jobs at low pay during their off-duty hours, thus throwing city laborers out of work.

The first serious incident occurred in July 1769, when a redcoat, John Riley, was jailed for hitting a local butcher who had insulted him. A near riot followed as twenty of Riley's comrades tried to rescue him from jail. Such episodes continued into early 1770. On March 2, the violence escalated when soldiers seeking revenge for an insult attacked workers at John Gray's ropeworks. Street fights intensified over the next few days.

On March 5, the bloodiest incident occurred, the so-called Boston Massacre. A young apprentice taunted the British sentry at the Customs House, who hit the boy with his gun. When a crowd gathered, shouting at the sentry, "Kill him, kill him, knock him down," Captain Thomas Preston led seven soldiers in his defense. The crowd grew larger, throwing snowballs, ice, and sticks at the soldiers and threatening them with clubs. Then someone hit a redcoat with a club, knocking the gun out of his hands. Preston's men fired, killing five townspeople and wounding six. The dead became martyrs, with March 5 commemorated as "Massacre Day" in the years ahead. The incident crystallized the colonists' opposition to standing armies. Nevertheless, when Captain Preston and six soldiers were tried for murder, the jury found two soldiers guilty of manslaughter and cleared the others. The radical Whig lawyer John Adams defended them, saying that all Englishmen should have a fair trial.

Just as the crisis in Boston reached its head in spring 1770, the British government decided on partial repeal of the Townshend Act, removing its duties except tea. The duties had raised under £21,000 in revenues, but cost hundreds of thousands of pounds sterling in trade as a result of the non-importation movement. As in the case of the Stamp Act, British officials backed away from a specific revenue measure without abandoning their right to levy taxes. Following Parliament's action, merchants in New York City and other colonial ports, eager to resume trade, cancelled their boycotts except on tea. Imports into the thirteen colonies from England rebounded over the next several years, increasing from £1.3 million in 1769 to £4.2 million in 1771.

The Gaspée Incident

For two years, the conflict between Great Britain and the colonies abated, then flared again in 1772. Trouble began this time in Rhode Island, when more than one hundred men burned the British schooner *Gaspée,* wounding its commander, William Dudingston. Avidly enforcing the Sugar Act, the *Gaspée* had harassed merchant vessels sailing through Narragansett Bay. The Crown named a Commission of Inquiry to locate the perpetrators and send them to England to be tried for high treason. Though the Commission identified none of the *Gaspée*'s attackers, colonists viewed the policy of taking defendants to England for trial as a serious threat to their constitutional rights.

In response, the Virginia assembly appointed a Committee of Correspondence to monitor British policy and facilitate communication among the provinces. Within a year, Committees of Correspondence in all thirteen provinces coordinated opposition to Britain's restraints.

The Boston Tea Party

The final showdown began in 1773, when Parliament passed the Tea Act to bail out the nearly bankrupt East India Company. Though some colonists purchased British tea, the boycott on the product was still in effect and many purchased cheaper, smuggled Dutch tea. To sell the company's huge surplus, the government dropped a heavy import duty into England on tea headed for America, but retained the Townshend duty, which Lord North insisted on keeping to uphold Parliament's power to tax the colonies. The company also received a monopoly in the colonies, with the right to choose certain provincial merchants as agents. The company selected consignees in the ports of Charleston, Philadelphia, New York, and Boston, to whom it promptly dispatched nearly 600,000 pounds of tea.

The Tea Act was doubly offensive to American Whigs as it renewed opposition to the duty and caused outrage over favoritism and privilege. One radical called the act "a dirty trick" and accused Lord North of "low cunning" for trying to break American resistance by reducing the price of tea. Before the tea ships arrived in Charleston, Philadelphia, and New York, militants convinced the East India Company's agents to resign. In Boston, the consignees, two of them sons of pro-British Governor Thomas Hutchinson, declined to quit. When three ships arrived, members of the Boston Committee of Correspondence, led by Samuel Adams, prevented them from unloading. Adams, the cousin of John, had been the chief agitator in Boston since the Stamp Act. A skilled politician and writer, though failed businessman, he kept the pot simmering against British policies and Governor Hutchinson. Now, with the Boston committee, he brought matters to a head: in a series of meetings, thousands of residents of Boston and surrounding towns met to refuse the tea. On December 16, 1773, when customs officials and Hutchinson denied the ships clearance to leave port, radicals ill-disguised as Mohawks boarded the ships, broke open the tea chests, and dumped them overboard. The destruction cost nearly £10,000.

For the British, the Boston Tea Party required stern action. London decided that steps must "be taken to secure the Dependence of the Colonies," and in particular, "to mark out Boston and separate that Town from the rest of the Delinquents." George III believed that the Americans must be forced to submit, because they increasingly assumed the "independency which one state has of another, but which is quite subversive of the obedience which a colony owes to its Mother Country." In 1774, Parliament passed four Coercive Acts, which the colonists called the Intolerable Acts. They closed the port of Boston until residents paid for the destroyed tea and altered the provincial charter to limit the power of town meetings and create a Crown-appointed, instead of elected, provincial council. Further, the acts expanded the governor's control over the courts, allowed the removal of trials of royal officials to England or to another colony, and permitted quartering of troops in private buildings if a colony failed to provide suitable barracks. The Crown appointed General Thomas Gage, commander of the British army in North America, as Massachusetts governor, thus threatening the colonists with military force.

Americans also considered the Quebec Act (1774) intolerable, though London did not intend it to punish the Bostonians. The Quebec Act helped keep the loyalty of French Canadians by confirming religious freedom to Roman Catholics in the province, allowing them to hold public office. It denied the Canadians an elected assembly, however, designating an appointed governor and council to make laws. Residents of the thirteen colonies abhorred the act because it extended rights to "papists" and undermined representative government. It also gave control of the Ohio Valley to the Quebec government, thus curbing the ambitions of speculators in other colonies.

The First Continental Congress

Though the British government expected the Coercive Acts to isolate Boston and convince other provinces to be obedient, the policies actually pushed Americans toward more unified resistance. After the port of Boston closed, residents faced severe unemployment and food shortages. Neighboring towns provided supplies and harbored refugees looking for work. Sam Adams and the Boston Committee of Correspondence called for an immediate boycott of British trade. Instead the other provinces favored a Continental Congress to consider what action to take. The Massachusetts assembly proposed a meeting in Philadelphia on September 1, 1774, to which all of the thirteen colonies except Georgia sent delegates. The fifty-five representatives included Richard Henry Lee, Patrick Henry, and George Washington of Virginia; Sam and John Adams of Massachusetts; and John Dickinson and Joseph Galloway of Pennsylvania.

The primary purpose of the First Continental Congress was to obtain repeal of the Coercive Acts and other restrictions. The Congress wanted Parliament to recognize the rights of Americans, but was not ready to declare independence. Some of its leadership, notably Galloway (who later became a loyalist), argued for a moderate course, but the Congress was committed to action. It confirmed the Suffolk County Resolves forwarded to Philadelphia by a local Massachusetts convention. The Resolves blasted the Coercive Acts as "gross infractions of those rights to which we are justly entitled by the laws of nature, the British constitution and the charter of this province." The laws should "be rejected as the attempts of a wicked administration to enslave America." Everyone qualified to fight should learn "the art of war as soon as possible, and . . . appear under arms at least once a week." By endorsing these Resolves, the Congress took a militant stance.

Further, the Continental Congress passed non-importation, non-exportation, and non-consumption resolutions, ending all trade with Great Britain and Ireland, and exports to the West Indies. It also banned importation of slaves. If the British had hoped to divide the colonies by closing Boston, expecting other cities to pick up its trade, the plan backfired when all of the colonies closed their ports. The boycott would continue until repeal of the Coercive Acts. Congress set up the Continental Association to enforce the ban on trade through elected local committees, called Committees of Observation and Inspection, or Committees of Safety. The groups would expose violators of the boycott as "enemies of American liberty," publicizing their names and interrupting their business. Almost every town and county in the thirteen colonies elected these committees, which soon took on other functions of local government, including raising militias and collecting taxes. This transfer of authority from colonial governments to the Committees of Observation was revolutionary, for Americans were vesting sovereignty in themselves rather than in Parliament.

Resistance Becomes a War for Independence

Over the winter of 1774–1775, the rift widened between the thirteen colonies and Great Britain. George III and his ministers considered the colonies in rebellion, yet the colonists themselves were unprepared to declare independence.

Lexington and Concord

The British instructed General Gage to take forceful action. Headquartered in Boston, he decided to seize the patriots' stores of food and ammunition at Concord, which he had learned about from an informer. Militant Bostonians discovered Gage's plan from their own spies, so they were ready to spread the alarm on the night of April 18th, 1775, when 700 redcoats mustered on Boston Common. Paul Revere and William Dawes escaped the city to raise the colonial militia and alert leaders Sam Adams and John Hancock, who were staying at Lexington, on the route to Concord. The Massachusetts Provincial Council, just a few weeks before, had resolved to resist any advance by Gage's troops.

As the British marched the sixteen miles to Concord, they heard church bells and saw lights in windows. Soon after sunrise on April 19th they reached Lexington, where they met about seventy armed militia, nearly half of the town's adult males. The Lexington company,

Map 5.1 Battles in Eastern Massachusetts Paul Revere and William Dawes left Boston during the night of April 18th, 1775, to alert colonial leaders that the British troops were marching to destroy military supplies at Concord. The map also shows the location of the Battle of Bunker Hill two months later.

led by Captain John Parker, had formed only a few weeks earlier, so their training was incomplete. But they were willing to defend, in the words of their town meeting, their "natural, constitutional and chartered rights." In the face of six companies of British infantry, Captain Parker attempted to disperse his troops. The British officer, Major John Pitcairn, wanted to disarm the Americans, not engage in battle. As the British advanced, a shot rang out, then several shots, and a British volley. Pitcairn tried to stop his troops, but the carnage continued for fifteen to twenty minutes, leaving eight Lexington men dead and ten wounded. Only one British soldier was wounded and none killed.

The British reached Concord at about eight o'clock in the morning, long after the patriots had hidden most of their military stores. Following a brief skirmish in which the Americans inflicted more casualties than the British, the redcoats headed back to Boston. The march became a harrowing escape for their lives. Hundreds of colonial militia from throughout the Massachusetts countryside rushed to battle. These farmers used guerrilla tactics, shooting from behind trees, walls, rocks, and buildings. The British countered the guerrillas by sending advance parties to clear houses along the route. Using their famed skills with the bayonet, the redcoats killed the occupants and set fire to the homes. By the end of the day, British losses totaled seventy-three dead and 200 wounded or missing, while Massachusetts counted forty-nine killed and forty-three wounded and missing.

Battle of Lexington, engraving by C. Tiebout after the drawing by E. Tisdale. The artist evokes the confusion and shock of the first battle of the Revolution.

In the days that followed the battles of April 19th, New England went to arms. Over 20,000 volunteers streamed to Cambridge. A large proportion of these soldiers soon returned home, but many stayed, expecting their wives, mothers, and sisters to work the family farms and defend the towns. One group of about thirty-five women, dressed in men's clothes and armed with muskets and pitchforks, guarded a bridge on the route British reinforcements might travel from Canada. As Abigail Adams, the wife of John Adams, later wrote, "We are in no wise dispirited here. If our men are all drawn off and we should be attacked, you would find a race of Amazons in America."

Troops from throughout New England besieged Gage's redcoats in Boston. Nathanael Greene, a young ex-Quaker, led 1,500 troops from Rhode Island. Connecticut promised 6,000 men and New Hampshire sent 2,000. From these earliest days of conflict, African American men served in the militia units. Without a unified army, each colony separately raised troops, selected officers, and secured provisions. By May 1775, the New England forces surrounding Boston numbered about 17,000. Ethan Allen and his Green Mountain Boys of Vermont captured Fort Ticonderoga, the British garrison on Lake Champlain in northern New York.

The Second Continental Congress

On May 10, 1775, the Second Continental Congress met in Philadelphia. While the delegates remained unwilling to support independence, they were disappointed by Parliament's refusal to change its course. They faced the prospect of executing a war already in progress, convinced that British troops had fired the first shots and committed atrocities. To ensure that all of the colonies backed the war and to place the military under the control of Congress, they appointed George Washington of Virginia as commander-in-chief of the Continental army. Designating a southerner to head the military, which in June 1775 consisted of New Englanders, broadened the appeal of the Massachusetts cause. At the same time, Washington was himself a delegate to Congress and steadfastly committed to civilian control of the armed forces. Despite his limited military experience, Washington proved to be an excellent choice. His military bearing, determination, dignity, physical stamina, and ability to learn from his mistakes suited his role as commander-in-chief.

To serve under Washington, Congress appointed thirteen generals. Its four major generals were Artemas Ward of Massachusetts; Philip Schuyler of New York; Israel Putnam of Connecticut; and Charles Lee, a veteran officer of the British army and recent immigrant to Virginia. The adjutant general was Horatio Gates, also a veteran British officer and Virginia planter.

"An Open and Avowed Rebellion"

Before Washington could arrive in Massachusetts, his troops engaged in the Battle of Bunker Hill. Learning that the British planned to seize the hills overlooking Boston, a detachment of the patriot army began to fortify the Charlestown heights. By mistake, the men built defenses on Breed's Hill rather than on the higher and less exposed Bunker Hill. This lapse might have isolated the detachment from the rest of the army had the British moved more quickly. Instead of attacking immediately, however, General Gage and the man who would soon replace him as commander of British forces, William Howe, foolishly allowed the Americans to complete their fortifications and obtain reinforcements. The British regulars lined up in proper European formation to storm Breed's Hill. Boston residents climbed to their roofs to watch. While the redcoats shot as they advanced up the hill—to little effect—the patriots waited until the enemy was within range of their guns. The redcoats failed on their first two assaults, losing many officers and troops, then with reinforcements took the hill when the Americans' ammunition gave out. The patriots retreated, pounded by artillery from British ships. While the British won the battle, their losses were staggering, as more than 40 percent of their combatants were killed or wounded.

During the year following Bunker Hill, many colonists became Whigs. The lives lost on battlefields in eastern Massachusetts undercut advocates of restraint. Still, given opposition from many delegates, the Continental Congress could not declare independence. During the summer of 1775, Congress asked the king for peace while preparing for war. In July, it approved a petition to George III, called the Olive Branch Petition, asking that he resolve their dispute with Parliament. Upon receipt of the petition in August, outraged by the colonists' armed resistance, the king proclaimed the thirteen provinces in "an open and avowed rebellion." In December, Parliament cut off all trade with the colonies, making American ships and any vessels engaging in commerce with the mutinous provinces subject to confiscation. For many Americans, these actions proved that the British government meant to crush the colonies militarily and economically.

The Continental Congress further alienated the British by ordering General Philip Schuyler to invade Canada. The congressmen hoped to make Canada the fourteenth British colony in rebellion. They expected to obtain help from French Canadians and perhaps even France itself, but even more, they wanted to prevent a northern attack. The American invasion of Canada was a failure from the start. Schuyler, suffering from illness and indecision, assembled troops and provisions too slowly, wasting valuable summer days. In September, much too late, Brigadier General Richard Montgomery took charge and moved the army north via Lake Champlain.

Concurrently, Washington dispatched a small army led by Benedict Arnold and Daniel Morgan over a rugged route through Maine. Their march took so much longer than predicted that the men had to eat their dogs and soap. When the combined American forces finally attacked Quebec in a blinding December snowstorm, they were defeated with heavy casualties, including Montgomery dead and Arnold wounded. The army remained in Canada until May 1776 when British reinforcements arrived, pushing the patriots back into New York. For Congress, the campaign was a tragic error. The thirteen colonies lost 5,000 troops to battle, desertion, and disease, and an enormous amount of supplies.

Taking Sides

The deepening conflict forced colonists to decide whether or not to support the revolutionary Whigs. Some people remained neutral, either because they cared little about the issues involved or because, like the pacifist Quakers, they were opposed to violence on religious grounds. Loyalists rejected the Revolution for a variety of motives. Some believed that the king and Parliament were right, or at least had reason to expect the colonists to pay their share toward imperial administration. During the course of the war, about 80,000 loyalists departed for Britain or other British colonies. Many more, numbering perhaps several hundred thousand, continued to live among their patriot neighbors. Tories included Crown officials, Anglican clergy, and merchants with close ties to Britain. Some of the best known loyalists were wealthy gentlemen and officeholders: Governor Thomas Hutchinson and Chief Justice Peter Oliver of Massachusetts; Joseph Galloway, speaker of the Pennsylvania Assembly; and Frederick Philipse, landlord of a 50,000-acre manor in New York.

Many Tories were not rich or intimately tied to Great Britain, for the Revolution became a power struggle within American society, not just one between the colonies and London. The tenants of New York manors, for example, took the opposite side of their landlords. Thus, residents of Frederick Philipse's manors became Whigs, while tenants of the patriot Livingstons and Schuylers supported the British. In Maryland, the loyalists gained widespread backing in Eastern Shore counties where farmers, suffering from economic decline and lack of political power, regarded the patriot elite as their enemies. The South Carolina backcountry divided along lines drawn during the 1760s, with the more affluent former Regulators supporting the Whigs, and their opponents, the "lower sort," casting their lot with the British.

Of considerable concern to white Americans were the loyalties of enslaved African Americans. Of the 2.5 million people in the thirteen colonies in 1775, about 500,000 were blacks. As the rhetoric of revolution reached African American slaves, increasing numbers escaped. On Maryland's Eastern Shore, loyalist whites made common cause with the bondpeople of Whig planters: in fall 1775, a Dorchester County committee reported that "the insolence of the Negroes in this county is come to such a height, that we are under a necessity of disarming them. . . . The malicious and imprudent speeches of some among the lower classes of whites have induced them to believe that their freedom depended on the success of the King's troops."

A chief source of unrest, the patriots believed, was the November 1775 proclamation of Lord Dunmore, royal governor of Virginia, declaring "all indented [sic] servants, Negroes, or others [owned by rebels] free, that are able and willing to bear arms, they joining His Majesty's Troops." Whigs considered this proclamation foul play, an attempt to start an insurrection. They increased slave patrols and warned of harsh punishments to those who ran away or took up arms against their masters. The penalty for slave rebellion, of course, was death. Nevertheless, African Americans aided the British by joining the army and employing their firsthand knowledge of the Chesapeake Bay. Some served as pilots along its tributaries, while others delivered fresh provisions to the British ships by foraging plantations at night.

African Americans also supported the Revolution, but received little welcome from the Whigs. As the Americans created an army from volunteer forces besieging Boston, they excluded slaves and even free blacks from participating. From 1775 through much of 1776, when white enlistments seemed adequate, the patriot leaders, many of them slaveowners, were unwilling to exchange freedom for military service. By 1777, however, when recruiters found it difficult to fill their quotas, the states north of Virginia began accepting free blacks and slaves. Officially, Virginia took only free African Americans, but some masters sent slaves as substitutes for themselves. An estimated 5,000 African Americans served in the Continental army and state militias or at sea on American privateers. At the end of their service, many but not all of the enslaved African Americans who fought for independence received freedom. Some masters who had pledged liberty to their slaves if they served as substitutes broke the promises after the war.

Estimates of the total number of Americans who joined the Whig forces range from 100,000 to 250,000. Most signed up for tours of duty lasting several months or a year, not for the duration of the war. An ardent Boston patriot, for example, a poor shoemaker named George Robert Twelves Hewes, served at least six different stints for a total of twenty months. Ordinary people like Hewes did their best to support both the patriotic cause and their families. Thus, Washington and his generals constantly faced the problem of expiring enlistments, a condition that severely hampered execution of the war. The inability of Congress to pay soldiers adequately also hindered recruitment and retention of troops. As time went on, the American troops became better trained and disciplined, but originated from less privileged rungs of society. By 1778, most of the states had to adopt

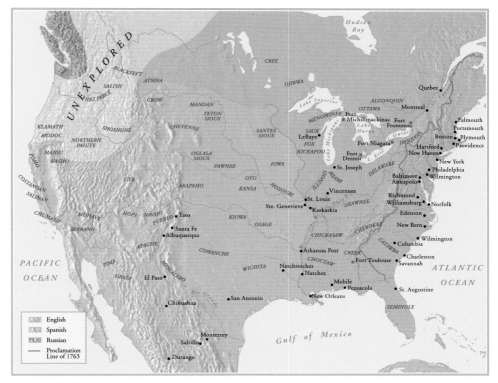

North America in 1764

Significant changes in European claims to regions in North America resulted from the Seven Years' War. The Treaty of Paris of 1763 divided former French territory between Great Britain to the east of the Mississippi River and Spain to the west. The British also gained Spanish Florida.

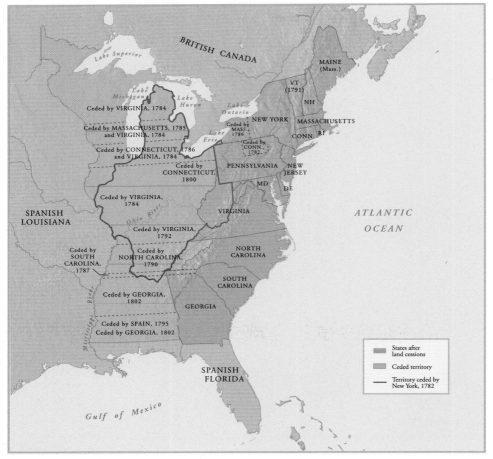

Western Land Cessions, 1782–1802

A number of states claimed territory west of the Appalachians based on their colonial charters. For example, under Connecticut's charter, which defined the Pacific Ocean as its western boundary, residents claimed part of Pennsylvania as well as western lands.

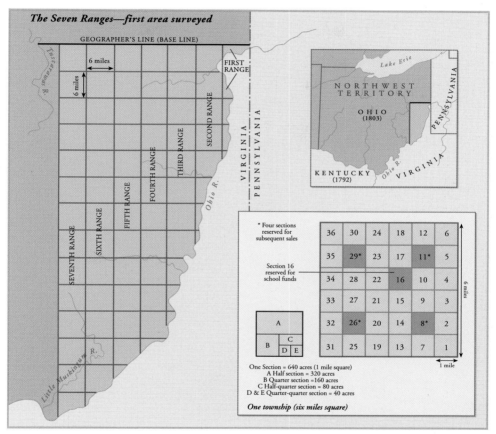

Land Ordinance of 1785

This map shows the plans for dividing land in eastern Ohio into townships and lots. The minimum price was $1 per acre.

Western Exploration, 1803–1807

At about the same time Meriwether Lewis and William Clark led the Corps of Discovery along the northern route to treat with Native Americans, explore the natural resources, and locate a northwest passage, Zebulon Pike traveled north along the Mississippi River and west to the Rocky Mountains.

conscription to fill their quotas. Men were drafted by lottery, but could pay a fine or hire a substitute, loopholes that contributed to disproportionate service by the poor.

Women took part in the American war effort by operating farms and businesses in their husbands' absence, defending their homes and families against marauding enemy soldiers, supplying food and clothing for the troops, and joining the army. Perhaps several hundred women put on uniforms to become soldiers. These troops included Deborah Sampson of Massachusetts, who enlisted under the name Robert Shurtleff. She fought in battle, but was discovered when she received a wound; after the war she collected an army pension. Others performed unofficial short-term service as spies. The most substantial contribution of women to the American military was that of the Women of the Army, as George Washington called them. Numbering perhaps 20,000 over the course of the war, they served as nurses, cooks, laundresses, and water carriers. They were regular members of the army who drew rations and were subject to military discipline. Some saw action in battle, particularly women in artillery crews who carried water to swab out the cannon after each firing. The story of "Molly Pitcher" evolved from women like Mary Hayes of Carlisle, Pennsylvania, who took the place of fallen soldiers.

Independence and Confederation

During the winter and spring of 1776, fighting continued between Great Britain and the thirteen colonies. Though the Canada campaign was a disaster, the Americans gained success in their siege of Boston. They sledged the heavy guns from Fort Ticonderoga about 300 miles, installing them in March 1776 on the Dorchester Heights. Instead of storming the artillery, the British withdrew from the city, sailing to Nova Scotia in preparation for an invasion of New York City.

In 1776, London undertook a huge effort to put down the revolt. It sent across the Atlantic Ocean 370 transports with supplies and 32,000 troops, of whom many were German mercenaries (called Hessians because the largest proportion came from the principality of Hesse-Cassel). The British intended these soldiers to join General William Howe's 10,000 troops from Nova Scotia, take New York City, and destroy Washington's army. The British navy, with seventy-three warships and 13,000 sailors in American waters, would bombard seaports and wreak havoc on colonial shipping.

As the British military descended upon New York in midsummer 1776, the Continental Congress finally declared independence. The force of events propelled most moderate delegates to cast their vote for a complete break. In January 1776, Thomas Paine, a recent immigrant from England, had published *Common Sense*. Though his arguments were familiar to Congress and readers of political tracts, Paine convinced the American public of the need for independence. *Common Sense* sold more than 100,000 copies within a few months, reaching hundreds of thousands of people as copies changed hands and nonreaders listened to Paine's words read aloud. Paine used language that appealed to ordinary Protestant Americans, employing biblical arguments that churchgoing farmers and craftspeople could appreciate, and avoiding Latin phrases and classical references. He

In this painting, *The Declaration of Independence*, by John Trumbull, the drafting committee stands at center: from left to right, John Adams, Roger Sherman, Robert Livingston, Thomas Jefferson, and Benjamin Franklin.

wanted to demonstrate that the time for compromise had passed, that the proper course was to shed the British monarchy and aristocracy to create an American republic. "We have it in our power to begin the world over again," he wrote. The bloodshed that began at Lexington justified rejection of the king: "No man was a warmer wisher for a reconciliation than myself, before the fatal nineteenth of April, 1775, but the moment the event of that day was made known, I rejected the hardened, sullen-tempered Pharaoh of England for ever." Pragmatically, Paine argued that the colonists must break their ties with London if they expected aid from France and Spain. He pointed out the importance of American exports, which "will always have a market while eating is the custom in Europe." He exclaimed, "'TIS TIME TO PART . . . there is something very absurd, in supposing a continent to be perpetually governed by an island."

Through the spring of 1776, sentiment for independence increased. News that the British had engaged German mercenaries heated the debate. The provincial assemblies of Georgia, South Carolina, and North Carolina gave their delegates in Congress permission to support the break, while Rhode Island declared independence on its own. Virginia proposed that Congress separate from Britain, taking measures "for forming foreign alliances and a confederation of the colonies." But in June, the New York, Pennsylvania, Delaware, and Maryland assemblies, controlled by moderate factions, were still not ready to condone a split. Nevertheless, Congress appointed a committee to draft the Declaration of Independence, of which Thomas Jefferson, a wealthy thirty-three-year-old Virginia planter and lawyer, was the principal author. A graduate of the College of William and Mary and a serious intellectual, he had been an active opponent of British policies since first elected to the Virginia assembly in 1769.

The Declaration set forth Congress's reasons for separating from the government of George III; the revolutionaries focused on the king's offenses because they had already denied the sovereignty of Parliament. It held "these truths to be self-evident: That all men are created equal; that they are endowed by their Creator with certain unalienable rights; that among these are life, liberty, and the pursuit of happiness." (See the Appendix for full text.) Employing the philosophy of John Locke and other Enlightenment writers, Jefferson continued, "that, to secure these rights, governments are instituted among men, deriving their just powers from the consent of the governed; that whenever any form of government becomes destructive of these ends, it is the right of the people to alter or to abolish it, and to institute new government." Congress placed the blame for the breach on the king, listing his misdeeds: refusing to approve necessary laws passed by the colonial assemblies, dissolving legislatures and courts, stationing a standing army, interrupting trade, and imposing taxes without colonial consent. Most recently, Congress announced to the world, George III had declared "us out of his protection and wag[ed] war against us. He has plundered our seas, ravaged our coasts, burned our towns, and destroyed the lives of our people. He is at this time transporting large armies of foreign mercenaries to complete the works of death, desolation, and tyranny already begun." In reference to Lord Dunmore's proclamation, the congressmen accused the king of exciting "domestic insurrection among us." For these reasons and more, Congress declared the thirteen colonies, now to be called the United States of America, "free and independent states" having "full power to levy war, conclude peace, contract alliances, establish commerce, and do all other acts and things which independent states may of right do."

On July 2, 1776, all delegations to Congress approved independence except New York's, which had not received new instructions so was forced to abstain. Completing revisions two days later, Congress adopted the Declaration. For many Americans, independence ended the problem of fighting a government that they continued to recognize as sovereign. When the Continental troops heard the Declaration read on July 9, they cheered, as did civilians throughout the states. However, the battles to defend this independence still lay ahead. General Washington cautioned "every officer and soldier . . . that now the peace and safety of his Country depends (under God) solely on the success of our arms."

To mount sufficient military force to win the war, the states needed unity. In mid-July 1776, Congress began debating the Articles of Confederation, a plan for permanent union, which it approved and sent to the states for ratification more than a year later. The chief disagreement among the congressmen was one that remained central to American politics for two centuries, the power of the national government versus that of individual states. The Articles permitted less centralized authority than would the Constitution, which was drafted a decade later. Under the Articles, Congress had responsibility to conduct foreign affairs, make war and peace, deal with Native Americans residing outside the states, coin and borrow money, supervise the post office, and negotiate boundary disputes between states. The "United States" meant thirteen sovereign states joined together by a Congress with specific functions. Article 1 established the "confederacy" to be called the United States of America, not a sovereign nation. Article 2 held that "each State retains its sovereignty, freedom and independence, and every power, jurisdiction, and right, which is not by this confederation expressly delegated to the United States, in Congress assembled." The Congress could neither tax nor raise troops, but could only assess quotas on the states, a serious disadvantage in time of war. Even so, the Articles failed ratification until 1781, when the last of the thirteen states finally approved. Conflict over state claims on western lands held up ratification. In the meantime, Congress attempted to govern within the limits of the unratified Articles, but its inability to raise revenue and draft troops obstructed the American war effort, creating huge shortages of supplies and men.

War in the North, 1776–1779

For the American patriots, the Revolution was a defensive war. It lasted eight years, from 1775 to 1783, longer than any other in United States history until the Vietnam War. The Continental army was often outmatched, for it remained smaller than General Washington wanted; his troops constantly needed training as veterans left and new recruits arrived. But as the theater of war moved from one region to another, American generals obtained reinforcements from state militias and local volunteers. The British, despite considerable assistance from Tories, lacked enough reserves to subdue the rebellious North American seaboard. The sheer expanse of the thirteen states and the 3,000-mile distance from England made the British army's task extremely difficult, despite its formal training and Britain's larger population and wealth.

Invasions of New York

To conquer New York, and thus divide New England from the rest of the states, in July 1776, British troops landed on Staten Island. In August, they attacked Washington's army at Brooklyn Heights. The redcoats defeated the Americans badly, pushing them back to Manhattan Island, and then to White Plains. But they failed to take advantage of Washington's mistakes, which could have allowed them to surround his troops. In November, however, the British did hand Washington a humiliating defeat by capturing the 2,900 defenders of Manhattan's Fort Washington.

The Continental army retreated across New Jersey with the British and their German allies at its heels. The patriots crossed the Delaware River into Pennsylvania, allowing the British to occupy New Jersey towns. The British gathered Tory support by offering a pardon to anyone who would take a loyalty oath within sixty days. For the Whigs, as Thomas Paine wrote, these were "times that try men's souls." The army was in retreat, the New Jersey government had dispersed, and citizens who were skeptical of Washington's abilities rallied to the British.

Before the end of the year, however, fortunes changed. British plundering across New Jersey turned indifferent farmers into radical Whigs, who became guerrillas, ambushing the enemy and stealing supplies. Meanwhile, Washington devised a plan that bought him time, acting before the enlistments of a large proportion of his army would expire on December 31. He attacked 1,400 Hessians at Trenton on Christmas night, in the midst of a winter storm. Taking the enemy by surprise, the Americans captured more than 900 men. In early January, Washington took the offensive once again, having convinced many of his soldiers to extend their terms for six weeks. Pennsylvania and New Jersey militia, inspired by the victory at Trenton, reinforced his troops. Washington eluded a superior British army under Lord Cornwallis, then defeated a smaller force at Princeton. General William Howe withdrew most of his army to New York. In the words of one British officer, the Americans had "become a formidable enemy."

In 1777, as the British made plans to suppress the rebellion once and for all, their strategy for the upcoming campaign became confused. General Howe intended to take Philadelphia, not by crossing New Jersey, but by means of his brother Admiral Richard Howe's fleet. At the same time, London organized an invasion from Canada, to win back Fort Ticonderoga and divide the states. The campaigns were not coordinated and neither started before June, when British General "Gentleman Johnny" Burgoyne led his force of more than 7,000 British regulars, German mercenaries, Native Americans, and Canadians by boat down Lake Champlain. True to his reputation, Burgoyne overburdened his troops with baggage, including cartloads of personal clothing and champagne. Burgoyne easily took Fort Ticonderoga, then headed for Albany. The American forces under Philip Schuyler felled trees and rolled boulders into the path of Burgoyne's heavy column. Covering twenty-three miles of terrain that was difficult even without American sabotage took the British army twenty-four days. Short on supplies and horses, Burgoyne sent 800 troops to Bennington, Vermont, where General John Stark and his militia ambushed them by pretending to be Tories. Troops under British officer Barry St. Leger returned to Canada when they heard that Benedict Arnold was headed west to intercept them. The rebel forces, on the other hand, burgeoned with volunteers as British soldiers pillaged the countryside. In September, near Saratoga, Burgoyne encountered the American army under General Horatio Gates, who had replaced Schuyler. The Americans surrounded the enemy, firing upon them day and night. Burgoyne sent for help from New York City, but Howe had long since sailed with most of his troops to Philadelphia. Burgoyne's 5,800-man army thus surrendered at Saratoga on October 17, 1777.

The British Occupy Philadelphia

As Burgoyne marched toward disaster in New York, General Howe more successfully reached Philadelphia. In July, his 13,000 soldiers departed from New York City aboard a fleet of 260 ships, but instead of disembarking within a week along the Delaware River, they sailed south

Map 5.2 Northern Campaigns, 1776–1778 The major revolutionary battles of these years took place in New York, New Jersey, and Pennsylvania. The inset indicates battles in 1776, when the British invaded Long Island and New York City, pushing Washington's troops across New Jersey until they won crucial battles at Trenton and Princeton. The larger map illustrates British offensives in 1777, while the 1778 battle at Monmouth Courthouse appears on the inset.

to the Virginia capes then up the Chesapeake Bay to Head of Elk. Their voyage lasted over a month, costing Howe valuable time that might have permitted him to assist Burgoyne. Washington tried unsuccessfully, with an army of 11,000 at Brandywine, to block Howe's advance through southeastern Pennsylvania. The British occupied Philadelphia, dividing their forces between Germantown and the capital. On October 4, 1777, Washington attacked the British encampment at Germantown, inflicting serious damage though he was once again defeated. Elizabeth Drinker, a Quaker resident of Philadelphia, in her diary reported significant losses on both sides. She wrote, "this has been a sorrowful day at Philadelphia and much more so at Germantown and thereabouts." She recorded news of the Continental army's movements, fearing that the troops would carry the battle to her city. "The apprehensions of their entering," she believed, "will render this night grievous to many." Washington did not attack Philadelphia, so the enemy retained control of the capital until they withdrew the next June.

Even so, in 1777, the British had failed to put down the American rebellion during yet another season of war. Upon hearing that Burgoyne's army had surrendered, the Howe brothers resigned. General Henry Clinton became the new commander of British forces in North America. The redcoats wintered in relative comfort at Philadelphia while Washington's troops nearly starved and froze to death at Valley Forge, to the west of the city. In February 1778, Continental soldiers lacked adequate clothing and received just three pounds of bread and three ounces of meat to last a week. Some ate only "fire cakes," baked from a paste of flour and water. Nevertheless, they became a disciplined army at Valley Forge, under the Prussian officer Baron von Steuben, who rigorously trained the Americans in the European art of war.

Alliance with France

While February 1778 brought despair to the Americans, it also brought hope—in the form of an alliance with France. Already supporting the United States with economic and military assistance, the French government hoped to recoup the international status it had lost during the Seven Years' War. Convinced by the victory at Saratoga that the former colonies could win the war, the French signed two pacts with the United States. The first was the Treaty of Amity and Commerce, in which France recognized American independence and both nations pledged "a firm, inviolable and universal peace." The second was the military Treaty of Alliance, in which they agreed to fight Great Britain jointly until the Americans had won independence, pledged not to negotiate a separate peace, and confirmed their defensive alliance "forever." France renounced claims to its former colonies in North America, but could retain any of the British West Indies that it conquered.

In supporting the Americans, the French renewed their long struggle with Great Britain that had been suspended in 1763. France's entry widened the war, placing greater focus on the West Indies, whose sugar production made them more valuable than the North American mainland to the British. The following year, Spain allied with France, but refused to recognize or assist the American insurgents beyond providing limited financial aid. Unlike France, which denied interest in North America, the Spanish viewed the Americans as potentially dangerous competitors.

The Wartime Economy

Despite significant economic assistance from France and a much smaller contribution from Spain, the United States had grave economic problems during the war. The loss of British markets devastated farmers, merchants, and fishermen, as the embargo closed crucial ports in the West Indies and British Isles. The Royal Navy attacked and blockaded American harbors and ravaged ships at sea. On land, the armies laid waste to farms and towns.

For Congress, the chief economic problem was paying for the war. Without the power to tax, it printed money, a total of almost $200 million in paper bills by 1779. The states printed a similar amount, despite their ability to tax, primarily because printing money was easier than trying to collect revenues from a financially strapped populace. Unfortunately, as the war continued year after year, the demand for military equipment, food, medical supplies, clothing, and soldiers' wages persisted. This extraordinary demand for provisions coupled with the continuing emission of paper money sent prices soaring. By 1779, the paper money was nearly worthless, inspiring the slogan "not worth a Continental."

The depreciation of currency resulted in popular unrest, as a group of Philadelphia militia in 1779 demanded a more equitable military draft and regulation of food prices. They were angry that the burden of militia service fell disproportionately on the poor because others could pay fines to avoid the draft. At the same time, the prices of food and firewood skyrocketed. In just two months, August and September 1779, the price of beef, flour, and molasses rose by more than 80 percent. The protesters, according to one broadside posted along the streets, blamed "a few overbearing Merchants, a swarm of Monopolizers and Speculators, an infernal gang of Tories" for the spiraling costs.

In the so-called "Fort Wilson Incident," armed members of the Philadelphia militia met at Burns's Tavern on October 4, planning to capture and exile from the city four suspected Tories. Several hundred militiamen marched their prisoners through the streets to the fife and drum of the Rogue's March, ordinarily played by the military when a soldier was discharged dishonorably. The militia was ridiculing the reputed Tories, all four of them wealthy citizens. When rumors raced through the capital that the militia planned to arrest others, about thirty gentlemen who thought they might be targets armed themselves and gathered at the house of lawyer James Wilson. Though a member of Congress, Wilson was suspect because he opposed price regulation. The militia marched past "Fort Wilson," gave three cheers, then shots rang out. Though it is unknown who shot first, both sides subsequently exchanged fire. After cavalry broke up the battle, six people lay dead and seventeen wounded, the majority of them militia.

The Fort Wilson Incident terrified many people because lower-class patriots had directed armed force against the Whig elite, protesting the policies of their own government. Henry Laurens, a wealthy South Carolina merchant and member of the Continental Congress, wrote, "we are at this moment on a precipice, and what I have long dreaded and often intimated to my friends, seems to be breaking forth—a convulsion among the people."

Continental Currency

The Continental Congress, which acted under the Articles of Confederation throughout the war, lacked the ability to tax. Because the states were reluctant to raise money through taxation to support the war, Congress funded military spending through loans and printed money. Before the Revolution, colonies had printed paper currency. For example, New York and Pennsylvania issued paper money as loans, thus putting needed money into circulation and obtaining public revenue from the interest.

Continental money, as noted in this example, promised the bearer the equivalent in Spanish dollars. Congress thus rejected the English system of pounds, shillings, and pence to adopt the Spanish denomination. This was a logical step because Spanish coins manufactured from Mexican and South American silver and gold had commonly circulated in colonial British America despite the official English currency. Unfortunately, Continental dollars quickly lost value as Congress printed millions to fund the war. By April 1781, $168 Continental was the equivalent of one silver dollar.

Courtesy, American Antiquarian Society

The War Moves West and South

The failure of the British army to defeat Washington's troops and the entry of France into the war led the imperial government to rethink its military strategy. Protection of Caribbean sugar islands from the French navy gained top priority. With redeployment of forces to the West Indies, British General Clinton had to consolidate his army, so in June 1778, he pulled his occupation forces out of Philadelphia, marching across New Jersey toward New York. Washington's army caught up with Clinton at Monmouth Courthouse, where the battle, fought in traditional European style, was indecisive. The British escaped to New York.

The Frontier War

In the west, from New York to Georgia, fighting devastated the backcountry. When the Revolution broke out, many Indians supported the British, who still held garrisons in the west and had more gunpowder and provisions than the patriots. Yet Native Americans responded in various ways to "this dispute between two brothers," as neutral Iroquois called the Revolution in 1775. "The quarrel seems to be unnatural," they said; "you are two brothers of one blood." Just as colonists divided among radical Whigs, Tories, and neutrals, so did the Native Americans. Even within some tribes, factions separated those who favored the British or the Americans, or wanted to avoid any involvement. The militant Indians who sided with Great

Britain considered the threat of white settlers crossing the Appalachians as most dangerous to their future. Many attempted to form pan-Indian alliances to fight their own wars of independence against land grabbers from the east.

Beginning in 1776, Indians attacked Anglo-Americans from the Georgia frontier to the Great Lakes. The Cherokees raided the southern backcountry and planned a major assault on Tennessee, but ran short of gunpowder and were defeated by Whig militia in fall 1776. Many Cherokees, Choctaws, Creeks, Shawnees, Iroquois, and others did not give up, however, but rather planned in 1779 "a general invasion of the Frontiers" coordinated by Henry Hamilton, the British lieutenant governor of the Illinois country. George Rogers Clark, a surveyor, heard of plans for the Indian and British offensive. To Patrick Henry, he wrote, "the Case is Desperate but Sir we must Either Quit the Country or attack Mr. Hamilton." In 1779, with a small force, Clark assaulted Fort Vincennes and obtained the British surrender, thus ending the pan-Indian campaign.

Despite Clark's victory at Vincennes, the Kentucky-Ohio frontier remained embattled throughout the war. The same was true of Pennsylvania and New York, where after 1777 most Iroquois and Delawares abandoned their neutrality to ally with the British. In 1778 and 1779, Major John Butler, his son Captain Walter Butler, and the Mohawk leader Theyendanegea, also known as Joseph Brant, led Tory and Native American forces against white settlements. The loyalists and Iroquois burned houses, barns, fields, and orchards, ran off livestock, and killed or captured settlers over a swath of frontier ranging from fifty to a hundred miles wide. In summer 1779, General Washington sent General John Sullivan with 4,000 troops, who retaliated by burning Iroquois villages, orchards, and fields of corn. At Newtown, New York, Sullivan defeated a contingent of about 700 loyalists and Indians. His scorched-earth policy seriously damaged most of the Iroquois towns; displaced Indians suffered through the winter of 1779–1780 on short rations. But the next spring they renewed their assaults.

Because many Anglo-Americans had trouble distinguishing between Indian friends and foes, Native Americans who allied with the United States or remained neutral throughout the war fared little better with the Whigs than those who sided with the British. In March 1782, frontier militia massacred ninety-six paci-

New York State Historical Association, Cooperstown

Joseph Brant, by Gilbert Stuart. The Mohawk leader, who was educated among whites and traveled to Great Britain in 1775, convinced many Iroquois to ally with the British.

fist Indian men, women, and children at the Moravian mission of Gnadenhutten in Ohio. Another group, the Catawbas of South Carolina, performed extensive service for the patriots. They searched for loyalists and escaped slaves, supplied food to the rebels, fought the Cherokees in 1776, and battled the British, who destroyed their town in retaliation. After the war, the South Carolina assembly compensated the Catawbas for their loyalty and livestock, refusing to abet the governor's plan to lease out their reservation. The Mahicans of Stockbridge in western Massachusetts, who fought in the American army, returned home to find that whites had taken over their land.

The Southern Campaigns

While the Revolution ravaged the frontier, the main theater of war remained east of the Appalachians, where in 1778, the British inaugurated a new strategy. Retaining troops in New York City, they invaded the south, counting on loyalist support in Georgia, the Carolinas, and Virginia to restore colonial governments to the Crown. The British also expected the large numbers of enslaved African Americans in the south to weaken patriot defenses. In November 1778, General Clinton sent 3,500 troops under Lieutenant Colonel Archibald Campbell to Georgia, where they joined 2,000 soldiers from Florida. They captured Savannah and Augusta, but had trouble conquering the backcountry. Then, with 10,000 troops, the British turned to Charleston, where in May 1780 they compelled the American general Benjamin Lincoln to surrender 5,500 men. The British fanned out through South Carolina, as many residents pledged their loyalty to the king. In July 1780, General Horatio Gates arrived to build a new southern army. Disaster struck once again, when Gates placed too much responsibility on untrained militia in action against Lord Cornwallis at Camden. The battle was a rout; even the regular Continentals were dispersed, and Gates—the hero of Saratoga—was disgraced.

The tide turned after General Nathanael Greene replaced Gates as commander of the southern army. The British contributed to the turnaround, as they became more insistent in demanding oaths of allegiance from Carolinians who preferred to keep out of the fray. This provoked a backlash, particularly because the British army stretched itself so thin that it withdrew protection from the people who took the oaths, thus exposing them to punishment by the Whigs. The redcoats and Tories also plundered, outraging many southerners and pushing them into the American camp. Most notorious was Banastre Tarleton's Tory Legion, which executed prisoners of war and destroyed houses and fields, leaving many families homeless. "Bloody" Tarleton created new revolutionaries, who joined Greene's army or the smaller irregular brigades led by Thomas "The Gamecock" Sumter, Colonel Andrew Pickens, and Francis Marion, "the Swamp Fox." During 1780 and 1781, Greene rebuilt the southern army using both traditional and guerrilla forces.

While not welcome as soldiers in South Carolina and Georgia, African American slaves played an important role in the southern campaigns, acting as spies and counterspies for each side. One man, Antigua, received freedom by act of the South Carolina assembly for himself, his wife Hagar, and child in reward for "procuring information of the enemy's

Map 5.3 Southern Campaigns, 1778–1781 In late 1778, the British decided to invade the South, where they were no more successful in ending the war. They agreed to peace after their defeat to the Americans and French at the Battle of Yorktown in Virginia.
View an animated version of this map or related maps at http://history.wadsworth.com/ayerscompact2/.

movements and designs." Throughout the South, African Americans provided much of the supporting labor for both armies, as they built fortifications, worked in lead mines, constructed and repaired roads, produced arms and ammunition, and drove wagons. American officers complained about the chronic shortage of black laborers, because Whig slaveowners jealously guarded their strongest and most talented slaves to work on their plantations. Further, thousands of African Americans took advantage of General Clinton's 1779 proclamation offering freedom to those who joined the king's service.

A practice of rebel leaders highlighting their ability to dissociate their own fight for liberty from the plight of enslaved African Americans was to offer recruits enlistment "bounties" in slaves, much as other states promised bounties in land. In South Carolina, Thomas Sumter offered one African American bondman or woman to each private who would enlist for ten months. A colonel would receive three mature blacks and one child. The practice was adopted by Andrew Pickens as well, and supported by General Greene, who expected to pay the bounties from slaves confiscated from loyalist estates. Because sufficient numbers of African Americans owned by Tories were lacking, regiments reported "pay" in arrears, some with grotesque precision. One payroll noted a deficit of 93 3/4 mature slaves and "Three Quarters of a Small Negro."

In fall 1780, Lord Cornwallis decided to head north, for while the British had destroyed two American armies and taken control of South Carolina and Georgia, the time had come to conquer the entire South. As his forces marched toward North Carolina, however, they met heavy resistance. In several battles, the conflict became a civil war, as Americans fought on both sides. In October 1780, just to the south of the state line at King's Mountain, Whig frontier units defeated an enemy force, of which only Patrick Ferguson, the commander of the loyalists, was British. In January 1781, at Cowpens, General Daniel Morgan crushed Tarleton's Tory Legion by making the most of his sharpshooting frontiersmen. Morgan lined up the riflemen in front of his disciplined Continentals. The sharpshooters fired several volleys at Tarleton's troops then withdrew to back up the regulars, who took the brunt of the fighting.

When Cornwallis learned that Tarleton's legion was lost, he chased the Americans into North Carolina, abandoning most of his equipment and supplies to move quickly. In March, Cornwallis met Greene at the Guilford Courthouse, where the American general used Morgan's Cowpens tactics, though less effectively because his successive lines of irregulars and Continentals were spread too far apart. Though the battle ended indecisively, one-fourth of Cornwallis's troops lay wounded or dead. Having discarded tents, medical equipment, and food—and cut off from his base in South Carolina—the British general withdrew to the North Carolina coast where he sought naval support.

Meanwhile, Greene moved south to reconquer South Carolina and Georgia, where the British still had 8,000 men in arms. Because these troops were spread out in numerous towns and forts, Greene's 1,500 Continental soldiers and the guerrilla brigades of Sumter, Pickens, and Marion could pick off the garrisons one by one. Greene wrote to Washington in May 1781 that if the enemy "divide their force, they will fall by detachments, and if they operate collectively, they cannot command the country." By July, the Americans had pushed the redcoats and Tories back to a narrow strip of territory between Charleston and Savannah, which the British held until their evacuation the next year. Despite initial disastrous defeats, the Whigs prevailed in the Carolinas and Georgia by recruiting irregular forces and employing them strategically. The great sweep of territory controlled by the former thirteen colonies proved impossible for the British army to subdue.

The surrender of Cornwallis at Yorktown in October 1781 effectively ended the war. The general had moved into Virginia, replacing Benedict Arnold as commander of the British forces there. Arnold, the former American officer, had turned traitor, joined the British army, and most recently captured Richmond. With an army of about 8,000 men, Cornwallis intended to concentrate British military efforts in Virginia, so requested more troops from New York. General Clinton refused. Their squabbling and delay allowed the Americans and the French to surround Cornwallis's camp on the Virginia peninsula by land and sea. Several times before, the French forces had collaborated with the Americans, but their joint efforts had resulted in failure. This time, soldiers under the Comte de Rochambeau and French fleets commanded by the Comte de Grasse and Comte de Barras played a decisive role in defeating Cornwallis. Washington's army marched south from New York to join American and French troops assembled in Virginia. The operation was a marvel of military cooperation for the eighteenth century; it even included the construction of bake ovens outside New York City to camouflage Washington's departure. With 17,000 men and heavy artillery, the American and French forces won the British surrender, finally placing the seal on American independence.

The Peace Settlement

In negotiating the peace, the United States had to reckon with both its adversary Great Britain and its ally France, which in turn was beholden to Spain. American peace commissioners Benjamin Franklin, John Jay, and John Adams, whom Adams called "militia diplomats," shrewdly worked one European nation against the other to obtain a desirable settlement. They ignored Congress's instructions to take advice from France because they understood that French and Spanish goals were different from their own. France had little interest in a strong American nation; Spain particularly feared its territorial expansion. Thus, in violation of the 1778 treaty with France, the American diplomats negotiated separately with the British, obtaining recognition of independence and most other provisions they requested.

The British and American peacemakers approved preliminary articles of peace on November 30, 1782; the Treaty of Paris signed on September 3, 1783 was essentially unchanged. The new nation would extend from approximately the present United States–Canada boundary on the north, to the Mississippi River on the west, to the thirty-first parallel on the south. The American diplomats also secured fishing rights off Newfoundland and the St. Lawrence River, of particular interest to New Englanders. Further, the British agreed to evacuate their troops promptly from the United States "without causing any destruction or carrying away any Negroes or other property of the American inhabitants." For its part, Congress would urge state governments to return confiscated property to the loyalists. Prewar debts owed by citizens of each country to citizens of the other would be honored: they should "meet with no lawful impediment to the recovery of the full value in sterling money."

The treaty was a success on paper for the United States, but left France and Spain dissatisfied and pro-British Native Americans "thunder struck." In coming decades, the Americans would struggle to enforce its provisions. The French gained little from the war except the separation of the mainland colonies from Great Britain. The Spanish had wanted to keep the Americans out of the Mississippi Valley and hoped to obtain the return of Gibraltar from the British. They instead accepted East and West Florida and the Mediterranean island of Minorca. Native Americans were furious that their British allies had signed away their lands.

While U.S. possession of the trans-Appalachian region remained disputed for decades, the provision that most immediately caused trouble was the one dealing with enslaved African Americans. Even before the final treaty was signed, American slaveowners claimed that the British military forces were taking their "property." The situation was complicated, for thousands of African Americans had fled behind British lines to find freedom and some had fought against their former masters. The British ruled that blacks who sought refuge before the signing of the provisional treaty in November 1782 could not be considered the property of Americans because they were already free, but slaves who escaped after that date would be returned to their masters. General Washington, Congress, and state governments tried but failed to convince the British to return all blacks to their former masters. At least 20,000 African Americans, including those who accompanied loyalist owners as well as the ex-slaves of Whigs, left with the British military. Some went to Nova Scotia, where they received a generally unfriendly welcome from white residents, while many others were transported to Florida and the West Indies. In the Sugar Islands most of the newly freed blacks were quickly re-enslaved.

Conclusion

The War of Independence was a success as American Whigs cast off a monarchy to create a new government in which many people, not a king and nobility, held power. They rejected as tyranny British efforts to impose revenue taxes without approval of representative assemblies and to curb rights such as trial by jury. The patriots used a variety of tactics including economic boycotts, riots, mass meetings, and petitions. Their local associations assumed governmental authority, providing the basis for republican rule.

Against many odds—including opposition from large numbers of loyalists—the thirteen British colonies won independence, created a confederation of sovereign states, and obtained claims to the vast trans-Appalachian territories. French financial aid and military support were crucial to victory. The Whigs avoided military dictatorship, preserved individual rights for white Americans, and established the framework for a future democratic society. Yet not all Americans reaped immediate benefits. While wartime ideology challenged slavery in the North, the vast majority of African Americans remained enslaved. And though the Revolution offered women new, temporary roles in the economy and military—and more permanent educational opportunities after the peace—their political and legal status was essentially unchanged. The Treaty of Paris ignored the territorial rights of Native Americans.

Of immediate importance to the nation's leaders, however, was establishing a stable government. The 1780s presented a series of challenges to the new republic.

RECOMMENDED READINGS

Calloway, Colin G. *The American Revolution in Indian Country: Crisis and Diversity in Native American Communities* (1995). Focuses on eight Indian communities to demonstrate the diversity of Native American experiences during the Revolutionary War.

Foner, Eric. *Tom Paine and Revolutionary America* (1976). A readable "life and times" of the author of *Common Sense.*

Gross, Robert A. *The Minutemen and Their World* (1976). An interesting study of how revolutionary fervor developed in Concord, Massachusetts.

Higginbotham, Don. *The War of American Independence: Military Attitudes, Policies, and Practice, 1763–1789* (1971). Straightforward military history of the Revolution.

Hoffman, Ronald, and Albert, Peter J., eds. *Women in the Age of the Revolution* (1989). Very good essays on women's status and contributions to the War of Independence.

In Search of Early America: The William and Mary Quarterly, 1943–1993, comp. Michael McGiffert (1993). Compilation of classic essays published in the foremost journal of early American history.

Morgan, Edmund S., and Morgan, Helen M. *The Stamp Act Crisis: Prologue to Revolution,* 2nd ed. (1996). A close examination of a crucial episode in the pre-revolutionary decade.

O'Shaughnessy, Andrew Jackson. *An Empire Divided: The American Revolution and the British Caribbean* (2000). Evaluates the differences that led West Indies planters to stay within the empire while mainland colonists rebelled.

Quarles, Benjamin. *The Negro in the American Revolution,* 2nd ed. (1996). The classic text on African Americans during the war.

Young, Alfred F., ed. *The American Revolution: Explorations in the History of American Radicalism* (1976). Important essays on the role of ordinary Americans in the Revolution.

> **Additional resources, exercises, and Internet links related to this chapter are available on the American Passages Web site: http://history.wadsworth.com/ayerscompact2/**

Toward a More Perfect Union
1783–1788

The American Patriots had won victory on the battlefield and, at least on paper, in negotiating the peace. The new country soon discovered, though, that independence
brought severe tests as well as opportunities. In 1786, Dr. Benjamin Rush of Philadelphia
summarized in a pamphlet the tasks facing the United States:

> There is nothing more common than to confound the terms of *the American revolution* with those
> of *the late American war*. The American war is over: but this is far from being the case with the
> American revolution. On the contrary, nothing but the first act of the great drama is closed. It
> remains yet to establish and perfect our forms of government; and to prepare the principles,
> morals, and manners of our citizens, for those forms of government. . . .

Having fought for liberty and self-government, Americans now had to create an effective
political framework to protect those rights. Their first government was a confederation of
small republics in which property-holding white men elected representatives. But questions
remained about how to avoid the opposite evils of tyranny and anarchy, questions that
inspired fiery debates and even rebellion during the 1780s.

American leaders had understood since 1776 that the task of creating a workable government lay before them. They were less prepared for other problems that arose soon after
the peace. With limited powers under the Articles of Confederation, the Congress faced challenges in demobilizing the army, conducting trade outside the confines of British mercantilism, paying the war debt, coexisting with Spanish colonies in Louisiana and Florida, dealing
with Native Americans, and supervising white settlement in the West. Despite Congress's
competent action on some of these issues, the need for a more powerful central government
became clear. Just four years after the conclusion of peace, delegates from the states met in
Philadelphia to draft the new Constitution, which became law upon ratification in 1788. This
Constitution has endured, with relatively few amendments, for over two centuries.

Politics and Change in the New Republic

In contrasting "the American revolution" with "the late American war," Rush made a distinction that many people have debated since the 1780s. Rush thought the revolution had
to continue because the government was not yet "perfect"—the states had too much power,

CHRONOLOGY

1783	Protest of Continental army officers at Newburgh, New York • Great Britain closes British West Indies to American ships • Massachusetts Supreme Court finds slavery unconstitutional
1784	Rhode Island and Connecticut pass gradual abolition laws • Spain closes port of New Orleans to Americans • Spain signs treaty of alliance with the Creeks • United States forces Iroquois to cede rights in Northwest Territory with Treaty of Fort Stanwix
1785	Native Americans yield lands in Ohio with Treaty of Fort McIntosh • Congress passes land ordinance for the Northwest Territory
1786	Shawnees sign Treaty of Fort Finney • Country party takes control of Rhode Island assembly • Virginia statute for religious liberty • Annapolis convention fails • Western Confederacy rejects treaties ceding lands in the Northwest Territory • Massachusetts farmers close county courts
1787	Shaysites attack the federal arsenal at Springfield, Massachusetts • Constitutional Convention meets in Philadelphia • Congress passes Northwest Ordinance • Constitution signed and sent to the states for ratification
1787–1788	Publication of *The Federalist* essays • Ratification of the Constitution by eleven states

leading to disunity and inertia. Others have framed the question in a different way: to what extent did the War of Independence bring about basic changes in politics and society? The war was revolutionary for propertied white men, but less so for women, African Americans, religious minorities, and the poor.

Republican Politics

Under the Articles of Confederation, the United States consisted of thirteen sovereign states rather than one nation. In framing the Confederation, representatives from the states had refused to transfer sovereignty to a central government. Only state assemblies, elected by the voters, could impose taxes; the central government, or Congress, would be an agent of the states. This decision was based on republican theory, that only in a small republic could representatives act according to the will of its citizens. If the territory were large, the interests and desires of the people would be too diverse, making harmony impossible. State officials, guarding their power, feared that a strong national government would be dominated by factions with interests opposite their own. Each state had an equal vote in Congress and sent delegates "appointed in such manner as the legislature of each State shall direct." Congress had responsibility to conduct foreign affairs, declare war and peace, and coin money, but could not levy taxes or raise troops. During the 1780s, its dependence on the states for funds brought the Confederation to a standstill. For years, Congress sought an amendment of the Articles to permit a national tax, but failed to obtain the required unanimous consent of the states.

The structure of the state governments reflected their framers' concept of republicanism. Most of the state constitutions resembled the old colonial governments, but incorporated changes that made them more responsible to the people. Most had two-house legislatures and a governor, but gave the largest share of power to the lower house of assembly, elected annually by the voters. The radical Pennsylvania constitution of 1776, more democratic than others, included no governor or upper house of assembly (senate), which was designed to represent the wealthier segment of society. Georgia also excluded the upper house and denied its governor any power. Even states that retained the governor eliminated his veto over legislation or allowed the assembly to override with a two-thirds vote. All of the states produced written constitutions as a protection against the kind of changes they believed the British had made in their unwritten constitution before the Revolution.

During the late 1770s and 1780s, as Americans formulated and revised state constitutions, they also developed the method by which frames of government were written and approved, the constitutional convention. Pennsylvania radicals called the first state convention in 1776, explaining that its members would be "invested with powers to form a plan of government only, and not to execute it after it is framed." Then, in 1780, Massachusetts voters demanded a convention to write a new constitution rather than accept a document their assemblymen had prepared. The constitution was ratified by the people (voters), who thus claimed to be sovereign—the ultimate source of political power—because the frame of government originated with them. Within a few years, other states adopted the same process, recognizing that a constitution should not be written by a governmental body—the legislature—that the constitution created. As one theorist argued, "Conventions . . . are the only proper bodies to form a Constitution, and Assemblies are the proper bodies to make Laws agreeable to that Constitution." Remarkably, in Massachusetts in 1780, every free man, even those without property, could vote on the new constitution. The document they approved limited suffrage to propertied men.

State constitutions also provided some protection for the liberties many Americans had defended in the Revolution. Virginia included a model Declaration of Rights that other states copied loosely. Most state constitutions offered freedom of worship, required search warrants, and banned excessive fines and quartering of troops in private dwellings. Only some of the states, however, guaranteed trial by jury and the rights of free speech, press, and assembly. A few opposed monopolies and imprisonment for debt.

The state constitutions were radical in the context of eighteenth-century politics because they vested power in the voters and lower houses of assembly. Nevertheless, the definition of who was qualified to cast ballots and hold office remained traditional. John Adams spoke for most politicians of his time when he wrote that only property holders should be counted among the sovereign people who could choose and serve as magistrates because the purpose of government was to safeguard property. "It is dangerous," Adams wrote, ". . . to alter the qualifications of voters. There will be no end to it. New claims will arise. Women will demand a vote. Lads from 12 to 21 will think their rights not enough attended to, and every man, who has not a farthing, will demand an equal voice." Voters, according to republican theory, must have a stake in society. Wives, slaves, servants, and unpropertied laboring men

Map 6.1 North America in 1783

The peace treaty ending the American Revolution gave the United States most of the territory from the Atlantic Ocean to the Mississippi River, south of the St. Lawrence River and Great Lakes, and north of Spanish Florida. The new nation obtained claims to the region west of the Appalachians primarily because Great Britain, France, and Spain had more urgent goals. The treaty left several borders vague, however, and the United States had difficulty enforcing several provisions. Spain refused to recognize the 31st parallel as Florida's northern border and closed the Mississippi River to American trade. See Map 6.2 for the area Spain ceded to the United States in 1795. Problems with Britain were more long-lived. Until 1796, the British refused to evacuate nine military posts, including Michilimackinac, Detroit, and Niagara. Britain controlled the west through these forts, both militarily and through diplomatic alliances with the region's Native Americans. The imprecise border between Maine and Canada nearly caused war between the United States and Britain two generations later, when the boundary dispute was resolved diplomatically in 1842.

were dependent on others and thus unqualified for suffrage. Yet in most places, women and free African Americans who owned property were also barred from voting, by law or by informal pressure. One exception was New Jersey, where the 1776 state constitution extended the vote to "all free inhabitants" who held sufficient property; in 1807, the legislature fell into line with other states by disenfranchising all women and blacks.

Women's Rights

Republican politics brought little change to women's lives. A married woman was still subject to the English common law that gave control of her property and earnings to her husband and denied her the right, without his permission, to make a will, sign contracts, sue in court, or act as a guardian. Despite independence, the American lawmakers refused to cast off this English tradition. Women were also barred from positions of high status. They could serve as ministers among Quakers and some Baptists but in no other churches; they taught school only at the primary level. None were lawyers or wealthy merchants, though some became successful shopkeepers. Women also lost ground in medicine. As medical courses at the college level became available to men, doctors with formal training displaced lay practitioners, including some midwives. Change occurred most noticeably in Boston, New York, and Philadelphia, where affluent clients demanded the new college-trained obstetricians.

In the post-revolutionary years, increased support for female education marked the most positive alteration in women's lives. This change accompanied the more general perception that a republic needed an educated people. Though women were denied entrance to all colleges, a number of academies opened their doors to provide secondary-level education to well-to-do girls. The school curricula included the three R's, English composition and grammar, geography, music, dancing, and needlework. The young women did not receive instruction in Latin, Greek, or advanced science and mathematics, the courses their brothers took to prepare for college.

Discussion of the need for better female education became intertwined with ideas about women's roles in the new nation. Beginning in 1784, Massachusetts writer Judith Sargent Murray

Courtesy, Winterthur Museum

"Keep Within Compass," published during the era of the new republic (c. 1785–1805), warned young women to remain within traditional female roles despite the revolutionary change in government.

published a series of essays, later compiled in a book titled *The Gleaner,* in which she argued that young women should prepare to support themselves in case they found no suitable husband or their spouse died. "Our girls," she wrote, "are bred up with one particular view: . . . an establishment by marriage." Murray believed that young women should learn a vocation for independence, but also justified advanced female education on the grounds that girls with developed minds would become better wives and mothers. Dr. Benjamin Rush pointed out that improved schooling would help women fulfill their duties in running households and preparing sons to be virtuous, wise leaders of the republic. He wrote, "our ladies should be qualified to a certain degree, by a peculiar and suitable education, to concur in instructing their sons in the principles of liberty and government." Nurturing incorruptible future leaders, or "republican motherhood," was women's principal responsibility under the new government, not voting or holding office.

The Question of Abolishing Slavery

The revolutionary rhetoric of freedom and self-determination unleashed a public debate over the legitimacy of slavery. African Americans fueled the discussion by escaping to the British and serving in the American army. In doing so, African Americans made whites more aware of the hypocrisy of fighting a war of independence while they kept other human beings in chains.

In the north, the first significant opposition to slavery had developed among Pennsylvania and New Jersey Quakers well before the Revolution. Since the seventeenth century, individual members of the Society of Friends had argued that black bondage violated basic Christian concepts, particularly the belief that all humans are equal in the eyes of God. For decades, these Quaker abolitionists failed to convince their meetings that slavery was wrong because many wealthy, powerful Friends held slaves. But after 1750, the Society of Friends became the first American religion to denounce perpetual bondage as a sin and to prohibit members from holding slaves. The Quakers then spearheaded an emancipation movement that gained strength among other whites in the 1770s and 1780s, contributing, along with escapes by African Americans, to the growth of free black communities in Philadelphia, New York, and other northern towns. In addition, by the 1780s, slavery was less important economically in northern states than in the south, thus the combination of religious conviction, natural rights concepts of liberty and equality, and pressure by African Americans could undercut its viability. Prospective owners, already sensitized by guilt, grew wary of purchasing slaves, who were likely to demand emancipation or run away. Instead, northern employers hired workers from among the growing numbers of free laborers, including many African Americans.

In Pennsylvania and New England, state governments acted against slavery by the mid-1780s. The Pennsylvania assembly passed the first abolition law in 1780, its preamble reflecting the ideas that inspired many abolitionists of the revolutionary era:

> When we contemplate our abhorrence of that condition to which the arms and tyranny of Great Britain were exerted to reduce us, when we look back on the variety of dangers to which we have

Pennsylvania Abolition Society Broadside

In 1775, ten Philadelphia men founded the first abolition society in America. They were mostly Quaker craftsmen and shopkeepers who were determined to sway public opinion against slavery and liberate enslaved people through legal and political action. Interrupted by the American Revolution, they reorganized in 1784, after Pennsylvania passed its gradual abolition act of 1780. PAS members then focused on enforcing its provisions, in particular making sure that free African Americans were not re-enslaved.

The abolition society distributed this diagram of a slave ship as part of a broadside against the international slave trade. The illustration shows the lower deck, with compartments (starting from the left) for men, boys, women, and girls. The text of the 1789 tract described the situation of the enslaved Africans, "packed, side by side, almost like herrings in a barrel, and reduced nearly to the state of being buried alive."

The Library Company at Philadelphia

been exposed, [we are grateful for] the manifold blessings which we have undeservedly received. . . . We conceive that it is our duty, and we rejoice that it is in our power, to extend a portion of that freedom to others.

The act was less comprehensive than its heartiest supporters wished. As a result of compromises required for passage, the Pennsylvania act abolished slavery gradually—so gradually that under its provisions no black Pennsylvanian would achieve freedom until 1808. The law provided that children born to slave mothers after March 1780 would be freed when they reached age twenty-eight. Slaves who had been born before that date would remain in bondage.

The Pennsylvania act was more effective than expected, as many enslaved blacks, exasperated that the law failed to free them, escaped their masters. Hundreds of slaveholders conformed to the spirit of the law by manumitting their slaves, regardless of birth date, at about age twenty-eight. Though these owners benefited from the labor of African Americans during their prime years, still, the manumissions helped to bring about the early end of slavery in the state. Also significant was the work of the Pennsylvania Abolition Society, which tested the limits of the 1780 abolition act by providing legal counsel to African

Americans to defend their liberty. The number of slaves in Pennsylvania declined from almost 7,000 in 1780, to 795 in 1810.

Elsewhere in the north, the Massachusetts supreme court in 1783 decided that slavery was incompatible with the state's 1780 constitution, which said all men are free and equal, though it did not specifically outlaw perpetual bondage. As blacks sued for freedom, the courts ruled on their behalf, and so by 1790, Massachusetts reported no slaves on the federal census. The Connecticut and Rhode Island legislatures in 1784 followed Pennsylvania's example by passing gradual abolition laws, and Vermont and New Hampshire also banned the institution. New York and New Jersey passed gradual abolition acts in 1799 and 1804 respectively.

During the 1780s, considerable support for abolition also developed in the Chesapeake region, though enslaved African Americans comprised almost 40 percent of the population. Southern states, like their northern counterparts, continued the First Continental Congress's prohibition of the slave trade. Some people expected cessation of the trade to result in the gradual death of slavery in Virginia and Maryland—a mistake because the African American population there grew naturally by reproduction. Involuntary bondage would persist without positive action for abolition.

Thomas Jefferson exemplified the troubled and confused state of mind of many white Americans about slavery. Though he remained a slaveholder throughout his life and held racist beliefs, Jefferson claimed to support a strategy for gradual abolition in Virginia. The plan, never considered by the assembly, would have freed and educated African American children born after the law went into effect and, when adults, removed them to a separate territory. Relocation of blacks would ensure that whites would keep political power after emancipation.

Efforts for general abolition failed south of Pennsylvania, yet some progress occurred when Virginia (in 1782), Delaware (in 1787), and Maryland (in 1790) made private manumission easier. New laws permitted slaveholders who were inspired by antislavery beliefs to free their slaves. A private abolition movement took fire in areas of the Upper South where Quakers and Methodists were numerous and planters were changing from tobacco to wheat as their chief crop, thus requiring fewer field hands. Though declining demand for labor played a role in their decision, still, slaveholders had the choice of whether to emancipate or sell their bondpeople. A market for slaves existed in the Carolinas and Georgia, where abolitionist sentiment had little impact.

The rise in the number of free African Americans in the Upper South was a measure of opposition to slavery. The free black population in Delaware rose to more than 8,000 by the end of the century; in Maryland to 20,000, and in Virginia to nearly 13,000. Even with impressive numbers of manumissions, however, in 1800 emancipated blacks were just 8 percent of all African Americans in the region.

Defining Religious Liberty

The issue of religious freedom also confronted the architects of the new state governments. Revolutionary ideals led many to challenge laws that forced people to attend and financially support an established church. Before the Revolution, the colonies had varied widely in the relationship of church and state. Congregational churches were tax-supported in Massachusetts, New Hampshire, and Connecticut, while the Church of England (Anglican) was established in the Carolinas, Virginia, Maryland, and New York. In contrast, Rhode Island, New Jersey, and Pennsylvania protected a great diversity of religions, giving none of them public funds. All of the colonies, however, placed limits on who could serve in political office.

The break with Great Britain had the greatest impact on the established Church of England, called the Protestant Episcopal church in the United States after the Revolution. With independence, some of its parishes dissolved, as missionaries departed because the church hierarchy in England stopped paying their salaries. Many Anglican clergymen and laypeople in New England and the Mid-Atlantic region became loyalists, helping to fuel the Whig movement for disestablishment. All of the states in which the Anglican church was established promptly ended government support except Virginia, which finally acted in 1786. Its assembly passed Thomas Jefferson's statute for religious liberty, stating, "no man shall be compelled to frequent or support any religious worship, place or ministry whatsoever, nor shall be enforced, restrained, molested, or burthened in his body or goods, nor shall otherwise suffer on account of his religious opinions or belief."

Nevertheless, the movement to end discrimination stalled, and in the 1780s, religious tests for political office remained common. Most Americans, who were overwhelmingly Protestant, thought that only Christian men, preferably Protestants, should govern. State and local laws required observance of the Sabbath, outlawed gambling and other entertainments, and proclaimed days of thanksgiving and prayer. The states most resistant to disestablishment were the old Puritan strongholds in New England. Massachusetts, New Hampshire, and Connecticut required tax support for Protestant churches well into the nineteenth century.

Challenges to the Confederation

Despite the dominance of the states, the Confederation Congress had important functions that required far more unity and power than it possessed. Of all Congress's difficulties, the inability to tax was most damaging, resulting in the Confederation's quick demise.

Military Demobilization

One of the most remarkable aspects of the American revolutionary experience—in light of revolutions since that time—was the absence of a serious military challenge to civilian control. George Washington was committed to popularly elected government and thus ignored suggestions that he become a military ruler. Even so, the United States faced two problems concerning the armed forces. During the war, Congress failed to pay or supply the army properly, but had promised generous pensions and bounties to entice men to sign up for the duration of the war. The second question confronting Congress was whether to establish a peacetime army, an issue that had both ideological and financial significance.

For two years after the Battle of Yorktown in 1781, the Continental army continued to exist, with Washington encamped at Newburgh, New York, where his troops monitored the British army still in New York City. American officers and enlisted men voiced grievances because they needed food, clothing, and wages. Soldiers rioted and insulted their officers, while many simply went home with no compensation except their weapons. Officers at Newburgh drew up a list of complaints for Congress, demanding as much of their back pay as possible and a full reckoning of the entire sum they were owed. The officers suggested that they receive lump sums instead of the promised pensions of half-pay for life. They seemed so disgruntled that Washington remained at Newburgh instead of going home to Mount Vernon as he had planned.

The officers' discontent became more threatening when several politicians, who favored a strong central government, recognized an opportunity to pressure the states into giving Congress the power to tax. In what became known as the Newburgh conspiracy, Robert Morris of Philadelphia and Gouverneur Morris and Alexander Hamilton of New York hatched a plan to use the officers' protests to strengthen the Confederation. Washington would not cooperate, stating that the army was a "most dangerous instrument to play with," even to obtain a national tax. In early 1783, rumors spread that the officers were ready to take "manly" action against the government unless their demands were met. The crisis ended when Washington pledged to negotiate for their back pay and pensions and the officers swore their loyalty to Congress. For its part, Congress agreed to pay troops three months' wages at discharge, while officers would receive pensions of five years' full pay in government bonds. A group of eighty enlisted men stationed at Lancaster, Pennsylvania, found the offer unacceptable, so they mutinied and marched on Philadelphia, barricading the State House where Congress met. Though the soldiers backed down without violence, the frightened congressmen fled to Princeton.

Restitution of military pensions, back wages, and bounties took until the 1790s because Congress lacked the funds to discharge its debts. Soldiers who had been promised land bounties in the west had to wait fifteen years for surveys, in large part because Native Americans refused to give up the territory. By the 1790s, most veterans had long since sold their rights to speculators for a fraction of their worth.

The issue of a standing army squared revolutionary ideology against the need for defense. One of the chief causes of the Revolution had been the peacetime quartering in New York and Boston of the British army, which patriots called a "MONSTER of a standing ARMY." But now the United States faced threats from the Spanish in Florida and Louisiana, the British in Canada, and Native Americans everywhere along the frontier. In April 1783, Congress appointed a committee to consult Washington and other generals on military requirements. The commander-in-chief argued that the United States had to be prepared against its enemies. He suggested retaining 2,600 Continentals in one artillery and four infantry regiments. He also advised Congress to organize a national citizens' militia that would stay in training for ready defense. In 1784, Congress dismissed Washington's plan, stationing a total of eighty men at two forts in New York and Pennsylvania. For reasons of principle and finances, the Confederation government virtually disbanded the army during an interval of peace, a pattern the nation would follow well into the twentieth century.

Economic Troubles

The Confederation Congress failed to solve the problem of its war debt, which by 1790 amounted to an estimated $10 million owed to other countries and $40 million owed to Americans. During the war, the government had issued paper currency to pay for goods and services. It abandoned this policy because of rampant inflation. Congress turned to the states, which refused to contribute sufficient funds, then borrowed from France and from American merchants and farmers for military provisions. It also deferred payment on soldiers' wages. As the principal and interest mounted on these promissory notes and bonds, Congress requested an amendment to the Articles to permit a national duty of 5 percent on all imports. The legislators tried for five years to obtain the necessary unanimous agreement of the states, but failed on each attempt.

One long-lasting consequence of the war's inflationary crisis was conflict between urban and rural interests over public finance. The spiraling cost of food and fuel in the late 1770s had hurt city residents much more than farmers. In public debate over currency and credit, farmers wanted access to government loans based on the value of their land and its production, similar to the colonial land banks that had allowed them to use real estate as collateral for loans. Though the provincial currency issued by the land banks had been fairly stable, in the 1780s, merchants and urban artisans recalled the more recent inflation of the Revolution. They believed that paper currency based on real estate would send prices sky-high. At the same time, merchants knew that the economy would stagnate if specie (gold and silver) were required for every transaction, so they embraced an alternative method of generating paper currency, the bank.

The first bank in the United States was the Bank of North America, created in 1781 in Philadelphia. Robert Morris proposed the institution, based on the Bank of England, as a way to help solve the wartime fiscal crisis. Morris obtained support from Alexander Hamilton, Thomas Paine, and a committee of Congress for his plan; both the Congress and state of Pennsylvania chartered the institution. Instead of issuing paper currency through a land office, as farmers wanted, the bank issued currency in the form of short-term loans to merchants. These bank notes were backed by gold and silver plate and coins that investors deposited in return for a share of the bank's profits. The attraction for stockholders was that formerly idle gold and silver assets could now earn interest. The Bank of North America earned regular profits during its first two decades, beginning with an 8.74 percent dividend to investors in 1782. If people doubted the security of the bank, they could redeem their bank notes. Bank advocates believed that once a few people tested its soundness and received specie, others would trust the bank and accept the bank notes as currency.

In fact, the Bank of North America followed a conservative course that kept it solvent financially but made it unpopular with many people. The bank's manager, Thomas Willing,

Robert Morris and Gouverneur Morris

In 1783, Charles Willson Peale painted this portrait of Robert Morris (right) and Gouverneur Morris, the superintendent of finance and his assistant, who were unrelated. Robert Morris, born in Liverpool, England, was a wealthy Philadelphia merchant who supervised procurement of military supplies during the Revolution. He was one of the founders of the Bank of North America, the country's first bank, which was modeled after the Bank of England and was intended to help relieve the wartime economic crisis. Gouverneur Morris, who came from a wealthy New York family, excelled as Robert Morris's assistant in the finance office. Both men became frustrated by Congress's weakness and the repeated failure to gain approval of a national tax. They joined with other nationalists in the Newburgh conspiracy to use the army's discontent over unpaid wages to force adoption of a more centralized government. When Alexander Hamilton became the first secretary of the treasury, he adopted a number of Robert Morris's ideas, including the national bank and federal assumption of state debts.

Charles Willson Peale, Gouverneur Morris and Robert Morris, 1783. Oil on canvas. 43⅜ x 51⅜" (110.5 x 131.4 cm) Acc. # 1969.20.1. Courtesy of the Pennsylvania Academy of the Fine Arts, Philadelphia. Bequest of Richard Ashhurst.

lent money only to good credit risks in the mercantile community, thus angering artisans and farmers who viewed the bank as a monopoly created by Congress to benefit the commercial elite. Also, Willing refused to liberalize the bank's loan policy by taking advantage of confidence in the bank's strength. Instead of expanding the money supply as later banks did, the Bank of North America made loans only up to the amount of specie in its vaults.

The Bank of North America helped the mercantile community through a time of uncertainty. Commerce had suffered during the Revolution as merchants lost connections with trading partners in Great Britain and the British West Indies. In 1783, Americans expected to reestablish those ties as well as enter new markets in Europe and the French and Spanish colonies. With their newly won independence, they gained release from the restrictions of British mercantilism.

But being part of the mercantilist system had brought advantages as well as constraints. The British closed the ports of the British West Indies to American ships, a sharp blow for New England and the Middle Atlantic states, which before the war had found a major market in the islands for exports of fish, grain, flour, lumber, and livestock. To Great Britain and its colonies, the United States was now a foreign country. Americans could sell provisions in the islands and purchase rum, sugar, and molasses, but everything had to be carried on British ships. West Indies planters complained because this resulted in higher prices; American shipowners had to find new routes. On the other hand, Britain was eager to purchase tobacco from the Chesapeake and to sell to Americans all the manufactures they would buy. U.S. merchants had access by treaty to ports in France and the French colonies, but were barred from trading in New Spain. Gradually, Americans developed trade with Germany, the Netherlands, Scandinavia, and even China. By the end of the 1780s, U.S. exports recovered to approximately their prerevolutionary level.

The road to recovery was rocky, however, because in the immediate postwar years American demand for British manufactures far outstripped exports. During the Revolution, American artisans had attempted to supply metal goods and textiles, but had been unable to match British quality and prices. With peace, British manufacturers extended generous credit to American consumers for clocks, watches, furniture, textiles, clothing, mirrors, and other goods. When depression hit in fall 1783 because of the loss of the West Indies market, American farmers, merchants, and shopkeepers found themselves seriously in debt. In New England, for example, the balance of trade with Great Britain was so uneven that exports covered only 13 percent of imports. While the economy improved after mid-1785, many farmers had difficulty escaping from debt.

Indeed, estimates of the gross national product suggest that the Revolution had an extended negative impact on the American economy. Data available for 1774 and 1790 indicate that income declined by over 40 percent, close to the decrease Americans experienced during the Great Depression of the 1930s.

Foreign Affairs

Though the United States had won both the war and the peace, its leaders soon learned that they received little respect among European nations. Despite the boundary provisions of the Treaty of 1783, Spain and Great Britain took advantage of the Confederation's weakness to trespass on territory in the west. The Spanish and English gained allies among Native Americans who were losing their lands to the steady stream of white settlers crossing the Appalachians.

During the 1780s, Spain tried to restrict expansion of the United States. The Spanish government had refused to accept the treaty boundaries granting the region between the Appalachians and the Mississippi River to the United States. With settlers rapidly filling the area, Spain feared for its control of Louisiana and East and West Florida; it wanted to extend its territory north from West Florida to the Ohio River. The Spanish pursued this objective in a number of ways. They retained forts north of the 31st parallel, which the United States claimed as its southern border. Then, in 1784, the Spanish government closed the port of New Orleans to Americans, apparently hoping to detach from the United States the region that later became Kentucky and Tennessee. Settlers in the trans-Appalachian region protested vigorously because they needed access to the New Orleans market for their goods. Some threatened to secede from the United States unless Congress convinced Spain to reverse its decision; a few, including James Wilkinson, a former Continental army officer, actually negotiated with the Spanish. Reporting on a journey in the west, George Washington wrote, "the western settlers (I speak now from my own observation) stand as it were upon a pivot; the touch of a feather would turn them any way."

Congress directed John Jay, the secretary of foreign affairs and a New Yorker, to negotiate with Spain to reopen the port. The Spanish diplomat, Diego de Gardoqui, refused to budge, instead offering to open other Spanish ports to U.S. commerce if Americans would relinquish demands for free navigation on the lower Mississippi. With the permission of Congress, Jay agreed to a treaty that provided commercial advantages for eastern merchants but closed New Orleans to westerners for a generation. The west and south erupted in opposition, blocking approval of the Jay-Gardoqui Treaty. The lower Mississippi River remained closed until 1788 when the Spanish permitted Americans to use New Orleans upon payment of duties.

The Spanish government also cooperated with Native Americans to slow the influx of Anglo-American settlers into contested territory. Spanish colonists in the Floridas remained few, so they depended upon good relations with the Creeks, Choctaws, and Chickasaws who controlled the region. Groups of Creeks who had migrated to Florida, and were called Seminoles by the British, could mobilize at least twice as many soldiers as the Spanish. Contrary to Spain's traditional policy of considering Native Americans as subjects to the Crown, its colonial officials in 1784 signed written treaties of alliance with the Indians.

Most threatening of these pacts to the United States was the one with the Creeks, which their leader Alexander McGillivray arranged. The son of a Scottish trader and a French-Creek woman, and educated in Charleston, McGillivray could negotiate his way in both European and Indian societies. To protect Creek lands from settlers streaming in from Georgia, he offered the Spanish "a powerful barrier in these parts against the ambitious and encroaching Americans" in return for an alliance and weapons. The Creeks called the invading Georgians "Ecunnaunuxulgee," or "people greedily grasping after the lands of the red people." With Cherokees and Shawnees to the north, the Creeks battled Anglo-Americans through the 1780s, thus slowing settlement on the southwest frontier.

The Confederation government also had difficulty establishing its claims against the British and the Indians of the Ohio Valley. In the treaty of 1783, the British had promised to remove their troops from forts in the Great Lakes region. Through the 1780s, however, they refused to withdraw, hoping for return of the territory. They barred American ships from the Great Lakes and allied with Native Americans who wanted to halt white settlement. British diplomats justified these actions with the excuse that Americans had failed to pay prewar debts to British creditors and return confiscated loyalist property.

Great Britain's neglect of its Indian allies in negotiating the peace led the U.S. government to treat them as a conquered people. With great bravado, considering the Confederation's small army, American commissioners said to the Ohio Indians, "You are mistaken in supposing that . . . you are to become a free and independent nation, and may make

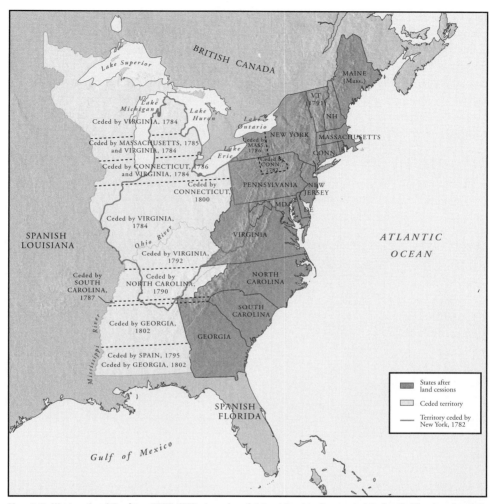

Map 6.2 Western Land Cessions, 1782–1802 A number of states claimed territory west of the Appalachians based on their colonial charters. For example, under Connecticut's charter, which defined the Pacific Ocean as its western boundary, residents claimed part of Pennsylvania as well as western lands.

what terms you please. . . . You are a subdued people." Other officials announced, "We claim the country by conquest." Under threat of arms, a group of Iroquois yielded rights in the Northwest with the Treaty of Fort Stanwix (1784); Wyandots, Delawares, and others ceded Ohio lands in the Treaty of Fort McIntosh (1785); and Shawnees gave up territory in the Treaty of Fort Finney (1786). Many Native Americans refused to recognize these treaties because the Indian negotiators lacked authority and had been forced to sign.

Soon, frontier warfare made U.S. officials realize that they were the ones who were "mistaken" in presuming that the Indians had been "subdued." Theyendanegea (Joseph Brant), the pro-British Mohawk leader, rallied Indians against white settlement in the Northwest. In 1786, he urged potential allies, "the Interests of Any One Nation Should be the Interests of us all, the Welfare of the one Should be the Welfare of all the others." Their resistance convinced Secretary of War Henry Knox that the United States must change its tactics or risk a general Indian war. He suggested that Congress return to the policy of purchasing lands, instead of demanding them by conquest. The congressmen agreed, incorporating into the Northwest Ordinance of 1787 the futile promise that the Indians' land "shall never be taken from them without their consent."

The Northwest Ordinances

Despite war with the Indians and the presence of British troops, the Confederation Congress moved forward with legislation to create the Northwest Territory. The issue of western lands had divided the thirteen states even during the Revolution. Some states claimed

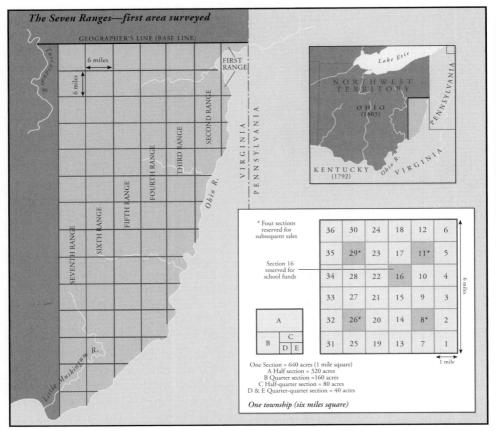

Map 6.3 Land Ordinance of 1785 This map shows the plans for dividing land in eastern Ohio into townships and lots. The minimum price was $1 per acre.

territories from their colonial charters, while others, such as Maryland and New Jersey, had never possessed such claims. Titles stood in conflict with one another, as in the case of the region north of the Ohio River, which Virginia claimed in its entirety and Connecticut and Massachusetts claimed in part. States lacking rights to western lands believed that all should be ceded to the Confederation because together the states had won the trans-Appalachian territory in the Revolution. Virginia, whose charter rights were oldest, resolved the issue in 1781 by agreeing to transfer to the United States the region north and west of the Ohio River, the area that later became the states of Ohio, Indiana, Illinois, Michigan, and Wisconsin. Virginia offered cession on the condition that the territory eventually be divided into states that would join the Confederation on an equal basis with the original thirteen. The trans-Appalachian lands south of the Ohio River remained temporarily under the control of Virginia, North Carolina, and Georgia.

Congress passed three ordinances to establish guidelines for distributing land and governing the Northwest Territory. Wealthy speculators who had purchased rights from Native Americans had significant influence over the shape these ordinances took. Thomas Jefferson was principal author of the first ordinance, which passed Congress in 1784. This law gave settlers a great deal of autonomy in establishing a territorial government. The Northwest would be divided into seven districts, with the settlers of each to govern themselves by choosing a constitution and laws from any of the existing states. When any district reached the population of the smallest of the original thirteen states, it would be admitted as a state to the Confederation on equal terms. Congress retained responsibility for selling the public lands.

The second ordinance, passed in 1785, set the rules for distributing lands. The influence of speculators was apparent, for the minimum price of a lot was $640, payable in specie or its equivalent, a sum far beyond the means of many potential settlers. All property would be surveyed before sale, laid out in townships six miles square. Each lot would contain 640 acres sold at a minimum of one dollar per acre, with better land offered at a higher price. The government retained lots for public schools and for distribution to Revolutionary War veterans. Because of the relatively high cost, Congress found few individual buyers. In fact, many land-hungry squatters simply set up their farms without government approval, sometimes purchasing rights from neighboring Indians, sometimes not. So Congress accepted a deal offered by a group of New England speculators, the Ohio Company, agreeing to sell them 1.5 million acres for $500,000 in depreciated bonds, or less than ten cents per acre in hard money. Given the Confederation's debt, the sale was welcome.

Congress further cooperated with the Ohio Company in drafting the Northwest Ordinance of 1787. In response to speculators' demands, the law established firmer congressional control over the territory, providing settlers less self-government than under the 1784 ordinance. Initially, a governor, secretary, and three judges appointed by Congress would administer the government. When 5,000 adult males resided in the territory, they could elect an assembly, but the governor held a veto over its actions. Men were eligible to vote if they owned at least fifty acres of land. Three to five states would be created from the Northwest Territory, with each state qualified to enter the union when its population reached 60,000. New states would have equal status with the original thirteen. The ordinance of 1787 also included provisions for individual rights that the Congress and the Ohio Company hoped would attract purchasers. They expected many settlers to come from New England. The ordinance protected private contracts, religious liberty, trial by jury, and habeas corpus (protection against illegal imprisonment). It prohibited slavery from the region forever. Thus, while catering to the interests of speculators, the Northwest Ordinance also extended rights won during the Revolution to new settlers in the west. Further, it limited the spread of slavery and determined that western territories would achieve the status of states rather than remain colonies.

Political and Economic Turmoil

Political strife under the Articles of Confederation disappointed Americans who had high hopes for their republic. Instead of harmony, economic interests clashed; the states failed to satisfy everybody. Many elites thought the United States was becoming too democratic and anarchic—as farmers revolted, government failed to control the violence, and some legislatures approved the insurgents' demands.

Creditors Versus Debtors

As a result of the postwar depression, farmers throughout the United States faced economic hardship. Many had eagerly purchased British manufactures, expecting to pay for the new clothes and consumer goods by selling their grain and livestock to the West Indies. British merchants offered easy credit to stimulate sales; American merchants and shopkeepers passed the credit on to farm families who would pay with the fall crop.

The house of cards collapsed when the British government closed the West Indies to American ships. English mercantile houses called in their debts in specie only, starting a chain of default that extended from London to the frontier. Americans lacked the gold and silver that the British demanded, but merchants refused to accept payment in farm products because they had no market for the goods. So they took farmers to court: in many places, the number of debt cases rose dramatically. For example, in Hampshire County, Massachusetts, from 1784 to 1786, the court heard 3,000 debt cases. Almost one-third of the county's adult males were prosecuted for insolvency.

State governments aggravated the situation by imposing taxes to repay war bonds in full, a policy that worked to the advantage of wealthy speculators who had bought up the bonds from farmers and artisans at a large discount. The Massachusetts government particularly favored mercantile interests, levying on farmers high taxes that also had to be paid in specie. When farmers defaulted, the courts sold their land and cattle, often at only one-third to one-half value. If their assets failed to cover the debts and back taxes, the farmers were imprisoned until they or someone else paid the sum. Often men sat in crowded jails with insufficient ventilation, heat, or food because they owed small debts. Ordinary folk became angry as they feared imprisonment and the loss of their farms.

Farmers Demand Reform

Protesters mobilized as they had in the prerevolutionary period, at first meeting in county conventions to draw up petitions to the state assembly. In Massachusetts, they demanded changes in the state constitution to make the government more responsive to their needs and less costly to run. They wanted abolition of the state senate, which represented the commercial elite; lowering of property qualifications to hold office; and transfer of the capital from Boston to a more central location. Inland towns found it difficult to send representatives to the assembly because expenses were so high. The farmers also demanded paper money and tender laws, the latter enabling them to settle debts and taxes with goods rather than specie. Both would ease the credit crisis. During the Revolution, the yeomen had benefited from inflation and were able to pay off prewar debts with cheap dollars. While they stopped short of demanding a return to high inflation, they hoped for a gentle upswing in prices and a larger money supply to help them settle their debts.

When state legislatures emitted paper money or passed tender laws, as in Rhode Island, North Carolina, New York, and Georgia, little unrest ensued. In Rhode Island, political parties channeled conflict, for after the Country party ousted the Mercantile party in spring 1786, the new assembly issued paper money with stiff fines for creditors who refused to accept it. Elites elsewhere referred to "Rogue Island," even suggesting that the state be abolished and divided between Massachusetts and Connecticut. In other states, mercantile factions maintained control of the government. They detested paper money because debtors would pay in depreciated bills; they opposed tender laws because of the lack of a market for grain and livestock. Merchants argued that paper currency issued as loans on farm property (rather than as notes based on gold and silver deposited in banks) was immoral because it would lose value, allowing debtors to violate contracts by paying back less than they had borrowed. Creditors asserted that their property rights were at risk.

Shays's Rebellion

When state governments failed to help, debtors in New England, New Jersey, Pennsylvania, Maryland, Virginia, and South Carolina protested militantly. Events moved furthest in Massachusetts. In fall 1786, armed Massachusetts farmers closed down county courts to prevent further hearings for debt. Perhaps one-fourth of potential soldiers in the state were involved, calling themselves the "Regulators," after the Carolina insurgents of the 1760s. Their opponents first labeled the rebels "Green Bushers" because they wore a sprig of evergreen—the Massachusetts symbol for liberty—then called them Shaysites when Daniel Shays, a forty-year-old veteran of Bunker Hill and Saratoga, emerged as leader. The government frantically requested aid from Congress, which complied by requisitioning $530,000 and 1,340 soldiers from the states. When the states failed to cooperate, the powerlessness of the Confederation was clear.

The Massachusetts government acted on its own, taking measures that further alienated angry farmers. The assembly passed the Riot Act, which prohibited armed groups from gathering in public and permitted sheriffs to kill rioters who refused to disband. The legislature also suspended habeas corpus, allowing officials to jail suspected insurgents without showing cause. The farmers refused to back down, as one warned, "I am determined to fight and spill my blood and leave my bones at the courthouse till Resurrection." They protested that the suspension of habeas corpus was "dangerous if not absolutely destructive to a Republican government." Nevertheless, in November 1786, the state government sent 300 soldiers to arrest rebel leaders; when that failed to stop the farmers from closing the courts, Boston merchants raised private funds to outfit 4,400 troops. Residents of Boston and coastal towns who feared the inflationary consequences of paper money filled the ranks. Revolutionary general Benjamin Lincoln commanded the army; in January 1787, they marched to Worcester to protect the county court.

The Granger Collection, New York

Daniel Shays and Job Shattuck, from the cover of a pamphlet supporting Shays's Rebellion.

Lincoln's army forced the Shaysites to choose between submission and armed rebellion, for a middle ground of petitions and court closings was no longer viable. The farmers amassed their own troops, estimated at 2,500 men, with Shays in charge of one regiment. They unsuccessfully attacked the federal arsenal at Springfield for weapons to assault Boston, then regrouped to await the merchants' army. Shays was convinced that their cause was just; in a newspaper interview he confidently stated that he "knew General Lincoln was coming against him, but as he would bring with him nobody but shopkeepers, lawyers, and doctors, he could easily defeat him." Lincoln attacked Shays by surprise in a blizzard, dispersing the rebels within half an hour.

The aftermath of Shays's defeat was more divisive and bloody than the engagements between the armies. The assembly declared a state of "open, unnatural, unprovoked, and wicked rebellion," giving the governor the power to treat the Shaysites as enemies of the state. The legislators passed the Disqualification Act, which barred people implicated in the revolt from voting and holding office for three years, teaching school, or keeping inns and taverns. Many of the insurgents escaped to New York and Vermont. Others, including individuals who had not been involved, were imprisoned. Militant Shaysites prolonged the conflict by raiding homes and kidnapping people who had sided with the government. As a result of the uprising and repression, voter turnout skyrocketed in the April 1787 election. A much greater number of western Massachusetts towns sent delegates to the legislature than they had in previous years, making the new assembly somewhat more responsive to rural debtors. While refusing to approve paper money, it enacted a tender law and quickly restored the civil rights of the insurgents.

The Movement for Constitutional Reform

The Confederation's helplessness in response to spreading armed rebellion strengthened the hand of nationalists like Robert Morris and Alexander Hamilton, who had been arguing for a more powerful central government. By 1787, Congress had lost much of its authority, and representatives stopped attending, often preventing action for lack of a quorum. Because it had failed to obtain a national tax and could not force the states to send requisitioned funds, the Confederation was broke. In 1785, Congress stopped interest payments on the French debt and in 1787 ended those on the principal. Nor could it reimburse American creditors. In 1787, Congress transferred responsibility for the national debt to the states.

The Philadelphia Convention

In September 1786, when Shays's Rebellion was still gathering steam, representatives gathered for a convention in Annapolis, Maryland, to discuss amending the Articles to give Congress power to regulate trade. The convention failed when only five state delegations arrived on time. Several of the delegates, including Alexander Hamilton, James Madison, and John Dickinson, called for another convention to meet in May 1787 at Philadelphia to consider a more thorough revision of the Articles. By early 1787, the disorder in Massachusetts and the growing concern about state emission of paper money built support for constitutional reform. In February, Congress endorsed a change. Twelve states—all but Rhode Island where farmers controlled the legislature—sent delegates to Philadelphia.

Though the appointed day was May 14, 1787, the convention failed to start until May 25 when enough representatives finally arrived. State legislatures had delayed choosing their delegations and travel was slow. Among the first were Virginia's representatives, who used the extra time for planning. James Madison, a thirty-six-year-old planter, slaveholder, and intellectual who had served in the Virginia assembly and Congress, came to the convention well prepared. A shy man who avoided public speaking, Madison nevertheless took a dominant role in the proceedings, for which he has been called the father of the Constitution. Propelled by the breakdown of Congress and the problems he witnessed in state government, Madison wanted to reform the Confederation to create a stronger central government. He believed that state constitutions with powerful assemblies were too democratic, giving too much influence to the common people. As a consequence, these legislatures collaborated with debtors by circulating paper money, which Madison considered an attack on property. The people should be represented adequately, Madison thought, but their power must be constrained. The United States needed a new constitution that would place authority in the hands of well-educated, propertied men. Another Virginia delegate was George Washington, whose popularity and prestige made his support for the convention crucial. He presided over the proceedings, but participated little in the debates.

A total of fifty-five men served at the Constitutional Convention between opening day and adjournment four months later. Twenty-one were practicing lawyers, another thirteen had been educated in the law, seven were merchants, and eighteen were farmers or planters; nineteen owned African American slaves. Most were relatively young men under the age of fifty, and many had served in the Revolution and had held political office. Benjamin Franklin, now eighty-one years old and ailing, was a member of the Pennsylvania delegation. Several heroes of the Revolution were absent, including Thomas Jefferson and John Adams, who served as ministers to France and Great Britain, respectively. Samuel Adams was not chosen as a delegate and Patrick Henry refused to participate because he "smelt a rat." Most of the delegates supported a plan to place more power in the national government.

The Great Compromise

The convention can be divided into two periods. During the first seven weeks, the matter overshadowing all discussion was the power of "large" versus "small" states. After this issue was resolved, delegations formed blocs in new ways, according to concerns about the executive, slavery, and commerce. The basic question that the convention avoided debating at length was whether to amend the Articles of Confederation or write an entirely new constitution. Madison, who thought the Confederation beyond repair, moved the convention along with a document he had drafted in advance, called the Virginia Plan, which scrapped the Articles. Madison was able to set the convention's agenda because at the outset no other delegate had prepared an alternate design.

The Virginia Plan proposed a powerful central government, dominated by a National Legislature of two houses (bicameral). The lower house would be elected by qualified voters and would choose the members of the upper house from nominations by state legislatures. The number of delegates from each state depended upon population. This bicameral National Legislature was empowered to appoint the executive and judicial branches of the central government and to veto state laws.

Several states opposed the Virginia Plan because it gave greater representation in the National Legislature to states with large populations. Delaware, Maryland, New Jersey, and Connecticut feared the power of Virginia, Pennsylvania, and Massachusetts, which together comprised almost one-half of the American people. If the Virginia Plan were adopted, just four states could dominate the legislature. In dividing on this issue, states considered the possibility of future population expansion as well as present size. Thus states with unsettled territories mostly sided with the large states, while those without room for growth chose the opposite camp.

The small states preferred a constitution that retained the structure of the Confederation Congress, but expanded its powers. In mid-June, William Paterson introduced the New Jersey Plan, which proposed a one-house, or unicameral, Congress in which the states had equal representation. Congress would appoint an executive council which in

Independence National Historical Park

This painting of the Constitutional Convention of 1787 by an unknown artist shows George Washington presiding. Because the convention met in secrecy, the artist used his imagination to paint the scene.

turn would choose a supreme court. As in the Virginia Plan, the authority of Congress was much enlarged, with powers to tax, regulate commerce, and compel states to obey its laws. The large states objected to this plan, arguing that Delaware (population 59,000) should not have as much power as Virginia (population 748,000).

The debate over representation in Congress brought the convention to an impasse. It made little progress toward a new constitution until the issue of state representation was resolved. The large states had the votes in the convention but knew that ratification would be impossible if the Virginia Plan prevailed. The Delaware delegation threatened to walk out until Connecticut formally proposed what has become known as the "great compromise." The plan established a bicameral Congress, with representation in the lower house based upon population. This body, called the House of Representatives, would be elected directly by the voters every two years and have the sole right to initiate revenue bills. Thus, the idea that people with a stake in society should elect the representatives who taxed them was incorporated into the document. In the upper house, called the Senate, states would have equal representation; each state legislature would choose two senators for six-year terms. The bicameral Congress resolved the division between the small and large states and also satisfied those who wanted to limit the influence of ordinary voters. Senators were expected to come from the wealthier, more established segments of society; their long terms and appointment by state legislators would shield them from public opinion. Both houses of Congress had to approve legislation.

The compromise between the large and small states created a government that was both national and federal. It was *national* because the House of Representatives was popularly elected, with not more than one representative per 30,000 people. Upon ratification, the United States would become a single nation rather than a confederacy of states. By expanding legislative powers, the sovereign people vested more authority in the central government. Congress received the powers to tax, coin and borrow money, regulate commerce, establish courts, declare war, and raise armed forces. States were specifically forbidden from keeping troops without the permission of Congress, making treaties, coining money, and issuing paper currency. At the same time, the new Constitution established a *federal* government, one in which the states retained rights, including equal representation in the Senate. Congress was forbidden from giving one state preference over another when levying taxes and regulating trade, nor could it impose export duties, prohibit the slave trade until 1808, or carve a new state from any state's territory without permission. Approval by three-fourths of the states would be necessary to amend the Constitution. But despite these provisions, many Americans believed that the states—the small republics—had lost too much power. The struggle for ratification revolved in large part around this issue.

The Executive, Slavery, and Commerce

Once the question of state representation was solved with the "great compromise," the convention made greater headway. Factions within the convention shifted from one debate to the next.

The power of the executive was a concern to people living in a world dominated by kings and princes. Delegates wanted to ensure that their government remained a republic, that it would not become a monarchy or dictatorship. At the same time, they believed that the executive branch should serve as a check on the legislature. The convention debated several questions affecting the executive's power. Should there be a single president or an executive board? While some argued that a plural executive could prevent one person from usurping power, the convention chose a single president, expecting to limit his authority in other ways. Length of term also stimulated discussion, for the longer the term the greater a president's autonomy. The convention reached agreement on a four-year term, without specifying the number of times he could be reelected.

The question of how the president would be chosen was divisive, between those who preferred direct election by the people and those who wanted Congress or the state legislatures to make the choice. Once again, the issue of states' rights reared its head. A committee appointed by the convention devised an ingenious but complicated formula to satisfy all sides: an "electoral college" was empowered to elect the president and vice president, with each state allotted as many votes as it had representatives and senators. Thus, even the smallest state received three votes and the large states were represented according to population. The state legislatures could determine how to choose the electors. The electoral college would never meet together as a group. The electors of each state gathered within their states to cast votes, which they sent to Congress for counting. If no candidate received a majority, the House of Representatives made the selection from among the five candidates with the most votes.

Of the Philadelphia convention's decisions on the executive, most crucial to the endurance of the Constitution was the balance of power between the executive and legislative branches. The convention gave the president a veto power over laws passed by Congress. The legislators could override the veto if two-thirds of both houses approved. Congress also had authority to remove the president by impeachment and trial for treason, bribery, and "other high Crimes and Misdemeanors." While Congress received power to declare war and raise troops, the president served as commander-in-chief. Only with the "advice and consent" of the Senate could the chief executive negotiate treaties and appoint ambassadors, Supreme Court justices, and other officials.

Slavery was a major factor in the convention's deliberations, though the words "slavery," "slave," and "slave trade" appeared nowhere in the 1787 Constitution. African American bondage affected the debates on representation in Congress, the election of the president, and the regulation of commerce. The southern states wanted to include slaves in a state's population when computing delegates to the House of Representatives and votes in the electoral college. Northerners protested that this gave white southerners an unfair advantage (illustrated in Table 6.1) because enslaved people could not vote. As part of the "great compromise," the convention decided that five enslaved Americans

Table 6.1 Enslaved Population in the United States, 1790

	Total	Slaves
New England	1,009,206	3,763
Middle Atlantic	1,017,087	45,210
Maryland and Virginia	1,067,338	395,663
Lower South	726,626	237,141

First page of the United States Constitution of 1787.

would count as three free persons for apportioning representation and direct taxes among the states. Since three-fifths of slaves living in the Chesapeake and Lower South numbered 380,000 people, the power of white voters south of Pennsylvania was significantly magnified.

Political bargaining resulted in additional provisions that upheld slavery. The convention approved a fugitive slave clause, which prevented free states from emancipating slaves who had escaped from masters in other states. The delegates also adopted a provision that forbade Congress from prohibiting slave importation for twenty years (with no requirement that it ban the slave trade after that time). North and South Carolina and Georgia demanded the option of importing people from Africa because they expected settlement to continue into western Georgia and the present states of Alabama, Mississippi, and Tennessee. Northern delegates, who might have pushed the convention toward the abolition of slavery, did almost nothing to promote that end.

Instead of trying to eliminate slavery under the new government, the northerners made the regulation of commerce their priority. The Lower South obtained the twenty-year protection of the slave trade when New England delegates promised their support in return for a compromise on international trade. The southern states suspected that the national government, if dominated by northerners in the future, would place heavy taxes on tobacco, rice, and indigo—the South's main exports. Southerners thought that navigation laws could also work to their detriment, because northern merchants owned most American shipping. If Congress passed legislation requiring that all exports be transported in American ships, southerners would lose the choice of using a foreign, perhaps cheaper, carrier. Northerners, on the other hand, wanted Congress to have the authority to negotiate trade agreements on an equal basis with other nations. Congress could then retaliate if a country imposed restrictions such as closing ports. The convention settled these matters, first by forbidding Congress from imposing export duties, then with a deal that empowered Congress to regulate commerce. In return for South Carolina's vote for the latter provision, New England agreed to extend the slave trade for twenty years.

The Philadelphia convention created a Constitution that shifted important powers to a national government, but still vested a great deal of authority in the states. The framers painstakingly created checks and balances among the branches of government. They required direct popular election of only the House of Representatives, giving that body the right to initiate taxes. The convention incorporated flexibility into the document, which had been absent in the Articles of Confederation, by permitting amendment with approval of two-thirds of both houses of Congress and three-fourths of the states. The document shielded some individual rights, though critics argued that many were omitted. The Constitution protected trial by jury in criminal cases and habeas corpus. It banned religious tests for holding office under the United States, ex post facto (retroactive) laws, and bills of attainder, which extinguished a person's civil rights upon sentence of death or as an outlaw. While codifying the principles of self-government and individual liberties, however, the convention denied them to almost one-fifth of the American population by embedding slavery within the fabric of the new government.

Ratification

After the delegates to the Philadelphia convention signed the Constitution on September 17, 1787, they quickly sent it to the Confederation Congress, which forwarded it to the states after little debate. One congressman from Virginia, Richard Henry Lee, tried to bury the document by adding amendments, but was overruled. Article 7 of the document required ratification by nine state conventions. States refusing to ratify could remain independent or unite together under another frame of government. Advocates of ratification knew that prompt action was necessary to forestall an effective opposition movement.

The group favoring ratification was not particularly well organized but had two advantages over its opponents. One advantage came from the choice of a name, the Federalists, for it undercut the ground on which their adversaries stood. James Madison, Alexander Hamilton, John Jay, and other supporters of the Constitution argued in favor of the federalist provisions that reserved powers to the states as well as the nationalist elements of the prospective government. While others denounced the Constitution because it transferred too much power to the national government from the states, the Federalists claimed the document provided balance. The critics were obliged to take the negative name of Antifederalists, which misrepresented their position in favor of states' rights.

The second advantage of those favoring ratification was that many advocates of a strong central government resided in the coastal cities and towns, where public opinion was easier to mobilize than in outlying areas. Most newspapers supported the Constitution. For example, in New York, where the ratification battle became intense, Hamilton, Madison, and Jay published in the newspapers a series of eighty-five essays that provided a detailed argument in favor of the Constitution. The essays also gained wide attention outside New York, and in spring 1788, the authors published them in book form as *The Federalist,* which is considered a major work in American political theory.

Most Federalists gained their livelihoods as merchants, shopkeepers, professionals, artisans, and commercial farmers. As creditors and consumers, many favored the Constitution because it stopped state emission of paper currency. Federalists desired a government that would foster the growth of a market economy and facilitate trade with other countries. They believed a national government would provide the stability and strength that were lacking under the Confederation, enabling the United States to gain stature among the nations of Europe. Some frontier settlers, seeking military defense against Native Americans, also supported the Constitution.

The Federalists, who viewed commercial development more favorably than the Antifederalists, thought the purpose of government was to arbitrate among opposing interests. Federalists believed that society benefited when people pursued individual goals. They considered elusive the republican ideal of a community in which everyone could reach consensus because they had similar needs. Madison argued in *Federalist #10* that people possess different interests because they have unequal abilities and thus varying success in accumulating property. People by nature also have "different opinions concerning religion, concerning government, and many other points." In a free society, they form factions on the basis of their conflicting ideologies and "the various and unequal distribution of property." He wrote:

> A landed interest, a manufacturing interest, a mercantile interest, a moneyed interest, with many lesser interests, grow up of necessity in civilized nations, and divide them into different classes, actuated by different sentiments and views. The regulation of these various and interfering interests forms the principal task of modern legislation, and involves the spirit of party and faction in the necessary and ordinary operations of the government.

Madison claimed that the Constitution would be beneficial because a large republic contained more safeguards than a small one. In an extended polity, so many factions exist that the ability of a single interest to monopolize power is reduced. With the national government, "you take in a greater variety of parties and interests; you make it less probable that a majority of the whole will have a common motive to invade the rights of other citizens."

Antifederalists disagreed with this analysis, both because they favored small republics and because they feared the actions of men who would likely dominate the central gov-

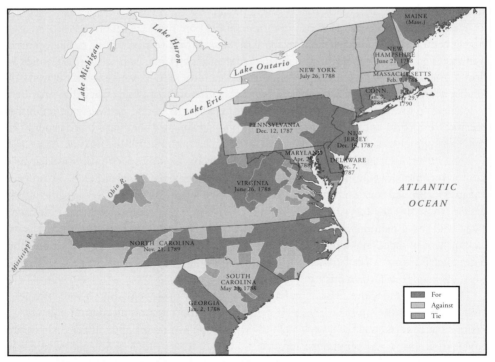

Map 6.4 Ratification of the Constitution The pattern of support by relatively small states is visible in the votes of Delaware, New Jersey, Georgia, and Connecticut. In Pennsylvania, Massachusetts, and New York, the more populated urban areas supported ratification.

ernment. Small farmers, many of them debtors who considered the mercantile elite their enemies, wanted nothing to do with this Constitution. At the core of their opposition was the belief that power should remain in the states. The Antifederalists understood that, despite equal representation in the Senate, the new government was fundamentally different from the Articles. They argued that a republic must be geographically small with a homogeneous population in order to meet the needs of its people. They believed the new central government would be too large and too remote, that the interests of citizens of the thirteen states were too diverse. A congressman could never know the will of 30,000 constituents; with so few persons elected to Congress and such large electoral districts, affluent well-known candidates would have the advantage over ordinary men who ran for office. Thus, even the House of Representatives, the branch of government closest to the people, would become the domain of the rich. To the Antifederalists, the Constitution lacked sufficient barriers against corruption and abuse of power. At the least, term limits on the president and senators were required to prevent these officials from keeping their offices for life. Annual elections (instead of every two years) would make the House of Representatives more responsive to the voters.

Antifederalists also pointed to the omission of a bill of rights as cause for rejecting the Constitution. They advocated freedom of speech, press, assembly, and religion; jury trials for civil cases; judicial safeguards such as the right to a speedy trial and to confront accusers and witnesses; and prohibitions against unwarranted searches and seizures. The Federalists answered that a bill of rights would be superfluous because state constitutions offered these protections (some did, but in no case was protection comprehensive), and because a bill of rights was needed against a powerful king, not when the people themselves were sovereign. This latter argument ignored the vulnerability of the individual to the will of the majority. The Federalists used poor judgment in failing to incorporate a bill of rights into the 1787 Constitution, for the Antifederalists gained momentum as a result. Omitting these rights, for which the patriots had fought, turned many Americans against the proposed frame of government.

Nevertheless, ratification proceeded rapidly at first as state legislatures called elections for the state ratifying conventions. Delaware was the first to ratify when its convention approved the Constitution unanimously on December 7, 1787. In Pennsylvania, where resistance was potentially heavy in the backcountry, Federalists moved quickly, securing approval by a two-to-one margin. New Jersey and Georgia then ratified unanimously. When Connecticut accepted the new government in January 1788 by a three-to-one vote, five states had joined the union. All of these states except Pennsylvania were relatively small and recognized the advantages of joining a union in which they had equal representation in the Senate.

Then the conventions became more acrimonious. North Carolina and Rhode Island rejected the document outright and New Hampshire put off its decision. Maryland and South Carolina ratified easily, but the vote in Massachusetts was close, as animosities from Shays's Rebellion colored the debate. Turnout for the Massachusetts convention was huge, as farmers in the central and western regions of the state believed the Constitution represented the interests of the eastern elite. The convention barely ratified the document by a vote of 187 to 168, recommending a series of amendments to protect individual rights and limit the powers of Congress. In June 1788, New Hampshire finally acted, becoming the ninth state to ratify, the number required to establish the new government. Nevertheless, two states remained crucial, Virginia and New York, whose size and economic importance made their approval necessary if the Constitution was to succeed. Virginia ratified in late June after a fierce debate, recommending to the first Congress a series of amendments, including a bill of rights. New York approved in late July, also with recommended changes, after New York City threatened to secede from the rest of the state if rural districts failed to accept the document.

Conclusion

The period from 1783 to 1788 was a crucial time for the United States, as it fixed the limits of revolutionary change and established a new government. Americans initially tried a political framework of thirteen small republics in which assemblies held the power to tax. All of the states (except New Jersey) restricted the vote—and political sovereignty—to propertied white men. "Republican motherhood" defined women's political role in the new nation. And despite a robust antislavery movement in the north, most African Americans remained enslaved.

The Congress, with little power under the Articles of Confederation, failed to solve its most pressing problems—the national debt, trade, and protection of U.S. borders against Spain and Great Britain. Even Congress's chief success, the legislation for governing and distributing land in the Northwest Territory, was marred by high land prices, delays in surveying, settlement by squatters, favoritism toward speculators, and conflict with Native Americans. When national government came to a halt and farmers rose in armed rebellion, nationalists demanded a constitution in which educated, propertied men like themselves would determine national economic policy and foreign affairs. These nationalists, who assumed the name Federalists, crafted the Constitution of 1787 to shift power from the states to a central government. The Antifederalists fought the new Constitution despite the "great compromise," which provided states equal representation in the Senate. The lack of a bill of rights intensified opposition. The Federalists prevailed, however, and with ratification by eleven states by July 1788, the United States began a new experiment in republican government.

RECOMMENDED READINGS

Beeman, Richard, Botein, Stephen, and Carter, Edward C., eds. *Beyond Confederation: Origins of the Constitution and American National Identity* (1987). These essays provide an excellent introduction to the Confederation period and the making of the Constitution.

Berlin, Ira, and Hoffman, Ronald, eds. *Slavery and Freedom in the Age of the American Revolution* (1983). Important essays on change, or lack thereof, in the status of African Americans during the Revolutionary era.

Doerflinger, Thomas M. *A Vigorous Spirit of Enterprise: Merchants and Economic Development in Revolutionary Philadelphia* (1986). A very good study of Philadelphia merchants and their impact on economic growth in the emergent United States.

Greene, Jack P. *Peripheries and Center: Constitutional Development in the Extended Polities of the British Empire and the United States, 1607–1788* (1986). Links the constitutional structure of Britain and its colonies to the Constitution of 1787.

Hamilton, Alexander, Jay, John, and Madison, James. *The Federalist Papers* (1788). Defense of Constitution of 1787; seminal treatise of American political thought.

Hoffman, Ronald et al., eds. *Native Americans and the Early Republic* (1999). Essays focusing on the impact of the Revolution and founding of the new republic on white-Indian relations.

Kenyon, Cecilia M. "Men of Little Faith: The Anti-Federalists on the Nature of Representative Government," *William and Mary Quarterly*, 3d ser., 12 (1955): 3–43. Insightful essay on the men who opposed ratification of the Constitution of 1787.

Kerber, Linda K. *Women of the Republic: Intellect and Ideology in Revolutionary America* (1980). Evaluates the impact of the Revolution on attitudes toward women.

Rhoden, Nancy L., and Steele, Ian K., eds. *The Human Tradition in the American Revolution* (2000). Biographical essays of famous and more ordinary Americans during the Revolutionary era.

Richards, Leonard L. *Shays's Rebellion: The American Revolution's Final Battle* (2002). A recent study of the western Massachusetts revolt that challenges earlier interpretations.

Additional resources, exercises, and Internet links related to this chapter are available on the American Passages Web site: http://history.wadsworth.com/ayerscompact2/

7

The Federalist Republic
1789–1799

Af
fter Ratification, the Federalists took leadership in creating the new government. Everyone expected George Washington to become president. The three authors of *The Federalist*, Alexander Hamilton, James Madison, and John Jay, who had been so important in achieving the Constitution, went on to play a central role in making it work. John Adams and Thomas Jefferson, who were serving as ministers to Great Britain and France during the convention, returned home to become, respectively, vice president and secretary of state.

Though many Federalists disagreed with specific parts of the Constitution, they accepted compromise and knew the weak Confederation had to be replaced. In the flush of victory over the Antifederalists, they set to the task of remedying the nation's ills. Differences soon became clear, however, between Hamilton on the one side, and Madison and Jefferson on the other, as the first administration tackled the national debt and foreign policy. As a result of their conflict over policy, varying interpretations of the Constitution, and competition for power, the nation's first political parties developed.

The New Government

The first national elections went well, from the Federalist point of view, considering the whirlwind of Antifederalist opposition to the Constitution. The great majority of representatives and senators in the first Congress were Federalists. They fulfilled Madison's image of well-to-do men of national reputation and experience in politics. Many had served in the Constitutional Convention and signed the document. Most had military or political experience during the Revolution and Confederation period; just a few came from lower-class backgrounds. While the first congressmen were revolutionaries, they were also elites who believed that the country's interests coincided with their own. They wanted a stable government to foster economic growth.

George Washington Becomes President

The choice of George Washington as president was a foregone conclusion, though he would have preferred to stay at his Mount Vernon estate in northern Virginia. In February 1789, members of the electoral college met in their state capitals to cast unanimous votes

C H R O N O L O G Y

1789	First Congress meets • Inauguration of George Washington as president • French Revolution begins • Judiciary Act of 1789
1790	Site on Potomac River chosen for permanent capital • Congress approves the funding and assumption plans • Samuel Slater builds first water-powered textile mill in the United States • First national census • Nootka Convention
1791	Bank of the United States is established • Native Americans of the Ohio Valley destroy Arthur St. Clair's army • Ratification of Bill of Rights
1793	France declares war on Great Britain and Spain • Washington begins second term • Proclamation of Neutrality • Genêt Affair • Britain seizes U.S. merchant fleet • Eli Whitney invents cotton gin
1794	Battle of Fallen Timbers • Whiskey Rebellion
1795	Senate approves the Jay Treaty • Treaty of Greenville • Treaty of San Lorenzo
1797	John Adams becomes second president
1798	XYZ Affair becomes public • Congress passes Alien and Sedition Acts • Kentucky and Virginia Resolutions
1798–1800	Quasi-War with France
1799	The Fries Rebellion • Napoleon takes power in France

for the former commander-in-chief. Washington's leadership during the war, his dignity and character, and his support for republican government made him the obvious choice. He might have tried to grasp power during the shaky Confederation, like a Napoleon or Stalin, but he did not. The first president's commitment to the success of the Constitution ensured the nation's survival during the early years. John Adams, elected vice president, received fewer than half as many votes as Washington.

The president-elect's trip from Mount Vernon to New York City, the temporary federal capital, became an eight-day triumphal march. In large and small towns along his way—Alexandria, Baltimore, Wilmington, Philadelphia—crowds of people, troops of infantry and cavalry, and local officials feted him with ceremonies, cannon fire, and banquets. Philadelphia citizens erected a Roman arch, crowning the revolutionary hero with a laurel wreath. In New Jersey, throngs saluted his military victories at Trenton and Princeton. On April 23, 1789, Washington crossed into Manhattan on a festooned barge, welcomed by thousands of cheering New Yorkers. He took the oath of office a week later.

The president and Congress, aware that they were setting precedent, initially placed a great deal of emphasis on titles and the comportment of officials. In this republic, in a world of monarchies, how should they be addressed? Should the president keep his door open or remain detached? While the questions may seem trivial, they indicate the novelty of this republican experiment. Adams, with diplomatic experience in Europe, urged Congress to adopt titles like those of other nations. A Senate committee suggested, for example, that Washington be called "His Highness the President of the United States of America, and Protector of their Liberties." After much debate, Congress dropped the notion of titles, preferring a more republican style. Washington and his successors have been addressed simply as "Mr. President."

For his part, the president wondered how to dignify his office and accomplish his work. He could easily have spent all of his time meeting with visitors, entertaining, and dining out. On the other hand, he did not want complete separation from the people. Washington's personality tended toward aloofness. He decided to hold a one-hour reception once a week, invite a few visitors to dinner, and sometimes attend the theater.

Washington also developed, by trial and error, the way in which the chief executive would deal with Congress. Early in his administration, in advance of negotiating a treaty with the Creek Indians, he attended the Senate to request their "advice and consent," as the Constitution seemed to direct. The senators were unprepared to discuss Washington's proposal, leading to embarrassment on both sides. The president resolved never to consult in formal session again. Instead, he set the precedent of private informal meetings with members of Congress. Heads of executive departments, such as the secretary of the treasury, would attend congressional hearings, not the president. And in the case of treaties, the executive would seek the Senate's consent *after* negotiations were complete, not advice—at least formally—beforehand.

Beyond titles and modes of operating, Congress and the president needed to establish executive departments and courts, and draw up a bill of rights, to fill gaps in the written Constitution. In creating executive departments, which included War, Treasury, State (foreign affairs), and the attorney general, the most crucial constitutional question concerned who would be able to remove the heads of departments from office. Some senators hoped to restrict the president's power by requiring Senate approval before officeholders could be fired, thus making them more accountable to the legislature. In rejecting this proposal, Congress clarified one aspect of the Constitution's balance of powers.

With the Judiciary Act of 1789, Congress put some flesh on the skeleton outlined in Article III of the Constitution, which stated that the "judicial power of the United States shall be vested in one Supreme Court, and in such inferior courts as the Congress may from time to time ordain and establish." Congress might have created a full-blown national court system, but supporters of states' rights opposed such enhancement of national power. Thus, the Judiciary Act, the result of compromise, established a Supreme Court of six justices and a system of federal inferior courts, which were few in number and restricted primarily to consideration of federal crimes. State courts retained original jurisdiction in most civil and criminal cases, with the U.S. Supreme Court taking appeals from the highest state courts. John Jay became the first chief justice.

The Bill of Rights

During its first months, Congress took up the question of amending the Constitution to satisfy criticisms voiced during ratification, objections that by the summer of 1789 still kept North Carolina and Rhode Island out of the Union. More than the original document, the first ten amendments, called the Bill of Rights, represented the will of the American people.

The ratification campaign had elicited a mountain of proposals for amending the Constitution. Opponents offered two major grounds for altering the document or abandoning it altogether. Antifederalist leaders believed it took too much power from the states and from themselves as leaders of state and local governments, while popular opinion feared the loss of personal freedoms to a strong national government.

James Madison became the chief proponent of the Bill of Rights in Congress, despite his earlier advocacy of the Federalist position that the amendments were unnecessary. In order to get elected to the House of Representatives, he had promised his Virginia constituents to obtain the safeguards. Madison took his vow seriously, pushing his reluctant Federalist colleagues to the task. Antifederalist leaders, who wanted to scrap the Constitution entirely, now denied support to the Bill of Rights because they knew protection of individual freedoms would garner popular support.

After much negotiation between the Senate and the House, on September 25, 1789, Congress sent to the states for ratification a total of twelve amendments. By December 15, 1791, three-quarters of the states approved the ten amendments known as the Bill of Rights, thus putting them into effect. Of the two amendments not approved at the time, one was a rule concerning congressional salaries that was not ratified for two centuries, until 1992, and the other was a complicated formula for computing representation in Congress that was never adopted. Of the Bill of Rights, Articles 1 through 8 enumerated basic individual rights, while the intention of Article 9 was to protect any personal freedoms omitted from this list. Article 10 directed that "powers not delegated to the United States by the Constitution, nor prohibited by it to the States, are reserved to the States respectively, or to the people." It addressed concerns that the national government might assume powers that were not mentioned in the Constitution. Passage of the Bill of Rights by Congress attracted enough support to bring in the two remaining states; North Carolina ratified the Constitution in November 1789 and Rhode Island followed suit in May 1790.

The First Census

Congress also promptly ordered a census of the American population, which the Constitution required within three years of Congress's first meeting and every ten years subsequently. The census, the founders expected, would provide an accurate enumeration for apportioning delegates to the House of Representatives and electoral college. Congress set August 1790 as the date of the first census, appointing marshals to complete their work within nine months, which actually stretched to eighteen. The first census was less complicated than later ones, with just six questions: name of head of household, number of free white males aged sixteen years and over, number of free white males under sixteen, number of free white females, number of other free persons, and number of slaves. The separate listing of enslaved persons was required by the clause of the Constitution that counted three-fifths of slaves for representation and taxes. The distinction between free

Table 7.1 The U.S. Population, 1790

United States	Total 3,929,625	Slaves 697,624
New England	1,009,206	3,763
Maine (part of Massachusetts)	96,643	0
New Hampshire	141,899	157
Vermont	85,341	0
Massachusetts	378,556	0
Rhode Island	69,112	958
Connecticut	237,655	2,648
Middle States	**1,017,087**	**45,210**
New York	340,241	21,193
New Jersey	184,139	11,423
Pennsylvania	433,611	3,707
Delaware	59,096	8,887
Southern States and Territories	**1,903,332**	**648,651**
Maryland	319,728	103,036
Virginia	747,610	292,627
North Carolina	395,005	100,783
South Carolina	249,073	107,094
Georgia	82,548	29,264
Kentucky	73,677	12,430
Tennessee	35,691	3,417

whites and blacks came from cultural values rather than some practical use. The census did not include Native Americans who lived outside areas settled by whites.

While sketchy and incomplete, the 1790 census served as a baseline for measuring the growth of a dynamic, expanding people. President Washington reported to Congress a total of 3.9 million people, of whom 60,000 were free blacks and almost 700,000 were slaves. The census covered the territory included in the thirteen original states and also Vermont, Kentucky, and Tennessee, which became states respectively in 1791, 1792, and 1796. It did not encompass the area north of the Ohio River where at least 4,000 white settlers had taken up land.

During the 1780s, the white population of the country had swelled by an extraordinary 44 percent, mostly through reproduction; in the 1790s, the increase remained high at 36 percent. After the Treaty of Paris, European immigrants once again began crossing the Atlantic Ocean, with the majority coming from Ireland. From 1783 to 1799, 156,000 Europeans entered the United States, of whom 69 percent were Irish, 14 percent were English, Scottish, and Welsh, and 6 percent were German. The African American population also grew quickly during the 1780s and 1790s, at a rate of 32 percent per decade.

Especially striking in the 1790 census are the small numbers of enslaved African Americans in New England and Pennsylvania compared with Maryland, Virginia, and the Carolinas, the result in part of northern abolition. This sectional difference would grow in the nineteenth century as the North focused more on commerce and developed a manufacturing sector, while the South cast its fate with agriculture, adopting cotton as its major crop.

Opposing Visions of America

Almost immediately during Washington's first administration, political divisions arose between sides favoring commerce versus agriculture. Two divergent conceptions of the nation's future emerged among supporters of the Constitution. During the early 1790s, two political parties developed, though leaders avoided calling them that because public opinion considered parties "evil," or detrimental to unified republican government. As events unfolded in foreign and domestic affairs, the two parties contested one issue after another.

Hamilton Versus Jefferson

Alexander Hamilton, appointed by Washington as secretary of the treasury, saw the future greatness of the United States in commerce and manufacturing. Born in the West Indies, Hamilton attended King's College in New York City, then served as Washington's aide-de-camp during the Revolution. Highly intelligent, full of energy and enthusiasm, he was a major proponent of the new Constitution. Appointment to the Treasury allowed Hamilton to promote his concept of a strong nation modeled on Great Britain, but his efforts to foster commerce and manufacturing aroused resistance among former allies, particularly Madison and Jefferson, leading to bitter partisan disputes.

Hamilton's party took the name Federalist though it was really nationalist. It favored commercial development, a national bank, high tariffs to spur manufacturing, and a strong central government based upon a "loose" interpretation of the Constitution, which allowed expansive powers to Congress and the president. The Federalists favored the British, abhorred the French Revolution after 1792, and were generally suspicious of power wielded by ordinary folk. They were somewhat critical of slavery, however, and gained the allegiance of free blacks. Because their power base lay in New England and the Middle States, the Federalists had little enthusiasm for western expansion and sometimes supported the right of Native Americans to retain their lands.

The Republican party, in contrast, favored a "strict" interpretation of the Constitution, opposing a strong central government and federal privileges for manufacturing and commerce. It thought Hamilton's plans for funding the national debt, the bank, and protective tariffs infringed upon states' rights and helped the "few" at the expense of the "many." It disdained the British model and charged Hamilton with advocating a return to monarchy. With their power base in the south, west, and northern cities, the Republicans rejected efforts to abolish slavery and were ardent expansionists on the frontier. They had little sympathy for Indian rights.

Thomas Jefferson became the chief spokesman for the Republican party, though James Madison collaborated in its growth. Jefferson, a wealthy planter and slaveholder, author of the Declaration of Independence, former minister to France, and now Washington's secretary of state, argued that Hamilton wanted too much national power. He believed the root of Britain's effort to destroy American liberty in the 1760s and 1770s had been commercial speculation and greed. Manufacturing in cities created poverty, dependency, and political corruption. Instead, the United States, with limitless land, should foster an agrarian society of small producers. A virtuous republic was one made up of small farmers whose goal was to produce enough to support their families. Commerce should exist primarily to allow them to sell their surplus in Europe and purchase manufactured goods in return. The farmers should be educated to participate wisely in republican government. Their self-sufficiency and education would make them virtuous, to act for the good of society rather than solely for their own gain.

Paradoxically, a large proportion of the Republicans were not small farmers. Many of the leaders were southern plantation gentry like Jefferson and Madison, or old Antifederalist elites. The party drew together people who had opposed ratification of the Constitution as well as those who favored it but abhorred the government's direction under Washington and Hamilton. The Republicans received solid backing from farmers, especially in the south and west, and from urban craftsmen and small traders who watched wealthy speculators and merchants benefit from Hamiltonian policies.

Funding the National Debt

In becoming secretary of the treasury, Alexander Hamilton's primary challenge was the Revolutionary War debt. A strong nationalist, he viewed the debt more as an opportunity to enlarge national power than as a financial hurdle. The United States owed $10 million to foreigners, particularly to the French, and $40 million to Americans. The states also owed $25 million in domestic debts. To continue the War of Independence when funds were depleted, Congress and the states had issued certificates to merchants, artisans, and farmers for supplies and to soldiers for wages. After the war, many ordinary folks could not wait for the government to pay—or lost hope that the money was forthcoming—so they sold their certificates to wealthy speculators for a fraction of face value. Often the sellers received only 10 to 15 percent, rates that reflected the risk speculators were taking during the shaky Confederation period.

In his Report on Public Credit of January 1790, Hamilton formulated a plan by which the U.S. government would honor at face value all Revolutionary War debts, including those of the states. His "funding" proposal involved the exchange of new federal securities for the old debt certificates. He planned to pay off foreign creditors as soon as possible, but retain the domestic debt, paying only interest and a small amount of the principal each year. A customs duty on imports and an excise tax on whiskey would cover the interest; post office income would gradually reduce the principal. Hamilton's funding plan would tie wealthy Americans to the new government through their continuing investment. His "assumption" plan, by which the federal government assumed state war debts, expanded this strategy by reorienting the loyalty of investors from the states to the nation.

Congress eventually passed Hamilton's proposal, though with great opposition. Many people, including Madison, thought that repaying the domestic debt at face value was unfair, that speculators received a windfall at the expense of the poor. The split between Hamilton and Madison began over this issue. Critics argued that funding allowed the "few" to benefit from the hardships of the "many," who had lost money when they sold their war bonds and who would pay again through import duties and the excise tax. Opponents feared the expansion of national power, and became convinced that the Treasury secretary was upsetting the balance between the central government and the states. Assumption raised additional questions because some states had more debt remaining than others. Massachusetts and South Carolina were keen on having the federal government assume their large debts, while Virginians opposed the plan, because they had satisfied most of the state's debt. Despite these divisions, the funding and assumption program passed Congress in July 1790, as part of a bargain struck by Hamilton, Jefferson, and Madison to situate the nation's permanent capital on the Potomac River, in Maryland and Virginia.

Planning Washington, D.C.

The choice of the Potomac for the nation's capital was controversial. While everyone agreed that a central location was necessary, regional interests surfaced as congressmen recognized its potential economic and political benefits. They also debated the question of the temporary capital. Should New York City or Philadelphia host the federal government until the permanent site was ready? The complicated negotiations over funding and assumption resulted in moving the temporary capital from New York to Philadelphia as well as locating the new city on the Potomac.

President Washington and his fellow Virginians supervised the development of the capital. The Residence Act of 1790 gave the president authority to select a ten-mile-square location somewhere along the Potomac; he chose the land on both sides of the river that included Alexandria, Virginia, and Georgetown, Maryland. The fed-

The Granger Collection, New York

Pierre Charles L'Enfant's intricate design for Washington, D.C., 1791, far outstripped the country's financial resources and interest in creating a national capital.

eral city would be built in neither of those towns, but on open land on the east bank of the river. Washington appointed a surveyor, three commissioners to manage the project, and Pierre Charles L'Enfant to design the layout of the capital and its major buildings. L'Enfant's grandiose street plan and Greek and Roman architecture expressed an exalted vision of the republic. The commissioners named the federal city "Washington" and the entire district "Columbia."

The president expected to finance construction by selling lots in the capital, thinking that land prices would skyrocket as citizens valued proximity to the seat of government. Instead, land sold poorly and lack of money undermined the project. At one of the failed auctions, even the participation of the president and a parade of two brass bands and an artillery troop could not foster sales. When the commissioners suspended construction temporarily for insufficient funds, L'Enfant protested and was fired. His plan for grand boulevards, public squares, fountains, and imposing buildings was retained, but its execution would wait. For a decade the enterprise limped along, saved by grants from Maryland and Virginia. In 1800, when the government moved to Washington, the president's mansion was still unfinished and only one wing of the Capitol had been built.

The National Bank

The cornerstone of Hamilton's new commercial order was a national bank, to be patterned after the Bank of England. The Bank of the United States and its branches would hold the federal government's funds and regulate state banks. The chief purpose of the national bank was to expand the money supply, thereby encouraging commercial growth.

The Bank of the United States, which Congress chartered in 1791 for twenty years, would have assets of $10 million, including $2 million in government deposits. Private investors could purchase the remaining $8 million in stock. As the bank prospered, stockholders would receive dividends on their funds. Thus, Hamilton created a way for wealthy Americans, who had just profited from funding the Revolutionary War debt, to benefit further. Because the government was a major stockholder, it also received dividends that could be used to pay off the national debt. The bank made loans to merchants beyond the value of its stock of gold and silver (specie), thus increasing the supply of money, a critically important move for an economy short of specie. The bank notes circulated as currency; the federal government supported their value by accepting them for taxes. To Hamilton and his commercial backers, the Bank of the United States was essential for economic growth. The majority of the House of Representatives agreed, by a vote of thirty-nine to twenty, but the tally indicated important regional differences that fueled growth of political parties. Among northern congressmen, thirty-three voted for the bank and one against, while only six southern delegates supported and nineteen opposed Hamilton's bill.

The plan had many opponents, who variously considered the bank immoral, monopolistic, or unconstitutional. Some believed that all paper money should be based on gold and silver. "Every dollar of a bank bill that is issued beyond the quantity of gold and silver in the vaults," John Adams said, "represents nothing, and is therefore a cheat upon somebody." The wild frenzy to purchase the bank's stock—in which 25,000 shares sold in two hours and then the shares were bid up to 1,300 percent of their face value—reinforced fears that the national bank would undermine republican virtue. Jefferson called the bank's stock "federal filth." Others charged the bank with monopoly, complaining that merchants could secure short-term loans to finance their commercial ventures, but farmers and artisans could not obtain mortgages for purchasing property or making improvements.

In Congress, Madison opposed the national bank on the constitutional grounds that the federal government lacked the power to create corporations, a strict interpretation of the Constitution. In particular, Madison said, the Tenth Amendment would deny the central government any power not expressly given. Hamilton and his supporters countered with a loose interpretation, that some powers of the federal government are implied. In the case of the bank, for example, the Constitution delegated to Congress and the president the power to lay and collect taxes, pay debts, regulate commerce, and coin and regulate money. It also provided the authority to "make all laws which shall be necessary and proper for carrying into execution the foregoing powers. . . ." Hamilton argued that the bank was a method by which the United States could fulfill its functions, and because some means was necessary, the power to establish the bank was implied. Though President Washington was initially unsure, he accepted Hamilton's reasoning and approved the bill.

Jefferson, like Madison, was convinced that the national bank was unconstitutional. By 1791, the secretary of state realized the political and economic consequences of the funding act—channeling more power to the federal government and more money to the rich—and thought the bank could only further these trends. He said he had been "duped" by Hamilton and "made a tool for forwarding his schemes" in accepting the assumption of state debts in return for the capital on the Potomac. He now believed that the Treasury secretary's program "flowed from principles adverse to liberty," as Jefferson told the president. It was "calculated to undermine and demolish the republic." Hamilton chafed at this criticism, stating "that Mr. Madison, cooperating with Mr. Jefferson, is at the head of a faction decidedly hostile to me and my administration; and actuated by views, in my judgment, subversive of the principles of good government and dangerous to the Union, peace, and happiness of the country."

Encouragement of Manufacturing

While the Treasury secretary won congressional support for the bank and funding the national debt, he was much less successful in his plan for industry. In 1791, the United States lacked a solid manufacturing base. Hamilton proposed high protective tariffs on certain goods to discourage Americans from buying imports and thus spur U.S. production. He also advocated bounties, or subsidies, on selected products to encourage entrepreneurs. Hamilton believed that a strong nation needed self-sufficiency in manufactures, especially for military defense, but failed to obtain congressional support for the subsidies. Madison contended that granting bounties would expand the power of Congress, while others argued that they were like monopolies and too expensive. A North Carolina congressman advised, "Establish the doctrine of bounties, [and] . . . all manner of persons—people of every trade and occupation—may enter at the breach, until they have eaten up the bread of our children."

In the 1790s, U.S. manufacturing remained on a small scale. Americans appreciated the quality of British imports; what they did not import, they produced themselves or purchased from neighboring artisans. Industry could not be stimulated overnight, for it required technology and the willingness of businessmen to invest time and capital for the long term. While some master craftsmen enlarged their shops and hired more workers, mechanized factories with mass production still lay in the future.

During the colonial and revolutionary periods, urban entrepreneurs had attempted large-scale textile manufacturing to provide employment for poor women and independence from British imports, but these efforts were short-lived and not mechanized. The "factories" had consisted of workhouses, in which large numbers of impoverished widows produced thread and yarn at traditional spinning wheels. Other businessmen used a "putting-out" system, whereby they distributed flax and wool for spinning at home.

In 1788, the Pennsylvania Society for the Encouragement of Manufactures and the Useful Arts introduced spinning jennies to their textile factory in Philadelphia. The jennies threatened to displace home spinners by producing cheaper yarn and thread. In 1790, however, the factory and its wooden jennies went up in flames, as did other early textile mills in the Delaware Valley. While the promoters believed that home spinners were sabotaging the factories, the fires may well have been accidental because the mills were highly flammable.

Samuel Slater, a twenty-two-year-old millworker and recent immigrant from Great Britain, in 1790 instituted a new phase in American cloth production by building a textile mill in Pawtucket, Rhode Island, using water power to run the spinning machines. From memory he constructed a spinning frame, a machine that produced stronger threads than the jenny produced. He had left Britain illegally; to keep its advantage in textile making, the government prohibited emigration of craftworkers or export of drawings of the machines. No satisfactory power loom yet existed, so Slater's mill performed only the first two steps of cloth production: carding, or preparing the cotton fibers for spinning, and spinning the thread. Slater then used the putting-out system of distributing the thread to families, who produced the cloth at home. Though Slater established additional mills in Rhode Island and Massachusetts, his workforce stayed fairly small, with about a hundred millworkers in 1800.

Rare Books Division, The New York Public Library Astor, Lenox and Tilden Foundations

Until after 1815, households performed one or more steps in textile manufacturing. Here a family works together, with the wife spinning thread, which the husband then wove on his loom. Women also wove cloth, but men rarely—if ever—used a spinning wheel.

Alexander Hamilton tried an ambitious industrial program in Paterson, New Jersey, with the Society for Establishing Useful Manufactures. The society hoped to create an industrial town on the Passaic River where skilled craftsmen recruited from Britain would produce a variety of cloth and clothing, blankets, carpets, shoes, hats, pottery, metal wire, and paper. After obtaining a state charter from New Jersey, the society sold stock that sold quickly and appreciated in value. The project lost capital, however, when major stockholders sold their shares to make a fast profit. The managers failed to obtain reliable machinery and workers, closing shop in 1796.

While the results of Hamilton's plans were disappointing, the United States did make progress during the 1790s toward industrialization. In 1790, Congress passed patent legislation, giving inventors exclusive rights to their work for seventeen years, and Slater initiated water-powered textile manufacture. Then, in 1793, while visiting a Georgia plantation, Eli Whitney, a New Englander, built the cotton engine, or gin. The device, which separated cotton fibers from husks and seeds, greatly increased the productivity of cotton cultivation, swelling the demand for African American slaves and fertile land in the Southwest, and spurring cloth production in the North. Because the gin could be duplicated easily, Whitney failed to make a fortune from the machine. In 1798, he further laid the basis for industrial growth by attempting to manufacture guns with interchangeable parts. After receiving a government contract for 10,000 weapons, he specified that each part be made identical to its counterparts so that it could be exchanged from one rifle to another, allowing less-skilled workers to build and repair the firearms. At this early date, however, such rigid standards were impossible to meet, and as a result, parts needed filing to fit together smoothly.

An inventor who would have benefited from Hamilton's proposed bounties was the Delaware-born artisan Oliver Evans, who apprenticed as a wagonmaker and became fascinated by machines. In 1772, at age seventeen, he heard that the Scottish inventor James Watt had improved the steam engine a few years earlier. Evans began building his own model but, for lack of money, thirty years passed before he actually installed a high pressure steam engine in his gypsum fertilizer factory in Philadelphia. This was the first such application of steam power to an industrial setting. In the meantime, in the 1780s, Evans also developed the idea of automating mills. He devised water-powered machinery for large grist mills that allowed one worker instead of three to supervise all the steps of producing flour. Evans obtained exclusive rights from the states of Pennsylvania and Maryland for his system of automated elevators, conveyors, and hoppers. With insufficient capital, however, he was unable to pursue many of his designs, including steam carriages and trucks, a machine gun, refrigeration, central heating, and gas lighting.

Expansion and Conflict in the West

While Alexander Hamilton's financial policies aided commerce in the east, dynamic growth also occurred in the west. The expansion of settlers from east to west challenged the ability of the new government to keep their loyalty. In particular, Hamilton's excise tax on whiskey weighed heavily on westerners. The young nation also contended with Native Americans who were losing lands to the settlers; the British military, who kept forts in the northwest; and the Spanish, who contested U.S. territorial claims and rights to navigate the Mississippi.

Kentucky and Tennessee

During the 1780s, the region west of the Appalachians and south of the Ohio River developed quickly, as families left Virginia and North Carolina in search of fertile land and lower taxes. Even before the Revolution ended, settlers crossed the mountains in large numbers: Kentucky swelled from 150 settlers in 1775 to 61,000 whites and 12,500 enslaved blacks in 1790; Tennessee reported 32,000 whites and 3,500 slaves in the latter year.

White settlement of Kentucky and Tennessee proceeded quickly as state governments, speculators, and frontiersmen defeated the Cherokees, who claimed ancestral rights to the territory. Understanding that they were renting the land rather than selling it, in 1775 a group of Cherokee leaders, including Attakullaculla and Oconostota, traded 27,000 square miles to Richard Henderson and his associates for a cabin of consumer goods. Called Henderson's Purchase, the sale involved most of Kentucky and was illegal in Indian and English law. With the outbreak of the Revolution, most Cherokees joined the British, fighting for return of their lands. Receiving little help from Britain, the Cherokees were defeated in 1777 and forced to sign away even more territory.

Young militants led by Dragging Canoe, Bloody Fellow, and others, assisted by loyalist whites who intermarried and became members of the tribe, rejected these land cessions. In the 1780s and early 1790s, the militant Cherokees, called Chickamaugas, allied with Creeks and Shawnees against settlers along the frontier from Kentucky to Georgia. On both sides, fighting was vicious, with men, women, and children burned, scalped, and shot; and, as in so many cases, the whites failed to distinguish between enemy Indians and those who wanted peace.

The Washington administration attempted to end the hostilities with the Treaty of Holston in 1791, but gave responsibility for negotiating with the Cherokees to Governor William Blount of the Tennessee Territory, a land speculator the Indians called "dirt king" for his greed after land. Blount ignored Washington's promise to the Cherokees that if they ceded territory on which the whites had settled, the United States would guarantee their remaining lands. Instead, Blount required a cession of more than 4,000 square miles in return for an annual payment of $1,000 and no guarantee. When Blount surveyed the border without Cherokee witnesses, the treaty fell apart and war continued. In 1794, after Dragging Canoe died and the Spanish stopped supplying the Indians because of war in Europe, the Chickamaugas met defeat.

By the end of the war, parts of Kentucky and Tennessee had passed the initial stages of settlement. Early on, groups of settlers had gathered in frontier stations consisting of two-story log houses connected by a high wall to create a fort against Indian attack. As the population grew and the threat from Native Americans declined, families moved away from the stations. In the early years, all family members worked to provide food, clothing, shelter, and a few amenities such as soap and rough-hewn furniture. They needed to become familiar with their new environment. One Kentucky pioneer described how "the women the first spring we came out, wo'd follow their cows to see what they ate, that they might know what greens to get. My Wife and I had neither spoon, dish, knife, or any thing to do with when we began life. Only I had a butcher knife." The settlers grew corn, tobacco, hemp, cotton, vegetables, and fruits; raised cattle, sheep, horses, and pigs; hunted and fished. Soon they produced a surplus to trade for necessities they could not make themselves, such as nails, rifles, ammunition, needles, tools, and salt, as well as to pay taxes and fees. They sold furs, ginseng, agricultural produce, and livestock. As fertile lands such as Kentucky's Bluegrass region yielded bountiful crops, farmers sought markets by way of the Mississippi River and the port of New Orleans. Because transporting crops overland through the mountains was much more difficult and expensive than sending them downstream, southwestern farmers demanded that the federal government convince Spain to end its restrictions on lower Mississippi shipping.

Map 7.1 Conflict in the Northwest Territory, 1790–1796 Native Americans continued to resist U.S. settlement in the Ohio region. They defeated U.S. forces in 1790 and 1791, but lost the Battle of Fallen Timbers in 1794. British forts in the Northwest Territory supported the Ohio Indians until that time.

Though the population increased and a market economy developed in the 1790s, the trans-Appalachian region had few schools or church buildings. Most children, if taught at all, learned reading and arithmetic at home. In towns where schools existed, boys might attend for a few months but girls stayed at home. The exception were the children of wealthy families who entered academies with secondary school curricula. One man remembered the experience of most residents of Kentucky in the 1790s: "Our preachers and teachers were, in general, almost as destitute as the people at large, many of whom could neither read nor write, did not send their children to school, and of course, kept no books in the house."

Religion was the frontier's chief cultural institution. Throughout the region, Presbyterian, Baptist, and Methodist ministers held services in private homes. Baptist lay ministers farmed beside their neighbors through the week, then led services on Sunday. Methodist circuit riders traveled from one congregation to another, conducting worship services, baptisms, marriages, and prayer meetings. The churches expected members to avoid sin, including fighting, excessive drinking, adultery, and even celebrating the Fourth of July. If members committed offenses and failed to express regret, they were expelled, a serious consequence for people who had few social outlets. In addition to church, social activities included barn raisings, corn huskings, and log rollings. These events caused trouble when whiskey and frivolity led church members astray, as with one couple a Kentucky Methodist church expelled for "Disorderly Conduct." Another man was "Excluded from this Church for Fighting & Drinking to Excess."

The Ohio Country

White settlement moved more slowly north of the Ohio River, partly because the U.S. government kept tighter control in the Northwest Territory, but more because Native Americans resisted strongly. Delawares, Shawnees, Iroquois, and many others refused to cede lands that the federal government wanted to sell to land-hungry easterners. In the 1780s, the United States obtained a series of cessions, but from just some of the people who owned the land. Indians who were not party to the agreements rejected them. Forming a confederacy to withstand U.S. invasion, Ohio Indians attacked whites who risked settling in the region. This northern Indian confederacy allied with the Chickamaugas and Creeks in the south, establishing a pan-Indian defensive that gained help from the Spanish in the south and the British in the north. At one meeting in 1787, the Native Americans agreed to merge their forces "for a general defense against all Invaders of Indian rights."

In the early 1790s, President Washington challenged the northern confederacy by sending two expeditions, both of them unsuccessful. Arthur St. Clair, governor of the Northwest Territory, led the second invasion in 1791, in which 600 of his 1,400 men died. Washington believed that the disaster resulted from the use of militia, so instructed General Anthony Wayne to raise 5,000 regulars. Wayne trained the troops for two years, then on August 20, 1794, defeated the Native Americans decisively at the Battle of Fallen Timbers. Though the British had customarily given aid to the Ohio tribes, this time they closed the gates to Fort Miami, denying refuge to the retreating Indians. A year later, when it became clear to the Native Americans that their alliance with the British had ended, they signed the Treaty of Greenville ceding to the United States most of the land in present-day Ohio.

The Whiskey Rebellion

In 1794, the Washington administration also sent troops against western Pennsylvania farmers, who since 1791 had resisted the whiskey tax. Washington and Hamilton decided to take advantage of the unrest to demonstrate the power of the new central government. Farmers throughout the west resented the tax on spirits, for distilling whiskey from grain made their produce less bulky, thus less expensive to transport to eastern markets. They also used the whiskey instead of cash and consumed a good portion of it themselves. In much of the trans-Appalachian region, officials failed to collect the excise at all.

The administration found willing officials in western Pennsylvania, however, and there proceeded to enforce the law. The Pittsburgh area farmers held protest meetings and refused cooperation with the collectors. They tarred and feathered collaborators, burned barns, and destroyed stills of people who paid the tax. The farmers charged that the tax favored large distillers and was collected unevenly. Rebels left notes signed "Tom the Tinker" to warn distillers who registered for the tax that their stills would be "fixed" (that is, ruined) unless they joined the revolt. The insurgents understood their fight as a struggle for "the virtuous principles of republican liberty." But the whiskey tax was only one of the farmers' complaints, which included failure to open up the Ohio country and removal of Spanish trade restrictions on the Mississippi.

Events came to a climax in July 1794. When officials continued to collect the tax and arrest resisters, 500 men surrounded the excise inspector's home, exchanged gunfire killing several people, and burned the house. The official and his family escaped. In the days that followed, rebels set more buildings on fire, raised liberty poles, attacked collectors, and rumored secession. The uprising spread to central Pennsylvania, Virginia, Maryland, and Ohio. Washington sent commissioners to obtain oaths of submission, but when the insurrection continued, he called up 13,000 eastern militia, who marched west with the president briefly in command. By the time the soldiers reached western Pennsylvania, the revolt was over, as the show of force intimidated the rebels. The administration had demonstrated that armed resistance to federal policies would not be tolerated.

The Spanish Frontier

As settlers from the United States migrated across the Appalachians and traders extended their commercial networks, they came into contact with the Spanish. The 1790s marked the high point of Spain's control in North America, its provinces extending from East Florida across the Gulf Coast to Louisiana, Texas, New Mexico, and California. The Spanish government continued to view these borderlands of their empire as a buffer against American and British designs on Mexican silver. Spanish officials recog-

Courtesy, Museo Naval, Madrid and Robin Inglis

Dances held by Native Americans for Alejandro Malaspina at Nootka Sound, 1791. Drawing probably by Tomás de Suria.

nized the phenomenal population growth of the United States. One warned that Americans were "advancing and multiplying . . . with a prodigious rapidity," while another took a dim view of the American frontier people, whom he considered "nomadic like Arabs and . . . distinguished from savages only in their color, language, and the superiority of their depraved cunning and untrustworthiness."

Nevertheless, the Spanish decided to open their territory to Americans, hoping to bolster the small settler populations. Spain offered free land in the Floridas and Louisiana, and even changed official policy to allow Protestants to keep their religion as long as they took an oath of allegiance to the Crown and had their children baptized Catholic. Because Spain could not provide desired consumer goods or adequate markets, it also relaxed mercantilist restraints, allowing plantation owners in the borderlands to sell their sugar, cotton, and indigo in the United States. These new immigration and economic policies facilitated later U.S. acquisition of the Floridas and Louisiana. Jefferson said prophetically, in 1791, that Spain had provided "the means of delivering to us peaceably, what may otherwise cost us a war."

Farther west, in New Mexico, the Spanish finally achieved peace with the Comanches and Apaches. Abandoning the attempt to make them subjects of the Crown, Spain signed a treaty recognizing their sovereignty. The Indians had forced the Spanish to set aside the goal of complete domination and to provide such gifts as guns, ammunition, clothing, mirrors, paint, tobacco, and sugar. Still, the Spanish sent prisoners of war to Cuba as forced laborers and settled other Apaches on reservations called *establecimientos de paz,* or peace establishments. Many Apaches refused to live on the reservations, however, steadfastly maintaining their independence. But the fighting stopped, making Texas, New Mexico, and Arizona safer for travel and economic development. Finally, settlers could journey directly between San Antonio, Santa Fe, and Tucson without fear of attack.

For several decades, fearing Russian and British incursions along the Pacific coast, Spain had expanded settlement in California. The government sent missionaries and soldiers north from Baja California in 1769 to set up missions and presidios along the coast from San Diego to San Francisco. José de Gálvez organized the effort, enlisting Junípero Serra, a zealous Franciscan priest, to establish the missions. Though fewer than 1,000 Hispanics lived in California by 1790, the missions controlled most of the arable land along the Pacific. With military force and by conversion, they put thousands of California Indians to work on mission lands. Before Spanish colonization, the region's native people possessed neither firearms nor horses; they lived in small villages with neither elaborate political structures nor much experience with war. In the earliest years after Spanish settlement, the natives lacked unity to avenge the crimes of Spanish soldiers or to refuse to serve as agricultural laborers. In 1775, however, one group burned the San Diego mission, followed by rebellions of other coastal Indians.

As elsewhere in North America, the California Indians declined sharply in population after contact with Europeans. People who went to work in the missions lived an average of ten to twelve years; their high death rate probably resulted from close quarters and exposure to disease. According to one missionary, "they live well free but as soon as we reduce them to a Christian and community life . . . they fatten, sicken, and die." The native population in the mission region along the Pacific coast declined from approximately 60,000 in 1769 to 35,000 at the end of the century.

The Spanish also looked to the Pacific Northwest, which they investigated in 1774, four years earlier than the British explorer Captain James Cook. After Cook publicized the trade for sea otter furs, however, British and American merchants sailed to Nootka Sound, at Vancouver Island, challenging the Spanish claim to the area north of San Francisco. The traders made huge profits by purchasing the silky black otter pelts from the Tlingit, Haida, Nootka, and Chinook peoples, to sell in China for tea, porcelain, and silk. The Indians had formerly hunted the sea otter on a limited basis for fine clothing and food. When the Spanish seized two British ships, England threatened war. Spain signed the Nootka Convention (1790), yielding its sole claim to the Pacific Northwest and returning the confiscated vessels. Over the next several years, the two countries tried but failed to negotiate a northern boundary of California. Of more concern to Spain, Great Britain, and the United States during the 1790s was the outbreak of war in Europe and the Atlantic, in the wake of revolution in France.

Foreign Entanglements

In 1789, the United States rejoiced when the French abolished noble privileges and formed a constitutional monarchy. Americans believed that France had followed their example, for during the first phase of the French Revolution, its moderate leaders included friends of the United States, notably the Revolutionary War hero, the Marquis de Lafayette. In 1792, however, radicals took control and executed King Louis XVI the next year. The international situation became perilous when the French Republic declared war on Britain and Spain. The king's execution and thousands of deaths by guillotine during the second phase of the revolution cost the French support in the United States, particularly among Federalists, who feared the consequences of ordinary people, "the mob," taking power. Republicans, while not defending the excesses, remained sympathetic toward France because they hated monarchical Britain more.

Neutrality

The European war presented Americans with a tricky situation, for they had connections with both France and Britain that were potentially dangerous. The U.S.-France commercial and military alliance of 1778 remained in force. While it did not require the United States to enter the war, the French Republic expected favorable trade policies and informal military assistance. Though Secretary of State Jefferson favored France and despised Britain, he agreed that neutrality was essential. American commerce was closely tied with Britain, whose navy could sweep U.S. ships from the sea. Hamilton was particularly concerned that British imports remain high because tariffs paid the lion's share of interest on the national debt. With all of this in mind, President Washington made the only reasonable decision, issuing his Proclamation of Neutrality in April 1793. The message warned citizens to avoid hostile acts against either side, including sale of weapons and privateering. Washington sought the belligerents' recognition of the U.S. right to trade in nonmilitary goods.

American neutrality quickly hit shoals with the activities of Edmond Genêt, the new minister from France. Citizen Genêt, as he was called in republican France, had arrived in Charleston several weeks before Washington proclaimed neutrality. He enlisted American mercenaries to man privateers and obtained ships to sail under the French flag against British shipping. The privateers, with largely American crews, seized British vessels, taking them to U.S. ports. There the French consuls sold the ships and their cargoes, paying the mercenaries with part of the proceeds. The French claimed this right under the 1778 alliance. The Washington administration, fearful of British reprisals and outraged by this violation of U.S. sovereignty, closed the ports to Genêt's privateers and requested his recall. The government prohibited foreign belligerents from arming vessels in U.S. ports and recruiting U.S. citizens in American territory; set the limit of U.S. territorial waters at three miles; and forbade foreign consuls from holding admiralty courts in U.S. cities to auction confiscated ships.

The Washington administration had greater success protecting the nation's sovereignty from French designs than from those of the British. The American republic's weakness became all too clear when the Royal Navy began impressing—recruiting by force—U.S. citizens from merchant ships. Then, in November 1793, the British ordered a total blockade of the French West Indies. Any ship intending to trade there would be confiscated. The blockade was timed to coincide with their invasion of St. Domingue, or Haiti, where enslaved blacks had risen up against their French masters in 1791. The British kept the blockade a secret until after U.S. ships headed for the Caribbean. Over the winter, their navy seized more than 250 American vessels, whether they were aimed for French, British, or neutral ports. The British impounded ships, cargoes, and even the sailors' possessions. Because international correspondence was so slow, Washington received no intelligence of the blockade and confiscations until March 1794.

The United States and Britain seemed headed for war. Exacerbating the crisis was the British refusal to vacate their forts and their aid to Native Americans in the Ohio country. Britain also helped Native Americans resist settlement in the west. In fact, in 1794 the governor of Canada, Lord Dorchester, told a group of Indians that they could expect war to break out between the United States and Britain within a year. With British victory, Dorchester promised, the Native Americans could reclaim the lands they had lost north of the Ohio River.

The Jay Treaty

The crisis abated when the British ended their total blockade of the French islands, now permitting Americans to trade foodstuffs and consumer goods but not war material. Rather than take retaliatory action, the president sent John Jay, chief justice of the Supreme Court, as special envoy to England. Jay's instructions were to convince the British to evacuate their forts in the west, pay for African American slaves who had left with their army after the Revolution, end impressment, open the British West Indies trade to American ships, and compensate recent shipping losses in the Caribbean.

Jay was unable to secure compensation for slaves, convince the British to stop impressment, or obtain recognition of all the neutral rights that Americans demanded. He did gain British withdrawal from the western forts by June 1, 1796, payment for confiscated ships in the Caribbean, and the opening of trade in the British West Indies to American vessels of 70 tons or less. He agreed, however, that American shippers would not export from the United States certain tropical products, including cotton, molasses, sugar, coffee, and cocoa, and that Americans would repay British creditors for pre-revolutionary debts.

Dramatizing the intense party rivalries of the 1790s, this pro-Federalist cartoon shows President Washington leading troops against French radicals, as Thomas Jefferson and Citizen Genêt try to hold him back. The dog graphically shows its disapproval of a Republican newspaper.

Washington received Jay's treaty in March 1795, keeping its contents secret until the Senate debate in June. Twenty Federalist senators voted to ratify while ten Republicans refused. The Federalists struck the provision forbidding U.S. merchants from exporting tropical crops. If they had agreed to this section, American trade would have faced a serious obstacle, particularly with the development of cotton. Thus, the Senate approved the treaty by exactly the two-thirds needed and sent it to the president, who signed the treaty as amended.

When the Jay Treaty became public, Republicans flew into a rage. Their opposition in large part was political: they abhorred *any* treaty with the British and privately bemoaned Jay's success on important issues. Publicly, they complained about his failures on impressment, neutral rights, and compensation for slaves. The Jay Treaty greatly hastened the growth of political parties, as Republicans gained support from former Federalists, particularly in the south. While Hamilton defended the treaty, opponents roared that it surrendered American independence to the former imperial tyrant. John Jay was burned in effigy; mass meetings, petitions, and demonstrations protested the treaty throughout the country.

By spring 1796, however, the tumult was over, in part because news arrived that Thomas Pinckney had concluded an agreement with Spain the previous October. The Treaty of San Lorenzo opened the Mississippi River to free navigation, allowed Americans to use the port of New Orleans without charge, and fixed the boundary between the United States and West Florida at the 31st parallel as specified in the Treaty of Paris.

Washington Retires

With the threat of war temporarily eased, the west open for settlement and trade, and a flourishing economy, the success of the republic seemed more certain. General Wayne's defeat of the Ohio Indians, the Jay Treaty, and Pinckney's diplomatic success gave westerners—and westward-looking Americans—resolution of their major problems: cession of lands in Ohio, removal of the British from the forts, free access to the Mississippi, and the right of deposit at New Orleans. Eastern merchants and farmers benefited from the lifting of trade restrictions in the British West Indies. Wartime demand for provisions in Europe and the Caribbean drove up farm prices and stimulated production. By the end of the century, American exports and shipping profits were almost five times their 1793 level. As a major neutral maritime nation, the United States assumed a greater place in world trade. With increased transportation profits, merchants invested more heavily in ships. The shipbuilding boom created demand for lumber, rope, and other supplies; wages for craftsmen and laborers rose, though so did the cost of living. Americans took advantage of their newfound prosperity to buy British imports, which in turn paid tariff income toward the national debt. Hamilton's funding plan was a success—the nation's credit was firm—despite resistance to the whiskey tax.

As the election of 1796 approached, George Washington announced his retirement, raising the question of his successor. The president had served two terms, his health had declined, and the battle over the Jay Treaty left him exhausted and angry. In his Farewell Address, Washington surveyed the accomplishments of his administration and gave the nation advice. The United States should avoid as much as possible becoming entwined in international affairs, he counseled. The European war demonstrated how perilous such involvement could be and how difficult it was to escape. "The great rule of conduct for us in regard to foreign nations is, in extending our commercial relations to have with them as little *political* connection as possible," Washington urged. His other major argument concerned factions. The outgoing president warned against parties based on sectional differences—North against South or East against West. And he cautioned against parties more generally, that the "disorders and miseries which result [from factionalism] gradually incline the minds of men to seek security and repose in the absolute power of an individual." In lamenting "the spirit of party," Washington blamed the Republicans for failing to support his administration. They had undercut his authority and the ideal of a consensual republic.

The Adams Presidency

Though Washington's successors appreciated the wisdom of his "great rule" of foreign policy, they had less enthusiasm for his advice on factions. In 1796, the parties yet lacked full-scale national organization, and candidates did not campaign. But the contest was very much alive, as Federalists supported the policies of Hamilton and Washington, while Republicans opposed them.

Election of 1796

In the third presidential election under the Constitution, both parties had sufficient cohesion to offer national tickets: the Federalist candidates were John Adams for president and Thomas Pinckney for vice president; the Republicans put up Thomas Jefferson for president and Aaron Burr, a senator from New York, for the second spot. The results of the electoral college vote were close: Adams 71, Jefferson 68, Pinckney 59, Burr 30, and a number of other candidates totalling 48. As specified by the Constitution, Adams became president and Jefferson, vice president. Americans quickly realized the problem of this procedure for electing the executive, as the president represented one party and the vice president the other. In any event, the Federalists kept control of the presidency, though barely, and they increased their votes in Congress by a small margin, to 64 Federalists versus 53 Republicans.

For many Americans, John Adams possessed credentials from service in the Revolution and the new republic that made him a worthy heir to Washington. He had contributed to prerevolutionary agitation in Boston, served as a delegate to the Continental Congress, promoted the Continental navy, and assisted Jefferson in drafting the Declaration of Independence. He had helped negotiate the 1783 Treaty of Paris, and in 1785, became the first U.S. minister to Great Britain. While Adams was a skilled diplomat, an avid student of government, and entirely honest, he lacked Washington's charisma, military bearing, and understanding of executive leadership. As a lawyer, Adams's style was more intellectual and independent. He preferred to make decisions on his own, without consulting the cabinet or congressional leaders.

Like Washington, Adams denounced parties. He began his administration with the hope, soon abandoned, that he might bridge the gulf between Federalists and Repub-

John Adams

Independence National Historical Park

Elected the second president of the United States in 1796, Adams was the sole non-Virginian and the only president to serve a single term among the first five chief executives. He was also the only president whose son (John Quincy Adams) served in the nation's highest elected office until George W. Bush (son of George H. Bush) became president in 2001.

Both the presidential elections of 1796 and 1800 between John Adams and Thomas Jefferson were close. While each had contributed mightily to gaining independence from Great Britain and establishing the new nation, neither served as the symbol of national unity as had George Washington in 1789. Party spirit had grown during the 1790s, undermining even Washington's position. Differences between Adams and Jefferson became public in 1791, despite their earlier long-term collaboration. After both men had served as president, they renewed their correspondence and friendship. They died on the same day, July 4, 1826, the fiftieth anniversary of independence.

licans. Jefferson rebuffed the chief executive's peace overture and directed the Republican opposition from his post as vice president. After the first few days of the Adams administration, the president and vice president never consulted one another.

"Quasi-War" with France

The second president inherited an international situation that had worsened by the time he assumed office in March 1797. The French, now ruled by a dictatorial executive board called the Directory, declared that the Jay Treaty revoked the 1778 alliance. They confiscated American merchant ships and cut off diplomatic relations. Once again, the United States seemed destined for war.

Called by Adams into special session in May 1797, Congress authorized the mobilization of 80,000 militia, completion of three war vessels, and fortification of harbors. Adams also appointed a commission of three men to negotiate with France: John Marshall of Virginia, Elbridge Gerry of Massachusetts, and Charles Cotesworth Pinckney of South Carolina. Their assignment was to prevent war, stop the confiscation of American ships carrying nonmilitary cargoes, and obtain compensation for recent losses. In France, the commission corresponded with French Foreign Minister Talleyrand through three intermediaries, who later became known to the American public as X, Y, and Z. The French agents told the commissioners that, like other petitioners to the Directory, they must pay a bribe even to be heard. The amount specified in this case was $250,000. The Directory also required an apology from Adams for criticizing France, a huge loan, and assumption by the U.S. government of any unpaid debts owed by France to American citizens. The commission refused these conditions and returned home. Their experience became known as the XYZ Affair.

In spring 1798, Adams received delayed correspondence that his envoys had been rebuffed. When he called for additional troops and warships, Congress responded by giving him more than he requested. Jefferson denounced the military buildup as "insane"; Republicans demanded to see evidence of France's treachery. When Adams made the commission's dispatches public, war fever engulfed the nation. The cry in the 1798 congressional elections became, "Millions for defense, but not a cent for tribute." Two patriotic

Preparation for War to Defend Commerce (1800), illustrating construction of the frigate *Philadelphia*. During the 1790s the United States tried to remain neutral in the European wars while prospering from international trade.

songs "Adams for Liberty" and "Hail Columbia" were widely sung, the latter serving as the unofficial national anthem. Congress expanded the regular army and war fleet, established the Department of the Navy, authorized naval vessels to protect American merchant ships, suspended commerce with France, and revoked the French alliance. George Washington assumed command of the army, with Alexander Hamilton in charge of field operations. To pay for all of this, Congress levied a direct tax of $2 million on dwelling houses, land, and slaves.

Without declaring war, the United States engaged France in hostilities from 1798 to 1800. In what was known as the Quasi-War, the U.S. Navy dominated the French, defeating their warships and sinking privateers. The British navy helped by protecting U.S. carriers. While some congressmen feared a French invasion and thereby justified further military preparations, French naval losses to Great Britain and the United States quickly removed that threat.

The Alien and Sedition Acts

The Federalists rode the crest of patriotism in 1798, using their majority in Congress to pass a series of acts that limited the rights of immigrants and critics of the administration. Congressional sponsors argued that the laws were necessary wartime measures. Their practical purpose, however, was to destroy the Republicans by undermining popular support and closing newspapers. The Federalists tried to take advantage of the Quasi-War to link their opponents with the enemy. This strategy worked in the short term, as the pro-French Republicans lost votes in the 1798 congressional election, but proved suicidal for Adams's party after the fear of invasion had passed.

The Federalist design resulted in four restrictive laws. The Naturalization Act of 1798 lengthened the period of residence needed for citizenship from five to fourteen years. The legislation was intended to stop the flow of Irish immigrants who, because they were anti-British and pro-French, swelled the number of Republican voters. The Alien Enemies Act established procedures in the event of declared war or invasion for jailing and deporting citizens of the enemy nation who were considered likely to spy or commit sabotage. The Alien Act, which had a term of two years, allowed the president to deport any non–U.S. citizens "he shall judge dangerous to the peace and safety of the United States, or shall have reasonable grounds to suspect are concerned in any treasonable or secret machinations against the government thereof." Like the Naturalization Act, this law potentially threatened Irish immigrants, but Adams refrained from using it.

The Federalists did enforce the fourth law, the Sedition Act, with serious results. Its term lasted until March 3, 1801, the day before the next president would be inaugurated. Thus the Federalists ensured that if the next chief executive were a Republican, he would not be able to retaliate without obtaining a new statute. In vague language, the Sedition Act made it illegal for "any persons [to] unlawfully combine or conspire together, with intent to oppose any measure or measures of the government of the United States" or to interfere with the execution of a law. Nor could a person "write, print, utter or publish . . .

any false, scandalous and malicious writing or writings against the government of the United States, or either house of the Congress . . . or the President." In effect, this law permitted imprisonment and fines for criticizing the government. It was an obvious infringement upon freedom of speech and freedom of the press.

Nevertheless, the administration enforced the law. Adams believed that the Sedition Act was constitutional, that people who censured his policies threatened the future of the republic. The prime targets for prosecution were Republican newspapers, including the Philadelphia *Aurora,* edited by Benjamin Franklin's grandson, Benjamin Bache, who was one of Adams's most powerful critics. The official authorized to administer the act was Secretary of State Timothy Pickering, a staunch Federalist, who methodically reviewed the Republican papers for actionable offenses. He even ordered an inquiry into the private correspondence of a Republican congressman who reputedly called Adams a traitor; in this case, however, the investigation was dropped. Under the law, the Federalists indicted and tried at least seventeen people for sedition. They timed cases to reach court in the fall of 1799 or the following spring, with the goal of silencing the Republican press during the 1800 election. Some papers folded and others closed temporarily while their editors were imprisoned. All but one of the cases were prosecuted in New England and the Middle Atlantic states, where the Federalists controlled the courts and could pack juries.

The Republican Opposition Grows

Passage of the Alien and Sedition Acts and the jailing of Republican spokesmen shifted the political winds. In late 1798, the Kentucky and Virginia legislatures approved resolutions that protested the Alien and Sedition Acts on the grounds that they were unconstitutional. The Kentucky and Virginia Resolutions, drafted anonymously by Thomas Jefferson and James Madison, respectively, argued that these laws violated the First Amendment and granted powers to the national government not delegated by the Constitution. The Virginia assembly resolved that "in case of a deliberate, palpable, and dangerous exercise of other powers, not granted by the [Constitution], the states . . . have the right, and are in duty bound, to interpose, for arresting the progress of the evil." Virginia and Kentucky sent their resolutions to other legislatures, none of which agreed that states could declare a federal law unconstitutional. Rhode Island, for example, responded that the federal courts held the power to determine constitutionality; "that for any state legislature to assume that authority would be . . . Hazarding an interruption of the peace of the states by civil discord, in case of a diversity of opinions among the state legislatures." Nevertheless, the resolutions contributed toward a theory of "nullification," the idea that a state had the right to veto a federal law it considered unconstitutional. This theory was based upon the strict interpretation of the Constitution that denied, as in the controversy over the national bank, implied powers to the central government.

With the Alien and Sedition Acts, the Federalists made a strategic error. Where formerly the Republicans could be branded as a faction creating animosity and disunity, they now became legitimate defenders of revolutionary principles. The Republican party justified its opposition by warning that the Federalists were on the road to tyranny. The Sedition Act, the Virginia Resolutions argued, impeded free investigation of the actions of government officials and "free communication among the people thereon, which has ever been justly deemed the only effectual guardian of every other right."

The administration fanned the flames of indignation with its heavy-handed reaction to a tax rebellion among German Americans in eastern Pennsylvania, a group who had previously favored the Federalists or stayed out of politics entirely. The Republicans took advantage of the rural Pennsylvanians' aversion to the 1798 federal property tax to win their votes in the congressional election. They circulated petitions against the tax, the defense buildup, and the Alien and Sedition laws, petitions that Congress ignored. By early 1799, the people of Northampton and Bucks counties held public meetings and stopped tax assessors from doing their work. In March, after the U.S. marshal jailed eighteen suspected tax resisters in Bethlehem's Sun Tavern, John Fries, a fifty-year-old auctioneer of upper Bucks County, led a band of 140 armed men to release the prisoners.

The Fries Rebellion ended quickly, as the rebels considered the magnitude of their offense. Fries announced that he would pay the tax and would even welcome the assessor to his house for dinner. Nevertheless, the president decided to make an example of the episode. He dispatched troops that failed to march until almost four weeks after the resistance had ceased. The army descended upon the countryside, entering houses and arresting sixty men. One army officer wrote "that every hour's experience confirms me more and more that this expedition was not only unnecessary, but violently absurd." Contrary to the Judiciary Act of 1789, the prisoners were taken to Philadelphia for trial. Fries and two others were found guilty of treason by a Federalist court and sentenced to hang, but were subsequently pardoned by the president. The Republicans added the administration's unwarranted use of force to their arsenal of charges against the Federalists.

Conclusion

George Washington had warned in his Farewell Address that "the spirit of Party . . . agitates the Community with ill founded jealousies and false alarms, kindles the animosity of one part against another, foments occasionally riot and insurrection. It opens the door to foreign influence and corruption. . . ." He invoked the ideal of consensual community, challenging his fellow citizens to work together for the good of their country. The flaw of this conception was that Americans could not agree on which policies were best for everyone. The interests of farmers, merchants, and artisans, of residents of the north, south, and west, often diverged. The Federalist and Republican parties grew out of different visions of the nation's future. During the 1790s, the Federalists retained control of the central government, confident that their vision was correct. They denounced parties, identifying their government with the republic as a whole. When they tried to eliminate factions by silencing their adversaries with the Sedition Act, ironically they legitimized the party system in the eyes of many Americans.

RECOMMENDED READINGS

Anderson, Margo J. *The American Census: A Social History* (1988). A very good source on the first federal census of 1790.

Cayton, Andrew R. L., and Teute, Fredrika J., eds. *Contact Points: American Frontiers from the Mohawk Valley to the Mississippi, 1750–1830* (1998). Essays about Indian-white relations in the backcountry from the prerevolutionary period through the early republic.

Cochran, Thomas C. *Frontiers of Change: Early Industrialism in America* (1981). A good introduction to industrialization in the early republic.

Elkins, Stanley, and McKitrick, Eric. *The Age of Federalism* (1993). Detailed narrative of the Washington and Adams administrations.

McCullough, David. *John Adams* (2001). An excellent biography of the second president.

McGaw, Judith A., ed. *Early American Technology: Making and Doing Things from the Colonial Era to 1850* (1994). Original essays on technology from agriculture to turnpikes.

North, Douglass C. *The Economic Growth of the United States 1790–1860* (1966). Includes a useful analysis of U.S. trade amid international conflict.

Onuf, Peter S., ed. *Jeffersonian Legacies* (1993). Wide ranging essays on Thomas Jefferson's character and politics.

Slaughter, Thomas P. *The Whiskey Rebellion: Frontier Epilogue to the American Revolution* (1986). An excellent book on the struggle between Alexander Hamilton and western Pennsylvania farmers over excise taxes.

White, Richard. *The Middle Ground: Indians, Empires, and Republics in the Great Lakes Region, 1650–1815* (1991). Influential study of Indian-white relations from New France through the War of 1812.

Additional resources, exercises, and Internet links related to this chapter are available on the American Passages Web site: http://history.wadsworth.com/ayerscompact2/

8

The New Republic Faces a New Century
1800–1815

Americans confronted the nineteenth century with a variety of fears. For the Federalists, the growing Republican opposition warned that the evils of democracy and anarchy stood ready to take control. For the Republicans, the Alien and Sedition Acts and Federalist repression of the whiskey rebels and John Fries underscored the need for change. Both parties, still members of the revolutionary generation, thought in terms of the ideals for which they had fought against the British. They also measured events against what was transpiring elsewhere in the world. By 1800, the French Revolution and Napoleon Bonaparte's rise to power dismayed Americans. The never-ending European war threatened to involve the United States for twenty years, and finally did in 1812. The revolt by slaves in the French West Indies horrified southern slave owners.

Though Thomas Jefferson's presidency proved to be less revolutionary than many Federalists expected, the new century brought indelible changes to American politics and society. The Federalist party shriveled and died, the Louisiana Purchase expanded the nation's territory to the Rocky Mountains and beyond, slavery became more firmly embedded in the southern economy, and the republic fought once more against Great Britain. The Second Great Awakening, the series of religious revivals that began in the late 1790s and gained steam after the turn of the century, influenced the ways in which many people interpreted these events.

Religion in American Society

During the first decade of the nineteenth century, religion absorbed the energies of many different groups: frontier settlers and Native Americans caught up in revivals, organizations to provide welfare relief in towns and cities, new sects like the Shakers, and free African Americans who built separate churches as the cornerstone of their communities. Many people believed that renewed emphasis on religion would transform the nation through individual faith and communal action.

The Second Great Awakening

As the century began, people throughout the country sought spiritual renewal. Among New England Congregationalists, the revivals spread from one town to another between 1797 and 1801. The national Methodist conference of 1800 held in Baltimore witnessed

CHRONOLOGY

1800	Washington, D.C., becomes national capital • Gabriel's rebellion • Convention of 1800 with France • Jefferson's election as president • Rise of Handsome Lake as a Seneca prophet
1801	Adams's "midnight appointments" • John Marshall becomes chief justice • Tripolitan War • Cane Ridge, Kentucky, camp meeting
1802	Judiciary Act of 1801 repealed
1803	*Marbury v. Madison* case • Great Britain and France resume war • Louisiana Purchase
1804	Lewis and Clark expedition departs from St. Louis • Aaron Burr kills Alexander Hamilton • Twelfth Amendment ratified • Haiti founded • Reelection of Jefferson as president
1805	*Essex* decision in Britain
1806	Non-Importation Act
1807	Burr tried for treason • *Leopard-Chesapeake* affair • Embargo Act
1808	Federal ban on importation of slaves • Madison elected as president
1809–1811	Tecumseh organizes pan-Indian resistance to land cessions
1809	Giles's Enforcement Act • Embargo repealed; replaced with Non-Intercourse Act • Treaty of Fort Wayne
1810	Annexation of West Florida
1811	Charter of national bank expires • Battle of Tippecanoe
1812	U.S. declares war on Great Britain • Hull surrenders Detroit • Madison elected to second term
1813	Perry defeats British navy on Lake Erie • Battle of the Thames
1814	Battle of Horseshoe Bend • British burn public buildings in Washington, D.C. • Americans repel invasion on Lake Champlain • Hartford Convention • Treaty of Ghent

an outpouring of religious fervor. These flames heralded a series of revivals—the Second Great Awakening—which lasted into the 1830s. In accepting the message of revival, large numbers of Americans embraced evangelicalism—the belief that they must take their message of salvation to others. They expected to create a more godly nation through conversion and good works.

In particular, eastern clergy worried that people on the frontier, with few churches, would let sin take control of their lives. As Americans streamed west across the Appalachians, by 1810, Ohio had 230,000 settlers, Kentucky and Tennessee had 668,000, and the Mississippi and Louisiana territories had 117,000. Evangelical ministers feared for the nation because so many westerners were unchurched. The clerics expressed their dread in terms of millennialism, the belief that the millennium—Christ's second coming—was at hand, as foretold in Revelation, the last book of the Bible. Pastors urged their congregations to prepare for the millennium by supporting missionary efforts in the West. They believed that Americans throughout the country must embrace Christianity and convert Native Americans and the people of other lands.

Circuit preachers and missionaries traveled throughout the frontier; the churches they started were often the first social organizations in new communities. The great western revivals of 1800–1815, which built upon this work, began when several Presbyterians summoned the first camp meeting, a religious gathering held outside over the course of several days. People came together, miles from their homes, to hear revivalist preachers. The most famous of the early camp meetings took place in August 1801, at Cane Ridge, Kentucky, where Presbyterian, Methodist, and Baptist clergy preached for about a week to a throng numbering about 20,000. From wagons and crude tents, the crowds listened to the spiritual message that Jesus Christ could save all people from their sins. People reacted emotionally and physically to this message, some jerking their heads or entire bodies, others falling to the ground in a faint.

Reminiscent of the Great Awakening in the South during the 1750s and 1760s, the camp meetings spread through Kentucky, Tennessee, and southern Ohio, gathering new congregations. The Methodist and Baptist churches, which placed less importance on the

Collection of the New York Historical Society

Methodist Camp Meeting, engraving by E. Clay. During the Second Great Awakening, itinerant preachers held outdoor revivals that often lasted for several days.

fine points of religious doctrine and a well-educated clergy than did the Presbyterians, benefited most from the revivals. The Methodists and Baptists saw extraordinary growth among ordinary people. As one minister wrote, "the illiterate Methodist preachers actually set the world on fire, (the American world at least) while [pastors of other denominations] were lighting their matches!"

Religion was important to black Americans, whether they remained enslaved or had achieved freedom. In the South, African Americans responded enthusiastically to revivalist preachers. The Methodists and Baptists welcomed free and enslaved blacks into their congregations as equals in spirit though not in governing the church. In hostile northern cities, free black communities depended upon separate churches for leadership and communal fellowship.

Growth of Sects

The period around 1800 witnessed the expansion of several dissenting sects: the Shakers, the Society of the Public Universal Friend, and the Universalists. They are called sects, rather than denominations, because they were new and fairly small. They held distinctive beliefs that set them apart from mainstream religions, yet had a significant influence on intellectual and social movements of their times.

The Shakers, whose official name was the United Society of Believers in Christ's Second Coming (the Millennial church), came to America in 1774, when Mother Ann Lee arrived from Britain with eight disciples. They left England to escape mob attacks and imprisonment. The group grew slowly at first, but expanded after Lee's death in 1784, as they reaped followers from revivals, especially Baptists. The sect offered an avenue for people who had been spiritually reborn in the Awakening and sought a distinctive way to represent that rebirth in their lives.

From visions, Mother Lee believed that she embodied Christ's Second Coming, that the millennium had already arrived. As Christ had appeared as a man, and Lee (called Mother of the New Creation) came as a woman, God had both male and female elements. The Shakers believed in salvation by confession of sin, equality regardless of sex or race, opposition to slavery and war, and assistance to the poor. They abstained from sexual relations. In Shaker communities, which by 1809 existed from Maine to Kentucky, men and women ate, slept, and worked separately. They followed a strict discipline and aspired to economic self-sufficiency. Shakers sat on straight-backed chairs, cut their food into square pieces, and walked along paths laid out in right angles. But in religious worship, they abandoned this right-angle order. In a large open space without pulpit or pews, worshippers danced, shouted, and sang. The Shakers influenced other groups to organize communal, utopian experiments during the years after 1815.

A similar but smaller sect was the Society of the Public Universal Friend, founded by Jemima Wilkinson of Rhode Island. Disowned by Quakers in 1776 for joining the Baptists, Wilkinson became ill, believed that she died, and then returned to life as the Public Universal Friend. Her mission was to convince others to repent their sins and prepare for the millennium. Like Mother Lee, Wilkinson preached celibacy, peace, and opposition to slavery. She traveled sidesaddle on horseback, attracting a coterie of believers in New England and Pennsylvania. As one convert said, Wilkinson was "the Messenger of Peace . . . Travelling far & wide to spread the glad tidings & news of Salvation to a lost and perishing & dying World who have all gone astray like Lost Sheep." In 1788, upon gathering over 200 Universal Friends, she organized a community called Jerusalem in western New York. The Universal Friends neither organized a communal economy like the Shakers nor continued to seek new members. Nevertheless, the community survived well past Wilkinson's death in 1819.

Another sect, the Universalists, rejected the Calvinist belief that only a minority of people, the elect, could attain salvation. They preached that "it is the purpose of God, through the grace revealed in our Lord Jesus Christ, to save every member of the human race from sin." The American Universalist Church, established in 1779 by an Englishman, John Murray, found a sympathetic audience among ordinary people caught up in the Second Great Awakening in New England and on the frontier. Its message of universal salvation had wide influence, though the Universalist Church itself remained small.

Revivalism among Native Americans

While the Second Great Awakening and dissenting sects claimed the imagination and souls of white and black Americans, a new wave of revivals drew together Native Americans. Among the Iroquois living on reservations in western New York and the Shawnees, Creeks, Cherokees, and other nations retaining lands in the trans-Appalachian region, prophets warned of imminent doom unless people changed their ways. Native Americans had continued to lose lands to whites throughout the area from the Appalachians to the Mississippi; by 1812, settlers in the region dwarfed the Indian population by seven to one. Decline in the numbers of fur-bearing animals caused economic hardship, while conflict over whether to cooperate with the United States created political factions within tribes.

Like the Delaware prophet Neolin in the 1760s, the new nativists blamed loss of land and power on the Indians' failure to maintain traditional rituals and on their adoption of wicked practices from the whites. Among many prophets, Handsome Lake of the Senecas (a nation of the Iroquois) and Tenskwatawa of the Shawnees wielded the greatest influence in the first decade of the nineteenth century.

Handsome Lake, a respected warrior and leader of the Allegany Senecas, fell ill in 1799, seemed to die, then came back to life saying that he had a vision in which messengers told him to become a prophet. In a series of revelations over several years, Handsome Lake received a message of impending catastrophe and a means to salvation. He told his people to stop drinking alcohol and practicing witchcraft; instead they should perform their ancestral rituals. The prophet also advocated peace. He embraced the U.S. acculturation policy by which Quakers tried to convince the Iroquois to adopt white farming methods and gender roles, but he opposed further large-scale land cessions, the whiskey trade, social dancing in couples, and gambling with cards. Other Indians opposed acculturation, which required

Tenskwatawa, the Shawnee Prophet

With his brother Tecumseh, Tenskwatawa organized pan-Indian resistance to white settlement in the Great Lakes region. He was one of a series of nativist prophets, including the Delaware Neolin and Seneca Handsome Lake, who challenged their followers to reject alcohol and Euro-American customs. The Shawnee Prophet and Tecumseh opposed accommodationist leaders who sold Indian land and, during the War of 1812, the brothers unsuccessfully allied with Great Britain against the United States.

National Art Gallery, 1985.66. 279. Smithsonian Institution

George Catlin painted this portrait of Tenskwatawa in 1830, nineteen years after the Battle of Tippecanoe. It is one of many paintings produced by Catlin and other artists in the 1830s of individual Native American leaders and scenes demonstrating Indian customs, such as dances and the hunt. Unlike many Indians of the time, the prophet is wearing skins rather than a cloak. He has silver earrings, armbands, and a gorget at his throat, but not a peace medal indicating alliance with the U.S. or British government. In contrast, the drawing of Tecumseh later in this chapter shows the Shawnee leader wearing a military coat and British peace medal.

women to leave the fields and take up spinning, and men to farm rather than hunt. They viewed the policy, accurately, as a way to justify further expropriation of hunting lands.

Handsome Lake served as a political leader of the Iroquois only briefly, from 1801 to 1803, but his spiritual message remained strong in the years that followed. Most influential was his drive against liquor. A former heavy drinker himself, the Seneca prophet advised, in the words of a white observer, that "the Whiskey is the great Engine which the bad Spirit uses to introduce Witchcraft and many other evils amongst Indians." Many Iroquois abstained from hard drink. One Quaker visitor "noted with satisfaction that in the course of our travels among all the Indians on the Allegheny River . . . we have not seen a Single individual the least intoxicated with Liquor—which perhaps would be a Singular Circumstance to Observe in traveling among the same number of white Inhabitants."

Also influential was Tenskwatawa, called the Shawnee Prophet, who became prominent among the people of the Great Lakes and Ohio Valley. With his brother, Tecumseh, he inspired a nativist movement to resist the U.S. government's acculturation policy and land grabbing. To avoid fiery destruction, he warned, Indians must revitalize their traditional ceremonies, avoid liquor, and reject the new gender roles. One of the prophet's visions promised that the whites would be destroyed if his people obeyed these instructions.

African Americans

As slavery ended in the North, blacks faced discriminatory practices that kept the racial caste system in place, including segregation in churches and schools, and restriction from politics and many occupations. Despite this racism, northern blacks created new lives, institutions, and communities that offered a potent draw to African Americans in the South. Southern blacks also considered more violent means to end bondage, as in the case of Gabriel's revolt in Virginia.

Free Blacks in the North

By 1800, Pennsylvania, New York, and all of New England had passed gradual abolition acts or ended slavery outright. New Jersey in 1804 became the last northern state to pass a law for gradual emancipation, which, like those of other states, freed children henceforth born to slave mothers, but retained slaves born before that date in perpetual bondage. The black children who benefited from the law would be required to serve their mother's owner, much like indentured servants, until a certain age—in New Jersey, twenty-five for males and twenty-one for females.

Despite the gradual nature of these emancipation laws, slavery declined rapidly in the northern states. Responding to their slaves' requests for freedom and to the spirit of the abolition acts, owners freed people whom the laws left in bonds. Masters usually required some additional years of service for the promise of freedom. Frequently, blacks negotiated agreements for themselves or family members. In 1805, a New York slave, Margaret, obtained her owner's pledge of freedom in eight years if she behaved "as she always has done in an

Table 8.1 Number of Enslaved African Americans, 1800 and 1810

	1800	1810
New England	1,339	418
New York	20,903	15,017
New Jersey	12,422	10,851
Pennsylvania	1,706	795
Delaware	6,153	4,177
Maryland & District of Columbia	107,707	115,056
Virginia	346,968	394,357
North Carolina	133,296	168,824
South Carolina	146,151	196,365
Georgia	59,406	105,218
Kentucky	40,343	80,561
Tennessee	13,584	44,535
Mississippi Territory	3,489	17,088

Table 8.2 Free Black Population in Northern Cities

	1790	1800	1810
Philadelphia	1,849	6,028	8,942
New York City	1,036	3,333	7,470
Boston	766	1,174	1,484

orderly manner as a servant ought to do." A New Jersey man promised to pay his owner $50 per year for four years in return for his release. When masters proved recalcitrant, blacks often forced the issue by running away.

The northern cities became magnets for escaped slaves. In addition, humanitarian concerns touched some southern masters, including George Washington, who freed his slaves in his will. Some owners in Delaware and the Chesapeake region, who held more slaves than they needed, emancipated their slaves, then sold them as indentured servants in the North. Between 1790 and 1810, the free black population of Philadelphia and New York City soared, while that of Boston also grew, though more slowly.

Reverend Richard Allen, a former slave, was founder of the African Methodist Episcopal Church and a leader of the Philadelphia black community.

Moorland-Spingarn Research Center, Howard Universit

Philadelphia and New York City became centers of free African American culture, with churches fostering autonomous community growth. In Philadelphia, responding to hostility, freed men and women organized separate congregations in the 1780s and 1790s. Reverend Richard Allen, for example, led black worshippers from St. George's Methodist Episcopal Church when whites insisted on segregated seating. Allen described the scene as they were forced to move during prayer:

> We had not been long upon our knees before I heard considerable scuffling and loud talking. I raised my head up and saw one of the trustees, H_____ M_____, having hold of the Rev. Absalom Jones, pulling him off his knees, and saying, "You must get up, you must not kneel here." . . . we all went out of the church in a body, and they were no more plagued by us in the church.

Allen purchased a blacksmith's shop, converted it into a church, calling it Bethel. By 1803, the black Methodist church had 457 members, the result of revivals and Allen's fervent preaching. But while the evangelical message of Methodism appealed to African Americans, and "Mother" Bethel grew, the congregation found relations with the hierarchy of the white Methodist church difficult. In the early decades of the nineteenth century, black Methodists in Philadelphia, Baltimore, Wilmington, and New York struggled against white control, finally seceding to form separate denominations. In 1816, Philadelphia's Bethel became the first congregation of the African Methodist Episcopal church.

Urban black churches provided mutual aid, fellowship, and avenues for leadership. One benefit of belonging to a New York congregation became obvious to an eighty-year-old woman after a fire destroyed her home. When asked where she would find shelter, she answered, "O a sister in the church has promised to take me in." Shunned by white organizations, effectively barred from politics, and lacking equal opportunity for employment, African Americans created alternatives through the church.

Like white urban residents, freed men and women formed mutual benefit societies. The names African Americans chose for these organizations demonstrated pride in their African heritage. Philadelphians, for example, formed the Free African Society, Daughters of Ethiopia, Angola Society, Sons of Africa, and many others. The official purpose of these societies was to collect dues to provide relief to poor widows and children, but, just as important, the groups facilitated community involvement.

With little money or access to capital, few African Americans, perhaps one in ten, scraped together the funds to purchase a house, shop, or farm. In the first decades of the nineteenth century, many blacks were still completing terms of servitude, while others, though free, lived and worked in white households as domestic servants. Even if they established their own households, women generally washed clothes or performed domestic service for others. Most men were mariners or hired as common laborers. The African American community provided additional opportunity by employing its own. Residents supported black shoemakers, carpenters, food retailers, hucksters, barbers, hairdressers, seamstresses, tailors, cooks, bakers, schoolteachers, and ministers. In Philadelphia, a few African Americans achieved considerable wealth and fame. By 1807, James Forten employed thirty men—blacks and whites—to produce sails for the city's shipbuilders. Robert Bogle developed the idea of catering parties, weddings, and funerals, while Frank Johnson became the city's premier musician. He performed on trumpet and violin, composed dance music and songs, and organized a band that played at balls and public events.

Northern blacks faced daily challenges in their quest for economic success and equal status. But they revered their African roots. The word African in the name of most mutual aid societies and churches testified to their pride of origins, though many of the founders were two, three, even four generations removed from ancestral lands.

African Americans in northern cities also knew of recent struggles by slaves in St. Domingue and elsewhere; a large number of blacks in Philadelphia and New York City had come from the French island with their masters who fled the black revolt. During the 1790s, blacks on St. Domingue led by Toussaint L'Ouverture, a former slave, defeated local whites and the French, Spanish, and British armies. In 1802, Napoleon tried once again to take control of the island, but failed when disease decimated his forces. In 1804, the victorious rebels of St. Domingue established Haiti as an independent nation. Most white Americans dreaded the importation of black revolt. Thomas Jefferson opposed trade with the island, stating, "We may expect therefore black crews, and supercargoes and missionaries thence into the southern states. . . . If this combustion can be introduced among us under any veil whatever, we have to fear it."

Slave Rebellion in the South

With more than 850,000 enslaved blacks in the American South in 1800, one-third of the population, whites had reason to be concerned about slave insurgency. After St. Domingue erupted, Georgia and the Carolinas declared black emigrés from the West Indies a threat, prohibiting their entry. South Carolina, in reopening its international slave trade in 1803, made every effort to avoid admitting rebels. The state excluded blacks from the West Indies and South America, and any who had ever lived in the French West Indies. Every man imported from another state needed a certificate indicating that he had not "been concerned in any insurrection or rebellion."

In August 1800, the worst fears of white southerners were nearly realized when an enslaved blacksmith named Gabriel organized an armed march against the capital of Virginia. With about 600 supporters from Richmond and surrounding counties, Gabriel planned a full-scale insurrection. His strategy included seizing guns from an arsenal, taking Governor James Monroe hostage, and forcing concessions from town officials. Gabriel expected poor whites to join him because they, like slaves, lacked political power. The attack failed when a torrential rainstorm washed out bridges, making travel impossible. Efforts to try again another day collapsed when two informers passed word of the conspiracy to authorities who rounded up suspects. Though Gabriel eluded capture for more than three weeks, he was arrested and hanged, as were twenty-six others implicated in the plot.

White Americans still held the revolutionary belief that all men and women desired freedom. Masters took seriously the threat of slave revolt. After Gabriel's rebellion, Governor Monroe observed about enslaved African Americans, "Unhappily while this class of people exists among us we can never count with certainty on its tranquil submission." In 1802, Virginians discovered additional conspiracies, with rumors of more violence heightening tensions. In 1805, after four whites had been poisoned in North Carolina, officials burned a slave woman alive, hanged three other slaves, and whipped and cut off the ears of another. Gabriel's plot, the St. Domingue uprising, and what appeared to be an upsurge of murders and arson by blacks convinced southern lawmakers to enact more stringent slave codes. South Carolina and Georgia tightened requirements for slave patrols and defined as treason any collaboration in slave rebellion. Hardening attitudes toward slavery snuffed out southern antislavery societies that were already faltering. On a more positive note, as the twenty-year constitutional restriction on prohibiting the slave trade expired, Congress officially banned the importation of slaves after January 1, 1808.

Jefferson's Republic

In 1800, the federal government moved from the nation's cultural capital in Philadelphia to an unfinished village on the Potomac: Washington, D.C. The ruling party also changed, as voters voiced their dissatisfaction with the Federalists by electing Thomas Jefferson and a Republican Congress. Jefferson's promise of reduced government and taxes appealed to a pop-

Map 8.1 The Election of 1800
The election Thomas Jefferson called "the revolution of 1800" was close, with Jefferson receiving 73 votes to John Adams's 65. The Federalist ticket, headed by Adams and Charles Cotesworth Pinckney, obtained considerable support from the Carolinas and mid-Atlantic as well as New England.

ulace concerned about other things besides national politics—their finances, their souls, and local communities. Events prevented the young nation from wrapping itself in isolation, however, for its economic prosperity depended a great deal upon international commerce, a trade severely hampered by the ongoing European war.

The Election of 1800

Most recently, the United States had been involved in the Quasi-War with France, in which the French navy initially ravaged the American merchant fleet. Congress had expanded the army, authorized the U.S. Navy to protect commercial ships, and revoked unilaterally the American-French treaty of 1778. The Federalists swept the congressional elections of 1798 on the crest of anti-French fervor; they tried to use war fever against the Republicans through the Alien and Sedition acts. Instead, the backlash of concern about civil liberties swelled the opposition.

As the 1800 election approached, many Federalists expected to take advantage of the unresolved difficulties with France in continuing to paint the Jeffersonian Republicans as pro-French, hence un-American. Nevertheless, President John Adams moved to end hostilities. He nominated a three-man commission, including William Vans Murray (minister to the Netherlands), Chief Justice Oliver Ellsworth, and Governor William R. Davie of North Carolina, to make peace with France. The commission received instructions that proved impossible to fulfill: its mission was to obtain French agreement that the 1778 alliance had ended and indemnities for confiscated American ships. In March 1800, Murray, Ellsworth, and Davie met with Napoleon, who had no intention of paying compensation. The commissioners reached an accord only by ignoring their instructions. The Convention of 1800, signed in France in October and ratified reluctantly by the U.S. Senate in February 1801, echoed provisions of the 1778 commercial treaty in calling for "a firm, inviolable, and universal peace." The Convention voided the defensive alliance of 1778, however, thus eliminating the French claim to U.S. support against Great Britain. The pact also included a vague confirmation by the French of neutral rights in international trade, but provided no restitution to American shippers, a failing that opponents said made the convention worthless. In fact, it had value in normalizing relations between the two countries.

The chief beneficiary of reduced tensions with France was Thomas Jefferson, named in May 1800 as Republican nominee for president, with Aaron Burr of New York for vice president. John Adams received the Federalist nomination for reelection, with Charles Cotesworth Pinckney of South Carolina as his running mate. Many Federalists opposed Adams for making peace with France. When the electoral votes were tallied, Jefferson and Burr each received 73 votes, Adams had 65, Pinckney 64, and John Jay 1. In lining up votes in the electoral college, the Republicans had failed to take account of the constitutional election procedures that lacked provision for party slates. The Constitution directed that each elector cast two votes, with the candidate receiving the highest number elected president and the runner-up vice president. The electors had no way of designating which candidate they supported for president and which for vice president. The Federalists avoided the difficulty by having one elector vote for John Jay, thus giving Pinckney one less vote than Adams.

If Burr had simply yielded to Jefferson in 1800, the problem would have been resolved without complication. The tie sent the election to the House of Representatives, which had a Federalist majority. Each state delegation received one vote. Some of the Federalists hatched a plan to support Burr, thinking that they might be able to control him as president. Hamilton opposed the plot vigorously, contending "Burr loves nothing but himself; thinks of nothing but his own aggrandizement, and will be content with nothing, short of permanent power in his own hands." The former secretary of the treasury advised his party to make a deal with Jefferson to keep the system of public credit and the navy, retain Federalist appointees in office, and remain neutral in the war between Britain and France. The House of Representatives required thirty-six ballots over six days before the Federalist delegate from Delaware, James A. Bayard, shifted his position to break the tie.

Jefferson's "Revolution"

The third president assumed a conciliatory stance toward the Federalists as he took office. On March 4, 1801, Jefferson delivered his inaugural address to the new Congress, which the Republicans dominated in the House by 69 votes to 36, and in the Senate by an 18–13 majority. He gave the address almost in a whisper, for he was not a good public speaker. The speech reflected his Republican beliefs: emphasis on the power of state governments, freedom of religion and the press, majority rule but protection of minority rights, low government expenditures, and reduction of the federal debt. Jefferson upheld the Convention of 1800 with France implicitly by stating that he desired amity and trade with foreign nations and "entangling alliances with none." His most famous statement, "We are all republicans, we are all federalists," attempted to get beyond the partisan battles that had bedeviled his two predecessors. He later described his election as "the revolution of 1800" that "was as real a revolution in the principles of our government as that of 1776 was in its form; not effected indeed by the sword, as that, but by the rational and peaceable instrument of reform, the suffrage of the people." Despite bitter political enmity, American leaders had created a party system by which power could be contested in elections rather than through bloodshed. With the election of 1800, the Constitution passed a crucial test, with peaceful transfer of power from one party to its opponents.

The new president worked to put his principles into action, to create an agrarian republic in which the federal government kept its role to a minimum. The location in Washington, D.C., seemed the ideal setting for a weak government. In 1800, the town had fewer than 400 dwellings, which one government official described as mostly "small miserable huts." The Capitol was incomplete, with wings for the Senate and House but no center. What existed was poorly constructed: the acoustics were dreadful, the roof leaked, and the heating was "noxious." The president's house was not yet finished in 1814 when the British burned it. Construction materials littered the grounds during Jefferson's administration to the extent that, according to one guest, "in a dark night instead of finding your way to the house, you may, perchance, fall into a pit, or stumble over a heap of rubbish." Cows grazed on what later became the Mall; hogs ran through the city's streets.

Washington, D.C., remained a village in part because the federal government was small, and Jefferson had no interest in seeing it grow. In 1802, federal personnel throughout the country numbered under 10,000, of whom 6,500 served in military posts. Of the nonuniformed officials, fewer than 300 worked in the Capital. The president and Supreme Court each had one clerk, Congress employed thirteen, and the attorney general had none. The central government had relatively little to do, for state and local governments or voluntary associations took primary responsibility for keeping law and order, maintaining roads and bridges, supervising the militia, and providing welfare relief and schools.

Jefferson's lack of attention to building Washington, D.C., revealed his approach to the presidency. In contrast to Federalist efforts to reflect the grandeur of European courts and capitals, he adopted informality and frugality. Jefferson dealt with members of Congress and foreign diplomats personally, inviting small groups for dinner and conversation. He avoided making speeches, sending written messages to Congress. With only one clerk, he handled many documents himself.

The change of political power from the Federalists to the Republicans raised questions about office holding and political spoils. At the highest level of executive appointments, the cabinet, Jefferson assumed his right to appoint trusted supporters. He named James Madison of Virginia, his closest ally, as secretary of state, and Albert Gallatin of Pennsylvania as secretary of the treasury. Other members of the cabinet included Levi Lincoln of Massachusetts as attorney general, Henry Dearborn of Massachusetts as secretary of war, and Robert Smith of Maryland as secretary of the navy.

The question of whether or not to retain bureaucrats was more difficult. Jefferson supported the idea of a civil service in which public officers held their positions on the basis of merit; during the election crisis he suggested that he would allow officeholders to keep their jobs. When he learned that Washington and Adams had appointed only six Republicans to about 600 positions, however, the new president replaced about one-half of the Federalists with Republicans. Most infuriating were the "midnight appointments," as Jefferson characterized them—the appointments Adams made as a lame duck after he knew that the election was lost. In February 1801, the Federalist Congress had passed a new Judiciary Act creating these additional judgeships and other offices, all of which Federalists received. Jefferson called upon the new Republican Congress to repeal the law.

Jefferson and Gallatin placed high priority in decreasing government expenditures, taxes, and the national debt. Gallatin opposed all spending by the federal government, including military. With support of the Republican Congress, the administration cut the defense budget in half. It repealed all excise taxes, including that on whiskey, relying primarily on import duties for income.

Jefferson's plan to reduce the navy and remain clear of international conflicts hit a snag when Yusuf Karamanli, the leader of Tripoli in North Africa, declared war on the United States. Karamanli demanded payments from the United States to "protect" American merchant carriers from pirates. To end this extortion, in 1801 Jefferson sent naval vessels to blockade Tripoli and protect shipping. The United States experienced a major loss when the ship *Philadelphia* ran aground while pursuing pirates, but when a small force of U.S. Marines and Arab mercenaries seized Derna, the Tripolitans agreed to peace. The war had propelled military expenditures upward, however, and convinced Jefferson of the navy's value, thus hindering somewhat the administration's plans for reduced government spending.

The Judiciary

Although the Republicans had captured the presidency and Congress in 1800, the judiciary remained firmly in the hands of the Federalists. Adams and the outgoing Congress had tried to solidify their party's power in the courts with the Judiciary Act of 1801, which amended the act of 1789. By appointing additional federal judges, the new law ended the onerous requirement for Supreme Court justices to ride from state to state holding circuit courts twice a year. The act also reduced the number of justices on the Court from six to five, thereby denying Jefferson the opportunity to make an appointment when a seat became vacant. The Republican Congress, in early 1802, repealed this law, reinstating the Judiciary Act of 1789, thus forcing some federal judges out of their jobs and the Supreme Court back to the circuit.

Jefferson's bitter relationship with the Supreme Court resulted in part from his antipathy toward Chief Justice John Marshall, his distant cousin, whom Adams had named to the bench in early 1801. Like Jefferson, Marshall was tall, informal in manner, and a native of Virginia. He had joined the patriot forces in 1775, serving until 1781. He attributed his nationalism to that service, saying he became "confirmed in the habit of considering America as my country, and congress as my government." Marshall began a successful law practice after the war, served as a Virginia assemblyman, supported ratification of the Federal Constitution, then became the leading Federalist in his state. In the legal environment of the new republic, many colleagues appreciated his originality in building cases on logic and natural law rather than depending upon English precedent. On the Supreme Court, too, Marshall followed his own lights, creating the legal basis on which the power of the Court rests. During his long, illustrious career, which lasted until 1835, Marshall solidified the authority of the judicial branch of the federal government.

Marshall's most important decision, *Marbury v. Madison* (1803), commenced in a suit by William Marbury, nominated by Adams as a justice of the peace but not commissioned by the Jefferson administration. Marbury sued under the Judiciary Act of 1789, which granted the Supreme Court the power to require Secretary of State Madison to hand over Marbury's commission. Given the partisanship involved, most observers expected Marshall and his Federalist court to direct Madison to comply. Instead, the chief justice said that he could not remedy Marbury's situation, though he wished to do so, because the Congress had erred in giving the Court such authority. Marshall declared the provision of the 1789 Judiciary Act unconstitutional, thus establishing the Supreme Court's power of judicial review.

Jefferson decided that the federal judiciary, still dominated by Federalists and growing in power under Marshall, had to be controlled. Because federal judges constitutionally held their seats for life, "during good behavior," the president suggested to congressional Republicans that they start impeachment proceedings against objectionable Federalists. The Republicans impeached John Pickering, an official of the federal district court of New Hampshire, who was an alcoholic and insane, but who had not to anyone's knowledge committed any high crimes. The Senate found him guilty anyway and removed him from his position. Next, in January 1805, the House of Representatives impeached Samuel Chase of Maryland, an associate justice of the Supreme Court and extreme Federalist who castigated Jefferson's administration. But the prosecution failed to convince two-thirds of the Senate that Chase should be expelled from office for misconduct and other charges. Some moderate Republicans refused to adopt Jefferson's strategy to eject troublesome opponents. Thus ended Congress's attempt to remove Federalists from the bench by impeachment.

Domestic Politics

Jefferson and the Republicans gained in popularity as they steered a course more moderate than the "revolution" of 1800 had promised. The president had reduced taxes and attempted to limit the judiciary, but did not dismantle the Federalist edifice of national power, including the military and the national bank. He mixed republican theory, based upon a nation of small farmers, with practical politics aiding commerce. His policies, combined with booming exports, steadily increased Republican support, as many Federalist voters switched parties. In the election of 1802, the Republicans won 102 seats to the Federalists' 39 in the House of Representatives; the Republican margin in the Senate was 25 to 9.

Looking forward to the next presidential election, Congress acted promptly to avoid the deadlock that had occurred in 1800. The Republicans wanted a formal way to keep the Federalists from conspiring once again to elevate the Republican candidate for vice president to the presidency. The Twelfth Amendment to the Constitution, which required the electors to draw up distinct lists for president and vice president, was ratified by September 1804.

The election of 1804 demonstrated the demise of the Federalists as a national party. Jefferson defeated the Federalist presidential candidate, Charles Cotesworth Pinckney, by 162 electoral votes to 14.

Jefferson had replaced Aaron Burr as his running mate with George Clinton, also of New York, thus keeping the ticket balanced geographically. For his part, Burr ran for governor of New York against the Republican candidate, Morgan Lewis, but lost by a landslide. Alexander Hamilton played a decisive role in the defeat by publicly denouncing his longtime enemy. Burr challenged Hamilton to a duel. When the two faced each other at Weehawken, New Jersey, in July 1804, Burr shot Hamilton to death. In doing so, the vice president ended his own political career as well as the life of one of the architects of the American nation-state.

The Louisiana Purchase

Jefferson had boosted his popularity prior to the 1804 election with the Louisiana Purchase, which marked the greatest success of his presidency. In pursuing the deal with France, he deviated from one of his beliefs—in limited power of the central government—to obtain land for his agrarian republic. Long interested in the west, he scored a diplomatic coup that doubled the size of the United States and reduced Spain's dominance west of the Mississippi River.

The Bargain with Napoleon

The chain of events leading to the Louisiana Purchase began in 1800, when France signed a secret treaty with Spain for lands in western North America. France would get back the territory it had ceded to Spain in 1763. When Jefferson and Madison heard in 1801 of the impending transfer, they sent the new U.S. minister to France, Robert R. Livingston, with instructions to prevent the exchange or at least obtain West Florida. The Americans wanted to prevent France from controlling the Mississippi Valley; the dilapidated Spanish empire

Plan of New Orleans, 1801

The French founded New Orleans in 1718 and retained control until 1763, when the Spanish took possession as a result of the Seven Years' War. New Orleans was the capital of colonial Louisiana under both the French and Spanish.

Located on swampy land on the east side of the Mississippi River and about 107 miles from its mouth, the town and surrounding agricultural lands were frequently devastated by floods and hurricanes. In 1803, when the United States purchased Louisiana, New Orleans had a mixed population of free and enslaved blacks, Native Americans, French, Spanish, and U.S. citizens.

The key location of New Orleans near the mouth of the Mississippi emphasized its economic importance to Americans west of the Appalachians. When Spain closed the port once again in 1802, Americans feared a strategic loss. During the War of 1812, the British also recognized the significance of New Orleans to the expanding United States, when they unsuccessfully attacked the city in January 1815.

Courtesy, Archivo General de Indias, Seville, and the Spanish Colonial Research Center, University of New Mexico

caused trouble enough. In October 1802, the Spanish suspended once again the right of Americans to deposit goods for export at New Orleans. The Americans thought, incorrectly, that Napoleon was behind the ban. Many wanted to take New Orleans by force. Jefferson wrote to Livingston, "The day that France takes possession of N. Orleans . . . we must marry ourselves to the British fleet and nation." Jefferson pushed for negotiations, however, not war.

In response to Livingston's overtures, Napoleon decided to sell the entire Louisiana Territory to the United States. The French leader's zeal to construct an American empire had cooled with the loss of his army in St. Domingue. In documents dated April 30, 1803, the United States agreed to pay France $15 million, to respect the rights of the French and Native Americans living in the territory, and to recognize the French residents as American citizens. Spain was furious because Napoleon had promised not to sell the region to the British or the Americans. Jefferson ignored the Spanish objections, but worried, as a strict constructionist, that the Louisiana Purchase was unconstitutional because the federal government had no specific power to acquire territory. He put aside these concerns, confident that it was right to avoid war and add vast lands for expansion of the American republic. "By enlarging the empire of liberty," the president argued, the nation could maintain its agrarian foundations, thus avoid descent into vice, luxury, and decay. A successful republic was dependent upon broad property holding, for virtuous, independent, middling farmers made ideal citizens. The Louisiana Purchase, Jefferson believed, would extend the life of the republic by providing space for generations of ordinary planters. While some Federalists disagreed, most Americans celebrated the end of friction over the Mississippi River and New Orleans. Western farmers could get their products to market; eastern merchants prospered from the trade.

Disputes with Spain

When U.S. officials gained formal possession of Louisiana in December 1803, the Spanish had only recently transferred control to the French. The ceremonies took place in New Orleans, a city of 8,000 that had been reconstructed in Spanish style since several great fires a decade earlier. With a cathedral, theater, impressive city hall, and mansions, New Orleans served as the cultural and economic center of the lower Mississippi Valley. In population, it was larger than other towns of the Spanish borderlands. The entire white population of the Louisiana Territory was approximately 50,000, including French, Spanish, Germans, English, and Americans.

Beyond Spain's objection to the U.S. purchase of Louisiana, the two nations also disputed the territory's boundaries, because the treaties transferring ownership were vague. Thomas Jefferson pushed for the most generous interpretation for the United States. He demanded West Florida, with an eastern boundary at the Perdido River, the present boundary between Alabama and the Florida panhandle. The president also thought his new acquisition extended in the southwest to the Rio Grande, incorporating all of Texas and part of New Mexico, and in the northwest to the Rocky Mountains. Spain, on the other hand, said the Louisiana Territory included only a constricted region along the west bank of the Mississippi from northern Missouri to the Gulf of Mexico.

In 1804, Jefferson sent troops to West Florida, hoping to convince Spain by threat of force to give up or sell the province. Americans already outnumbered Spanish residents in the territory, which later comprised parts of Mississippi, Alabama, and Louisiana. Jefferson also wanted East Florida. He decided not to attack, and instead attempted to purchase the Floridas over the next several years, but failed.

➤ The Lewis and Clark Expedition

To strengthen U.S. claims to the West, Jefferson sponsored an exploratory mission to the Pacific Ocean. Several times since 1783, he had tried to organize expeditions for scientific knowledge and to promote American interests in the region. As president, he now had the authority and financial resources to support this major undertaking. By the early nineteenth century, however, others had surveyed parts of the territory. In 1792, an American sea captain Robert Gray explored the Columbia River, and George Vancouver, a British naval officer, sailed the northwest coast. A few years later, fur traders working for the Spanish government ascended the Missouri River to present-day North Dakota, while British traders from Canada began moving west.

Even before buying Louisiana, the president had decided to send an expedition west; the purchase gave the project greater urgency. He appointed his private secretary, Meriwether Lewis, as captain of the enterprise. Lewis chose his friend William Clark to be his partner. Lewis and Clark had served in the army together in the old Northwest, so both were familiar with frontier conditions. Jefferson selected Lewis for his scientific interests as well as his wilderness experience. The president wanted "a person who to courage, prudence, habits & health adapted to the woods, & some familiarity with the Indian character, joins a perfect knoledge of botany, natural history, mineralogy & astronomy."

Jefferson had a long list of goals for his explorers. They were to travel to the source of the Missouri River to find the elusive northwest passage, fill in huge blanks in geographic knowledge of the West, and bring back descriptions of unknown species of plants and animals. He also hoped they would make peaceful contact with Native Americans to expand commercial networks for fur traders. Lewis and Clark more than fulfilled their assignment, keeping daily journals of their experiences, including descriptions of Indian societies and culture, systematic weather records, and observations of flora and fauna, as well as a detailed map of their journey. Their relations with the people of the Northwest were for the most part amicable.

Lewis and Clark received commissions as army officers to lead the Corps of Discovery of about forty men who departed from St. Louis in May 1804. During that summer and fall they traveled up the Missouri River, using poles and tow ropes against the current. They battled the hot sun, diarrhea, and mosquitoes; several men deserted and one died, the only member of the Corps to perish during the entire trip. The adventurers met with the leaders of Indian nations along the way, telling them that the United States had taken possession of the territory from the Spanish. They arrived in the Mandan and Hidatsa villages of what is now North Dakota, where they spent the winter of 1804–1805.

In April 1805, the Lewis and Clark expedition set out with their guide Sacagawea, a Shoshone woman, and her French husband and infant son. They proceeded up the Missouri River, made an arduous crossing of the Rockies, and reached the mouth of the Columbia River before winter. On the way back, the corps divided in two, with Clark leading a party southeast along the Yellowstone River and Lewis taking a northern route through Montana. They joined forces once again in North Dakota, then returned to St. Louis by September 1806. They had been away so long that many assumed they had been killed by the Spanish or Native Americans.

Spies and Infiltrators

Spanish officials in fact had tried to intercept Lewis and Clark, whom they correctly suspected of making allies for the United States among the western Indians. General James Wilkinson, commander of U.S. troops in the west, governor of the Louisiana Territory, and a double agent known to the Spanish as "Agent 13," had tipped off New Spain about the expedition. The governor of New Mexico sent out search parties but failed to find Lewis and Clark. They did stop the mission of Thomas Freeman and Peter Custis, who in 1806 started from Louisiana to find the source of the Red River. Another Spanish party nearly intercepted Zebulon Pike, whom Wilkinson had dispatched to explore and spy in the region that is now Kansas, Colorado, and New Mexico. Pike became lost in the southern Rockies, was rescued by Spanish soldiers, arrested, then released.

Map 8.2 Western Exploration, 1803–1807 At about the same time Meriwether Lewis and William Clark led the Corps of Discovery along the northern route to treat with Native Americans, explore the natural resources, and locate a northwest passage, Zebulon Pike traveled north along the Mississippi River and west to the Rocky Mountains.

Both the United States and Spain knew they were playing for high stakes. The United States could use exploration of the west and alliances with Native Americans to help confirm their claims to broad boundaries of the Louisiana Territory. The Spanish had by far superior documentation for Texas, New Mexico, Arizona, California, and western Colorado. But they also denied American rights to what is now western Louisiana. Jefferson sent General Wilkinson with troops to the undefined boundary between Louisiana and Texas; the Spanish dispatched Lt. Col. Simón de Herrera to defend eastern Texas. The two officers avoided fighting by establishing a neutral zone until diplomats could negotiate the border.

Still concerned about protecting their silver mines in Mexico, the Spanish took steps to increase settlement in Texas. They welcomed Indian exiles—Cherokees, Choctaws, and Alabamas—from lands overrun by American settlers east of the Mississippi, but the Hispanic population failed to grow significantly. New Spain officials specifically barred U.S. citizens from Texas, under threat of arrest and imprisonment. The Americans, one Spanish official feared, "are not and will not be anything but crows to pick out our eyes." Anglo-American traders continued to infiltrate Texas, however, to trap animals and bargain for horses with the Comanches and other Indians.

The Burr Conspiracy

While Lewis and Clark were reconnoitering the far Northwest, Aaron Burr conceived a plot to create a separate nation in the West. He contacted the double agent James Wilkinson, various unhappy politicians, and representatives of foreign governments. Burr suggested a variety of plans to those who would listen, including an invasion of New Spain, an attack on Washington, D.C., and secession of the West. Wilkinson cooperated with Burr at first, then turned informer when the conspiracy became public knowledge. Jefferson ordered Burr's arrest for treason, while applauding Wilkinson's "fidelity." Burr tried to escape to Europe, but was captured and taken to Richmond, Virginia, where he was tried in 1807.

The Burr conspiracy case, presided over by Chief Justice Marshall and involving three prosecutors and six defense lawyers, might have been called the trial of the century. An unbiased jury could not be found; one juror said before the case was heard that Burr should be hanged. The principal actors in the trial were Marshall, who ignored his responsibility as an impartial judge to favor the defense, and Jefferson, who directed the prosecution from afar. Because Marshall upheld a definition of treason that required actual gathering of troops, not just conspiracy, the case against Burr collapsed. Jefferson blamed Marshall and considered trying to impeach him, but found insufficient congressional support.

More Foreign Entanglements

The renewal of war in 1803 between Great Britain and France portended trouble for the United States. American merchants flourished, as they took advantage of neutrality and wartime demand for provisions in Europe and the West Indies. But their ships became vulnerable to the British navy and French privateers.

A Perilous Neutrality

Great Britain and France each wanted to prevent the United States from provisioning the other. In particular, the British intended to stop American traders from carrying foreign sugar, coffee, and other tropical products to Europe, even though the merchants conformed technically to British guidelines by taking the goods first to U.S. ports, then reexporting. In the *Essex* case of 1805, British courts stiffened their rules, stating that merely carrying Spanish and French goods to U.S. soil for reexport was insufficient, that only commodities originally meant for sale in the United States, then subsequently redirected to Europe, would be considered exempt from seizure. Few reexported cargoes met the new guidelines. With the *Essex* rule, the Royal Navy stepped up its confiscations of American ships. Then, in 1806 and 1807, the British and French established blockades of each other's harbors, in combination eliminating neutral trade with Europe and the British Isles. The British insisted that neutral ships sail to Britain first for inspection and licensing before trading in Europe. Napoleon's Berlin and Milan Decrees banned trade with Britain and threatened neutrals who obeyed the British rules with seizure.

After the British destroyed the French and Spanish navies in 1805 at Trafalgar, off the coast of Spain, the British restrictions and impressment of sailors were by far the most troublesome to Americans. Many Federalists and some Republicans cried for war. But Jefferson and the congressional majority looked for ways to avoid hostilities. With a trimmed federal budget and small military, the Republicans were unprepared for war. Congress passed a Non-Importation Act (1806) banning specified British goods, while the president opened negotiations with Great Britain to end impressment and recognize neutral trading rights. No agreement satisfactory to both sides could be reached. Then, in June 1807, the British ship *Leopard* fired upon the American frigate *Chesapeake* for refusing to submit to a search for British deserters. The *Chesapeake,* hit twenty-two times, managed to respond with only one shot. The *Leopard* boarded her, impressing four men.

The Embargo of 1807

As Americans briefly clamored for war, Jefferson closed U.S. ports and territorial waters to British vessels and recalled American ships from the Mediterranean, where they would have been trapped had war begun. The British refused to stop impressing American sailors. They challenged Jefferson's port closure by firing on coastal towns in Maine and sailing in Chesapeake Bay. The president resisted a declaration of war, but placed military posts and gunboats on alert. He chose economic warfare instead. Unfortunately, this policy destroyed the commercial boom that had meant high prices for farmers and employed thousands of sailors.

At the urging of President Jefferson and Secretary of State Madison, Congress passed the Embargo Act in December 1807. The law prohibited exportation to all other countries. The administration hoped in particular to defang the former parent country by withholding provisions to the British Isles and West Indies. A by-product of non-exportation would be a severe drop in imports of British manufactures. Jefferson and Madison argued that the boycott would hurt all warring parties, but Britain worst. During 1808, the administration faced difficulty enforcing the embargo because ships, especially from New England, left harbor pretending to sail to American coastal ports but headed for foreign destinations instead. The trade with the British West Indies continued illegally. Federal agents also had little success in preventing smuggling into Canada. In January 1809, the government resorted to an extreme measure, Giles's Enforcement Act, which empowered the president to use the militia against smugglers. The act effectively ended trade.

The embargo had considerable impact on the U.S. economy. Agricultural prices declined, leading to farm foreclosures. According to official records, exports declined by 80 percent in 1808, though smuggling certainly lessened the effect. The U.S. Treasury suffered a loss in customs revenue, its chief source of income. The embargo stimulated further technological development of the textile industry, particularly in weaving cotton cloth with power looms.

With stern enforcement under Giles's Act, New Englanders became more strident in their demands for termination of the embargo. Jefferson became convinced that civil war was possible, but refused to support repeal. Republicans in Congress moved anyway, on March 1, 1809, replacing the embargo with a Non-Intercourse Act, which reopened trade with all countries except Great Britain and France. If either of the two belligerents changed its policy to favor neutral rights, the United States would resume commerce with that nation as well. While the new law banned trade with major markets, loopholes offered generous opportunities for smuggling.

Congress made this shift just days before the close of Jefferson's presidency. Jefferson thus ended his administration without solving the nation's international troubles, which Americans increasingly defined as an effort by Britain to subjugate its former colonies. As he returned to Monticello, however, the president could reflect favorably upon the goals he had achieved—lower taxes and national debt, smaller government, open doors to immigrants, and peace. He also took pride in an accomplishment he had not foreseen in 1801, the purchase of the Louisiana Territory. Jefferson's administration was remarkable for what it did— and for what it did not do, considering his opposition to Hamiltonian policies in the 1790s. Under Jefferson, the Republicans left intact the national bank, the federal administrative structure, and armed forces. Considering the war-torn world in which the young nation found its way, however, the Republican commitment to minimal government left the United States militarily unprepared.

Madison and the War of 1812

When Britain continued to impress American sailors and seize ships, Jefferson's successor had two choices: accept humiliation or declare war on Great Britain. The British argued that they acted from necessity, as Napoleon conquered Europe. Americans upheld their rights as neutrals to sell provisions to both sides. They considered British impressment of 6,000 seamen as a violation of national sovereignty and human rights. Between 1809 and 1812, these conflicts developed into war.

The Election of 1808

Despite the embargo, Jefferson retained enough popularity to win a third term, had he chosen to run. When he withdrew, he designated James Madison, the secretary of state, as his successor. James Monroe, who had served as governor of Virginia and minister to Great Britain, challenged Jefferson's choice, but congressional Republicans endorsed Madison. Dissenting Republicans, called the Tertium Quids, gave Monroe some support, but his candidacy died quickly. George Clinton accepted renomination for vice president. The Federalists put up Charles C. Pinckney and Rufus King, hoping that the effects of the embargo might reverse their party's decline.

The Federalists improved upon their performance in 1804 and 1806, gaining twenty-four seats in Congress, but still had much less than a majority. The electoral vote for president was 122 for Madison and 47 for Pinckney. While Americans suffered from the embargo, most were unprepared to desert the Republicans. In electing the new president, citizens ratified Jefferson's political philosophy and policies, which Madison had helped formulate. The third and fourth presidents had jointly founded and nurtured the Republican party; together they had adjusted their ideals to meet the practical needs of the expanding nation. The country could expect a continuation of Jeffersonian policies, though the retiring president withdrew entirely from decision making.

In another way, however, the new administration presented a real departure. Madison brought his elegant wife Dolley Payne Madison with him to the executive mansion, which was still unfinished when they arrived. They made a remarkable couple, as one observer noted:

> Mr Madison was a very small man in his person, with a very large head—his manners were peculiarly unassuming; and his conversation lively, often playful. . . . Mrs. Madison was tall, large and rather masculine in personal dimensions; her complexion was so fair and brilliant as to redeem this objection, in its perfectly feminine beauty. . . . There was a frankness and ease in her deportment, that won golden opinions from all, and she possessed an influence so decided with her little Man.

The first lady transformed the president's house into a proper executive mansion. She served as hostess to frequent teas and dinner parties, inviting Federalists and Republicans to socialize together.

Heading for War

After Madison's election, the European struggle continued to embroil the United States. While both Britain and France were hostile to free trade, the British dominated the seas, and as a consequence had substantial impact on U.S. commerce. Over the period to 1812, as Napoleon pushed across Europe, invaded Russia, and met defeat, he became inconsequential as a threat to the Americans. Indeed, his attempt to install his brother Joseph Bonaparte as king of Spain in 1808 undermined Spanish control in the New World. In West Florida, Anglo-Americans who had earlier pledged allegiance to Spain, in 1810 commandeered the Spanish fort at Baton Rouge, declared independence, and petitioned Madison for annexation by the United States. The president promptly claimed West Florida as part of the Louisiana Purchase and American troops occupied Baton Rouge. When Louisiana became a state in 1812, it included the western part of West Florida from Baton Rouge to the Pearl River.

In 1811, Madison appointed James Monroe, his former rival for the presidency, as secretary of state. Monroe took office hoping to reach an accord with the British, but soon decided that they wanted nothing less than to put the United States back into its colonial yoke. Great Britain adhered to its Order in Council that American exports go to England before shipment to Europe; the Royal Navy continued to impress American seamen. When Napoleon partially lifted his blockade in 1811, the United States resumed trade with France. Madison tried to convince the British to drop their restrictions as well, but instead they pounced on American ships headed for French ports.

In 1811, Tecumseh attempted to unite northern and southern Indians to defend their remaining lands east of the Mississippi River. This portrait, which was based on sketches made c. 1811, is from Benjamin Lossing's *Pictorial Field Book of the War of 1812* (1869).

Events in the West also intensified anger toward Britain, because Anglo-Americans believed that the British in Canada were stirring up Native American discontent. In fact, while some Indians traded with the British, many natives distrusted the whites of both Canada and the United States. An alliance between militant Indians and the British took time to evolve, as each group moved independently toward war with the Americans. The nativist message of Tenskwatawa, the Shawnee Prophet, and his brother Tecumseh found widespread support as a result of the Louisiana Purchase, expanding white settlement, and sales by accommodationist Indian leaders of a large proportion of native lands still remaining east of the Mississippi.

The nativists were spurred into action by the Treaty of Fort Wayne (1809), which turned over 2.5 million acres to the United States. Tecumseh met with William Henry Harrison, governor of the Indiana Territory, to request that the treaty be annulled. Failing that, the Indian leader went south to seek support from the Creeks, Cherokees, and Choctaws. He found allies among militant factions of Creeks and Seminoles. These factions, called the Red Sticks, opposed the accommodationists among their own people who sold land to the

United States and adopted Anglo-American ways of life. Tecumseh's effort to create a pan-Indian movement throughout the trans-Appalachian west ultimately failed, however, because by 1811, large white populations in Tennessee, Kentucky, and Ohio formed a barrier between north and south.

In November 1811, William Henry Harrison decided to cut short Tecumseh's efforts for unity. The governor did not believe the Indian leader's assurance that whites were "unnecessarily alarmed at his measures—that they really meant nothing but peace—the United States had set him the example by forming a strict union amongst all the fires that compose their confederacy." Harrison led a force against Prophetstown, the village Tenskwatawa had founded several years before on the Tippecanoe River. Before Harrison struck, the prophet attacked the encamped soldiers at night, but suffered casualties and withdrew. Harrison also lost men, but burned the town and claimed victory in what became known as the Battle of Tippecanoe. The nativists subsequently rebuilt their settlement; Harrison's action had little effect except to drive them closer to the British.

The War of 1812 Begins

When news of the battle reached Washington, many officials interpreted it as evidence that a British-Indian alliance already existed. The outcome, they mistakenly believed, showed that the British were weak, incapable of sustaining their allies. "War Hawks" in Congress, including the newly elected Speaker of the House Henry Clay of Kentucky and Representative John C. Calhoun of South Carolina, advocated preparations for war. They represented a new generation who had not participated in the Revolution and perceived Britain's actions as restoring colonial status. In Calhoun's words, his generation had to prove to "the World, that we have not only inherited that liberty which our Fathers gave us, but also the will and power to maintain it." By April 1812, President Madison agreed. The Federalists, only one-fourth of Congress and primarily from New England, opposed conflict with Great Britain in part to obstruct administration policy, in part for commercial interests. The Republicans were divided. Opponents claimed that Madison intended to wage war for territorial expansion in Canada and Florida.

The nation was ill-prepared when Madison issued his war message on June 1. Military funding would prove difficult because the charter of the national bank had been allowed to expire in 1811 due to politics and state banking interests, leaving state banks but no central agency as a source of loans. Lack of federal taxes beyond import duties, which fell sharply when the British blockaded the Atlantic coast, further limited the country's resources. The failure of New England leaders to provide their share of funds—indeed merchants' provisioning of the enemy and the desire of some New Englanders for a separate peace—severely hampered the war effort. The governors of Massachusetts and Connecticut refused to send their militia. Not everyone in New England opposed the war, however, for the majority of representatives from Vermont, New Hampshire, and Maine (still part of Massachusetts) voted in favor of the June 1812 declaration of war. Large numbers of the region's young men enlisted in the army.

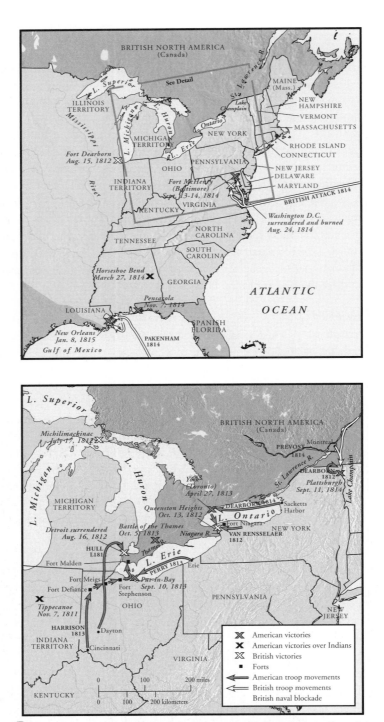

Map 8.3 The War of 1812 Many of the battles occurred in the Great Lakes region, on the U.S.-Canadian border, shown in detail at bottom. View an animated version of this map or related maps at http://history.wadsworth.com/passages2e

Despite military deficiencies and lack of national unity, the Madison administration pushed forward into battle. Madison offered an armistice if the British stopped impressment, but they refused. Canada, with only 5,000 regular soldiers, seemed the logical target. The redcoats there had little hope for reinforcements as long as Napoleon marched through Europe.

U.S. military leaders planned three advances, one from Lake Champlain to Montreal, a second at the Niagara River, and the third from Fort Detroit east through Upper Canada. With American victories, they hoped, Canada would fall, forcing Britain to recognize U.S. rights. The Americans moved first in the west, where they expected more support from local militia than from New England. Both the Canadians and the United States needed control of the Great Lakes to retain access to lands farther west. General William Hull received orders to lead about 2,000 troops against Fort Malden, opposite Detroit, under command of British General Isaac Brock and reinforced by Tecumseh and his men. Hull dawdled long enough to allow more British soldiers to arrive. He failed to take Fort Malden and surrendered Detroit. The British and Native Americans then took control of much of the region by capturing Fort Michilimackinac, to the north, and Fort Dearborn, at the present site of Chicago. Another blow came for the United States in October, when the army lost the Battle of Queenston, opposite Fort Niagara, after the New York militia refused to leave American soil to assist the regular troops. William Henry Harrison, commissioned a general, reinforced Fort Wayne against Indian attack. The Americans held

Anne S. K. Brown Military Collection, Brown University Library

"The Fall of Washington or Maddy in full flight," an anonymous English cartoon, 1814. Two British sailors ridicule President Madison and Secretary of State Monroe as they escape the burning capital with state documents.

Fort Harrison (Terre Haute, Indiana) and other points along a line from Sandusky, Ohio, to St. Louis, and undermined Tecumseh's war effort by destroying Indian towns and corn-fields in Ohio, Indiana, and Illinois.

During this frustrating campaign against Canada, James Madison stood for reelection. Some critics claimed that he had started the conflict to win another term. His opponent was DeWitt Clinton, a New York Republican. Clinton tried to gain support from both political parties by advocating peace to the Federalists while telling the Republicans that Madison had failed to prosecute the war hard enough. The president won by an electoral tally of 128 to 89; he obtained substantial Republican majorities in the House and Senate.

In contrast to the army's failures in 1812, the tiny U.S. fleet had surprising success against the mighty Royal Navy. The *Constitution* sank the British *Guerrière* in August; two months later the *United States,* captained by Stephen Decatur, took the *Macedonian;* in December the *Constitution* destroyed the *Java.* The American defeats of an enemy consid-ered master of the seas greatly bolstered public opinion.

Victories and Losses, 1813–1814

On land, however, 1813 began with another disaster for the Americans, as the British and Native Americans killed and captured nearly an entire force of 900 troops at Frenchtown, south of Detroit. The United States managed to hold Fort Meigs and Fort Stephenson in northern Ohio. But to destroy British control of Lake Erie and territory to the west, the army needed naval support. The United States began building ships at Presque Isle, Penn-sylvania (now Erie), and on September 10, 1813, Oliver Hazard Perry defeated the British squadron at Put-in-Bay, establishing American dominance of the lake. This naval victory cleared the way for General Harrison to attack Fort Malden, from which the British and Indians hastily retreated toward Niagara. The Americans caught up with them at Mora-viantown on October 5, winning a decisive victory known as the Battle of the Thames. Tecumseh died on the battlefield; his brother Tenskwatawa continued to fight alongside the British during the rest of the war, but with little success. To the east, the U.S. Army had burned York (Toronto), the capital of Upper Canada. But the Americans met defeat in an offensive against Montreal and lost Fort Niagara.

In the Mississippi Territory, the nativist Red Sticks waged civil war against Creek lead-ers who accommodated Anglo-American demands for land. The fratricidal conflict became a war against the United States in July 1813 when 180 American militia struck a much smaller group of Red Sticks. A month later, the nativists killed about 250 settlers who had taken cover in a stockade called Fort Mims. The Red Sticks, with 4,000 warriors but lack-ing adequate arms, faced overwhelming odds against the combined forces of U.S. troops, accommodationist Creeks, and Cherokee allies. Three armies entered Red Stick territory, destroying homes and dispersing families. The turning point came in March 1814, when General Andrew Jackson, with 3,000 militia and Indian allies, defeated 1,000 Red Sticks in the Battle of Horseshoe Bend, killing 800. The surviving militants escaped to Florida, where they joined nativist Seminoles and continued to fight. Despite the fact that accommodationist Creeks assisted Jackson's troops in the battle, the United States forced them to cede more than 20 million acres of land, including much of what was to become Alabama and a fifth of present-day Georgia.

In the summer of 1814, the British turned greater attention to the war in America, having defeated Napoleon in April. They sent 10,000 experienced redcoats to Canada, threatening New York until the American naval victory on Lake Champlain in September cut short the British invasion. Britain also sent forces to Chesapeake Bay, where in August they attacked the nearly defenseless Washington, D.C. Redcoats burned the Capitol and the president's mansion, shortly after the Madison household fled saving official documents and the Gilbert Stuart portrait of George Washington. The enemy promptly left the capital, and the U.S. government returned.

The British then assaulted Baltimore. Despite heavy bombardment of Fort McHenry by the Royal Navy, the redcoats failed to take the city. James Monroe, who was by then secretary of war as well as secretary of state, took credit for Baltimore's stand. Francis Scott Key memorialized the scene of flaming rockets and exploding bombs in his poem "The Star Spangled Banner," which was later set to the tune of a popular English song and, in the early twentieth century, became the national anthem. The British sailed south to the Gulf Coast, intending to block off the Mississippi River. In late 1814, Andrew Jackson captured Pensacola, Florida, then organized the defense of New Orleans.

The Hartford Convention

Over the course of the war, sentiment had grown in New England for secession, as the British tightened their blockade of the region and occupied the Maine coast. The Massachusetts governor secretly contacted the British about a separate peace. In late 1814, a group of Federalists organized the Hartford Convention to find a more moderate course to remedy their loss of power within the Union. The convention issued a report supporting the right of states to declare federal laws unconstitutional (similar to the Virginia and Kentucky Resolutions of 1798) and arguing that states should be responsible for their own defense. The Hartford delegates called for significant amendments to the Constitution: removal of the three-fifths clause that counted slaves in apportioning delegates in the House of Representatives and electoral college; a two-thirds majority in Congress to declare war and admit new states; a one-term limit on the president and ban on residents from the same state succeeding one another in the office (obviously targeted at Virginia); and prohibition of naturalized citizens—who were largely Republican—from federal positions. These proposals, calculated to damage Republican power bases in the south and west and among new immigrants in the cities, fell on deaf ears when news of the peace treaty arrived from Europe.

The Treaty of Ghent

Peace came as both the British and the United States recognized that the end of the twenty-year struggle in Europe eliminated the rationale for war in America. The defeat of Napoleon removed Britain's need to regulate neutral trade and impress seamen. Both sides could also see that they had little hope of victory. Britain might continue its blockade and smother U.S. commerce, but to what purpose? Conquest of the former colonies, now expanded into the west, would require huge expenditures of manpower and funds. Victory at New Orleans would plug the Mississippi, but in late 1814 success was still uncertain. News arrived, as the British considered terms for peace, that the Americans had repelled the offensives at Lake Champlain and Baltimore. While some Britons desired revenge, more wanted to resume trade.

Madison authorized John Quincy Adams, Albert Gallatin, Henry Clay, and two others to meet the British peace delegation in August 1814 at Ghent, in what is now Belgium. After several months of stalemate, the negotiators agreed on Christmas Eve, 1814, to return to the status quo at the outbreak of war. The British dropped their demands for part of Maine and an independent Indian territory north of the Ohio River, while the Americans stopped insisting that the British renounce impressment, which had ceased.

Battle of New Orleans

Bad weather in the Atlantic delayed until February the ship bringing news of the Treaty of Ghent. In the meantime, British forces prepared to move against the Gulf Coast. A fleet of sixty ships and 14,000 men planned to attack Mobile, seize control of the coast and the rivers, then move against New Orleans.

For Americans unaware of the peace treaty, such a plan posed a serious threat. New Orleans, distant and disconnected from the cities of the east coast, lay vulnerable to invasion. Once the British established a foothold there, troops could move up the Mississippi River. Moreover, a British invasion threatened to bring free and enslaved African Americans, French and Spanish settlers, Native Americans, and even pirates into the conflict throughout the Gulf territories, igniting rebellions against white farmers and traders.

The commander in charge of the American forces, Andrew Jackson, was especially sensitive to the dangers settlers faced on the Gulf Coast. A Tennessee lawyer, planter, and militia leader, he had defeated the Red Sticks at Horseshoe Bend. He repelled the British at Mobile, then raced to New Orleans before the British troops could arrive. The Americans got there first, in December of 1814. When six hundred free blacks volunteered to help defend the city, Jackson gratefully accepted their offer.

A series of attacks by the British damaged the American forces but did not take New Orleans. The British general in charge, Sir Edward Pakenham, unleashed a frontal assault on January 8, 1815. Two Congreve rockets, launched by the British to signal the beginning of the assault and to frighten their opponents, screamed into the air. Jackson's troops, dug in behind earthworks, fired directly into the charging British troops; wave after wave of the onslaught fell as American troops took turns firing and reloading. In less than an hour it was over: Pakenham and two of his generals lay dead, along with over 2,000 of their troops. The Americans suffered only thirteen dead and a few dozen wounded or missing. Nearly a month later, word of Jackson's remarkable success reached the nation's

Capital. "ALMOST INCREDIBLE VICTORY!!!," headlines trumpeted. Nine days later word of the Treaty of Ghent, ratified two weeks before the Battle of New Orleans, arrived in Washington.

Conclusion

With its simple provision to reinstate the *status quo ante bellum,* the Treaty of Ghent might appear to make the War of 1812 meaningless. The losses of lives and dollars, and disaffection of New England, all seem for nothing. Yet most Americans celebrated the peace, knowing they had withstood Britain's attempt to treat them as colonials. A second generation of Americans had proven they could survive a struggle with what was probably the world's most powerful nation. In addition, the United States had defeated Tecumseh's pan-Indian movement in the West, effectively ending Native American power east of the Mississippi.

Much had changed from 1800 to 1815. The Federalists transformed themselves from the architects of the national government in the 1790s to advocates of narrow sectional interests. Thomas Jefferson and James Madison, who had upheld states' rights, moved in the opposite direction during their administrations. Without denying their commitment to limited government, a skeleton military, low taxes, and republican principles, they expanded "the empire of liberty" by purchasing Louisiana and forcing Native Americans from their lands. Jefferson and Madison used every means short of armed conflict to protect commerce, then went to war when all else failed. In purchasing Louisiana, Jefferson relaxed his philosophy of strict interpretation of the Constitution in hope that the additional territory would extend the life of his agrarian republic. Madison facilitated the growth of nationalism by exacting respect from Great Britain. With the Atlantic world at peace once again, residents from Maine to Louisiana concentrated on making money and building their communities, all with a greater sense that they belonged to an American nation.

RECOMMENDED READINGS

Andrews, Dee E. *The Methodists and Revolutionary America, 1760–1800: The Shaping of an Evangelical Culture* (2000). An excellent study, including important chapters on the role of women and African Americans.

Coles, Harry L. *The War of 1812* (1965). A readable, one-volume study.

Dowd, Gregory Evans. *A Spirited Resistance: The North American Indian Struggle for Unity, 1745–1815* (1992). Demonstrates the significance of religion in Native American resistance.

Ellis, Joseph J. *American Sphinx: The Character of Thomas Jefferson* (1996). A highly readable study of a complex president.

Freeman, Joanne B. *Affairs of Honor: National Politics in the Early Republic* (2001). A provocative study of the means of political conflict, including dueling.

McCoy, Drew R. *The Elusive Republic: Political Economy in Jeffersonian America* (1980). Insightful exploration of Jeffersonian politics and thought.

Moulton, Gary E., ed. *The Journals of the Lewis and Clark Expedition.* 7 vols. (1983–1991). Most comprehensive edition of manuscript maps and journals.

Nash, Gary B. *Forging Freedom: The Formation of Philadelphia's Black Community, 1720–1840* (1988). Insightful study of the challenges of freedom for one community of African Americans in the North.

Smelser, Marshall. *The Democratic Republic, 1801–1815* (1992). A useful, lively overview of the period.

Waldstreicher, David. *In the Midst of Perpetual Fetes: The Making of American Nationalism, 1776–1820* (1997). Study of popular political culture, including the ways in which African Americans and women participated in celebrations yet were excluded from voting.

Additional resources, exercises, and Internet links related to this chapter are available on the American Passages Web site: http://history.wadsworth.com/ayerscompact2/

Passages
1815–1855

The United States redefined itself during the forty years after 1815. The boundaries of the nation, the character of its population, the nature of its economy, and the religious beliefs of its people all took new shape. Some of the changes confirmed what the architects of the young nation had expected several decades before; other changes proved to be surprises and the bitterest of disappointments. The speed and scale of transformation astonished everyone.

In 1815, the young United States held only eighteen states, with Louisiana standing exposed at the western boundary, Florida in the hands of the Spanish, and an unsettled line between Canada and the United States. The western half of the continent remained only vaguely known to Anglo-Americans and seemed too far away to be of importance any time soon. Even within the country's sketchy borders, American Indians populated large and rich areas in both the north and the south.

Four decades later, the continental boundaries of the nation had expanded beyond recognition. Florida had come into the Union from Spain. War with Mexico had brought in vast territories from Texas to California. Negotiation with Great Britain had defined the northern boundary from Maine to Oregon. Military and economic pressure on the American Indian nations had driven them across the Mississippi River. A new state entered the Union about every two and a half years; by the end of the 1850s, thirty-three states—including two on the Pacific coast—claimed a place in the nation.

The population exploded. The number of Americans grew from 8.4 million in 1815 to 31.4 million by the end of the 1850s. Nearly 4 million of those people were held in slavery, while 3 million people had crossed the Atlantic from Europe in a mixture of hope and desperation. People spread out across the expanse of the burgeoning country, establishing farms and towns far from the older cities of the East. About half the population of an average town moved every ten years. By the end of the period the United States claimed 5 million more people than England, and the new country boasted eight cities of more than 150,000 inhabitants—more than any other country in the world.

Large changes altered the scale of life, tying people together as few could have imagined in 1815. Steamboats transformed water transportation in the 1810s, canals boomed in the 1820s, and railroads arrived in the 1830s. The United States claimed over 35,000 miles of railroad track by the end of the era. In the 1840s, the first telegraph wires carried information from one city to another in a clatter of keys; by the late 1850s, telegraph wires stretched across the Atlantic Ocean. Novels sold tens of thousands of copies in a few months. Newspapers, confined to just a few major cities in 1815, became staples of American life in the 1830s and 1840s, read and published in hundreds of communities of every size. Daguerreotypes and colorful lithographs decorated homes that had been empty of pictures a generation earlier.

The United States became integrated ever more tightly into the international economy. The capacity of ships arriving in American ports doubled in the 1830s, doubled again in the 1840s, and then again in the 1850s. American vessels plied the Atlantic with cargoes of cotton and wheat for England and Europe. Clipper ships sailed around South America and into the Pacific, carrying prospectors and immigrants along with tea. The United States, anxious about European intervention in Latin America and the Caribbean, claimed the hemisphere as a place under its jurisdiction and protection.

Americans created lodges, clubs, and societies of every sort. Baptists, Methodists, and Presbyterians vied with one another for converts. Reform groups emerged to stamp out alcohol and war, to encourage education and humane treatment of the unfortunate, to improve diet and health, to bring the end of slavery. Women accounted for many members of these organizations, lending their energy and intelligence to activities beyond the home. Political parties mobilized nearly all adult white men, sweeping them up as Democrats, Whigs, Free Soilers, Know-Nothings, and Republicans. Men swore allegiance to their party, expressing their passions and beliefs in slogans, songs, and parades. On election days, as many as eight out of ten eligible voters went to the polls, publicly proclaiming their support for their candidates.

The expansion of the United States was the expansion of the largest and most powerful slave society in the modern world. Slavery grew stronger with each passing decade, embracing an ever larger part of the continent to the south and west, holding more people within its bonds, accounting for a larger share of the nation's exports. As the years passed, the discussions in the churches, the reform organizations, and the political parties increasingly turned to sectional conflict. Rivalry and distrust between the North and the South infected everything in the public life of the country.

The years between 1815 and 1855, then, did not witness a smooth passage through an "industrial revolution" or "growth of the common man" or "westward expansion." Rather, these years marked a passage filled with rapids and countercurrents and waterfalls. Panics and depressions, internal and external wars, massive migration and immigration, freedom and slavery—all came tumultuously.

Exploded Boundaries
1815–1828

The sudden climax of the War of 1812 surprised everyone. The leaders of the United States had wondered whether a large and lightly governed republic could survive in the rough-and-tumble world of international conflict. When the new country held its own in the war against England, the most powerful military force on earth, Americans gained a new confidence. President James Madison, ending his term in 1816, announced that the Constitution had proven itself able to "bear the trials of adverse as well as prosperous circumstances."

James Monroe, another in a long line of Virginia Republicans, easily won the national election of 1816. He bore the reputation of being an honest and dependable man, less intellectually distinguished than Jefferson or Madison. Monroe and his wife set a new tone for the presidency, with greater emphasis on etiquette, style, and entertaining, on embodying and celebrating the new national stature of the United States. The Monroes had the executive mansion painted a brilliant white to cover the smoke stains from its burning during the war with England; the residence became known as the "White House." After his election, Monroe toured the Northeast, including New England. A Boston journalist, impressed, talked of a budding "Era of Good Feelings," an era without party rancor, a strong contrast to the bitter conflict of earlier decades. The term was an exaggeration but many people wanted to believe a new era of cooperation had begun. President Monroe relished the role of peacemaker and conciliator.

Newly secure, the United States entered upon a period of territorial expansion and economic growth no one could have foreseen just a few years earlier. Throughout the country, steamboats, canals, and turnpikes tied the countryside to the cities and the cities to one another. White settlers, freed from concern about the British and emboldened against the American Indians, pushed west in vast numbers, taking enslaved African Americans with them across the South. Such rapid growth led many Americans to worry that their society was changing too fast, that selfishness and ambition had come to rule.

New Borders

The borders of the United States had been fluid and in doubt throughout the nation's brief history. In every direction other nations and peoples contested American boundaries. To the north, English power loomed in Canada. To the west, American Indians resisted efforts by

CHRONOLOGY

1815	Battle of New Orleans • *Enterprise* first steamboat from New Orleans to Pittsburgh
1816	Monroe elected president; "Era of Good Feelings" begins • Clay calls for "American System" • Second Bank of the United States chartered • Indiana admitted to the Union
1817	Mississippi admitted to the Union
1818	Jackson invades Florida • Erie Canal begun • Illinois admitted to the Union • National Road completed
1819	Transcontinental (or Adams-Onís) Treaty with Spain • *Dartmouth College v. Woodward* and *McCulloch v. Maryland* • Financial panic and depression • Alabama admitted to the Union • Auburn penitentiary established
1820	Missouri Compromise • Monroe elected president • Maine admitted to the Union
1821	Missouri admitted to the Union
1822	Denmark Vesey Rebellion, Charleston
1823	Monroe Doctrine announced
1824	Contested election of John Quincy Adams • Lafayette's visit • *Gibbons v. Ogden*
1825	Completion of Erie Canal
1826	Kidnapping of William Morgan

whites to buy or seize their ancestral lands. To the south, the Spanish held on in Florida. Moreover, many states had little economic dealing with one another, trading instead with England, Europe, and the Caribbean. As a result, states defended sharply conflicting policies, and their economies did not connect with one another very effectively. The peace after 1815 provided an opportunity for the United States to establish its borders more securely and to integrate itself more fully.

Native Peoples

President Monroe worked to establish clearer borders for the young nation. He succeeded in his dealing with Great Britain, when the two countries clarified the boundaries between the United States and Canada. The Rush-Bagot Treaty of 1817 calmed conflict on the Great Lakes and the Convention of 1818 fixed the border with Canada at the 49th parallel.

Relations with American Indians proved much more challenging. By the early nineteenth century, the American Indians had lived in contact with European culture for more than two hundred years. The native peoples had long combined their ancient practices with newer ones. Commercial hunting expeditions covered ever-expanding territory, tracking animals to trade with white trading partners. Trade networks stretched over thousands of miles.

Indians' clothing reflected the combination of cultures, as they combined moccasins with woolen breeches, imported cloth turbans, and jewelry made of melted silver coins. The intermingling worked both ways, for considerable numbers of English and Scots

Map 9.1 Lands Ceded by American Indians The United States negotiated one treaty after another with American Indians in the decades after 1815, acquiring land and pushing the natives of these areas to the west.

traders lived among the Indians. Many men of European background adopted Indian dress and language and married into native families. African Americans, too, often took refuge with the Creeks and Seminoles, so that by 1815 mixed ancestry had become common.

The removal of the British troops after the War of 1812 dealt a strong blow to the hopes of the American Indians. Alliances with the British, both actual and threatened, had helped hold back the white Americans. Now that the alliance with England had been destroyed, the United States quickly sought to exert firm control over the eastern half of the continent. Andrew Jackson, triumphant general in the war, was placed in charge of negotiating with the Creek, Cherokee, Chickasaw, and Choctaw nations of Alabama, Florida, and Mississippi after the peace of 1815. Jackson used heavy-handed treaties to force Indians from their former lands. Many of the natives resisted the removal, objecting that the treaties extracted by Jackson had been signed by Indians who had no authority to make such concessions.

The various native peoples identified themselves by the location of their villages, their languages, and their traditional enemies, and often fought with one another, but whites insisted on lumping these diverse people into groups that could be more easily dealt with. Jackson and other officials relied on particular American Indians as allies in war but then deliberately punished all the tribes in the region regardless of earlier promises. Such policies weakened the power of Indian leaders and left their people little choice but to accept bribes and annual grants of money in return for their lands. As soon as Jackson managed to secure lands from the Creeks, Cherokees, and Chickasaws, white settlers rushed into the territories, hungry for the fertile land and the fortunes it could build. Such incursions occurred across millions of acres in North Carolina, Kentucky, and Tennessee as well as in Alabama, Mississippi, and Georgia; in each state, the Indians were pushed to the hilly and mountainous lands least desirable for farming. The U.S. government made it easy for white settlers to buy land and sold about a million acres a year throughout the next decade. Not surprisingly, tensions steadily mounted between the ancient residents of the land and those who now claimed it.

As in the South, white settlement in the Northwest was made possible by the subjugation of the native peoples. After northern Indians' disastrous losses in the War of 1812, they posed little threat to white settlers. The U.S. government quickly established a series of forts throughout the Northwest to intimidate any American Indians and to make sure that the British and Canadians did not regain a foothold. The growing numbers of white farmers made it difficult for Native Americans to hunt for a living. President Monroe exulted in the "rapid and gigantic" spread of white settlers into the Northwest, an expansion the "rights of nature demand and nothing can prevent." The president argued that "the earth was given to mankind to support the greatest number of people of which it is capable, and no tribe or people have a right to withhold from the wants of others more than is necessary for their own support and comfort." Whites who moved to the Northwest confronted only scattered remnants of native peoples, trading with white merchants for food, sometimes begging from homesteaders.

The American Indians strove to adapt to white ways while maintaining their identity; the Cherokees, in particular, won praise for their "civilized" customs. One Cherokee, Sequoyah, devised an alphabet in his people's language in 1821. The wealthiest Cherokees purchased African American slaves and built substantial cotton plantations. No matter what accommodations they made, the American Indians suffered repeated conflicts with whites who relied on sheer numbers, trickery, violence, and the law to dispossess Native Americans of their land claims.

The Spanish in Florida

Like the American Indians, the Spanish who remained in Florida after 1815 had become vulnerable. Without the assistance of the British, they found it nearly impossible to resist American incursions into their territory. White Americans, for their part, felt they had a right, even an obligation, to drive the Spanish from the mainland, in part because Protestants had long distrusted the Catholic, monarchical Spanish. Many Americans thought it inevitable that Florida and Mexico would become part of the United States. To make relations even more volatile, sixty miles from the southern border of the United States stood the so-called Negro Fort, occupied by runaway slaves and their Indian allies.

In the spring of 1816 Jackson warned the Spanish commandant of Pensacola that the stronghold was "occupied by upwards of two hundred and fifty negros many of whom have been enticed away from the service of their master—citizens of the United States." The fugitives would "not be tolerated by our government," Jackson warned, "and if not put down by Spanish Authority will compel us in self Defence to destroy them." Spain was eager, in fact, to be rid of the fort as well, but did not have the military power to overthrow it. The Spanish feared, correctly, that Jackson would use the refuge as a pretext to invade Florida. Indeed, the Americans sent an expedition against the fort; a projectile hit a powder magazine, killing 270 of the men, women, and children inside.

In 1818, Jackson's forces also punished groups of Seminoles, who, with their Creek allies, had launched raids against white settlers in south Georgia and then fled into Florida. The American soldiers burned a Seminole town, only to see their foes retaliate by attacking a boat of soldiers, women, and children on the Apalachicola River, killing all but a few on board. Though his authorization from Washington was doubtful, Jackson invaded Spanish territory, executed a Creek prophet and two British men he accused of abetting the Indian cause, and overran the weak Spanish presence in the most important outposts. Some in Congress wanted to punish Jackson for what they considered his unauthorized attack. Jackson rushed to Washington to defend himself and his honor. Enraged by the appointment of a Senate committee to investigate his conduct during the war, Jackson threatened to slice off the committee chairman's ears. Unimpressed, the Pennsylvania Senator commented, "I have passed [Jackson's] lodging every day and still have my ears." Jackson also swore that he would kill Speaker of the House Henry Clay in a duel because of his speeches challenging Jackson's actions in Florida. In contrast, many white Americans thronged the cities where Jackson appeared along the way, celebrating him as a decisive hero rather than castigating him for being the military despot Henry Clay claimed. The congressional hearings on Jackson's behavior in the war had little effect except to make Jackson suspicious of the men in power in Washington.

Meanwhile, American and Spanish officials negotiated. The U.S. delegation was led by the brilliant and tenacious John Quincy Adams, son of the former president. With Jackson's military victories giving force to his words, Adams held out until the Spanish, in return for 5 million dollars in compensation of private claims, ceded to the United States all territories east of the Mississippi River. In this, the Adams-Onís Treaty of 1819, the Spanish kept the vast territory from Texas to present-day California, while the United States claimed a northern border that ran unbroken to Oregon and the Pacific Ocean. Adams called his handiwork the Transcontinental Treaty, for it stretched the borders of the United States from the Atlantic to the Pacific.

Building a National Economy

The end of the Napoleonic Wars in 1815 unleashed the economies of Europe and the countries that dealt with Europe, including the United States. American prosperity grew as the population boomed, as people moved across the expanse of the continent, and as transportation advances knit once isolated settlers and small towns together. Slavery expanded along with free labor, farms along with factories, the East along with the South and the West. People made their livings in new ways and participated in an economy of ever-expanding scope.

Leading members of the Republican party, long known for their opposition to federal power, began to view the central government more favorably after the victory of 1815. Young Republicans such as Henry Clay of Kentucky and John C. Calhoun of South Carolina urged Congress and the president to encourage the growth of enterprise with the aid of the government, creating roads, canals, a strong navy, and a national bank. In their eyes, the war with Great Britain had shown the dangers of a sprawling American nation, its resources scattered, its defenses thin. The future of the country, Clay and Calhoun believed, lay in commerce and industry. The government should ally itself with the forces of trade. These nationalists called their vision the "American System." Despite the excitement among many Americans, representatives from New England joined with Virginia and North Carolina to reject projects supported by the mid-Atlantic and western states. They considered the projects too expensive and too threatening to local power.

Adopting some ideas of the "American System," President Monroe urged Congress to use protective tariffs to protect American manufacturing, to build roads to tie the newly expanded markets and farms together, to connect the abundant rivers and lakes in the United States with a system of canals to integrate "the whole coast from its southern tip to its northern extremity in one continued inland navigation." Monroe hoped his plan would be supported by a broad and nonpartisan consensus. He eagerly waited for agreement to develop.

Banks, Corporations, and Law

No country needed credit more than the United States. Because far too little cash spread across its vast and growing territory, much business within the country rested on nothing more than trust and promises. Credit relations became tangled and fragile; the fall of one borrower could bring down a chain of lenders. Throughout the years before and during the War of 1812, states chartered banks to help alleviate the problems caused by a shortage of cash. More than 200 such banks had been founded by 1815 and nearly 400 by 1818, issuing notes that served as currency in cash-starved areas. Thomas Jefferson worried that "our citizens are clamoring for more banks, more banks."

Many influential men, including the recently elected President Monroe, supported a new national bank to stabilize the economy and distribute scarce money more uniformly. Advocates of the bank argued that the notes of state banks varied far too much in soundness and value, making the economic system dangerously unstable. The expanding country's economic system needed a central institution to coordinate the flow of money. Accordingly, in 1816 Congress chartered the Second Bank of the United States. Based in Philadelphia, it was authorized to establish branches wherever it wished. The new national

What now seem the "natural" boundaries of the continental United States were by no means obvious in 1815. As it stood, somewhat surprised in its lack of defeat by the powerful British in the War of 1812, the United States still had poorly defined and dangerous borders in almost every direction. The boundaries of Maine, the enormous area west of the Great Lakes, and Oregon remained contested with Great Britain in the north. Though we now think of the relationship between the United States and Canada as the very model of peaceful coexistence, at the time many people worried about this British territory looming over the United States. To the south, Spain (and runaway slaves and the Seminoles) controlled Florida and much of the Gulf Coast. The territory, so close to the booming areas of the South, posed a threat to slavery as well as to the territorial ambitions of the United States. To the west, the territory that would become Mexico remained contested, still in the process of defining its own nationhood. In the five years after the peace of 1815, the United States eagerly negotiated treaties with Great Britain and Spain to clarify and stabilize the young nation's borders. The settlement of the treaties helped create the conditions for rapid growth and economic development.

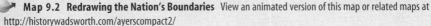

Map 9.2 Redrawing the Nation's Boundaries View an animated version of this map or related maps at http://historywadsworth.com/ayerscompact2/

bank was an amalgam of public and private enterprise: the federal government deposited its funds in the bank and appointed a fifth of the directors, but the bank ran as a private business. For the privilege of being the only such institution authorized to operate on a national basis, the bank handled, without fees, the funds of the federal treasury. The bank pumped large amounts of paper currency into the system in an attempt to feed the voracious hunger of the postwar economy, especially in the new states of the West.

The local, state, and federal courts of the United States also encouraged the growth of business in the years after the peace of 1815. Courts increasingly favored market forces over custom and stability in property relations, shifting the advantage from farmers and landowners to developers. Those who wanted to dam rivers for factories or build roads enjoyed increasing precedence over those threatened by floods, fires, or disruption caused by development. The courts assumed that the public good from the growth of business outweighed the stability favored by older notions of justice. Because many people bitterly protested this shift in emphasis, state legislatures sometimes sought to curb the power of business interests.

The Supreme Court under Chief Justice John Marshall issued a number of important decisions following the War of 1812 that also hastened economic development. Marshall was more concerned with establishing the power of the federal government than with furthering the economy, but by creating a more uniform legal environment that transcended the restrictions of particular states, the Court accelerated the growth of business. One decision of 1819 made bankruptcy laws more uniform across the country; another, *Dartmouth College v. Woodward,* sheltered corporations from legislative interference; yet another 1819 ruling, *McCulloch v. Maryland,* established the constitutionality of the Bank of the United States and protected it from state taxation. A fourth case in this period, *Gibbons v. Ogden* (1824), limited the rights of states to interfere in commerce with either special favors and monopolies or restrictive laws. "In all commercial regulations," Marshall pronounced, "we are one and the same people." In this new legal environment, increasingly emulated by state courts and legislators, business flourished in the years immediately following the end of war.

Roads and Canals

Americans threw themselves into a frenzy of road and turnpike building after 1815. New York alone chartered 300 companies that began construction of 5,000 miles of gravel roads. Investors, states, and even the federal government built thousands of miles of private roads—turnpikes—charging tolls to offset the roads' notoriously high maintenance costs. Some road builders laid logs side-by-side to provide a durable surface, though these so-called corduroy roads took a heavy toll on horse, wagon, and rider and wore out quickly besides. In 1818, the U.S. government opened the "National Road," connecting the Potomac River at Cumberland, Maryland, with Wheeling, [West] Virginia, on the Ohio River. The road was the best that technology could provide at the time, with excellent bridges and a relatively smooth stone surface. The road attracted so much business, however, that traffic jams slowed movement to a crawl and the road quickly fell into poor condition. Even on good roads, it often cost more to move bulky items such as corn or wheat than the price the products could bring at market.

Businesses and state governments began to plan dependable canals with controllable locks and a steady flow of water. Because Baltimore and Philadelphia enjoyed close con-

The Erie Canal, connecting the Hudson River with Lake Erie, demanded a monumental engineering effort. It soon paid its way, however, as shippers and farmers rushed to use the new waterway.

nections with the West, benefiting from heavily used turnpikes, New York City merchants worried that their dominant position in the East would be lost if they did not establish fast and inexpensive connections as well. Fortunately for New York, a flat passage broke through the Appalachian Mountains within the state's borders. New Yorkers believed that a canal through this area, connecting the Hudson River to Lake Erie, would far surpass any other kind of transportation. Such a canal would be ten times longer than any other canal then in existence: 364 miles through swamps and solid rock, through places where virtually no white settlers had bothered to migrate.

The mayor of New York City and future governor of the state, De Witt Clinton, became the foremost advocate of the canal, certain it would make his city "the great depot and warehouse of the western world." People scoffed at the money thrown away in "Clinton's Big Ditch." But the largely untrained engineers learned as they went along. Aqueducts had to span rivers and gorges, aqueducts tight and strong enough to withstand the weight of the water and the boats they carried. Locks had to be constructed of heavy timbers and even heavier stone. The canal, 4 feet deep and 40 feet wide at the top, was dug by hands, backs, and shovels. Thousands of laborers, many of them foreign-born, moved with the canal, enlivening and sometimes frightening the more sedentary settlements on the route. Year after year, the canal edged toward Lake Erie, transforming the

Steamboat

Steamboats began to ply the Mississippi River and other major waterways in the 1810s and 1820s, accelerating trade and fueling the growth of cities along the way. This boat is being loaded at Natchez, Mississippi, one of the earliest outposts of the new cotton economy in what would eventually be remembered as the "Old" South, even though it did not exist long enough to really deserve the name. The technology of the steamboat had been known before the War of 1812, but the end of the war opened the rivers of the United States to a rapidly increased trade. Though steamboat technology steadily improved so that steamboats become safer, larger, and more comfortable, they remained dangerous by their very nature. Built light and carrying large tanks under extreme pressure, streamboats were vulnerable to submerged obstacles and often exploded without warning and without obvious cause.

© Bettmann/Corbis

countryside along the way; by 1819, the canal stretched for seventy-five miles. As soon as workers completed a segment, boats crowded upon its waters, the tolls they paid financing the portions yet unfinished.

The completion of the Erie Canal in 1825 demonstrated that Americans could accomplish great things. The constructors of the canal, bragged one speaker, "have built the longest canal, in the least time, with the least experience, for the least money and to the greatest public benefit." Soon after De Witt Clinton ceremoniously poured water from Lake Erie into the Atlantic, thousands of boats were traveling along the canal between Buffalo and New York City, pumping half a million dollars of tolls into the state coffers, sending a surge of prosperity along its route. By 1834, approximately nine boats passed through major locks on the canal each minute. Other states looked enviously upon the glorious and profitable Erie Canal and began their own plans and excavations.

Not everyone saw such transformations of the land in glowing terms. A contemporary satire mocked the pleasures of being dragged "along a muddy ditch, hour after hour, in constant dread of lifting your head above your knees for fear of having it knock'd off your shoulders by a bridge!" Although the canal had been envisioned as primarily a freight service, from the beginning more than 40,000 passengers traveled on the new waterway. Settlers, tourists, salesmen, and evangelical ministers took advantage of the convenience and low cost of the canal to reach new lands and wider audiences for their products.

Steamboats

Canals, though useful and exciting, reached only a limited part of the vast North American continent. Rivers offered faster and cheaper travel, especially along the Mississippi, Missouri, and Ohio. But their limitations were obvious as well. The rivers could be dangerously fast in some seasons and so slow as to be impassable in others. They often froze for months in the winter. Strong currents ran in only one direction. Those who wanted to transport goods northward had to push their boats against the current, sometimes with poles, sometimes by dragging the boats with ropes as the crews walked along the shore, sometimes merely by grabbing trees and bushes on the banks. It took three or four months to drag a boat upstream. Others simply sold their craft for scrap in New Orleans and walked back to Ohio or Illinois, a long and arduous trip.

Not surprisingly, people dreamed of using steam engines to drive riverboats. Robert Fulton's steamboats had traversed the quieter waters of the Northeast since 1807, but Fulton did not manage to build one for the rigors of the Mississippi until 1811. The War of 1812 slowed development of the steamboats, since engines could not be imported from England, but innovation resumed with the war's end. As soon as Jackson won New Orleans in 1815, the *Enterprise* churned its way upriver from Louisiana all the way to Louisville, Kentucky. Dozens of other craft soon joined, competing with one another. In 1817, the journey from New Orleans to Louisville took twenty-five days; in 1819, fourteen days. "If any one had said this was possible thirty years ago," a journalist marveled, "we should have been ready to send him to a mad-house." Though the shallow, high-powered, and top-heavy steamboats showed a dangerous propensity to explode, run aground, and slam into submerged obstacles, no one thought of going back to the old way of travel. Based on contemporary estimates, 40 percent of steamboats built prior to 1849 sank, burned, or exploded, frequently killing large numbers of passengers. To grasp the extent of the hazards of steamboat travel, a comparable rate of carnage today would involve six to nine serious accidents per motorist per year.

The increasing speed and frequency of the steamboats encouraged the growth of villages and towns along the rivers. Huge stacks of wood carted in from the countryside appeared wherever the steamboats regularly stopped for fuel; new stores sold the goods transported on the river; muddy villages dreamed of becoming major cities. Indeed, the populations of Louisville, Pittsburgh, and Cincinnati doubled or more than doubled between 1815 and 1825, developing into centers not only of trade but also of meatpacking and flour milling.

Regional Growth

As the American economy grew, different parts of the country specialized economically. The more the regions integrated with one another, ironically, the more they differed. When roads, canals and steamboats lowered the cost of shipment, it made more sense for

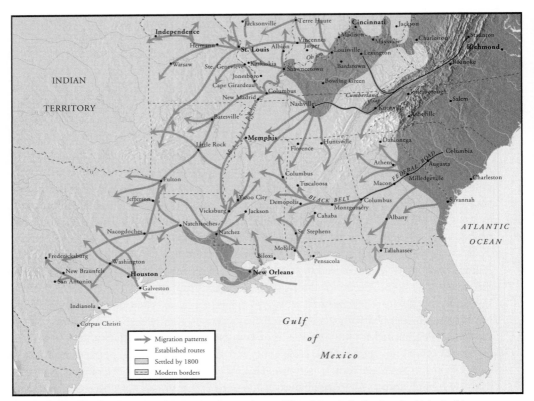

Map 9.3 Migration Patterns in the Southeast White southerners followed rivers and valleys into the rich lands of the Southwest, with the wealthier among them relying on slaves to clear the lands for new plantations.

particular places to specialize in what they produced best. As a result, the South, Northeast, and Northwest, all pursuing growth and development, followed paths quite different from one another.

The different regions of the United States cannot be understood in isolation from one another. The South, for example, did not stand outside the political, cultural, and economic events that transformed the rest of the nation. Slavery played a critical role in the history of the entire country, producing the cotton that fueled the growth of the Northeast's textile factories and providing a large market for the farms of Ohio, Illinois, and Indiana. The South, moreover, changed as much as any part of the country in these years and often played a leading role in the nation's politics and foreign affairs. Unlike most texts, therefore, this one does not set the South apart in a separate chapter but integrates its history into the story of the United States.

The Creation of the Cotton South

The demand for cotton in England took off after 1815, when cotton became, for the first time, the clothing of choice for large numbers of the world's people. Cotton clothes were cheaper, easier to create, and more comfortable in warm weather than those made from wool or linen. No place in the world was as prepared to supply the burgeoning demand for cotton as the American South. Small farmers as well as planters from the older states of the southern seaboard saw opportunity in the new states of Alabama and Mississippi, especially now that Andrew Jackson had opened Mobile as a port for southern Alabama. Many white farmers also moved to western Tennessee and parts of Louisiana. The steamboat and the cotton gin gave southern planters powerful new tools, while slaves could clear and cultivate land for new plantations far more quickly than would have been otherwise possible. Slaveowners in the older states of the Atlantic seaboard, faced with what they considered a surplus of labor, eagerly sold slaves to planters moving to the "new" lands. One million slaves were sold from the states of the Upper South in the three generations after the ratification of the Constitution. This domestic trade, comprised of a complex network of traders, provisioners, and insurers, constituted as much as 13.5 percent of the total southern economy.

The expansion of the cotton kingdom broadened and deepened the slave trade. Many planters in the East took advantage of the opportunity to sell slaves "down south," especially as the price of slaves—stagnant or declining before 1815—began to rise. Hundreds of thousands of slaves endured forcible migration to the new states of the Southwest in the 1810s and 1820s; some moved in groups along with their owners to new plantations, but many were sold as individuals to slave traders in the East, who then shipped or marched them to slave markets in New Orleans, Mobile, and other cities in the Southwest. The families of many enslaved African Americans were broken apart, as slave traders eagerly bought those in their teens for the hard work of clearing land for plantations from virgin forest.

The movement west was not a simple march from the east, but rather followed the geographic and political contours of the areas recently acquired from the American Indians. The first settlements began along the rivers that made it possible to transport cotton to market and in those places where the Creeks and other Indians exercised no claims. The new plantation districts were disconnected from one another, centering on Montgomery in Alabama, Jackson in Mississippi, and Memphis in Tennessee, all areas taken from the natives of the region since 1814. Small farmers occupied the land farthest from the rivers, supporting themselves with hunting and foraging as well as with growing small amounts of cotton. Young lawyers and editors headed out for the Southwest as well, eager to make their mark in the river towns and county seats growing up across Alabama and Mississippi.

"The Alabama Feaver rages here with great violence and has carried off vast numbers of our Citizens," wrote one North Carolina planter in 1817. "I am apprehensive, if it continues to spread as it has done, it will almost depopulate the country." The fever proved contagious, "for as soon as one neighbour visits another who has just returned from the Alabama he immediately discovers the same symptoms which are exhibited by the person who has seen the allureing Alabama." Even established men in the older states put their plantations up for sale; others saw the new states as a place for their grown children to get a fresh start. The combined population of Alabama, Mississippi, and Louisiana more than tripled between 1810 and 1820, growing from 117,000 people to 357,000.

The new plantations concentrated on cotton at the expense of everything else. Southerners who had just come into the vast and apparently inexhaustible lands of the Creeks and Seminoles worried little about conservation. The finest plantations clung to the rivers, for water offered the only way to get the ever-expanding cotton crop to market. Flatboats carried the bulky product to barges waiting at the docks of Natchez and Vicksburg on the Mississippi or to ships waiting in the bays of Mobile and New Orleans. Food and other provisions for the plantations came down the rivers from the new farms and cities to the north. A new national economy knitted together the enormous expanse of the young United States.

Some ambitious young men from northern states moved to the new cotton lands, the place in the United States, it seemed, where the greatest fortunes could be made in the shortest amount of time. Virgin land could produce a cotton crop in only one year; in two years, a plantation could be in full production. But most of the new residents came from older plantation states. Young southern men were especially eager to move and make their mark. Their wives, mothers, and daughters were often much less enthusiastic about migrating to Mississippi or Alabama, for it meant being removed from the kin who gave

Arise! Arise! and weep no more dry up your tears, we shall part no more. Come rise we go to Tennessee. That happy Shore To old virginia never — never — return. —

Abby Aldrich Rockefeller Folk Art Center, Williamsburg, VA

The rapid spread of cotton plantations fueled the domestic slave trade. These enslaved people are being marched from Virginia into Tennessee.

those women much of their happiness and social standing. The lure of the Southwest over-rode concerns husbands may have felt for their wives' opinions, however, for the new states offered a chance at the independence they considered synonymous with manliness. They sought to build a world as much as possible like those of Virginia or Carolina, only more prosperous.

Emergence of the Northwest

The area west of the Appalachians, north of the Ohio, and east of the Mississippi—the "Northwest"—was growing at an even faster pace than the Southwest. "Old America seems to be breaking up, and moving westward," one man wrote in 1817 as he watched people move down the Ohio River. The 280,000 white settlers of 1810 in Ohio, Indiana, and Illinois grew to 784,000 ten years later. In the first two decades of the new century, the trans-Appalachian population grew from about 300,000 inhabitants to more than two million. This immigration in the North bore considerable similarities to its southern counterpart. First of all, many of the settlers to the Northwest came from the states of the Upper South; large parts of southern Ohio, Indiana, and Illinois were settled by people from Virginia, Kentucky, Tennessee, and North Carolina. Some southern migrants to the North professed themselves eager to move out of states with slavery, while others merely

Map 9.4 Migration Patterns in the Northwest As in the South, migrants in the North wove their way into the West. New Englanders and New Yorkers followed a northerly path, while other people flowed in from the south, all of them following rivers, canals, and major roads.

followed the easiest routes to good land. People from New England and New York filled the towns and farms of the northern parts of the new states of the Northwest. In 1824, Illinois voters defeated, by fewer than 2,000 votes, a proposition to hold a constitutional convention to authorize the continuance of slavery in the state.

As in the South, young people dominated migration to the Northwest. Migrants to both regions abandoned areas back east where land had become too expensive, crowded, or depleted. As in the Southwest, settlers to the Northwest did not move in a simple westward wave, but rather flowed up the rivers and spread from there, sometimes back towards the East. People often emigrated in groups, whether of families or of larger communities. "We are seldom out of sight, as we travel on this grand track towards the Ohio," one traveler noted, "of family groups behind, and before us, some with a view to a particular spot, close to a brother perhaps, or a friend who has gone before, and reported well of the country." Family farms clustered closer together in the Northwest than in the Southwest because the absence of a large slave workforce meant that landholdings remained relatively small.

Most white settlers proved dissatisfied with the first land they claimed, for about two out of three migrants moved again within a few years. Rumors always circulated about richer land a bit farther west, about a new town certain to be a major city, about opportunity just over the horizon. Many people who had moved once found it easy to move again. Those who remained in a community became its "leading citizens," consolidating land into larger farms, setting up grist mills and sawmills, running for office, establishing the small towns that served as county seats and trading centers. In many cases, storekeepers were among the first to arrive and among those whose fortunes flourished best. Storekeepers became the bankers and wholesalers of their communities, often buying considerable amounts of land along the way, boosting the towns growing around the stores, churches, and schoolhouses. Courthouses were built early on to formalize land sales and taxation.

Farm and Factory in the Northeast

While the economies of the West and the South were being transformed by settlers and slaves, the economy of the East underwent its own fundamental change. Since the colonial years, people outside the major cities—more than nine out of ten Americans—had made in their own homes much of what they needed. This local production grew stronger when trade dried up during the war with England; in the war's wake, more than two-thirds of the clothes Americans wore were made in their own homes. The year of 1815, in fact, saw the peak of household manufacturing. Local blacksmiths, tailors, cobblers, and other artisans supplied what families could not produce for themselves, while local gristmills and sawmills processed crops and lumber.

Farms averaged a little over a hundred acres, about half improved and the other half occupied by wood lots for fuel and timber. Forests often dominated the farms of younger families, while mature families proudly claimed large areas of cultivation, the products of years of labor. Women and men, children and adults shared and divided the work among themselves. Farm families cleared their fields at spring thaw, manuring, plowing, and planting as soon as danger of frost passed. Livestock and poultry needed constant attention; sheep had to be washed and sheared and geese plucked in the spring. Farm families reaped flax in June, enjoyed a brief respite in August, and then pushed hard for the fall harvest. In winter, men and boys cut wood, while women and girls spun thread and wove cloth for clothes. The garden and dairy were the responsibility of women and girls, the cash crops the responsibility of men. Farmers, chronically short of cash, bartered among themselves and with merchants.

After 1815, the farms in many parts of New England, New York, and Pennsylvania would be tied ever more tightly into the economies of the towns and cities. Farm families produced more cash crops and bought more things with money rather than through barter. Women, especially widows and other single females, worked in their homes to produce palm hats, portions of shoes, or articles of clothing that merchants from nearby cities gathered and had assembled in workshops. These women added such work to their farm work, laboring in the evenings and throughout the winters. With so many young men leaving New England for the West, many communities found themselves with considerable numbers of young women who might never marry as well as older women who could not count on the support of sons. Piecework offered these women a chance to contribute to the economies of their households in a way the older farm economy had not, bringing in scarce cash. It was important to everyone in their families that those wage-earning women did not have to leave home to earn those wages.

The expanded cash economy thus overlapped with and conflicted with an older, more self-contained economy. Families sought opportunity in new jobs and new markets, even as they feared that the increasingly dense networks of trade would depress the value of their crops, make seasonal farm labor even more difficult to acquire, entice young people from the farm, and undermine local artisans. Rural folk both welcomed and worried over the changes. Although it would be generations before cities and factories dominated the economies of the Northeast, in the meantime, farms, towns, and small factories grew ever more interconnected.

The textile industry of New England stood as the most dramatic example of industrial growth. The cost of cotton clothing fell faster than the cost for any other product as machinery and cheaper cotton lowered the price. Francis Cabot Lowell of Boston designed a power loom in 1813, recreating from memory a machine he had seen on a recent trip to England. The same year, Lowell and a partner, Nathan Appleton, spent over $400,000 to open the first factory in the United States that could integrate all the steps of making cloth under a single roof: the Boston Manufacturing Company, in Waltham, Massachusetts, where a waterfall with a ten-foot drop offered free power. An expanded group of investors in the enterprise—the Boston Associates, they were called—pooled the resources of the city's most prominent merchant families.

Unlike earlier factories, that of the Boston Associates used unskilled labor and machines even for weaving, the most expensive part of the process. Lowell and Appleton, concerned

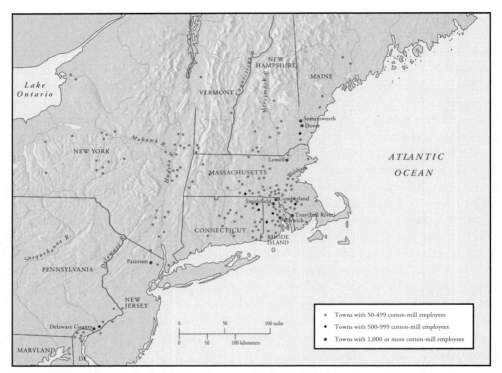

Map 9.5 Cotton Mills in the Northeast The cheap cotton of the South combined with the cheap labor and abundant water power of the Northeast to create the United States's first industrial economy in small towns and cities located on streams.

that the introduction of factories into the United States might create the same alienated and despised working class they saw in England, recruited young New England farm women and girls as operatives. Young females had experience in producing yarn and cloth at home and they would work hard for low wages. Many were eager to earn money for themselves, to move out of crowded homes, and to send money back to their families. As Appleton put it, the young women supplied "a fund of labor, well educated and virtuous" for the factory.

The operatives, considering millwork a three- or four-year commitment before they married and began families of their own, worked fourteen hours a day, six days a week. When they signed a contract with the agents who received a dollar a head for each worker they could recruit, the young women agreed to stay with the mill for at least twelve months or to be put on a blacklist that would prevent them from getting a job elsewhere. The factory was unlike anything the young women had ever confronted: "You cannot think how odd everything seemed," one mill girl recalled; even those who had spun and woven for years could not be prepared for the "frightful" sight of "so many bands, and wheels, and springs in constant motion." Leaving the factory in the evening, an operative could still hear the noise of the mill in her head, "as of crickets, frogs and jewsharps, all mingled together in strange discord."

The Early Textile Mills

The complex machinery, whirring spindles, and ceaseless web of threads to be pieced together when they broke took a toll on the health and safety of the young workforce of the early textile mills of New England. Women and girls were considered especially well-suited for this work because of their quick fingers and their familiarity with fabrics and thread. Most of the young women who came into the mills were adolescents and young women eager to get out on their own for a while before they married, and were able to contribute to the family income in a way not possible if they had stayed at home. New England at this time had a skewed sex ratio with a preponderance of females, as many of the younger men fled the hard farming of their native region to the easier lands of upstate New York and farther west.

The social and economic ground for industrialization had been broken in the Northeast. Mills, most of them small, grew up along the streams of Connecticut and the Delaware Valley of Pennsylvania and New Jersey, turning out not only textiles but also metal and wood products. These mills, like their bigger and more visible counterparts in Lowell, depended on low wages paid to workers without many other options. Many potential workers, competitors, and outside observers worried about the effects of the factories, even as investors and other supporters saw in the new buildings the hope for a richer and more productive American society.

Consequences of Expansion

The enlarged boundaries of the American nation, as exciting and promising as they seemed, brought troubles almost immediately. The newly integrated economy proved vulnerable to fluctuations in currency and to outside pressure. The rapid spread of slavery in the South threatened northerners who did not want to see the institution expand into new territories in the West. The resulting political fight over the future of slavery inspired slaves to launch a revolt in South Carolina. The leaders of the United States came to feel that their new status in the world called for an emboldened foreign policy, one that proclaimed an enlarged role for the United States in its hemisphere.

In all these ways, the explosive growth of the country in the fifteen years after 1815 brought consequences few could have imagined.

The Panic of 1819

In 1819, a series of events abroad and at home combined to bring a sudden halt to some of the growth in the economy of the United States. Prices for cotton lands in the Southeast, the most sought-after property in these years, skyrocketed as world demand for cotton cloth increased every year. Southern cotton rose to such an extent that in 1818 and 1819 British manufacturers turned to cotton from other sources, especially India. American cotton prices tumbled, along with the value of the land that produced it. And cotton was not the only crop whose value rapidly declined: tobacco plummeted from 40 cents a pound to 4 cents, wheat fell from $2.41 a bushel to 88 cents. State banks built on inflated, even fraudulent, credit wavered and then crashed. One year after authorizing the first military pensions for veterans of the Revolution, 16 percent of the federal budget was consumed by pensions just as financial crisis deepened. The Panic of 1819 had begun.

The panic proved a sudden and sobering reminder of just how complicated and interdependent the economy of the nation was becoming. The cities were hit the hardest. About half a million workers lost their jobs as business ground to a halt. Americans shuddered to see "children freezing in the winter's storm—and the fathers without coats and shoes." In the streets where new goods had been piled now wandered people without homes or food. Charitable groups opened soup kitchens. Wherever they could, families who had moved to towns and cities returned to the countryside to live with relatives. Things were not much safer in the country, however, where the failure of banks meant that apparently prosperous farmers saw household goods, farm animals, and the people they held as slaves sold in humiliating auctions.

Many people, including congressmen, began to call for the revocation of the charter of the Second Bank of the United States. States had chafed throughout the two years of the bank's life at what they considered its dictatorial power. Several states tried to limit that power by levying extremely high taxes on the branches of the Bank of the United States in their states, but it was at this point that the Supreme Court ruled in *McCulloch v. Maryland* that the laws of the federal government "form the supreme law of the land."

Despite the panic, James Monroe was reelected to the presidency in 1820 in one of the quietest and most lopsided elections in the nation's history. The Federalist party, fatally crippled by its opposition to the War of 1812 and its support of the Hartford Convention, offered no effective opposition. Neither did Monroe face an organized contest from others within his own Republican party, which was divided along sectional lines. He received every electoral vote but one. Most Americans seemed to blame someone other than President Monroe for the Panic of 1819 and the lingering hard times that followed it. The Era of

Good Feelings somehow managed to survive in the White House—though, it turned out, not in the halls of Congress.

The Missouri Compromise

The recent admission of the new states of the Southwest and Northwest had left a precarious balance in the Senate between slave states and free, though northern states held a strong, and growing, preponderance in the House of Representatives. The Missouri territory posed a special challenge to the balance. Slavery had quickly spread in Missouri, stretching along the richest river lands. If Missouri were admitted with slavery—as its territorial legislature had decreed—then the slave states would hold a majority in the Senate. Slavery in Missouri, an area of the same latitude as much of Illinois, Indiana, and Ohio, seemed to violate the assumption long held by many people in the North that slavery, if it grew at all, would expand only to the south.

The three-fifths clause of the Constitution, northerners complained, gave the slave states twenty more members of Congress and twenty more electors for the presidency than they would have if only white population were counted. The South seemed to be getting extra representation unfairly.

The debates over slavery in Missouri in 1819 and 1820 were not debates between fervent abolitionists in the North and fervent proslavery advocates in the South. Neither of those positions had yet been defined. Instead, white northerners and southerners of all political persuasions agreed that as many blacks as possible should be shipped to Africa. White Americans who could agree on little else about slavery did agree that blacks and whites could not live together in the United States once slavery had ended. That was the message of the American Colonization Society, founded in 1816 and based in Washington, D.C. Many Americans shared the sentiments of a New Hampshire member who wrote, "This is not their country. . . . O let them breathe the air of the land of their fathers. . . . Send them home." The society bought land in Africa—naming the new country "Liberia"—and sent about 12,000 free African Americans there over the next fifty years. Disease took a terrible toll, however, and many died. Fewer African Americans migrated. In Philadelphia, they even staged protests against the notion of colonization.

In the meantime, slavery caused problems for the political system. A New York congressman, James Tallmadge, Jr., introduced an amendment to the bill that would admit Missouri as a state permitting entry only if it admitted no more slaves and if those slaves in the territory were freed when they became twenty-five years old. More than eighty of the North's congressmen supported the Tallmadge amendment and only ten opposed it. In the Senate, though, the slave states prevailed by two votes. A deadlocked Congress adjourned in March of 1819 to meet again in December.

During the months in between, politicians worked behind the scenes to prepare for the debates and decisions of December. The Union, so celebrated and expansive in the wake of the war with Britain, so peaceful for whites since the Creeks, Seminoles, and Cherokees had been quelled, now seemed in danger of breaking apart from within. Both northern and

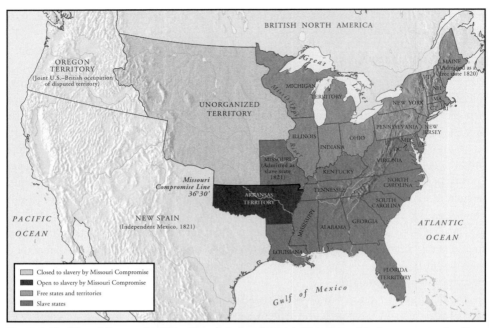

Map 9.6 The Missouri Compromise The conflict over the fate of slavery in Missouri proved the first great sectional conflict over the issue. Under the provisions of the Missouri Compromise, Missouri entered the Union as a slave state while Maine entered as a free state. Slavery was prohibited in the remainder of the Louisiana Territory.

southern politicians talked openly of ending the Union if need be. Simmering northern resentment, held in check for decades, was suddenly announced, even celebrated. Southerners felt betrayed. In their eyes, slavery was a thing they had inherited, something for which they bore no blame, an institution that would fade away naturally if it were left alone. White southerners thought northerners irresponsible and unrealistic to attack as the Tallmadge amendment did. The denial of Missouri statehood seemed to southerners nothing less than an assault on their character.

In northern states, where abolitionist societies had been relatively sedate, people suddenly announced the depth of their distaste for the institution. Furious meetings erupted in towns and cities across the North, turning out petitions and resolutions in large numbers. Slavery, these petitions thundered, was a blot on the nation, a violation of the spirit of Christianity, an abomination that must not spread into places it had not already ruined. The antislavery advocates of the 1820s expected colonization and abolition to occur simultaneously and gradually. But they were also determined to stop the spread of slavery toward the northern part of the continent.

After weeks of debate, a compromise emerged from the Senate: Missouri, with no restriction on slavery, should be admitted to the Union at the same time as Maine, thereby ensuring the balance between slave and free states. Slavery would be prohibited in all the lands acquired in the Louisiana Purchase north of the southern border of Missouri at 36° 309 latitude. Such a provision excluded the Arkansas territory, where slavery was already established, but closed to slavery the vast expanses of the Louisiana Territory—the future states of Iowa, Minnesota, Wisconsin, the Dakotas, Nebraska, and Kansas. Any slaves who escaped to the free states would be returned. Many of the northern men who voted for the measure found themselves burned in effigy back home and defeated when it came time for reelection. The South was no more satisfied than the North, furious to hear itself vilified in the national capital it had long dominated.

The debate broke out again when the Missouri constitutional convention not only authorized slavery but decreed that the state legislature could never emancipate slaves without the consent of their masters; the proposed constitution also pronounced that free blacks would never be permitted to enter the new state. The national House of Representatives refused to admit Missouri under this document, and the denunciation by both sides began again where it had paused. Finally, in early 1821, Henry Clay managed to fix a majority in the House in favor of a bill that would admit Missouri as long as the new state promised to pass no law barring the entry of a citizen from any other state. Exhausted, Congress ratified the law.

Northern and southern states had become wary and distrustful of one another as they had never been before. In a real sense, the debates over slavery in Missouri created "the North" and "the South," uniting the new states of the Northwest with the states of New England, New York, and Pennsylvania as they had not been united earlier, forging a tighter alliance between the new states of the Southwest and Virginia, the Carolinas, and Georgia. To the North, the South seemed greedy and corrupt; to the South, the North seemed greedy and hypocritical. The country became polarized as never before.

Vesey's Revolt

In Charleston, South Carolina, the heart of South Carolina's richest plantation district, a free black man named Denmark Vesey had closely followed in the papers the debates over the Missouri controversy. What he read there reinforced what he had seen in the Bible and the documents of the American Revolution: slavery was immoral. Vesey, a middle-aged mulatto of large stature who had bought his freedom twenty years earlier, stood as a commanding presence among the African American people of the low country. A skilled carpenter and preacher, Vesey traveled up and down the coast and into the interior, berating those blacks who accepted racial insult. Many African Americans were attracted to him; most were afraid to oppose him regardless.

Vesey drew not only upon his own strengths, but upon those of a powerful ally, a man known as Gullah Jack. This man, an Angolan, had arrived in South Carolina near the turn of the century, one of the 40,000 slaves brought into the state right before the end of the legal slave trade in 1807. Gullah Jack still looked very much the part of the conjurer he was, with huge whiskers, tiny arms, and unusual gestures setting him apart from American-born blacks.

The conspirators hoped to seize the city's poorly protected guardhouse, stores, and roads before the whites could gather themselves in opposition. House slaves would kill their white owners. Once Charleston was secure, the rebels, Vesey planned, would sail to Haiti, where Toussaint L'Ouverture had staged a black rebellion decades earlier and where slavery had been abolished. But a house servant broke under the pressure and alerted Charleston whites to the danger only two days before the revolt planned for June 16, 1822. The governor ordered out five military companies, and Vesey called off the attack. Over the next two months, white authorities hanged thirty-five alleged conspirators and banished thirty-seven more from the state. Few of the rebels would reveal the names of their allies, going to their deaths with the secrets of the revolt secure. Denmark Vesey was one of those killed.

Charleston Mayor James Hamilton bragged that "There can be no harm in the salutary inculcation of one lesson, among a certain portion of our population, that there is nothing they are bad enough to do, that we are not powerful enough to punish." Despite such boasts, white southerners blamed Vesey's Rebellion on the agitation against slavery by northern congressmen in the Missouri debate. "The events of 1822," a leading South Carolinian observed, "will long be remembered, as amongst the choicest fruits of the agitation of that question in Congress."

The Monroe Doctrine

The instability of the Spanish regime in Europe, exacerbated by the Napoleonic Wars, sent aftershocks into the colonies in the New World. Throughout the first and second decades of the nineteenth century, one struggle after another disrupted Latin America. Seeing Spain vulnerable in Europe and abroad, leaders in the colonies of the Western Hemisphere—Simón Bolívar in Venezuela, José de San Martín in Argentina, and Miguel Hidalgo in Mexico— pushed ahead with their long-simmering plans for national independence. By 1822, Chile, Mexico, Venezuela, and the Portuguese colony of Brazil had all gained their independence.

Neither the United States nor Great Britain wanted to see France fill the vacuum left by Spain in the New World. A French or Russian empire would pose a potentially dangerous economic and military threat much greater than any posed by the fading Spanish regime. Accordingly, in March of 1822 President Monroe urged Congress to recognize the new republics of Latin America. Throughout the next year, as the French army invaded Spain, the U.S. minister in England proposed that the United States and England jointly declare that neither country would annex any part of the tottering empire of Spain nor permit any other power to do so. Encouraged by former presidents Jefferson and Madison, Monroe wanted to make the joint declaration, but Secretary of State John Quincy Adams persuaded him that it would be more fitting and dignified for the United States to declare its policy independently instead of coming "in as a cock-boat in the wake of the British man o'war." Adams's policy was directed more against outside intervention in Latin America than in favor of the new republics, which he considered weak and unlikely to endure an attack by a major power.

Accordingly, in December of 1823 the president used his annual message to Congress to announce what would eventually become known as the Monroe Doctrine: "The American continents, by the free and independent conditions which they have assumed and maintained, are henceforth not to be considered as subjects for future colonisation by any European power." The North American republic had exerted its first claim to recognition by the great powers of the world, making a show of acting independently even though Great Britain was the real power. The Russians and Spanish denounced the American policy as "blustering," "arrogant," "indecent," and "monstrous," meriting only "the most profound contempt." They tolerated the doctrine because the European powers, exhausted by wars among themselves, had little desire to expand their involvement on the other side of the world. The leaders of the Latin American revolts welcomed the warning to the European powers, but were less certain about the United States's own intentions toward Latin America. The Monroe Doctrine, after all, did not say that the United States would not interfere in the Western Hemisphere, only that it would not permit European countries to do so.

The Reinvention of Politics

Two events of 1824 threw into sharp relief the accomplishments and dangers of the emerging nation. The first event was the thirteen-month tour of the United States by one of the heroes of the American Revolution: the Marquis de Lafayette. The second event was the presidential election of 1824. While Lafayette's visit tied the country together with bonds of memory and celebration, the election showed that Americans had become far more divided than had seemed possible only four years earlier.

Lafayette's Return

Lafayette sailed into New York and was met, fittingly enough, with a steamboat, symbol of the strides the United States had made since Lafayette's departure decades earlier. He spent tumultuous and tearful days in New York, where old comrades and young admirers poured out to see the living embodiment of the sacrifices and bravery of the Revolutionary War. Then Lafayette, along with his son, George Washington Lafayette, and his traveling companion, a radical young Scotswoman named Frances Wright, set out to see the rest of the United States. They went first to New England, visiting with John Adams, then down the coast to Philadelphia, Baltimore, Washington, Charleston, and then New Orleans. From there, they went up the Mississippi and on to Nashville, where he met Andrew Jackson.

Everywhere Lafayette traveled, the people tried to outdo what had been done before; the hero met with booming guns, torchlight parades, thousands of children dressed in the colors of France, beautiful young women, illuminated pictures, banquet after banquet, speech after speech. Some moments stood out: when the general cried, alone, at the grave of Washington at Mount Vernon, and when he traveled to Monticello to meet with Jefferson.

Congress, knowing that the marquis was in serious financial difficulties, presented him with a gift of $200,000 (an enormous sum at the time) and a township of public land. Lafayette met with Cherokees in Georgia. Slaves, hearing of the patriot's opposition to slavery, lined the roads wherever he went to cheer him on.

A toast announced what Americans most admired in Lafayette, "the great apostle of liberty whom the persecutions of tyranny could not defeat, whom the love of riches could not influence, whom popular applause could never seduce." The Frenchman, in other words, was admired for his selflessness at the time of the American Revolution, for putting the cause of liberty before his own self-interest, for putting himself at risk in the pursuit of freedom. Such a posture of noble self-sacrifice was what Americans valued most in their public men and what they expected of those to whom power was given. In Lafayette, they could celebrate the best in themselves. While remembering their own Revolution and celebrating Lafayette, the 18th Congress defeated a resolution to express its sympathy with revolutionaries in Greece attempting to throw off Ottoman rule. Although backed by Henry Clay and Daniel Webster, one of the resolution's opponents remarked that America would persuade others by "the moral influence of its example," not by actively supporting democratic movements abroad.

The Election of 1824

Many people felt that they saw the worst of the country in the presidential election going on while Lafayette toured the country. Few eligible voters had bothered to cast a ballot four years earlier when James Monroe had won the presidency without opposition, for his election seemed foreordained. But politicians and observers expected a more interesting contest in 1824. Many thought the next president would be William Crawford, secretary of the treasury, a Georgian and apparent heir to the Virginia dynasty. Others focused on John Quincy Adams, an experienced statesman, New Englander, and the secretary of state—the office from which many presidents had come. Others looked to John C. Calhoun of South Carolina, an impressive secretary of war and advocate of a strong national government. Yet others placed their bets on Henry Clay of Kentucky, Speaker of the House of Representatives for many years and one of the most visible members of Congress. Finally, Andrew Jackson of Tennessee hoped to parlay the widespread fame he won in the wars against the English and the Indians into the presidency.

Several of these men realized they did not command sufficient national support to win the election outright. They hoped, however, to prevail if the election went into the House of Representatives, where the top three candidates would vie if no candidate won in the electoral college. Cliques spread rumors, and alliances of convenience flourished. Openly partisan newspapers sang the praises of their man and published lacerating rumors about his opponents. The most novel was John Henry Eaton's successful press campaign to portray Jackson as a patriotic soldier, quietly tending his farm while Washington politicians schemed to block his election by ordinary voters because of his lack of polish and his incorruptible character.

While the Marquis de Lafayette serenely toured the United States, local and state politicians worked feverishly in taverns, caucuses, and newspaper offices. Many American voters seemed disenchanted with the crass politicking, though, and relatively few voted in 1824. Jackson's popular vote nearly equaled that of Adams and Crawford combined, but the election was thrown into the House of Representatives because no candidate received a plurality in the electoral college. The House could choose among the top three candidates: Jackson, Adams, and Crawford.

Since his fourth-place finish put him out of the running, Clay, the Speaker of the House, sought to strike the best deal he could with the other candidates, assuring himself of maximum power, visibility, and opportunities in subsequent elections. Clay, considering Jackson unworthy of the post and a potential military despot, discussed his future with Adams. When the vote came to the House of Representatives in early 1825, Adams won the presidency—taking the three states Clay had won in the electoral college. Two weeks later, Henry Clay received the appointment of secretary of state. "So you see," Andrew Jackson fumed, "the Judas of the West has closed the contract and will receive the thirty pieces of silver." Throughout the muddy little city of Washington, people speculated about the promises the upright John Quincy Adams had made to win the presidency. People often mentioned the cold sweat that broke out on his face when he received word of his election.

Adams wanted a stronger national government, internal improvements, and a tariff to protect American industry. But he could not mobilize support for his positions, either within Washington or among the voters. Adams refused to use patronage to persuade or coerce people to go along with his plans. His administration bogged down into factionalism and paralysis, always with the shadow of his supposed "corrupt bargain" with Clay darkening his reputation. Things seemed far removed, indeed, from the glorious days when Lafayette sacrificed for the American Revolution.

New York politicians sought to harness ambition into useful and organized forms in the 1820s, pioneering the development of the party system. Aaron Burr converted a simple patriotic club in New York City, the Society of Saint Tammany, into the beginnings of a major political machine. De Witt Clinton invented the "spoils system," in which it became the expectation that an incoming officeholder would remove those appointed by his predecessor and put his own supporters in their place. Martin Van Buren, a young lawyer and politician from New York, nicknamed the "Little Magician," combined the city machine and the spoils system into a powerful statewide organization. He used newspapers in Albany and New York City to spread the word of the party to the fifty small newspapers he controlled throughout the state, which also published vast numbers of handbills, posters, and ballots at election time. He built a large network of party men, many of them lawyers who traveled widely in the state and knew many of their counterparts. Van Buren's goal was to combine party unity with personal advancement for party members, creating a powerful and self-reinforcing cycle.

Martin Van Buren opposed John Quincy Adams in the presidential contest of 1824 because Adams's nationally sponsored canals, roads, education, and other services would cut into the power of state government and state politics, elevating what Van Buren saw as dangerous federal power over power closer to home. Partly for this reason, Van Buren cast his lot in 1824 and the years thereafter with Andrew Jackson, who shared Van Buren's preference for localized power. As the next presidential election came closer, Van Buren, now a senator, worked ever more energetically for Jackson, hoping to spread the model of New York politics to the nation as a whole.

The Adams Twilight

The second half of John Quincy Adams's administration proved unhappy and unproductive. Neither Adams's talents nor his devotion to the Union had faded, but the public mood seemed little interested in either. The "corrupt bargain," in which Henry Clay allegedly conspired to hand the presidency to Adams, still hung over the White House in 1827. In the eyes of many, Adams had proven himself unfit for office, not only with his reputed bargain, but also, false rumor persisted, by procuring a young American girl for the Russian czar when Adams served as a fourteen-year-old member of the U.S. diplomatic corps in St. Petersburg. The president's elite education and even his purchase of a billiard table and chess set for the White House were disparaged by opponents as symbols of "aristocracy." Adams's many and diverse opponents organized against him and his policies almost from the beginning of his administration. It soon became clear that the president would be able to accomplish little of his ambitious agenda of internal improvements, a national university, and western exploration, ideals that might have won support in earlier years.

Supporters of Andrew Jackson of Tennessee, John C. Calhoun of South Carolina, and William Crawford of Georgia gradually joined forces in anticipation of the election of 1828, when they hoped to unseat Adams and his vision of an active and centralized government. The struggle, Calhoun wrote to Jackson, was between "power and liberty." The champion of power had had his turn, Adams's opponents believed; now it was time for the champions of liberty to step forward. After some jockeying, Andrew Jackson emerged as the man to challenge Adams.

Adams's supporters warned of the dangers of electing a raw and rough "military chieftain" such as Andrew Jackson to the presidency. Jackson's opponents distributed a handbill marked with eighteen coffins, each one representing a man Jackson had supposedly killed in a duel or ordered executed under his military command. The most incendiary charge, however, was that Jackson had married a woman married to another man, leading her to commit both bigamy and adultery in the process. The facts of the case were unclear—it appears that Rachel Jackson was a religious woman, trapped in a bad marriage, who thought she had received a divorce when she married Jackson—but the anti-Jackson forces made the most of any suspicions to the contrary.

Anti-Masons

Charges of conspiracy and corruption raged throughout American politics in the 1820s. Some of the suspicions seemed confirmed by events in New York. As the economy of that state prospered along with the Erie Canal, so did fraternal organizations of every sort. The

Ancient Order of Masons did especially well, claiming almost 350 lodges in the state. The Masons' exclusive society, surrounded by elaborate ritual and strict secrecy, many non-Masons felt, contradicted American ideals of democracy and openness, taking men away from their families and undermining organized religion. Since Masons were obliged to show business or political preference to a brother over "any other person in the same circumstances," some of those outside the order feared that Masons might win undue influence in their town, state, or country. As proof, they pointed out that every New York governor but one between 1804 and the late 1820s belonged to the Masons.

Suspicion of the Masons exploded when a brother named William Morgan turned against the order and decided to publish its secret rituals. Local Masonic leaders used their influence with county officials to harass and jail Morgan, who was later kidnapped in September 1826. He disappeared; many said he had been murdered. The investigation soon stalled, however, as Masonic law enforcement officers and others dragged their feet. Despite twenty trials and three special prosecutors, only a few convictions resulted and those convictions brought only minor jail terms. Congregations split and communities divided into warring factions over the Masons. Alleged Masonic skullduggery proved a convenient way to explain personal and political setbacks. A local Episcopal rector recorded his dismay: "I have lived here in the midst of fire, and . . . it has scorched my ears." Fury against the Masons soon spread from New York to the rest of the country, forcing one lodge after another to dissolve.

By 1827, nearly a hundred "Morgan committees" had met and formed in New York and began to spread across the entire northern half of the country, attracting men of reputation and prestige. Within two years, the "Anti-Masons" had established more than a hundred newspapers. They held public meetings and launched lobbying campaigns, bypassing local elites and inventing new means of pressuring legislatures directly. Unlike earlier reform organizations, such as those that supported Sunday schools and the distribution of Bibles, the Anti-Masons thrived on controversy. They devoted themselves to changing public opinion, to mobilizing people against a powerful entrenched force. They succeeded: Masonry lost more than half its members and created virtually no new lodges for the next fifteen years. So great was the Anti-Masons' success, in fact, that the movement's leaders dreamed of creating a new party to purify and energize American politics.

Birth of the Democrats

Even while the struggle over the Masons unfolded, Senator Martin Van Buren of New York was building a political coalition behind Andrew Jackson. Van Buren traveled throughout the United States, hammering out a new coalition of ambitious state politicians willing to back Jackson. The members of the coalition called themselves "Democratic Republicans," eventually to be shortened to "Democrats." Their candidates did extremely well in the off-year congressional elections of 1827, exploiting people's disapproval of the ineffectual Adams administration. The Democrats controlled both the House and the Senate.

Throughout 1827 and 1828, Van Buren and the other party leaders organized voters as they had never been organized before. Although Jackson himself was a prominent

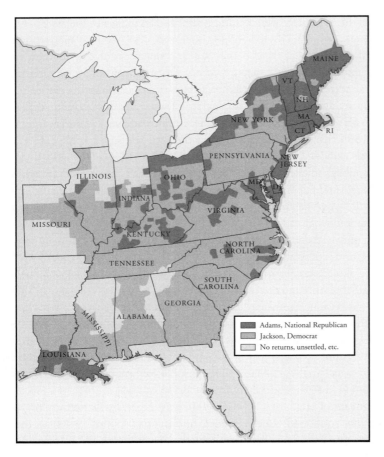

Map 9.7 **The Election of 1828**
Andrew Jackson overwhelmed John Quincy Adams almost everywhere except in Adams's native New England.

Mason, Van Buren adopted techniques not unlike those pioneered by the Anti-Masons in these same years. Using every strategy at their disposal—bonfires, speeches, barbecues, parades, professional writers, and the first campaign song—these Jacksonians claimed that they had found a true man of the people to strip the office from the aristocratic Adams. In towns across the country, "Old Hickory"—Jackson was supposedly as hardy as that toughest of trees—was celebrated with hickory poles, brooms, sticks, and trees. The National Republicans, as Adams's supporters became known, sniffed at what they considered the unseemly display that diverted attention from real issues, but they could not deny the power of the new methods to win voters' attention.

In the meantime, American politics became more democratic and inclusive. Most legislatures across the Union lowered property requirements for voting and made judicial offices elective rather than appointed. Voters seemed restless, hungry for someone to give direction and force to public life. Voting turnout in 1828 doubled that of the 1824 election. The dramatic confrontation of men and styles contributed to widespread voter interest, while politicians at every level and on both sides made sure voters went to the polls.

Jackson won easily over Adams, winning 178 of the 261 electoral votes, capturing the critical mid-Atlantic states and all the states of the South except Louisiana and Kentucky. The election proved bittersweet for Jackson, though, for his wife died soon afterward. Jackson blamed the slanderers of the other party for Rachel's death, for she had fallen ill after seeing an editorial denouncing her. The president-elect passed the weeks before his inauguration in sadness and bitterness.

Conclusion

The United States saw enormous economic change between 1815 and 1828. New states in both the Southwest and the Northwest joined the national and international economies. The nation's armies conquered and removed diverse peoples among the Native Americans. Cotton poured from Alabama and Mississippi in ever-growing amounts, while food flowed from Indiana and Illinois. Banks proliferated with the expanding population, and the Second Bank of the United States lent stability to the system. The major ports along the east coast grew as they had never grown before, connecting the expanding United States with the economies of England and Europe. New factory buildings went up along the streams and rivers of the Northeast, producing by water power what hands had made only a few years earlier. Turnpikes and roads covered the country in an increasingly dense network. Such changes seemed to mark the beginning of a new kind of security and prosperity for the United States.

As the economy and territory grew, however, Americans had to reckon with the consequences of their expansion. The political system churned as people from different areas of the country and different economic factions jockeyed for power. Democracy turned out to be far messier than the Founding Fathers had imagined, creating new kinds of political figures, new kinds of political parties, and new kinds of politcal conflicts that threatened to pull the nation apart almost as soon as it came together.

RECOMMENDED READINGS

Appleby, Joyce. *Inheriting the Revolution: The First Generation of Americans* (2000). Paints a wonderful picture of these years.

Cashin, Joan E. *A Family Venture: Men and Women on the Southern Frontier* (1991). Tells the story of the southwestern migration in a compelling way.

Dangerfield, George. *The Awakening of American Nationalism, 1815–1828* (1965). A classic interpretation of the postwar era.

Davis, David Brion. *The Problem of Slavery in the Age of Revolution, 1770–1823* (1975). Gives a magisterial overview of the international struggles with slavery.

Freehling, William W. *The Road to Disunion: The Secessionists at Bay, 1776–1854* (1990). Portrays the drama of sectional conflict throughout this era.

Horwitz, Morton J. *The Transformation of American Law, 1780–1860* (1977). Puts forward a strong and controversial argument about the law and commerce.

Larson, John Lauritz. *Internal Improvement: National Public Works and the Promise of Popular Government in the Early United States* (2001). The best treatment of this important subject.

Lewis, James E. *The American Union and the Problem of Neighborhood: The United States and the Collapse of the Spanish Empire, 1783–1829* (1998). Provides a fresh interpretation of this complicated relationship.

Mathews, Jean. *Toward a New Society: American Thought and Culture, 1800–1830* (1990). Offers a subtle interpretation of cultural history of this period.

Rohrbough, Malcolm J. *The Trans-Appalachian Frontier: People, Societies, and Institutions, 1775–1850* (1978). Tells this complex story well.

Saunt, Claudio. *A New Order of Things: Property, Power, and the Transformation of the Creek Indians, 1733–1816* (1999). Makes comprehensible the great complexities in the lives of American Indians in these crucial decades.

Sellers, Charles G. *The Market Revolution: Jacksonian America, 1815–1846* (1991). Gives a stirring portrayal of the period with economic change at the center.

Sheriff, Carol. *The Artificial River: The Erie Canal and the Paradox of Progress, 1817–1862* (1996). Offers a compelling account of the canal's origins, building, and effects.

Additional resources, exercises, and Internet links related to this chapter are available on the American Passages Web site: http://history.wadsworth.com/ayerscompact2/

10

The Years of Andrew Jackson
1829–1836

Tumultuous change came to the United States in the years Andrew Jackson served as president. Elections became sweeping public events that involved men of every class. Voters and leaders hotly debated and contested the role of government in American life. Religious revivals swept up entire communities in devotion and prayer. Working people created labor unions, and abolitionists launched a bold crusade against slavery.

Growing democracy was not the full story of these years, however. The people of the Creek, Choctaw, Cherokee, Seminole, Sac, and Fox nations were driven from their homes in the South and in the old Northwest. A crisis threatened to ignite a military struggle between South Carolina and the federal government. The revolt of Nat Turner and debates over slavery in Virginia unleashed a proslavery reaction throughout much of the South. The defeat of Mexico in Texas opened a vast new territory to slavery as well as to the settlement of free Americans. Few decades in American history witnessed more important and more fundamental changes.

Accompanying this rapid expansion of boundaries of every sort was considerable anxiety that American society threatened to spin out of control. The government held little power, and people worried that many Americans had moved beyond the influence of church, family, school, or employer. Some Americans began to suggest ways to contain the consequences of change. They offered political compromise, reform societies, and new ideals of the home as ways to counteract what they saw as threatening chaos.

Andrew Jackson Takes Charge

Andrew Jackson, still dressed in black in mourning after the recent death of his beloved wife Rachel, traveled by steamboat from Nashville to Washington in the winter of 1829 to begin his presidency. The entire nation watched to see what sort of changes this new kind of leader might make, what sort of America he might help create.

The People's President

Once he arrived in Washington, Jackson began to assemble his cabinet, balancing North, South, and West. Martin Van Buren, leader of Jackson's successful campaign the year before, became secretary of state, a position traditionally reserved for the man next in line

CHRONOLOGY

1828	Tariff of Abominations • Calhoun's *Exposition* • Election of Jackson
1829	David Walker's *Appeal* • Mexico tries to abolish slavery in Texas
1830	Indian Removal Act • *The Book of Mormon* • Finney's revivals begin in Rochester • Anti-Masonic party holds first national party convention
1831	Nat Turner's rebellion • Garrison's *The Liberator* • Jackson reorganizes cabinet, Van Buren over Calhoun • Mormons migrate from New York to Ohio
1832	Bank War begins • Nullification Crisis • Virginia debates over slavery • Jackson reelected
1833	Formation of American Anti-slavery Society • Force Bill against South Carolina • Compromise Tariff • Slavery abolished in British Empire
1834	Whig party organized • National Trades Union formed
1835	Arkansas admitted to the Union • Revolution breaks out in Texas • Abolitionists' postal campaign • War against Seminoles and runaway slaves in Florida
1836	Congress imposes gag rule • Battle of the Alamo; Texas Republic established • Treaty of New Echota • Election of Martin Van Buren

for the presidency. Vice President John C. Calhoun, ambitious for the presidency himself, chafed at the appointment but could do little to change it; he and his wing of the party had to satisfy themselves with the appointment of one of their number as secretary of the treasury. The most controversial appointment, however, proved volatile for reasons that had little to do with political partisanship. Jackson wanted a close friend in the cabinet, someone in whom he could confide, and he chose an old Tennessee associate and influential editor, John Eaton, as his secretary of war.

Eaton, a widower in middle age, had married Peggy O'Neal Timberlake, an attractive and witty twenty-nine-year-old daughter of a well-known innkeeper in Washington. She was rumored to have driven her last husband to suicide, forcing him to defraud the government to pay debts she had run up. She was also rumored to have had sex with Eaton before their marriage—along with, one contemporary smirked, "eleven doz. others!" Eaton had asked Jackson's opinion of the marriage beforehand, receiving the old general's blessing; the president liked outspoken women and knew from bitter experience the power that unfounded rumors could hold. Jackson, in a gesture of friendship and support as the gossip flew, offered Eaton the cabinet position, apparently hoping he would decline. Unfortunately for Jackson, Eaton accepted. The decision electrified Washington.

Despite his rambunctious youth, Jackson disdained official Washington's fondness for strong drink, endless banquets, and overheated social life. He had witnessed that high life during his time as senator from Tennessee and he held it in contempt when he returned to the capital; he preferred instead to attend the city's churches. Jackson considered him-

The Missouri Compromise

The conflict over the fate of slavery in Missouri proved the first great sectional conflict over the issue. Under the provisions of the Missouri Compromise, Missouri entered the Union as a slave state while Maine entered as a free state. Slavery was prohibited in the remainder of the Louisiana Territory.

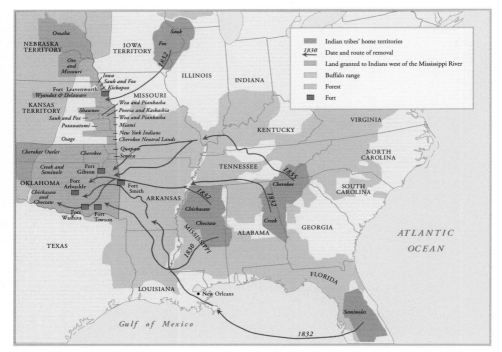

Removal of the American Indians
In the early 1830s, the Indians of the North and South were "removed" to reservations in Oklahoma and Kansas.

The Growth of Railroads

A vastly expanded transportation network tied the United States together. The system exaggerated sectional differences by unifying the Northeast with the Northwest, creating the reality and perception of a "North" with interests different from those of a "South" stretching from the Atlantic to the Mississippi and beyond.

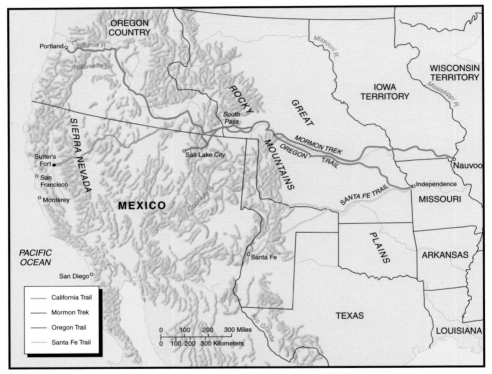

Trails to the West

The trails to Oregon and California looked straightforward enough on a map but proved immensely challenging, even deadly, in practice.

self an outsider despite his power and popularity, an outsider determined to reform Washington, to make the city worthy of the nation it was supposed to serve.

As the inauguration day of March 4 neared, Washington's population doubled as men who considered themselves important in General Jackson's election arrived in the city to claim their fair share of glory, excitement, and jobs. They drank all the whiskey the city had to offer, slept five to a bed, and generally offended the more genteel residents of the capital. At the inauguration, 30,000 people crowded in to see the new president. After Jackson's brief address, members of the excited audience followed him back to the

One of the most famous men in the United States due to his exploits in the War of 1812, Andrew Jackson of Tennessee seemed to many people an inspiring leader. Others, however, saw him as a "military chieftain" dangerous with the power of the presidency.

White House—as one observer put it, "country men, farmers, gentlemen mounted and dismounted, boys, women and children, black and white, carriages, waggons and carts all pursuing him." They surged into the White House, spilling barrels of orange punch, standing with muddy boots on expensive chairs to get a better look at the proceedings, smashing thousands of dollars worth of china. Servants attracted the mob outside by moving the liquor. Jackson, suffocated by admirers and disgusted by the scene, climbed out a rear window and went for a steak at his boardinghouse.

Jackson and the "Spoils System"

Many people in Washington were as appalled at the events that followed the inauguration as they were with the inauguration itself. As the new administration got under way, Jackson and his advisors cleaned house in the federal government, removing those officials whose competence, honesty, or loyalty to Jackson and the Democrats were suspect. Although such a policy had become established practice in several major states, including Van Buren's New York, Jackson was the first president to make such sweeping changes on the federal level. He envisioned himself purging an arrogant bureaucracy of corruption, establishing the democratic practice of "rotation in office." As officeholders quaked and fretted, Jackson's lieutenants decided which custom houses and federal offices would be cleansed. Some of the incumbents clearly deserved to lose their jobs, having served jail terms, embezzled funds, or succumbed to drink, but others were guilty only of being active partisans for the other side in the recent election.

Jackson removed about 900 of 10,000 men from their offices and removed them in an especially brash spirit. One Jackson supporter unwisely announced to the Senate that the Jacksonians saw "nothing wrong in the rule that to the victors belong the spoils of the enemy." This proclamation gave an enduring notoriety to what from then on would be called the "spoils system," a system that Jackson envisioned as reform, not cynical politics. A Washington woman observed, "Oh how dreadfully a parent must feel when he looks on his children gathered round him, and knows that one word spoken by a stranger, may reduce them to beggary. Such is the situation of hundreds . . . men too far advanced in life to be able to enter on new paths of industry."

Jackson further infuriated opponents by appointing partisan newspaper editors to important posts, leading to charges that Jackson was corrupting, rather than cleansing, American government. One key appointment, the collector of the Port of New York, did indeed prove disastrous, as the man eventually fled the United States with $1.2 million of the people's money. Over the course of Jackson's two terms he replaced only about 10 percent of all officeholders, not many more than his predecessors had, but Jackson also recognized the power of the postal system to aid partisan political aims. He elevated the postmaster general to a cabinet level position and worked to appoint friendly editors as local postmasters where they solicited subscriptions to Democratic publications and were frequently accused of misrouting or destroying rivals' pamphlets and newspapers.

The festering conflict within the administration over the so-called Eaton affair proved just how important matters of symbolism could be. The wives of the other cabinet members, Vice President Calhoun's wife, and even Emily Donelson—Jackson's daughter-in-law and hostess of the White House—refused to be in the same room with Peggy Eaton. But Jackson would not be swayed in his support for John and Peggy Eaton. The new cabinet found itself bitterly divided between pro-Eaton and anti-Eaton factions. Jackson labored to mend fences, calling an influential pastor to the White House and trying to find evidence to prove Mrs. Eaton's virtue. Nothing proved effective, though, and Jackson decided that the real villain of the story was Vice President Calhoun and his unbending wife Floride. By contrast, Martin Van Buren, a widower, cemented his friendship with the president by treating Mrs. Eaton with ostentatious respect. Jackson, embittered by the refusal of his other advisors to stand by Mrs. Eaton, largely abandoned his official cabinet and relied instead on an informal group of advisors, his so-called Kitchen Cabinet, and on Van Buren, the only winner in the Eaton episode.

Struggles over Slavery

The years around 1830 saw several issues surrounding slavery come to a head. Southern states, worried about the rapidly growing population and power of the North, sought to define the limits of federal power. Feeling themselves neglected and abused by northern interests, South Carolina leaders tried to secure greater autonomy. At the same time, free blacks in both the North and South worked to replace the colonization movement with a

The young wife of Secretary of War John Eaton became the center of a scandal that rocked Washington during Andrew Jackson's first term.

campaign to end slavery and create freedom for African Americans in America. Even as these struggles unfolded, the largest slave revolt in the history of the United States erupted in Virginia. Combined, these events demonstrated that slavery and the issues on which it touched would bedevil the confident and boisterous young country far into the future.

The Tariff of Abominations, Nullification, and States' Rights

Before the election of 1828, Martin Van Buren and other Democrats had sought to broaden support for Jackson, whose strength lay in the South, by passing a tariff favorable to the economic interests of New Englanders and westerners. After elaborate deal making, the Democrats enacted a major tariff. But it came with a high cost: southerners were furious with what they called this "tariff of abominations," for it raised the price they would have to pay for manufactured items and threatened markets abroad for southern cotton. John C. Calhoun, like other South Carolina planters, feared not only that the tariff would bleed the state dry economically but that it would set a precedent for antislavery forces who might gain control of the federal government at some future date.

Accordingly, in the summer and early fall of 1828, a few months before he would take office as Jackson's vice president, Calhoun sought to find a principled way to reconcile his national ambitions and his local concerns. Rather than argue only against the tariff itself, Calhoun asserted the general rights of individual states within the Union. To do so, he returned to what he called "the primitive principles of our government," the foundations on which everything else rested. Calhoun insisted that interests had become so diverse in the United States that laws appropriate for one state or section might well harm another. Rather than merely letting the majority run roughshod over the minority, Calhoun believed, it made more sense to let a state "nullify" a national law within its own borders. Such nullification was constitutional, he said, because the federal system did not locate sovereignty in any one place, but rather divided it among the states and the nation. Should three-fourths of the states agree that a law must apply to all the country, then that clear majority could overrule the nullification. Calhoun thought he was finding a way to preserve order in an increasingly contentious Union. The document in which he laid out his ideas, the *South Carolina Exposition,* appeared in December of 1828; the pamphlet was published anonymously because it was too politically dangerous for the vice president of the United States to be publicly on record for nullification.

Calhoun's declaration of principles came at a celebration of Thomas Jefferson's birthday at the Indian Queen Hotel in Washington. Southern and western Democrats hoped that the gathering would reveal the strength of the alliance between the two sections, both of which wanted greater autonomy from the federal government. President Jackson, Vice President Calhoun, and Secretary of State Van Buren were all present. Van Buren urged the president to make clear his own position on nullification and states' rights. No one was really sure what Jackson thought on the issue, since he was identified as a southerner but had made his reputation fighting for the Union against the British. As the officeholders went around the table, one toast after another proclaiming the rights of the states, Jackson became ever more steely. When it was his turn, the president stood, lifted his glass, and—staring at Calhoun—pronounced words filled with a meaning obvious to those present: "Our Federal Union—it must be preserved." Van Buren climbed on a chair to see how Calhoun would respond to this rebuke. "The Union—next to our liberties the most dear," he retorted, his glass trembling, "may we all remember that it can only be preserved by respecting the rights of the states and distributing equally the benefits and burdens of the Union." There was no going back.

South Carolina planters persuaded themselves that they would have to do something soon. They watched with growing alarm as the newspapers told of the success of British abolitionists in ending slavery in the British West Indies—the place from which many elite white South Carolina families had come generations earlier. With the memory of Denmark Vesey's plan of 1822 and an 1829 revolt in the low country still fresh in their memory, white Carolinians felt they could display no weakness on the slavery issue. Unlike other southern states, where stark geographic differences between low country and hill country often divided voters and encouraged party differences, South Carolina witnessed broad agreement among its electorate on this crucial issue. Throughout the state, raucous crowds gathered to call for a fight against the federal government on the tariff. Those South Carolinians who favored a more conciliatory stance toward the federal government could not generate nearly as much support for their position.

When the toasts at the Indian Queen Hotel revealed that President Jackson had no sympathy for nullification, the leaders of the movement in South Carolina were surprised and disappointed. After all, Jackson, like them, was a planter and slaveholder and would suffer economically along with the South Carolinians. Jackson considered the tariff to be for the good of the nation as a whole. The tariff provided money for defense and prevented federal debt. The South Carolina challenge would limit the power of the U.S. government to make law for the country in matters that transcended state boundaries. Jackson did not believe the United States could afford to permit such divisiveness to impair its strength in the world of nations. Jackson, the old general, would tolerate no opposition on such matters.

Nullification, Jackson announced, would not stand. He could not have been any clearer: nullification was "incompatible with the existence of the Union, contradicted expressly by the letter of the Constitution, unauthorized by its spirit, inconsistent with every principle on which it was founded, and destructive of the great object for which it was formed." Disunion was treason, he warned, and would be treated as such; Congress passed a "Force Bill" to permit him to use military power to keep South Carolina in line. Recent opponents of Jackson such as Henry Clay and Daniel Webster were pleased—and surprised—at Jackson's nationalism; they had not expected such convictions from a Tennessee planter. Southerners in general were caught in a difficult position, disapproving of South Carolina's radicalism but distrustful of the centralizing precedent of the Force Bill.

Congress twisted and turned on the issue, not wanting South Carolina to get its way but unwilling to see Jackson use arms. After much debate, Congress, under the leadership of Henry Clay, offered compromise in early 1833: the tariff would be slowly but steadily lowered over the next decade, giving northern manufacturers time to adapt. South Carolina, secretly relieved, declared itself the victor and accepted the compromise tariff; in a final display of states' rights defiance, though, the Carolinians nullified the Force Bill. Jackson ignored them, recognizing the emptiness of the gesture.

Free Blacks and African American Abolitionism

Even as the white leaders of South Carolina struggled to define the extent of their powers within the Union, free blacks and slaves struggled to define their freedom. Communities of several thousand free blacks lived in every major northern city, establishing their own churches, newspapers, school, and lodges.

In many towns and cities along the coast of the Northeast, as many as 25 percent of all free black household heads worked as sailors. The dangers, poor pay, and family hardships opened seafaring posts for African Americans, though black men serving on whalers out of New England received equal shares in the profits with divisions made on the basis of skill rather than race.

More numerous were free African Americans in the Upper South slave states, especially Maryland and Virginia. Some had been emancipated during the decades after the Revolutionary War, when slavery seemed to be dying and when the ideals of the new nation and Christianity persuaded some masters to free their slaves. Although free blacks in the Upper South scattered throughout smaller towns and rural areas, they generally tended to gather in cities as they did in the North. The cities strung along the Atlantic and Gulf coasts—Norfolk, Savannah, Charleston, Mobile, and New Orleans—all contained several thousand free blacks. Outside of these cities, few free blacks lived in the deep South.

Free African Americans stayed in the South to be closer to family members held in slavery and because, ironically, southern cities held greater economic opportunity than the North. Because whites deemed many jobs in the South "nigger work," below the dignity of whites, black southerners dominated some fields of work. Black men constituted most of the barbers and teamsters, for example, while black women found work as laundresses and domestics. Free blacks in the South had to be careful, making sure that local officials kept records of their freedom, but they could acquire property and educate their children. They stayed in contact with African Americans in the North through newspapers, letters, and word passed by the many black sailors who plied the eastern seaboard.

Free blacks throughout the country debated the merits of leaving the United States altogether, as many whites encouraged them to do. The colonization movement struggled in the 1820s. Few black Americans were willing to be shipped to a place they had never seen; only about 1,400 black Americans went to Liberia in the 1820s. African Americans came to see in colonization an attack on their hard-won accomplishments in the United States, for their leaders insisted that people of color had earned a place in this country. Rather than spending moral energy and money on removing black people, they argued, Americans should work instead on making the United States a fairer place.

David Walker proved to be an important figure in this movement. Walker had lived in Charleston at the time of Denmark Vesey's conspiracy in 1822, becoming familiar with the long tradition of revolt and resistance in the Carolina low country. After the suppression of Vesey, Walker moved to Boston. There, he established a used-clothing store, one of the few businesses open to African Americans in the North. Walker did well in the business, bought a home, joined the African Methodist church, and became a black Mason, an organization that fought against slavery and the slave trade. He gave his support to *Freedom's Journal,* an anticolonization paper published by black people in Boston and New York City between 1827 and 1829.

In 1829, Walker released his *Appeal . . . to the Colored Citizens of the World.* Americans, whatever their skin color, had never read such a document. Walker denied that slaves felt or owed any bond to their masters. He called for black spiritual self-renewal, starting with African Americans' recognition of just how angry they were with their lot in the United States. They needed to channel that anger with God's love, Walker urged, making a group effort to end slavery immediately. He did not call for violence but for black Americans to be full Americans in both government and economy. Condemning Henry Clay's support for removing all free blacks to Africa, Walker accused Clay and those supporting colonization of concocting a "plan to get those of the colored people, who are said to be free, away from those of our brethren whom they unjustly hold in bondage, so that they may be enabled to keep them the more secure in ignorance and wretchedness. . . . For if the free are allowed to stay among the slaves, they will have intercourse together, and . . . the free will learn the slaves *bad habits,* by teaching them that they are MEN . . . and certainly *ought* and *must* be FREE."

Within weeks of its publication, Walker's *Appeal* appeared in Savannah, where it was seized, and then in Milledgeville, Georgia (the state capital), then in Virginia, North Carolina, South Carolina, and New Orleans. The *Appeal* created panic and repression wherever it appeared. Southern whites worried at this evidence of invisible networks of communication and resistance among the slaves, free blacks, and, perhaps, sympathetic whites in their midst. Events in Virginia bore out their worst suspicions.

The Crisis of Slavery in Virginia

Nat Turner was a field hand, born in 1800, who felt that God had called him for more than the lot of a slave. Well known even in his youth for his intellectual abilities and his effectiveness as a preacher, on Sundays Turner traveled throughout the countryside around Southampton County, Virginia, coming to know most of the slaves and free black people who lived there. Praying and fasting, Turner saw visions: drops of blood that formed hieroglyphics on leaves, black shadows across the white moon. These things, he became certain, foretold a slave revolt, of the time "fast approaching when the first should be last and the last should be first." Turner, unlike Gabriel in Richmond in 1800 and Vesey in Charleston in 1822, chose to build his revolt around a small group of select lieutenants rather than to risk spreading the word broadly. Their plan was to begin the rebellion on their own and then attract compatriots along the way.

On August 22, 1831, Turner and his band began their revolt. They moved from one isolated farmhouse to the next, killing all the whites they found inside, including children. They gathered horses and weapons. Turner rode at the end of the group, praying for guidance on what plan they should follow. As the night went on, Turner's men had killed about seventy people, starting with the family of Turner's master. By morning, word had rushed to Richmond of the unimaginable events in Southampton. Whites huddled together in Jerusalem, the county seat, and troops arrived to put down the revolt. Blacks, many of whom had no connection with the rebellion, were killed by infuriated and frightened whites hundreds of miles away from Southampton. Turner's troops were all captured or killed, but he managed to escape and to hide in the woods of the county for two months. Once captured, Turner narrated a remarkable "confession" in which he told of his visions and prophecies. He had no regrets and no doubts that God would stand in judgment of the people who held other people in slavery. At his hanging in November, he showed no signs of remorse.

White southerners saw in Nat Turner their worst nightmares. Here was a literate slave, allowed to travel on his own, allowed to spread his own interpretation of the Bible to dissatisfied slaves eager to listen to Turner's prophecies. The crackdown was not long in coming, as delegates to the state assembly gathered in Richmond a month after Turner's execution. In a series of remarkable debates, these white Virginians, some of them sons and grandsons of Thomas Jefferson, John Marshall, and Patrick Henry, openly admitted the

Nat Turner

In 1831, Americans hungered for news of Nat Turner. In the absence of photographs or of artists on the scene, people were left to imagine what Turner might have looked like—just as they imagined what his motives might have been. A white lawyer took down Turner's "confessions," which sold many copies throughout the nation. In those notes, Turner attributed his acts to directives from God and proclaimed his confidence that he acted properly. Whites scoffed at such claims, assuming that Turner must have been simply insane. In this drawing, Turner is imagined as a sort of biblical character, inspiring a small band of lieutenants. This was in fact the way Turner worked, entrusting his plans to a small group of trusted men until the moment of the revolt, when they launched out on their journey from one white household to the next and gathered allies along the way. The swamp setting is a bit fanciful, however, portraying Virginia as a dark tropical region. Turner did apparently hope to escape into Virginia's Great Dismal Swamp, but most of his planning and raids took place on a considerably less exotic landscape.

The Granger Collection, New York

debilitating effect of slavery on Virginia. They worried most about slavery's influence on whites, worried that slavery kept the economy from developing as it did in the North. Delegates from western Virginia, where relatively few slaves lived, expressed their misgivings most freely, but even large slaveholders from the East admitted slavery's negative effects. Petitions flowed into Richmond, particularly from the western counties where whites resented the domination of the state by the wealthy minority of tidewater slaveholders, urging the legislators to take a decisive step to rid Virginia of slavery. Defenders of slavery warned that the debates, published in the newspapers and discussed on the streets and in the shops and homes across the state, might result in more revolts. Enslaved Virginians were not an "ignorant herd of Africans," one delegate warned, but an "active, intelligent class, watching and weighing every movement of the Legislature, with perfect knowledge of its bearing and effect."

Some delegates urged that the state purchase all slaves born after a certain date—1840 was proposed—and colonize them in Africa or sell them to plantations farther south. Others argued that the state could not afford such a step, that the Virginia economy would collapse without slavery, that slaves born before the date of freedom would revolt, that property rights guaranteed in the Constitution made it ridiculous to talk about taking slaves from their owners. Others went much further, arguing that slavery was not wrong at all but rather God's plan for civilizing Africans otherwise lost to heathenism and barbarism. The disparate regions of Virginia found themselves in deep conflict; some discussed separating themselves from the rest of the state if one policy or another were followed. The lawmakers, starkly divided, ultimately decided that it was "inexpedient" to take any step at all against slavery at that time, that it would be left for subsequent legislatures to begin the process that would free Virginia from slavery. In the meantime, they passed harsher laws to limit the movement and gathering of free blacks and slaves.

Political Turmoil and the Election of 1832

Andrew Jackson made fervent enemies as well as devoted followers throughout his presidency. No one could be neutral about him, for he seemed to touch everything in American life. The election of 1832 saw voters and leaders mobilize in opposition or support of Jackson, latching on to a wide range of issues. The president, furious at any resistance, lashed out, determined that his work not be wasted. The nation had never seen such political conflict, as citizens debated issues of the economy, states' rights, and morality.

Taking Sides

In September 1831, the first national political convention in U.S. history met in Baltimore. It was convened by the Anti-Masons. Despite their origins and their name, the Anti-Masons were concerned with the state of American politics in general, not merely with the threat posed by the Masons. They attracted an impressive list of ambitious and accomplished young men to their convention, including many who believed the Jackson White House was too pro-southern and too callous with the American Indians. The Anti-Masons found little appeal in John Quincy Adams's National Republicans, for that party seemed to be stuck in the past and hapless against the strong Jacksonian Democrats. The Anti-Masons promised to become a powerful third party, a wild card in an already tumultuous American politics.

The Jacksonians held their own convention the following spring. Jackson, fed up with the controversy over Peggy Eaton and alienated from Calhoun, early in 1831 asked all the members of his cabinet to resign. When the president reconstituted the cabinet, he replaced pro-Calhoun men with men more to his own liking. Van Buren, who had suggested the purge as a way of cleaning house before the election of 1832, was nominated by Jackson to be the new ambassador to Great Britain. Calhoun, in revenge, cast the Senate vote that rejected Van Buren's appointment. Van Buren and Jackson got the last laugh when the convention of 1832 filled the vice presidential slot with Van Buren and removed Calhoun from the ticket. Calhoun, it became clear, would never be Jackson's choice for president; Van Buren had supplanted him as heir apparent.

Other kinds of resentments also fueled the conflict of the early 1830s. As prices and rents rose more quickly than wages, urban working people found themselves falling behind. These working men and women felt their contributions slighted in the new economy, their labor no longer bringing the recognition and rewards it deserved. Workers formed unions to defend their rights. In the early 1830s trades' associations appeared in New York, Boston, Baltimore, Washington, and Louisville. They sponsored newspapers, lobbied legislatures, and supported one another during strikes. By the mid-1830s, between 100,000 and 300,000 men and women belonged to unions.

A number of labor and political leaders, recognizing the power of such numbers, sought to mobilize the organized workers into politics. While union members generally liked Andrew Jackson's blows against monopoly, they thought he pulled up short in his attack on privilege. They sought to push the political system into doing more to protect working people. Some unions became deeply engaged in politics and put forward their own candidates.

The Bank War

Despite the tariffs intended to serve their interests, most people in the Northeast felt they had received little from Andrew Jackson's first term. They viewed him with distrust and growing anger, perceiving in Old Hickory an enemy to moral and commercial progress, a defender of the backward South and West against the East. The fate of the Second Bank of the United States stood as the key issue in this regard. Many merchants and others deemed it a stabilizing force in the American economy, holding an otherwise decentralized money system in place. It was the job of Nicholas Biddle, the president of the Bank of the United States, to make sure that state banks kept plenty of metal currency—specie—on hand

From "The Union," 1835, courtesy of The New York Public Library

A Voice from the People!
Great Meeting in the Park!!

This poster sought to mobilize New York City's working people in favor of a new labor party.

with which to pay the national bank when asked to do so. Such rules kept the state banks from putting out too many notes, from inflating the currency with paper money unsupported by gold or silver. When the economy fell into trouble, on the other hand, Biddle and the Bank of the United States would lessen their demands on the state banks, preventing panics and deflation.

While businessmen appreciated this role of the bank, many other Americans distrusted it. In their eyes, this largely private institution enjoyed far too much power for its own good or the good of the country. Why should privileged stockholders in the bank, they asked, profit from the business of the federal government? Why should the national notes be allowed to depress the value of state notes, with their origins closer to home?

For many voters, objections to the Bank of the United States were as much objections to banking and commerce in general as to any specific policies of the national bank. The whole business of banking seemed suspect, with its paper money, its profits seemingly without labor, its government-supported monopolies, its apparent speculation with public money. Andrew Jackson shared these feelings of mistrust. As a young man, he had lost a considerable amount of money to a speculator, and nothing he saw as president changed his mind about those who dealt in the mysteries of currency. He disliked monopoly, he disliked paper money, and he disliked the Bank of the United States.

The issue came to a head in 1832 as Henry Clay and other National Republicans, joined by South Carolina nullifiers such as Calhoun, sought to use the bank as a way to defeat Jackson for the presidency. A few months before the election in the fall, the bank's supporters steered its application for rechartering through Congress. Jackson heard of the news while he was ill in bed. "The bank," he told Martin Van Buren, "is trying to kill me, *but I will kill it!*" He vetoed the recharter, proclaiming that the bank was "unauthorized by the constitution, subversive of the rights of the States, and dangerous to the liberties of the people."

Jackson's opponents, in turn, saw the president, not the bank, as the usurper of American rights. How dare he single-handedly overturn what the people, in the form of Congress, had declared to be their will? Henry Clay and other opponents argued that his action posed a far greater threat to the American people than did the bank. If the president could force his way into the lawmaking process, the division of powers laid out in the Constitution would be violated and the Union would risk falling under the despotic rule of a president who would be king.

Before the bank could deploy its enormous financial resources to gather the two-thirds majority necessary to override his earlier veto, Jackson quickly moved all federal funds from the Bank of the United States to state banks. The newly appointed secretary of the treasury followed Jackson's plan and put the government deposits in seven state banks— promptly dubbed "pet banks" by opponents of the new strategy. Congressmen of both parties denounced Jackson's move. Biddle and his bank's supporters fought on for two more years, but without the government's deposits they had little leverage. Jackson's lieutenants efficiently mobilized the votes they needed in Congress to prevent the renewal of the

The Bank of the United States as a Monster

This elaborate cartoon conveyed a simple message but with many subtleties that informed people at the time could have decoded. Each of the heads of the "hydra" is labeled with the name of a state, representing the way the "monster" of the Bank of the United States had slithered its way into every corner of the nation. The largest head at the center of the hydra, that of Nicholas Biddle, is labeled "Penn" for Pennsylvania. The soldier on the right has dropped his axe, discovering that splitting one of the heads of the hydra only reveals another inside. President Jackson, elderly and yet still vigorous and determined, wields a sword labeled "veto," killing with a manly thrust a frightening opponent that seemed too formidable for anyone else to conquer. Vice President Martin Van Buren seems to be trying to help, albeit ineffectually. He contributes mainly by exclaiming "Well done general!"

GENERAL JACKSON SLAYING THE MANY HEADED MONSTER.

bank's charter. The Bank of the United States, deprived of government support, began a slow death.

The election of 1832 turned around these broad issues about the fate of the nation. Jackson portrayed himself as the champion of the common man fighting against a bloated aristocracy of privilege and monopoly. Clay, the candidate of the National Republicans, portrayed himself as the defender of the Union against an arrogant and power-hungry president, a man who had shown a disregard for morality and justice in his dealing with the American Indians and enacting the spoils system as well as with the bank. William Wirt, the candidate of the Anti-Masons, declared himself the opponent of conspiracies, corruptions, and subversions larger and more insidious than the bank, all the more dangerous for not being clearly defined.

Despite the challenges on the bank and by the Anti-Masons, Jackson won by a considerable margin, losing South Carolina to a nullifier, Vermont to the Anti-Masons, and the rest of New England and a few other states to Clay. Emboldened by his majority at the polls, the president went on the offensive.

Those opposed to Jackson began to call themselves "Whigs." Like their British namesakes, the American Whigs saw themselves as the counterbalance to otherwise unchecked monarchical power—in this case "King Andrew I," "the most absolute despot now at the head of any representative government on earth."

The Indian Peoples and the Mexican Nation

Andrew Jackson's administration focused much of its energy on the native peoples of North America. The American Indians held immense areas of the South and the West when Jackson took office, land that many whites wanted and demanded. The southwestern border of the United States remained tantalizingly ambiguous as well. Mexico governed its Texas province loosely and many white Americans coveted that land. Both of these situations would undergo explosive change under Andrew Jackson.

Jackson and the American Indians

Andrew Jackson had announced, and acted upon, his attitudes toward the Indians years before he took office as president. The steady pressing of white population onto the rich lands of the Cherokee, Chickasaw, Creeks, Seminoles, and Choctaws, he thought, left the people of those nations with two choices. They could either become "industrious Citizens" who accepted the sovereignty of the states that claimed the lands on which they lived, or they could "remove to a Country *where* they can retain their ancient customs, so dear to them, that they cannot give up in exchange for regular society." If they could adapt themselves to agriculture and law, they might remain where they were, protected by the laws they pledged to obey; if they could not adapt, they would have to leave. Their only other choice, Jackson thought, was extinction.

White people had mixed feelings about the Indians. Americans of European descent considered the Indians admirable in many ways, dignified and free, able to learn and prosper. Not a few "white" and "black" families were proud to claim some Indian ancestry. Andrew Jackson, for his part, adopted a Creek infant, Lyncoya, educated him, and brought him to live with him and his wife. In fact, the death of Lyncoya from tuberculosis in 1828, at age sixteen, hastened Rachel Jackson's heartbreak and decline. Many other white Americans, including some in Congress, had long contributed time and money to the Indians, helping to build and staff schools, sending seed and agricultural implements to ease the transition to farming.

By the late 1820s, the "civilized tribes" had adapted themselves to the dominant society. Many of the tribes were led by chiefs of mixed descent, leaders who lived in cabins, houses, and even mansions. Men such as John Ross negotiated land settlements and profited from such deals but also attempted to create systems of political representation and law. He joined the Methodist church and courted any political party he believed best advanced Cherokee interests. The wealthiest Indians, especially the Cherokee, bought African American slaves. The children of the Indian leaders and others went to schools established by white missionaries, who persuaded a considerable number of Indians to convert to Christianity. The Cherokees published a newspaper that included articles in both their own language and in English.

Despite these adaptations, the Indians of the Southeast showed no desire to leave the land on which they lived in the late 1820s. In their view, they had already given up more land than they should have—millions of acres over the preceding twenty years—and were determined to hold on to what remained. "We would not receive money for land in which our fathers and friends are buried," they declared. Most whites, especially those who lived nearby and coveted the rich cotton lands under the Indians' control, bristled at the continuing presence of the native inhabitants. Many white people longed to banish the American Indians to land on the other side of the Mississippi River, where, it seemed, whites would not want to live for a very long time, if ever.

In 1827, the Cherokees held a national convention and drew up a written constitution, patterned on that of the United States. They desired both to declare their sovereignty over their lands and to show whites just how devoted they were to American values. But the new constitution, U.S. courts ruled, violated the law of both the nation and the state of Georgia, which petitioned the federal government to remove the Cherokees. An already volatile situation worsened when gold was discovered on the Indian lands and white prospectors rushed in. The Georgia legislature declared the Cherokees' laws null and void, placing Georgia law into effect instead. The Cherokees suddenly found themselves even more vulnerable than before. White settlers invaded northern Georgia, taking Cherokee property.

Jackson told the Indians he was their friend, even their "father," but that he could do nothing to stop their mistreatment except to move them beyond the Mississippi River, where, he promised, they would be safe. The Indians and their supporters, mostly religious people in the North, responded bitterly to such claims, arguing that the rights of the Constitution should certainly extend to people who had lived in North America since time immemorial. Many northern men and women who first organized to oppose Indian removal and participated in local and regional protests would later act together to oppose the expansion of slavery. But the Jacksonians quickly pushed through the Indian Removal Act of 1830. Two Supreme Court decisions in favor of the Cherokees, in 1830 and in 1832, proved to be without effect, since they depended on the federal government to implement them and Jackson had no intention of doing anything of the sort.

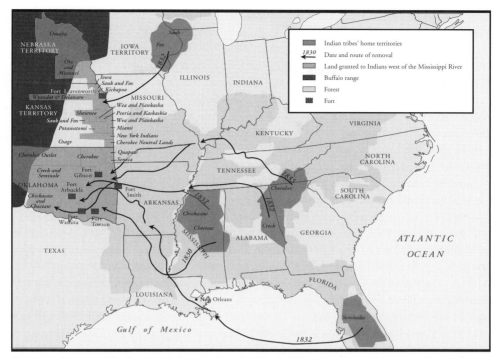

Map 10.1 Removal of the American Indians In the early 1830s, the Indians of the North and South were "removed" to reservations in Oklahoma and Kansas.

In the face of the impending removal, most of the Indian peoples split into pro-assimilation, "progressive," factions and anti-assimilation, "conservative," factions. They debated fiercely and sometimes violently among themselves. Missionaries and federal agents dealt primarily with the progressives, but many other Indians resisted, often by moving far into the backwoods. Many thousands of each nation remained behind, either those who had passed into white or black society through marriage or those who lived outside areas of heavy settlement.

Agents, some of mixed blood, swindled the Indians as they prepared for the removal. The Choctaws, the first to move, underwent horrific experiences, suffering greatly and dying in large numbers as they traveled in the worst winter on record with completely inadequate supplies. The Creeks, too, confronted frauds and assaults. The Indians who moved sold whatever they could not take with them, usually at a great loss. Wagons and carts carried the old and the sick, while women and children drove livestock along the trail. Soldiers usually accompanied the Indians, along with an agent to hand out whatever support the government provided. Some of the migrants used steamboats to travel up or down the Mississippi River and then to Oklahoma along the Arkansas or Red River, while others proceeded over land. "To see the remnant of a once mighty people fettered and chained together forced to depart from the land of their fathers into a country unknown to them," an Alabama newspaper admitted, "is of itself sufficient to move the stoutest heart."

The Cherokee removal was the most prolonged. After years of negotiating, the government struck a bargain with a small and unrepresentative number of the Cherokee in the Treaty of New Echota in 1836. While groups of several hundred at a time left, including some of the wealthiest, 17,000 refused to leave by the deadline. General Winfield Scott then led 7,000 troops against them, driving people from their homes empty-handed, marching them to stockades and shipping them out by rail and water. About a quarter of all eastern Cherokees died in what they called the Trail of Tears. Some Cherokees remained in the mountains of North Carolina and Tennessee, but the power of the eastern Indians had been destroyed.

The Seminoles fought against removal as long as they could. Led by Osceola, the son of an English trader and the husband of an escaped slave, the Seminoles tried to break the will of the whites by killing soldiers and civilians and by burning their crops and homes. The Second Seminole War launched by the federal government to remove the 5,000 Indians began in 1836 and dragged on for six years. The conflict proved both unpopular and unsuccessful. About 36,000 U.S. soldiers fought and 1,500 died; many more suffered debilitating disease. The federal government spent $20 million in the fight, even though few white people wanted to settle on the Seminoles' land. The United States captured Osceola only by deception at a supposed peace conference. He died in captivity a few months later, after which some Seminoles finally migrated to Oklahoma. But most of the Seminole people, able to use the swampy landscape to hide, were never driven out of Florida.

Fighting also erupted in the Illinois Territory between white settlers and the Sac and Fox Indians. These people, under the leadership of Black Hawk, saw their lands along the Mississippi River taken over by whites while the Indians were on a hunting expedition in 1832. The whites burned the Indians' huts and plowed under their fields. In retaliation, the Sac and Fox destroyed white settlements. A large contingent of volunteers (including a young Abraham Lincoln), regular troops, and allied Indians set out after Black Hawk and his people, who also had allies from other Indian nations. Eventually, the whites outnumbered Black Hawk and overran his camp, killing nearly 500 as they tried to cross the Mississippi River. Taken prisoner, Black Hawk refused to repent, telling his captors that he "has done nothing for which an Indian ought to be ashamed. He has fought for his countrymen, the squaws and papooses, against white men who came, year after year, to cheat them and take away their land." Black Hawk's words and deeds, widely reported in the newspapers of the country, attracted considerable sympathy among whites in the East. Andrew Jackson met with Black Hawk and pardoned him; the chief's autobiography became a best-seller. The United States, using its defeat of the Sac as an example, found it much easier to induce the other Indians of the Old Northwest to cede 190 million acres for $70 million.

Conflict with Mexico

Speculators and settlers from the United States continually moved into Mexican Texas in the 1820s and 1830s. Sometimes the Mexican officials encouraged the newcomers; at other times, they sought to slow American settlement. Seeking the end of slavery in Mexico, they wanted settlers but they did not want the slaves white settlers often brought with them. The key leader in the American migration was Stephen F. Austin, a Virginia-born entrepreneur who first arrived in Mexico in 1821 on the heels of Mexican independence. Throughout the 1820s, Austin, negotiating with the changing Mexican governments, oversaw the arrival and settlement of hundreds of Americans. While the Mexican laws on slavery shifted repeatedly, most of the American settlers—the great majority of them southerners—argued that they had to have slaves if Texas were to develop as they and as Mexican leaders hoped. The Americans, with the tacit approval of local officials, improvised laws and took advantage of loopholes to keep slavery in fact if not in name.

American settlers and the Mexican government came into increasing conflict, as provincial officials attempted to collect tariffs and slow immigration into the district. Austin and the other Americans petitioned the Mexican government to let them become a separate Mexican state under its own administration, but they were rebuffed when Antonio López de Santa Anna took control of the government. In the 1830s, as Santa Anna consolidated his power in Mexico, his attempts to centralize control in Mexico City led to revolts in the Yucatan and Zacateces as well as in Texas. In Santa Anna's eyes, the Texans were clearly inviting an expansionist United States to take this province away from Mexico; he sent in troops to meet the threat.

In 1835, a convention of Texans voted to fight against Santa Anna, offering large amounts of land to all who would come help in the struggle. Volunteers and money flowed into Texas from throughout the United States, where people had been watching the events in that area with great interest. Southern states in particular sent hundreds of men. Nevertheless, they were greatly outnumbered by the Mexicans, who decimated the Americans at several battles. As the Mexican army sought to occupy San Antonio, 188 rebels—including Davy Crockett of Tennessee, famous for his frontier exploits and for his service in Congress—took refuge in the Mission of the Alamo. Most of the people inside were American, but they were joined by *tejanos,* Mexicans of the province who allied themselves with the revolt for independence. The defenders of the Alamo held out against 3,000 Mexican soldiers for nearly two weeks in 1836, until the Mexicans finally stormed the mission and killed all inside except three white women, two white children, and an African American slave. The Mexicans stripped the bodies of the insurrectionaries and burned them. After the Alamo, support for the rebellion grew rapidly in the United States, where it came to be seen as a moral struggle between the forces of freedom and the forces of autocracy. "Remember the Alamo" became the rallying cry.

Santa Anna seemed on the verge of victory until Sam Houston, the general of the American forces, surprised the larger Mexican force at San Jacinto in April of 1836. Rushing toward the Mexican camp, a force of 900 Texans and *tejano* cavalry commanded by Juan Seguín won a decisive battle in only eighteen minutes. Santa Anna himself was captured a day later. As a prisoner, he signed treaties removing Mexican troops from Texas, granting Texas its independence, and recognizing the Rio Grande as the boundary. The Mexican Congress, when they heard of this capitulation, announced that they would not be bound by its terms.

Texans and many Americans elsewhere urged the U.S. government to annex the new republic before it could be retaken by the Mexicans. That plea unleashed a heated and pro-

The Alamo

A small force of Americans and *tejanos* were overwhelmed at the Alamo mission in San Antonio. Although the Mexican army won the battle, its victory unleashed the support of the United States. Almost from the moment of the battle, the Alamo became the object of mythmaking. The press of the United States turned the men inside the mission into valiant heroes and imagined their deaths in ways that embodied the highest standards of masculine self-sacrifice. The newspapers back east talked little of the *tejanos* and instead celebrated the white soldiers in the Alamo as the vanguard of American civilization and decried the Mexicans as bloodthirsty and inhuman mercenaries defeating the men from the United States through sheer numbers.

The Granger Collection, New York

tracted debate between advocates of American expansion and those who thought such a step would be immoral and impolitic. Much of the debate raged between southerners, who saw Texas as a vast new empire, and northerners, especially abolitionists, who opposed annexation because it would lead to slavery's expansion. The fate of Texas was to be a key political issue for the next decade.

Revival

The power and influence of Protestant churches surged to a new level in the Jacksonian era. Far more than in any previous generation, the Jacksonian years saw the churches take leading roles in every facet of life and in every part of the Union. Revivals pulled in scores of new members, firing them with the desire to remake their lives. Many of those who experienced the spiritual rebirth of the revivals sought ways to demonstrate their faith and their hope for America. A radical new movement against slavery gathered force with stunning speed. At the same time, other Americans sought purer forms of religion itself, listening to prophets who spoke of new churches and new possibilities. Everywhere in the late 1820s and early 1830s, religion seemed on people's lips.

Revivalism

Since the late eighteenth century, revivals led by the major Protestant denominations had periodically inflamed the United States. In those revivals, people who had never declared their faith in Jesus Christ or who had fallen away from the church made public expressions of their faith. Thousands of people gathered in the North, South, and West, in town and countryside, to pray and hear ministers tell them of God's love and forgiveness. Hearing of these gifts, and aware of their own sinfulness, men and women sometimes fell to the ground as if stricken. Others cried and screamed. The churches that devoted themselves to spreading the Gospel—known as "evangelical" churches because they sought to bring others to their faith in Scripture—periodically experienced revivals or "awakenings" when numbers of people expressed or renewed their faith. This revivalism burst out again in the mid-1820s.

Desires for personal relationship with God and a sense of community often linked new religious leaders with recent scientific advances to encourage beliefs in spiritualism, magnetic healing, phrenology, and mesmerism. Science and religion were not seen by those in the early nineteenth century as incompatible, as both the supernatural and scientific could explain the individual's role in creation. Samuel Gridley Howe, director of the New England Asylum for the Blind, chose to monitor a local deaf and blind girl to determine if morality and faith were inborn to humans. He chose Laura Bridgman, a local girl who had recently survived scarlet fever but lost her sight and hearing. She learned to read and became a celebrity, with as many as a thousand people turning out to see her as part of the asylum's efforts to raise money. She was also listed as a major attraction in contemporary tourist guides, so wealthy travelers from around the nation and Europe stopped in Boston to see her.

Many ministers and churches across the country were swept up in the religious awakening of the 1820s, but one man embodied its new and aggressive spirit: Charles Grandison Finney. Finney, a young attorney from Utica, New York, who had not regularly attended church until encouraged to do so by his fiancée, suddenly found himself struck with the power of God's love. "An overwhelming sense" of his wickedness brought Finney to his knees. "I wept aloud like a child [and] the Holy Spirit descended upon me in a manner that seemed to go through me body and soul," he recalled. "I could feel the impression like a wave of electricity, going through and through me." Finney spread the word of the Bible in the plain and straightforward language of everyday life. He told people that they had it within their power to take the first step toward God, that God would listen. Finney told people to seek out salvation, to throw themselves open to the mercy of Jesus.

Finney found in the new cities of western New York a receptive audience among young men, on their own in a rapidly changing America, and among women of every age. The churches, these people believed, had grown cold in the hands of the established ministry and needed a revival of spirit. They wanted a Christianity of activity, of prayer meetings, of spreading the word any way they could. Finney's influence grew in strength and numbers as women prayed with one another. The district of upstate New York that lay along the path of the Erie Canal became known as "The Burned-Over District," as one revival after another surged through its towns and farms.

The revivals took on a new scale and urgency in 1830 as they ignited Rochester. Like other rapidly growing towns and cities along the Erie Canal, Rochester was ripe for revival. Many people worried that the people of the young city barely knew one another, that husbands and wives, workers and employers, rich and poor were drifting apart. Politics appeared a morass of selfishness; alcohol seemed to drown hopes of social progress and family happiness; men seemed more concerned with their businesses, lodges, and politics than with their souls. When Finney came to town in 1830, accordingly, he was met by a populace hungry for something to stir them up, hungry for a new message.

Women's prayer groups met daily and traveled from home to home in efforts to bring the word of Jesus. Women pleaded with their husbands to listen to the Reverend Finney. Employers made it clear to the men who worked under them that it would be noticed whether or not they attended the revival. These efforts, combined with Finney's masterful sermons and hopeful message, transformed Rochester, bringing hundreds of people into the church who had not come before and reclaiming many who had strayed. All the Protestant denominations worked together, setting aside for a while their differences on baptism and other doctrines.

Such a powerful revival seemed evidence to many people that America could be changed by faith. As they watched saloons shut down, families brought together, and shops and stores closed while the revival was in progress, it appeared that the way was being prepared for God's kingdom on earth. If the United States could be adequately reformed, these people believed, the day of redemption could be hastened. The American Tract Society, eager to improve the nation's moral state, had delivered roughly 5 million gospel tracts by 1828, one for every three people in the United States and the equivalent to 90 million pamphlets today. It was up to Americans themselves to purge their country of sin, to make themselves better, and then to help others see the way as well. Such faith bred a demand for immediate reforms. When the means of change lay so close at hand, only a prayer away, delay seemed a rejection of God's love.

The Birth of Mormonism

Like many American families of these years, that of Joseph Smith could not find a secure place. His father dreamed of bringing his family out of poverty, moving them from one community to another. Young Joseph, like hundreds of other people in upstate New York, looked for treasure rumored to have been buried long ago in the mountains; he watched with concern for his soul, too, as revivals came and went without his conversion. Smith reported that he felt the presence of an angel, however, who told him "that God had work for me to do, and that my name should be for good and evil among all nations, kindreds, and tongues. He said there was a book deposited, written upon gold plates, giving an account of the former inhabitants of this continent, and the source from which they sprang. He also said that, the fullness of the everlasting Gospel was contained in it." Smith claimed that the angel directed him to the location of the sacred writings.

Smith began to transcribe what he had found; sitting in a tent divided by a partition, he read the plates to an assistant on the other side. *The Book of Mormon* took shape, telling of a struggle between the chosen ones and their persecutors, of a promised land reserved for the righteous. North America, the book said, had been visited by Jesus in the distant past but the people had lost their way and fallen into disputation. Those people had been cursed by God for their sins and marked with dark skins; their descendants were the American Indians, who had forgotten their lost paradise.

After 1830 Joseph Smith and several followers traveled throughout New York selling copies of what they called the "Gold Bible." They were met with hostility virtually everywhere they went, but they slowly gathered converts to their Church of Jesus Christ of the Latter-Day Saints. Many of the new members were poor, including some free blacks, but others had considerable resources. The most important converts were two brothers, Brigham and Joseph Young. As the movement gathered momentum, hundreds of people joined the church; entire congregations of churches of other faiths joined the Mormons and gladly contributed everything they owned to the church's common fund. The faithful moved first to Ohio and then to what Smith believed to be the original Eden: Missouri. But other settlers made no secret of their disapproval of the Mormons, firing shots, throwing stones through windows, and burning the crops of the Latter-Day Saints. One opponent depicted Mormonism as "the only form of religion in this country which refuses to conform either to the spirit of progress and improvement . . . which characterizes the age in which we live." The Mormons found no peace for the next decade. They were constantly harassed by non-Mormons who feared the growing number of converts and the local economic power that came from the church members' pooled resources and hard work.

Character Development

For generations before the 1820s, Americans had relied on authority and reputation to keep their families and communities stable. Young men and women remained in their parents' households well into their twenties, subordinate to the demands and expectations of their fathers. Workingmen served for years as apprentices and journeymen to master artisans, slowly learning the craft and gradually working toward independence. Men and women carefully cultivated their reputations, projecting a polished image of themselves. Churches aided stability, encouraging deference to the authority of God and institution.

The early nineteenth century saw a new emphasis in American life, a new focus on what people called "character." In a society so mobile, so disconnected from traditional sources of stability and identity, people felt the need for new ways of ensuring appropriate behavior. Americans looked to new kinds of institutions suited for a new age, institutions that could better deal with strangers, new people, those cut off from older forms of social stability. Americans turned first to families, imparting to them primary responsibility for creating virtuous children and husbands.

Women at Home and Beyond

Women had long been recognized as the foundation of a good family. Women directly produced a large portion of the food farm families consumed, while town-dwelling families depended on women for running the household—especially hard work in the days before indoor plumbing and electricity. During the era of the Revolution and early republic, women had been encouraged to raise virtuous children befitting a nation of free people. Churches had long depended on women as the source of spiritual energy and admirable role models.

Women became central in yet another way. As Americans looked about them, they became concerned that little seemed to be holding their society together. People moved far beyond the reach of government and beyond the eyes of their parents. Men and women married at younger ages and left home far earlier than their parents had. The opening of land in the West undermined one of the principal forms of control exercised by fathers in earlier generations: the promise of passing on the family farm to sons who stayed at home. Now, sons could acquire land in the West with or without the support of their parents. Daughters might marry earlier and begin families of their own. The American population skyrocketed as so many young families established themselves.

The new economy, too, caused concern for many. Increasingly, men and women seemed pulled in different directions, away from a sole focus on the family farm or family artisan shop. Men found new opportunities in town, in businesses that kept offices or shops in a central area. Young men often worked for wages for a number of employers rather than serving for many years with one master. Middle-class women, too, saw their lives change, especially in towns and cities. Bakeries, butcher shops, clothiers, and candlemakers began to offer, more easily and cheaply, some of the things that women had long labored to produce at home. Schools and academies became more common, providing a place for children to receive education beyond the bounds of the home. Young women from poorer backgrounds came into cities looking for jobs as maids and laundresses, taking away some of the household burden for women well off enough to hire them. Families in towns and cities had fewer children with each passing decade. Women's lives remained hard, as each birth threatened serious illness or death, but those lives began to change in important ways.

As ministers, journalists, and other opinion makers looked upon the changing nature of the households of the Northeast, they began to articulate an ideal of what has been called "domesticity." Families should seize the opportunities provided by the new situations, they said, and help lessen some of the costs created by the new order. Women could put their minds to higher purposes, focusing more on nurturing their children in spirit and mind as well as in body. Women would become the moral center of the household, the guardians of good thoughts, clean living, and a sense of safety for children and husbands.

While the world beyond the household seemed increasingly threatening and disorienting, women could make the home a place of refuge and renewal.

Many middle-class women welcomed this message and this mission. It fit well with their own experiences and their own aspirations. In a time when public life made almost no provisions for female participation and when women found virtually no well-paying jobs open to them, the elevation of the home promised an elevation of women's role. Men believed what they said: they thought women naturally better than themselves, more moral and feeling, more intuitive and spiritual. Men worried about the coarseness and callousness of the tumultuous marketplace even as they enjoyed the sense of freedom, excitement, and possibility it offered. Middle-class fathers wanted their children shielded from the hard world as long as possible, if only so they would be better able to handle the world when they emerged after their nurture at home.

Domesticity asked something of men as well. If the home were to be a haven, the center of society, men would have to make a greater investment in those homes than had their fathers. Men needed to acknowledge the feelings of their wives more, speaking in tones of respect and affection, respecting their wishes about sex and children. Fathers were expected to spend more time with their children, providing a firm male model to accompany the softer nurture of their wives. Drinking and cursing had no place at home.

Such models of domesticity did not emerge overnight, of course. The 1820s saw only the beginnings of a crusade to make all American homes fit this model. The effort began in towns and cities, making only gradual inroads into the raw and growing countryside. It was stronger in the Northeast than in the South and in the West. Working-class families could not afford this idealized model even if they wanted to follow its example. Women who had to work for others all day had little time to devote to their own families. Women who worked in their own homes mingled the market and the household in a way the creators of the domestic ideal deplored. Men who could not be certain of their next day's wages could not afford to keep children out of the workforce into their late teens. Slave families struggled to stay together in any way they could and could only imagine what it might be like to live in the homes held up as ideal in these years. Nevertheless, that ideal was celebrated and elaborated with each passing year, growing along with the booming towns and cities of the North.

An Eruption of Reform Movements

The same Americans who promoted the Christian, middle-class home as their ideal looked to other institutions and reforms in the 1820s to help remake American society. They sought to extend the ideals of character, self-control, and education to those who seemed to fall beyond the good effects of family and household. They worried about hungry children, desperate fathers, and distraught mothers. They noticed increasing numbers of women selling themselves on the city streets. They decried bulging jails and streets full of people without homes. They worried over the many young men and women who seemed adrift in this rootless new society. Reformers tapped the domestic impulses of improvement for the society as a whole.

Groups of reform-minded people mobilized themselves in the Northeast to counter these problems. Some of their efforts grew out of the churches, while others grew out of the ideals of the American Revolution and the marketplace. The American Bible Society intended to ensure the moral tone of American life and counteract what its founders feared was a dangerous trend towards irreligion and political licentiousness. The society launched an ambitious drive to put Bibles in every American home, pioneering steam presses and national systems of distribution, and ultimately issuing over 32 million Bibles. Individual denominations and publishers produced a range of Bibles to reach audiences of varying wealth and sophistication. The churches launched an ambitious drive to put Bibles in every American home, distributing a million Bibles each year.

The American Sunday School Union wrote and published materials for children to be used in Sunday schools across the country. Those schools, while based in churches, taught reading and writing as well as religion. They put the churches at the center of community life, giving children beyond the reach of traditional schooling a chance to learn some of the skills and attitudes necessary for spiritual and economic success. The American Tract Society produced millions of short inspirational pamphlets to reach those who might not set foot in a church or pick up a Bible. The new organizations prided themselves on being national in reach, extending to the Northwest and Southwest, knitting Americans together with a common faith. They preached nothing controversial, claiming only to spread the good news of the Protestant Christian faith. They depended on the hard work of women, who filled the membership rolls and helped raise funds.

Reformers created a new kind of institution—the "penitentiary"—in these years for those apparently most in need of reform: criminals. In a penitentiary, unlike a common jail, criminals would be locked in individual cells, free from the contamination of others, alone with their conscience and the Bible. There, reflecting on their crimes, they would become "penitent" and would emerge as better people. They would undergo some of the moral nurture they had obviously missed as children and would be ready to take their place in the economy of wages, self-discipline, and delayed gratification growing in the United States.

The most prominent penitentiaries were built in New York and Pennsylvania in the 1820s. Reformers argued over whether prisoners should be isolated at all times, the Philadelphia model, or whether they might be allowed to work together in silence, as they did at Auburn in New York. In either case, Americans were proud of their penitentiaries, among the first in the world, holding them up as examples of what the enlightened new nation could do. Almost every state in the nation, South as well as North, soon built its own penitentiary. Foreign observers such as Alexis de Tocqueville of France traveled to the United States to assess this innovation.

Alongside penitentiaries, asylums for the deaf and blind, for the insane, for orphans, and for the poor began to appear in the 1820s, replacing more informal kinds of care. Dorothea Dix became famous throughout the United States for her often lonely crusade on behalf of people otherwise forgotten. Dix lobbied ceaselessly for the construction of cleaner, healthier, and more hopeful kinds of institutions for those who could not care for themselves. Each institution placed its faith in strict order, in moral teaching, and in faith in the inherent good of human nature.

Abolitionism

While the great majority of white northerners thought Christians should seek holiness mainly in their own hearts, others were equally certain that society itself could and should be changed. To many, slavery seemed the place to start.

William Lloyd Garrison played a central role in the emergence of the new antislavery movement, bringing the attention of whites to what had been largely a crusade by African Americans. At the age of twenty-two, Garrison became the editor of the first newspaper dedicated to the prohibition of alcohol. Believing in the necessity of ending slavery as well as drunkenness, Garrison joined the colonization movement and soon became editor of its paper as well.

In the late 1820s Garrison attended the anticolonizationist meetings held by African Americans in eastern cities, including the group that published the first antislavery newspaper, *Freedom's Journal.* He experienced a mounting desire for a more aggressive antislavery crusade as he saw the limitations of the colonization movement and as he witnessed the passion of people such as David Walker. The balding and bespectacled young Garrison sought out other financial supporters and a partner to launch a paper of his own: *The Liberator.* It called for the immediate start toward emancipation, explicitly rejecting colonization. In 1831, the paper's first year, it had only six subscribers, but it acquired fifty-three by the following year, most of them African American. "I *will* be as harsh as truth," Garrison announced, "and as uncompromising as justice. On this subject, I do not wish to think, speak, or write, with moderation. . . . I am earnest—I will not equivocate—I will not excuse—I will not retreat a single inch—AND I WILL BE HEARD." He was.

Two hundred antislavery societies emerged in the early thirties. Ground that had been prepared by the evangelical crusades of the preceding few years proved fertile for the antislavery cause. Some northern church members argued

The Granger Collection, New York

William Lloyd Garrison played a key role in persuading many northern whites that slavery was morally wrong and should be brought to an immediate end.

that it was the duty of good Christians to cast out slaveholders and to work for immediate emancipation, to use the enormous power of the church as a force for freedom. These "immediatists" called for slaveholders to recognize the truth of what the abolitionists were saying, to free their slaves immediately, hire them as free workers, and help repay the former slaves for their years of unpaid toil. These early abolitionists hoped to convert the slaveholders by persuasion and prayer, by church and newspaper—not by law and force.

The American Anti-slavery Society formed in Philadelphia in 1833. Looking to the example of Great Britain, where the major denominations supported the antislavery movement that was at that moment triumphing over slavery in the British West Indies, the members of the society expected American church leaders to take the lead against American slavery. The North would have to be converted before it could expect the South to follow. To convert the North, antislavery organizations held out the prospect of a free South, where 2 million freed slaves would constitute an "immense market" for the products of Northern "mechanics and manufacturers." These abolitionists expected the former slaves to remain in the South; they spoke little of the competition the freedpeople might provide to the workers of the North. Similarly, the antislavery people believed a free South would prosper, with planters and free whites flourishing as they had never flourished before; the South, they claimed, would "exhibit the flush of returning health, and feel a stronger pulse, and draw a freer breath."

The antislavery organizations proved volatile inside as well as out. Far more than any other organizations in the United States at this time, the antislavery cause brought together male and female, black and white, patrician and working class, Quaker and Unitarian, Baptist and Methodist, radical and moderate, political and anti-political people. Each of these groups had its own vision of how the abolitionists should spend their energies and influence. Black abolitionists, in particular, wanted the organizations to do more to help black communities in the North. Black women such as Maria W. Stewart published pamphlets that cried out that it "is of no use for us to wait any longer for a generation of well educated men to arise. We have slumbered and slept too long already; the day is far spent; the night of death approaches . . . Let every colored man throughout the United States, who possesses the spirit and principles of a man, sign a petition to Congress, to abolish slavery in the District of Columbia, and grant you the rights and privileges of common free citizens." Rejecting calls for removal of freedpeople to Africa, Stewart denied that "we can never rise to respectability in this country. They would drive us to a strange land. But before I go, the bayonet shall pierce me through."

The antislavery societies used pamphlets, leaflets, and other literature as their major weapons. Rapid innovations in printing lowered the cost of producing such materials, which flooded post offices and streets. The postal campaign reached its peak in 1834 and 1835, when a million pieces went out through the mail, much of it to the South, where the abolitionists hoped to appeal directly to ministers and others who might be willing to listen to their pleas. That literature, white southerners furiously protested, virtually invited slaves to follow Nat Turner's example. Georgia slaveholders offered a $12,000 reward for the capture of wealthy merchant Arthur Tappan, who, along with his brother Lewis, funded much of the postal campaign against slavery. Arthur received a slave's severed ear in the mail. Mobs in Charleston seized sacks of mail from northern cities and burned them in the streets.

The pamphlets infuriated people in much of the North as well. Mobs, led by some of the wealthiest merchants of northern towns but constituted in large part by white working people, rose up violently against the abolitionists. In 1835 mobs destroyed the home of African Americans, pelted antislavery speakers, and dragged William Lloyd Garrison himself through the streets of Boston at the end of a rope. The leaders of that mob announced that they had assaulted Garrison "to assure our brethren of the South that we cherish rational and correct notions on the subject of slavery." Many white Northerners believed the abolitionists to be hypocrites who cared nothing for America and everything for their own sanctimonious souls. Antislavery speakers risked a mob every time they spoke; one man counted over 150 attacks made on him. Abolitionists' churches were blown up and their school buildings dragged into swamps.

The persecution, ironically, strengthened the abolitionist cause. Denunciation and harassment only made the abolitionists more certain of the need for their efforts, of the moral decay caused by slavery. The 200 antislavery societies of 1835 grew to over 500 in 1836. The reformers flooded Congress with petitions calling for the end of slavery in the District of Columbia, sending over 300 petitions signed by 40,000 people. The acceptance of these petitions by the House, southerners argued, besmirched slaveholders' honor and threatened to incite slaves to rebellion. The petitions should be rejected out of hand. Congress sought to avoid conflict by merely tabling the petitions, but the compromise pleased no one.

Over the next decade, Northerners of even a mild antislavery bent chafed at this "gag rule," which they saw as a clear violation of American freedom in the interests of slavery. Former President John Quincy Adams fought back in 1837 by attempting to present a petition from 22 slaves. Representatives from Georgia and Alabama demanded that Adams be expelled and the petition "taken from the House and burnt or the southern states would withdraw from the House." In their fury to squelch any petitions to Congress on the subject of slavery, southern representatives failed to notice that the petition from the slaves did not advocate abolition. Angered and embarrassed at Adam's trickery, one Mississippian decried this "outrage that has no parallel in parliamentary history" and condemned Adams as one who "rejoiced in the alarm and excitement he occasions like the midnight incendiary who fires the dwelling of his enemy, and listens with pleasure to the screams of his burning victims."

Conclusion

The years of Andrew Jackson changed America in profound ways. No longer would politics be a matter of remote personalities in Washington, for now a two-party system mobilized and articulated voters' desires. No longer would slavery be a matter beyond debate, for the nullification crisis, Walker's *Appeal,* Turner's revolt, and the emergence of an abolitionist movement made slavery a concrete and burning issue. After bitter debate and resistance, the power of the American Indians of the eastern United States had been broken and their people removed from homes they had occupied beyond memory. The aggressive young churches of the Second Great Awakening ensured that the Protestant faith became a matter of public action and testimony. The culture of the United States had become sharply divided over matters both public and private, as full of conflict as it was of possibility.

RECOMMENDED READINGS

Bay, Mia. *The White Image in the Black Mind: African-American Ideas about White People, 1830–1925* (2000). Provides an extremely helpful perspective.

Feller, Daniel. *The Jacksonian Promise: America, 1815–1840* (1995). Offers an upbeat overview.

Freehling, Allison Goodyear. *Drift Toward Dissolution: The Virginia Slavery Debate of 1831–1832* (1982). Presents an interpretation of the crisis in Virginia.

Freehling, William. *Prelude to Civil War: The Nullification Crisis in South Carolina, 1816–1836* (1966). The standard account of the subject.

Johnson, Paul. *A Shopkeeper's Millennium: Society and Revivals in Rochester, New York, 1815–1837* (1978). Tells the story of revivals in an exciting way.

Hinks, Peter B. *To Awaken My Afflicted Brethren: David Walker and the Problem of Antebellum Slave Resistance* (1997). Reveals the crucial role black Americans played in the creation of the abolitionist movement.

Laurie, Bruce. *Artisans into Workers: Labor in Nineteenth-Century America* (1989). An excellent synthesis of this complicated history.

Mayer, Henry. *All on Fire: William Lloyd Garrison and the Abolition of Slavery* (1998). A comprehensive and fascinating biography.

Roberts, Randy, and Olson, James S. *A Line in the Sand: The Alamo in Blood and Memory* (2001). Relates a sophisticated understanding of this challenging topic.

Roediger, David R. *The Wages of Whiteness: Race and the Making of the American Working Class* (1991). Boldly interprets the uses the white working class made of the notion of "race."

Walters, Ronald. *American Reformers, 1815–1860* (1996). A fine analytical synthesis.

Watson, Harry L. *Liberty and Power: The Politics of Jacksonian America* (1990). A helpful and balanced interpretation of a subject that has been much debated by scholars.

Weber, David J. *The Mexican Frontier, 1821–1846: The American Southwest under Mexico* (1982). Tells the complex history of this region before war brought it into the United States.

 Additional resources, exercises, and Internet links related to this chapter are available on the American Passages Web site: http://history.wadsworth.com/ayerscompact2/

11

Panic and Boom
1837–1845

In 1837 the largest financial panic and depression the nation had ever experienced descended on the United States. The hard times shaped reform, literature, politics, slavery, and foreign policy.

It was not surprising that economic troubles stimulated political conflict, but the reform spirit also flowered during these hard years. Men and women energetically championed public education, abstinence from alcohol, antislavery, and a host of other improvements to American life. The popular press burgeoned, along with art, photography, and literature. A few leading thinkers articulated a bold and distinctive American philosophy, one that bore the marks of its tumultuous time.

The hard times in the East drove westward expansion. These were the years in which the mass migration to the Pacific began, as pioneers began to push across the West to Oregon and California. Politics churned as the nation worried over the consequences of its rapid territorial growth.

Economic Crisis and Innovation

The late 1830s and early 1840s produced a surprising mixture of bad and good economic news. The economy fell into prolonged depression, but at the same time the creative energies of the American economy flourished. Courts and legislatures fostered an environment favorable to business, while inventors and investors plunged ahead despite the failures they saw all around them. In fact, the most important economic development of the entire century—the railroad—emerged from these years of turmoil.

Panic and Depression

Andrew Jackson sought to leave a comfortable legacy to his handpicked successor, Martin Van Buren, but even the inauguration ceremony in March 1837 accentuated the great disparities between the two men. Whereas Jackson's gaunt figure symbolized his sacrifices on the frontier and battlefield, Van Buren seemed the plump embodiment of a life spent in political office. Whereas Van Buren's inaugural speech inspired little enthusiasm in the crowd of 20,000, the mere sight of ex-President Jackson roused great cheers. Though Van

CHRONOLOGY

1837	Financial panic • *Charles River Bridge v. Warren Bridge* decision • Grimké sisters lecture to mixed audiences • Elijah P. Lovejoy murdered in Alton, Illinois • Horace Mann becomes first secretary of Massachusetts State Board of Education • Ralph Waldo Emerson, "The American Scholar"
1838	John Quincy Adams successfully defeats attempt to annex Texas
1839	Depression worsens • Daguerreotypes introduced to the United States
1840	Congress passes Independent Treasury Act • Harrison elected president • Frederick Douglass escapes from slavery • American Anti-slavery Society splits • Washingtonian temperance movement emerges • James G. Birney runs for president as candidate for Liberty party
1841	Harrison dies; John Tyler becomes president • Brook Farm founded • California sees arrival of first wagon train • Oregon fever • P. T. Barnum opens the American Museum • *Amistad* case heard before the Supreme Court
1842	Edgar Allan Poe, "The Murders in the Rue Morgue"
1843	Oregon sees arrival of first wagon trains
1844	Methodist Episcopal church divides over slavery • James K. Polk claims the United States's claim to "all Oregon" • Baltimore-Washington telegraph line • Samuel F. B. Morse patents the telegraph • Edgar Allan Poe, "The Raven"
1845	Texas and Florida admitted to the Union • Baptist church divides over slavery

Buren had been a principal architect of the so-called spoils system, he replaced few office-holders on the lower levels of government and made few changes in Jackson's cabinet. The new president seemed content to carry on Jackson's work.

Within weeks of Van Buren's inauguration the American economy hit stormy waters. An unprecedented amount of silver poured into American banks in the mid-1830s from abroad, fueling intense investment. Britain's economy expanded rapidly, increasing the demand for cotton, encouraging southern planters to buy land and slaves on credit, and boosting available credit for investment in American projects such as canals and turnpikes. British investors bought up state bonds and securities, while British exporters offered generous credit for purchase of a wide array of manufactured goods. American merchants, land speculators and state governments indulged in a feast of easy credit and seemingly endless profits.

Unfortunately, poor harvests in Britain disrupted the American economy when British firms demanded repayment of loans just at the time that prices for American cotton declined because of record production and reduced English demand. As a result, a major New Orleans cotton broker failed when it could not make its payments to British banks or pay debts in excess of a million dollars owed to J. & L., Joseph & Co., one of the nation's largest exchange brokers located in New York City. The collapse of Joseph's triggered panic. As a city official noted "everybody will fail—all Hell will fail." Desperate merchants

The irony of a Fourth of July celebration during hard times fills this cartoon, in which symbols of poverty and decay pile on one another.

and creditors tried to extract cash from debtors, credit evaporated, and thousands lost their jobs. Lots in Manhattan that had sold for $480 in September 1836 fell to $50 in seven months.

Despite the role of international trade in bringing on the crisis, many people blamed the problems on Jackson's banking policy, especially the practice of accepting only specie, not paper money, for the purchase of public lands. They looked to Van Buren to lead the repeal of this strategy, but Jackson made it clear to Van Buren that he did not want to see his work undone. Delegations of merchants came to the White House to plead with Van Buren, but to no avail. A "run" began on the banks; customers withdrew a million dollars in specie in only two days in early May. The panic of 1837 had begun. Soon it spread to every city and region of the country.

The panic quickly affected working people as well as the rich. Jobs dried up and many urban families had no idea of where they would get their next meal. In New York City, a poster warned that "Bread, Meat, Rent, Fuel—Their Prices Must Come Down. The Voice of the People Shall be Heard, and Will Prevail." Thousands of people gathered for a public meeting in the freezing weather. Told that a nearby warehouse held 50,000 barrels of flour, the protesters stormed the building; they took what they could and broke open hundreds of barrels. The riots continued for days until the police managed to regain order.

The panic of 1837 was followed by a better year in 1838, then by another panic in 1839. In the wake of that second panic, the stagnation of the economy spread more deeply

Museum of the City of New York

and more widely, not ending until 1843. Labor unions weakened as workers grew afraid to risk their jobs. States' plans to finance canals, roads, and other public projects crashed. Nine states defaulted on the bonds with which they intended to finance those improvements, leading furious European investors to shun American investments. Governors and legislators found themselves under attack from voters angry that the states had permitted themselves to go so far into debt. Visions of a "glorious future" had vanished from the public imagination, a Chicago lawyer lamented.

Van Buren admitted that allowing state banks to hold federal funds had apparently fueled the speculation, but he would not even consider reinstating a national bank. Instead, he proposed what came to be known as the Sub-Treasury Plan or the Independent Treasury Plan. In that system, public funds would be disbursed by the secretary of the treasury as the economy seemed to dictate and banks would be kept out of the picture. It would be two more years before the plan passed, but by then it could do neither the country nor Martin Van Buren much good. The Whigs quickly won state-level offices and looked forward to harvesting more.

The Charles River Bridge Case

Even as the panic unfolded, some of the questions raised by the economic changes of the early 1830s worked their way through the American court system. American law still embodied many assumptions from the centuries before corporations and far-flung economic enterprises challenged local power.

The Charles River Bridge of Boston, for example, had been granted a franchise by the state legislature in 1785. The owners of the bridge charged a toll for everyone who crossed. As the population of Boston and Charlestown grew rapidly, so did the traffic and the tolls on the bridge. The bridge, which cost about $70,000 to build and improve, was bringing in $30,000 a year by the late 1820s. Another bridge also chartered by the state, the Warren Bridge, went up across the Charles, only 260 feet away. No sooner was the new bridge built than the traffic on the older bridge declined by more than half. The managers of the Charles River Bridge sued in court, claiming that their original charter implied a monopoly that the state had violated by building a competing bridge. Throughout the 1830s, the case proceeded to the U.S. Supreme Court and was heard in 1837.

The Chief Justice of the Supreme Court, Roger B. Taney, shared the Jacksonian animosity against monopolies. His decision in the *Charles River Bridge* case held that a state charter did not imply monopoly. Should old charters be permitted to hinder modern improvements, the country "would be obliged to stand still." The charters had perhaps been necessary in the past, he admitted, but by the 1830s such props no longer seemed necessary to attract capital investment. Taney's decision in the *Charles River Bridge* Case reflected a growing consensus among Democrats and Whigs that older forms of economic privilege had to make way for innovation and investment. It would take decades, and many political struggles, for the law to adapt to the new forms of American economic enterprise, but the process had begun.

Railroads

By the 1830s, Americans had devised several means for dealing with the vast spaces of their continent. Thousands of miles of canals cut across the East, while steamboats plied the waters of the North and South. Such means of transport, while cheap and dependable, remained relatively slow and limited in their reach. Inland cities longed for fast overland connections with the outside world, and they knew of experiments with railroads in England and the United States over the last decade. When New Jersey sponsored a bold rail and canal connection between New York and Philadelphia in 1831, it ordered a custom-built locomotive from an English company—the *John Bull*. The railroad became an immediate success, carrying over 100,000 passengers in 1834. That same year, Ralph Waldo Emerson noted in his journal the "uncomputed mechanical advantages" that "rides on the rail-road." He marveled that "men & trees & barns whiz by you as fast as the leaves of a dictionary."

American companies emulated and improved upon the English designs. By 1841, ten American railroad shops had sprung into existence. Those shops soon began changing the English designs, making the engines more powerful and the rails cheaper. Railroad companies quickly grew into some of the largest and most complex American businesses. Employing hundreds of people, they pioneered management and engineering innovations. In this era of panics and credit scarcity, how did rail companies finance the enormous expense of men, machinery, and maintenance? Major manufacturers such as Matthew Baldwin expanded their locomotive works by attracting wealthy investors to join the firms as partners, whereas smaller, more specialized manufacturers plowed all profits back into new equipment. Governments—state, local and federal—also provided financial assistance. As an example, the state of Pennsylvania chartered 2,333 corporations by legislation between 1790 and 1860 and two-thirds of these entities were transportation companies.

Railroads almost immediately became the key form of transportation in the United States. Rail transport grew cheaper as the network expanded and trains could run when canals had frozen over. By 1840, American companies and states had spent $75 million dollars to build 3,300 miles of track, surpassing Great Britain; by 1850, the country claimed nearly 9,000 miles of railroad. New industries rose to serve the trains as iron, coal, and steel burgeoned with the railroads' demand. The railroads consumed prodigious amounts of wood for their ties, trestles, and boilers. Workers building and running the railroads operated in large gangs and frequently suffered from disease. Recruiters for companies in Illinois wrote of desertions when rumors of cholera appeared and the men would "scatter like frightened sheep." Accidents and misbehavior were common: "North bound freight ran into a drove of cattle, went down an embankment . . . nine cars with it," read one account. "Two engines delayed 24 hours, while engineers and firemen went off on a drunken spree."

Despite such challenges, railroads gave farmers quick and certain access to markets, and towns prospered or died depending on their rail connection. Local artisans often

Map 11.1 The Growth of Railroads A vastly expanded transportation network tied the United States together. The system exaggerated sectional differences by unifying the Northeast with the Northwest, creating the reality and perception of a "North" with interests different from those of a "South" stretching from the Atlantic to the Mississippi and beyond.

found themselves undercut by cheaper finished goods from city merchants, while eastern farmers soon faced competition from the produce of rich Midwestern soils.

Railroads appeared in every region of the United States but not in a uniform network. Beginning from many different entrepreneurial efforts and adapting to widely varying terrain, railroads did not adapt a standard distance between the rails, or guage. As a result, trains could not travel from North to South; cargo had to be unloaded and reloaded. The South's trains focused on connecting coastal cities with inland plantations and farms, while in the North and West railroads ran from city to city, knitting together a network of economic development that benefitted a wider area. In this way, railroads accelerated the growth of differences between the South and the rest of the country.

Telegraph poles marched alongside the railroads, preventing gruesome crashes on single-track lines and speeding the flow of information just as the railroads sped the flow of people and goods. Like the locomotive, the telegraph was the product of inventors in several different countries but received a major impetus from America. Samuel F. B. Morse patented his version of the electronic telegraph in 1840. Morse struggled with the invention for more than ten years, devising the code of dots and dashes that bears his name as well as devising ways to make the current travel farther. In 1842, he received half of a $60,000 research grant from Congress to run an experimental line from Washington to Baltimore. (The other portion of the grant provided $30,000 dollars to study animal magnetism or mesmerism, one of the great fads of the early decades of the century). Observers of the first public tests in 1844 were astonished by the telegraph: "Strange and wonderful discovery, which has made the 'swift-winged lighting' man's messenger, annihilated all space, and tied the two ends of a continent in a knot." Following its success, the telegraph spread across the country with great speed. In the four years after its initial test, more than 5,000 miles of wire had been strung with another 3,000 under construction.

Life in the New Slave South

The South, though increasingly dominated by slavery, remained an integral part of the United States. Southern cotton drove national economic growth and southern politicians controlled much of the nation's government. The South was a prosperous place for white people, whose average per capita incomes, while lower than those of northern whites, exceeded those of almost every other society in the world and were catching up to those in the North.

Thanks to the rapid expansion of newspapers and the telegraph, white southerners took part in all the national conversations about race, slavery, and politics. The growing connections between the regions, in fact, emphasized the differences between the North and the South. As people in each region read the hard words those across the Mason-Dixon line frequently said about them, their distrust of one another grew.

And as increasing numbers of people such as Frederick Douglass escaped to the North, northerners became ever more aware of their region's complicity in perpetuating slavery. The single profound difference between the North and South, slavery, became ever more significant as it grew ever stronger.

African Americans and the South

By the 1830s, slavery had spread over an enormous area stretching from Maryland to Texas. The decade had seen the domestic slave trade grow at a feverish rate, for the new planters of Mississippi, Alabama, and Louisiana eagerly imported slaves to clear land and plant cotton. By the time of the panic of 1837, Alabama, Mississippi, and Louisiana grew more than half the nation's cotton. American slavery became ever more diverse as it expanded. Enslaved people worked in hemp, wheat, rice, corn, sugar, and tobacco fields as well as cotton fields. They worked with livestock and racehorses, practiced trades such as carpentry and blacksmithing, and labored on the docks of New Orleans, Mobile, and Memphis and in the shipyards of Baltimore. Some slaves lived where their families had dwelled for generations; others cleared new land along the Mississippi frontier. Some knew the white people among whom they lived quite well; others belonged to absolute

The slave trade grew into a vast business in the years before the Civil War. Many people, including those who did not own slaves themselves, made their livings from supplying slavetraders with food, shelter, transportation, insurance, and banking. As this map shows, the trade ran strongly from the Upper South to the Lower South, from east to west. Although slavery remained firmly entrenched in states such as Virginia, Kentucky, and North Carolina, the demand for slave labor was so strong in the new plantation districts of Alabama, Mississippi, and Louisiana that slaveholders sold off "surplus" slaves to the traders who came through their counties each year. Traders gathered slaves in the cities of the Chesapeake, especially Alexandria, Virginia, to ship them around the Florida Keys to ports on the Gulf Coast, especially New Orleans. Meanwhile, other slaves were sold "down the river" from places close to the border with the North to the plantations surrounding Vicksburg, Natchez, and Baton Rouge. Other slaves were forced to walk or to take trains across the middle of the South. All along, even more slaves were bought and sold within states, being moved from one county to another in ways that do not appear on this disheartening map.

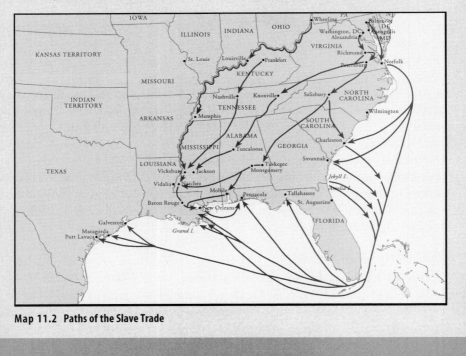

Map 11.2 Paths of the Slave Trade

strangers. Some worked in large groups of black people; others worked alone or beside whites.

Southern culture mixed English, African, Scots-Irish, Caribbean, French, Indian, and Hispanic influences into a rich and complex blend. Language, food, music, and religion took on new shapes as black and white cultures interacted. In the meantime, African

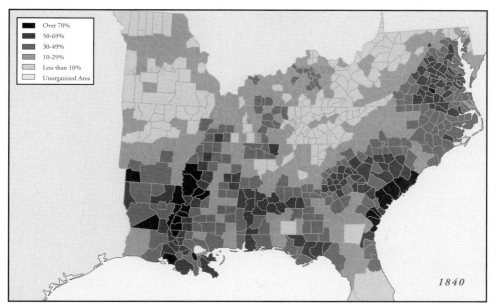

Map 11.3 The Spread of Slavery Slavery moved to the lands taken from the American Indians in Georgia, Alabama, and Mississippi, even as the institution remained strong in the older plantation areas of the Atlantic coast.

Americans prided themselves on the stories, songs, and dances they knew to be particularly their own, on the styles of the baskets, quilts, and clothes they sewed, or the way they carried themselves. Black culture remained distinct and vibrant, even as it influenced the larger American culture.

African American families tended to rely on a broader range of kin than did white families. Grandparents, aunts, and uncles often played significant roles in child rearing in black families. When people of actual blood relation were unavailable, southern slaves created "fictive kin," friends and neighbors given honorary titles of "brother" or "aunt" and treated as such. These arrangements permitted slave families considerable resiliency and variety.

Enslaved Americans generally lived in a relatively small community of others. About a quarter of all held in slavery lived on farms with fewer than nine slaves, whereas another quarter lived on the 3 percent of southern plantations that held more than fifty slaves. The remaining half lived on plantations with somewhere between ten and forty-nine bondspeople. African Americans often found wives or husbands on nearby farms, visiting one another on evenings and weekends.

Plantations and Farms

White slaveowners in the American South tended to live on the same plantation as their slaves, but wealthier whites put day-to-day control of their plantations in the hands of professional overseers. These overseers were often ambitious young men of middling background who used the overseer position as a stepping stone to their own plantation. Slaves could and did appeal to the owner if they thought the overseer unfair. Since a master might indeed trust a well-known slave more than a new overseer, the position involved tact as well as brute force.

On larger plantations, where slaves often worked in groups called gangs, trusted male slaves served as "drivers." Such drivers tended to be especially strong and skilled, commanding respect from whites as well as blacks. Although whites held the ultimate threat of force, they much preferred to keep the work moving smoothly, with as little trouble as

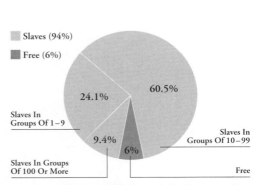

Pattern of Black Population

- Slaves (94%)
- Free (6%)

60.5% — Slaves In Groups Of 10–99
24.1% — Slaves In Groups Of 1–9
9.4% — Slaves In Groups Of 100 Or More
6% — Free

Chart 11.1 Patterns of Black Population in the South
Most black people lived on large plantations with more than ten other enslaved people, even while others were scattered on much smaller farms and in towns and cities.

possible. The driver could help both sides, protecting fellow slaves from abuse and assuring that the work got done efficiently. Drivers frequently found themselves caught between the two competing sets of demands, however, and slaves often resented or even hated drivers.

About three out of four enslaved people worked mainly in the fields. Almost all of them went to the fields during the peak times. Women, who worked in the fields alongside men, also served in the house as cooks and domestics. Slaves were well known for controlling the pace of work, reporting their tools broken or "lost" when they were forced to work too fast or too long. They traditionally had Sundays to garden for themselves, do their domestic chores, or hunt.

Slaves' lives were by no means simple. Lines of power often became complicated and tangled on plantations and farms, with masters, mistresses, sons, overseers, and drivers claiming authority. Slaves tended to work at several different jobs over the course of the year. Some slaves were respected as purveyors of healing or religious knowledge from Africa; some slaves were admired for their musical ability; others won recognition for their ability to read and preach the Gospel. These abilities did not always correspond with the opinions of whites, who frequently underestimated the abilities and character of the people among whom they lived.

Whites told themselves that they provided "their people" a better life than they would have known in Africa. Indeed, southern masters explained the justice of slavery to themselves and to the North by stressing their Christian stewardship for the slaves. As one clergyman wrote to his fellow slaveholders in the early 1840s, slaves "were placed under our control . . . not exclusively for our benefit but theirs also."

Throughout the 1830s and 1840s, southern slaveholders and ministers prided themselves on their Christian mission to the slaves. Most masters would not permit their slaves to learn to read, but they did arrange to have Bible selections read to their slaves. Although many slaves eagerly accepted the Gospel in the white-dominated churches, others resented the obvious and shallow uses the masters made of the sermons, telling the slaves to accept their lot and to refrain from stealing food. Such slaves displayed their deepest religious feelings only in their own worship, in the secret meetings in brush arbors and cabins in the slave quarters. There, they prayed to be free and to be united in heaven with those they loved.

Largely oblivious to the lives their slaves led beyond their sight, masters pointed to the physical condition of the slaves as evidence of their concern for "their people." Compared with slaves in other places in the hemisphere, it was true, those of the American South were relatively well-fed and healthier. They had limited and monotonous diets, but generally consumed enough nutrients. Slaves received ineffective or dangerous health care, their houses were small and drafty, and their clothing was limited to a few rough garments per year, but none of these conditions endangered slaves' physical survival. Slaves in the United States,

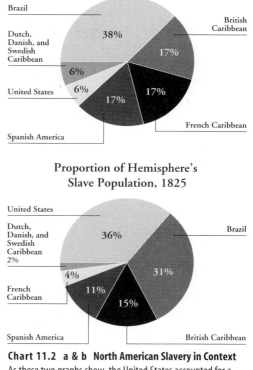

Chart 11.2 a & b North American Slavery in Context
As these two graphs show, the United States accounted for a relatively small proportion of all enslaved people brought from Africa into the Western Hemisphere, but because of the longer life spans of North American slaves, over a third of the enslaved population of the New World lived in the United States.

working in relatively healthy settings and benefiting from a balanced ratio between men and women, generally lived longer than did their counterparts elsewhere in the hemisphere.

On the other hand, many slaveowners did not refrain from having their slaves whipped on small provocation, branded, shackled, or locked up in sweltering enclosures; slaves suffered sexual abuse. Partly because expectant mothers were often kept in the fields until the last minute, about a third of all black babies died before they reached their first birthday. American slavery, compared with slavery elsewhere, whatever ameliorating features it might have had, was a harsh institution.

The Politics of the White South

In the South as in the North, the Whigs portrayed themselves as the party of progress and prosperity. The lawyers, editors, and merchants who set up shop in the hamlets and towns of the South proved receptive to such views. The young men who followed such professions eagerly joined organizations such as the Masons, temperance groups, and political parties. They prided themselves on their broad views of national issues. In their eyes, only the Whigs reflected such enlightened perspectives. The large planters on the richest lands were also attracted to the Whigs. The Whigs drew, too, on the farmers in the mountains of the Upper South, men determined to develop connections to outside markets.

The Democrats, on the other hand, found their strongest supporters among the middling farmers and planters of the South. These men tended to resent and fear taxes on their lands and slaves. They admired the Democrats' aggressive approach to removing the American Indians and western expansion. Southerners distrustful of northerners and of commerce found the minimal-government pronouncements of the Democrats appealing.

In the South both the Whigs and the Democrats declared themselves the friends of southern slavery, but they differed in their emphases. The Democrats pledged that they would protect slavery by extending the power of the government as little as possible. The Whigs, on the other hand, argued that the best way to protect slavery was for the South to develop its region's economy and build strong economic and political bridges to the North.

Reform Takes Root

The wild swings of the economy of the 1830s seemed to drive Americans to improve their society. They could see dangers all around them but they could also glimpse how things could be better. The new machinery of railroads, telegraphs, and printing presses held out exciting new possibilities for spreading the word, for pulling people together for common purposes.

Some Americans took practical routes to progress, focusing their efforts on schools and alcohol, whereas others explored philosophy and literature. Some used the new printing machinery of the age for entertainment, whereas others turned to the fight against social evils.

Public Schools

Many Americans had become dissatisfied with the way young people were schooled in the United States. No state had a statewide school system, and local districts ran their own affairs, often wretchedly. The rich attended private schools or employed tutors, whereas the parents of poorer children had to sign oaths declaring themselves "paupers" before their children could benefit from charity schools. Parents from the middle classes, charged a fee according to the number of children they had, sent their offspring to schools often taught by untrained teachers. Hundreds of districts, especially in the South, created no schools at all. Many American children never went to school in the 1820s and 1830s and those who did often attended for only a short time.

Reformers argued that unequal and inadequate education would not suffice in America, a country dependent upon informed democracy. These reformers wanted free schools. Taxes and other state support would make it possible for all children to go to public schools. The rich would be more likely to send their children to such schools, reformers reasoned, if their tax dollars were supporting them; the poor would be more likely to send their children if they were not stigmatized as paupers. Buildings and teachers could be improved with the increased support.

A Massachusetts lawyer and Whig politician, Horace Mann worked relentlessly to make rich citizens, especially manufacturers, see that a tax in support of schools was a wise investment. Think how much better workers would be, he argued, if they could read and calculate. Think to what good use women could be put as teachers, he argued, instilling future citizens with their virtues of cooperation and peacefulness. Mann gradually persuaded influential people in Massachusetts of the practicability of common schools. In 1837, he became the first secretary of the Massachusetts Board of Education.

When Mann took over, many schools were in session for only a couple of months a year. He transformed that system during his tenure. The minimum school year stretched to six months, buildings and teacher training improved significantly, and teachers' pay increased by more than half.

Women teachers became common in the Northeast. Oberlin College in Ohio admitted women in 1837, making it the first coeducational institution in the country. Females attended new "normal schools" that provided teacher training; they read educational journals, received professional supervision, and taught with uniform textbooks. These standards spread throughout the North and the West in the 1840s and 1850s, as did McGuffey's Readers. These books, which sold an astonishing 9 million copies between 1836 and 1850, blended Christian piety and the virtues of hard work. Though each book aimed at a specific grade, the underlying message was always the same: "God has given you minds which are capable of indefinite improvement."

The Washingtonians

Americans had long waged campaigns against intemperance, but the fight against drink took on a new urgency in the depression years of the late 1830s and early 1840s. Many people, religious and otherwise, saw alcohol as the scourge of American life. "You cannot go into hardly any man's house," an English visitor wrote, "without being asked to drink wine, or spirits, even in the morning." Men drank at work, farmers routinely turned their grain into whiskey, and rum was a major part of New England commerce. Americans aged fifteen or older consumed an average of 40 gallons of beer, spirits, and wine per capita.

The Washingtonian movement, named in honor of George Washington, gave great force and visibility to a crusade against alcohol. Whereas earlier temperance movements had mainly enlisted those who were already opposed to alcohol, the new movement marked an effort by drinkers to reform themselves. Earlier attempts at temperance had often pitted middle- and upper-class reformers against members of the working class, but the new movement grew among people in the lower ranks of American society. Older reform attempts had been largely the efforts of men, but now women became active.

The Washingtonians began in Baltimore in 1840, when six drinkers pledged to one another to quit drinking and to persuade other drinkers to do the same. Word of the new movement quickly spread up the eastern seaboard, and by 1843 the Washingtonians claimed millions of adherents. Unlike earlier temperance efforts led by upper class or religious leaders, Washingtonians prided themselves on an egalitarian ethos: "Exclusiveness was never intended to constitute . . . Washingtonianism. We write plain things for plain people." Partly as a result of the new organization, Americans' consumption of alcohol plummeted in the 1840s.

"Martha Washington" societies, for women only, grew rapidly, challenging the men's movement both in size and in fervor. These female temperance advocates were not well-to-do ladies stooping to help the fallen, but rather the wives of artisans and small businessmen. They helped families in distress to get back on their feet. They also provided a new edge to the temperance crusade, reminding men that drunkenness was more often than not a male failing and that it was the wives and children of drunkards who suffered most from their neglect, cruelty, and even violence.

Abolitionism Strengthened and Challenged

By the late 1830s the American Anti-slavery Society claimed over a quarter of a million members, primarily in the Northeast and Midwest. The first female abolitionist speakers— the Grimké sisters, Angelina and Sarah—were prize recruits into the antislavery ranks, for they were the daughters of a prominent South Carolina slave-owning planter. By telling New England audiences of their own experiences with slavery, the Grimkés held a credibility that white northern abolitionists could not match. In 1837, the Grimkés decided to exert their power in a new forum by lecturing to mixed audiences of men and women. Although some people strenuously objected to such an elevation of women in the public sphere, the Grimkés spoke to over 40,000 people in nine months in 1837 and 1838. "*All moral beings have essentially the same rights and the same duties,* whether they be male or female," Angelina Grimké admonished an audience. The female slaves of the South, who "now wear the rion yoke of slavery in this land of boasted liberty and law . . . are our countrywomen—*they are our sisters.*"

As it grew stronger, the antislavery cause met with more determined opposition. When abolitionist Elijah P. Lovejoy offended readers of his religious paper in St. Louis— denouncing a local judge who prevented the trial of a mob who had burned a black man alive—citizens of Alton, Illinois, invited Lovejoy to move to their town. Alton prided itself on being a progressive place, but soon some prominent members of the community, angered at Lovejoy's paper for its dissemination of "the highly odious doctrines of modern Abolitionism," held a public meeting demanding that he quit printing such ideas. Lovejoy only intensified his attacks on slavery. Mobs destroyed two of Lovejoy's presses and vowed to tar and feather him, but he persisted. A mayoral candidate in Alton whipped a mob to a frenzy to destroy a replacement press as it was offloaded from the train in September. In November 1837, as his fifth press arrived, a battle erupted and

The Dangers of Drink

This print was a popular one in the United States early in its national history because many people considered alcohol the greatest threat to the country. In this one image, viewers could trace the devastating effects of drinking on a young man and his family. Everyone knew the excuses people told themselves about drinking. At first, in the lower left corner, the very young man shares a drink with a friend. He then proceeds to make weak excuses, such as drinking to "keep the cold out." From there, it is a short step to losing control, having "a drink too much," and becoming "riotous." At the "summit," the star of the story has become a "confirmed drunkard," wasting his life with equally drunken friends. His drinking leads quickly to poverty and then to desperate crime in order to support the habit. Finally, despairing, he turns to suicide as the only way out. Meanwhile, an abandoned wife and child, homeless, suffer on their way to the poor house. This was America's first war on drugs and it struck many of the same themes as those of later crusades.

From the Collections of the Library of Congress

Lovejoy was killed as he and his assistants fought the crowd. The mob shattered his press, and local law officers arrested the defenders of Lovejoy for inciting the violence.

Abolitionists debated the proper response to such opposition. William Lloyd Garrison counseled his allies to offer no resistance to violence. He and his supporters renounced all allegiance to the established parties and churches, which had long since shown themselves tolerant of slavery. Other abolitionists, by contrast, used whatever means they could to bring slavery to an end, including political parties.

The differences among the abolitionists came to a head at the annual meeting of the American Anti-slavery Society in 1839. They differed most visibly in their attitudes toward the role of women. Women constituted perhaps half of all members of the antislavery organizations, but some male abolitionists sought to keep females in a subordinate role and prevent women members from voting, speaking publicly, or serving on committees with men. Unable to resolve their differences, the abolitionists split. The more conservative group, based in New York, created the Liberty party to run a candidate for president in the upcoming election of 1840. Garrison's organization maintained a more radical stance on the role of women and mocked those who sought "to sustain and propagate those eternal, immutable principles of liberty, justice, and equality" by denying "woman her right as a human being to speak and act with brethren on the anti-slavery platform."

Whatever their differences, abolitionists barraged Congress with petitions demanding that slavery be ended in the District of Columbia. Former President John Quincy Adams, now a congressman from Massachusetts, used all his parliamentary skill to fight the gag rule that prevented Congress from recognizing antislavery petitions; he finally succeeded in getting it overthrown in 1845. Adams also successfully defended Africans who had seized a slave ship bound for Cuba, the *Amistad,* and landed in Connecticut. Supported by a large network of abolitionists, Adams took the case before the U.S. Supreme Court and won not only the acquittal of the Africans for murdering the ship's captain but their freedom as well.

Black antislavery speakers greatly strengthened the antislavery cause. Speakers such as Henry Brown, Henry Bibb, Solomon Northup, Sojourner Truth, Harriet Tubman, and Ellen Craft electrified audiences. Slavery, they made clear, was nothing like the benign institution portrayed by its defenders. Public speakers such as Henry Highland Garnet urged listeners to "strike for your lives and liberties. Let every slave throughout the land do this, and the days of slavery are numbered. Rather die freemen than live to be slaves. Remember that you are FOUR MILLIONS! . . . Let your motto be resistance! resistance! RESISTANCE!"

Although white abolitionists valued the contributions of their black compatriots, they urged black speakers not to make too much of a fuss when confronted with the insults and indignities

The Granger Collection, New York

One of the most influential and famous Americans of the nineteenth century, Frederick Douglass fought tirelessly against slavery and in favor of a wide range of social reforms.

faced by black people in the North. African American abolitionists chafed under the restrictions they faced from fellow reformers and enemies alike; they demanded greater rights for northern as well as southern blacks. Their experiences showed the extent to which race was a national problem.

One of the most remarkable Americans of the nineteenth century burst into visibility in the early 1840s. Frederick Douglass had grown up in Maryland. Like other places in the Upper South, Maryland's economy was diversifying in the 1830s and 1840s as commerce intensified and railroads spread. Douglass learned to read from his mistress, though it was against the law for her to teach him. He carried with him a copy of *Webster's Spelling Book* and *The Columbian Orator,* a book of speeches, including a slave's persuasive argument with his master to set him free.

Sent to Baltimore by his owner, Douglass worked in the shipyards, continued to read widely, and plotted his escape to freedom. After several attempts, Douglass finally borrowed the papers of a free black sailor and rode a train to freedom. Douglass found himself in New York City, alone and without any notion of what he should do. A runaway slave might be hunted down by a slavecatcher for a reward. Fortunately for Douglass, he met a black man who introduced the young runaway to the New York Anti-slavery Society. After white abolitionists saw the skill with which he spoke, they sent Douglass to travel throughout the North with William Lloyd Garrison.

Development of an American Culture

European visitors had long scoffed at the failure of the United States to create anything they considered "culture." During the first desperate decades of the nation's experience, filled with war, economic panic, and political conflict, few Americans found opportunity to do philosophy, write novels, produce ambitious paintings, or carve sculpture. But in the 1830s and 1840s, the new country experienced a sudden outburst of creativity in everything from the most elevated philosophy to the most popular amusements.

Transcendentalism

Leading thinkers saw the possibilities of improvement everywhere, not just in education or reform. Several of those thinkers came out of Unitarianism, a form of liberal Christianity especially strong in New England. Unitarianism encouraged people to emphasize feeling rather than dogma. Several young people raised within the Unitarian church took these ideas further than their elders intended, rejecting much Christian doctrine. A belief in the literal truth of the Bible, these youthful critics argued, trapped religion in the past. Better to appeal directly to the heart from the very beginning. These thinkers wanted religion to transcend churches and denominations.

Women played an active role in the effort to create an American philosophy, with Margaret Fuller becoming especially important. Fuller, raised in the Unitarian church in Cambridge, Massachusetts, received a fine education. But she felt herself adrift, full of "unemployed force," after her male classmates went on to college. She read widely and taught school with two other important figures in the revolt against Unitarianism: Elizabeth Peabody and Bronson Alcott. These three, like Horace Mann, believed that children were innately good and that education should be designed to let that goodness flourish. They argued that school, like church, should not be permitted to get in the way of people's natural connection with nature and with one another.

They soon took their lead from Ralph Waldo Emerson. Emerson had grown up around Concord, Massachusetts. Though descended from a distinguished ministerial family, he was raised by a widowed mother and forced to work his way through Harvard College. Uncomfortable as a minister and dissatisfied as a schoolteacher, Emerson set out for Europe. There he met exciting English intellectuals whose stirring ideas were to

From the Collections of the Library of Congress

Ralph Waldo Emerson was America's first popular intellectual, a combination of poet, lecturer, entertainer, and minister.

influence him deeply: Samuel Coleridge, Thomas Carlyle, and William Wordsworth. These writers, caught up in European romanticism with its rejection of the austere logic of the Enlightenment, provided Emerson with a perspective far removed from the cool Unitarianism on which he had been raised. Emerson perceived humankind as deeply tied to nature, filled with its rhythms and longings. He published such ideas in his first book, *Nature* (1836), a work that gained him considerable attention from the like-minded young people of New England.

But it was Emerson's address before the Phi Beta Kappa initiates at Harvard in 1837 that announced his arrival to a larger audience. Emerson worried over the state of the nation after the panic of 1837. The panic directly touched one of Emerson's friends in Concord, Henry David Thoreau, who graduated from Harvard in the panic year and could find no decent job. Emerson, older than Thoreau, had finally achieved some economic security in the summer of 1837, thanks to an inheritance, but he was well aware of the difficulties facing even the Phi Beta Kappa graduates of Harvard during August of that hard year.

Emerson titled his speech "The American Scholar." He argued that the scholar should be a man of action, a man of nature, a man of risk and endeavor. Books and poetry held tremendous power, Emerson admitted, but it was in activity, in striving, that the American scholar became truly American. It was time to set the teachings of Europe aside long enough to find America's own voice, Emerson told the graduates.

Echoes of these ideas were also heard in the South. William Gilmore Simms, a leading essayist, novelist, and poet from South Carolina, traveled throughout the South delivering lectures to communities, universities, and learned societies on diverse topics such as "English Literature" and "The Philosophy of History." Like Emerson, Simms saw southern scholars as armed with "the sufficient spear of truth" who "shall compel the deference of sordid politicians."

Speakers developed these ideas throughout the late 1830s, enjoying growing fame and influence through public lectures. Railroads made it feasible for the first time for speakers to cover a large amount of territory. Public speaking generally paid much better than any kind of writing. The growth of newspapers and other printing facilitated advertising, getting word of the lectures out beforehand and spreading summaries of the lectures to those unable to attend. People flocked to the lectures. In the lecture hall, Emerson exulted, "everything is admissible, philosophy, ethics, divinity, criticism, poetry, humor, fun, mimicry, anecdotes, jokes, ventriloquism. . . ."

Emerson's home in Concord became the gathering place for a group who came to be called the transcendentalists, who sought to "transcend" the mundane into the mystical knowledge that every human possessed if he or she would listen to it. Margaret Fuller became the editor of the *Dial,* the transcendentalist magazine, while Elizabeth Peabody opened a bookstore catering to the interests of the group. Bronson Alcott and about eighty others founded Brook Farm, one of the many utopian communities that tried to get off the ground in the 1830s and 1840s. Brook Farm put people to work in the fields in the morning and on their books in the afternoon. The community produced both crops and an impressive weekly newspaper. Its schools stood as examples of enlightened education. The experiment failed economically after a few years, but for a while Brook Farm offered the possibility of combining intellectual excitement, physical work, and social responsibility in a way the transcendentalists craved.

Since the transcendentalists believed that people should establish a close connection to nature, Henry David Thoreau decided to conduct an "experiment in human ecology." He wanted to see—and show—how a modern man could live in harmony with nature. In 1845, he built an isolated house in the woods near Walden Pond, carefully calculating the cost of nails and other supplies and keeping a thoughtful journal. He strove to be self-sufficient and self-contained. The experiment proved important for the book Thoreau eventually published about his experience, *Walden: Life in the Woods* (1854).

Emergence of a Popular Culture

The transcendentalists were not alone in their craving for intensity. American painters, sculptors, and writers found an increasing audience for their works in the 1830s. And so did entrepreneurs who sought out the largest audiences they could find with spectacle and controversy.

Thomas Cole was the key figure in the emergence of American painting. Though born in England, he came to the Ohio frontier as a small child. Cole taught himself to paint but went to England and Italy to perfect his art. He returned to the village of Catskill in New York to paint the Hudson River Valley in the late 1830s and early 1840s. Soon, other painters, such as Asher Durand and Frederick Church, joined Cole in their fascination with the stirring American landscape, creating what became known as the Hudson River School.

Cole also turned to richly symbolic allegorical painting. His journey to Europe had struck him by its contrasts, "both the ruined towers that tell of outrage, and the gorgeous temples that speak of ostentation." He believed America, by contrast, "to be the abode of virtue." He embodied his notions of the cycles of civilization and personal life in two powerful allegorical series, *The Course of Empire* and *The Voyage of Life.* Engravings of these series became popular fixtures in American homes.

Other important artists followed their own paths through the American landscape. George Catlin spent much of the 1830s living among the American Indians of the Great Plains, making hundreds of drawings and paintings. As a young man he was moved by the sight of an Indian delegation visiting Philadelphia and vowed that "nothing short of the loss of my life shall prevent me from visiting their country and becoming their historian." In Catlin's paintings, easterners thought they might catch the last glimpse of a disappearing people.

Audiences could also view vanishing wildlife in the remarkable watercolors of John James Audubon. Audubon, born in Haiti and educated in France, settled on the Kentucky frontier as a merchant after he married. He loved the American wilderness too much to stay in his shop, though, and he launched out on daunting journeys to record the environment and appearance of the birds of the young nation. After ten years of work Audubon produced *The Birds of America, from Original Drawings, with 435 Plates Showing 1,065 Figures* in four immense volumes, completing the project in 1838.

The most famous artistic production of antebellum America was a statue: Hiram Powers's *The Greek Slave,* completed in 1846. Powers grew up in the raw country of Ohio but moved to Italy as he prospered. There, Powers sculpted his statue of a nude young woman bound in chains. The young woman represented, Powers said, a Greek girl captured by the Turks in the Greco-Turkish war. As such, she represented Christianity and whiteness, unbowed by the evil and darkness surrounding her. Powers sought, and received, the endorsement of a

The New York Museum/Art Resource, NY

Hiram Powers's statue The Greek Slave became an American sensation, attracting large crowds and many imitators.

group of American clergymen, removing any qualms audiences might have. *The Greek Slave* served as the model for hundreds of miniature copies that appeared in the drawing rooms of the finest homes.

The same drawing rooms also contained a novelty of the age: daguerreotypes. This form of photography developed in France but arrived in the United States in 1838 soon after its creation. Within a few years, more than eighty young photographers practiced their craft in New York City alone and by 1850 as many as 10,000 daguerreotypists had set up shop. This early photography was cumbersome and required long periods of stillness before the camera, but the American people hurried to studios to have their portraits done.

Engravings based on paintings and photographs soon filled the publications coming off the presses. For the first time, illustrations could be produced cheaply. Etched metal plates replaced crude woodcuts for the mass production of lithographs of popular subjects such as Bible stories, sporting events, shipwrecks, and railroad disasters.

Seeing the opportunity afforded by this emergence of a popular audience for print, American writers worked hard to fill the hunger. One especially gifted author, Edgar Allan Poe, skillfully navigated between the market and his art. Poe wrote short stories, the kind of writing most in demand, but he brought to the form a kind of self-consciousness few had demonstrated before. Poe tapped into a widespread fascination with the occult, seances, and ghosts, filling his work with ruins, shadows, and legends. Works such as "The Murders in the Rue Morgue" marked the first appearance of the detective story. Throughout the 1840s, Poe published stories such as "The Masque of the Red Death," "The Pit and the Pendulum," and "The Tell-Tale Heart" and poetry such as "The Raven." Plagued by ill health, however, Poe did not survive the decade.

P. T. Barnum exploited the public fascination with the macbre and fanciful and opened his American Museum in New York in 1841. Barnum displayed oddities that strained the limits of belief but that could not be completely disproved. He displayed an aged black woman who he claimed was 161 years old and had been George Washington's nurse. Thousands turned out to gaze at her infirm body and hear her tales of "dear little George." Unlike earlier museums, Barnum's museum frankly offered entertainment, including magicians and midgets such as the famous Tom Thumb and the Feejee Mermaid, actually a monkey skeleton attached to the bones of a large fish. The fact that the "curiosities" were often attacked as fakes by scientists did not seem to deter visitors: Barnum's American Museum flourished for the next twenty years and his public tours with Swedish singer Jenny Lind enraptured millions and habituated Americans to a culture of celebrity and publicity stunts.

The Transformation of American Politics

Popular politics had been building in the United States since the 1820s, when Andrew Jackson electrified the electorate and when states lowered the obstacles of political participation. The two major parties, the Democrats and the Whigs, had experimented with ways to mobilize voters and to retain the power they won. The system grew throughout the 1830s, but no one was prepared for what happened in 1840.

The Election of 1840

The contest of 1840 should have offered an easy contest for the Whigs. Much of the nation remained mired in depression. Van Buren offered little effective leadership during the economic crisis and many people held him to blame for the hard times. But the Whigs were not as strong as they might have been. Their party had been built piece by piece in the 1830s in reaction to Andrew Jackson. As a result, the party was a crazy quilt of interests and factions. In 1836, the party had even permitted three candidates to run against Van Buren because no one man could command the party's full allegiance. Party leaders vowed that they would not make the same mistake in 1840.

The Whigs were determined to find the one man who stood for the common beliefs that unified Whigs beneath their surface differences. Those beliefs turned around faith in commerce, self-control, Protestantism, learning, and self-improvement. Most important, the Whigs wanted to make an active response to the depression plaguing the nation by putting money in circulation, building internal improvements, and strengthening banks. The trick was to find a candidate who embodied their beliefs without appearing to be "aristocratic" or hungry for power.

The Whig party found such a man in William Henry Harrison. Harrison had made his name as a general—most notably in his defeat of an Indian confederacy in the Battle of Tippecanoe in 1811—and later served in the House of Representatives and in the Senate. He had won fame without gathering many political liabilities and was identified with no particular position.

Seeking to balance their ticket, the Whigs chose Senator John Tyler of Virginia. Tyler shared few beliefs with his fellow Whigs, but his embrace of slavery helped mollify southerners. Moreover, his name made a nice pairing in the phrase that soon became famous: "Tippecanoe and Tyler, Too." One Whig warned that the combination of Harrison and Tyler had "rhyme, but no reason in it."

The Democrats were relieved that the Whigs had nominated Harrison. Democrats considered the old general a nonentity; one reporter commented sarcastically that if Harrison were merely given some hard cider and a small pension he would contentedly sit out the rest of his days in a log cabin. (He actually lived in a mansion and was a rich man.) The sarcasm backfired, though, for many Americans saw log cabins and home-brewed cider as evidence of American virtue and self-reliance. The Whigs, long frustrated at their reputation as snobs and elitists, seized on hard cider and log cabins as symbols of their party's loyalty to the common American.

All over the country, Whig speakers displayed paintings, signs, flags, and models of log cabins at huge outdoor rallies while freely dispensing cider to thirsty crowds. Harrison himself went out on the campaign trail, the first presidential candidate to do so. A new kind of American political style was being forged. For the first time, women became

Map 11.4 The Election of 1840

The remarkable success of the two-party system in transforming the American political landscape was dramatized by the election of 1840. Slavery had torn at the nation ever since the Missouri Compromise, with the rapid spread of the institution all the way past the Mississippi River into Missouri, Arkansas, and Louisiana and the sudden rise of abolitionism in the North. Looking at this map, however, one would never know that these momentous things had happened. The great majority of states contained areas where either the Whigs or the Democrats dominated, the two areas balancing out almost evenly in most states so that both parties competed for every vote. The Whig party faced a difficult balancing act, for the map shows that the party won in Massachusetts and Connecticut, where antislavery was strong, and in the areas of Alabama and Georgia where plantation slavery dominated. National leaders had somehow to appeal to both constituencies if they were to remain in power.

prominent at these rallies, encouraging their husbands, fathers, and suitors with smiles, waving kerchiefs, and riding in parades with pro-Harrison banners they had sewn. The Whigs embraced causes many women supported, such as temperance and allegiance to the church.

The Democrats had no idea of how to respond to the hard cider and log cabin campaign. Martin Van Buren proved an easy target for a Whig campaign that emphasized homespun values. The president's portly figure and penchant for silk vests and doeskin gloves made the Democrats' long-standing claims of representing the common man look hypocritical. Andrew Jackson himself came out to campaign, firing the same charges against the Whigs that had worked so well in the past, charges of elitism, hostility to slavery, and softness on the bank issue. Even these charges failed. Harrison won nineteen of the twenty-six states, bringing about half a million new voters to the Whigs. Voter turnout surged to a level almost unimaginable just a decade earlier: Eight of every ten eligible voters went to the polls. After 1840, elections would demand the combination of active campaigning, the search for potent symbols, and boisterous public displays that had proven so successful in that year.

Tyler, Webster, and Diplomacy

The Whig celebration did not last long. Harrison, determined to prove his fitness despite his age, expounded the longest inaugural speech in American history in March 1841. Unfortunately, the weather was bitterly cold; Harrison contracted pneumonia and died exactly a month after taking office. John Tyler had become president even though he shared few of the prevailing ideals of the Whigs in Congress. Efforts on the part of Whig leaders to expand the power and reach of government with tariffs, banks, and internal improvements proved fruitless in the face of Tyler's opposition. Whig leaders in Congress responded by gathering in the Capitol gardens and excommunicating him from the party. Whig newspapers denounced him as "His Accidency" and the "Executive Ass." All but one of the members of the cabinet Tyler inherited from Harrison resigned in protest.

The only member to stay on, Daniel Webster, the secretary of state, did so because he feared his rival Henry Clay's ascendancy if he resigned and he did not think it proper to step down until important negotiations with England were complete. Conflicts between the two countries had broken out over the boundary between the United States and Canada. In 1837, armed men had fought along the border as Americans aided a rebel movement trying to overthrow British control of Canada; later, a Canadian militia burned an American steamboat carrying supplies for the insurgents, generating intense anger in the northern United States. Armed battle also erupted in the "Aroostock War" over the disputed boundary between Maine and New Brunswick.

Conflict had long been building between the British and the Americans, too, over the African slave trade. Great Britain insisted that its vessels be permitted to search American ships off the coast of Africa to prevent the transportation of slaves to British colonies. Americans resented the intrusion in its affairs and refused. The issue threatened to explode in 1841, when American slaves seized the slaving ship the *Creole,* which was taking them from Virginia to New Orleans. The slaves steered the vessel to the Bahamas and claimed their freedom under British law. Much to the anger of southern whites, the British gave sanctuary to the slaves.

Daniel Webster met with the British representative, Lord Ashburton, to settle these issues before they flamed up into a war that neither nation wanted. After extensive debate, the United States and Great Britain decided on a new boundary that gave each about half of what each had claimed in Maine and in the area to the west of Lake Superior. The Webster-Ashburton Treaty also established joint American-British patrols to intercept ships carrying slaves from Africa. Though the treaty stipulated that the United States must maintain a minimum presence totaling eighty guns along the African coast, Tyler's secretary of the navy undercut American effectiveness by sending only four ships mounting eighty guns instead of the approximately fifteen schooners better suited for the task. In 1850, while the U.S. Navy had captured only seven slavers since beginning the patrols, the British had captured over 500 ships and freed over 38,000 Africans.

The Challenge of the West

Americans of every sort kept their eyes to the west. Railroads, telegraphs, canals, and roads strained in that direction; population restlessly flowed there. But thoughtful people recognized that the lack of borders and limits posed threats as well as potential. When everything seemed possible, people placed few checks on their appetites. Every boundary was contested, every obstacle attacked.

The "Wests"

The hard times in the East made moving west seem an increasingly attractive option. Horace Greeley, the most influential newspaper editor of the day, warned people looking for a job in the midst of the depression not to come to the city but rather to "go to the Great West." To people in New England, migration to the West in the 1840s often meant migration to the lands of the northern plains and surrounding the Great Lakes. To people from Virginia and Kentucky, migration to the West might mean heading to the free states of Ohio, Indiana, or Illinois or, more often, to Mississippi, Louisiana, and Texas. For people from the cities of the East, the destination might be a booming new city such as Indianapolis, Chicago, or Detroit.

One "West" that captured the imagination of Americans in these years lay in Oregon and California, word of whose beauty and wealth had slowly filtered east throughout the preceding decade. Although many people considered it nothing less than suicide to attempt to cross the Rockies and what was considered "The Great American Desert," a growing stream of families decided to take the chance. Echoing earlier tall stories of the frontier, Peter H. Burnett, organizer of the "Great Migration" of 1843, regaled listeners with tales of Oregon's wealth and fertility. "In Oregon, pigs are running about under great acorn trees, round and fat, and already cooked, with knives and forks sticking out of them so you can cut off a slice." Most of those who moved to the Pacific coast gathered in northern Missouri or southern Iowa. They set out in early May across undulating plains, with water and firewood easy to find, their wagons pulled by oxen. The settlers gradually ascended to Fort Laramie, at the edge of the Rockies. By July, they had reached the Continental Divide, the point at which rivers on one side flowed to the east and those on the other flowed to the west. On the trail for more than three months by this point, the settlers had covered two-thirds of the distance of their journey.

From the Divide, the settlers heading to California split off from those going to Oregon. Both faced enormous difficulties in the remainder of their trip. They raced the weather, for early mountain snowstorms could be deadly. Some of the mountainous areas were so steep that wagons had to be dragged up one side and let down the other with ropes, chains, and pulleys. Finally, by October, 2,000 miles and six months after they had left Missouri or Iowa, the settlers crossed one last ridge and looked down on the sparkling valleys of Sacramento or the Willamette River.

Migration to the Pacific began slowly, with only a few dozen families making the treacherous journey between 1840 and 1842. The numbers mounted between 1843 and 1845,

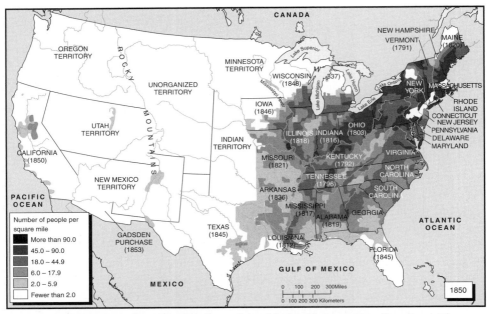

Map 11.5 Population Expansion, 1830–1850 The population of the United States moved steadily westward at the same time that the Northeast became ever more densely settled. The population of the South remained thinner because plantations did not concentrate people as the family farms and towns of the North did.

when over 5,000 people passed through Utah on their way to Oregon and California. Throughout the 1840s, the great majority of migrants chose Oregon over California as their destination. Even so, distances still mattered: from the 1840s until the completion of the transcontinental railroad in 1869, Oregon grew from a few hundred white settlers to more than 100,000. By comparison, in the same period, Iowa's population jumped from a few thousand to 1.2 million. Oregon came to seem a respectable place for literate and upright Protestant families to settle, whereas California seemed a gamble, attractive mainly to single men willing to take their chances in a boom economy that could go bust.

Manifest Destiny

In 1842, the Great United States Exploring Expedition returned from a journey of 87,780 nautical miles. It had circumnavigated the globe, located Antarctica, and explored the Pacific coast. The captain of the expedition reported that Oregon was a treasure trove of "forests, furs, and fisheries." If the United States did not use its military to occupy the territory all the way to the 54°40′ boundary, it would be risking much more than the Oregon territory itself. California might throw off the light Mexican rule under which it rested and join with an independent Oregon to create a nation "that is destined to control the destinies of the Pacific." The Tyler administration sought to

Map 11.6 Trails to the West The trails to Oregon and California looked straightforward enough on a map but proved immensely challenging, even deadly, in practice.

downplay this report, not wanting to disrupt negotiations still pending on the boundary of Maine and Wisconsin.

The forces of expansion proved too strong for the administration to contain, however. In 1845, newspaper editor John Louis O'Sullivan announced that it was the "manifest destiny"—the clear and unavoidable fate—of the United States "to overspread the continent allotted by Providence for the free development of our yearly multiplying millions." In other words, God intended white Americans to fill in every corner of the continent, pushing aside American Indians, Mexicans, English, or anyone else.

The Democrats in Congress and President Tyler supported this expansion, focusing first on Texas. If the United States did not quickly annex Texas, Democrats contended, it might fall under the sway of the British and become not only a barrier to further American migration but also a bastion of antislavery. If, by contrast, the United States acted quickly, Texas could attract not only slaveholders and their slaves but also emancipated slaves, keeping them away from the North and the other attractive lands such as California and Oregon.

Midwestern Democrats, for their part, agreed that expansion was essential to the American future. The country simply could not afford to have major ports and potential markets sealed off. These Democrats had their eye on Oregon.

In 1844, James K. Polk, a former governor of Tennessee, got the Democratic nomination for president after an acrimonious convention and nine ballots. The Democrats appealed to both northerners and southerners with a program of aggressive expansion, attempting to counter fears of slavery's growth not by rejecting Texas but by embracing Oregon.

Politics in Turmoil

In 1844, the Whigs nominated Henry Clay for president on a program explicitly opposed to expansion. The apparently clear-cut choice between Clay and Polk soon became complicated, however. Clay announced that he would not oppose Texas annexation if it could be done peacefully and by consensus. Such a strategy backfired, attracting few advocates of expansion but alienating antislavery people in the North. Although Polk only won 49.6 percent of the vote, hardly a ringing endorsement of aggressive expansionism, his diaries indicate that he entered office with a clear vision of annexing large areas of Mexican territory, Texas, and Oregon.

Meanwhile, the early 1840s witnessed bloody battles over religion. A growing stream of immigrants from Ireland, the great majority of them Catholic, flowed into northern cities. In Protestant eyes, the Roman Catholic church posed a direct threat to American institutions. That church's hierarchy was undemocratic, critics charged. In 1844 the largest anti-Catholic riot of antebellum America broke out in Philadelphia; several Catholic churches burned to the ground while local firemen, rather than fight the blaze, simply hosed down the surrounding buildings to prevent the fire from spreading. Because the Democrats proved far more sympathetic to the Irish than did the largely Protestant Whigs, the political differences between the parties now became inflamed with ethnic conflict.

Slavery, too, became an even more explosive issue in the early 1840s. In 1844 the Methodist church divided over slavery, and the Baptists split the following year. Southern church leaders were angry that many of their northern brethren refused to believe that American slavery was part of God's plan and bitterly resented their northern brethern's passage of a clause demanding no communion with slaveholders. Five hundred thousand southerners formed the Methodist Episcopal Church, South, while Baptists from nine southern states created the Southern Baptist Convention. Questions about slavery moved beyond laws and the Constitution into debates about sin, evil, and God's plan for the nation. As New York Governor William Marcy explained to John C. Calhoun, "I can fight your battles so long as you make the Constitution your fortress, but if you go to the Bible or make it a question of ethics, you must not expect me or any respectable member of the free states to be with you."

The conflicts over slavery exerted immediate political consequences. The abolitionist Liberty party won 62,000 votes in 1844. In New York, in fact, the Liberty party's strong

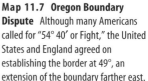

Map 11.7 Oregon Boundary Dispute Although many Americans called for "54° 40' or Fight," the United States and England agreed on establishing the border at 49°, an extension of the boundary farther east.

showing took enough votes from Clay to give the state to Polk. And those electoral votes proved the difference in the national election, as Polk won the presidency by the narrowest of margins.

Even before Polk took office the Senate voted to annex Texas, an independent republic since 1836, as soon as Texas consented. Texas gave its approval in the fall of 1845 and won its vote in Washington at the end of that year. The Democrats sought to quiet concerns among northerners by also annexing Oregon. Though Americans, including some northern Democrats in Congress, clamored for all of Oregon to its northernmost boundary with Russian territory, chanting "Fifty-four Forty or Fight," Polk secretly negotiated with Britain to set the boundary at the 49th parallel, an extension of the northern U.S. boundary from the east. Northern Democrats who had supported Polk on Texas felt betrayed and cheated by this southern conspiracy to "strangle Oregon." Their resentment of Polk's handling of Oregon would smolder, ready to flare again.

Conclusion

The years between 1837 and 1845 bore the mark of the largest economic depression in the nation's history up to that time. Widespread dissatisfaction with the Democrats' handling of the economy laid the foundation for the remarkable Whig victory of 1840, when

William Henry Harrison—and Tyler, too—campaigned under the banner of the log cabin and cider. The depression also drove settlers to the West and forced politicians to focus the energies and anxieties of the country on faraway opportunities and dangers.

Despite these economic problems, Americans remained profoundly optimistic about the long-term prospects of their nation. Painters, philosophers, and poets spoke in a confident new American vernacular. Reformers pushed hard for improvements in education, temperance, antislavery, and much else. Popular culture such as novels, magazines, and Barnum's museum entertained thousands of people. Many Americans focused so much on the future precisely because they had no desire to acknowledge the immediate problems surrounding them.

RECOMMENDED READINGS

Ballesein, Edward J. *Navigating Failure: Bankruptcy and Commercial Society in Antebellum America* (2001). Paints a compelling portrait of the financial turmoil of these years.

Fehrenbacher, Don E. *The Slaveholding Republic: An Account of the United States Government's Relations to Slavery* (2001). A magisterial overview of this important subject.

Genovese, Eugene. *Roll, Jordan, Roll: The World the Slaves Made* (1974). Stands as the most powerful portrayal of American slavery.

Hine, Robert V., and Faragher, John Mack. *The American West: A New Interpretive History* (2000). A fresh interpretation of a crucial American region.

Holt, Michael F. *The Rise and Fall of the American Whig Party: Jacksonian Politics and the Onset of the Civil War* (1999). A remarkable act of scholarship, describing important political change in every part of the nation.

Johnson, Walter. *Soul by Soul: Life Inside the Antebellum Slave Market* (1999). The best study of the vast domestic slave trade.

Kaestle, Carl F. *Pillars of the Republic: Common Schools and American Society, 1780–1860* (1983). The most thorough and balanced account of education reform.

Larson, John Lauritz. *Internal Improvement: National Public Works and the Promise of Popular Government in the Early United States* (2001). A valuable interpretation of one of the most important changes in these decades.

Licht, Walter. *Industrializing America: The Nineteenth Century* (1995). An extremely helpful overview.

Reiss, Benjamin. *The Showman and the Slave: Race, Death, and Memory in Barnum's America* (2001). Tells the fascinating story of the connection between popular culture, commerce, and race.

Stevenson, Brenda E. *Life in Black and White: Family and Community in the Slave South* (1996). Paints a subtle picture of both white and black southerners.

Von Frank, Albert J. *The Trials of Anthony Burns: Freedom and Slavery in Emerson's Boston* (1998). Tells a stirring story of what slaves and the abolitionists were up against.

Additional resources, exercises, and Internet links related to this chapter are available on the American Passages Web site: http://history.wadsworth.com/ayerscompact2/

12

Expansion and Reaction
1846–1854

The years of territorial expansion, population growth, and prosperity that accompanied a triumphant victory in a war with Mexico also proved to be years of unprecedented danger and foreboding for the United States. Heightened expectations of a transcontinental empire led to political conflict. Massive immigration from Europe fueled social conflict. Literature took on a more pessimistic tone. Female activists discovered that progress for women would come only as a result of prolonged effort. The attempt to open the West to settlement divided southerners and northerners. A stopgap compromise on slavery satisfied neither side.

War with Mexico

Spanish territory to the south of the United States had been a major concern for generations. Throughout the 1820s American leaders had struggled with the promise and danger posed by Mexican independence and the annexation of Texas; throughout the 1830s and 1840s Americans had aided Texans in their fight against the Mexican army. The United States longed for the territories Mexico controlled in western North America, but Mexico pledged to keep those lands. No one could be sure that the United States could defeat Mexico in a large-scale war, but President Polk seemed determined to find out.

The United States at War

The Mexican government had never recognized the independence of Texas, which Texans claimed as a result of their defeat of Santa Anna in 1836. President James K. Polk raised the stakes by insisting that the border between Texas and Mexico lay at the Rio Grande, not at the Nueces River farther north. Even before the formal annexation of Texas took effect in 1845, Polk ordered American troops under the command of General Zachary Taylor to cross the Nueces.

Polk had his eyes not only on the border with Texas but on larger prizes still: the sale of California and New Mexico. Polk ordered John C. Frémont, leading an army expedition to map rivers within U.S. borders, to California. Frémont, acting on instructions to seize California "in the event of any occurrence," supported the "Bear Flag Rebellion," an armed

CHRONOLOGY

1846	Mexican War begins; Stephen Kearny occupies Santa Fe; Zachary Taylor takes Monterey • Border between Canada and United States established at 49th parallel • Wilmot Proviso ignites sectional conflict • Bear Flag Republic in California proclaimed • Hiram Powers completes statue *The Greek Slave*
1847	Taylor defeats Santa Anna at Buena Vista; Winfield Scott captured • Veracruz and Mexico City • Mormons reach Great Salt Lake Valley
1848	Gold discovered in California • Treaty of Guadalupe Hidalgo • Attempts to buy Cuba from Spain • Free-Soil party runs Van Buren for president • Zachary Taylor elected president • Seneca Falls Convention • Oneida community established • Regular steamship trips between Liverpool and New York City • Mormons settle in Great Basin
1849	California seeks admission to Union • "Forty-niners" race to California • Cotton prices invigorate South • Cholera epidemic returns
1850	Nashville Convention attempts to unify South • Fugitive Slave Law • Taylor dies; Millard Fillmore becomes president • Compromise of 1850 • Nathaniel Hawthorne, *The Scarlet Letter* • First land-grant railroad: Illinois Central • John C. Calhoun dies
1851	Herman Melville, *Moby-Dick* • Maine adopts prohibition • Woman's rights convention in Akron, Ohio • Indiana state constitution excludes free blacks
1852	Franklin Pierce elected president • Harriet Beecher Stowe, *Uncle Tom's Cabin* • Daniel Webster and Henry Clay die
1853	Gadsden Purchase • Nativism increases
1854	Know-Nothings win unexpected victories • Whig party collapses • Republican party founded • Kansas-Nebraska Act • Ostend Manifesto encourages acquisition of Cuba • Henry David Thoreau, *Walden* • High-point of immigration • Railroad reaches Mississippi River

struggle by American settlers against the Mexican government. Disrupted, the Mexican provinces might be sacrificed more easily and more cheaply to the United States.

The president prepared for war in Texas, seizing on a skirmish between Mexican and American troops north of the Rio Grande as a convenient excuse. He declared that Mexico had started a war when it "invaded our territory and shed American blood on the American soil." Even though northern Whigs continually denounced the war and its motives, Whig congressmen believed they had to support appropriations for the soldiers in the field. The final vote for war was overwhelming, with only fourteen Whig congressmen and two senators opposing the president. While unpopular in New England, the war stirred widespread support in the South and West. Tasked to raise four regiments, enough volunteers to fill fourteen regiments swamped recruiters in Illinois. Thirty thousand men responded in Tennessee, earning the state the nickname the "Volunteer state."

Sixteen hundred American troops under the leadership of Colonel Stephen Kearney took Santa Fe in New Mexico with no casualties late in the summer of 1846. California proved to be a greater struggle, partly because Mexican settlers there put up more of a fight and partly because Frémont—now commanding a volunteer unit comprised of Indian mercenaries, Bear Flaggers, and sharpshooters—provoked fights and stimulated enraged Californios to drive the Americans from Los Angeles. In any case, the American forces won control of California a few months after they had taken New Mexico. The United States Army, under Zachary Taylor and Winfield Scott, achieved a series of victories in Mexico itself in 1846 and 1847, including an impressive amphibious landing at Veracruz by Scott's forces that ended in the conquest of Mexico City and "the halls of Montezuma."

Though the Mexicans outnumbered the Americans, the regular U.S. forces enjoyed impressive leadership from their officer corps. The Mexican War familiarized Americans with names like Ulysses S. Grant, Jefferson Davis, and Robert E. Lee. Nevertheless, Polk distrusted his two leading generals—Taylor and Scott—suspecting, correctly, that they might capitalize on their military success to seek the presidency. Soldiers were recruited throughout the nation, but in the 1840s as many as 40 percent of recruits were recent immigrants and 35 percent were illiterate. Conditions of service were harsh, with savage discipline, irregular pay, and poor supply. At any period during the Mexican War, one-third of the men on the muster rolls had deserted, the highest rate of desertion among American wars. Though it lost a high proportion of its men—about 14,000 of the 105,000 who fought—the United States Army proved remarkably effective.

The Consequences of War

Many northerners worried about the expansion of slavery that might accompany victory over Mexico. To put such concerns to rest, David Wilmot, a first-term Pennsylvania Democrat in favor of the war, made a bold move: when a bill to appropriate 2 million dollars to end the war and purchase California and Mexican territory north of the Rio Grande came before Congress in 1846, Wilmot offered a "proviso," or condition, that declared slavery could not be established in any territory the United States might win from Mexico as a result of the war. Still smarting over perceived mistreatment of their interests by Polk and aware of growing rejection of slavery's expansion among their section's voters, northern Democrats saw the proviso as "our *declaration of independence* from southern dictation, arrogance, and misrule." It passed the House by a vote of 83 to 64, with congressmen, with few exceptions, voting along sectional rather than party lines. The Wilmot Proviso eventually went down to defeat and the war proceeded, but from 1846 on, the opponents of slavery increasingly distrusted Polk and southern political leaders.

Henry David Thoreau protested the war with Mexico. As he wrote in his essay "On Civil Disobedience," Thoreau considered the Mexican War "the work of comparatively few individuals using the government as their tool." Thoreau decided to signal his disgust with the American government by refusing to pay his taxes. He spent only one night in jail before his friends paid his taxes for him, but Thoreau's essay proved influential later in American history when protesters looked for inspiration and justification.

The war between the United States and Mexico ranged over an enormous territory, though the main battles occurred deep within Mexico. While the navy blockaded the Mexican coastlines, General Winfield Scott landed at Veracruz, marched more than 200 miles inland, and seized the capital, Mexico City, forcing a negotiated settlement to the war.

The small military of the United States coped with unprecedented challenges in equipping and supporting an army thousands of miles from supply bases. With the army short nearly 40 percent of authorized strength at the war's beginning, Congress more than doubled the size of the army and called upon the states to provide 50,000 volunteers. Overcoming the challenges of geography and distance, the junior officers and congressmen who managed and supplied U.S. troops in the Mexican War

unknowingly conducted a dress rehearsal for similar difficulties during the Civil War.

The Mexican War was the first reported to Americans using telegraph and express riders to speed information of battles back to newspaper editors who competed fiercely to "scoop" their rivals with the latest news. The president reacted furiously to leaks of secret cabinet meetings and the *New York Herald's* publication of the still-secret Treaty of Guadalupe Hidalgo that ended the war. Attempting to frighten editors, Congress confined the *Herald's* reporter for leaking the treaty. His editor responded by releasing the names of congressmen who regularly slipped confidential stories to the press. The government backed down, and political reporting in Washington was changed permanently.

Map 12.1 War with Mexico, 1846–1847
View an animated version of this map or related maps at http://history.wadsworth.com/passages2e.

The war with Mexico limped to an end in late 1847 and the beginning of 1848. American troops controlled Mexico City, the Gulf Coast, and all the northern provinces claimed by the United States, but the Mexican government refused to settle on terms of peace. President Polk, General Winfield Scott, and peace commissioner Nicholas Trist bickered over the treaty. Northerners and southerners viewed one another with undisguised distrust and distaste. Some Americans urged Polk to lay claim to all of the conquered country, others insisted that the United States should seize no territory at all from the war, and many, such as John C. Calhoun, driven by racial fears, wanted to limit seized territories to the sparsely settled regions to prevent "the fatal error of placing these colored races on an equality with the white race." Trist, on his own in Mexico, finally signed a treaty in Guadalupe Hidalgo that brought the negotiations to an end in February 1848.

Mexico, for $15 million and the abandonment of American claims against the Mexican government and its people, agreed to sell California, New Mexico, and all of Texas above the Rio Grande. When the treaty finally appeared before Congress for ratification the following month, many doubted that it would pass. Declining popular support for the war derailed plans to send an additional 30,000 troops to occupy northern Mexico. The various cliques, however, swallowed their disagreements long enough to ratify the treaty in March. A prominent newspaper pronounced the treaty "a peace which every one will be glad of, but no one will be proud of." The Mexicans signed the treaty in May and the war finally closed, with Mexico surrendering nearly 600 million acres of territory to the United States.

War and Politics

James K. Polk did not seek reelection in 1848. The Democrats, scrambling to find someone to unite the northern and southern branches of the party, decided on Lewis Cass of Michigan. Cass, a rather colorless man except for his red wig, spoke for the majority of northern Democrats who sympathized with white southerners in their determination to keep black people enslaved. He called for "popular sovereignty," for people in the territories to make their own policies on slavery. Antislavery Democrats walked out of the Democratic convention and called their own convention in Buffalo, New York, where they nominated former president Martin Van Buren as the Free-Soil candidate for the presidency.

Abolitionists who had supported the Liberty party were intrigued to see a candidate who might win a substantial number of votes. Antislavery "Conscience Whigs" also threw their support behind Van Buren. These various groups forged a working alliance for the election of 1848, declaring their solidarity behind the name of the Free-Soil party and its stirring motto: "fight on and fight forever" for "Free soil, free speech, free labor, and free men."

The mainstream Whigs found themselves in an awkward spot, for they had fervently opposed the Mexican War but now sought to capitalize on the popularity of General Zachary Taylor. Taylor had several advantages as a candidate. He had no troubling political past. Though he was a slaveholding planter, he had opposed the war with Mexico before he had been sent there to lead American troops. Just what he thought

Map 12.2 The Election of 1848
The balanced strength of the two-party system across the entire country was demonstrated by this election, in which the candidates won northern and southern states in almost equal numbers.

about anything was quite unclear, but with his lack of connection to recent bitter party squabbles, Taylor appealed to voters in both sections who desired to "see the times of Washington, Monroe, and the younger Adams return, when the government was administered for the benefit of the country not of a faction."

Taylor won the election in the electoral college, but the popular vote revealed little consensus. Taylor, with 1,360,000 votes, won eight slave states and seven free ones, while Cass won eight free states and seven slaveholding ones, with 1,220,000 votes. Although the Free-Soilers' prospects as a third party appeared bleak, Van Buren came in second in several important states and his vote total was large enough to gain the respect of northern Democrats and send twelve men to Congress.

Americans on the Move

Americans moved in massive numbers in the years around 1850. As the economy improved, transportation developed, boundaries became settled, and gold beckoned, people flooded to the states of the old Northwest and the old Southwest as well as to Texas, Oregon, and California. The suffering of Ireland and political conflict within Germany drove millions across the Atlantic, filling the cities and farms of the East.

Rails, Sails, and Steam

The late 1840s and early 1850s saw the emergence of the fastest-growing rail lines and the fastest ships in the world. Private investors poured tens of millions of dollars into rail expansion. The federal government aided railroads with free surveys and vast grants of land. The major cities of the eastern seaboard competed against one another to attract as many rail lines as possible. Owners of mines and factories subsidized new railroads, as did Wall Street speculators and investors from Great Britain.

Railroads proved more important for some parts of the country than for others. Railroads flourished in New England and New York, where the density of population and manufacturing permitted the new technology to work most efficiently. Midwestern states such as Ohio, Illinois, and Indiana also showed themselves well-suited to the railroads. Chicago had no railroads at all in 1850, but by 1860 twelve lines converged in the city. Three of those lines stretched from Chicago all the way to New York City; a trip that had taken ten days before the railroad now took only a day and a half. Daily, 120 trains moved in and out of Chicago, some hauling as many as forty cars loaded with freight.

Rural areas as well as cities immediately felt the effects of the railroad. Farmers now found it profitable to ship their produce to a city a hundred miles away. Previously, crops spoiled or were weather damaged in transit, or the cost and hazards of the journey eliminated the profit. Farmers specialized, becoming dairymen, vegetable growers, and fruit producers. Corn, wheat, hogs, and cattle flowed out of Ohio, Illinois, Indiana, and Wisconsin. The older farms of New England, New York, and Pennsylvania turned to specialty products such as cheese, maple sugar, vegetables, and cranberries. These products rode the railroad tracks to market, tying countryside and city together. In 1843, Margaret Fuller noted that Chicago and Buffalo, linking the West and the Erie Canal system, were the "two correspondent valves that open and shut all the time, as the life-blood rushes from east to west, and back again from west to east."

In the South, still recovering from failed improvement schemes and loan repudiation after the economic crises of the late 1830s, railroad building trailed off in the 1840s. While spending levels did not match that of the North, states such as Virginia aggressively pursued rail construction beginning in 1847, and had spent over $15 million dollars by 1860 in loans to corporations and the building of two state-owned lines. North Carolina reversed decades of opposition to state supported improvements in 1849, building a major line and subsidizing plank roads, private rail lines, and navigational aids. With an uneven and fragmented system of railroads, most southern commerce and passengers relied instead on the steamboats that plied the Mississippi and other major rivers. The riverboats grew in size, number, and ornateness throughout the period. The 1850s marked the glory days of these riverboats, with cotton bales stacked on every square inch of deck.

Elsewhere, packet steamships carried mail, freight, and passengers up and down the eastern seaboard and over the Great Lakes. Over 57 million newspapers, pamphlets, and magazines and nearly 48 million letters criss-crossed the nation in 1847. Beginning in 1848, Americans could count on regular steam travel between New York and Liverpool, England. These innovations in transportation, exciting as they were, came at a steep cost. "I never open

Clipper Ship

Graceful and fast, American clipper ships raced around South America and across the Pacific. New England merchants had conducted lucrative trade with Asia since the beginning of the century. American ships ventured to Canton and Shanghai for tea, silks, furs, ginseng, and glassware. In 1852, reflecting the growth of Asian trade, over 150 various types of vessels rested at anchor in Honolulu. These wooden ships with towering expanses of canvas sails were the fastest craft of their day. Experiments with steam power and iron hulls would eclipse the great clipper ships by the 1860s, but their beauty and speed, preserved in memory and in thousands of contemporary prints and paintings, lingered even after they were replaced by more economical ships that carried larger cargoes.

The Granger Collection, New York

a newspaper that does not contain some account of disasters and loss of life. This world is going on too fast. Oh, for the good old days of heavy post-coaches," one diarist observed.

Clipper ships enjoyed a brief but stirring heyday in the late forties and early fifties. Clippers used narrow hulls and towering sails to attain speeds that had yet to be reached by any other sailing vessels of their size. They sailed from New York to San Francisco, all the way around South America, in less than a hundred days. Although they were to be displaced after 1855 by uglier and more efficient steamships, for a few exciting years the clipper ships thrived on the high prices, small cargoes, long voyages, and the desperate need for speed fueled by remarkable discoveries in California.

The Gold Rush

The natives of California had long known of the gold hidden in the rocks and creeks of that vast territory. White American settlers, too, had found gold deposits in the early 1840s. But it was a discovery in January of 1848 that changed everything.

In 1839, John Sutter had emigrated from Switzerland to the area that became Sacramento, where he established a large fort, trading post, and wheat farm. Sutter hired a carpenter named James Marshall to build a mill on the American River. While working on the project,

Marshall happened to notice "something shining in the bottom of the ditch." He realized that the nugget, about half the size of a pea, was gold. Sutter, Marshall, and the other men on the place tried to keep the find a secret, but word leaked to San Francisco. There, sailors abandoned their ships, soldiers deserted their barracks, and clerks left their shops to look for gold along the American River. Newspapers stopped publishing and local governments shut down as Mexicans, Indians, and Americans in California rushed to the foothills. By the end of 1848, such men had gathered nuggets and dust worth about $6 million.

Back east, people remained calm, even skeptical, about the discovery until 230 ounces of almost pure gold went on display in the War Department in Washington and the president confirmed, in his State of the Union address in December 1848, that "the accounts of the abundance of gold in that territory are of such extraordinary character as would scarcely command belief." The gold rush began: "The coming of the Messiah, or the dawn of the Millennium could not have excited anything like the interest," one newspaper marveled. By the end of 1849, over 700 ships carrying over 45,000 easterners sailed to California. Some of the ships went around South America; others transported their passengers to the Isthmus of Panama, which they crossed by foot and canoe.

About 55,000 settlers followed the overland trails cut across the continent. Some traveled alongside the continuing stream of settlers to Oregon; others followed trails directly to the goldfields from destinations as far south as Mexico. Whether they went by sea or land, the participants in the gold rush were quite different from other immigrants to the West. The "forty-niners" tended to be either single men or groups of men from the same locality. Most of the men who flooded into California had little interest in settling there permanently. They intended to find their share of the gold and move on. Once in California, men of all classes, colors, and nations worked feverishly alongside one another in the streams and mountainsides. Disease and miserable living conditions hounded them, sending thousands to their deaths. Others, like Ramón Navarro of Argentina, kept diaries to record their wild swings of riotous wealth and desperate poverty punctuated by violence in the boomtowns of California. Like the vast majority of miners, after three years Navarro found wealth elusive and returned to South America no richer than when he arrived.

When some Chinese men returned home from California flush with American riches and stories of the "Golden Mountain," the fever spread in Asia. About 70 percent of the Chinese immigrants came from Guangdong Province, where many peasants and artisans had become impoverished and desperate enough to launch the dangerous journey. Young men, in particular, thought California might offer a way to attain the wealth they needed to acquire a farm and a wife back in China. Migrants could buy tickets from brokers on credit, with high interest. Upon their arrival in California, the Chinese immigrants discovered that they had to borrow yet more money from Chinese merchants in San Francisco to be transported to the goldfields. The miners worked continuously in hopes of paying off that debt, but the costs seemed worth the potential reward.

California held hope for African Americans, too. Most of the black migrants to California left from the coastal cities of New England. California beckoned with the promise of an

American West where color really might not matter so much. Although abolitionists, black and white, warned that even California might not be safe for black migrants, several thousand African Americans decided to take the chance.

Whatever their race, few miners discovered a fortune. The average miner in 1848 found about an ounce of gold a day, worth around $20, or about twenty times what a laborer back east made with a daily wage. As the number of competing miners skyrocketed over the next few years, however, the average take declined until it reached about $6 a day in 1852. Mining became more mechanized, and soon the biggest profits went to companies that assaulted the riverbeds and ravines with battalions of workers, explosives, and crushing mills.

Although miners of every background

A diverse population of men rushed to the California goldfields in 1849. Recent immigrants from China worked alongside Indians, whites, and African Americans.

went bust, California as a whole flourished. Towns appeared wherever people gathered to look for the gold. Men who tired of mining turned to farming instead, or teaching school or building houses. The largest fortunes were made supplying the miners. Men such as Levi Strauss, a dry goods salesman from New York, created tough denim jeans and Collis P. Huntington, later founder of the Central Pacific Railroad, met arriving ships and bought all the shovels on board for marked-up sale to miners. San Francisco was the big winner: by 1850, it had grown into a brash and booming city of 35,000 diverse residents.

The Mormon Migration

A different kind of westward movement was already in full force as the California gold rush got underway. These migrants were members of the Church of Jesus Christ of Latter-day Saints, or Mormons. In the face of relentless persecution, Joseph Smith, the founder of the church, had led his flock to Illinois. There they established the town of Nauvoo, which by the mid-1840s had become the largest city in Illinois with over 15,000 people. But conflict erupted when Smith decreed that polygamy was God's will, that men within the church would marry several wives, and he created the Nauvoo Legion, an armed force to protect his followers. When Smith ordered the destruction of a Mormon press that printed a poster condemning polygamy, the paper's owners signed warrants for his arrest. In June 1844, a mob of non-Mormons broke into the jail where Smith was being held and killed both him and his brother.

After struggle among the elders, Brigham Young, a young loyalist of Joseph Smith, emerged as the new leader of the Mormons. Young decided to move to a place beyond the reach of

Persecuted in Illinois in the 1840s, the Mormons launched a mass migration to the Great Salt Lake in the state they called "Deseret."

the Mormons' many enemies. Young knew about the Great Salt Lake, a place cut off from the east by mountains and from the west and south by deserts. The Mormons abandoned Nauvoo in the spring of 1846 as anti-Mormons pounded the town with cannon, destroying the Great Temple. In a well-coordinated migration, 15,000 Mormons moved in stages to the Great Salt Lake. When they first arrived, in 1847, the valley presented a daunting picture of rock and sagebrush, but the settlers irrigated the land, turning it into a thriving community.

When frosts, insects, and drought ruined much of the crop in the spring of 1848, Young announced that the Mormons would pool their labor and their resources even more than before. They designed an ambitious city with wide streets surrounding a temple that would "surpass in grandeur of design and gorgeousness of decoration all edifices the world has yet seen." Young concentrated control of the city and its farms in his own hands and in those of his fellow church leaders.

As some non-Mormons settled at the Great Salt Lake, Young decided that a form of government other than the church must be established. He oversaw the creation of a state called "Deseret," a Mormon term meaning "honeybee." The Mormons began a successful campaign to attract new converts from Europe, Asia, and Latin America. In 1849, the residents of Deseret, with Brigham Young as territorial governor, petitioned Congress for admission into the Union as a new state—a status it was not to achieve for another half century.

Although polygamy was practiced by no more than 15 percent of Mormons, in 1852 the church decreed that plural marriage was a fundamental church doctrine. The pronouncement provoked outrage across the country and led President Buchanan to order the military to prepare for an attack on Salt Lake City.

The High Tide of Immigration

Even as Americans moved west, a vast immigration from Ireland surged into the eastern United States. Irish immigration was not new; about a million people had left Ireland for the United States between 1815 and 1844. But the situation in Ireland changed much for the worse beginning in 1845, when a blight struck healthy potato fields, turning the leaves black almost overnight and filling the air with "a sickly odor of decay." This, the Great

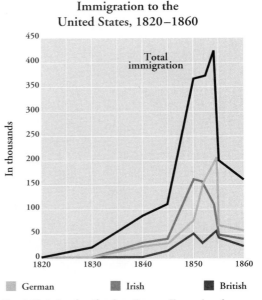

Chart 12.1 Immigration from Europe The number of immigrants from Ireland grew markedly in the late 1840s and early 1850s as a result of the Great Potato Famine. German immigration reached its peak a few years later as political turmoil erupted there.

Potato Famine, which would last for nearly a decade, destroyed the basic food for most of the Irish people. Over a million people died; another 1.8 million fled to North America. In all, about a fourth of the island's population departed, with more people leaving in the eleven years after 1845 than in the preceding 250 years combined.

The Irish emigrants tended to be young, single, poor, unskilled, and Catholic; they came over in the dead of winter, with virtually no money or property. Although some Irish immigrants spread throughout North America, most congregated in the cities of the North and Midwest. They lived from day to day on whatever money they could earn. Most men worked on docks, others in canal and railroad construction; women worked as domestics and as unskilled laborers in textile mills. Desperately poor and widely despised, the Irish figured prominently in arrest reports and on penitentiary rolls.

The high tide of Irish immigration occurred just before the peak of German immigration. Over a million Germans came to America between 1846 and 1854, many of them dislocated by a failed revolution in Germany in 1848. The Germans tended to be farmers who brought some money with them and established farms in the Midwest. The Germans, more than the Irish, were divided by wealth, generation, politics, regional background, and religion. Combined, the Irish and German immigrants accounted for almost 15 percent of the entire population of the United States.

The Quest for Perfection

The late 1840s and early 1850s, though relatively peaceful and prosperous, led a number of people to resist the drift of American life. Some became so disenchanted that they established utopian communities where they could experiment with alternative ways of organizing labor, power, and sexuality. Others launched a crusade for woman's rights.

Perfect Communities

Most of the hundred or so utopian communities created in the United States between the Revolution and the Civil War were founded in the 1840s. Some communities were secular in origin and some religious. They all insisted that people truly dedicated to social improvement had to flee corruption and compromise. Though several prophets and leaders emigrated from Europe to the New World in hopes of establishing religious utopias, most of the idealistic communities grew directly from American origins.

The most notorious American communal experiment emerged in 1848. It was in that year that John Humphrey Noyes and his 250 followers created the Oneida Association in upstate New York. Noyes had become convinced that it was possible for humans to be "perfected," made free of sin. Most controversial, he argued that people in a state of perfection should not be bound by conventional monogamous marriages; all belonged to one another sexually in "complex marriage." He gathered a small group of disciples around him who put such beliefs into action, practicing birth control by having males withdraw during intercourse.

Oneida experimented not only with sex but also with economic cooperation. Everyone performed the full range of labor. The women of the group cut their hair, wore pantaloons rather than skirts, and played sports with their male compatriots. Unlike other utopian communities, Oneida focused its energies on manufacturing rather than farming. The community produced an improved and profitable steel animal trap. Later, Oneida transformed itself into a profitable business corporation specializing in silverware.

The utopian communities testified to the freedom the United States offered. People took advantage of the isolation offered by the enormous space of the young country to experiment with communities based on religious, sexual, or philosophical principles. The proliferation of such communities also testified, however, to how full of longing many Americans seemed for communal relations in a society changing from the influences of immigration, technological advances, and political conflict.

Woman's Rights

The seeds for the organized movement for woman's rights in the United States had been planted in 1840, when women attending the World's Anti-Slavery Convention in London, England, found themselves consigned to seats in a separate roped-off area. One of the delegates was Elizabeth Cady Stanton. Listening to the debates over the place of women in antislavery, Stanton felt "humiliated and chagrined, except as these feelings were outweighed by contempt for the shallow reasoning of the opponents and their comical pose and gestures." Stanton discovered an important ally at the London meeting: Lucretia Mott, a devout Quaker and feminist. The two women vowed that they would start a movement back in the States for woman's rights, but they did not soon find the opportunity they sought. Stanton devoted her time to raising her family in Boston. In 1847, she moved with her family to Seneca Falls, New York.

While living in Seneca Falls, Stanton grew frustrated with the narrowness of life in a small town and the limitations placed on women there. Meeting with Lucretia Mott again, Stanton told her friend how miserable she had become. The two women joined with three of Mott's Quaker friends to plan a convention in July in Seneca Falls, although only Mott had had any experience in organizing a reform meeting. Stanton recalled that they "felt as helpless as if they had been suddenly asked to construct a steam engine."

Women's Rights National Historical Park, Courtesy of Seneca Falls Historical Society

Elizabeth Cady Stanton, one of the founders of the woman's rights movement, about the time of the Seneca Falls Convention of 1848.

Casting about for a way to express their grievances most effectively, and rejecting the "reports of Peace, Temperance, and Anti-Slavery" as "too tame and pacific for the inauguration of a rebellion such as the world had never before seen," they decided to model their "Declaration of Rights and Sentiments" on the Declaration of Independence. It began with a ringing statement: "The history of mankind is a history of repeated injuries and usurpations on the part of man toward woman, having in direct object the establishment of an absolute tyranny over her." The Declaration demanded the right to vote and insisted on woman's full equality with men in every sphere of life, including property rights, education, employment, divorce, and in court. The organizers worried about how many people might attend the meeting—held in an obscure town during a busy season for farmers—but over a hundred people came, including a considerable number of men. Of those men the most prominent was Frederick Douglass. Douglass's newspaper, the *North Star,* was one of the few papers to give the convention a positive notice.

The organizers of the Seneca Falls Convention succeeded in their major role: getting Americans to talk about woman's rights. Word of the Declaration spread among the many women's groups working in other reform organizations. Stanton, Mott, and their allies determined that they would hold a convention each year to keep the momentum going.

At the Akron meeting in 1851 a black woman spoke. She had escaped slavery in New York in 1827 and supported her family by working as a domestic. In 1843, she had a vision in which she was commanded to carry the word of God; she renamed herself "Sojourner Truth." In Akron, Truth celebrated women. "I have plowed and reaped and husked and chopped and mowed, and can any man do more than that?" she asked. The campaign for woman's rights developed a complex relationship to abolition and to African Americans. The movement might have offered a rare opportunity for women such as Sojourner Truth to be heard, but white woman's rights advocates generally phrased their demands for equal rights in terms of education and refinement that neglected black women and their needs.

Not all activist women, moreover, dedicated themselves to woman's rights. More conservative women devoted their energies to acquiring public funds for orphanages, shelters for "fallen" women and the poor, using their connections to important men in state legislatures, on city boards, and in prosperous businesses to raise money and garner support. They asked for laws to criminalize seduction and to change property laws, to oppose Indian removal, restrict slavery, support colonization of free blacks in Africa, and stop the sale of liquor. They often proved successful and effective with these indirect means and saw little need for agitating for the vote for women.

Popular Culture and High Culture

The ever-growing acceleration of printing presses and railroads in the 1850s meant that Americans enjoyed more access to books, newspapers, plays, and lectures every year. People hungered for education and entertainment of all sorts. Performances of Shakespeare became widely popular, for example, as audiences flocked by the thousands to theaters in places as diverse as Philadelphia, Vicksburg, and San Francisco to see *Hamlet* and *King Lear*. But not all the products of popular culture proved as elevating.

Mass Appeal

Several authors, now forgotten, reached remarkably large audiences with their writing. Some achieved success by playing on the nativism and anti-Catholicism of these years with polemics such as *Maria Monk's Awful Disclosures,* supposedly by one Maria Monk of the Hotel Dieu Nunnery of Montreal. That titillating volume, imagining sordid behavior by priests and nuns, sold over 300,000 copies in the first twenty-five years after its publication in 1836. George Lippard composed a serialized melodrama entitled *The Quaker City; or the Monks of Monk Hall, A Romance of Philadelphia Life, Mystery, and Crime.* It sold 60,000 copies in 1844 and at least 10,000 copies annually for ten years. Lippard paraded the worst aspects of American life in order to stir his fellow citizens to reform them; instead, he merely entertained them.

Other authors used the new capacities of mass printing to produce an ever-growing flood of self-help books. Catherine Beecher reprinted an edition of her *Treatise on Domestic Economy* every year in the 1840s and into the 1850s. The book offered a comprehensive guide to women on how to live their lives in the new domestic world, providing tips on topics as diverse as etiquette and how to wash feathers (carefully). The book was more than a how-to compilation, however; it told women that their work stood at least equal in importance to the work their husbands did outside the home.

One of the most influential books of the era bore the intriguing title of *Ten Nights in a Bar-Room*. In that book, first published in 1854 and eventually selling more than 400,000 copies, Timothy Shay Arthur described how the weakness of drink dragged down not only the main characters who wasted their nights in a bar, but also their families, their neighborhoods, and even "a nation of drunkards."

In their popular reading, Americans showed themselves both excited and frightened by the large social changes through which they were living. Whether the books fed fear and suspicion or offered strategies for dealing with the new challenges—or both—Americans liked stories told in bold colors.

Hawthorne, Melville, and Whitman

While popular authors dealt with the changes around them in melodramatic and obvious ways, more enduring writers crafted literature of greater subtlety. Yet the books these more gifted writers produced were very much attuned to their time and place. Nathaniel Hawthorne's *The Scarlet Letter* and Herman Melville's *Moby-Dick* were ironic, dark, and complex allegories, but Walt Whitman's *Leaves of Grass* evoked a determinedly hopeful vision. All three captured a key part of the American mood in the 1850s. Their lives as well as their work bore the unmistakable marks of the times in which they lived.

Nathaniel Hawthorne's father died at sea and left his family to do the best it could with limited resources. Hawthorne went to Bowdoin College in Maine and then returned to his mother's home and set up as a writer. Quiet and ambitious, he did not marry until he was thirty-eight years old. He read almost indiscriminately, gulping down popular crime fiction as well as the latest literary products of Europe. Though he himself was not morose, Hawthorne was fascinated by the lingering consequences of sin. He turned to the history of New England as the setting for his best work, finding there an allegory for the struggles of his own age.

Hawthorne became an active supporter of the Democratic party. He wrote for the Democratic papers and won a job in the Salem customs house. Hawthorne's political experiences in the late 1840s embittered him, however, for his Whig opponents not only sought to remove Hawthorne from his post but also charged him with corruption. It was at this point that Hawthorne wrote *The Scarlet Letter,* a symbolic story about revenge and its costs. Though set in the colonial era, the novel opened with a biting portrayal of the Salem customs house and its petty (Whig) politicians. The novel propelled Hawthorne into literary fame.

After the arrival of Hawthorne's long-delayed prosperity, he and his family moved to Lenox, Massachusetts. There he met a younger writer, one who admired Hawthorne for his willingness to write complicated stories of guilt. The young author was Herman Melville. He had left school at the age of fifteen, tried his hand at writing, but, in need of work that paid better and more certainly, went to sea. His experiences gave him the subjects for most of his writing. His first two books, *Typee* and *Omoo,* adventure stories of the sea, did quite well. But Melville was not satisfied to write such books; he envisioned nothing less than an American epic.

Melville's masterpiece, about a ship captain's search for the great white whale "Moby-Dick," created a peculiarly American idiom: part Old Testament, part adventure story, part how-to book, part encyclopedia. Good and evil swirled together in *Moby-Dick.* Unlike *The Scarlet Letter, Moby-Dick,* published in 1852, did not do well on the market. Melville, disenchanted, made his work more cynical and biting. His novel *The Confidence-Man,* published six years after *Moby-Dick,* dwelt on the swindling, corruption, and self-deception that seemed at the heart of the United States in the 1850s. Few people at the time noticed Melville's bold experiments and he gradually fell silent.

Walt Whitman also labored on an epic work, *Leaves of Grass,* throughout the early 1850s. The collection of poems reflected America at mid-century in all its diversity, roughness, innocence, and exuberance. This poetry included everything and everyone, speaking in a language stripped of classical allusion and pretension. As Whitman wrote in the preface to this book, anyone who would be a poet in the mid-nineteenth century must "flood himself with the immediate age."

Whitman took the raucous city of New York as his subject. For him, cities were frontiers, full of democracy and possibility. Whitman participated fully in the life of the city, writing as a partisan Democratic journalist, running a shop, working as a building contractor, spending days in the public library, moving from one editing job to another, attending boisterous political meetings—all the while jotting notes for a new kind of epic poetry taking shape in his head.

As he invented a poetical style to match his kaleidoscopic vision of American life, Walt Whitman also invented an image of himself as the poet who would take in and express everything. Both his life and his poem would be "A Song of Myself." Whitman's book was literally self-made; in 1855 he set some of the type and hired friends—printers of legal work—to publish the book for him.

Leaves of Grass came out to no public recognition whatsoever. Whitman sent a few copies to people he admired, however, including Ralph Waldo Emerson. The reply could not have been more heartening: "I find it the most extraordinary piece of wit and wisdom that America has yet contributed." But most readers of the book, including several leading literary figures who read it on Emerson's recommendation, considered it vulgar, even obscene, shapeless, and crude. The hopeful words of *Leaves of Grass* soon became lost in years when a darker vision of the United States prevailed.

Slavery and a New Crisis in Politics

The decade of the 1850s began with many signs of change and progress. The economy kicked into high gear. People flooded to the recently acquired territories of California and Oregon as well as to the upper and lower Mississippi region. Clipper ships, steamships, and railroads expanded their reach. Abolitionists, perfectionists, and feminists worked for the improvement of American society. Despite the generally positive turn of events, however, a persistent undercurrent of fear and anxiety wore at even the most privileged Americans.

The Crisis of 1850

Some of Americans' anxiety emanated from the new golden land of California, where lawlessness became rampant. The men who had left everything back east or in Europe to come to the goldfields showed little respect for the property rights—and even lives—of the Mexicans, Indians, or white men who were there before. In the eyes of many, anarchy threatened if California could not form a government quickly. As gold fever spread, the military governor urged the president to grant the territory a government as soon as possible. A territorial convention created such a government in 1849, helping to restore order, but one of the provisions of the new constitution created great disorder of another kind back in the United States. The new constitution declared that "neither slavery nor involuntary servitude . . . shall ever be tolerated in this state."

This straightforward statement exacerbated conflicts that had been brewing in Washington ever since the Wilmot Proviso three years earlier. White southerners of both parties considered the admission of a free California a grave threat to their own status in the Union, giving the Senate a free-labor majority. John C. Calhoun, the most vocal and extreme spokesman for the South, urged his fellow white southerners to band together. If they did not cooperate, Calhoun argued, they would be overwhelmed by the numbers and the energy of the free states of the North and the West. Southern congressmen talked of commercial boycotts, even of secession.

Southern Whigs had put Zachary Taylor forward for the presidency in 1848, assuming that, as a southerner himself, he would support the expansion of slavery. Wishing to avoid further rancorous debates over slavery in Congress, Taylor chose to send an agent secretly to California urging local leaders to design their government and submit their plan to Congress. To the disbelief and disgust of southerners, Taylor urged that California be admitted as it wished to be admitted, without slavery. But Taylor's support of the proposed California constitution unleashed a bitter debate in Congress. White southerners argued that to deny the South an equal representation in the Senate was to risk war between North and South. To give in on California was to lose the sectional balance on which their very safety rested. The most aggressive white southerners wanted to go on the offensive before northerners in Congress had time to act; in October 1849, they called a convention of the southern states to meet in Nashville in June of 1850.

A fabled session of Congress occurred as a result. In January 1850, the three most famous legislators of the first half of the nineteenth century—John C. Calhoun, Henry Clay, and Daniel Webster—assumed leading roles in the great national drama. Calhoun played the role of the southern protagonist, delivering fiery warnings and denunciations on behalf of the white South; Clay reprised the role of the Great Compromiser that had made him famous in the Missouri controversy thirty years earlier; Webster played the role of the conciliator, persuading the an-

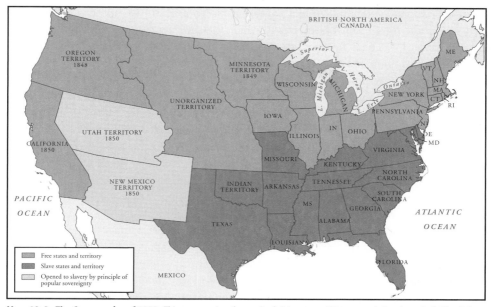

Map 12.3 The Compromise of 1850 This compromise, the result of elaborate and bitter negotiation, brought California into the Union as a free state, leaving the territories of Utah and New Mexico open to the (slim) possibility of slavery.

gry North to accept, in the name of the Union, the South's demand for respect. Clay and Webster rehearsed their lines in a private meeting before Clay presented his bill to Congress.

Clay's bold plan addressed in one inclusive "omnibus" bill all the issues tearing at the United States on the slavery issue. Balance the territory issue, he suggested, with other concerns that angered people about slavery. Leave slavery in the District of Columbia, but abolish the slave trade there. Provide a stronger law to capture fugitive slaves in the North, but announce that Congress had no power to regulate the slave trade among the states. Admit California as a free state, but leave undetermined the place of slavery in the other territories won from Mexico. Advocates on both sides hoped the compromise would buy time for passions to cool.

Clay made his plea with his characteristic eloquence and power. The eloquence appeared to have little effect, however, for the same bitter arguments went on for months after Clay's speech. In March, Calhoun, too ill to speak himself, wrote an address in which he conceded nothing; three days later, Webster claimed to speak "not as a Massachusetts man, nor as a northern man, but as an American." Webster found himself widely denounced in the North as a traitor, buckling under to the slave mongerers. Moreover, President Zachary Taylor—like Clay and Webster, a Whig—refused to support their compromise. William Seward of New York denounced the compromise as "radically wrong and essentially vicious."

The Nashville Convention of southern states, meanwhile, turned out to be ineffective, since six states sent no representatives, and the representatives who did come disagreed on the proper course of action. While a South Carolinian argued that "unite, and you shall form one of the most splendid empires in which the sun ever shone," most delegates still believed slavery was best preserved by remaining in the Union. In nine days of deliberations, the convention took no stand on the pending compromise; the representatives waited to see its provisions.

The omnibus bill appeared doomed. A series of unanticipated events, however, aided the compromise. Both Calhoun and Taylor died a few months apart. Millard Fillmore was now president, and Fillmore supported the omnibus bill. Webster resigned to serve as Fillmore's secretary of state, and Clay, after 70 addresses to the Senate defending the omnibus bill, left Washington to recover. Younger, less prominent, members of Congress steered the various components of the compromise through committees and votes. The compromisers were led by Stephen A. Douglas, a promising young Democrat of Illinois. The majority of northern and southern senators and representatives tenaciously voted against one another, but each part of the compromise passed because a small group of conciliatory congressmen from each side worked together. By September the various components of the compromise of 1850 had become law.

The problem of slavery, of course, would not go away merely because of a political compromise. The fugitive slave component of the Compromise of 1850 proved especially troubling. The Fugitive Slave Act directly implicated white northerners and insulted them with blatantly unjust provisions. The commissioners, who were appointed by a federal circuit judge and who decided the fate of black Americans accused of being runaway slaves, for example, received ten dollars if an accused fugitive were returned to his or her master but only five dollars if freed. Marshals and sheriffs could force bystanders to aid in the capture of an accused fugitive; if bystanders refused, they faced a substantial fine or even a jail term. The alleged runaway could not even testify in his or her own defense or call witnesses. Perhaps most horrifying of all was this provision: no matter how many years before slaves had escaped, no matter how settled or respectable they had become, they could be captured and sent back into bondage.

Most northern whites offered no opposition, and many, such as Daniel Webster, considered the law "essential to the peace of the country." Most of the two or three hundred alleged fugitives prosecuted under the law were ruled to be runaways and sent south. But abolitionists raged at the Fugitive Slave Law and they were not alone. Many northerners were furious. Armed opposition to the slavecatchers immediately arose in cities across the North; mobs broke into jails to free ex-slaves; one slaveowner who came north to claim his property was shot. Ralph Waldo Emerson spoke for many when he asserted that "as long as men have bowels, they will disobey." The Fugitive Slave Law, far from calming the conflict between North and South, made it more bitter.

African Americans and the White North

The years surrounding the crisis of 1850, ironically, were also the years in which black minstrel shows reached their peak of popularity. The traveling troupes of minstrels offered the strange ritual of white men in blackface simultaneously ridiculing and paying homage to the creativity of African American culture. Although white people of all classes and backgrounds attended the minstrel shows, the quick-paced, humorous, and flashy skits and songs held special appeal for members of the white working class. Over the preceding decades, those workers had seen the value of their labor eroded by mechanization and immigration. In their eyes, the minstrel shows offered both a comforting dramatization of their own racial superiority and a way to associate imaginatively with carefree and fun-loving "black" people.

White northerners revealed their ambivalences about African Americans in other ways as well. Whites who argued that the new territory of the West must be free soil frequently insisted on the exclusion of free blacks. Ohio, Indiana, Illinois, and Oregon passed laws barring free blacks from entering or settling within their boundaries. Whites in cities associated black people with poverty and crime while unaware or unconcerned that recent immigrants had displaced blacks from jobs as stevedores, boatmen, and day laborers. A considerable majority of northern whites showed little interest in attending antislavery rallies.

Harriet Beecher Stowe's *Uncle Tom's Cabin or Life Among the Lowly* helped change white attitudes toward African Americans. Stowe had been writing throughout her life, but had not become prominent. In 1849, her infant son died of cholera in Cincinnati; the next year she moved back to New England. There, people talked angrily of the new Fugitive Slave Law. "You don't know how my heart burns within me at the blindness and obtuseness of good people on so very simple a point of morality as this," she wrote to her brother Henry Ward Beecher.

Stowe put her objections to the law and its effects into a story printed serially in a moderate antislavery newspaper beginning in June 1851. Stowe based her portrayals of black people on the African Americans she had known in Cincinnati, where they worked for her as domestic servants. They told Stowe of the terrors of being sold south to Louisiana, of their vulnerability to sexual exploitation. Stowe also drew on firsthand narratives of escape. She switched the usual roles of the freedom narratives, however, making a woman—Eliza—the active heroine and a man—Uncle Tom—the one left behind to endure slavery. The love of a mother for her children drove the story. The image of Eliza crossing the partially frozen Ohio River, baby in her arms, grew into one of the most powerful and familiar scenes of American culture.

The novel's 300,000 editions drove eight steam presses night and day to meet the demand in 1852 alone and eventually sold over 6.5 million copies in the United States and around the world, the best-selling novel of the nineteenth century. *Uncle Tom's Cabin* became the subject of the most popular play in American history. Readers and theatergoers were shocked at stories of cruelty, violence, and sexual abuse. Stowe used techniques commonly found in domestic novels—the sanctity of the family, the power of religion, the triumph of endurance—to show that black people had the same feelings as white people.

That *Uncle Tom's Cabin* and minstrel shows reached their peak of popularity at the same time gives some idea of the confusion and ambivalence with which white northerners viewed African Americans in the early 1850s. Stowe's story was based on an antislavery message, but thousands of whites laughed at other whites in blackface. Only events could force northerners to decide what they really thought.

Minstrelsy

© Bettmann/Corbis

White men in blackface mimicked southern slaves for white audiences in the era, acting out ambivalent feelings of contempt and envy. Minstrelsy centered on comedy, dance, skits, and song. On the eighteenth- and nineteenth-century stage, black characters normally were played by whites who painted their faces black and danced, mimed, and parodied exaggerated sexuality and foppishness to amuse white audiences, many of whom were recent immigrants. Crude racist humor combined with idealized plantation scenes of abundance and sloth to portray blacks as simultaneously foolish and sly, responding to their oppression with bemusement and a dance step. Ironically, black dance styles drawn from Africa would evolve into complex tap routines that became a staple of the American stage. These shows were wildly popular in all sections of the country and created stereotypes of black behavior and comic style that persisted well into the twentieth century in movies, radio, and television.

Politics in Chaos

The same years that saw struggle between the North and the South over race and slavery also saw profound conflicts over other issues. The high tide of immigration in the early 1850s unleashed a political backlash as nativists organized themselves against the newcomers from Ireland and Germany. Meanwhile, the booming economy drove other Americans to lust for expanded territory beyond the bounds of the continental United States. And an effort by political leaders to quiet struggle between the North and the South by expanding in the West triggered the most violent conflict the nation had yet seen between the forces of slavery and antislavery.

The Know-Nothings

Franklin Pierce, the Democratic candidate for president in 1852, was a northerner friendly to the white South. Pierce's opponent—Winfield Scott—proved to be less impressive despite his fame as a general in the war with Mexico. The death of Henry Clay and Daniel Webster in 1852 left the Whigs adrift and directionless. Pierce crushed Scott in every state except four. "General opinion seems to be that the Whig party is dead and will soon be decomposed into its original elements," one diarist commented in the wake of the election.

Many influential Whigs took the 1852 election as a sign that the Democrats would always succeed by appealing to the lowest common denominator. The real, substantive issues that had originally shaped the two parties—banks, the tariff, and internal improvements—no longer distinguished them from one another. Neither did slavery and sectional issues sharply define the two parties, for each tried to appease voters in both the North and the South. Even the broader cultural orientation of the two parties had blurred in 1852, as the Whigs appealed to the burgeoning foreign-born vote and Protestant nativists grew disgusted with the Whigs.

In the eyes of many white Protestants, the new arrivals, especially from Ireland, appeared impossible to assimilate. "They increase our taxes, eat our bread, and encumber our street," commented one American diarist. The immigrants threatened to drive down wages because they were willing to work for so little. They also threatened to thwart enforced temperance. That movement gained momentum in 1851, when Maine became the first state to enact statewide prohibition of alcohol. The immigrants often received the right to vote in state and local elections soon after they landed, with Irish Catholics supporting the Democratic party and opposing prohibition, while English and German and Irish Protestants supported the Whigs and frequently voted in favor of prohibition.

In the face of such challenges to their values and power, "native Americans" organized against the immigrants. The most powerful manifestation of nativism appeared in New York City in 1849, when Charles Allen founded the Order of the Star Spangled Banner. Its membership was restricted to native-born white Protestants sworn to secrecy. When asked about the order by outsiders, members were instructed to say "I know nothing"—and thus they became popularly known as the "Know-Nothings." The order grew slowly at first, but it drew on deeply held and deepening prejudices.

The Know-Nothings moved into politics in 1854 in a way few expected. Mobilizing as many as 1.5 million adherents organized from local lodges to a national council, they did not announce their candidates beforehand, but rather wrote them in on the ballots, taking incumbents by complete surprise. The Know-Nothings won virtually all the seats in the legislature, the governor's chair, and the entire congressional delegation in Massachusetts with this strategy. By 1855, they dominated New England and displaced the Whigs as the major opponents to the Democrats through the Middle Atlantic states, in much of the South, and in California. Democrat and Whig leaders denounced "the 'Know Nothing' fever" that disrupted the campaigns and strategies of the parties.

No one in the major parties had anticipated such a turn of events. The Whigs, after all, had long attracted the nativists, fervent Protestants, and temperance advocates to which the Know-Nothings now appealed. But these disgruntled voters proved extremely receptive to the Know-Nothing appeal. The Know-Nothings, unlike the Whigs, left control of the party close to the grassroots. They offered a revitalized political party, one more receptive than the Whigs to the anti-Catholic and anti-immigrant desires of its constituents and one that would attack problems rather than compromise on them. Many rural districts voted heavily for the Know-Nothings as a way to get back at the cities that had dominated the major parties for so long. Voters blamed standing politicians for corruption and sought a new organization free from the control of the "wire pullers" who ran campaigns from smoke-filled backrooms. "Thousands flocked into the order, not that they approved its principles," one observer noted, but as "the only chance for restoring the government, from a state of corruption, to comparative health and soundness." For such reasons, the Know-Nothings made strong showings in the South as well as the North.

The appearance of the Know-Nothings reflected a deep-seated change in the American political system. The party system began disintegrating at the local and state level, with the Whigs fading in some states as early as 1852 and in others not until three years later. Voters defected from the Whigs and Democrats to both the Know-Nothing and Free-Soil parties.

A Hunger for Expansion

The same forces of commerce and transportation that tied together the vastly expanded United States in the late 1840s and early 1850s pulled Americans into world affairs. American ships set out not only for England, but also for South America, Asia, Australia, New Zealand, and Tahiti. The ships carried lumber and hides, tea and silks, missionaries and scientists. American whaling ships patrolled the South Pacific, stopping for fuel and food at islands scattered over a vast territory. Some entrepreneurs, such as the American Guano Company, even rushed to mine 200 foot-high mountains of bird droppings piled up on remote Pacific islands. The droppings, called guano, offered a nitrogen-rich fertilizer much in demand on the farms and plantations of the eastern United States. American traders eager to break into the Asian market appeared in Japanese ports.

These exchanges in far-off ports often depended on the Hawaiian Islands as way stations. On a single day in 1852, for example, 131 whaling ships and eighteen merchant ships were tied up in Honolulu. Such trade came at a horrifying cost to the native population because of disease. Over the seventy-five years since the first contact with outsiders in the late eighteenth century, the Hawaiian population had declined from about 300,000 residents to only about 73,000. Around 2,000 foreigners lived in Hawaii by the early 1850s, a good many of them Americans. Though politicians and editors talked of annexing the islands for the United States, opposition on the islands and in Washington postponed any action.

Some well-placed Americans gazed at yet more Mexican territory with covetous eyes, urging the Pierce administration to acquire Baja California and other parts of northern Mexico. Mexico was not interested, though. Proponents of expansion had to settle for much less than they had wanted: after long wrangling, in 1853 the United States paid $15 million for a strip of Mexico to use as a route for a southern transcontinental railroad. This was the Gadsden Purchase, named for the American diplomat who negotiated it. The purchase defined the final borders of the continental United States.

Cuba seemed the most obvious place for further expansion. Many Americans believed that Cuba should be part of the United States. Cuba was rich and growing, its slave trade flourishing even after the slave trade to the United States had ended. Abolitionists and others talked of freeing Cuba both from slavery and from the Spanish, whereas white southerners talked of adding this jewel to the slave empire.

The United States offered to buy Cuba from Spain in 1848, but met a rude rebuff. Franklin Pierce, pressured by the southerners in his party and in his cabinet, in the early 1850s renewed the effort to "detach" Cuba from Spain. American diplomats in Europe created a furor in October 1854 when they clumsily wrote the "Ostend Manifesto," a statement of the policy they wanted the administration to follow: gain Cuba peacefully or by force. When the "manifesto" was leaked to the press, the Pierce administration was widely vilified. London newspapers derided the manifesto as the "pursuit of dishonorable objects by clandestine means." Pierce publicly renounced any intention of taking over Cuba. The movement to expand the United States into the Caribbean came to a temporary halt.

Kansas-Nebraska Lets Loose the Storm

As the Cuban episode revealed, Franklin Pierce proved to be an ineffectual president. The best hope for the Democrats, Stephen A. Douglas determined, was to deflect attention to the West. Douglas called for two kinds of action: organizing the territories of the West, especially the Kansas and Nebraska area, and building a railroad across the continent to bind together the expanded United States with the route running through his home state of Illinois. The two actions were interrelated, for the railroad could not be built through unorganized territory. Partly to get southern votes for the territorial organization and partly because he believed that slavery would not survive in the northern territories, Douglas wrote a bill invalidating the Missouri Compromise line. He proposed that the people of the new territories decide for themselves whether or not their states would permit slaves and slaveholders. Adopting the phrase, "popular sovereignty," Douglas put it forward in the Kansas-Nebraska Bill.

Douglas's plan unleashed political and sectional resentments that had been bottled up by prior compromises. Six prominent Free-Soil senators, including Salmon P. Chase, Charles Sumner, and Joshua Giddings, denounced the plan as a plot by a "Slave Power" to make Nebraska a "dreary region of despotism, inhabited by masters and slaves." Northern ministers publicly protested the pending legislation, while newspapers throughout the North scornfully attacked the proposal. Despite the widespread opposition, however, the opponents of the Kansas-Nebraska Bill could not coordinate their efforts sufficiently to stop its passage.

The fight over Kansas-Nebraska inflamed northern resentment as never before. Many northerners determined that they could no longer trust southerners to keep a bargain and that northerners were no longer obligated to enforce the Fugitive Slave Act because the Kansas-Nebraska Act had nullified the Compromise of 1850. Attempts to arrest and extradite Anthony Burns, a fugitive slave in Boston, created such a turmoil that the mayor called out 1,500 militia to line the streets along the route between the courthouse and the ship that was to take Burns back to slavery in Virginia.

The Kansas-Nebraska Act sparked a chain reaction. It divided the Democratic party across the North; it upset the fragile balance of power between North and South in Con-

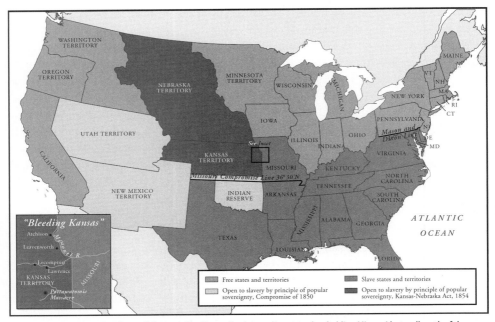

Map 12.4 Kansas-Nebraska and Slavery The Kansas Territory, adjacent to slaveholding Missouri but well north of the Missouri Compromise line, stood as a place both slaveholders and Free-Soilers felt they could claim as their own.

gress; it provided a set of common concerns and language to unite disgruntled northern Whigs, Democrats, Free-Soilers, and abolitionists. Northern voters punished Democrats who had supported the Kansas-Nebraska Act as the party lost 66 of the 91 free-state House seats it had gained in 1852. As northern Democrats lost seats, southerners gained control of the party, fueling further resentment of southern dominance. The Know-Nothings took advantage of the widespread disillusionment with the two major parties to campaign against Catholics, immigrants, and corruption issues apparently unrelated to slavery.

Over the next two years the northern political system churned as voters looked for a party that would reflect their concerns and also have a chance of winning power. The Know-Nothings began to fade almost as quickly as they had emerged. They came to seem just another political party led by ambitious politicians who exploited patronage for personal gain. Violent gangs that terrorized immigrants under the Know-Nothing banner alienated many voters, and Know-Nothing legislators proved unable to control or punish Catholics as they had promised.

In 1854, a party was founded in Wisconsin to unite disgruntled voters. The new party appealed to former Whigs, Free-Soilers, Know-Nothings, and even Democrats fed up with their pro-southern party. This new party called itself the "Republican" party. Its platform announced that "no man can own another man" and it would not permit slavery in the territories or in new states.

Conclusion

The late 1840s and early 1850s saw the United States energized by victory over Mexico and the acquisition of vast new territories, by railroads and clipper ships, by westward migration, and by the arrival of millions of immigrants. As northern family farms spread during the good times, however, so did plantation agriculture and slavery. The gold of the West brought not only wealth but also lawlessness. The cities of the Atlantic coast seemed full to overflowing with immigrants from Ireland and Germany, whereas the cities of the Pacific burgeoned with immigrants from China and restless men from back east. Politicians seemed corrupt and helpless in the face of these changes. Each political compromise only seemed to make things worse. The parties that had held the country together for a quarter of a century began to buckle under the stress.

RECOMMENDED READINGS

Anbinder, Tyler. *Nativism and Slavery: The Northern Know-Nothings and the Politics of the 1850s* (1992). Provides a full and balanced account.

Fehrenbacher, Don E. *The Slaveholding Republic: An Account of the United States Government's Relations to Slavery* (2001). Carefully analyzes this troubling issue.

Faragher, John Mack, and Hine, Robert V. *The American West: A New Interpretive History* (2000). A superb synthesis.

Fellman, Michael. *The Unbounded Frame: Freedom and Community in Nineteenth-Century American Utopianism* (1973). A helpful overview of perfectionist communities.

Foos, Paul. *A Short, Offhand, Killing Affair: Soldiers and Social Conflict During the Mexican-American War* (2002). A dark work on a neglected war.

Griffith, Elisabeth. *In Her Own Right: The Life of Elizabeth Cady Stanton* (1984). Tells the compelling story of this crucial leader of the woman suffrage movement.

Hedrick, Joan D. *Harriet Beecher Stowe: A Life* (1994). Gives a detailed portrait of the author of *Uncle Tom's Cabin.*

Lott, Eric. *Love and Theft: Blackface Minstrelsy and the American Working Class* (1993). Provides an original and challenging analysis.

Miller, Kerby A. *Emigrants and Exiles: Ireland and the Irish Exodus to North America* (1985). Contributes a full account of the origins and impact of this migration.

Morrison, Michael. *Slavery and the American West: The Eclipse of Manifest Destiny and the Coming of the Civil War* (1997). Details this complicated story.

Potter, David M. *The Impending Crisis: 1848–1861* (1976). Stands as the best overview of American politics from the wake of the Mexican War to the outbreak of the Civil War.

Reynolds, David S. *Beneath the American Renaissance: The Subversive Imagination in the Age of Emerson and Melville* (1988). A brilliant exploration of the "classic" era of American literature.

Rohrbough, Malcolm J. *Days of Gold: The California Gold Rush and the American Nation* (1997). Offers a fresh and exciting account of its subject.

 Additional resources, exercises, and Internet links related to this chapter are available on the American Passages Web site: http://history.wadsworth.com/ayerscompact2/

Passages
1855–1877

Americans of the 1850s had no idea that the Civil War awaited them. They could not imagine that a vast war, larger than any Europe had known, could overwhelm the new republic. New farms and plantations, after all, spread rapidly in expectation of more boom years like the 1850s. Villages and workshops developed throughout the North, while cities, fed by millions of immigrants from Europe, grew at harbors and along railroads and rivers. In the South, cotton and slavery created a per capita income for white southerners higher than that of any country in Europe except England. Slavery, it was clear, would not collapse of its own contradictions any time soon; the institution had never been more profitable. Telegraphs, newspapers, steamboats, and railroads tied the North and South together more tightly every year.

The two sections viewed each other as aggressive and expansionist, intent on making the nation all one thing or another. The North claimed that the slaveholder South would destroy the best government on earth rather than accept the results of a fair election. The white South claimed that the arrogant and greedy North would destroy the nation rather than acknowledge what the Constitution had established. Both sides were filled with righteous rage, accepting violence to gain the upper hand, whether that involved capturing fugitive slaves or applauding John Brown's failed insurrection. Americans could not stop the momentum they had themselves created. Despite desperate efforts at compromise and delay, the war came.

Once the war could no longer be avoided, most people threw themselves into the conflict alongside their neighbors, regardless of whatever doubts they had held before. Confident that the war would be brief, young men on both sides enlisted to teach their enemies a lesson. Both the North and the South proved excellent at war. They innovated freely and successfully, fought relentlessly, discovered effective generals, and mobilized women as well as men. Indeed, the North's strengths and the South's strengths balanced so that the war went on for four years, killing 630,000 people, a proportion of the population equivalent to 5 million people in the United States today and a number larger than the country was ever to sacrifice in another war.

Throughout the conflict, from Lincoln's election to his death, the role of slavery remained both powerful and unclear. Lincoln announced that the war was for Union, not abolition. The Confederacy announced that the war was for independence, not merely slavery. Enslaved

Americans in the South, however, forced slavery as an issue on both the Union and the Confederacy, risking their lives to flee to Union camps, undermining plantations and farms. Lincoln and much of the North came to see that ending slavery would end the Confederacy and help redeem the death and suffering. Two hundred thousand black men enlisted as soldiers and played a key role in bringing Union victory.

The North and the South struggled with themselves even as they fought one another. The North broke apart along lines of class, ethnicity, party, and locale. By 1864 a considerable portion of the northern population wanted the war to end, with compromise if necessary. The opponents of Lincoln expected to overwhelm him in the election that fall and even Lincoln shared that expectation. The white South broke apart along lines of class, locale, and gender. Poor soldiers deserted; upcountry communities shielded the deserters and resisted the Confederate government; impoverished white women rioted and resisted. Slaves rushed to the Union army at the first opportunity, every escape weakening the southern economy and Confederate morale.

Events on the battlefield, through 10,000 conflicts large and small, exerted their own logic and momentum. The Union army grew stronger as the Confederate army thinned and weakened. The victories of Grant and Sherman in 1864 destroyed the South's best hope of a negotiated peace. The relentless spread of the Union army throughout the South divided the Confederacy into smaller and smaller pieces, each helpless to aid the other. When Lee's army fell into defeat, the Confederate nation dissolved almost immediately.

Whatever Lincoln's plans for reuniting the nation, those plans ended at Ford's Theater in April of 1865. Lincoln's successor, Andrew Johnson, took the most cautious route possible, limiting the scope of black freedom in every way he could. The white South's resolve, indeed, seemed greater than any power the Union wielded in the South. African Americans struggled to make their freedom real: they mobilized politically, founded churches and schools, and reconstituted families. They demanded rights as Americans and did all they could to secure those rights. Black southerners found many white northern allies but many more white southern enemies who quickly turned to violence, as well as white northerners who supported or tolerated the violence. The years of 1866 and 1867 were full of a promise and a terror no one could have imagined ten years before. In many ways, the Civil War had not yet ended; its consequences had hardly begun.

For the next decade, Reconstruction in the South gradually receded. The process left blacks with greater political rights in law because of the Fourteenth and Fifteenth Amendments, but a more limited role in the day-to-day process of governing. The presidency of Ulysses S. Grant was a disappointment because the hero of the war proved unable to provide effective leadership, sectional reconciliation, or honest government. An economic collapse in 1873 helped the Democrats restore the national political balance and hasten the end of Reconstruction. The disputed election between Rutherford B. Hayes and Samuel J. Tilden in 1876 saw the abandonment of black southerners to the rule of those who believed in white supremacy. The Civil War had preserved the Union and abolished slavery, but the unsettled problem of race cast a long shadow into the future.

Broken Bonds
1855–1861

The United States had never seemed stronger than at the beginning of 1855. The economy was booming, settlers pushed into the West, railroads spread at a relentless rate, and immigrants streamed into American farms and factories. Churches, schools, asylums, and reform organizations grew faster than ever.

But the signs of danger were not hard to see. The conflict between the North and the South grew more bitter with each passing political crisis. Every year brought a clash more divisive than the one before. Disputes between North and South broke out in the Kansas Territory, in the village of Harpers Ferry, and finally in the contest for president. The party system, weakened by nativism and loss of faith by voters, seemed powerless to stop the disintegration.

North and South Collide

Conflict between the North and the South had been a staple of American politics for decades before 1855. Territories proved a persistent problem, but northerners and southerners also argued over the tariff, nominees for high office, and religion. The arguments grew hot, but eventually calmed down until the next outbreak. Events of the late 1850s, however, broke the pattern. New crises came before the old ones could dissipate. The crises embroiled every political, economic, moral, and practical difference between the North and the South.

The White South Fortifies Itself

Slavery had never been stronger in the United States than it was in the 1850s. The three and a half million slaves of the South extended over a vast territory stretching from Delaware to Texas. Theorists devised ever more elaborate and aggressive defenses of slavery, no longer depicting it merely as a necessary evil or an unfortunate inheritance from the English. Rather, they claimed, slavery was an instrument of God's will, a means of civilizing and Christianizing Africans otherwise lost to barbarism and heathenism. Southern physicians went to great lengths to prove that Africans and their descendants were physically and intellectually inferior to whites.

CHRONOLOGY

1855	Proslavery and free-soil forces clash in Kansas • Massachusetts desegregates public schools
1856	John Brown's raid in Kansas • James Buchanan elected president • Congressman Preston Brooks canes Senator Charles Sumner
1857	Financial panic and depression • *Dred Scott* decision • Lecompton Constitution • Baltimore–St. Louis rail service completed • Hinton R. Helper, *The Impending Crisis of the South* • Mass revivals
1858	Lincoln-Douglas debates • Frederick Law Olmsted begins design for Central Park in New York City
1859	John Brown's raid on Harpers Ferry • Vicksburg convention calls for reopening of African slave trade • Kansas ratifies free-soil constitution
1860	Democratic convention divides • Abraham Lincoln elected president • South Carolina secedes from the Union
1861	Mississippi, Florida, Alabama, Georgia, Louisiana, and Texas secede • Montgomery Convention creates Confederate States of America • Lincoln inaugurated • Firing on and surrender of Fort Sumter

Some defenders of slavery argued that slavery was *better* than free labor, more humane and Christian. If the hypocritical and self-righteous men of the North would admit it, white southerners argued, free labor exacted a great cost. Men, women, and children went hungry when unemployment, ill health, or old age struck. In the South, by contrast, slaveholders cared for their slaves even when those slaves had grown too old or feeble to work. The South's relative lack of schools, orphanages, asylums, and prisons, the defenders of the region insisted, testified not to backwardness but to a personalized society where individual responsibility replaced impersonal institutions.

Some white southerners in the late 1850s argued for the expansion of American territory in Cuba or Central America, places where slavery could flourish. William Walker, a young Tennesseean, dreamed of personal glory and a new territory for slavery. After several attempts at "filibustering," small-scale military efforts, in Mexico, Walker took advantage of a civil war to gain power in Nicaragua in 1855 and 1856. President Pierce granted diplomatic recognition of Walker's government, but Central American leaders united against him, cholera wiped out his dwindling, poorly supplied army, and Cornelius Vanderbilt, furious at Walker's revocation of Vanderbilt's Nicaraguan steamship charter, cut off his support from Washington. White southerners enthusiastically supported several attempts by Walker in the late 1850s to take Nicaragua, but he failed repeatedly, and finally was executed by a firing squad in Honduras in 1860.

Despite the agitation of a few editors and politicians for the reopening of the African slave trade, most white southerners wanted above all to keep and protect what they had, not jeopardize slavery by brashly expanding it. Not only would a renewed slave trade with Africa ignite the opinion of the world against the South, but it would also drive down slave prices and create new problems of discipline and revolt. The white South prided itself on

Chart 13.1 Cotton and the American Economy Even as the economy of the entire nation boomed, cotton accounted for an ever-growing proportion of American exports to the rest of the world.

having created a stable and prosperous society during its two and a half centuries of slavery and did not want to endanger that society.

Moreover, the slave economy boomed in the late 1850s. Planters took advantage of improved cotton gins, river boats, railroads, and new kinds of seed to double, in the 1850s alone, their production of cotton. The claim of southern politicians that "Cotton is King" proved no empty boast. Even though northern factories and farms grew rapidly in the 1850s, cotton still accounted for fully half of all U.S. exports. Without cotton, many thousands of northern and British workers would have had no jobs.

The prosperity created by the cotton boom resonated throughout the southern economy. Southern cities grew quickly, attracting immigrants and businesses. Although the South could not keep up with the North, it actually did quite well by international standards. Considered as a separate economy, the South stood second in the world in the number of miles of railroad, sixth in cotton textile factories, and eighth in iron production. Slaves proved to be adaptable both to factories and cities. The number of slaves in cities declined in the 1850s mainly because the demand for slaves in the countryside was so strong.

(a)   (b)

Chart 13.2 a & b Slaveowning in the South About three-fourths of southern white families owned no slaves in 1860. More than half of those who did possess slaves claimed four or fewer.

A Yeoman Farm

Non-slaveholding whites in the antebellum South, living on farms such as this one in Texas, comprised approximately 75 percent of the white population. Most owned small plots of land they farmed themselves with the aid of their family and local networks of kin and community for access to market goods. They are frequently referred to as yeomen farmers, an ideal of the self-sufficient farm household as one of the cornerstones of American democracy.

Access to arable land and the prospects to purchase slaves became issues of increasing concern through the 1850s. Land exhausted by tobacco or cotton or that was tied up in large holdings of wealthier farmers raised the stakes of access to western lands. In many areas back east in Virginia and the Carolinas, poorer white families and younger sons found themselves unable to move from laborers and farm tenants to land ownership. While many southern yeomen families migrated to southern Illinois, Indiana, and Missouri to break ground in areas without slavery, many others considered the opportunity to own slaves part of their political birthright and supported slavery's expansion even if they owned no slaves themselves.

Painting of a block house in New Braunfels, by Carl G. von Iwonski. Courtesy of the Daughters of the Republic of Texas Library

The southern economy, then, was not weak or weakening in the 1850s. On the other hand, the South was not urbanizing or industrializing nearly as quickly as the North. The South did not create a large class of entrepreneurs or skilled workers, nor did the region invest much money in machinery to make its farms and plantations more efficient. The southern plantation economy, in effect, was too profitable for its own good. The short-term gains of the 1850s, reflected in the escalating value of slaves, dissuaded wealthy southerners from investing in businesses that might have held greater potential for long-term development.

Northerners considered the southern economy the reverse image of the North: sick rather than healthy, backward rather than dynamic. Critics of the South argued that slavery victimized not only slaves but also "poor whites." In the antislavery portrayal, the Slave Power's domination began at home, where haughty self-proclaimed aristocrats lorded over ignorant whites, bullying them into supporting parties and policies that worked against their own interests. Antislavery advocates charged that slaves degraded white labor in the South and substituted a cheap sense of racial superiority for actual accomplishment.

The most effective criticism of the South in this vein came from a southerner: Hinton Rowan Helper, the son of a small slaveholding farmer in western North Carolina. In the late 1850s, a northern press, with aid from the Republican party, published Helper's book, *The Impending Crisis of the South*, which argued that the South's growth, prosperity, and cultural development were being held back by slavery. Helper deployed statistics from the census to prove his case, showing that land values, literacy levels, and manufacturing rates in the South were substantially lower than those in the North. He warned of the devastation caused by slavery, "It must be continually fed by new fields and forests, to be wasted and wilted under the poisonous tread of the slave." He proposed that slaveholders be taxed to colonize all free blacks in Africa or Latin America.

There is little indication that many southern whites agreed with Helper's assessment of them as ignorant, illiterate, and degraded. Most whites saw slavery as an avenue for their own advancement, not a hindrance. Many men and women bought a slave before they bought land. Slaveowners included women, shopkeepers, industrialists, lawyers, ministers, and even a few free blacks. No investment seemed to offer a more certain return than a slave, especially in the 1850s when slave prices rose rapidly. Although that rise in prices meant that a growing proportion of white people would be unable to afford a slave, most non-slaveholding whites apparently reconciled themselves to their situation or determined that they, too, would eventually join the slaveowning ranks. Many white southerners' livelihoods depended on servicing the slave trade, through insurance, medical care, and transport. The slave trade generated tens of millions of dollars in the antebellum South.

Politics reinforced the sense among southern white men that they lived in a fair and democratic society. Although many non-slaveholders in mountainous districts across the South voted against the large slaveholding districts, most southern white men voted in concert with the richest men in their immediate neighborhoods. In the eyes of the poorer men, their wealthy neighbors could act as spokesmen and brokers for the community in the state capital.

Southern whites identified themselves most of all as white people, tied to other whites by blood and heritage. Whites held black people in contempt, despite their knowledge that many African Americans were more intelligent, hardworking, and Christian than many whites. To be white was to be the inheritor of all the accomplishments of the ancients, of Christendom, and of the modern world. Such attitudes were reinforced at every level, from the daily rituals of life to the writings of leading thinkers from Europe. White southerners railed against the Republicans because that party threatened this bond of race between the white North and the white South. A senator from Mississippi outlined the rising threat to a large audience, "twenty years ago this [antisouthern] sentiment was confined to a few fanatics, now it pervades all classes, ages, and sexes of society."

Despite the solidarities of racial thinking, important political differences divided southerners. At one extreme were the so-called fire-eaters, virulent defenders of the South and slavery. These men were diverse. Some lived in cities, others on plantations. Some, such as J. D. B. DeBow, wanted to make the South more industrial and modern, whereas others rejected such development as a Yankee blight on the rural South. Whatever their differences, these men saw themselves as the voice of honesty. Men such as Robert Barnwell Rhett and Edmund Ruffin argued that the abolitionists and their Republican supporters intended to destroy the South. The only sane response, they believed, was to agitate the slavery issue constantly, to refuse to yield an inch in the territories or anywhere else.

At the other end of the political spectrum in the South were the former Whigs and Know-Nothings. They considered the Democrats, especially the fire-eaters, great threats to the future of the South and slavery. Former leaders of the Whigs and the nativist American party did their best to pull their allies into a new party opposed to the Democrats and attractive to a "thoughtful, sedate, constitution-abiding, conservative class of men." The many Unionists in the Upper South, in cities, and even in some of the richest plantation districts felt drawn to this position. The editors of the former Whig and American papers warned voters that the Democrats would sell out the South in Kansas, that the Democrats talked a tough game but always ended up caving in to the North.

Bleeding Kansas

The Kansas-Nebraska Act declared that settlers would decide for themselves, by "popular sovereignty," what kind of society they would create. But partisans from both the North and the South determined to fill the territory with settlers of their own political persuasion. "Come on, then, Gentlemen of the slave States," New York's Senator William H. Seward proclaimed soon after the Kansas-Nebraska Act passed, ". . . We will engage in competition for the virgin soil of Kansas, and God give the victory to the side which is stronger in numbers as it is in right."

The Massachusetts Emigrant Aid Company announced that it planned to raise $5 million to aid and encourage settlement in Kansas to ensure that the embattled territory became a free state. Advocates of slavery in Kansas believed that the forces of abolition would overwhelm the territory before slaveholders could move there. Fearing the exaggerated claims of the abolitionist press that 20,000 antislavery emigrants were moving to Kansas, advocates of slavery in Missouri depicted Kansas as "the unwilling receptacle of filth, scum, and offscouring of the East . . . to pollute our fair land."

Proslavery advocates in Missouri fought what they saw as Yankee invaders. On election day, they flooded across the border to vote in support of the proslavery candidates for the territorial legislature, casting roughly 3,400 more ballots than there were eligible voters. This action by the "border ruffians," as the northern press quickly labeled them, was not necessary, for southerners already accounted for six of every ten men settled in Kansas by 1855. In any case, the proslavery forces triumphed and took control of the territorial legislature in Lecompton. There, they passed a series of aggressive laws against free-soil advocates. Forbidding antislavery men to serve on juries or hold office, the legislature also decreed the death penalty for any person who assisted a fugitive slave.

The Granger Collection, New York

"Border Ruffians." The northern press depicted what it took to be the seedy character of the proslavery men who came over the border from Missouri into Kansas to support slavery.

Antislavery Kansans decided that their only recourse was to establish a rival government. They worked through the summer and fall of 1855 in Topeka to write a constitution of their own. Over the winter, the free-soil advocates "ratified" the constitution and elected their own legislature and governor. The free-soil delegates felt justified by the obvious injustice of their proslavery opponents.

Antislavery forces in New England and New York sent rifles to Kansas to arm what they saw as the side of righteousness. These arms became nicknamed "Beecher's Bibles" because Henry Ward Beecher's congregation, at his urging, funded part of their cost. Southerners, in turn, organized an expedition of 300 young men to reinforce their comrades. Not surprisingly, this volatile situation soon exploded into violence. On May 21, 1856, a group of slave-state supporters marched into the free-soil stronghold of Lawrence to execute warrants from the proslavery territory court against free-state leaders and two newspapers. They threw printing presses into the river, fired cannon at the Free State Hotel, and burned the hotel to the ground. Free-soilers labeled the episode the "sack of Lawrence."

The next day, in Washington, D.C., Representative Preston Brooks of South Carolina searched out Senator Charles Sumner of Massachusetts. Sumner had delivered a series of bitter speeches against slavery. Sumner attacked Brooks's relative and fellow South Carolinian, the elderly Senator Andrew P. Butler, for taking "the harlot, slavery" as his "mistress." Brooks, defending the honor of his family and his state, demonstrated his contempt for Sumner by striking him repeatedly about the head with a heavy rubber cane as Sumner wrote letters at his Senate desk. He did not return to his seat for two and a half years, the victim of shock. The empty seat became a symbol in the North of southern brutality; the incident became a symbol in the South of the only sort of response the arrogant North would respect. The *Richmond Enquirer* applauded Brooks's attack as necessary to keep in line "vulgar abolitionists in the Senate" who "dare to be impudent to gentlemen."

The next day, an event back in Kansas intensified the conflict. The episode swirled around one John Brown, a free-soil emigrant to Kansas. Brown had been a supporter of abolitionism since 1834 and followed five of his sons to Kansas in 1855. There, he became furious at the proslavery forces. He accompanied a group of free-staters to defend Lawrence, but they heard of the hotel's destruction before they arrived. Brown persuaded four of his sons and a son-in-law, along with two other men, to exact revenge for the defeat. The band set out for Pottawatomie Creek. There, acting in the name of the "Army of the North," they took five men from three houses and split open their skulls. The men had been associated in some way with the territorial district court, but no one was, or is, sure of Brown's precise motives. He was never punished for the killings.

In the wake of the "sack of Lawrence," the caning of Sumner, and the "Pottawatomie Massacre"—exploding in just a three-day period in May of 1856—the territory became known as "Bleeding Kansas." A new governor finally helped quiet the conflict in September, but the legitimacy of the territorial government remained an issue of heated contention. The South won a hollow victory when it seized the first election for the territorial government in Kansas. That government would soon pass, but the symbolic value of Bleeding Kansas would long endure.

The Republicans Challenge the South

The events in Kansas proved a disaster for the Democrats. In one state after another, Democratic representatives and senators lost office in the off-year elections of 1854. After a bitter two-month battle, a coalition of anti-Nebraska Democrats and nativists carried the Speakership of the House. To many Southerners, the Democrats seemed a mere tool of Stephen Douglas and his northern allies; to many Northerners, it seemed that Douglas's call for popular sovereignty was a cover for greedy slaveholders. President Franklin Pierce seemed incapable of leadership. The Democrats, needing someone who had not been tarnished by the events of the preceding two years, turned to James Buchanan, the "Old Public Functionary," to run in 1856. As minister to England, Buchanan had conveniently been out of the country during the entire Kansas mess.

Although Know-Nothings were able to agree at the local and state level on issues of corruption and anti-Catholicism, slavery split them as they attempted to organize a presidential campaign and to develop consensus on sectional issues. In February 1856, Know-Nothing unity ended in a controversy over slavery when fifty northern delegates from eight states walked out of the National Council and called for a separate convention of northerners in June. Southerners who had voted with the Know-Nothings had nowhere to turn

Voters turned out in near record numbers for the presidential election in 1856. The Republicans, organized in only a few states in the North in the spring, rapidly consolidated their message and rallied voters in New England and the Upper North. A shift in a few thousand votes in key states such as Pennsylvania, and the Republicans might have won. Democrats celebrated victory, but their leaders recognized that the growing population of the North and Midwest would decide control of the House of Representatives. Southerners, now firmly in control of the Democratic party, escalated their demands for opening western territories to slavery and for federal protection of slave property. Northern Democrats faced defeat in home districts when they supported such policies, weakening the party's ability to resist the Republicans. The distribution of voter support for the various parties illustrates the inability of Democrats, Know-Nothings, or Republicans to appeal as a national party with a platform that appealed across the growing sectional divide. As the Know-Nothings faded as a serious competitor, the two remaining parties struggled to increase their appeal in the Lower North and Midwest, key areas that would determine the victor in the next election.

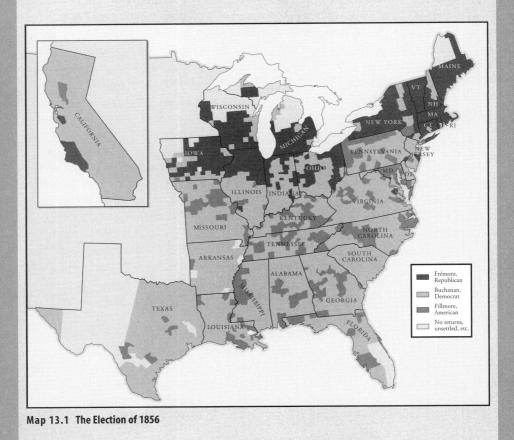

Map 13.1 The Election of 1856

The Election of 1860
This four-way election saw the North divided between Lincoln and Douglas, the South divided between Bell and Breckenridge.

Lincoln, Republican
Douglas, Democrat
Breckenridge, Democrat
Bell, Constitutional Union
"Fusion" tickets
No return, unsettled, etc.

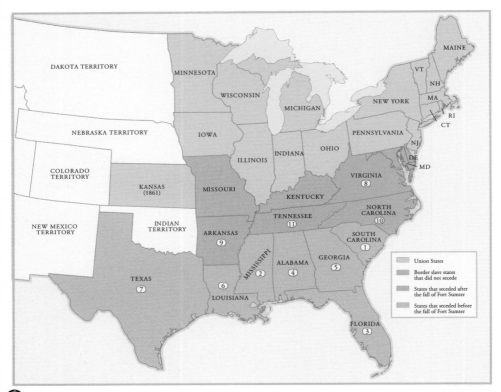

Southern Secession

The seven Gulf states seceded first, and on February 9th, delegates from these states met in Montgomery, Alabama, to create a provisional constitution, similar to that of the United States except in its explicit guarantee of slavery and states' rights. Advocates of secession traveled throughout the Upper South to convince voters and leaders to join the Confederacy. Regardless of the appeals to law and interpretations of the Constitution, the emotional heart of the debate white southerners conducted among themselves centered on three related issues: loathing of the prospect of racial equality, fear of servile insurrection and race war, and a surprisingly frank, if horrified, discussion of the inevitable miscegenation that would result if slavery were destroyed. While the language of states' rights appeared in these discussions, it focused on the states' rights to maintain slavery and preserve the standing racial order. Immediately after Lincoln called for troops to suppress the rebellion in South Carolina, Virginia, Arkansas, North Carolina, and Tennessee departed the Union. The other slave states—Kentucky, Maryland, Delaware, and Missouri—remained in the Union. Western Virginia would soon separate from the rest of the state and declare its loyalty to the Union. View an animated version of this map or related maps at http://history.wadsworth.com/ayerscompact2/.

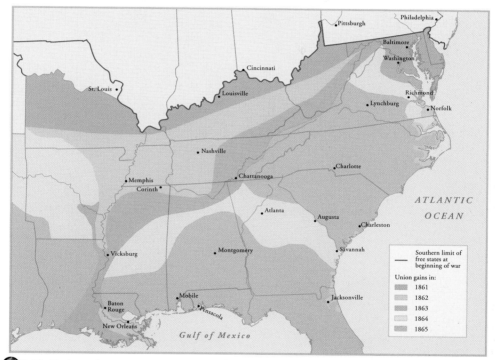

Pittsburgh

Philadelphia

Baltimore

Washington

Cincinnati

St. Louis

Louisville

Richmond

Lynchburg

Norfolk

Nashville

Charlotte

Memphis
Corinth

Chattanooga

ATLANTIC
OCEAN

Atlanta

Augusta

Charleston

Vicksburg

Montgomery

Savannah

Mobile

Jacksonville

Baton
Rouge

Pensacola

New Orleans

Gulf of Mexico

Southern limit of
free states at
beginning of war

Union gains in:
1861
1862
1863
1864
1865

The Territory of War

The Confederacy managed to protect large parts of its interior throughout the war, but the Union increasingly controlled the crucial rivers, rail lines, and ports.

View an animated version of this map or related maps at http://history.wadsworth.com/ayerscompact2/.

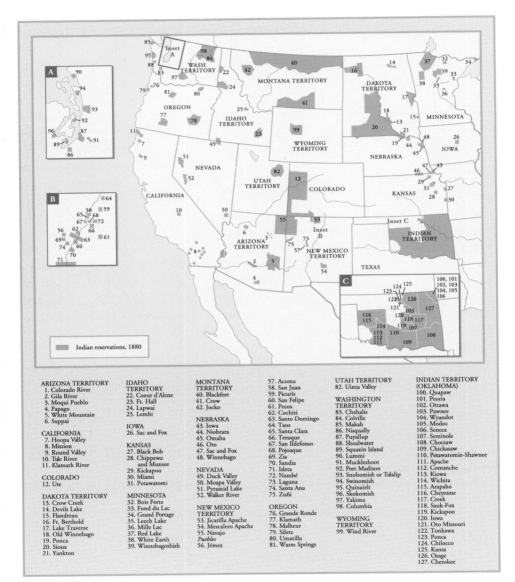

Indian Reservations, 1880

Indian Reservations in the West

Following the end of the Civil War and with the adoption of the peace policy of President Ulysses S. Grant, a network of Indian reservations spread across the West. This map shows how extensive the reservation system was.

but to the Democrats, but northerners could devote their attention to the new Republican party. The Republicans bypassed their most outspoken antislavery men for the 1856 nomination and turned to John C. Frémont, famed as an explorer of the West. He had taken almost no public positions and had accumulated almost no political experience. The Republicans thought they had found just the sort of vague candidate who would give few potential voters a reason to vote against him.

The new Republican party was antislavery but not pro-black; Republicans avoided talking about race. What they did talk about was the goodness of the North: the North, they argued, was everything the South was not, a place where hardworking white men could build a life for their families free from the threat of arrogant, powerful, and greedy slaveholders.

Abolitionists had succeeded in making slavery detested throughout the North and had created much of the anti-southern energy that flowed into the Republican party. But abolitionists distrusted that party. The Republicans seemed interested only in the welfare of the white North. They denied any intention of ending slavery in the South and even resurrected talk of colonization, the movement the abolitionists had abandoned twenty-five years earlier. The Republicans, although better than the pro-southern Democrats, still dissatisfied the abolitionists.

The Republicans talked of the "Slave Power," a political conspiracy of the most powerful slaveholders. Republicans saw everything from the three-fifths clause to the bloodshed in Kansas as the fruit of the Slave Power. How else to explain the long list of southern victories at a time when the North grew more populous and wealthy? Kansas and the caning of Sumner showed that the Slave Power, a Cincinnati paper raged, "cannot tolerate free speech anywhere, and would stifle it in Washington with the bludgeon and the bowie-knife, as they are now trying to stifle it in Kansas."

Republicans attacked Catholics as well, repeating the charges that nativists had made for decades. Ironically, rumors that Frémont was a Catholic quickly surfaced and refused to subside. Moreover, Frémont refused to give direction to the national campaign. To make matters worse, Millard Fillmore, the former president, ran under the banner of the American party, as the Know-Nothings called themselves. Fillmore hoped that the three-way election would split the electorate so that the final decision would rest with the House, where he would appear as a compromise candidate.

On election day in 1856, 83 percent of the eligible voting men went to the polls, one of the highest turnouts of the era. Although Buchanan won all of the South except Maryland, he received only 45 percent of the popular vote in the country as a whole. A difference of a few thousand votes in a few states would have denied Buchanan the election. The Democrats had won, but were filled with anxiety; the Republicans had lost, but were filled with confidence. It was clear to everyone that the American political system was in flux and transition.

Observers of all political persuasions believed that James Buchanan had it within his power to strengthen the Democrats in both the North and the South. His party, after all, still controlled the Senate. The Republicans, moreover, had drawn much of their power from the chaos in Kansas. Once Kansas had peacefully entered the Union as a free state under the banner of popular sovereignty, Democrats happily observed, no other territory awaited in which similar conflicts might be expected. Slavery, everyone seemed to agree, had no chance in Oregon, Nebraska, Minnesota, Washington, Utah, or New Mexico. The territorial issue that had torn at the country since 1820 might finally die down.

Dred Scott

In his inaugural address, James Buchanan mentioned a case pending before the Supreme Court, a case regarding a slave. Buchanan looked forward to the ruling, for he believed that the territorial issue was "a judicial question, which legitimately belongs to the Supreme Court . . . . To their decision, in common with all good citizens, I shall cheerfully submit, whatever they may be." That case had moved its way through various levels of courts for more than a decade. Dred Scott, born a slave in Virginia around 1800, had in the 1830s been taken by his master, an army surgeon named John Emerson, to territories far in the upper Midwest. Scott had married Harriet Robinson, the slave of a federal Indian agent.

Dr. Emerson bought Harriet and thus owned the two daughters she bore with Scott. When Emerson died in 1843, Scott and his family became the property of Emerson's widow, who moved to St. Louis. In 1846 the Scotts petitioned for their freedom, claiming that their residence in the free territory entitled them to free status.

A long series of postponements and delays dragged the case on into the early 1850s, when the legal environment had become much more divided by political controversy over slavery. Democratic judges and lawyers worked to deny the Scotts their freedom on the grounds that such a precedent would undermine the right of southerners to take slaves into the territories. A Republican lawyer agreed to carry the Scotts' case before the Supreme Court to counter the Democrats' aggressive claims. Unfortunately for the Republicans and the Scotts, five southern Democrats sat on the Court, along with two northern Democrats, one northern Whig, and one

The Granger Collection, New York

The Dred Scott case attracted the attention of the entire country in 1856. This northern newspaper depicted Scott and his family sympathetically, emphasizing family ties and the women of the family.

northern Republican. Presiding was Chief Justice Roger B. Taney (pronounced "tawney"), an eighty-year-old Marylander first appointed to the Court by Andrew Jackson in 1835.

The *Dred Scott* case came before the Supreme Court during the superheated months of 1856, when Kansas, the Brooks/Sumner affair, and the presidential election commanded the country's attention. Although the case could have been decided on relatively narrow grounds, the Democratic members of the Court wanted to issue a sweeping pronouncement that would settle once and for all the question of slavery in the territories. President-elect Buchanan pressured a fellow Pennsylvanian on the Court to side with the southerners. Two days after Buchanan took office in March of 1857, the Court announced its decision in the *Dred Scott* case. It took Chief Justice Taney two hours to read the opinion.

Taney spent half his time denying that Scott had the right to bring a case in the first place. Black people, Taney decreed, could not become citizens of the United States because "they were not included, and were not intended to be included, under the word 'citizens' in the Constitution." Taney declared that at the time the Constitution was written, throughout the "civilized and enlightened portions of the world," members of the "negro African race" were held to be "altogether unfit to associate with the white race . . . and so far inferior, that they had no rights which the white man was bound to respect." Therefore, Dred Scott had never been a citizen of Missouri and had no right to sue his mistress. Taney also decreed that Congress had never held a constitutional right to restrict slavery in the territories and that therefore the Missouri Compromise of 1820 was invalid. Two justices dissented from the majority's opinion, but the decision stood as the law of the land.

Southerners and many northern Democrats exulted that they had been vindicated by the *Dred Scott* decision, that the Republicans' demand for territories free of slavery was simply unconstitutional. Democratic editors claimed that the decision "vindicates and sustains the Democratic Party in the patriotism and wisdom of its course" as "*sectionalism* has been rebuked, and abolitionism staggered." The Republicans, however, sneered at the decision, which they saw as one more corrupt act by the Slave Power Conspiracy designed to turn the nation in "one great slave pen." They reprinted the dissenting opinions in the *Dred Scott* case and denounced the decision in the state legislatures they controlled throughout the North. They argued that the Founding Fathers had never intended slavery to be a permanent part of the United States and merely tolerated bondage because they expected it to die of its own weight. If the *Dred Scott* decision were followed to its logical conclusion, they warned, the United States would reopen the slave trade with Africa and even extend slavery into northern states where it had been banned.

The Republicans thought the Court's audacious statement "the best thing that could have happened" to the Republican party. As an abolitionist newspaper put it, the "fiercer the insult, the bitterer the blow, the better." The Republicans expected the *Dred Scott* decision to make their party stronger. The Republicans needed to sweep the government in 1860, they argued, to clean out corruption and conspiracy from the executive, Congress, and now the courts.

American Society in Crisis

The American economy boomed in the mid-1850s. Not only did cotton do well, but so did the farms, factories, railroads, and cities of the North and West. People cheered the laying of a telegraphic cable all the way across the Atlantic Ocean, an incredible feat that triggered celebrations in towns across the nation, including wild fireworks in New York City that set City Hall ablaze. Currier and Ives prints became the rage, brightening homes around the country with charming scenes of American life. The sale of newspapers, books, and magazines surged. Working people's organizations staged a comeback. Churches and schools spread with remarkable speed. The mileage of railroads tripled to more than 30,000 miles.

But underlying this prosperity ran a deep current of unease. Some people worried that Americans were growing soft and self-indulgent. Others felt guilt that as the economy boomed, slavery became stronger. Others despaired at the state of American politics, which seemed in disarray. The conflict between the North and the South embodied all these anxieties, giving them concrete shape.

Financial Panic and Spiritual Revival

Late in the summer of 1857, people warned that there had been too much speculation recently, that companies and individuals had borrowed too much money. The end of the Crimean War in Europe seemed ominous for the United States, for now the countries of the Old World could turn their energies toward growing their own food, undermining the heavy demand for American farm products that had buoyed the economy for several years. When a major insurance company went under in 1857, a panic spread among New York banks and railroad stocks plummeted along with western land values. Soon, banks and companies across the country began to fail.

Working people of all ranks lost their jobs. Not only unskilled laborers, domestics, and millworkers found themselves without work, but so did educated bookkeepers and clerks. Across the North, hundreds of thousands of people had no income and many were forced to rely on charity to feed and clothe themselves. Workers tried to organize, but employers shut down the mills and factories. As winter approached, many people wondered whether their families would survive through the cold months.

Southerners blamed northern financiers for bringing on the panic of 1857. Though the white and free black working people of southern cities suffered along with their counterparts in the North, white southerners bragged that their region quickly recovered from the panic. They also bragged that their slaves, unlike white workers, never starved or went without a roof over their heads: "The White Slave trade is more exacting and fraudulent than Black Slavery, . . . it is more cruel, in leaving the laborer to take care of himself and his family . . . which make his freedom an empty and delusive mockery."

Throughout the country, the panic and depression of 1857 caused people to pause and take stock of their situation. Some said that the political system had betrayed the country, that selfish politicians had allowed banking to become too loose or the tariff too strict—or vice versa, since no one could be certain. Others warned that Americans had grown too rich and lazy for their own good, becoming too wrapped up in their material welfare at the expense of everything and everyone else.

A wave of religious revivals emerged in response to the panic. They lasted for over a year, sweeping back and forth across the country. Unlike earlier revivals, the religious spirit emerged not in rural districts but in the largest cities of the Northeast. Unlike earlier revivals, too, those of 1857 attracted a conspicuously large number of men as well as women. In contrast to earlier revivals in rural areas, middle-class men in the commercial districts of larger cities met for daily prayer meetings, regularly covered in the press, that convened promptly at noon and with each member limited to a five-minute prayer to keep the group on schedule. The Young Men's Christian Association expanded rapidly during this time, providing young single clerks a venue for creating a "businesslike piety." The revivals also witnessed the first active participation of denominations such as the Episcopalians and Unitarians. It seemed to many people, in fact, that the revivals were the most heartening and significant in American history, showing that the people in the forefront of modern America were trying to change their ways. And as people read their newspapers they saw plenty that needed to be changed—especially in Kansas.

The Agony of Kansas

Most of the settlers who had arrived in Kansas in 1856 and 1857 were non-slaveholding migrants from the Upper South. They did not appear eager to establish slavery in Kansas. An open election, therefore, would likely install a constitutional convention in favor of free soil at the time Kansas became a state. The proslavery legislature elected in the earliest days of the territory, however, still controlled Kansas in 1857. Free-state advocates fought back, touring the North and raising money for the struggle against the Slave Power.

In November of 1857, the small band of proslavery delegates who still controlled the legislature proposed a new constitution. Kansas had to produce a constitution that the U.S. Congress would accept. The legislature provided that voters would choose between the constitution with slavery or without slavery. In either case, slaveowners already in Kansas would be permitted to keep their slaves. The Republicans portrayed the constitution as one more audacious act of the Slave Power, but in fact the "Lecompton Constitution" posed a serious problem for the Democrats. Northern members of the party could not support it without appearing too sympathetic to the South; they could not oppose it without alienating the southern Democrats that made up the bulk of the party's strength. President Buchanan knew well that 112 of his 174 electoral votes had come from the South and that, of the 165 Democrats in both houses of Congress, 100 were southerners.

Stephen Douglas refused to endorse the Lecompton Constitution as a violation of popular sovereignty, but President Buchanan urged its adoption. When challenged by Douglas to support the rights of voters in Kansas, Buchanan warned Douglas, "no Democrat ever yet differed from an administration of his own [party] without being crushed." The president persuaded himself that the constitution was in fact a moderate compromise,

The Panic of 1857

New York City symbolized for many Americans the consequences of the high living and corrupt practices that brought on the panic of 1857. "With fifty-seven suspended banks . . . hundreds and thousands of bankrupt merchants, importers, traders, and stock jobbers . . . with her rotten bankruptcies permeating and injuring almost every solvent community in the nation," raged one New Orleans newspaper, New York stood as "the centre of reckless speculation, unflinching fraud and downright robbery." This cartoon dramatizes the moral corruption that many people believed lay at the heart of the panic.

The panic had more immediate and concrete causes. The end of the Crimean War in Europe triggered a decline in overseas demand for American agricultural products and reduction in specie flows into the nation from European investors. A wave of bankruptcies caused bank closures as cash became scarce and banks shut their doors on investors when cash supplies ran out. Small businessmen and managers, with no prospects of sales, laid off workers or offered them payment in kind instead of wages. Ironically, the southern cotton economy rebounded sooner, as European demand for cotton recovered by 1858, while northern and midwestern grain farmers faced low prices for the next two years.

© Bettmann/Corbis

letting Kansas enter the Union as a free state in the long run while protecting the slave-holders who were already there. Once Kansas was a state, he reasoned, its legislature could decide what to do with those slaves. Most northern voters saw the matter differently: though it was obvious that the great majority of Kansans wanted to enter the Union as a free state, those antislavery Kansans would be forced to accept slavery.

Republicans could hardly believe that Buchanan had handed them such an easy way to portray him as a tool of the South. And neither could Stephen Douglas, who recognized that Buchanan's actions would create enormous problems for the Democrats. The Democrats fought bitterly among themselves for months, Douglas denouncing the president for supporting "trickery and juggle" and seeking to use the Senate to block the Lecompton Constitution, Buchanan using the powers of the presidency to mobilize senators against Douglas.

Moderate southern and northern Democrats warned that the South was destroying its only hope for continued success: a strong Democratic party in the North. When Kansas voters overwhelmingly rejected the Lecompton Constitution in 1858, they rejected Buchanan and the South as well. The Democrats suffered widespread defeat in the state elections that spring and lost control of the House. Northern Democrats, still weak from the loss of seats after the 1854 elections, lost again as only 32 of 53 free-state Democrats survived the 1858 contest and 12 of those were opposed to the Lecompton Constitution. Douglas himself faced a tough election battle and Buchanan did everything he could to destroy this rival in his own party. Running against a promising Republican candidate, Abraham Lincoln, Douglas needed all the help he could get.

The Lincoln-Douglas Debates

Abraham Lincoln was very much the underdog in the Illinois senatorial race of 1858. As a Whig in a heavily Democratic state, Lincoln had not found it easy to win or hold office in the 1840s and 1850s. He had lost repeatedly, occupying national office for all of two years: elected to the House of Representatives in 1846, Lincoln lasted only one term and was sent back to his law office in Springfield. There, Lincoln made a good living as a lawyer, drawing on his own abilities and the connections that came with his marriage to Mary Todd, a member of a prominent family. Lincoln's modest beginnings on the Kentucky and Illinois frontier lay comfortably in the past. Still, he longed for a major public office.

Though the short, portly, experienced, pragmatic, and famous Stephen Douglas seemed the opposite of the tall, thin, inexperienced, principled, and obscure Abraham Lincoln, the two men in fact shared a great deal. Douglas, too, had grown up poor. Douglas, although the most

2
Freeport
August 27

1
Ottawa
August 21

5
Galesburg
October 7

6
Quincy
October 13

4
Charleston
September 18

7
Alton
October 15

3
Jonesboro
September 15

Map 13.2 The Path of the Lincoln-Douglas Debates The two candidates followed a long and circuitous route—nearly 1,300 miles long, on rail, river, buggy, and horseback—through Illinois in their efforts to win the voters over to their vision of the American future.

prominent Democrat in the country, was actually four years younger than Lincoln. Both Lincoln and Douglas shared their constituents' moderate positions on most national issues.

Illinois's population was composed of many New England migrants in the northern half of the state, upcountry southern migrants in the bottom half, and German and Irish immigrants in Chicago. Both the factories and the farms of Illinois prospered in the 1850s, as did abolitionists, Know-Nothings, Whigs, and southern-leaning Democrats. The Illinois senatorial election of 1858 promised to throw all these groups into contention. At stake was this question: could the Democrats survive as a national party, with Douglas as their leader, or were they doomed to become a party of the South?

Douglas traveled by private railroad car from Chicago to Springfield, the state capital and Lincoln's base. All along the way, Douglas gave speeches to thousands of people, telling them that he was the voice of experience, principled compromise, and popular sovereignty. He also told them that Lincoln held "monstrous revolutionary doctrines" of abolitionism. To Douglas's great annoyance, Lincoln followed the senator to rebut his arguments and charges, sometimes appearing in the crowd, sometimes arriving the next day. Douglas, though reluctant to give the relatively unknown Lincoln a share of attention, finally agreed to hold seven joint debates in the late summer and early fall.

Lincoln was far from an abolitionist, refusing to join the antislavery Liberty and Free-Soil parties and staying with the Whigs longer than many of the men who became Republicans. He repeatedly brought up the *Dred Scott* decision from the previous year, however, arguing that it would permit slavery to spread into lands where Illinois men or their sons would otherwise migrate. The West must remain a region where "white men may find a home . . . where they can settle upon some new soil and better their condition in life." Douglas offered what he saw as practical, commonsense responses to such charges, arguing that slavery would not spread anywhere the majority of the white population did not want it to. A far greater and more immediate threat, Douglas argued, was that the Republicans would force the South into desperate acts by dragging moral issues into political contexts. Let the sovereign white people of each state decide for themselves whether they would have slavery or not, Douglas counseled. Douglas did not defend slavery, but he declared that "I care more for the great principle of self-government, the right of the people to rule, than I do for all the negroes in Christendom."

Lincoln charged that Douglas's strategy merely postponed an inevitable reckoning between the slave states and the free states. He argued that "a house divided against itself cannot stand. . . . Either the opponents of slavery will arrest the further spread of it, . . . or its advocates will push it forward till it shall become alike lawful in all the States, old as well as new." Notwithstanding Douglas's efforts to dismiss the morality of slavery as beside the point, that morality repeatedly surfaced in the debates. Lincoln argued that he, not Douglas, was the one defending true self-government. Douglas's policy permitted the forces of slavery to grow stronger and more aggressive, whereas Lincoln's would place slavery on the path toward "ultimate extinction." It would likely be several generations before that extinction occurred, Lincoln believed, but the process could begin in 1858.

Lincoln made a distinction between different kinds of rights. African Americans, he thought, had economic rights, but he did not believe in social equality between blacks and whites. He would not grant black men the right to intermarry with whites, serve on juries, or vote, but he did believe that black people had the right not to be slaves. Lincoln took the offensive, making Douglas appear more of a defender of slavery than at heart he was.

The election was close, but the state legislature, which elected U.S. senators in these decades, went to the Democrats and they returned Douglas to Washington. But Lincoln had become identified as the spokesman for a principled yet restrained antislavery. All across the North, in fact, the Republicans made impressive gains in 1858. In every state, many people wanted the nation to find some compromise. But the political environment did not have a chance to calm in 1859, for it was then that John Brown returned to the national scene.

John Brown and Harpers Ferry

John Brown had become famous in the three years since he had burst into prominence in Bleeding Kansas in 1855. Antislavery people back east, assured by journalists that Brown had not personally killed anyone at Pottawatomie, admired the hard man for his firsthand opposition to slaveholders. Thus, as he toured New England in search of funds to carry on the cause, he found willing listeners and open hands. Antislavery advocates were eager to contribute to the fight against slavery in Kansas, not realizing they were contributing to a fight against slavery much closer to home. Brown wrote letters to wealthy abolitionists requesting assistance for "an important measure, in which the world has a deep interest." Throughout 1857 and 1858, Brown planned for an attack on the federal arsenal at Harpers Ferry, Virginia. He had a thousand iron pikes forged to arm the slaves he believed would rise in rebellion once he and his men triggered the revolt. He tried to win the support of Frederick Douglass, who, while sympathetic, thought the plan doomed logistically. But Brown pressed on. One of his lieutenants moved to Harpers Ferry and even established a family there, preparing the way for the attack. In the meantime, Brown continued the fight against slavery in the West, freeing eleven slaves in Missouri, killing their master and leading them into Canada. Such exploits, though illegal, only heightened Brown's visibility and appeal in New England.

The assault on Harpers Ferry started in earnest in the summer of 1859, when Brown rented a farm seven miles away and assembled his men and munitions. To his disappointment, he could recruit only twenty-one men, five of them African Americans.

The raid began easily enough on Sunday, October 16, as Brown's men quickly seized the arsenal and a rifle-manufacturing plant. Brown and his men remained in the small armory building, waiting for word to spread among the slaves of Virginia that their day of liberation had come. The word spread instead among local whites, who quickly surrounded Brown's men, killing or capturing eight of them. Militia from Virginia and Maryland arrived the next day, followed soon after by federal troops. The troops rushed the armory. Ten of the abolitionist forces were killed, five (including Brown) wounded, and seven escaped. Brown was tried within two weeks and found guilty. He was sentenced to be hanged exactly a month later, on December 2.

The entire episode, from the raid to Brown's execution, took only about six weeks to unfold. Yet those six weeks saw opinion in both the North and the South change rapidly. Public opinion in the North and South, mixed at first, crystallized into sharply opposing viewpoints. Even those northerners who were appalled at the violence were also appalled at the speed with which Brown was tried and condemned. Even those southerners who read with reassurance early denunciations of Brown in the North were appalled when they realized that many northerners refused to condemn the raid. A senator from South Carolina denounced the raid as the result of "the miserable, intermeddling, nefarious spirit of many of the people of our associate States with [a] matter that concerns them not."

The campaign launched by John Brown and twenty-one black and white allies in 1859 failed in its immediate aims of unleashing a rebellion of the enslaved but succeeded in heightening the moral and political debate over slavery.

The rhetoric surrounding John Brown seemed almost cathartic, as both northerners and southerners said the worst they could imagine about the other. The many people of moderate sympathies on both sides watched, dismayed, as common ground eroded beneath their feet.

Brown had not set out to become a martyr. He fully expected to unleash a massive slave rebellion. Although his precise plans remain obscure, maps in his possession marked places where slaves outnumbered their masters and might overwhelm them with force. Brown wanted to play the role of Moses, leading the oppressed and chosen out of captivity. Once captured, however, Brown seemed to fit another role, that of Christ, selflessly dying for the salvation of others. In a letter to his wife he wrote, I "am sure I can recover all the lost capital occasioned by that disaster, by only hanging a few moments by the neck; & I feel quite determined to make the utmost possible out of a defeat." No longer the Old Testament figure of blood and vengeance, Brown now appeared to many in the North as a New Testament figure of suffering and dignified sacrifice. William Lloyd Garrison speculated that Brown planned "a desperate self-sacrifice for the purpose of giving an earthquake shock to the slave system and thus hastening the day of universal catastrophe." Many northerners came to believe that John Brown's body could be redeemed only with a return to the stern violence he had championed.

The North and South Call Each Other's Bluff

Everyone knew the election of 1860 held enormous meaning for the United States, but no one could be sure what that meaning might be. Would this be the election that brought all to their senses? Would the border states be able to control the election? Would northern voters suddenly realize the South meant what it said? The actual events proved far more threatening than most Americans had believed possible.

◗ The Election of 1860

White southerners automatically linked John Brown with the Republican party, though leading Republicans explicitly denied any connection. Southerners believed that "every village bell which tolled its solemn note at the execution of Brown proclaims to the South the approbation of that village of insurrection and servile war." The Republicans realized that they would be a purely northern party. Not only had any southern base of support disappeared, but Harpers Ferry and the public mourning and grief over Brown had made the Republicans far more attractive among northern voters than before.

The Democrats also felt the effects of Brown's raid. Meeting in Charleston in April 1860 to decide on their presidential nominee for the fall election, the northern Democrats nominated Stephen Douglas. The northern Democrats saw this as a compromise with the South. But southern Democrats demanded that the party explicitly support the rights of slaveholders to take their slaves into the territories. Northern Democrats could not afford to make that concession and still have a chance to win back home. The southerners proved heedless of this plea, however, and walked out of the convention. Several weeks later, the Democrats met in Baltimore and nominated Douglas. Southerners, walking out once again, declaring themselves the "purified" Democratic party, nominated John C. Breckinridge of Kentucky.

Before the Democratic convention met again in June, Unionists in both the North and the South tried to avert catastrophe by nominating a compromise candidate. Calling themselves the Constitutional Union party, they settled on John Bell of Tennessee. Many of these Unionists were former conservative Whigs and Know-Nothings who no longer had a political home. They advocated an end to agitation over slavery, "the Union as it is, the Constitution unchanged," to safeguard the "priceless heritage of our fathers." They counted on the other candidates to create a deadlock that would have to be settled in the House of Representatives. There, the Unionists hoped, legislators would gratefully turn to their compromise candidate.

As the Democrats tore themselves apart, the Republicans met in Chicago. There, in efforts to put southern concerns at rest, the Republicans announced their belief in the right of each state to decide for itself whether it would have slavery. The Republicans cemented their appeal to voters unconcerned with the slavery issue by calling for protective tariffs, internal improvements, and free homesteads for anyone who would settle the West. The Republicans were much stronger than they had been only four years earlier. Party strategists calculated that they need only win Pennsylvania and one other state they had lost to the Democrats in 1856 to wrap up the election. The states they needed to take were Illinois, Indiana, or New Jersey—all of them on the border with the South and all of them far more moderate on the slavery question than states farther north. Thus, the Republicans turned to a moderate who was a favorite son of one of the crucial states: Abraham Lincoln of Illinois.

A certain air of unreality surrounded the election of 1860. People did not know that the way they voted would bring on a civil war, or even secession. Although Stephen Douglas constantly warned of such a danger, both Breckinridge and Lincoln downplayed any such dire consequence. Ironically, all the years of conflict had persuaded both the North and the South that the other talked tougher than it would act. The parties staged loud and raucous political events that proved long on emotion and short on clearly defined positions. Lincoln said nothing and stayed close to home while his party leaders displayed split fence rails and touted his honesty.

The election of 1860 was actually two separate elections, one in the North and one in the South. Lincoln made no attempt to explain himself to the South; Breckinridge made little attempt in the North. They never met face to face. Bell spoke mainly to the already converted. Douglas, breaking with tradition, spoke from New England to Alabama, trying to warn people what could happen if they voted along sectional lines. While campaigning across the Deep South, he endured rotten fruit, insults, and injuries from a collapsed platform. Few men were willing to believe their opponents would have the nerve to act on their threats.

On election day, November 6, Lincoln won in every northern state except New Jersey, which divided between Douglas and Lincoln. Douglas won outright only in Missouri.

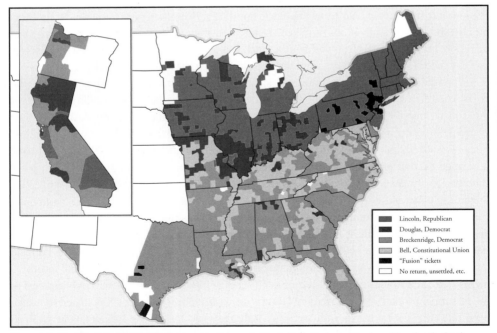

Map 13.3 The Election of 1860 This four-way election saw the North divided between Lincoln and Douglas, the South divided between Bell and Breckenridge.

Breckinridge won the entire South except the border states of Virginia, Tennessee, and Kentucky, which went with Bell. Even at this late stage of sectional division, voters did not fit into easy categories. It was hardly a contest between a rural South and an industrial urban North, for northern cities tended to vote for compromise candidates, not for Lincoln. Similarly, over half of southerners voted for Bell or Douglas, supporting the Union over the South.

Once the election returns were in, though, these complications seemed to evaporate. Even though Lincoln won only in the North, the election was not even close in the electoral college, where Lincoln won 180 electoral votes to Breckinridge's 72, Bell's 39, and Douglas's 12. In southern eyes, the North had arrogantly placed its own interests above those of the Union, insisting on electing a man who did not even appear on Southern ballots. In northern eyes, the South was to blame, walking out of nominating conventions and talking of disunion. The election of 1860 completed what John Brown's raid had started: the estrangement of North and South.

The South Debates Independence

The fire-eaters declared Abraham Lincoln's 1860 victory a sign that the North valued neither the Union nor the Constitution on which it was based. The South, they said, had every right, every incentive, to leave the Union. Although the Republicans claimed to work within the political system, Lincoln's supporters had violated an honored tradition of compromise.

Even though the Democrats still controlled the Senate and the Supreme Court, southerners believed that Lincoln would use the patronage of the federal government to install Republican officials throughout the South and possibly entice non-slaveholders with their free labor doctrines. Such officials could undermine slavery from within, eroding the authority of slaveowners. For years, Lincoln had talked of "a house" that had to be unified, of a nation that had to be all slave or all free. Would he not act to undermine slavery now that he was in power?

The nation's eyes turned to South Carolina. Influential men there, after all, had talked of secession since the nullification crisis nearly thirty years earlier. They believed that the same states that had created the Union could also dissolve that Union when it no longer served their purposes. The South Carolina legislature met on the day after Lincoln's election but did not secede immediately. Its members called for an election two months later to select delegates who would then decide the course the state should follow. In the meantime, they hoped, support for secession would grow. The next day, a local paper blustered, "the tea has been thrown overboard; the revolution of 1860 has been initiated."

States of the Deep South quickly lined up behind South Carolina. Carolina leaders, heartened by the response, seceded earlier than they had planned, on December 20. Southerners serving in Buchanan's cabinet began resigning and by the administration's annual New Year's Day reception, southerners in attendance all refused to shake Buchanan's hand or acknowledge the president. By February 1, Mississippi, Florida, Alabama, Georgia,

Louisiana, and Texas had joined the secession movement. On February 4, delegates from these states met in Montgomery, Alabama, and created a provisional constitution, similar to that of the United States except in its explicit guarantee of slavery and states' rights. On February 18, the convention inaugurated a provisional president, Jefferson Davis of Mississippi, and a vice president, Alexander H. Stephens of Georgia. Davis was a strong states' rights advocate but not a fervent secessionist. With an eye towards opinion in the crucial states of Virginia, North Carolina, Kentucky, and Tennessee, these leaders of the new Confederacy portrayed themselves as a calm and conservative people, not wild-eyed revolutionaries.

The advocates of secession knew they had to strike before Lincoln took office. Two bad things could happen if they waited to see what the new president did once in office. He might either attack the South by force or he might prove to be as moderate as he claimed to be. In the latter case, secessionists feared, white southerners would let the moment pass.

Many thousands of white southerners resisted secession. Some argued that secession was treason. Others warned that the South was committing suicide. Others argued that the southern states should wait until they could cooperate with one another more formally and fully. By presenting a united front to the North, these "cooperationists" insisted, the South would not need to secede at all. The North, recognizing that the South really was not bluffing, would grant concessions protecting slavery forever.

The arguments against immediate secession appealed to a large portion of southerners. Even in the southern states that rushed to secede in January of 1861, almost half of all votes went to delegates who had not supported immediate secession. The opposition to secession proved stronger still in the Upper South. Upper South moderates warned that their states would bear the brunt of any conflict between the Lower South and the North. And voters listened: more than a month after the first seven states seceded, secession lost in Virginia by a two-to-one margin. The secessionists were stymied, too, in Tennessee, North Carolina, and Arkansas. The leaders of these border states believed they could bargain between the Gulf Confederacy and the North, winning the concessions the South wanted while maintaining the Union.

Recognizing the need to convince the border states to join the secession movement, five states from the Lower South dispatched agents to the Upper South to advocate and justify disunion. These commissioners wrote numerous letters to local politicians and spoke to legislatures, public meetings and private gatherings of community leaders in their efforts to cajole and persuade. These conversations among southerners clearly highlight the importance of race and slavery as the foundation of the states' rights argument. Delegates, such as Stephen Hale of Alabama, warned Kentucky's governor that Lincoln's election "was nothing less than an open declaration of war, for the triumph of this new theory of government destroys the property of the South, lays waste her fields, and inaugurates all the horrors of a San Domingo servile insurrection, consigning her citizens to assassinations and her wives and daughters to pollution and violation."

Northerners, too, remained quite divided at the beginning of 1861. Many recent immigrants viewed the conflict as none of their business. Northern Democrats called for conciliation with the South and many argued they were "for peace and not war . . . war is no remedy . . . and horribly wicked when waged without any cause, and by one portion of our people against another." Many black Northerners warned that a war for the Union alone did not deserve black support. A war to end bondage would be worth fighting, they argued, but in 1861 only the most aggressive white abolitionists spoke of such a cause.

People had plenty of opportunity to air their opinions, for events did not move quickly after Lincoln's election. After the first flush of secessionist victory at the beginning of 1861, people throughout the nation watched and waited to see what would happen when the new president officially assumed office on March 4. In the meantime, no one appeared to be in charge. James Buchanan, as lame-duck president, could not do much, and neither could the lame-duck Congress.

Most Republicans, including Lincoln, viewed the rhetoric and even the votes for southern secession as negotiating strategies rather than actual steps toward dissolving the Union. The Republicans showed no inclination to bargain with the South over what remained the key question: federal support for slavery in the territories. Many recalled northern acceptance of defeat at the polls in 1856 and denounced southern rejection of the "lawfully elected administration." The tensions that had built up in the 1850s, Lincoln thought, could no longer be avoided. "The tug has to come," he argued, "and better now, than any time hereafter." If the North postponed action, Lincoln and other Republicans thought, the South would step up its efforts to gain new slave territories in the Caribbean and Central America, dragging the United States into war.

The First Secession

In the winter of 1861, the center of the conflict between the North and the South gradually shifted to two obscure forts in the harbor of Charleston, South Carolina. A Kentucky-born U.S. Army officer, Major Robert Anderson, worried that secessionists would attack his small federal force at Fort Moultrie in Charleston. Determined to avoid a war, on December 26 Anderson moved his small garrison from Fort Moultrie to Fort Sumter, a facility occupying a safer position in the center of the Charleston harbor. Tired of tension and stalemate, northern editors cheered Anderson's actions: "these are the times to develop manhood. God bless Major Anderson for setting us a good example." When South Carolina guns drove away a ship President Buchanan had sent with supplies for Anderson and his men, Buchanan chose not to force the issue. Meanwhile, South Carolina troops strengthened their position around the Charleston harbor.

Lincoln Becomes President

Men from both the North and the South worked frantically, but fruitlessly, to find a compromise during these weeks. Some urged the passage of a new constitutional amendment that would permit slavery forever; some urged the purchase of Cuba to permit slavery to expand; some urged that war be declared against another country to pull the United States together again. All the compromises were designed to placate the South. Abolitionists viewed such maneuvering with disgust and told their countrymen to let the South go. "If the Union can only be maintained by new concessions to the slaveholders," Frederick Douglass argued, "then . . . let the Union perish." Such views were not popular. Mobs attacked antislavery advocates throughout the North.

On February 11, Abraham Lincoln began a long and circuitous railway trip from Illinois to Washington, covering nearly 2,000 miles and using twenty separate rail lines, pausing frequently along the way to speak to well-wishers. At first, he played down the threat of secession—"Let it alone," he counseled, "and it will go down of itself." But as the train rolled on and the Confederate convention in Montgomery completed its provisional government, Lincoln became more wary. Warned of attempts on his life, Lincoln slipped into Washington under cover of darkness.

Lincoln assembled his government under the growing shadow of war. He sought to balance his cabinet with men of various backgrounds. The two most formidable cabinet members were Secretary of State William H. Seward, a moderate Republican, and Secretary of the Treasury Salmon P. Chase, a radical Republican inclined to take a harder line with the South. Fort Sumter stood as the most pressing issue facing the new administration. Any show of force to reclaim the fort from South Carolina, southern Unionists warned, and the secessionists would sweep border states such as Virginia into the Confederacy.

Lincoln, with Seward's advice, toned down the speech he delivered at his inauguration in March. He told the South that he had no intention of disturbing slavery where it was already established, that he would not invade the region, that he would not attempt to fill offices with men repugnant to local sensibilities. But he also warned that secession was illegal. It was his duty to maintain the integrity of the federal government, and to do so he had to "hold, occupy, and possess" federal property in the states of the Confederacy, including Fort Sumter. Lincoln pleaded with his countrymen to move slowly, to let passions cool.

People heard in Lincoln's inaugural what they chose to hear. Republicans and Unionists in the South thought it a potent mixture of firmness and generosity. Skeptics, on the other hand, focused on the threat of coercion at Fort Sumter. If Lincoln attempted to use force of any kind, they warned, war would be the inevitable result. Lincoln did not plan on war; he was trying to buy time, hoping that compromisers in Washington would come up with a workable strategy.

The Decision at Fort Sumter

But there was less time than Lincoln realized. On the very day after Lincoln's speech, Major Anderson reported to Washington that he would be out of food within four to six weeks. Initially unsure as to the wisdom of retaining the fort, Lincoln finally decided that he had to act: he would send provisions but not military supplies to Fort Sumter. By doing so, Lincoln would maintain the balance he promised in his inaugural speech, keeping the fort but not using coercion unless attacked first. He sent a note to South Carolina's governor

South Carolina troops fire cannon at the federal forces under the command of Major Robert Anderson. Although no one was killed in the assault, the shots opened the Civil War.

The Granger Collection, New York

of his intent to provision the fort, a note perceived by Confederate leaders not as a courtesy, but an ultimatum.

The president recognized that the Confederacy was determined to act. Jefferson Davis and his government had decided a week earlier that any attempt to reprovision the fort would be in and of itself an act of war. Davis believed that no foreign power would respect a country, especially one as new and tenuous as the Confederate States of America, if it allowed one of its major ports to be occupied by another country. The Union's resupply of the fort would mean the Union still controlled it.

The Confederate government decided that its commander in Charleston, P. G. T. Beauregard, should attack Fort Sumter before the relief expedition had a chance to arrive. The leaders understood the risks. The Confederate secretary of state warned Jefferson Davis that the attack would "lose us every friend at the North" and "wantonly strike a hornet's nest which extends from mountains to ocean, and legions, now quiet, will swarm out and sting us to death. It is unnecessary; it puts us in the wrong; it is fatal." Nevertheless, on April 12, at 4:30 in the morning, Beauregard opened fire on the Union garrison. The shelling continued for thirty-three hours. Anderson held out for as long as he could, but when fire tore through the barracks and his ammunition ran low he decided the time for surrender had come. Northerners agreed that the events in South Carolina could not go unanswered. Lincoln issued a call for 75,000 volunteers to defend the Union. Southerners agreed that they would have no choice but to come to that state's aid if the North raised a hand against their fellow southerners.

Conclusion

It was no accident that the slave states and free states experienced mounting animosity and distrust in the late 1850s. The rapid expansion of both the North and the South put the two regions on a collision course in the West.

Watching the events of those years unfold, however, it is clear that the conflict could certainly have taken other forms. Had Kansas been handled more adroitly by Buchanan and the Democrats, had Preston Brooks not caned Charles Sumner, had Chief Justice Taney not issued the *Dred Scott* decision, and had John Brown not given violence a martyr's sanction, the election of 1860 would not have become the watershed it did. This cascade of events washed the United States toward dissolution. Another cascade of events would soon push it into war.

RECOMMENDED READINGS

Crofts, Daniel W. *Old Southampton: Politics and Society in a Virginia County, 1834–1869* (1992). Provides a detailed account of the way politics worked in communities of the Upper South.

Charles B. Dew. *Apostles of Disunion: Southern Secession Commissioners and the Causes of the Civil War* (2001). Offers excellent coverage of debates about secession among southerners.

Fehrenbacher, Don E. *The Dred Scott Case: Its Significance in American Law and Politics* (1978). The classic account of this complicated episode.

Finkelman, Paul, ed. *His Soul Goes Marching On: Responses to John Brown and the Harpers Ferry Raid* (1995). Contains fascinating articles about this much-interpreted event.

Foner, Eric. *Free Soil, Free Labor, Free Men: The Ideology of the Republican Party Before the Civil War* (1970). Masterfully demonstrates the power of free labor ideology.

Holt, Michael F. *The Political Crisis of the 1850s* (1978). Stresses the dynamics of the two-party system in bringing on the Civil War.

Morrison, Michael A. *Slavery and the American West: The Eclipse of Manifest Destiny and the Coming of the Civil War* (1997). A subtle survey of this critical topic.

Stampp, Kenneth. *America in 1857: A Nation on the Brink* (1990). Shows the advantages of examining the simultaneous processes and events of this period.

Wyatt-Brown, Bertram. *Southern Honor: Ethics and Behavior in the Old South* (1982). Puts forward a powerful interpretation of white southern culture.

Zarefsky, David. *Lincoln, Douglas, and Slavery: In the Crucible of Public Debate* (1990). Recasts our understanding of these famous political debates.

Additional resources, exercises, and Internet links related to this chapter are available on the American Passages Web site: http://history.wadsworth.com/ayerscompact2/

Descent into War
1861–1862

At the beginning of 1861, Americans could not imagine anything like the war that soon consumed their nation. Events piled on one another in ways that no one could have anticipated. The men who voted for Lincoln did not think the South would secede, the architects of secession did not think the North would resist, and neither side thought the other would or could fight for long. Events proved no more predictable once the war began. Last-minute reinforcements and retreats changed the outcome of battles; news from the battlefield shaped every political and diplomatic decision.

War Begins: April 1861–July 1861

Neither the Union nor the Confederacy was ready for conflict in the spring of 1861. A number of states had yet to declare their loyalties and other states, communities, and families found themselves divided against themselves. In a matter of months, both the North and the South had to prepare for war.

Lincoln Calls for Troops

Two days after the Confederate flag went up over Fort Sumter on April 15, President Lincoln declared South Carolina in rebellion against the United States and called for 75,000 militiamen to help put the rebellion down. The president sought to appear restrained in his response. He demanded that forces gathering from the states of the Lower South "disperse and retire peacefully." He still hoped that Unionists in southern states besides South Carolina would rally to the nation's defense if he showed that he was no extremist. Lincoln also acted cautiously because he had not received the approval of Congress, which would not convene until July.

Lincoln's attempt to blend firmness and conciliation failed. Southern states saw the call to the militia as an act of aggression against South Carolina and state sovereignty. The Upper South states replied with defiance to Lincoln's requests for their troops on April 15, 1861. One Virginia representative responded to the president, "I have a Union constituency which elected me by a majority of one thousand, and I believe now that there are not ten Union men in that county to-day." Virginia seceded two days later. Although many

CHRONOLOGY

1861

April	15	Lincoln calls for 75,000 militia
April	17–May 20	Arkansas, Tennessee, Virginia, and North Carolina secede
May	29	Richmond becomes capital of Confederacy
July	21	Confederate victory at Bull Run (Manassas)
	25	Frémont takes command in the West
	27	McClellan takes command of Union forces near Washington
August	30	Frémont declares martial law, and frees slaves, in Missouri
September	6	Kentucky remains in the Union
November	1	McClellan assumes command of all Union armies
	6	Jefferson Davis elected president of Confederacy with six-year term
	7	Union capture of Port Royal, South Carolina
	8	Union navy seizes Confederate commissioners Mason and Slidell from British ship *Trent*
	19	Halleck replaces Frémont as Union commander in West
December	26	Union government releases Mason and Slidell
	30	Suspension of specie payments

1862

February	6	Union captures Fort Henry on Tennessee River
	16	Confederates surrender Fort Donelson to Grant
	22	Inauguration of Jefferson Davis
	25	Legal Tender Act in North authorizes "greenbacks"
		Confederates evacuate Nashville
	27	Confederate Congress authorizes martial law and suspends habeas corpus
March	8–9	*Virginia v. Monitor* in Hampton Roads, Virginia
	17	McClellan begins move to James River Peninsula
April	5	McClellan begins siege of Yorktown
	6–7	Grant wins dramatic victory at Shiloh
	16	Confederacy passes Conscription Act
	25	New Orleans surrenders to Admiral Farragut
May	8–9	Jackson's Shenandoah Valley Campaign
	20	Homestead Act passed by Union Congress
	31	Lee takes command of Army of Northern Virginia
June	6	Confederates evacuate Memphis
	26	Lee drives McClellan from Richmond in Seven Days' Battles
July	11	Halleck appointed general-in-chief of Union armies
	12	Border states reject Lincoln plan for gradual emancipation
	17	Second Confiscation Act
	22	Cabinet hears Lincoln's draft of Emancipation Proclamation
August	3	Union decides to evacuate McClellan's troops from peninsula
	29–30	Confederate victory at Second Bull Run (Manassas)
September	4–6	Lee invades Maryland
	17	Battle of Antietam (Sharpsburg)
	22	First Emancipation Proclamation
October	3–4	Union victory at Corinth
November	7	Burnside replaces McClellan as commander of Army of the Potomac
		Republicans lose widely in mid-term elections in North
December	13	Lee overwhelms Burnside at Fredericksburg
	16–20	Crisis in Lincoln's cabinet
	27–29	Sherman defeated near Vicksburg

people in Virginia still clung to hopes of avoiding war, two delegates to every one voted for secession on April 17. These Virginians, like white southerners of all inclinations and temperaments, refused to supply soldiers to confront another slaveholding state. Recognizing the importance of moving President Jefferson Davis and his government closer to their armies, the Confederacy immediately voted to move its capital to Richmond in May of 1861.

In the North, even in areas like New York City, which had opposed Lincoln's election, 250,000 people filled the streets in a Unionist rally. Democrat Stephen Douglas addressed a tumultuous Chicago crowd. "There are only two sides to the question," he proclaimed. "Every man must be for the United States or against it. There can be no neutrals in this war, only patriots—or traitors." Ohio's governor informed Lincoln that "without seriously repressing the ardor of the people," he would raise twenty regiments to defend the nation rather than the requested thirteen. A Harvard professor, born during Washington's presidency, exclaimed, "I never knew what a popular excitement can be . . . The whole population, men, women, and children, seem to be in the streets with Union favors and flags."

The States Divide

Arkansas, Tennessee, and North Carolina quickly followed Virginia's example. North Carolinians, who over the winter rioted against secession and shot Confederate flags from their staffs, considered Lincoln's actions a call to arms for southern men that "as by a stroke of lighting, . . . made the South wholly South." The Oklahoma Territory, too, aligned itself with the Confederacy. There, leaders of the Five Civilized Tribes, slaveholders themselves, used the opportunity to fight against the U.S. government that had dispossessed them from their homes three decades earlier. The leaders of other Indian nations sided with the Union, however, and began to fight for control of the Indian Territory.

State leaders elsewhere frantically struggled with one another. In Maryland, rioters attacked Massachusetts troops as they marched through Baltimore two days after the secession of neighboring Virginia—spilling the first blood of the war when twelve civilians and four Union soldiers died in the gunfire. Maryland bitterly divided, the southern portion of the state sympathizing with the Confederacy, with Baltimore, where free blacks outnumbered slaves by eleven to one, and the western portion generally supporting the Union. Should the United States lose Maryland, the District of Columbia would be completely surrounded by Confederate territory. Accordingly, Lincoln acted quickly to keep Maryland in line, jailing secession advocates and suspending the writ of habeas corpus so they could not be released. He admonished Baltimore leaders to send their "rowdies" home and if "they do attack us, we will return it, and that severely."

Kentucky, after months of determined attempts to remain neutral, decided for the Union in September after Confederate troops entered the state. Missouri officially remained in the Union but was ravaged from within for the next four years. Dissension took different form in the mountains of western Virginia. In June, delegates from fifty counties met in Wheeling to renounce the Virginia secession convention, begin the gradual abolition of slavery, and declare their loyalty to the Union. Lincoln recognized these breakaway counties as the legal government of Virginia and their legislative delegations

The seven Gulf states seceded first, and on February 9th, delegates from these states met in Montgomery, Alabama, to create a provisional constitution, similar to that of the United States except in its explicit guarantee of slavery and states' rights. Advocates of secession traveled throughout the Upper South to convince voters and leaders to join the Confederacy. Regardless of the appeals to law and interpretations of the Constitution, the emotional heart of the debate white southerners conducted among themselves centered on three related issues: loathing of the prospect of racial equality, fear of servile insurrection and race war, and a surprisingly frank, if horrified, discussion of the inevitable miscegenation that would result if slavery were destroyed. While the language of states' rights appeared in these discussions, it focused on the states' rights to maintain slavery and preserve the standing racial order. Immediately after Lincoln called for troops to suppress the rebellion in South Carolina, Virginia, Arkansas, North Carolina, and Tennessee departed the Union. The other slave states—Kentucky, Maryland, Delaware, and Missouri—remained in the Union. Western Virginia would soon separate from the rest of the state and declare its loyalty to the Union.

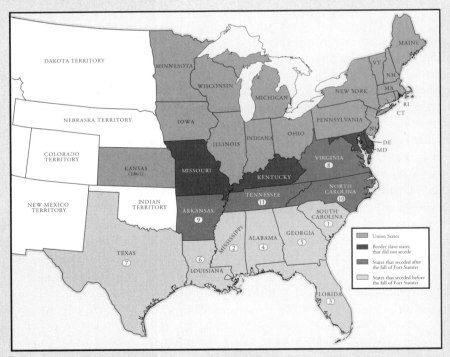

Map 14.1 Southern Secession View an animated version of this map or related maps at http://history.wadsworth.com/passages2e

were seated in July 1861. After a complicated series of conventions and elections, the state of West Virginia came into being in 1862 and joined the Union the following year.

As it turned out, the Union and the Confederacy divided about as evenly as possible. Virginia, Tennessee, North Carolina, and Arkansas, all of which went into the Confederacy, might well have decided to remain with the Union; had they done so, the Confederacy would have had little hope of sustaining a successful war against the North. Those states accounted for half of all manufacturing and half of all food production in the Confederacy. Maryland, Kentucky, and Missouri, on the other hand, might well have joined the Confederacy; had they done so, the Union cause would have been weakened, perhaps fatally. Kentucky and Missouri occupied crucial positions along the major rivers that led into the South. Even the dissidents balanced: eight states along the border provided 235,000 white and 85,000 black troops to the Union and 425,000 to the Confederacy.

Although Abraham Lincoln was criticized from every angle in these months, he managed to bring into the Union fold the states he had to win. Had he lost these struggles, he might well have failed in all the other struggles that awaited him.

The Numbers

In retrospect, the cards seemed heavily stacked in the North's favor. The Union, after all, had vastly greater industrial capacity, railroads, canals, food, draft animals, ships, and entrepreneurial talent, all the things a mid-nineteenth-century war required. The Union could also claim four times as many white residents as the South. And although the 3.5 million enslaved people who lived in the Confederacy were extraordinarily valuable to the South, everyone recognized that the slaves could become equally valuable allies for the North.

Since the South acknowledged the North's advantages, many people then and since assumed that the Confederates must have been driven either by irrational rage or heedless bravery. Neither the Confederates nor the North, however, expected the secession crisis to turn into a full-fledged war, much less a four-year war. When Lincoln called for the 75,000 militia, he called them for only ninety days' service. When southern boys and men rushed to enlist for the Confederacy in the spring of 1861, they assumed they would be back home in time to harvest their crops in the autumn.

Southerners considered themselves natural soldiers, caricaturing their new enemies as clerks and factory workers. Though the Union did have more city men and immigrants than the South, most northerners, like southerners, were young men raised on farms. Since both sides believed that their opponents were weak and divided, northerners and southerners thought the conflict would likely come to a swift, and peaceful, resolution. Commanders on each side recognized their lack of experience. Lincoln calmed General Irvin McDowell: "You are green, it is true, but they are green also, you are all green alike." In such a struggle, sheer numbers did not seem nearly as important as they eventually became.

The Strategies

The military strategies of both sides sought to minimize actual fighting. The South saw itself as purely on the defensive; it would wait for northern armies to invade and then defeat them. The North, for its part, counted on General Winfield Scott's "Anaconda Plan," named after the snake of that name that slowly squeezes its prey to death. That plan depended on sending an overpowering force down the Mississippi River in the fall, dividing the South in two. At the same time, the Union navy would seal off the South from outside supplies. Ground troops and land battles would be kept to a minimum.

The Confederacy possessed considerable military advantages. It occupied an enormous area, larger than today's United Kingdom, France, Italy, and Spain combined. It possessed dozens of harbors and ports, connected by an excellent system of rivers and an adequate network of railroads. The Confederacy's long border with Mexico made it difficult to seal off outside supplies. The Confederacy could wage a defensive war, moving its troops internally from one point to another, whereas the Union had to move around the perimeter. The many country roads of the South, known only to locals, would provide routes for Confederate surprise attacks or strategic retreats.

For a model of how such a defensive plan might work, Southerners looked to the American Revolution. Like the American colonies eighty years earlier, the Confederates did not have to win every battle nor conquer northern territory. Southerners thought they had only to keep fighting long enough for the North's political, economic, regional, and ethnic divisions to overwhelm its temporary unity. Indeed, the Confederacy enjoyed advantages the American colonies had not enjoyed. The new southern nation covered twice as much territory as had the colonies, and the North possessed nowhere near the military power of the British at the time of the Revolutionary War.

Leadership

There was also the matter of leadership. In 1861, many observers would have given the advantage to the Confederates in this regard. Abraham Lincoln, after all, had held public office for only two years before he assumed the presidency, and his only military service had been a brief service in the militia. Jefferson Davis, by contrast, had distinguished himself in the war with Mexico. He had been secretary of war under Franklin Pierce and had served in the United States Senate. Davis, unlike Lincoln, directed his forces' military strategy with the confidence born of firsthand knowledge and experience.

At the beginning of the war, too, it appeared that the South had the better generals. The southern leaders certainly had more experience: the average age of the Union generals in 1861 was thirty-eight; of Confederate generals, forty-seven. Robert E. Lee of Virginia had served as an engineer, an officer in the Mexican War in the 1840s, and superintendent of West Point in the late 1850s. He resigned his U.S. military commission and accepted command of Virginia's forces. Lee made the same tortured decision so many southerners made when secession finally came: "With all my devotion to the Union and the feeling and loyalty of an American citizen, I have not been able to make up my mind to raise my hand against my relatives, my children, my home."

Neither the Union nor the Confederacy felt a need for a commanding general. Many lesser generals still had to be named quickly, however. Military experience and ability did not always prove to be the major considerations in these appointments. About a third of Union generals and half their Confederate counterparts had not been professional soldiers, though most had undergone some military training; overall, the North and the South placed roughly similar proportions of professional soldiers in command. The South did enjoy an advantage among junior officers, as seven of the nation's eight military colleges were in the South. In 1861, one-third of Virginia regiments' field grade officers had graduated from the Virginia Military Institute. Lincoln, forced to unify a people far more divided than the white population of the Confederacy, chose generals from the ranks of various constituencies he needed to appease: abolitionists, Democrats, Irish, and Germans. Jefferson Davis did the same to bind ambitious politicians from the various states to the new Confederacy.

Neither the Union nor the Confederacy enjoyed a clear advantage in civilian leadership. Both Lincoln and Davis assembled cabinets that balanced geography, political faction, personality, and expertise. The Confederates had to create a government from scratch, including the design of flags, stamps, and money. Davis ran through several secretaries of war and secretaries of state before finding the two men on whom he felt he could rely, James A. Seddon and Judah P. Benjamin, respectively.

The Union enjoyed a head start in such matters, but the Republicans had many problems to iron out. Office seekers besieged Washington at the very time Lincoln was trying to keep the South in the Union; he felt like an innkeeper, he said, faced with customers demanding rooms in one wing while he tried to put out a fire in another. Lincoln's cabinet ended up containing men whom he barely knew and upon whom he was not always sure he could rely.

The First Conflicts

Battles began before anyone was ready. On the day following Lincoln's call for troops in April, federal officers in charge of the arsenal at Harpers Ferry and the naval yard in Norfolk, Virginia, sought to destroy the weapons under their command before secessionists could seize them. Despite their efforts, Virginia troops managed to recover valuable gun-making machinery, artillery, naval stores, and ships for the Confederate cause. A few weeks later, battles broke out along the B&O Railroad in what would become West Virginia, with Robert E. Lee, the new general for Virginia, leading an unsuccessful and embarrassing chase of troops under the command of George McClellan. Meanwhile, nearly 4,000 Confederates, most of them from Texas, pushed into New Mexico. They hoped to win the mineral riches of Colorado and perhaps even California for the Southern cause.

All these struggles showed both sides to be far from ready to fight a war in 1861. Not only were guns and uniforms scarce, but so were combat experience and even battlefield training.

Even those men who had attended West Point had learned more about engineering than they had about tactical maneuvers. The United States Army contained only about 16,000 men, and nearly 12,000 of them were scattered across the vast territory west of the Mississippi River. The militiamen who first responded to the calls of the Union and Confederacy had scarcely been trained at all.

Mobilization

Both sides took immediate steps to create new armies, organized within local communities and led by local men. The Confederate Congress authorized 400,000 volunteers in May of 1861. In its special session beginning in July of 1861, the Union Congress authorized 500,000 troops, each signing on for three years; 700,000 eventually enlisted under this

The Granger Collection, New York

Early in the war, Thomas Jonathan "Stonewall" Jackson was the most beloved Confederate leader, admired for his military daring and his devout religious belief.

authorization. Much mobilization took place on the local level. Prominent citizens often supplied uniforms, guns, and even food for the troops from their localities. Units elected their own officers. States competed to enlist the largest numbers of men. A private mourned his state's slow mobilization, "New York and Pennsylvania and New Jersey are alive, while I am ashamed to speak of the apathy in Massachusetts." Local newspapers sought to make sure that state-level leaders dealt fairly with local troops and officers.

Some Northerners wondered whether the many divisions among classes, occupations, religions, and ethnic groups would hinder the Union war effort. Such doubters took heart at the response to the crisis of 1861. Both workingmen and wealthy men eagerly signed up. Members of ethnic groups took pride in forming their own units; the Irish and Germans supplied over 150,000 men each, with the total of foreign-born in service totaling nearly half a million. Northerners congratulated themselves that patriotism and self-sacrifice had not been killed, as many feared, by the spirit of commerce so strong in the land. Editor Horace Greeley sketched the transformation of Northerners from "a sordid, grasping money-loving people" to one in whom the "fires of patriotic devotion" still burned.

Southerners, too, found reason to be proud in 1861. The leaders of the South had secretly worried that when push came to shove the non-slaveholders would not fight for a cause that many identified with the defense of slavery. But Southern boys and men were activated by the same impulses that drove their Northern counterparts: dreams of glory, youthful self-confidence, and a burning desire to impress family, friends, and young women with their bravery. At this point in the war, white Southerners talked less about slavery than they had before or than they would later. In their eyes, they fought to defend their farms and homes from "foreign" invaders.

Editors, politicians, and citizens of both the North and the South demanded that the conflict be wrapped up immediately. "ON TO RICHMOND" ran the headline in northern papers while General Beauregard informed Jefferson Davis of his troops' readiness "to meet the enemies of our country under all circumstances." Confident of victory, they itched for the fight that would settle things once and for all. Only a few, such as William T. Sherman, dissented. This "is to be a long war,—very long,—much longer than any politician thinks."

The First Battle

Northerners soon grew impatient with the passive Anaconda Plan of cutting the South off from the outside. With so many men eagerly signing on to fight, Northerners thought they should get the war over early, before the South had time to consolidate its forces. The Union already had 35,000 men poised in northern Virginia, about twenty-five miles away from a Confederate force of 20,000 under the command of P. G. T. Beauregard. Beauregard's troops protected an important rail junction at Manassas, along Bull Run (a "run" is a stream). Confederate and Union troops also watched one another warily in the Shenandoah Valley, about fifty miles to the west.

These troop deployments reflected a primary goal of each side in the early stages of the war: capturing the capital of its enemy. Union leaders thought that if they could win Richmond—the industrial, commercial, and administrative center of the South—the rest of the Confederacy would soon follow. Confederate leaders thought that if they could conquer the capital of the United States, forcing Lincoln and his cabinet to flee, European powers would recognize the Confederacy's sovereignty and legitimacy.

The officers of both the Union and the Confederacy had learned their strategy at West Point although few had ever commanded units above the regimental level. These officers usually attempted to concentrate their force in hopes of overwhelming the enemy at the point of attack. The Union tried to take advantage of its greater numbers of men and resources; the Confederacy sought to use its interior lines, knowledge of the Virginia landscape, and aggressive maneuvers to gain an advantage. Educated with the same texts and serving together in peace and war, leaders on both sides knew what the others hoped and planned to do.

In the first major battle of the war, the South's advantages outweighed the North's. Both sides attempted to coordinate their troop movements near Washington and in the Shenandoah Valley. The valley had long served as a major corridor between the North and the South. If that corridor was left unprotected by the Union, Confederate forces could rush up the valley and capture Washington. But if too many troops protected the valley, the North would tie up men and resources that could be used more effectively elsewhere. The Confederacy employed cavalry, under the command of the flamboyant young colonel

James E. B. (Jeb) Stuart, to move quickly up and down the valley, keeping the North off balance.

The Union, under the command of General Irvin McDowell, tried to concentrate most of its forces at Manassas by moving them from the valley. On July 21, the Northern troops were finally ready to attack. Congressmen and other spectators drove their carriages out from Washington to "see the Rebels get whipped." Union troops flooded over the battle-field, fording the creeks, flanking the strongest points in the Confederate lines. The Southern forces fell back to more defensible positions. When it looked as if the Confederates were to be routed, a Southern general pointed out Thomas J. Jackson to his men, "There is Jackson standing like a stone wall! Rally behind the Virginians!" "Stonewall Jackson," until recently an undistinguished mathematics professor at the Virginia Military Institute, had been christened.

The Confederate reinforcements that poured off the train at Manassas gave Beauregard a renewed spirit. The Union forces suffered confusion when the lack of a common uniform led some Northerners to mistake Confederates for their own troops. They began to pull back and then to run. Some civilian carriages got caught in the panicked flood of troops rushing back to Washington; the Confederates gleefully captured a New York congressman hiding in the woods and held him for the next six months in Richmond . . . as a prisoner.

The South had claimed its first victory. Each side had engaged about 18,000 soldiers, making Bull Run by a considerable margin the largest battle ever waged in the United States up to that time. Both the North and the South lost about 600 men. Nevertheless, the humiliating rout confirmed the Confederate belief that one Rebel could whip ten Yankees.

Key parts of Confederate lore emerged from Bull Run as well: the Rebel yell and the Confederate battle flag. The yell was not merely a scream or a roar, but a high wail, unnerving and strange. It served as the rallying cry for Southern troops for the rest of the war. The first flag of the Confederacy, the Stars and Bars, looked a great deal like that of the United States, leading to confusion in the heat of battle. After Bull Run, Beauregard designed a new flag—a square banner, red with a blue cross and white stars—to ensure that Southern troops did not fire on one another. It was that battle flag, never the official flag of the Confederacy, that later generations came to consider synonymous with the South.

For the next two years, the Battle of Bull Run emboldened Southern forces who fought in Virginia. The Confederacy, feeling itself invulnerable, fought aggressively, even recklessly, in the east. The Union fought cautiously, even tentatively, in Virginia. One Union soldier wrote home, "During the day one of the boys brought in a Virginia paper in which it stated that one 'Southerner could lick five Northern mudsills. It was not so comforting to feel we were to be killed off in blocks of five." Neither side forgot this conflict even though each side called it by different names. Northern forces generally named battles after physical features such as rivers and mountains; thus, they deemed this the Battle of Bull Run. Southerners usually named battles after nearby towns or villages; they called this one Manassas.

Women and War

Women had avidly studied the debates being waged in the newspapers. They had expressed their opinions in private conversation, in their letters, and in their diaries. Many had listened to the speeches on all sides. They had counseled their sons and husbands, sometimes urging their men on to join others of their community. They had worn cockades displaying their loyalties and had sung the latest songs. Once the speeches, songs, and toasts had come to an end and the fighting had begun, women became even more active.

© Corbis

Women in both the North and South quickly stepped forward as nurses, sometimes against opposition, to save lives and relieve suffering.

Within two weeks of the war's beginning, women on the two sides had formed 20,000 aid societies. These societies devoted themselves to supplying the armies' needs, especially clothing and medical supplies. One such organization in Alabama provided, in just one month, "422 shirts, 551 pairs of drawers, 80 pairs of socks, 3 pairs of gloves, 6 boxes and one bale of hospital supplies, 128 pounds of tapioca, and a donation of $18 for hospital use."

With the first battles, women claimed positions as nurses, even though men had served before as military nurses. Despite some initial grumbling by men, women converted themselves immediately into competent and devoted nurses. Dorothea Dix, long known as the champion of the mentally ill and other neglected people in the antebellum era, took matters in hand for the North. She became superintendent of nurses for the Union army, the highest executive appointment for a woman to date, organizing 3,000 women who volunteered to serve. Concerned both about the effectiveness and propriety of women ministering to young male strangers, Dix decreed that she wanted only "plain" women, women over thirty, and women who would dress in brown and black. Unfortunately, by war's end, Dix's prudery, enthusiasm, and mismanagement had alienated military doctors, most of the Sanitary Commission, and many of her own nurses.

Women's efforts soon became legendary. They labored until they could no longer stand, until their long dresses trailed blood from amputations and wounds. Kate Cumming and Phoebe Pember played leading roles in the Confederacy, and Clara Barton took her aid to the front lines of the Union and later founded the American Red Cross. Most women stayed closer to home, working in factories, doing piecework in their households, or tilling fields. As Northern farmers departed for the military, observers in the Midwest saw "more women driving teams" and more "at work in fields than men."

War Takes Command: August 1861–March 1862

The war spread across the continent in the fall, winter, and spring of 1861–1862. Armies consolidated command and launched campaigns thousands of miles from headquarters. Governments transformed their economies, invented or reinvented navies, conducted diplomacy, and cemented the loyalties of those at home. Families steeled themselves for a war longer than they had been willing to imagine.

McClellan Assumes Control

The North, while embarrassed by Bull Run, took from that defeat a determination to fight more effectively. Volunteers flooded into recruitment offices. Lincoln removed the leaders responsible for that battle and replaced them with George B. McClellan. Although short of stature and only thirty-four years old, McClellan exuded great authority. He was known as the "young Napoleon." McClellan had distinguished himself in the Mexican War and had studied military tactics in Europe. Moreover, he had already frustrated Confederate forces under Robert E. Lee in western Virginia. He now threw himself into reorganizing and reenergizing the Union troops under his command.

The press lavished praise on the young general. Already inclined toward grandiose visions of his abilities, McClellan developed an exalted sense of himself. The cocky commander considered Lincoln an "idiot" and his cabinet incompetent "geese." McClellan ignored, avoided, and insulted those men at every opportunity. McClellan wanted to make his army perfectly prepared before he risked it, and his reputation, in battle against Confederates whose numbers his spies consistently exaggerated. Meanwhile, months dragged by. Lincoln and newspaper editors became furiously impatient, but McClellan would not be moved.

The War in the West Begins

There was to be no waiting in the West. Four days after the battle at Bull Run, the Union installed a new commander in charge of the forces in Missouri: John C. Frémont, the "pathfinder of the West" and former Republican presidential candidate. Whereas the situation in Virginia unfolded slowly, the situation in Missouri burst into chaos in July and August of 1861. Guerrilla forces raged throughout the state. Confederate armies built up on the southern border, ready to attack in both the eastern and western parts of the state. Frémont decided that he had to protect the Mississippi River in the East and therefore left a weak force in the West. That force, outnumbered by the Confederates, staged a desperate attack, with terrible losses, at Wilson's Creek. As at Bull Run, the lack of a standard uniform color created deadly confusion. The Northern units fell into ragged retreat, exposing Missouri to Rebel incursions.

With the army so far from Washington, desperate for war materials and supplies, contractors took advantage of the situation, selling substandard goods to the Union army at inflated prices. With the populace of Missouri so divided in its loyalties, Frémont, who, a contemporary noted, had "all of the qualities of genius except ability," did not know whom to trust. Frantic, he declared the entire state under martial law, decreed the death penalty for captured guerrillas, and seized the slaves and other property of all Confederate sympathizers. Slaveholders in the border states of Kentucky and Maryland threatened to throw their allegiances to the South if Lincoln did not overrule Frémont.

The president, desperate to keep the border states within the Union, advised the general that the proclamation angered loyal slaveowners and threatened the loss of Kentucky and requested him to revoke his emancipation order. When Frémont resisted, demanding a public order overruling him, Lincoln felt that he had no choice but to remove Frémont from his post.

Events on the battlefield in the earliest stages of the war proved to be a poor guide to the long term. Although the North had been shaken by Bull Run and Missouri, it had lost neither Washington nor the border states. Although the South had apparently won at Bull Run, the Confederate forces, exhausted and bogged down in mud, had not taken advantage of the situation to attack the Union capital. Although slaveholders in the border states fumed at the Union government and military leaders, they remained in the Union. As a result, the South was deprived of a key strategic advantage: access to the Ohio River and a defensible border with the North. With the Union army able to move up and down the Ohio at will, the Confederates had to defend a vast, vague, and shifting border in Kentucky and Tennessee.

The war was not to be won by a decisive battle within a few months of the war's start. Instead, slower and less dramatic processes proved decisive. Armies and navies had to be built from scratch; economies had to be converted to wartime demands; households and families had to absorb growing sacrifices. These transformations began in earnest in the summer of 1861.

Paying for War

The Civil War, involving so many men over such an enormous territory, immediately became breathtakingly expensive. It was by no means clear how either side was going to pay. Although the Union and the Confederacy were, by any international standard, rich societies, neither had ever supported a large army or an active government. Taxes on imported goods and the sale of apparently endless public lands paid for what government there was. Ever since the Bank War of the 1830s, the federal and state governments did little to manipulate the currency. As a result, when the war came, the men responsible for paying for it had only a few options—loans, new taxes, or the creation of paper money.

Loans met the least resistance in both the North and the South, but this borrowing could provide only a third of the cost of the war. Taxes proved even less effective. The Confederacy quickly decided that it had no choice but to turn to paper money. As soon as it could find adequate engravers and printing presses, the South began producing millions of dollars in the new currency. Catastrophic inflation began to grow as early as the winter of 1861–1862. In Virginia, cash was scarce as women wrote husbands in the army for money and others turned away poorer friends, "I have no money by me at all" and "the wealthiest men in the county here have no money."

The situation was not quite as bad in the North, where taxes and bonds carried much more of the burden of financing the war, but the Union, too, was forced to issue paper money by the first winter of the war. People hoarded gold in anticipation of the deprivations a widened war would cause. New York banks felt they had no choice but to suspend specie payments in December of 1861. In February of 1862, the Union Congress reluctantly decided that it had no choice but to create paper money. The Legal Tender Act of that month permitted the treasury to release up to $10 million of the new currency, quickly dubbed "greenbacks." Over $450 million in paper notes circulated during the war, replacing the earlier system of state bank notes with a unified national currency.

The Confederate Homefront

Southerners watched helplessly as armies stripped their farms of food and livestock. They ministered to the bleeding young men dragged into their parlors and bedrooms. The residents of places where both Unionists and Confederates remained strong—such as Missouri and eastern Tennessee—became caught in internal civil wars that pitted roving gangs of thugs against one another. Governors received letters from women, their husbands and sons gone, who worried that they faced starvation if they did not get help soon.

Inflation ate away at the Confederacy like a cancer. The rapid rise in prices made currency worth less every day. The government issued war bonds that paid 8 percent interest per year at a time when inflation reached 12 percent per month in 1861. Speculators could make money simply by buying up supplies and holding them while prices escalated. Farmers faced the temptation to grow cotton despite the needs of the armies. Cotton stored well and everyone knew that cotton would fetch a high price after the war, no matter who won. As a result, land and labor that could have grown food bent under the weight of cotton. A Georgia newspaper blamed speculators, for "a conscienceless set of vampires . . . are determined to make money even if one-half of the people starve."

Confederate leaders worried that the plantations could not produce the food the armies so desperately needed if white men did not force the slaves to work. African Americans wanted to hunt, fish, or work for themselves and their own families rather than to labor for the white people. Plantation mistresses often discovered that slaves would not work when the master—and the whips and guns he wielded—no longer hung over the slaves. Accordingly, the Confederate Congress passed laws exempting from the draft white men to supervise slaves on larger plantations. That a government in such need of every available soldier felt compelled to write such laws revealed how central slavery remained even in the midst of war.

To many poorer Southerners, the law was another in a growing list of grievances. Resentment against wealthy men and women—mediated during peacetime by family ties, common church membership, careful manners, and democratic politics—quickly came to the surface in the context of war. Common people were quick to notice when plantation slaves labored over cotton rather than corn, when the well-to-do hoarded gold or dodged taxes. Wealthy young men sometimes entered the Confederate army as privates, but others considered an officer's commission their just due as gentlemen. Scions of plantation fortunes often did little to disguise their disgust or amusement at the speech or clothing of the poorer men alongside whom they fought. The poorer soldiers noticed, as did their wives.

Navies

The navies of the North and South had to adapt most quickly. Just as many battles, starting with Bull Run, broke out at rail junctions, so did the leaders on both sides recognize the centrality of ports and rivers. The North's Anaconda Plan depended on control of the waterways, stopping the shipment of the South's immensely valuable cotton crop, cutting the region off from importations of weapons and other manufactured goods, and dividing the Confederacy along the Mississippi River.

The Union enjoyed a great initial advantage in its number of ships, but many of those ships were scattered around the globe. It took months to bring them home. Moreover, most of the Union's vessels were deep-sea ships. With remarkable speed, however, the Union naval department built new craft and deployed them against the South. In the first months of the war, the Navy Department armed merchant ships and sent them to blockade Southern ports. By the end of 1861, over 260 vessels patrolled the coasts and the skilled workers of the shipbuilding towns of the east coast had 100 more under construction, including the North's first ironclad ships.

The South had virtually no ships at the beginning of the war, but the Confederate navy seized, acquired, or built roughly 125 ships each year, including over 400 steampowered ships. The Confederacy immediately contracted with large shipbuilding companies in England. Jefferson Davis authorized sailors to attack Northern ships on the high seas and turn them in for a share of the booty. For a few months, these "privateers" preyed on any unguarded ship they could find, but the Union navy quickly shut them down. The Confederates then used their naval officers to man ships that would attempt to sink rather than claim enemy ships. One intrepid officer, Raphael Semmes, escaped through the blockade in 1861 and seized eighteen Union ships before he was trapped at Gibraltar and forced to sell his ship and escape to England.

In the meantime, the North pushed its advantage. Larger ships began to blockade 189 harbors and ports from Virginia to Texas, patrolling 3,500 miles of coastline. Such enormous territory obviously proved difficult to control, especially because Northern ships periodically had to travel to ports hundreds of miles away for supplies and fuel. When Union craft left for such journeys, Southern blockade runners rushed into the unprotected ports. The Union navy decided to seize several Southern ports for use as supply stations.

The federal ships moved first in August, at Cape Hatteras in North Carolina, shelling the forts there and cutting off the supplies that dozens of blockade runners had brought

Confederate Ships Under Construction in England

The Confederacy depended on English shipyards, such as this one in Liverpool, to construct vessels to run the Union blockade, attack Union ships on the seas, and defend its ports. English willingness to construct and equip Southern ships waned as battlefield defeats reduced the prospect of Confederate victory. The most effective arm of the Confederate navy consisted of commerce raiders, which destroyed roughly 255 Union ships and doubled the cost of marine insurance for Northern merchants. Two of the most successful, the *Alabama* and the *Shenandoah*, built at the Laird shipyards in Liverpool, were hybrid sail and steam-powered ships that disrupted Northern commerce and destroyed merchant ships in the Atlantic and Pacific Oceans. The *Shenandoah* fired the last official shot of the war across the bows of a whaler in the Bering Sea on June 28, 1865, as part of a month-long campaign that resulted in the capture of twenty-four whaling ships. Not until August 2nd did her captain James Waddell learn the war had ended. Fearing prosecution for piracy, Waddell sailed the *Shenandoah* warily back to England, arriving off the Irish coast on November 5, 1865.

Williamson Art Gallery & Museum, Birkenhead, England

into the Confederacy. The Northern navy also took a station near Biloxi, Mississippi, from which it could patrol the Gulf of Mexico. The most valuable seizure, however, was Port Royal, South Carolina. Not only did that place offer an excellent harbor, but it stood midway between the major Southern ports of Charleston and Savannah. The 77 ships and 16,000 sailors and soldiers dispatched to Port Royal were the largest combined force yet assembled in American warfare.

Diplomacy and the Trent Affair

On the day after the capture of Port Royal, a Union ship stopped a British mail packet, the *Trent,* as it traveled from Cuba to St. Thomas. The *Trent* carried James Mason and John Slidell, Confederate commissioners sailing to London and Paris to negotiate for the support of the British and French governments. The captain of the Union ship, Charles Wilkes, after firing two shots across the bow of the British vessel, boarded it and seized the Confederate emissaries. When Wilkes arrived in Boston to deposit Mason and Slidell in prison, he met with a hero's welcome. Congress ordered a medal struck in his honor.

The excitement began to wane, however, when people realized the possible repercussions of Wilkes's actions. Despite the growth of the Union navy, Great Britain still ruled the oceans. British newspapers and politicians called for war against the arrogant Americans: "We are pretty well accustomed to Yankee bluster and hot headedness, but we cannot think that they will be so utterly blind as to provoke a collision with a power which with little difficulty could blow to the four winds their dwarf fleet."

The *Trent* affair reflected the uneasy state of international relations created by the war. The Confederacy hoped that England or France, even both, would come to its aid. The importance of cotton in the international marketplace was such, Southerners argued, that the industrial powers of Europe could not long afford to allow the Northern navy to enforce its blockade.

The situation in the winter of 1861–1862 proved more complicated than people had expected, however. International law did not offer a clear ruling on whether Captain Wilkes had acted legally. And neither did self-interest offer a clear guide as to whether England should declare war on the United States or aid the Confederacy. The factories of Britain had stockpiled cotton in expectation of the war and did not clamor for intervention as Southerners had hoped. Anger over the *Trent* affair was balanced by resentment of Southern assumptions about British dependence on cotton. Confederates who "thought they could extort our cooperation by the agency of king cotton" would be disappointed, British leaders warned. They considered aid given in response to blackmail "ignominious beyond measure," completely unacceptable. France and England watched one another warily, neither country eager to upset the fragile balance of power between themselves by taking the first step in America.

The Granger Collection, New York

Ulysses S. Grant distinguished himself in key battles in Tennessee and Mississippi in 1862. Many months and battles would pass, however, before Grant would assume command in the East.

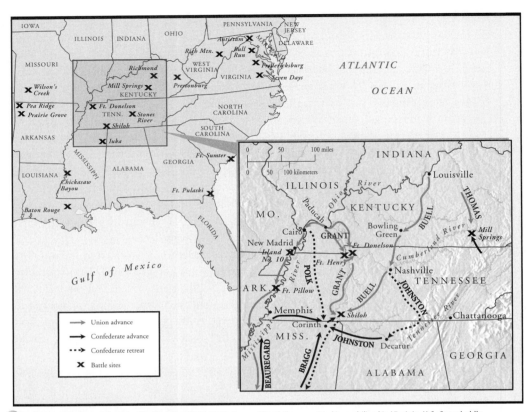

Map 14.2 Campaigns in the West in 1862 While Lee and McClellan remained immobilized in Virginia, U.S. Grant boldly pushed to the Mississippi border. View an animated version of this map or related maps at http://history.wadsworth.com/passages2e.

Public opinion within England and France divided, for it was by no means clear to most Europeans which side had the better claim to their sympathies. Lincoln repeatedly declared that the war was not a war to end slavery. That declaration, Lincoln believed, was necessary to cement the support of the border states, but it undercut the support of English and European abolitionists for the Union cause. The Confederates claimed to be fighting for self-determination, a cause with considerable appeal in Europe, but potential supporters often viewed Southern slaveholding with disgust and distrust. One Confederate agent in London blamed Britain's failure to recognize the Confederate state on the South's "pernicious adherence to the institution of slavery." Both the English and the French waited for events on the battlefields of North America to clarify issues.

The *Trent* affair, however, had to be settled at once. Its settlement came through diplomatic evasion and maneuvering. The U.S. officials decided that Wilkes had acted on his own, unauthorized by the government of the Union. Mason and Slidell were freed from prison and permitted to continue their journey. Although the Confederacy was jubilant at having "won," the underlying situation had not changed. Mason and Slidell found that though many powerful people elsewhere were sympathetic to the rebellious Southerners, they were unwilling to go to war against the United States.

The international situation remained tense and unsettled throughout the war. Leaders of both the North and the South could imagine situations in which England or France would intervene with weapons and supplies. Foreign intervention loomed as a fervent hope for the Confederacy and a great fear of the North.

The Rivers of the West

The Union felt starved for victories at the beginning of the hard winter of 1862. Northern troops remained bogged down in the eastern theater, but Union generals in the West moved aggressively. Deprived of control of the Ohio River when Kentucky sided with the Union, the Confederates under Albert Sidney Johnston desperately needed to stop the Union in the West. Troops under the command of Ulysses S. Grant, a relatively obscure general from Illinois, confronted a Confederate line of defense across southern Kentucky. Employing the Union's new river gunboats to great effect, Grant pushed down both the Tennessee and the Cumberland Rivers across the Kentucky border into Tennessee.

Important Confederate forts stood on both these rivers, but Grant hoped to overwhelm them by combined attacks on water and land. He assaulted Fort Henry on the Tennessee River in early February, easily overcoming the fort's defenses with the big guns on his river craft. The Union now commanded a river that flowed all the way through Tennessee into northern Alabama. Grant sent his boats steaming back up the Tennessee River to the Cumberland while he marched his men overland to Fort Donelson. There, the Confederates fought desperately, destroying several of the gunboats. Despite the Confederates' efforts, however, Grant pressed his advantage and overwhelmed Southern troops that attempted to break out of the fort and retreat to nearby Nashville.

When the Confederate general in charge of the 13,000 troops who remained in the fort attempted to negotiate with Grant (an old friend) for their surrender, Grant brusquely responded: "No terms except an unconditional and immediate surrender can be accepted. I propose to move immediately upon your works." Grant's phrase soon echoed through northern newspapers, jokes, and even mildly risqué love letters. Grant's first two initials, northern newspapers crowed, actually stood for Unconditional Surrender. Within days, Union troops pushed into nearby Nashville, the capital of Tennessee, making it the first great conquest of the war.

The Monitor and the Virginia

Even as Grant's troops seized their victories on the rivers of Tennessee, the Union navy continued its relentless attack on the eastern seaboard of the Confederacy. A well-planned amphibious assault allowed the Northern navy to consolidate its control of the North Carolina coast. The blockade steadily tightened.

Despite the Union's success, the Southern navy had reason for hope in early 1862. Confederate Secretary of the Navy Stephen Mallory had created an effective and innovative department. Mallory sought to take advantage of recent developments in shipbuilding and naval warfare such as steam power, the screw propeller, and armor. The Confederacy eagerly experimented, too, with mines in their harbors and developed the world's first combat submarine, the CSS *Hunley*.

Most important, the South examined the possibilities of iron-plated ships. In the years immediately preceding the Civil War, the French and British had been experimenting with such vessels, but the United States remained far behind. The Confederacy began building an ironclad almost from the very beginning of the war, converting a Union frigate, the USS *Merrimack*, captured in Norfolk in April of 1861.

Collection of President Franklin P. Roosevelt U.S. Naval Historical Center Photograph

In one of the most memorable episodes of the war, the two ironclad ships, the *USS Monitor* and the CSS *Virginia,* bruised one another in the harbor of Hampton Roads, Virginia, in March 1862. Though neither ship won, the Union's *Monitor* proved the superior vessel.

The confederacy added walls of two-feet-thick solid oak, covered with two-inch-thick iron plate, and installed an iron ram on the front to rip through the wooden hulls of enemy ships. It carried ten heavy guns. The Confederacy changed the ship's name from the USS *Merrimack* to the CSS *Virginia*.

The Union, for its part, hired a Swiss inventor to design a different kind of ironclad; his innovative plan called for a ship most of which would be submerged except for a rotating turret on top. Its inventor would refund the $275,000 cost to the government if the ship—condemned as a "cheesebox on a raft"—failed. It was by no means clear how such a craft might work in battle. No one was even sure it would stay afloat, much less fight effectively with its two guns. It was called the *Monitor*.

On March 8, 1862, the Confederates decided the time had come to unleash their new weapon. The *Virginia* attacked several Union ships occupying the harbor at Hampton Roads, Virginia. The ironclad sank two wooden ships and drove three others aground; their guns proved useless against the heavy iron sheathing.

In one of the more dramatic episodes of the young war, however, the Union happened to be sending its own ironclad to another Virginia port thirty miles away on the morning after the *Virginia* launched its attack. As soon as the sound of the guns in Hampton Roads reached the *Monitor,* it steamed down, arriving just in time. The two vessels pounded one another for hours. The imposing Southern ironclad had been neutralized and the blockade would continue. Although neither iron ship actually won the battle of March 9, the advantages of the Northern *Monitor* quickly became evident. Not only did that craft provide a much smaller target and a more maneuverable set of guns, but the *Monitor* required only half as much water in which to operate. The *Virginia* proved too big to retreat into rivers and too unwieldy for open seas. The Union began a crash campaign to build as many ironclads as possible, using the *Monitor* as its model. Britain, once the world's most formidable fleet, possessed only two ironclads. In the view of the *London Times,* "it would be madness" to engage "that little *Monitor*" with Britain's wooden fleet.

The Union on the Offensive: March–September 1862

The Union strategy had long pivoted around the effort to take Richmond. With apparently unlimited resources, Northerners expected to make quick work of Virginia. Although the Confederacy had put up a surprisingly effective campaign, the Union believed it would win the war in the spring and summer of 1862. As with all things in this war, however, events followed directions no one could foresee.

The Peninsular Campaign Begins

On the very day that the CSS *Virginia* emerged at Hampton Roads, Abraham Lincoln gave his approval of General George McClellan's long-delayed plan to win the war in the East. Rather than fighting in northern Virginia, McClellan would attack on the peninsula between the James and York Rivers farther south, using the Chesapeake Bay as a supply route. By moving the war away from Washington, McClellan argued, he would lessen the threat to the nation's capital and find better roads from which to attack Richmond.

Four hundred watercraft of every description began transferring Union soldiers to the tip of the peninsula at Fort Monroe, about seventy miles from Richmond. The transfer of 100,000 men took weeks to unfold. McClellan required several more weeks to arrange them "just so" in preparation for what he expected to be his triumphant march into Richmond.

Shiloh

In the meantime, U.S. Grant and his fellow general William T. Sherman pushed their troops ever deeper into Tennessee. The Confederates, under Albert Sidney Johnston, had retreated to Corinth, Mississippi, where they regrouped and joined with other units arriving by train from throughout the Confederacy. They planned to attack Grant to regain momentum, if not the enormous territory and strategic rivers they had lost at Fort Henry and Fort Donelson. Grant established his own base of operations only twenty miles away, at Pittsburgh Landing, Tennessee. To the surprise of the Union, Johnston attacked the larger Union force at Shiloh Church on April 6.

The scattered woods and rough terrain around Shiloh turned the battle into a series of brutal fights among desperate groups of scattered men with little coordinated leadership. Johnston, killed leading an attack, was replaced by Beauregard, who succeeded in pushing the Union men back two miles. The Confederates' dominance proved short-lived, however, for

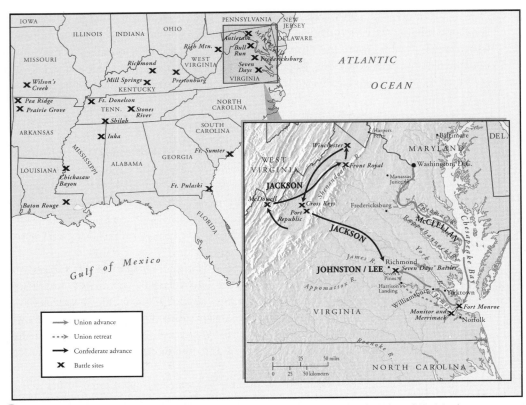

Map 14.3 Eastern Battles of 1862 George McClellan's long-awaited campaign to take Richmond, Virginia, the capital of the Confederacy, began in March of 1862. The vast maneuver unfolded over many months and ended with the brutal stalemate of the Seven Days. Stonewall Jackson's Valley Campaign kept the Union forces divided. View an animated version of this map or related maps at http://history.wadsworth.com/passages2e.

25,000 Northern reinforcements arrived overnight. The Southerners received no new men. The next day saw Grant and his army regain the ground they had lost, driving the Confederates back to Corinth. Though the Southern forces had been badly hurt, the Northern forces were themselves too exhausted and shaken to pursue.

The carnage at Shiloh exceeded anything anyone had ever seen. The bloodiest battle in the hemisphere up to that point, Shiloh exacted a horrible toll: about 1,700 killed and 8,000 wounded on each side. About 2,000 of the wounded men in both the Union and the Confederacy forces would soon die. Newspapers and generals debated the outcome of the battle for months, trying to decide the hero and the loser, but it eventually became clear that the Southern attempt to halt Northern momentum in the Mississippi Valley had failed. Frustrated with McClellan's inertia, Lincoln turned aside criticism of Grant, "I can't spare this man, he fights."

New Orleans

Yet another drama played itself out in New Orleans. There, a Union naval force under David Farragut determined to do what Confederates considered impossible: overwhelm their largest city and largest port from the Gulf. Confederates recalled that the mighty British of 1815 had been unable to take New Orleans and fully expected the same fate to befall the Yankees. The city lay under the protection of two forts claiming 115 guns as well as a river blocked with logs, barges, and thick cables. So safe did they consider New Orleans that Confederate troops abandoned the city to fight at Shiloh, leaving the port protected only by militiamen.

Farragut had his own weapons, however: 20 mortar boats, 17 ships with 523 guns, and 15,000 soldiers. The Union navy pounded the forts for days with the mortars, unsuccessfully. Frustrated, on April 24 Farragut audaciously led his ships, single file, past the forts and past Confederate ships that tried to ram the Union craft or set them on fire with flaming rafts. Once they had run this gauntlet, the Union ships had clear sailing right up to the docks of New Orleans. There, they confronted no resistance as 4,000 Confederate troops withdrew from the city.

Troops under the command of Benjamin Butler occupied New Orleans while Farragut continued to drive up the Mississippi River. He took Baton Rouge and Natchez, but Vicksburg held Farragut off. Riverboats coming from the north soon took Memphis as well, giving the Union control of all the Mississippi River except the area near Vicksburg. Northern forces used the river as a major supply route. Rather than a highway uniting the Upper and Lower South, the Mississippi became a chasm separating one half of the Confederacy from the other.

The Confederate Draft

The end of April, then, seemed to promise the early end to the war that people had expected at its outbreak. Although many of the battles had been close that spring, they all seemed to turn out in favor of the North. The first yearlong enlistments in the Confederate army were running out in April; many soldiers left for home. The Confederate Congress, fearful that its armies would be short of men as the Union stepped up its attacks, decided that it had no choice but to initiate a compulsory draft. All white men between the ages of eighteen and thirty-five were required to fight for three years. If men enlisted or reenlisted within the thirty days following passage of the law, they could choose the unit with which they fought.

Although the Confederacy eventually abolished substitution, a policy that allowed men with enough money to pay a substitute to fight in their place, it still permitted men from many occupations, such as teachers and apothecaries, to claim an exemption from military service. Governors appointed many men to positions in their state governments and militia so that they would be exempted from the draft. In Georgia and North Carolina, state and counties aided the families of poor soldiers by taxing slaves and large property owners.

The Confederacy also exempted one white man for every twenty slaves he supervised in the "twenty negro law." That law, like the draft in general, necessary though it was, divided Southerners more profoundly than anything else in the Civil War. A Mississippi private deserted to return home, refusing to "fight for the rich men while they were at home having a good time."

The Seven Days

"Every blow tells fearfully against the rebellion," a New York newspaper declared at the end of May. "It now requires no very far reaching prophet to predict the end of this struggle." From the viewpoint of the battlefields in Tennessee and Mississippi, the war did indeed seem to be nearing its end. And in Virginia George McClellan's troops, the pride of the Union and 100,000 strong, had pushed their way up the peninsula toward Richmond. By the end of May only five miles separated them from their destination.

Not that it would be easy for the Union troops to take Richmond. The river assaults that had worked so well two months earlier in Tennessee failed in Virginia. The Confederates were able to attack the river gunboats from the heights of Drewry's Bluff. Even the *Monitor* proved ineffectual when faced with an enemy one hundred feet above. Moreover, the Confederates had established imposing defenses around Richmond and concentrated many of their troops in the vicinity.

Defensive positioning proved more important in the American Civil War than in any prior conflict. Defenders gained their advantage from a new kind of weapon: the rifle. A rifle, unlike a musket, used a spiral groove in the barrel to put spin on a bullet, like a football pass, giving the bullet much greater stability and accuracy. A musket had been accurate at only about eighty yards, but a rifle could hit a target at four times that distance. Although the benefits of rifling had long been recognized, it was not until the 1850s that a French inventor, Charles Minie, devised a way to make it possible for a rifled gun to fire without requiring the grooves to be cleaned. Although the rifles still had to be loaded from the end of the barrel, preventing even the most skillful soldiers from firing more than three times a minute, rifles nevertheless made it much more difficult for attacking troops to overwhelm a defense.

Lincoln and McClellan believed that Washington faced a direct threat from Confederate troops in the Shenandoah Valley under the command of the increasingly impressive Stonewall Jackson. For three months in the spring of 1862, Jackson maneuvered his men up and down the valley, creating the impression that his forces were larger than they were and that they could attack anywhere, any time. As a result, the Union divided its forces, depriving McClellan's invasion of tens of thousands of soldiers that would have otherwise been available for the assault on Richmond.

The Union and the Rebel forces tested one another around Richmond in May and June, inflicting heavy casualties in battles that settled nothing. Robert E. Lee replaced Joseph Johnston, wounded in battle, as general of the Confederate forces in Virginia. Lee quickly proved himself aggressive and daring. He almost immediately planned an attack against the larger force under McClellan's command. Lee sent out J. E. B. Stuart, his cavalry leader, who rode all the way around McClellan's troops, reconnoitering their position and stealing their supplies. Stuart reported that part of McClellan's troops were vulnerable to attack. Lee brought Jackson and his men to join in an assault.

The resulting prolonged conflict around Richmond, which became known as the Seven Days' Battles, did not distinguish either side. Thirty thousand men had been killed and wounded. The Confederates' offensive did not work as planned and Jackson failed to carry out his part of the assault. For the North's part, McClellan, though possessing far more troops than his opponents' 90,000, believed himself outnumbered, wiring Lincoln that he faced 200,000 Confederates and "if this [army] is destroyed by overwhelming numbers . . . the responsibility cannot be thrown on my shoulders."

Slavery Under Attack

By the summer of 1862, the war seemed to have reached a stalemate. Both the Union and the Confederacy believed a decisive battle could still win the war. The North took heart because Union ships controlled the coasts and rivers on the perimeter of the South even as Union troops pushed deep into Tennessee and Mississippi. The Confederacy took comfort because vast expanses of rich Southern farmland and millions of productive slaves remained beyond the reach of Union control.

President Lincoln, while detesting slavery personally, feared that a campaign against bondage would divide the North. As the war dragged into its second year, however, even Northerners who did not oppose slavery on moral grounds could see that slavery offered the South a major advantage: slaves in the fields meant more white Southerners on the battlefields.

More important, black Southerners themselves pressed slavery as a problem on the Union armies. Wherever those armies went, slaves fled to the federals as refugees. The Union called the black people who made their way to the Union ranks "contrabands," a word usually used to describe smuggled goods. The term revealed the confusion among white Northerners about the status of the black people in their midst. Although some Union officers returned the slaves to their owners, other officers seized the opportunity to strike against slavery and use former slaves to further their war aims. The slaves "bring much valuable information" and "are acquainted with all the roads, paths, fords," and "haunts of secession spies and traitors."

Northern leaders confronted such issues most directly near Port Royal, South Carolina. When the Union forces overran the Sea Islands along the coast in 1862, the relatively few whites who lived there fled, leaving behind 10,000 slaves. Almost immediately, various groups of Northerners began to vie for the opportunity to reshape Southern society. The Sea Islands claimed some of the largest and richest plantations in the South, growing rare and expensive long-staple cotton. Union leaders felt it crucial that freed slaves prove they would work willingly and effectively. Female abolitionist schoolteachers journeyed down from New England, while men came from New York City and the Northwest to demonstrate that plantations run on the principles of free labor could be both productive and humane.

The former slaves valued the opportunity to learn to read and write and wanted land of their own, but they did not always appreciate lessons from the newcomer whites about

Missionaries at Port Royal

In Union hands since 1861, the Sea Islands of South Carolina attracted slaves from the mainland who joined the 9,000 slaves who remained when their masters fled the federal army. These islands quickly became a testing ground for Northern ideals. Abolitionists quickly realized that these slaves, among the most isolated groups in the South, would prove a test for creating a community to disprove theories of black inability to adapt to a free labor society.

Societies formed in cities such as Boston, New York, and Philadelphia to organize financial and educational support for the newly liberated men and women on the islands. Missionaries and teachers of both genders came to the islands to instruct the newly freed residents in matters both secular and religious. The first group that sailed from New York in March 1862 also brought men to manage the production and sale of cotton, several of whom clashed with the antislavery activists when their interest in a profitable crop exceeded their concern for black welfare. Although eager to seize plots of land to support themselves and their families, many former slaves associated cotton with servitude and refused to plant it. Politicians, ministers, and newspapermen reported the conditions and progress made at Port Royal as a measure of what the end of slavery would mean for blacks and for the South.

Corbis-Bettmann

religion and agriculture. Black people knew how to farm and knew their God. Not only in South Carolina, but wherever the Union army penetrated, officers and civilians sought to control black labor and rich land. Sometimes, federal officials decreed that the freedpeople could sign contracts with whomever they chose—but they had to sign contracts with someone. In other times and places, Union leaders permitted black people to take responsibility for some of the land they had worked as slaves. Some white Northerners proposed seizing land from former slaveholders to give to the former slaves.

General David Hunter, a man of abolitionist sympathies, took advantage of his position in Port Royal in the late spring of 1862 to organize a number of black military units and to declare slavery abolished in South Carolina, Georgia, and Florida. Hunter stated that Union soldiers would not act "as a police force for the protection of property." Lincoln revoked Hunter's proclamation. Lincoln did not envision the immediate emancipation decreed by Hunter, with no compensation to slaveholders and with former slaves living alongside their former masters. Lincoln thought that slavery must end gradually, with payments to the slaveholders for their loss of property. Ideally, Lincoln argued, the former slaves would be colonized beyond the borders of the United States, perhaps in Haiti or Liberia.

Lincoln also resisted those members of his party and his cabinet who thought that black men should be enlisted into the Union army. Such Republicans, often called "Radicals" for their support of black rights, passed laws that forbade Northern commanders to return refugee slaves to their former masters, and they ended (albeit gradually and with compensation) slavery in the District of Columbia.

Many Northern Democrats firmly opposed such expansion of the war's purposes and means, warning that abolition would only embitter and embolden the Confederates. McClellan, a strong opponent of Radical Republicans, believed emancipation would "disintegrate our present armies." Democrats sympathetic to the South, called "Copperheads" by their opponents, marched under the motto "The Constitution as it is and the Union as it was." They wanted slavery to remain in place so that the South would come back into the nation.

Lincoln sought to steer a course between the Radicals and the Copperheads. But in the summer of 1862 he moved closer to an assault on slavery. The Union army had strengthened its position in Kentucky and Missouri, and it no longer appeared that the border states could effectively align themselves with the Confederates. Similarly, Lincoln came to see that the Southern Unionists could not or would not organize effective opposition to the Confederacy from within. Lincoln decided that to win the war he would have to hit slavery. Responding to a Southern Unionist, the president wrote, "This government cannot much longer play a game in which it stakes all, and its enemies stake nothing. Those enemies must understand that they cannot experiment for ten years trying to destroy the government, and if they fail still come back into the Union unhurt."

On July 22, 1862, Lincoln and his cabinet authorized federal military leaders to take whatever secessionist property they needed and to destroy any property that aided the Confederacy. That meant that Union officers could protect the black men and women who fled to Northern camps, using them to work behind the lines. Lincoln decided to wait for a victory on the battlefield before announcing the most dramatic part of his plan: that as of January 1, 1863, he would declare all slaves in areas controlled by the Confederates free. Although this proclamation would free no slaves under Union control in the border states, it ruled out compromise that would end the war and bring the South back into the Union with slavery. Knowing that this announcement would unleash harsh criticism in the North, Lincoln wanted to wait until the North was flush with confidence before he announced this preliminary Emancipation Proclamation. When and where that victory might occur, however, was by no means clear in July of 1862.

Second Manassas and Antietam

Confidence actually ran higher in the Confederacy than in the Union during the second summer of the war. The Union, after all, could draw little solace from McClellan's sluggish performance in the ferocious Seven Days' Battles outside of Richmond in June. Lincoln placed Henry Halleck, who advocated a more aggressive stance toward southern civilians and their slaves, in charge of all Union troops. The president put John Pope, who had been fighting in the West, in charge of the new Army of Virginia. McClellan still commanded troops, but his role had been restricted. Pope issued a series of orders that signaled a new harder tone to the conflict. Troops would forage as needed, no longer guard Southern property, and hold local civilians responsible for damages caused by area guerrillas.

The new Union leaders decided to remove McClellan's troops from the peninsula of Virginia and consolidate them, under the joint command of Pope, with troops from the Shenandoah

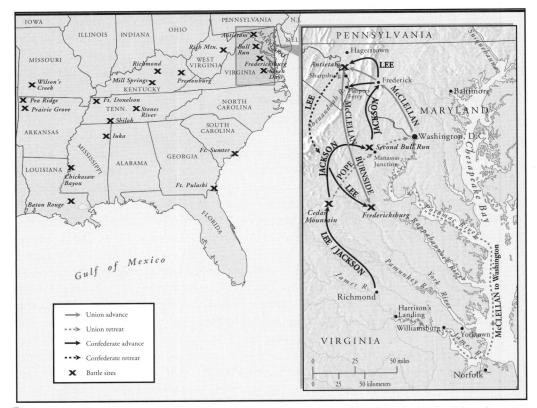

Map 14.4 Campaigns in Virginia and Maryland, 1862 As Union troops moved from the peninsula below Richmond to an area closer to Washington in August, Lee and Jackson used the opportunity to go on the offensive. Over the next several months, they clashed with Union forces at Manassas and Antietam in Maryland. View an animated version of this map or related maps at http://history.wadsworth.com/passages2e.

Valley. The forces began to move from the peninsula in August, creating a temporary opportunity for the Confederacy. Lee decided to attack Pope's troops while McClellan's were withdrawing. He hoped to occupy as much territory as possible, resting and resupplying his troops while complicating Union efforts to unify their forces.

Lee's plan worked better than he could have expected. Stonewall Jackson attacked Pope's men and pillaged a large federal supply depot at Manassas. Pope then fell under attack by James Longstreet's troops, who drove the new Yankee commander back into Washington. With McClellan no longer threatening Richmond and Pope posing no danger to northern Virginia, Lee decided to push into Maryland. He believed that large numbers of Marylanders would rush to the Confederate cause. Lee had another audience in mind as well: England and France. In the wake of Union indecision and defeat in the summer of 1862, leaders in both countries were leaning toward recognition of the Confederacy. A major victory in Northern territory, Lee felt certain, would prove that the South deserved the support of the major powers.

Lee acted so confidently because he knew he would face George McClellan again. On September 17, the two old adversaries fell into battle once more, this time at Antietam Creek, near Sharpsburg, Maryland. The Confederates had 35,000 men to McClellan's 72,000, but the Southerners held the defensive ground. The terrible battle ended in confusion and stalemate. More men were killed, wounded, or declared missing on this day than on any other day in the Civil War: 13,000 for the Confederacy and 12,000 for the Union. Lee had lost nearly a third of his army; McClellan, despite his numerical advantage, had been unable to shatter the enemy.

Neither side could be satisfied with the battle's outcome, but the North made the best of the situation. Lincoln decided that Antietam represented enough of a victory to justify his announcement of the preliminary Emancipation Proclamation. The European powers decided that they would withhold their support for the Confederacy for the time being. The Confederacy decided that it would pull back into Virginia to fight another day.

Things could have turned out very differently at this juncture. Had McClellan destroyed Lee's army, the Confederacy might have given up its claims for independence before slavery had been ended. Had Lee merely held his ground in Virginia after driving McClellan away from Richmond and Pope back into Washington, England and France might have offered mediation—and the North might well have accepted, again without the end of slavery. As it was, however, both the North and the South would fight again and again.

Stalemate

While Northerners and Southerners slaughtered one another in Maryland with little clear advantage gained by either side, Southern forces under the command of Braxton Bragg pushed far into Kentucky, determined to regain ground lost early in the war. Confederates believed that Kentuckians would rush to the Southern flag if given a chance. But Kentuckians had little confidence that the Confederates could prevail in Kentucky and did not want to risk all they had in support of a losing cause. Although the Confederates never suffered sharp defeat in Kentucky, they had too few men to occupy the state, and retreated after the battle of Perryville. Rather than risk losing his army, Bragg pulled his men into a more defensible position in Tennessee.

By the summer and fall of 1862, many men had died to little apparent purpose. Lincoln decided that generals in both the East and the West must be removed; George McClellan and Don Carlos Buell seemed too slow to react. Lincoln replaced Buell with William S. Rosecrans and replaced McClellan with Ambrose E. Burnside, an appealing man uncertain that he was qualified for the job. His doubts proved to be well founded.

In November, Burnside decided to establish a new base for yet another assault on Richmond. He moved his troops to Fredericksburg, Virginia, and launched an attack on a virtually impregnable Confederate position at Marye's Heights. With Southerners able to fire down on them at will from protected positions, over 12,000 Union soldiers were killed, wounded, or missing. Observing the suicidal Union charges, Robert E. Lee remarked to General Longstreet, "It is well that war is so terrible—we should grow too fond of it." At battle's end, both armies remained where they had been at the battle's beginning.

The North fell into mourning, humiliation, and anger at this sacrifice. Officers as well as enlisted men made no secret of their loss of faith in Burnside. Despondent, Lincoln responded to defeat at Fredericksburg, "If there is a worse place than Hell, I am in it." In Tennessee, Rosecrans felt that he had to move against Bragg to demonstrate Union resolve

After the slaughter at Marye's Heights in December 1862, Confederates stripped the bodies of Union soldiers of their boots and uniforms. Here, Northern burial parties inter their dead.

© Stock Montage, Inc.

and power. The two armies clashed on the last day of 1862 at Stones River near Murfrees-boro. The two sides, losing about a third of their men each, fought to a virtual draw.

The winter of 1862–1863 saw the North and the South precariously balanced, both against one another and within their own societies. On the battlefield, the South had made impressive showings at Fredericksburg and at Second Manassas, but the Northern army had held Kentucky and Maryland. The Confederacy still possessed Vicksburg, but Grant and Sherman were planning ways to take the city. Slaves ran to Union armies at every chance. The preliminary Emancipation Proclamation gave the Union effort a new purpose and new credibility with liberals in Europe, but Lincoln faced mounting criticism within his own party and a growing threat from disgruntled Democrats. The North needed victories.

Conclusion

The bloody sacrifice without decisive victory of the Seven Days and Antietam fed disillusionment on both sides. The governments in both the North and the South found themselves the objects of bitter criticism. Military officers squabbled among themselves and with civilian leaders. The only thing people could agree on was that the war would not end soon.

The preceding year and a half had seen events and changes no one could have predicted. Eighteen months after Lincoln had begun his journey to Washington to become president, war had become a way of life. The boundaries between the Union and the Confederacy had been firmly drawn. The governments of both sides had begun to function effectively. The first volunteer units of both armies had been mobilized. Both the South and the North had claimed military victories. The Confederacy recalled the battle at Manassas with pride, whereas the Union took comfort in the steady success of its navy and the capture of New Orleans. The first international crisis, the *Trent* affair, had passed without dragging a major European power into the conflict. But in late 1862 both the North and the South felt that their cause must be clarified and given greater purpose.

RECOMMENDED READINGS

Berlin, Ira, Fields, Barbarado, Miller, Steven F., Reidy, Joseph P., and Rowland, Leslie, eds. *Free at Last: A Documentary History of Slavery, Freedom, and the Civil War,* (1997). A monumental collection of first-hand testimony about emancipation.

Boritt, Gabor. *Why the Civil War Came* (1996). A useful overview of thinking on this much-debated historical topic.

Crofts, Daniel W. *Reluctant Confederates: Upper South Unionists in the Secession Crisis* (1989). Analyzes the crucial border states with keen insight.

Crowley, Robert, ed. *With My Face to the Enemy: Perspectives on the Civil War* (2001). Offers interpretations from leading historians of the conflict.

Eicher, David J. *The Longest Night: A Military History of the Civil War* (2001). The best one-volume military history of the war.

Freehling, William W. *The South vs. the South: How Anti-Confederate Southerners Shaped the Course of the Civil War* (2001). Serves as a synthesis of various forms of Unionism by black and white Southerners.

Jones, Howard. *The Union in Peril: The Crisis over British Intervention in the Civil War* (1992). Provides a fresh interpretation of a critical episode.

McPherson, James M. *Battle Cry of Freedom: The Civil War Era* (1988). Stands as the best one-volume account of the Civil War.

Paludan, Phillip Shaw. *A People's Contest: The Union and the Civil War, 1861–1865* (1988). Paints a compelling portrait of the North during war.

Royster, Charles. *The Destructive War: William Tecumseh Sherman, Stonewall Jackson, and the Americans* (1991). Offers an original and disturbing meditation on war.

Thomas, Emory M. *The Confederate Nation, 1861–1865* (1979). The standard account.

Additional resources, exercises, and Internet links related to this chapter are available on the American Passages Web site: http://history.wadsworth.com/ayerscompact2/

15

Blood and Freedom
1863–1867

The Civil War enveloped the entire nation, homefront and battlefield alike. The outcome of a battle could win an election or trigger a riot, while events at home affected the leaders' decisions of when and where to fight. In the North, the strong political opposition to Abraham Lincoln and his policies exerted a constant pressure on his conduct of the war. In the South, slaves abandoned plantations and white families' hardships led soldiers to rethink their loyalties.

The outcome of the Civil War was not predetermined by the North's advantages of population and resources. Deep into the war, events could have taken radically different turns. Slavery might have survived the conflict had the Confederacy won at particular junctions or, more likely, had the United States lost the will to push the devastating war to the South's full surrender and the immediate abolition of slavery. Even with the war's end the future course of the nation remained in doubt as Americans confronted the greatest rupture in their history.

People at War: Spring 1863

Both Northerners and Southerners expected the spring of 1863 to bring the climax of the Civil War. Much had been decided, organized, and mobilized over the preceding two years. Yet while generals and armies determined the result of battles, the women, slaves, workers, bureaucrats, draft dodgers, and politicians behind the lines would determine the outcome of the war.

Life in the Field

Soldiers eventually got used to the miseries of sleeping on the ground, poorly cooked food, driving rain, and endless mud. They learned to adapt to gambling, drinking, cursing, and prostitution, either by succumbing to the temptations or by steeling their resolve against them. They could toughen themselves to the intermittent mails and the arrival of bad news from home. Men recalled their initial mortification and humiliation of discovering the entire company infested with lice, a shame that turned to indifference when the sharper horror of wounds descended. Over time, veterans could even learn to absorb the deaths of men with whom they had shared so much.

CHRONOLOGY

1863

January	Second Emancipation Proclamation
March	Union Congress passes Conscription Act • Confederate Congress passes Impressment Act
April	Bread riot in Richmond
May	Culmination of Lee's victory over Hooker at Chancellorsville
June	Lee's army crosses Potomac
July	Union victory at Gettysburg • Vicksburg surrenders to Grant • Port Hudson surrenders to Union • Lee retreats across Potomac into Virginia • New York City draft riots • Black troops fight at Fort Wagner, South Carolina
October	Grant assumes control of Union forces in West
November	Lincoln's Gettysburg Address • Union victory at Chattanooga

1864

March	Grant assumes command of all Union forces
May	Battle of the Wilderness in Virginia
July	Union failure at Battle of the Crater near Petersburg
September	Sherman captures Atlanta • Sheridan's victories in Shenandoah Valley
November	Lincoln reelected president • Beginning of Sherman's march from Atlanta to the Atlantic

1865

February	Columbia, South Carolina, burned; Confederates evacuate Charleston
March	Congress creates Bureau of Refugees, Freedmen, and Abandoned Lands (Freedmen's Bureau) • Lincoln's second inauguration • Confederate army authorizes recruitment of slaves into army
April	Fall of Richmond to Union • Lee surrenders to Grant at Appomattox Court House • Lincoln assassinated
May	Jefferson Davis captured • Former Confederate states hold constitutional conventions through December; pass "black codes" • African Americans hold conventions in South
December	Thirteenth Amendment to Constitution ratified, abolishing slavery

1866

February	Johnson vetoes Freedmen's Bureau bill
April	Congress passes Civil Rights Act and Freedmen's Bureau renewal over Johnson's veto
May	Riots in New Orleans and Memphis
June	Congress approves Fourteenth Amendment • Ku Klux Klan formed

1867

March	Congress passes Reconstruction Act and Tenure of Office Act Constitutional conventions in Southern states
August	Johnson dismisses Secretary of War Stanton, triggering impeachment proceedings • First elections in South under Reconstruction Act

But the most stalwart of soldiers could not adapt to the constant threat of diseases such as diarrhea, dysentery, typhoid, malaria, measles, diphtheria, and scarlet fever. As bloody as the battles were, disease killed twice as many men as died from the guns of the enemy. Soldiers feared disease and many shared a New England private's opinion, "I tell you there is no *honor* in a man's *sickness,* but there is about a *wound.*" Many doctors of the Civil War

Ill and injured men filled the ground around the surgical and hospital tents where horrifying surgery often awaited them.

© Bettmann/Corbis

era used the same instruments of surgery on soldier after soldier, unwittingly spreading disease and infection. After every battle, screams filled the night as surgeons sawed off legs and arms, feet and hands, in often vain hopes of stopping gangrene.

Purposes

The North fought for ideals of union and democracy; the South fought for ideals of self-determination. Yet soldiers acted courageously not only because they believed in the official political purposes for which they were fighting, but also because they wanted to be admired by the people at home, because they wanted to do their part for their comrades, because they wanted to bring the war to a quicker end, and because they grew to hate the enemy.

Many men fought alongside their brothers, uncles, cousins. A steady stream of letters flowed back and forth between the units and the families and neighbors back home. Gossip, praise, and condemnation flourished. Any soldier who planned to return home knew that his deeds in the war would live with him the rest of his life. As a result, even fearful or halfhearted soldiers might throw themselves into battle to demonstrate their courage. A Southern mother, far from wanting her son home after three years of war, condemned his wrangling of a medical furlough. "You are bound by the duties of your position . . . Your time belongs to your Country." He was dead from wounds two months later.

Whereas about three-fifths of Civil War soldiers were over twenty-one at the age of enlistment, the largest single group of soldiers was eighteen. For those who passed the birthdays of their late teens or early twenties on the battlefields, the transition to manhood became inseparable from the war. A soldier from Illinois proudly wrote his family that "this war has made a man of your son." To be manly meant more than the simple ability to inflict violence on the enemy. It meant pride, responsibility, loyalty, and obedience. Every battle became a test of manhood, which had to be proven every time it was challenged under fire.

Courage developed, too, out of hatred. People on both sides spread the worst stories and rumors about one another. Newspapers printed exaggerated or fabricated atrocity reports about the enemy. While many were repelled by battlefield carnage, others took satisfaction. One Confederate artillery officer admired the "severed limbs, decapitated bodies, and mutilated remains" at Fredericksburg and declared that it did "my soul good" to ride over the bodies of the federal dead. Union troops also hardened their attitudes. A Wisconsin soldier informed his fiancée that his unit wanted to fight until "we kill them all off and cleanse the country." The longer the war went on, the more people felt they had to hate one another to justify so much bloodshed.

The sermons men heard in the camps told them they were fighting on the side of the right. The Old Testament afforded rich imagery and compelling stories of violence inflicted for good causes. Many Americans believed that God enacted His will directly in human affairs. As the war ground on, the leaders, the soldiers, and the civilians of both sides came to feel that events were more than the product of human decision or even courage. Surely, they told themselves, so much suffering and sacrifice had to be for a larger purpose.

The Problems of the Confederate Government

Convinced that greedy merchants were holding supplies of flour until prices rose even higher, poor women in Richmond, in the spring of 1863, broke open the stores of merchants accused of hoarding the precious staple, taking what they needed. After President Davis climbed on a wagon and threw coins at the crowd, he ordered a militia unit to prepare to fire on them. The threat of violence and of arrest, as well as the promise of free supplies, broke up the riot, but similar events occurred in several other Southern cities such as Atlanta, Columbus, and Augusta. No one could tell when even larger riots might erupt again. Fearing the consequences for morale, military officers in Richmond ordered the press and telegraph office to suppress news of the riot, but word of the riot soon spread.

The rioters were not the only ones who took what they needed. Confederate officers in the field forced reluctant farmers to accept whatever prices the army offered, in an increasingly worthless currency. In the spring of 1863, the Confederate government attempted to curb the worst abuses of this practice in the Impressment Act. If a farmer did not think the prices he or she received were fair, the case could be appealed before local authorities. In practice, however, this cumbersome system failed. Farmers hid their produce from officers and resented it when they were forced to sell. North Carolina's governor denounced impressments to the War Department in Richmond: "If God Almighty had yet in store another plague . . . I am sure it must have been a regiment or so of half-disciplined Confederate cavalry."

The Southern government could not afford to lose civilian support. Although the absence of political parties originally appeared to be a sign of the South's consensus, that absence eventually undermined what original consensus the Confederacy had enjoyed. Jefferson Davis, without a party mechanism to discipline those who spoke out against him, could not remove enemies from office. Davis's own vice president, Alexander Stephens, became a persistent and outspoken critic of the Confederate president's "tyrannical" policies, actively undermining support for Davis and even allying with avowed enemies of Davis and his policies.

The Confederate government faced a fundamental dilemma. The whole point of secession had been to move political power closer to localities, protecting slavery in particular and self-determination in general. The government of the Confederacy, however, had to centralize power. If the armies were to be fed and clothed, if diplomats were to make a plausible case for the Confederacy's nationhood, if soldiers were to be mobilized, then the Confederate government had to exercise greater power than its creators had expected or intended. Jefferson Davis continually struggled with this tension. For every Southerner who considered Davis too weak, another considered the president dangerously powerful.

The Northern Homefront

In the North, the war heightened the strong differences between the Democrats and the Republicans. The Democrats won significant victories in congressional elections in the fall and winter of 1862, testifying to the depth and breadth of the opposition to Lincoln and his conduct of the war. Wealthy businessmen were eager to reestablish trade with their former Southern partners, whereas Irish immigrants wanted to end the risk of the draft and competition from freed slaves. Many citizens of Ohio, Indiana, and Illinois, whose families had come from the South, wanted to renew the Southern connections that had been broken by the war.

The Union passed its Conscription Act in March of 1863 because disease, wounds, and desertion had depleted the ranks of soldiers faster than they could be replaced. When drafted, a man could appear for duty, hire a substitute to fight in his place, or simply pay a fee of $300 directly to the government. Poorer communities resented the wealthy who could avoid service. Demonstrations broke out in Chicago, Pennsylvania mining towns, rural

Black men had called for their inclusion in the U.S. Army from the beginning of the war. In the spring of 1863, the U.S. Colored Troops were formed and over 180,000 African American men fought for the Union over the next two years.

Vermont, and Boston. To avoid mob violence, state and federal governments often paid bounties—signing bonuses—to those who volunteered. More than a few men took the bounties and then promptly deserted and moved to another locality to claim another bounty.

The opposition to the Lincoln government raised crucial issues. With the North claiming to fight for liberty, what limitations on freedom of speech and protest could it enforce? A Democratic congressman from Ohio, Clement Vallandigham, tested those limits in the spring of 1863. Hating both secessionists and abolitionists, Vallandigham refused to obey a general's orders to stop criticizing the Lincoln administration. He was arrested, tried before a military court, and sentenced to imprisonment for the rest of the war. Lincoln was dismayed by these events. He commuted Vallandigham's sentence, sending him to the Confederates in Tennessee, hoping to make Vallandigham appear a Southern sympathizer rather than a martyr to the cause of free speech. Vallandigham quickly escaped to Canada, however, where he continued his criticisms. Ohio Democrats defiantly nominated Vallandigham for governor in the elections to be held in the fall of 1863. If things continued to go badly for the Union, who knew what kind of success a critic of Lincoln might find?

☛ African American Soldiers

Though Northern civilian and military leaders remained deeply divided and ambivalent about black freedom, it became clear to everyone that black men could be of great value to the Union. In May 1863, the War Department created the U.S. Colored Troops. African American men from across the North rushed to enlist as soon as they heard of the new black regiments.

At first, black recruits found themselves restricted to noncombat roles and a lower rate of pay: ten dollars a month versus the thirteen dollars a month and three-fifty clothing allowance given to white soldiers. Black men, though eager to serve, protested that they could not support their families on such amounts. African Americans knew, and coveted, the rights and privileges of other Americans. They wrote petitions and appealed to higher authorities, often in the language of the Declaration of Independence and the Constitution.

Confederate officials who expected black soldiers to make reluctant or cowed fighters soon discovered otherwise. In May of 1863, two black regiments stormed, seven times, a heavily fortified Confederate installation at Port Hudson, Louisiana. Soon thereafter, black soldiers found themselves on the other side of the barricades. At Milliken's Bend, Louisiana, they fought Confederates hand-to-hand. Northern newspapers echoed the words of praise from generals in the field: "No troops could be more determined or more daring."

Encouraged and frequently supported financially by their communities, African American men in the North went to the recruiting tables in great numbers. Frederick Douglass, the leading spokesman for black Americans, celebrated the enlistments: "Once let the black man get upon his person the brass letters, *U.S.;* let him get an eagle on his button, and a musket on his shoulder, and bullets in his pocket, and there is no power on earth which can deny that he has earned the right to citizenship in the United States." From Rhode Island to Ohio, black troops prepared to head south.

The Battlefields of Summer: 1863

Everything seemed in place for a climactic culmination of the war in the summer of 1863. The Union had almost severed the western half of the Confederacy from the eastern; the federal army had penetrated deep into Tennessee and stood on the threshold of Georgia. On the other hand, the Confederate army had toughened itself to its disadvantages and learned to make the most of the advantages it enjoyed.

Vicksburg and Chancellorsville

Union leaders needed all the help they could get in early 1863. Grant and Sherman remained frustrated in their goal of seizing Vicksburg; Rosecrans faced Bragg in Tennessee; Lee's army had yet to be decisively defeated despite the men, resources, and determination thrown into battle against him. Lee would face General Joseph Hooker, whom Lincoln had chosen to replace Ambrose Burnside. Throughout the spring, "Fighting Joe" Hooker energized his men and repaired some of the damage to morale and readiness inflicted at Fredericksburg. But no one knew if he would be able to handle Lee.

The Northern public was especially impatient with Grant and Sherman. Grant knew the delays threatened his command. Vicksburg, heavily fortified by both geography and the Confederates, seemed most vulnerable to attack from the southeast, but to get there Grant would have to find a way to move his men across the Mississippi River without landing them in swamps. Throughout the long wet winter, Grant had tried one experiment after another, including digging canals. Nothing worked.

Grant finally decided on a bold move: he would run a flotilla of gunboats and barges past Vicksburg under the cover of night to ferry his men across the Mississippi south of the city, where the land was better. The guns of Vicksburg stood two hundred feet above the river, ready to fire down on any passing craft, but the Union men covered their ships' boilers with sacks of grain and bales of cotton to protect them from the shelling. Most of the boats made it through. Grant had Sherman create a diversion, confusing the Confederates, and then fer-

Map 15.1 Vicksburg After months of frustration, Ulysses S. Grant and William T. Sherman found a way to attack Vicksburg from the south and east. Following great struggle, the Union generals were able to take the city on July 4, 1863. View an animated version of this map or related maps at http://history.wadsworth.com/ayerscompact2/.

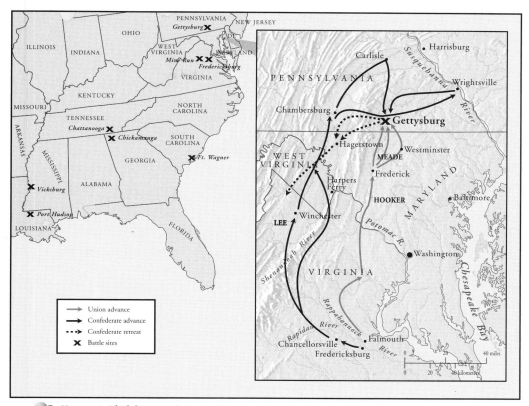

Map 15.2 Virginia, 1863 The battle of Chancellorsville, not far from Fredericksburg, was a great victory for the Confederates. But it marked just the opening stage of a long summer of fighting that would culminate at Gettysburg two months later. In that battle, the Confederates sorely missed General Stonewall Jackson, accidentally killed by his own troops at Chancellorsville.
View an animated version of this map or related maps at http://history.wadsworth.com/ayerscompact2/.

ried his entire army across the Mississippi. Grant's army remained vulnerable, cut off from his allies and his major supply base, but by mid-May, Grant had fought four battles, cost the South 8,000 dead and wounded, marched two hundred miles, and pinned 30,000 Confederates within Vicksburg's fortifications.

In the same week Grant made his landing near Vicksburg, Hooker began his attack on Lee, still based in Fredericksburg. Hooker commanded 130,000 men. Unlike Burnside, however, Hooker intended to outsmart Lee rather than try to overwhelm him with numbers. A large Union force would sweep around Lee and attack him from behind, even as another force attacked from the front. To keep from being bottled up in Fredericksburg, Lee would have to emerge from his well-entrenched defensive position. Lee met this bold move with an even bolder one. He would divide his forces and send Stonewall Jackson to attack Hooker's men from the rear, outflanking Hooker's own flanking maneuver.

On May 2, Jackson assaulted Hooker's troops near Chancellorsville. The outnumbered Confederates defeated the surprised and indecisive Hooker, achieving a major victory. Southern jubilation, though, ended the very night of this triumph, for nervous Confederate soldiers accidentally shot Stonewall Jackson while he surveyed the scene near the front lines. The surgeons removed his arm that evening and hoped that he might live.

While Jackson lay in his tent, fading in and out of consciousness, Lee managed to contain another assault on Fredericksburg and to push the Union troops away from their positions. The losses had once again been staggering—13,000 casualties, roughly 22 percent of the army—but Lee had overcome a larger opponent. After the last battles quieted, however, Jackson died. His death took with it Lee's most trusted general. Many on both sides shared the opinion of a New York paper: "Richmond papers scarcely exaggerate when they say the Confederacy could better have lost fifty thousand men!"

Gettysburg

Despite his victory at Chancellorsville, Lee recognized that the Confederacy was in trouble. Rosecrans still threatened to break through Tennessee into Georgia, Grant clawed his way closer to Vicksburg, and the Union blockade drew an ever tighter net around the coast. Some of his generals urged Lee to rush with his troops to Tennessee to defend the center of the Confederacy and pull Grant away from Vicksburg. But Lee decided that his most effective move would be to invade the North again, taking the pressure off Virginia and disheartening the Union. A successful strike into the North might even yet persuade Britain and France to recognize the Confederacy and give heart to Peace Democrats in the North.

In early June, Lee began to move up through the Shenandoah Valley into southern Pennsylvania with 75,000 men. Hooker seemed confused. When, after a minor dispute, Hooker offered his resignation to Lincoln, the president quickly accepted and put General George Meade in charge. Meade had to decide how best to stop the greatest threat the Confederate army had yet posed to the North. Washington and Baltimore lay in danger, along with the cities, towns, and farms of Pennsylvania. There, the Confederate troops enjoyed taking food and livestock from the rich land. Free blacks and fugitive slaves were also seized and forced south into slavery.

Although Lee and his men moved unchecked across the Potomac and deep into Pennsylvania, they found themselves in a dangerous situation. Lee had permitted Jeb Stuart's cavalry, his "eyes," to range widely from the main army; as a result, the Confederates had little idea where the Union army was or what moves it was making. For their part, Meade and his fellow officers decided to pursue Lee, but not too aggressively, looking for a likely time and place to confront the enemy.

On June 30, units from the Confederacy and the Union stumbled over one another at a small town neither side knew or cared much about: Gettysburg. On July 1, they began to struggle for the best defensive position near the town, fighting over the highest and most protected land. It appeared at first that the Southerners had the better of the first day's battle, but as the smoke cleared both sides could see that late in the day the Union army had consolidated itself on the most advantageous ground. Meade's men, after fierce fighting at the ends of their line, occupied a fishhook-shaped series of ridges and hills that permitted them to protect their flanks. The second day saw the Confederates slowly mobilize their forces for assaults on those positions and launch attacks late in the afternoon. The resulting battles in the peach orchard, the wheat field, Little Round Top, and the boulder-strewn area known as the Devil's Den proved horrific—with 35,000 men dead or wounded—but left the Union in control of the high ground.

Despite the Union's superior position, Lee decided on a frontal attack the next day. The Confederates hoped their artillery would soften the middle of the Union lines. The Confederates did not realize how little damage their guns had done until well-entrenched Union troops decimated waves of an attack led by George E. Pickett. Only a few Southern men made it to the stone wall that protected the Northerners, and even those Confederates quickly fell. It proved a disastrous three days for the Confederacy, which lost 23,000 men through death or wounds, about a third of its entire force. While the Union lost similar numbers of men, it had more to lose. The Northerners and their new general had fought a defensive battle; the Southern side, short on supplies and men, had gambled on an aggressive assault. Elation swept the North. "The glorious success of the Army of the Potomac has electrified all," a Northerner exulted. In the wake of Chancellorsville and Lee's apparently effortless invasion of Pennsylvania, he admitted, many Northerners "did not believe the enemy could be whipped."

The next morning, a thousand miles away, Vicksburg surrendered to Ulysses S. Grant. Unlike Gettysburg, where the battle had been fought in a place no one considered strategically important, Vicksburg held enormous tactical and psychological importance. It had been the symbol of Confederate doggedness and Union frustration. After six weeks of siege, after six weeks of near starvation behind the Confederate defenses, Vicksburg fell. The Mississippi River now divided the Confederacy while it tied the Union to the Gulf of Mexico.

Some Southerners, including Jefferson Davis, did not perceive Gettysburg as a defeat. In their eyes, Lee and his men had pushed deep into the Union, inflicted heavy losses, and damaged Northern morale without being trapped there. The losses at Gettysburg did embolden westerners to increase their complaints against the Confederate government's apparent fixation on the eastern theater. "Of what earthly use is this 'raid' of Lee's army into [the North], in violation of all the principles of war? Is it going to end the struggle, take Washington, or save the Mississippi Valley?"

Northerners at the time often agreed that Gettysburg had not been a decisive Union victory, pronouncing themselves more frustrated than satisfied with Meade, who had not destroyed Lee's army despite his greater numbers. During the Confederate retreat to Virginia, the Southerners found themselves caught between a swollen Potomac River and pursuing federal troops. Meade, his army exhausted and weakened, chose not to fight against the defenses Lee's men hurriedly put up against their pursuers. Meade could not know that the condition of the Southern troops was even worse than his own. Fortunately for the Confederates, the river soon calmed enough that they were able to escape back into Virginia.

The New York City Draft Riots

On the very day that Lee struggled across the Potomac to safety, riots broke out in New York City. Northern working people held complicated feelings about the war. Many of those who labored in the North's factories, mines, farms, and railroads had come to the United States in the last few years. These people, mostly Irish and Germans, volunteered in large numbers to fight for the Union cause. Between 20 to 25 percent of the Union Army consisted of immigrants, the great majority of them volunteers.

Despite their patriotism for their adopted country, many of the immigrants viewed black Americans with dread and contempt. Urban labor organizations divided over Lincoln's election and over the response to secession. Many Catholic Irishmen, almost all of them Democrats, proclaimed that they had no quarrel with white Southerners and that they resented the federal government's draft. The obvious effect of inflation on the wages of workers created strong resentments as well. Working people sneered at those men who had enough money to hire substitutes to fight in their place. Three hundred dollars, after all, constituted half a year's wage for a workingman.

Irish immigrants despaired at the losses among Irish-American units in the field. When their regiments were decimated at Fredericksburg, Gettysburg, and elsewhere, Irish people began to wonder if commanders valued their lives as highly as those of the native-born. When word came, just as the draft lottery was to take place in New York City on July 11, 1863, of the 23,000 men lost at Gettysburg, the fury of working people rose. On July 13, it exploded. Mobs began by assaulting draft officials, then turned their anger on any man who looked rich enough to have hired a substitute, then on pro-Lincoln newspapers and abolitionists' homes. They assaulted any African Americans they encountered on the streets, burning an orphanage, whipping men and women, and hanging victims from city lampposts. Lincoln was sickened by accounts of the riot and a city editor despaired, "Great God! What is this nation coming to?"

The police struggled for three days to control the riot. Eventually, troops (including all-Irish units) rushed from the battlefields of Pennsylvania to aid the police. The troops fired into the rioters; over a hundred people died and another 300 were injured. The working people got some of what they wanted: more welfare relief, exemptions from the draft for those whose families would have no other means of support, and an exodus of black people who feared for their lives.

Riots in New York City were triggered by an impending draft lottery and by news from Gettysburg that told of heavy Union losses there. Black Americans suffered the most from the riots.

Ironically, a few days after the New York draft riots, scores of black troops died during a bold nighttime assault on Fort Wagner near Charleston, South Carolina. Despite the bravery of the African Americans, the assault failed. The Confederates made a point of burying the African American soldiers in a mass grave along with their white officer, Robert Gould Shaw, intending to insult him and his memory. Instead, they elevated him to a Northern martyr. The *Atlantic Monthly* marked a change in Northern attitudes towards black soldiers: "Through the cannon smoke of that dark night, the manhood of the colored race shines before many eyes that would not see."

Chickamauga

After Gettysburg, Vicksburg, and the New York riots in July, events slowed until September, when Union General William Rosecrans left Chattanooga, near the Georgia border, and began moving toward Atlanta. His opponent, Braxton Bragg, hoped to entice Rosecrans into dividing his forces so that they could be cut off. The armies confronted one another at Chickamauga Creek—a Cherokee name meaning "river of death." The Confederates took advantage of Union mistakes on the heavily wooded battlefield, inflicting harrowing damage and driving Rosecrans back into Chattanooga. The Union troops were trapped there, the Confederates looming over them on Lookout Mountain and Missionary Ridge, with few routes of escape and limited supplies. The Northerners had gone from a position of apparent advantage to one of desperation.

Lincoln, judging Rosecrans "confused and stunned" by the battle at Chickamauga, used this opportunity to put Grant in charge of all Union armies between the Appalachian Mountains and the Mississippi River. In the fall of 1863, Grant traveled to Chattanooga, where Sherman joined him from Mississippi and Hooker came from Virginia.

The Gettysburg Address

The North's victories in the summer of 1863 aided Lincoln's popularity. The draft riots in New York City damaged the reputations of Democrats, whereas the bravery of black soldiers on the battlefields of Louisiana and South Carolina led white Northerners, particularly Union soldiers, to rethink some of their prejudices. In the fall of 1863, the Republicans won major victories in Pennsylvania and Ohio. Lincoln determined to make the most of these heartening events.

When Lincoln received an invitation to speak at the dedication of the cemetery at Gettysburg on November 19, he saw it as a chance to impart a sense of direction and purpose to the Union cause. The event had not been planned with him in mind and the president was not even the featured speaker. Edward Everett, a scholar and famed lecturer, had been asked weeks before to give the main address. But Lincoln recognized that a battlefield offered the most effective backdrop for the things he wanted to say.

Burial crews had been laboring for weeks on the Gettysburg battlefield. Thousands of horse carcasses had been burned; thousands of human bodies had been hastily covered with a thin layer of soil. Pennsylvania purchased seventeen acres and hired a specialist in rural cemetery design to lay out the burial plots so that no state would be offended by the location or amount of space devoted to its fallen men. Only about a third of the reburials had taken place when Lincoln arrived; caskets remained stacked at the station.

Lincoln, contrary to legend, did not dash off his speech on the back of an envelope. He had reworked and polished it for several days. The "remarks," as the program put it, lasted three minutes. Lincoln used those minutes to maximum effect. He said virtually nothing about the details of the scene surrounding the 20,000 people at the ceremony. Neither did he mention slavery directly. Instead, he spoke of equality as the fundamental purpose of the war. He called for a "new birth of freedom."

Lincoln was attempting to shift the purpose of the war from Union for Union's sake to Union for freedom's sake. He sought to salvage something from the deaths of the 50,000 men at Gettysburg. Democratic newspapers rebuked Lincoln for his claim, arguing that white soldiers had "too much self-respect to declare that negroes were their equals." But other Northerners accepted Lincoln's exhortation as the definition of their purpose. They might not believe that blacks deserved to be included as full participants in a government of, by, and for "the people," but they did believe that the Union fought for liberty broadly conceived. As battles and years went by, the words of the Gettysburg Address would gain force and resonance.

Just four days after Lincoln's speech, Grant gave the North new reason to believe its ideals might triumph. On November 23, Grant's men overwhelmed the Confederates on Lookout Mountain outside Chattanooga; two days later, Union soldiers accomplished the improbable task of fighting their way up Missionary Ridge because Confederate artillery could not reach opponents coming up directly from below. The Union, now in control of Kentucky and Tennessee, had a wide and direct route into Georgia. A clerk in the Confederate War Department reflected on the year's reverses: "calamity . . . utter ruin. Unless something is done . . . we are irretrievably gone."

England and France finally determined in late 1863 that they would not try to intervene in the American war. First Britain, then France detained or sold to foreign powers warships intended for the Confederacy. The Northern public, encouraged by events on the battlefield, supported Republican candidates in the congressional elections of 1863 more vigorously than had seemed possible just a few months before.

The Winter of Discontent: 1863–1864

The battles of the summer had been horrific. Both sides held their victories close to their hearts and brooded over their losses. The resolve and fury of summertime faded into the bitterness and bickering of winter. As the cycle rolled around again, people steeled themselves for a final push.

Politics North and South

Lincoln hoped to end the war as soon as possible, using persuasion as well as fighting to entice white Southerners back into the national fold. In early December 1863, Lincoln issued his proclamation of amnesty and reconstruction. To those who would take an oath of loyalty to the Union, Lincoln promised a full pardon and the return of all property other than slaves. Though he excluded Confederate leaders and high officers from this offer, Lincoln tried to include as many white Southern men as possible. As soon as 10 percent of the number of voters in 1860 had sworn their loyalty to the Union, he decreed, the Southerners could begin forming new state governments. Education and apprenticeship programs would aid former slaves in the transition to full freedom. He did not provide for African American participation in the new governments of the South.

Two factors worked against acceptance of Lincoln's policy. First, Northern Republicans and much of the public overestimated the extent and depth of Southern Unionist sentiment after years of war and occupation. Second, even in areas under federal control such as Tennessee and Kentucky, guerrilla bands and raiders terrorized the local population. Elections in parts of Tennessee were blocked by irregulars. "The people are warned . . . not to hold such an Election under pain of being Arrested and Carried South for trial," one observer reported. Civilians were often caught between threats. Those who failed to aid Union forces were perceived as "enemies of mankind" with "the rights due to pirates and robbers," whereas those who actively aided the federals were liable to find crops trampled, barns burned, and vigilante justice enacted by neighbors and guerrillas.

Abolitionists and their allies attacked Lincoln's reconstruction plan as far too lenient to the Rebel masters and not helpful enough for the former slaves. In the Wade-Davis bill of February 1864, Republican congressmen attempted to inflict more stringent conditions on former Confederates and offer more help to former slaves. They wanted to use the power of the national government to enforce a standard set of laws across the South and to require 50 percent, rather than 10 percent, of the population to swear the loyalty oath, an oath of past as well as future loyalty. They feared that too weak a plan of reconstruction would permit former slaveowners and Confederates to negate much of what the war might win. Congressmen and Secretary of the Treasury Salmon P. Chase worked behind the scenes in opposition to Lincoln's plan. With an eye toward the upcoming election and the need to entice Arkansas and Louisiana to rejoin the Union, Lincoln refused to sign the Wade-Davis bill.

Although Jefferson Davis did not have to worry about his own reelection in late 1863—the Confederacy had established the presidential term at six years—he did have to worry about congressional elections. They did not go well: 41 of the new 106 representatives expressly opposed Davis and his policies, while he held only a slight majority in the Senate. Just as Northern Democrats called for compromise and peace, so did some Southerners. When Davis took a hands-off policy, he was criticized for doing too little. When he tried to assert more control, he found himself called "despotic" by his own vice president. Editors savaged Davis as responsible for the South's worsening fortunes: "Had the people dreamed that Mr. Davis would carry all his chronic antipathies, his bitter prejudices, his puerile partialities, and his doting favoritisms into the Presidential chair, they would never have allowed him to fill it." The Confederacy stumbled through the winter and into the spring of 1864, desperately watching for signs that the North might be losing heart.

Prisons

Early in the Civil War, both sides had exchanged prisoners of war rather than spending men and resources to maintain prisons. Such arrangements worked well enough into 1863, but then things began to break down. The Confederates decreed that any former slave captured would be executed or re-enslaved, not taken prisoner. The Union, as a matter of principle, refused to participate in any exchanges so long as this policy remained in effect. Prisoners began piling up on both sides, and stories of mistreatment became more frequent and more horrifying.

Northerners who heard of the Confederate camp at Andersonville, Georgia, became livid. The camp was built early in 1864 when the Confederates decided to move prisoners from Richmond. Not only would prisoners be less likely to be rescued by Northern troops moving south, but they could more easily be supplied by railroad away from the heavy fighting in Virginia. The camp, built for 10,000 men in an open, partly swampy field, soon became overcrowded; it held 33,000 by August. Gangs of Northern soldiers controlled

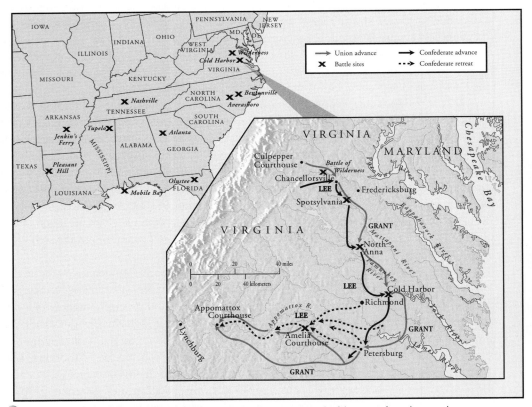

Map 15.3 Grant Against Lee in Virginia The two most important generals of the war confronted one another at one brutal battle after another between May 1864 and April 1865.

View an animated version of this map or related maps at http://history.wadsworth.com/ayerscompact2/.

daily life within the prison, routinely beating and robbing new arrivals. Of the 45,000 men eventually held at Andersonville, 13,000 died. The camp's commander, Colonel Henry Wirz, was the only Confederate official executed for war crimes after the war.

Even higher proportions died at smaller camps in North Carolina. Although Confederates held in Northern prisons were better supplied, even there, death rates reached as high as 24 percent with rations often short and men reduced to eating rats. Overall, about 16 percent of Northern soldiers died in prison, 12 percent of Southerners. Many in the North criticized Lincoln for refusing to reinstitute exchanges, but Lincoln would not sacrifice the former slaves. Moreover, he knew that exchanges helped the soldier-starved Confederacy more than they did the North.

Union Resolve

In March 1864, Lincoln gave new direction and purpose to the Union effort by putting Ulysses S. Grant in charge of all Northern forces. Grant and Lincoln agreed that the Union had to use its superiority in materiel, manpower, and navy to attack the Confederacy on every front at once, forcing the South to decide what territory it would sacrifice. While Grant would fight in Virginia, Lincoln left William T. Sherman in charge in Chattanooga. Sherman would attack the young railroad center of Atlanta, cutting the Gulf South off from the Upper South. The loss of Atlanta would chop the Confederacy into pieces too small to resist the Northern army.

In retrospect, the events of 1864 may appear anticlimactic. The Confederates seemed to face overwhelming odds. Yet Southerners recognized that everything turned around holding the Northerners off until the presidential election in the North. If the Southerners could inflict enough damage on the Union army, Northerners might elect someone willing to bring the war to an end through compromise. The Confederates knew, too, that the three-year terms of the most experienced veterans in the Union army expired in 1864. More than half of those veterans chose to leave the army, even though the war was not over. They would be replaced with younger, less seasoned soldiers. The Confederates also realized that Grant, new to his command, would be confronting Robert E. Lee, who was fighting with an experienced army. All things considered, it was by no means clear in 1864 that the Union would win in Virginia or win the war.

African Americans played an increasingly large role in Union plans, for over 180,000 black soldiers enlisted just when the North needed them most. By the spring of 1864, the means of recruitment, training, and pay for these soldiers had become well established. The Confederates, however, refused to recognize the same rules of warfare for black soldiers that they acknowledged for whites. In April of 1864, at Fort Pillow in western Tennessee, Confederate cavalry under the command of Nathan Bedford Forrest shot down black Union soldiers and their white commander who attempted to surrender.

With the election clock running, Grant set out in May 1864 to destroy Lee's army. The Battle of the Wilderness near Chancellorsville saw brutal fighting and horrible losses. Fire in the tangled woods trapped wounded men, burning them alive. Grant lost more men

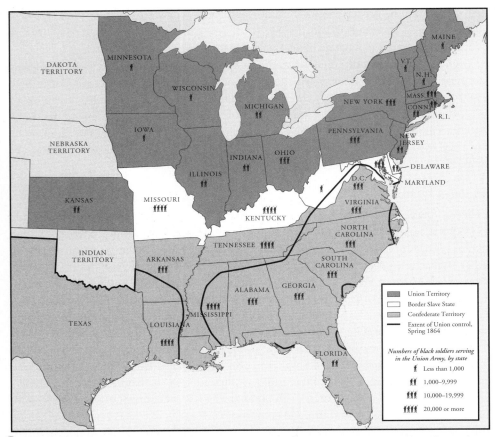

Map 15.4 Black Soldiers in the Union Army African American men streamed into the U.S. army from all across the country, but they were especially prominent in the occupied South where they had been enslaved.

than Hooker had in the battle of the previous year, but whereas Hooker treated such losses as a decisive defeat and retreated, Grant pushed on.

The two armies fought again and again over the next two months in the fields of Virginia. The Confederates turned the Union army back to the east of Richmond and rushed up the Shenandoah Valley to threaten Washington itself. While failing to take the capital, Confederate raiders "taxed" Maryland towns for thousands of dollars of greenbacks and burned the town of Chambersburg, Pennsylvania, when it refused to pay $500,000. The North repulsed the invasion and dispatched Philip Sheridan to the valley to make sure the Confederates did not regroup. With the Confederates pinned down in Petersburg, near Richmond, Pennsylvania coal miners volunteered to tunnel under the fortifications and plant explosives. Throughout July, they dug; finally, at the end of the month, they detonated a charge and blew an enormous crater in the Confederate lines. The attack that followed the explosion, however, failed. Union soldiers piled into the crater, where the rallying Confederates trapped them.

Fortunately for Lincoln, things were going better farther south. Throughout June and July, Sherman pushed relentlessly through north Georgia toward Atlanta. By the end of July, the Southern army had fallen back into Atlanta, preparing to defend it from siege. It seemed only a matter of time before the Union triumphed. But how much time? After rapidly advancing, federal troops slowed as they closed on Atlanta and many feared Sherman was "on the eve of disaster."

The Northern Election of 1864

The president had to fight off challenges even within his own party. Some Republicans considered Lincoln too radical; others considered him too cautious. Through adroit use of patronage, however, Lincoln managed to win renomination in June. The Republican party tried to broaden its appeal to Democrats by nominating Andrew Johnson, a former Democrat from Tennessee, to the vice presidency.

In the meantime, the Democrats confidently moved forward. They knew that in the eyes of his critics, Lincoln had caused the war, trampled on constitutional rights, consolidated too much power, and refused to end the war when he had a chance. The Democrats intended to take full advantage of such criticisms, especially by nominating George McClellan as their candidate. McClellan demonstrated that a person could oppose Lincoln's political purposes of the war without being a coward or traitor. McClellan and the Democrats portrayed themselves as the truly national party, for they were determined to restore the United States to its prewar unity and grandeur. McClellan said he would end the war if the South would reenter the Union—bringing slavery with it. It was a bargain that appealed to many in the North.

Just when it appeared that the Democrats would unseat Lincoln, however, news from the battlefield changed everything. Sherman swung around Atlanta and began destroying the railroads that made the small city an important junction. The Confederates, afraid they would be encircled and trapped within the city, set much of Atlanta on fire and abandoned it. Sherman and his army marched into the city on September 2. Two weeks later, Sheridan attacked the Confederates in the Shenandoah Valley, systematically destroying the valley's ability to support the Southern army again.

Even with these military victories, Lincoln won only 55 percent of the popular vote. Contrary to expectations, Lincoln carried the large majority of the armies' votes. In their letters, soldiers who identified themselves as Democrats rejected McClellan. A Vermont soldier who described himself as "a McClellan man clear to the bone" would not accept "peace by surrendering to the rebels"; instead "he would let his bones manure the soil of Virginia." Lincoln did much better in the electoral college, sweeping every state except three. The Republicans also elected heavy majorities to both houses of Congress and elected the governor and legislative majorities in all states except New Jersey, Delaware, and Kentucky. Lincoln believed the election validated the strength of republican govern-

PICTURING THE PAST
Politics & Diplomacy

To attract Democrats who supported the war, Lincoln and the Republican leadership renamed their party the National Union party and chose a Southern Unionist, Senator Andrew Johnson of Tennessee, as vice president. Though Lincoln won easily in the electoral college vote, he faced strong opposition throughout much of the North from George McClellan, who claimed 45 percent of the popular vote.

With the popular vote so close, in many states the outcome hinged on the votes of soldiers. In earlier wars, when soldiers departed home for service, they no longer voted, so no provision existed in law or practice for military personnel to vote away from their home polling site. By 1864, thirteen states permitted soldiers to vote in the field, while five continued to disenfranchise soldiers. Democrats had opposed absentee voting because they suspected soldiers would vote Republican, but hoped that General McClellan still enjoyed the favor of soldiers. Democrats lobbied senior generals while crying fraud. After three years of war, soldiers in the field, even those who considered themselves loyal to McClellan, would not support the Democratic peace platform. A Union colonel, a staunch Democrat, wrote his wife, "I have not come across an officer or a man that will vote for McClellan." This had always been considered a Democratic corps, but these formerly loyal Democrats voted for Lincoln by a factor of ten to one. Compare the distribution of votes for Lincoln in 1864 and 1860 (page 377) and note the areas where Lincoln gained and lost support.

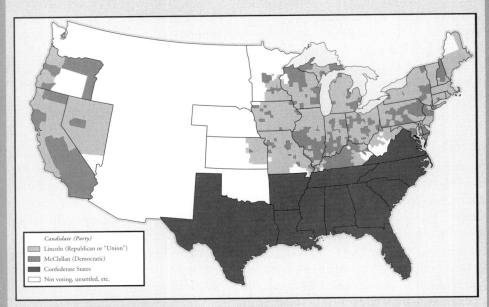

Candidate (Party)
- Lincoln (Republican or "Union")
- McClellan (Democratic)
- Confederate States
- Not voting, unsettled, etc.

Map 15.5 The Election of 1864

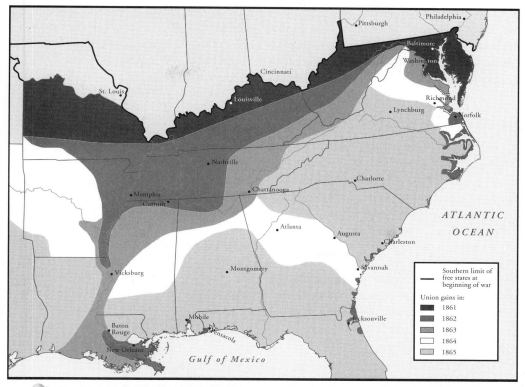

🐚 **Map 15.6 The Territory of War** The Confederacy managed to protect large parts of its interior throughout the war, but the Union increasingly controlled the crucial rivers, rail lines, and ports.
View an animated version of this map or related maps at http://history.wadsworth.com/passages2e.

ment: "We can not have a free government without elections; and if the rebellion could force us to forego, or postpone a national election, it might fairly claim to have already conquered and ruined us."

The March to the Sea

Jefferson Davis traveled through the Lower South after the fall of Atlanta, exhorting citizens to remain defiant. A week after Lincoln's election, Sherman set out across Georgia, provisioning his army along the way, taking the war to the Southern people themselves. Such a march would be as much a demonstration of Northern power as a military maneuver: "If we can march a well-appointed army right through [Confederate] territory," Sherman argued, "it is a demonstration to the world, foreign and domestic, that we have a power which Davis cannot resist." The triumphant army of 60,000 made its way across the state throughout the fall of 1864. Large numbers of deserters from both sides, fugitive slaves, and outlaws took advantage of the situation to inflict widespread destruction and panic.

Sherman arrived at Savannah on December 21. "I beg to present to you, as a Christmas gift, the city of Savannah," Sherman buoyantly telegraphed Lincoln. Contrasting with the devastation of the South, the president's annual message to Congress outlined a portrait of a North gaining strength with "more men now than we had when the war began . . . We are gaining strength, and may, if need be, maintain the contest indefinitely."

From War to Reconstruction: 1865–1867

As the war ground to a halt in early 1865, Americans had to wonder if they remembered how to share a country with their former enemies. They had to wonder, too, how different the country would be with African Americans no longer as slaves. Of all the changes the United States had ever seen, emancipation stood as the most profound.

War's Climax

Events moved quickly at the beginning of 1865. In January, Sherman issued Special Field Order 15, which reserved land in coastal South Carolina, Georgia, and Florida for former slaves. Those who settled on the land would receive forty-acre plots. Four days later, the Republicans in Congress passed the Thirteenth Amendment, abolishing slavery forever. Antislavery activists, black and white, packed the galleries and the House floor. Observers embraced, wept, and cheered. A Congressman wrote his wife that "we can now look other nations in the face without shame."

At the beginning of February, Sherman's troops began to march north into the Carolinas. Columbia, South Carolina, burned to the ground. Growing numbers of Confederate soldiers deserted from their armies. Lincoln met with Confederate officials at Hampton Roads on board the steamship *River Queen* to try to bring the war to an end, offering slaveowners compensation for their freed slaves if the Southerners would immediately cease the war. Jefferson Davis refused to submit to the "disgrace of surrender."

Corbis

This picture of Lincoln, taken four days before his assassination, shows the toll four years of war had taken on the fifty-six-year-old president.

At the beginning of March, Lincoln was inaugurated for his second term. Rather than gloating at the impending victory on the battlefield, Lincoln called for his fellow citizens to "bind up the nation's wounds." That same month, Congress created the Bureau of Refugees, Freedmen, and Abandoned Lands to ease the transition from slavery to freedom. Nine days later, the Confederate government, after hotly debating whether to recruit slaves to fight as soldiers if their owners agreed, finally decided to do so after Lee, desperate for men, supported the measure.

Appomattox and Assassination

The Confederates' slave recruitment law did not have time to convert slaves to soldiers, however, for Grant soon began his final assault on Confederate troops in Virginia. Petersburg fell on April 2, Richmond the next day. Lee hoped to lead his army to the train station at Appomattox Court House to resupply them, but on April 9 Grant intercepted Lee's men just short of their destination. Lee, with nowhere else to go and no ally to come to his aid, surrendered.

A number of Confederate armies had yet to surrender, and Jefferson Davis had yet to be captured, but it was clear that the war had ended. Cities and towns across the North erupted in celebration and relief as crowds filled the streets to sing, embrace, fire salutes, and wave the flag. Southerners began to straggle home. Two days later, Lincoln addressed a Washington audience about what would come next for the freedmen. He admitted that Northerners differed "as to the mode, manner, and means of Reconstruction" and that the white South was "disorganized and discordant."

Lincoln did not live to take part in the planning, for he was assassinated on April 14 by John Wilkes Booth, a failed actor and Southern sympathizer. Booth attacked Lincoln while the president sat with Mrs. Lincoln at Ford's Theater in Washington, shooting him in the back of the head and then leaping to the stage. Lincoln never recovered consciousness; he died early the next morning. After a long and frantic search, Booth was captured and killed in a burning barn.

The Costs and Consequences of the War

The North lost almost 365,000 men to death and disease in the Civil War, and the South lost 260,000. Another 277,000 Northerners were wounded, along with 195,000 Southerners. Black Americans lost 37,000 men in the Union army and another 10,000 men, women, and children in the contraband camps. Widows and orphans, black and white, Northern and Southern, faced decades of strug-

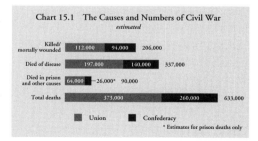

Chart 15.1 The Causes and Numbers of Civil War Deaths
Disease killed even more men than did the bullets of the enemy.

gling without a male breadwinner. Many people found their emotional lives shattered by the war. Alcohol, drug abuse, crime, and violence became widespread problems. The war's legacy lingered in people's minds. Forty-eight years after the war, a former army surgeon on his deathbed fretted "that leg must come off—save a leg—lose a life."

The Southern economy fell to its knees. Major Southern cities had been reduced to ash. Railroads had been ripped from the ground, engines and cars burned. Fields had grown up weeds and brush. Farm values fell by half. Livestock, tools, barns, and fences had been stolen or destroyed by the armies of both sides. Recovery was slow. In Georgia, for example, as late as 1870 the state recorded 1 million fewer pigs, 200,000 fewer cattle, and 3 million fewer acres under cultivation than in 1860. Just as damaging in the long run, lines of credit had been severed. Before emancipation, planters had used slaves as collateral for loans. Now, without that basis, few people outside the South were willing to loan money to planters or other investors.

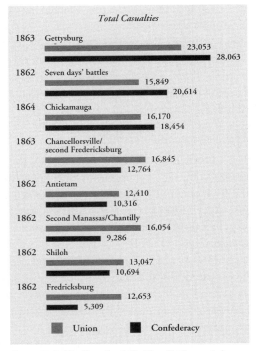

Total Casualties

1863 Gettysburg — 23,053 / 28,063
1862 Seven days' battles — 15,849 / 20,614
1864 Chickamauga — 16,170 / 18,454
1863 Chancellorsville/second Fredericksburg — 16,845 / 12,764
1862 Antietam — 12,410 / 10,316
1862 Second Manassas/Chantilly — 16,054 / 9,286
1862 Shiloh — 13,047 / 10,694
1862 Fredericksburg — 12,653 / 5,309

▉ Union   ▉ Confederacy

Chart 15.2 The Most Costly Battles Battles exacted horrible costs from early in the war until near its very end.

The Civil War did not mark a sudden turn in the Northern economy, but it did accelerate processes already well underway. The nationalization of markets, the accumulation of wealth, and the dominance of larger manufacturing firms all became more marked after 1865. Greenbacks, bonds, and a national banking system regularized the flow of capital and spurred the growth of business. The Republicans passed the Department of Agriculture Act, the Morrill College Land Grant Act, the Homestead Act, and the Union Pacific Railroad Act, all using the power of the federal government to encourage settlement of the West, strengthen public education, and spur economic develop-

Civil War deaths compared with U.S. deaths in other wars (estimated)

Civil War — 633,000
World War II — 407,000
World War I — 117,000
Vietnam War — 58,000
Korean War — 33,500
Mexican War — 13,000
Spanish-American War/Philippine Insurrection — 9,700
Revolutionary War — 4,500
War of 1812 — 2,200

Chart 15.3 Civil War Losses The Civil War exacted a horrible cost, far outstripping every other conflict in which the United States has fought.

ment. Despite the prosperity in the North, the hundreds of thousands of veterans faced many dislocations and readjustments as they returned to the farms, factories, and shops they had left months or years before.

Emancipation and the South

As the battles ground to a halt, slaves became former slaves. Some, especially the young, greeted freedom confidently, whereas others, especially the elderly, could not help but be wary of anything so strange, no matter how long and how much they had prayed for it. Some seized their freedom at the first opportunity, taking their families to Union camps or joining the army. Others celebrated when the Yankees came to their plantations, only to find that their owners and white neighbors retaliated when the soldiers left. Others bided their time. Some refused to believe the stories of freedom at all until their master or mistress called them together to announce that they were indeed no longer slaves.

Upon hearing the news, the freedpeople gathered to discuss their options. For many, the highest priority was to reunite their families. Such people set off on journeys in desperate efforts to find a husband, wife, child, or parent sold away in earlier years. For others, sheer survival was the highest priority. Freedom came in the late spring, barely in time to get crops in the ground. Some former slaves argued that their best bet was to stay where they were for the time being. They had heard rumors that the government would award them land. Between July and September of 1865, however, those dreams died. Union officers promised land to former slaves in Virginia, Louisiana, Mississippi, and South Carolina, but then Washington revoked the promises. The land would be returned to its former owners.

Former slaveowners also responded in many different ways. Some fled to Latin America. Others tried to keep as much of slavery as they could by whipping and chaining workers to keep them from leaving. Still others offered to let former slaves stay in their cabins and work for wages. The presence of black soldiers triggered resentment and fear among former slaveowners who marked the increased independence among blacks that was encouraged by "Negro troops." One slaveowner believed "the people of the South are in very great danger . . . I tell you most seriously that the whole south is resting upon a volcano."

African Americans had no choice but to compromise with white landowners. At first, in the spring of 1865, planters insisted that the former slaves work as they had worked before emancipation, in "gangs." In return for their work, they

North Wind Picture Archives

Former slaves on the move. Black Southerners took advantage of the presence of Union troops to leave the farms and plantations on which they had been held. Many set out to find family members.

Desolation of the South

After four years of war, little remained in many cities of the Confederacy. Atlanta, Columbia, and Richmond had been ravaged by fire; Vicksburg, Petersburg, and Fredericksburg had been pummeled by siege and battle. Union troops had destroyed railways, rivers were blocked by the refuse of war, and fields and farms had been stripped by the marauding troops of both sides or simply overrun by weeds. Roads, wagons, and riverboats were choked with civilian refugees, returning soldiers, and prisoners of war. In the countryside, even on farms and plantations untouched by combat, former slaves abandoned masters to seek family members and new opportunities.

Thousands of refugees from the countryside relied on federal aid and rations to survive. White women, particularly those from slaveholding families, found adjusting to defeat and emancipation trying. One woman from North Carolina bitterly lamented her transformation from "social queen" to "domestic drudge." African American women looked forward to working for the benefit of their own families.

© Bettmann/Corbis

would receive a portion of the crop, shared among all the workers. Many black people chafed at this arrangement, preferring to work as individuals or families. In such places, landowners found that they had little choice but to permit black families to take primary responsibility for a portion of land. The former slaves provided the labor and received part of the crop as a result. Planters, though reluctant to give up any control over the day-to-day work on their land, realized they had few choices. They possessed little cash to pay wage workers and no alternative labor.

The Bureau of Refugees, Freedmen, and Abandoned Lands—the Freedmen's Bureau—oversaw the transition from a slave economy to a wage economy. Its agents dispensed medicine, food, and clothing from the vast stores of the federal government to displaced white and black Southerners. The Bureau created courts to adjudicate conflicts and to draw up labor contracts between landholders and laborers. It established schools and coordinated female volunteers who came from the North to teach in them. Although many white Southerners resented and resisted the Freedmen's Bureau, it helped smooth the transition from slavery to freedom, from war to peace.

A Black School

As growing numbers of African Americans gained literacy after emancipation, they increasingly taught in their own schools. To gain access to schools for their children and themselves, former slaves migrated to cities and towns and frequently demanded construction of a schoolhouse as a condition for signing a labor contract. Less than a month after the fall of Richmond, over 1,000 black children and adults attended schools begun by the city's black churches. Across the South, blacks organized and collected money to buy land, constructed schools with their own labor, and funded teacher salaries from self-imposed taxes and tuition. Teachers often advocated racial equality before the law and suffrage, as well as encouraging black political mobilization. Many Northern blacks, including a large number of women, helped found the first black colleges in the South, such as Fiske, Hampton, and Tougaloo. By 1869, black teachers outnumbered whites among the 3,000 teachers in the South.

© Corbis

Black Mobilization

Black Southerners mourned the loss of Abraham Lincoln. Without his leadership, former slaves rightly worried, the forces of reaction might overwhelm their freedom. Southerners of both races watched to see what Andrew Johnson might do.

Throughout the South, former slaves and former free blacks gathered in mass meetings, Union Leagues, and conventions to announce their vision of the new order. They wanted, above all else, equality before the law and the opportunity to vote. They did not demand confiscation of land, nor did they speak extensively of economic concerns in general. Let us have our basic rights before the courts and at the ballot box, they said, and we will take care of ourselves. Such concerns and confidence reflected the perspective of the conventions' leadership: former free blacks, skilled artisans, ministers, and teachers. The great mass of Southern blacks found their concerns neglected.

Black Southerners agreed on the centrality of two institutions, however: the church and the school. At the very moment of freedom, they began to form their own churches. For generations, African Americans had been forced to worship alongside whites. For many ex-slaves, one of their first acts of freedom was to form their own churches. Before the war, 42,000 black Methodists in South Carolina attended biracial churches. By 1870, only 600 mostly elderly blacks remained. People who owned virtually nothing somehow built churches across the South. A black church in Charleston was the first building raised from the ruins of the city in 1865. Those churches often served as schools as well.

Andrew Johnson

In the meantime, events in Washington undermined the efforts of black Southerners to build a new world for themselves. Andrew Johnson wanted to attract moderates from both the North and the South to a political party that would change as little as possible. Johnson had been selected to run for the vice presidency because he was a Southerner who had remained true to the Union. As a result, both Northerners and Southerners distrusted Johnson. A longtime Democrat before the crisis of the Union, Johnson maintained a limited Jacksonian view of government. The new president's well-known disdain for the wealthy planters of the South appealed to equally disdainful Republicans in Washington. His public statements suggested a harsh peace for former slaveowners and Confederate leaders: "*Treason* is a crime, and *crime* must be punished." Unlike some Republicans, however, Johnson held little sympathy for black people or for expansion of the powers of the federal government. Johnson saw himself pursuing Lincoln's highest goal: reuniting the Union. He believed that reunification should start by winning the support of white Southerners.

Johnson could hardly have been placed in a more difficult position. Congress was not in session at the time of Lincoln's death and would not be for seven months, so Johnson used the opportunity to implement his vision of reunion. In what became known as "Presidential Reconstruction," Johnson offered amnesty to former Confederates who would take an oath of loyalty to the Union, restoring their political and civil rights and immunizing them against the seizure of their property or prosecution for treason. By 1866, Johnson granted over 7,000 pardons to wealthy Southerners and Confederate senior officers who applied individually for amnesty.

Johnson's plans for political reunion made no provisions at all for black voting. Indeed, his plan threatened to return the South to even greater national power than it had held before because the entire African American population would now be considered when the number of representatives was calculated, not merely as three-fifths of a people as before the war.

White Southerners could hardly believe their good fortune. The state conventions elected in 1865 flaunted their opinions of the North. Some refused to fly the American flag, some refused to ratify the Thirteenth Amendment, some even refused to admit that secession had been illegal. Former Confederates filled important posts in state governments. Georgia elected Alexander H. Stephens, the ex-vice president of the aborted nation, to Congress. Even Johnson recognized that far from inaugurating new regimes led by Unionist yeomen, "there seems, in many of the elections something like defiance."

The North erupted in outrage when the new state governments enacted the so-called "black codes," laws for the control of the former slaves. The Southern white legislatures granted only the barest minimum of rights to black people: the right to marry, to hold property, to sue and be sued. Most of the laws decreed what African Americans could not do: move from one job to another, own or rent land, testify in court, practice certain occupations. When the members of Congress convened in December of 1865, they reacted as many of their constituents did—with fury. To Northerners, even those inclined to deal leniently with the South, the former Confederates seemed to deny all the war had decided with this blatant attempt to retain racially based laws. And many Northerners blamed Johnson.

Johnson and the Radicals

It was not that most Northerners, even most Republicans, wanted the kind of policies promoted by Radicals such as Thaddeus Stevens, who called for land to be seized from wealthy planters and given to the former slaves, or of Charles Sumner, who wanted immediate and universal suffrage for blacks. But neither did they want the sort of capitulation that Johnson had tolerated. A Chicago editor spoke for his readers: "As for Negro suffrage, the mass of Union men in the Northwest do not care a great deal. What scares them is the idea that the rebels are all to be let back . . . and made a power in the government again." Moderates tried to devise plans that would be acceptable to both sides.

The moderates sought to continue the Freedmen's Bureau. The Bureau was understaffed and underfunded—only about 900 agents covered the entire South—but it offered some measure of hope for former slaves. The Bureau saw itself as a mediator between blacks and whites. Its commissioner, General Oliver Howard, advocated education as the foundation for improving living conditions and prospects for blacks. By 1869, approximately 3,000 schools, serving over 150,000 students, reported to the Bureau, and these numbers do not include the many private and church-funded schools throughout the South.

The Bureau insisted on the innovation of formal contracts between laborer and landlord. Although these contracts infuriated Southern white men, the Bureau ended up supporting landowners as often as black laborers. The moderates also attempted to institute a Civil Rights bill to define American citizenship for all those born in the United States, thereby including blacks. Citizenship would bring with it equal protection under the laws, though the bill said nothing about black voting. The Bureau struggled against strongly held prejudice. Its Mississippi commissioner despaired of a public that failed to "conceive of the Negro having any rights at all."

Republicans supported the Freedmen's Bureau and Civil Rights bills as the starting place for rebuilding the nation. But Johnson vetoed both bills, claiming that they violated the rights of the states and of white Southerners who had been excluded from the decision making. Republicans closed ranks to override Johnson's veto, the first major legislation enacted over a presidential veto.

To prevent any future erosion of black rights, the Republicans proposed the Fourteenth Amendment, which, as eventually ratified, guaranteed citizenship to all

American-born people and equal protection under the law for those citizens. The amendment decreed that any state that abridged the voting rights of any male inhabitants who were twenty-one and citizens would suffer a proportionate reduction in its congressional representation. This clause offered white Southerners the choice of acceptance of black suffrage or reduced Congressional representation. It also was the first Constitutional amendment to use the word "male," angering feminist abolitionists who challenged the Republicans' denial of suffrage based on sex. Johnson urged the Southern states to refuse to ratify the amendment, advice they promptly followed.

The Ku Klux Klan emerged in 1866, devoting itself to the maintenance of white supremacy in all its forms.

Throughout the second half of 1866 the North watched, appalled, as much that the Civil War had been fought for seemed to be brushed aside in the South. Not only did the Southern men who met in the state conventions refuse to accept the relatively mild Fourteenth Amendment, but they made clear their determination to fight back in every way they could against further attempts to remake the South. The spring of that year saw riots in Memphis and New Orleans in which policemen and other whites brutally assaulted and killed black people and burned their homes with little or no provocation.

It was in 1866, too, that the Ku Klux Klan appeared. Founded in Tennessee, the Ku Klux Klan dedicated itself to maintaining white supremacy. The Klan dressed in costumes designed to overawe the former slaves, hiding behind their anonymity to avoid retaliation. The Klan became in effect a military wing of the Democratic party, devoting much of its energy to warning and killing white and black men who dared associate with the Republicans.

Johnson toured the country in the fall of 1866 to denounce the Republicans and their policies. Even his supporters saw the tour as a "thoroughly reprehensible" disaster. The voters rejected both Johnson and the Democrats, as the governorship and legislature of every Northern state came under the control of the Republicans. In the next Congress, Republicans would outnumber Democrats sufficiently to override any presidential veto. The Republicans felt they held a mandate to push harder than they had before. They had only a few months, however, until their term ended in March, to decide what to do. They bitterly disagreed over the vote, land distribution, the courts, and education. Some wanted to put the South under military control for the indefinite future, whereas others sought to return things to civilian control as soon as possible. Finally, on March 2, 1867, as time was running out on the session, they passed the Reconstruction Act.

The Reconstruction Act

The Reconstruction Act placed the South under military rule. All the Southern states except Tennessee, which had been readmitted to the Union after it ratified the Fourteenth Amendment, were put in five military districts. Once order had been instituted, then the states would proceed to elect conventions to draw up new constitutions. The constitutions written by those conventions had to accept the Fourteenth Amendment and provide for universal manhood suffrage. Once a majority of the state's citizens and both houses of the national Congress had approved the new constitution, the state could be readmitted to the Union.

To ensure that Andrew Johnson did not undermine this plan—which soon became known as "Radical Reconstruction"—Congress sought to curb the president's power. With no threat of his veto after the 1866 elections, the Republicans could do much as they wanted. Congress decreed that it could call itself into special session. There, it limited the president's authority as commander-in-chief of the army and, in the Tenure of Office Act, prevented him from removing officials who had been confirmed by the Senate.

Johnson, characteristically, did not quietly accept such restrictions of his power. When he intentionally violated the Tenure of Office Act by removing Secretary of War Edwin Stanton in the summer of 1867, many in Congress decided that Johnson warranted impeachment. Matters stewed throughout the fall, while the first elections under the Reconstruction Act took place in the South.

Reconstruction Begins

After word of the Reconstruction Act circulated in the spring and summer, both black and white men claimed leadership roles within the Republican party. Black Northerners came to the South, looking for appointive and elective office. Ambitious black Southerners, many of whom had been free and relatively prosperous before the Civil War, put themselves forward as the natural leaders of the race. Such men became the backbone of the Republican party in black-belt districts.

White Southerners sneered at white Northerners who supported the Republican cause. They called them "carpetbaggers." These men, according to the insulting name, were supposedly so devoid of connections and property in their Northern homes that they could throw everything they had into a carpetbag—a cheap suitcase—and head south as soon as they read of the opportunities created by Radical Reconstruction. The majority of white Northerners who became Republican leaders in the South, however, had in fact moved to the region months or years before Reconstruction began. Many had been well educated in the North before the war and many held property in the South. Like white Southerners, however, the Northern-born Republicans found the postwar South a difficult place in which to prosper. Black people were no more inclined to work for low wages for white Northerners than for anyone else, and Southern whites often went out of their way to avoid doing business with the Yankees. As a result, when Reconstruction began, a considerable number of Northerners took up the Republican cause as a way to build a political career in the South.

White Southern Republicans, labeled "scalawags" by their enemies, risked being called traitors to their race and region. Few white Republicans emerged in the plantation districts, because they endured ostracism, resistance, and violence. "It costs nothing for a Northern man to be a Union man, but the rebuff and persecution received here . . . tells a horrible tale." In the upcountry districts, however, former Whigs and Unionists asserted themselves against the planters and Confederates. The Republican party became strong in the mountains of east Tennessee, western North Carolina, eastern Kentucky, north Alabama, and northern Georgia. Many whites in these districts, though unwilling to join with low-country African Americans or their white leaders, struck alliances of convenience with them. Black voters and white voters generally wanted and needed different things. Blacks, largely propertyless, called for an activist government to raise taxes to provide schools, orphanages, and hospitals. Most whites, on the other hand, owned land and called mainly for lower taxes.

Throughout the South, most whites watched, livid, as local black leaders, ministers, and Republicans mobilized black voters in enormous numbers in the fall of 1867. Membership in Union Leagues swept the region, with local leagues assisting with labor contracts and school construction as well as political activity. An Alabama league demanded recognition of black citizenship: "We claim exactly the same rights, privileges and immunities as are enjoyed by white men—we seek nothing more and will be content with nothing less." While many white Democrats boycotted the elections, the Republicans swept into the constitutional delegate positions. Although many black men voted, African American delegates made up only a relatively small part of the convention's delegates. They held the majority in South Carolina and Louisiana, but much smaller proportions elsewhere. About half of the 265 African Americans elected as delegates to the state conventions had been free before the war, and most were ministers, artisans, farmers, and teachers. Over the next two years, these delegates would meet to write new, much more democratic, constitutions for their states.

At the very moment of the success of the Southern Republicans, however, ominous signs came from the North. Republicans were dismayed at the election returns in the North in 1867, for the Democrats' power surged from coast to coast. Many white voters thought that the Radicals had gone too far in their concern with black rights and wanted officeholders to devote their energies to problems closer to home. Racism linked Democratic appeals against blacks in the Midwest with western diatribes against the Chinese and the specter of a nation menaced by a "Mongolian and Indian and African" alliance against ordinary white men. Integrated public schools and confiscation of plantation lands for former slaves were soundly defeated. The Republicans in Washington heard the message. They began scaling back their support for any further advances in Reconstruction.

Conclusion

The Civil War changed the United States more deeply than any other event in the nineteenth century. The conflict brought the deaths of over 625,000 soldiers. It saw bitter rioting in the streets and the first assassination of a president. It brought a major shift in the balance of power among the regions and an expansion of the federal government. Most important, the war brought what few Americans could have imagined at the end of 1860: the immediate emancipation of 4 million enslaved people.

Freedom emerged from the war through a circuitous route. The war began as a war for Union. As the deaths mounted and African Americans seized freedom at every opportunity, abolitionists and Republicans increasingly insisted that the war become a war to end slavery. Many white Northerners supported emancipation because it seemed the best way to end the war. Abraham Lincoln worked desperately to keep the support of both the advocates and foes of emancipation, knowing that moving too quickly would shatter the fragile support that kept him in office. The New York City draft riots and the close elections of 1863 demonstrated that many Northerners resisted the continuation of the war and its embrace of black freedom. Only Union success on the battlefield in late 1864 permitted Lincoln's reelection. His assassination made an already confused situation far more so, ending slavery and restoring the Union without a blueprint and without leadership.

The end of the fighting saw the conflict shift in the South, as people struggled to determine what freedom would mean. For black Southerners, the goal was autonomy and respect. For white Northerners, the goal was to reconstruct the South in an idealized image of the North. For white Southerners, the goal was the reassertion of the power they had held before the war, especially power over the black people in their midst. Such goals could not be reconciled. The era of Reconstruction would be devoted to the struggle among them.

RECOMMENDED READINGS

Berlin, Ira, Fields, Barbara J., Miller, Steven F., Reidy, Joseph P., and Rowland, Leslie S., eds. *Freedom* (1985–). A rich and fascinating multivolume documentary collection.

Blight, David W. *Race and Reunion: The Civil War in American Memory* (2001). Documents the role of politics, myth, and race in shaping how the Civil War is remembered.

Donald, David. *Lincoln* (1995). Stands as the most elegant biography.

Faust, Drew Gilpin. *Mothers of Invention: Women of the Slaveholding South in the American Civil War* (1995). Offers a challenging and interesting interpretation.

Fellman, Michael. *Inside War: The Guerrilla Conflict in Missouri During the American Civil War* (1989). Makes palpable the internal struggles in the border areas.

Foner, Eric. *Reconstruction: America's Unfinished Revolution, 1863–1877* (1988). A magisterial interpretation of the struggle over black freedom.

Gallagher, Gary W. *The Confederate War: How Popular Will, Nationalism, and Military Strategy Could Not Stave Off Defeat* (1997). Explores why the Confederacy could fight as long as it did.

Harris, William C. *With Charity for All: Lincoln and the Restoration of the Union* (1997). Offers a fresh assessment of Lincoln's attitudes toward the white South.

Hattaway, Herman, and Jones, Archer. *How the North Won: A Military History of the Civil War* (1983). Authoritatively describes strategy and tactics.

Litwack, Leon. *Been in the Storm So Long: The Aftermath of Slavery* (1979). Beautifully evokes the conflicting emotions and motives surrounding freedom.

Neely, Mark E., Jr. *The Union Divided: Party Conflict in the Civil War North* (2002). Examines the impact of political dissension in the North on war effort.

Roark, James L. *Masters Without Slaves: Southern Planters in the Civil War and Reconstruction* (1978). Describes the war from the perspective of those who lost the most in Southern defeat.

Rose, Willie Lee. *Rehearsal for Reconstruction: The Port Royal Experiment* (1964). A classic account of the first efforts to create Northern policy toward the freedpeople.

Additional resources, exercises, and Internet links related to this chapter are available on the American Passages Web site: http://history.wadsworth.com/ayerscompact2/

16

Reconstruction Abandoned
1867–1877

Republicans in 1867 believed that they had taken important steps toward a newer and more just society with their Reconstruction legislation. "We have cut loose from the whole dead past," said Timothy Howe of Wisconsin, "and have cast our anchor out a hundred years." But the struggle over black rights that had begun during the Civil War was far from over. The battle shifted from the halls of Congress back to the South. There, in the decade that followed, whites sought to recreate as many of the features of slavery as they could. Violence, brutality, election fraud, and raw economic intimidation ended the experiment in multiracial politics known as Reconstruction.

While racial prejudices were the main cause, other forces hastened the abandonment of Reconstruction. In the mid-1870s, a severe economic depression made African American rights seem a less urgent issue. White Americans feared that the national government was becoming too powerful; a renewed commitment to localism and states rights helped southern whites repress black aspirations. For many in the North, the hum of industry, the spread of railroads, and the rise of cities seemed more in tune with national progress than preserving the rights of former slaves. With a western frontier to open and Native Americans to subdue, the nation retreated from the principles for which the Civil War had been fought. By the disputed presidential election of 1876, it was evident that white Americans no longer wished to be involved with the fate of blacks in the South. After a decade of slow, painful withdrawal from a commitment to equality, an informal sectional compromise sealed the return of white rule to the South in 1877.

A Presidency Under Siege: Andrew Johnson Impeached

The struggle between the executive and legislative branches over the fate of the South continued unabated into the second half of 1867. As President Andrew Johnson sought to impede the Radical Reconstruction program, Republicans in Congress argued that he should be impeached and removed from office. When the president tried to oust Secretary of War Edwin M. Stanton in August 1867, cries for impeachment mounted. For the moment the Republicans could do little until Congress reassembled in December. After lawmakers gathered, the sentiment for removing the president had receded and it appeared

CHRONOLOGY

1867	Alaska purchase treaty signed
1868	Andrew Johnson impeached and then acquitted • Purchase of Alaska completed • Ulysses S. Grant wins presidency
1869	Ulysses S. Grant inaugurated as president • Transcontinental railroads link up • Licensing of women lawyers begins • Fifteenth Amendment passes Congress • "Gold Corner" scheme of Jay Gould and Jim Fisk • Woman suffrage enacted in Wyoming Territory
1870	Santo Domingo annexation treaty defeated • Ku Klux Klan terror raids in the South • First Greek letter sorority (Kappa Alpha Theta) founded
1871	Ku Klux Klan Act passes Congress • Tweed Ring exposed in New York City • Chicago fire burns three and a half miles of the city
1872	Liberal Republican movement challenges Grant • Grant wins reelection over Horace Greeley
1873	Panic of 1873 starts economic depression • Salary Grab and Credit Mobilier scandals • Mark Twain and Charles Dudley Warner publish *The Gilded Age*
1874	Woman's Christian Temperance Union founded • Democrats make substantial gains in the congressional elections • Sale of typewriters begins • Chautauqua movement for summer education starts
1875	Congress passes Civil Rights Act • Smith College and Wellesley College open to provide higher education for women
1876	Sioux defeat Custer at Little Big Horn • Centennial Exposition opens in Philadelphia • Tilden and Hayes are candidates in contested presidential election
1877	Hayes declared winner of presidency after series of compromises settles disputes • Reconstruction ends

that the president would survive for the rest of his term. As he had done so often in the past, Johnson defied Congress and precipitated a confrontation. After the Senate in January 1868 refused to accept his dismissal of Stanton, Johnson replaced him anyway. Presidential stubbornness, Republicans said, was a clear violation of the Tenure of Office Act.

Emboldened by Johnson's defiance, the solidly Republican House voted for his impeachment and leveled eleven charges against him. None of the specifications in the articles of impeachment alleged violations of criminal laws; they dealt instead with Johnson's Reconstruction policies and his obstruction of Congress. The trial came in March. Two months later the Senate failed to achieve the necessary two-thirds vote to convict Johnson. The impeachment attempt lost because moderate Republicans feared that if Johnson were convicted on political grounds it would set a bad precedent. Moreover, Johnson himself eased up on his obstructive tactics. With the 1868 presidential election looming, it seemed less urgent to oust a man who would soon leave office. True to his nature, Johnson did not become more conciliatory. He encouraged southern whites to resist Reconstruction and contributed to the denial of rights to African Americans that marked the 1870s. Few presidents have done less with their historical opportunities than Andrew Johnson.

The Purchase of Alaska

During the months of Johnson's impeachment and trial, Congress concluded a major territorial acquisition that completed expansion on the North American continent. In March 1867, the Russian minister to the United States (Washington did not yet rate an ambassador from the European powers) hinted to Secretary of State William H. Seward that the government of the Tsar in St. Petersburg wanted to sell Alaska. The Russians knew that they could not defend their northern possession against the British in Canada. Seward worked out a treaty with the Russians that was signed on March 30, 1867. The United States paid $7,200,000 for Alaska; on April 9, 1867, the Senate, by a vote of thirty-seven to two, agreed to the deal.

Paying for the Alaska purchase required Congress to appropriate money. The House did not take action on the problem until July 1868 after Johnson had been impeached. Since the United States had already occupied the territory, the lawmakers went along and passed the bill on July 14. The Alaska purchase was a major strategic and geographic victory for the United States. For the moment, the impulse for expansion eased and the nation turned to its internal affairs.

The Election of 1868

Both parties looked ahead to the first postwar presidential contest but the issues of the Civil War defined the race. The Republicans nominated the great hero of the conflict, Ulysses S. Grant. As the architect of Union victory, his popularity transcended partisanship. Republicans believed that they had selected a candidate "so independent of party politics as to be a guarantee of peace and quiet." In his official letter of acceptance, Grant said "let us have peace" and that phrase became the theme of the Republican campaign. The Republicans were not campaigning on any promise to expand Reconstruction or black rights.

The Democrats turned to the former governor of New York, Horatio Seymour. Along with his running mate, Frank Blair of Missouri, Seymour relied on racial bigotry and white supremacy as the keynotes of his appeal. To win, the Democrats agreed, they had to arouse "the aversion with which the masses contemplate the equality of the negro." Seymour went out to campaign; Grant stayed home. The Republicans won, but not by a landslide. Grant garnered 53 percent of the vote; Seymour totaled 47 percent. Although Grant carried the electoral college by a margin of 214 to 80, the signs were not good for a continuation of Reconstruction. White voters were less willing to help African Americans, and the high point of post–Civil War racial reform was in the past.

The Fifteenth Amendment and Woman Suffrage

After the 1868 election, Republicans pushed for the adoption of the Fifteenth Amendment to the Constitution. Under its terms, the federal and state governments could not restrict the right to vote because of race, color, or previous condition of servitude. Congress approved the amendment in February 1869 over Democratic opposition. The purpose of the change was to limit the legal right of the southern states to exclude African Americans, and Democrats assailed it as a step toward black equality and a social revolution. In fact, the new amendment did not assure African Americans the right to hold office, and it left untouched the restrictions that northern states imposed on the right of males to vote. Literacy tests and property qualifications remained in place in some states outside of the South. State legislatures endorsed the amendment promptly and it was added to the Constitution in 1870.

The big losers in the adoption of the Fifteenth Amendment were women who had hoped that they might share in some of the expansion of political rights. In fact, several of the major advocates of woman suffrage, such as Susan B. Anthony, opposed the amendment because it left women out. In Anthony's mind, black and Asian men should be barred from voting if women did not have the right of suffrage too. Despite his earlier support for woman suffrage, Frederick Douglass, the major black leader, contended that "this hour belongs to the negro," by which he meant black males.

At a meeting of the Equal Rights Association in May 1869, the sharp differences about how to achieve woman suffrage produce an open break. Two distinct groups of suffragists emerged. The National Woman Suffrage Association (NWSA) reflected the position of Susan B. Anthony and Elizabeth Cady Stanton that the Fifteenth Amendment should be shunned until women were included. The American Woman Suffrage Association (AWSA), led by Lucy Stone and Alice Stone Blackwell, endorsed the amendment and focused its work in the states. Amid this dissension one small bright spot appeared. The new territory of Wyoming granted women the right of suffrage in 1869. The goal of the Wyoming legislature was to make Americans notice its underpopulated territory, not to expand women's rights. Nonetheless, a forward step had been taken. The discord between the major suffrage groups, however, lasted for two decades and slowed the progress toward reform.

The Grant Era

Ulysses S. Grant came to the White House with almost no political experience. He believed that he should administer the government rather than promote new programs. "I shall on all subjects have a policy to recommend," he said in his inaugural address, "but none to enforce against the will of the people." He promised, unlike Andrew Johnson, to carry out the laws that Congress passed. Nineteenth century Americans did not expect a president to be an activist and neither did Grant himself. Those who hoped for a period of calm after the storms of Johnson's presidency were soon disappointed.

Grant's passive view of the presidency allowed Congress to play a dominant role in his administration. As a result, the executive office itself lost some of the authority Lincoln had given it during the Civil War. A generation passed before power shifted back toward the White House. Since Republicans were suspicious of strong presidents, that development aroused little protest from the governing party.

Hard choices confronted the new president. Southern Republicans begged for help from Washington to fight off resurgent Democrats. Yet, many party members in the North believed Reconstruction was no longer wise or practical. Support for black aspirations seemed a loser. As a result, the commitment to African Americans waned among Republicans. Within the party, differences also flared over the right of Republican leaders to hand out patronage. The government should follow a merit system of appointing officials said some Republicans; this idea became known as "civil service reform." Party regulars, who hated civil service reform, argued that Grant should side with them and defer to the wishes of congressional leaders when making appointments.

Grant tried to stay away from partisan battles. As a result, he followed a shifting policy in selecting his cabinet and making appointments. The president did not accept the advice of influential Republicans but depended instead on men who shared his cautious governing style. The president gave cabinet officers wide discretion to use merit rather than political connections in staffing their departments. Without the clear objective of a war before him, Grant seemed confused by the shifting demands of domestic politics.

The most immediate problem for Grant in his first year was the South. The Democrats were trying to split the Republicans by making common cause with those party members unhappy about their existing leadership. Playing down their racism and dislike of blacks, the Democrats argued that former Confederates should now be allowed to participate in public life. The strategy produced mixed results in 1869. Republicans did well in Mississippi and won a close race for governor in Texas. Democrats triumphed in Virginia and Tennessee. Overall, the results suggested that Republican strength was eroding as the Democrats got back into politics. Southern white Republicans and their black allies found that Washington often left them on their own to confront the resurgent Democrats.

The Railroads Meet

While politics dominated Washington, an event in Utah captured public attention. The national economy needed secure and efficient transportation to the West Coast. Throughout the 1860s, two transcontinental railroads had been laying tracks across the country. The Union Pacific had built westward and the Central Pacific eastward. The two lines faced imposing obstacles of money and geography. The Central Pacific had crossed the heights of the Sierra Nevada Mountains through rocky gorges and across treacherous rivers. Several thousand Chinese laborers did the most dangerous work. They tunneled into snowdrifts to reach their work sites and then toiled on sheer cliffs with picks and dynamite. Many died, all faced discrimination, and the railroad would not have existed without them. On the Union Pacific side, more than 10,000 construction men, many of them Irish immigrants, laid tracks across Nebraska and Wyoming.

On May 10, 1869, the two rail lines met at Promontory, Utah. Engine 119 of the Union Pacific placed its cowcatcher up against the cowcatcher of the Central Pacific's Engine No. 60. Railroad executives drove a golden spike into the ground with a silver sledgehammer after missing their target on the first few tries. The transcontinental lines were a reality. Loans and subsidies from the federal government to the railroads had enabled the lines to be built quickly. Following their completion, a period of railroad construction ensued. Soon the United States had one of the most developed transportation systems in the world.

With railroads in place, the entire West seemed open to settlement for white Americans eager to dominate the Great Plains. No longer did potential farmers think of this area as "The Great American Desert." The whole continent lay available. That meant, however, that hard decisions lay ahead regarding the Native Americans who had been pushed westward before the Civil War as well as the nomadic tribes of the Plains Indians already living in the area. These native residents of the West found their hunting grounds and traditional domains at risk as settlers appeared.

Grant's "Peace Policy"

Treatment of the Indians after the Civil War wavered between benevolence and cruelty. In the case of Grant, Native Americans found he treated them with more respect and insight than had many previous presidents. His administration pursued what became known as the "peace policy." While many western settlers advocated the extermination of the Indian tribes, most Americans applauded Grant's strategy of conciliation.

The approach took shape before Grant came to the White House. Advocates of the Indians contended that the hostile tribes should be resettled in Dakota Ter-

In the work of building the transcontinental railroad, the grueling labor of Chinese workers was indispensable. They worked for low pay in difficult conditions in a society that scorned them and often subjected them to harsh discrimination.

Chief Red Cloud of the Sioux sits in his regalia for a photographer. Fear and fascination were mingled in popular attitudes toward Native Americans after the Civil War.

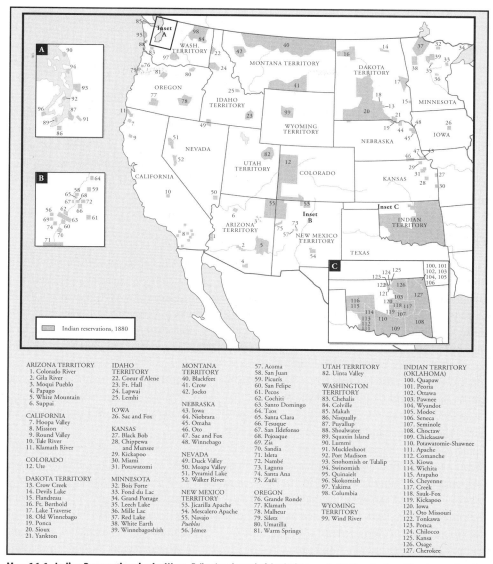

Map 16.1 Indian Reservations in the West Following the end of the Civil War and with the adoption of the peace policy of President Ulysses S. Grant, a network of Indian reservations spread across the West. This map shows how extensive the reservation system was.

ritory and in the Indian Territory (now Oklahoma). The government would stop treating the entire West as a giant Indian reservation. Instead, the government would allocate specific areas to the tribes. On these "reservations" Native Americans would learn the cultural values of white society, be taught to grow crops, and be paid a small income until they could support themselves. The plan was not yet in place when Grant became president.

The Peace Policy in Action

Grant's commissioner of Indian Affairs was Ely Parker, a Seneca. Congress appropriated $2 million for Indian affairs and set up a Board of Indian Commissioners to distribute the money. Indian agents were not to be political hacks; the Grant administration asked for nominations from Christian churches.

The peace policy blended kindness and force. If the Indians accepted the presence of Christian church officials on the reservations, the government would leave them alone. Resistance to the peace policy sparked the army to drive the Indians onto reservations. In its early months, the peace policy seemed a humane improvement over what had gone before. For the Indians, the new approach represented another attack on their way of life. They would not simply accept what whites offered to them without a final burst of armed resistance.

An Era of Scandals

Periodic corruption has marked American government throughout its history, but the post–Civil War era seemed particularly prone to such behavior. Scandals plagued the Grant administration. In the summer of 1869, two speculators, Jay Gould and Jim Fisk, manipulated the gold market to achieve huge profits for themselves. The price of gold rose until on September 24, 1869, when financial turmoil erupted. Investors who had promised to sell gold at lower prices faced ruin. Then the government sold its own gold supplies, the price of gold broke, and the market returned to its normal level. In the resulting inquiries about what had happened, the public learned that some members of Grant's family had helped Gould and Fisk carry out their plan. Whispers had it that Julia Grant, the president's wife, might have been involved. The story was not true, but doubts spread about the ethical standards of Grant's presidency.

To the odor of corruption was soon added a sense of White House confusion and incompetence. The administration talked of forcing Spain to give up Cuba and then backed away from the idea. The president wanted to annex the Dominican Republic (Santo Domingo). An agent of the president worked out a treaty of annexation with Santo Domingo's rulers, and the pact was sent to the Senate. Grant pushed hard for approval of the treaty, but the Senate, fearful of the influence of speculators and lobbyists, was suspicious of the president's goals. As a result, the treaty was defeated and the president embarrassed.

Grant's administration had more success in the resolution of American claims for maritime losses against Great Britain over the *Alabama,* one of several Confederate raiders that had been constructed in British shipyards during the Civil War. The *Alabama* had sunk numerous Union vessels. Charles Sumner, chair of the Senate Foreign Relations Committee, wanted to use the claims as leverage in an effort to acquire Canada. In 1871, the State Department worked out an amicable settlement of the issue that left Canada alone.

Grant and Congress

Other issues troubled Grant's relations with Congress. Congressional Republicans were split on issues such as the protective tariff and the currency. The mainstream of the party believed that a tariff policy to "protect" American industries against foreign competition was in the best interest of business, workers, and the party itself. A minority of Republicans called the protective policy wrong economically and a potential source of corrupt influence from the affected industries. On the currency, eastern Republicans favored the gold standard and what was known as "hard money," where every dollar was backed by an equal amount of gold. Western Republicans advocated an expansion of the money supply through paper money, or "greenbacks," and, when necessary, even the issuance of dollars backed by silver as an alternative to gold.

The civil service issue also split the party. The reliance on political clout to get a government job came under fire as reformers argued that competence and nonpartisanship were better ways to staff these positions. Republicans who wanted to reduce the tariff, rely on the civil service, and treat the South with more leniency defected from the Grant administration. They formed "Liberal Republican" alliances with Democrats in such states as West Virginia and Missouri. In the 1870s, "liberal" meant someone who favored smaller government, lower tariffs, civil service, and most important, an end to Reconstruction.

Grant and His Party

With his presidency under attack, Grant turned to the Republican leaders in Congress for support. These Republicans disliked the Liberal Republican program and its leaders. Angry Liberals threatened to bolt the party. Grant knew that he could never satisfy the demands of the Liberals on Reconstruction or the civil service. The Democrats could always outbid him on those issues, and endeavoring to court his Republican opponents would only weaken the party further. The president understood that he had to please his base to win reelection in 1872. Grant was not a gifted politician, but he could read that lesson clearly.

Toward the 1870 Elections

Following that logic, Grant conciliated mainstream Republicans. He dismissed cabinet officers who disagreed with him and aligned himself with party members willing to defend Congress and the White House. Officeholders who supported Liberal Republican candidates or Democrats were fired. Despite these actions, the elections went for the opposition. Liberal Republicans won races in West Virginia and Missouri. The Democrats added forty-one seats to their total in the House and picked up another six seats in the Senate. The Republicans retained control of both houses, but their position was weakening. Grant's enemies even thought he might be defeated in 1872.

The Ku Klux Klan in the South

By the summer of 1870, reports reached Washington of violence against blacks and white Republicans across the South. Roving bands of whites calling themselves the Ku Klux Klan (see Chapter 15) made the attacks. Throughout the South, the Klan stamped out chal-

A Cartoonist Attacks the Ku Klux Klan

The use of political cartoons to convey ideas about contemporary issues became more sophisticated after the Civil War. One of the great popular artists of the day was Thomas Nast. In the 1870s, his images attacked the refusal of southerners to grant real freedom to African Americans and the increasing reliance in the South on such terror organizations as the Ku Klux Klan and the White Leagues. Nash dramatized for his audience that southern whites, in or out of a hood, had the same goal—"a white man's government." These striking pictures helped sustain the Republican party during the presidency of Ulysses S. Grant. Unfortunately for blacks in the South, neither Nast nor the white political leadership in the North persisted in their commitment to equal rights. By the end of the decade, other cartoons depicted blacks in a degrading manner that justified white dominance and paved the way in time for racial segregation.

The Granger Collection, New York

lenges to white dominance. One Republican in Louisiana pleaded that "murder and intimidation are the order of the day in this state."

The Klan and its offshoots, such as the Knights of the White Camelia, White Leagues, and the White Brotherhood, acted as the paramilitary arm of the Democratic party to stamp out Republicanism through any means. In Tennessee a black Republican was beaten after he won an election for justice of the peace. His assailants told him "that they didn't dispute I was a very good fellow . . . but they did not intend any nigger to hold office in the United States."

The Klan stopped at nothing to eliminate its opponents. Leaders of the Republican party were hunted and killed. Four blacks died when the Klan attacked an election meeting in Alabama in October 1870. A "negro chase" in South Carolina left thirteen blacks dead. The Klansmen rode in white robes and hoods; their aim, they said, was to frighten their racial foes. The disguises also hid their identity from law enforcement. A wave of shootings and brutality undermined the chances of the Republican party to survive and grow below the Mason-Dixon line.

The Government and the Klan

Viewing the wreckage of their southern parties after the 1870 elections, Republicans recognized that the Klan's terror tactics had worked to intimidate voters and demoralize their leaders. But doing something posed problems. As 1871 began, the Republicans had less stomach for sending troops to the South to affect politics. As an Illinois newspaper observed, "the negro is now a voter and a citizen. Let him hereafter take his chances in the battle of life." Republican leaders asked themselves whether the cost of maintaining party organizations in the South justified the effort in the face of such resolute Democratic opposition.

The violence of the Klan presented a challenge that could not be ignored. Without firm action, the Republican party in the South might disappear. Congress adopted legislation to curb election fraud, bribery, and coercion in elections. When these measures proved inadequate, the lawmakers passed the Ku Klux Klan Act of 1871. This law outlawed conspiracies to deprive voters of their civil rights and banned efforts to bar any citizen from holding public office. The government also received broader powers to fight the Klan through the use of federal district attorneys to override state laws. As a last resort, military force could also be employed.

The Democrats labeled these laws an unconstitutional interference with the rights of the states. Their passage was "the crowning act of centralization and consolidation," said one critic. A Republican countered by saying: "Tell me nothing of a constitution which fails to shelter beneath its rightful power the people of a country."

Breaking the Power of the Klan

Republicans determined to end the lawbreaking and violence that the Klan embodied. The Justice Department, which had been established in 1870, argued that the threat the Klan posed to democratic government amounted to war. Officials in Washington mobilized federal district attorneys and United States marshals to institute prosecutions against the Klan. The legal offensive in 1871 brought results as in state after state Klan leaders were indicted. Federal troops assisted the work of the Justice Department in South Carolina. The Klan was discredited as a public presence in southern politics; its violence became more covert and less visible. Even though the prosecutions of the Klan showed that effective federal action could compel southern states to comply with the rule of law, sentiment in the North for such stern measures was receding. Reconstruction did not seem to be a noble crusade for human rights but part of a troubling pattern of corruption and excessive government power.

The Tweed Ring in New York

The willingness to use national power to push Reconstruction receded in part when Americans became convinced that politics everywhere were corrupt. The most celebrated example of wrongdoing in this period was the Tweed Ring, which dominated New York City during the late 1860s.

William Magear Tweed, Jr. had risen through various city offices and by the early 1870s was a member of the New York state senate. He was closely identified with the Democratic party organization that met at a political clubhouse called Tammany Hall to plan strategy. The expanding cities of the post–Civil War years offered politicians chances to make money from providing lucrative contracts and official services. Tweed and his allies turned these new opportunities to their personal advantage. They padded the city's accounts and extracted kickbacks from contractors doing business with the city.

There was more to Tweed, however, than just corruption. His power rested on the votes of the city's heavily Democratic population. Long loyal to the Democrats who shared their suspicion of Republican efforts to regulate moral behavior, Irish Catholic immigrants supported the party that helped them and respected their lifestyle and religious values. Their votes were crucial to keep New York in the Democratic column in presidential contests. Tammany made sure that city services and jobs were available to those who supported their organization at the polls. Tweed and his "ring" thus reflected larger changes in American cities and urban politics that began in the 1860s.

In fact's Tweed's moment at the peak of New York politics was brief. The *New York Times* devoted endless columns to exposing the misdeeds of the Democratic party and its leaders. More significant from a national perspective, a cartoonist named Thomas Nast used his art to make Tweed an object of scorn. Nast's drawing depicted Tweed as the leader of a band of criminals, a money-grubbing scoundrel who was unfit for public office. The cartoon devastated Tweed himself. As he told one editor: "I don't care a straw for your newspaper articles. My constituents don't know how to read, but they can't help seeing them damned pictures."

During mid-1871, an angry member of the Tweed Ring gave city account books to a reporter. The disclosure of how much had been spent on city projects stunned voters. A courthouse that had been projected to cost $250,000 came to $13 million. Within a year, Tweed had been indicted. He escaped conviction in his first trial but was later retried and found guilty on 204 counts. He fled the country and took refuge in Spain. Arrested there when an official recognized him from a Nast cartoon, he was returned to New York a broken man and died in 1878.

For many troubled Americans, Tweed's rise and fall symbolized the decline in ethical standards that had followed the Civil War. In the North, they thought that expanding the power of the government, as well as expanding the vote to all white males and many freed slaves, threatened the nation's political future. "We are in danger of going the way of all Republics," said one critic of the existing system. "First freedom, then glory; when that is past, wealth, vice, and corruption." That view was too gloomy, but it expressed the attitude of increasing numbers of middle-class citizens in the North.

Liberal Republicans Challenge Grant

Restoring ethical standards was the goal of the Liberal Republicans who wanted to field a candidate against President Grant in 1872. Only in that way could Reconstruction be ended and civil service reform achieved. Leading the campaign were Senator Carl Schurz, a Missouri Republican; Edwin L. Godkin, editor of *The Nation;* and Charles Francis Adams, the son of former president John Quincy Adams.

Liberals believed in smaller government and an end to the protective tariff. "The Government," wrote E. L. Godkin, "must get out of the 'protective' business and the 'subsidy' business and the 'improvement' business and 'development' business . . . It cannot touch them without breeding corruption." But Reconstruction was their main target. They saw what happened in the South as an unwise experiment in racial democracy. Jacob D. Cox, who had been secretary of the interior under Grant, maintained that "the South can only be governed through the part of the community that embodies the intelligence and the capital." In effect, black Americans in the South would have to look to whites in that region for protection of their rights and privileges.

The problem was that the Liberal Republicans did not have a good national candidate to run against Grant. Few party leaders were men with national stature. Schurz was a native of Germany and therefore ineligible to run under the Constitution. The race came down to Charles Francis Adams, Lyman Trumbull of Illinois, and Horace Greeley, editor of the New York *Tribune.* After six ballots, Greeley was the nominee. At sixty-one, Greeley was an odd choice. He favored the protective tariff, unlike most reformers, and he was indifferent about the civil service. His main passion was ending Reconstruction. Once a harsh critic of the South, he had now mellowed. His personal opinions, which included vegetarianism and the use of human manure in farming, made him an oddball to most Americans. "That Grant is an Ass no man can deny," said one Liberal in private, "but better an Ass than a mischievous idiot."

The 1872 Election

Grant was renominated on a platform that stressed the need to preserve Reconstruction. Voters in the North must safeguard what they had won during the Civil War. The Democrats were in a box. If they rejected Greeley, they had no chance to win. Picking him, however, would alienate southern voters who remembered Greeley's passion against the Confederacy. In the end, the Democrats accepted Greeley as their only alternative. The Liberal Republican-Democratic nominee made a vigorous public campaign, while Grant observed the tradition that the incumbent did not take part in the race personally.

The Republicans made their appeal on the issues of the war. One speaker told his audience that they could either "Go vote to burn school houses, desecrate churches and violate women or vote for Horace Greeley, which means the same thing." The black leader, Frederick Douglass, said of the impending contest: "If the Republican party goes down, freedom goes down with it." When the voters went to the polls, the outcome was a decisive victory for Grant and his party. The president swamped Greeley in the popular vote and in the electoral tally. There were still enough Republicans in the South to enable Grant to carry all but five of the southern states in one of the last honest elections the region would see for many years. The Democrats had reached a low point behind Greeley. Worn out by the rigors of the campaign, he died in late November. The triumph was a mixed one for Grant. He remained in the White House, but scandals would soon plague his second term.

A Surge of Scandals

As the excitement of the 1872 election faded, allegations of corruption in Congress surfaced. The first controversy turned on the efforts of the Crédit Mobilier Company (named after a French company) to purchase influence with lawmakers during the 1860s. The directors of the Union Pacific had established Credit Mobilier to build the transcontinental line. By paying themselves to construct the railroad, the participants in the venture sold bonds that were marketed at a large profit to investors and insiders. The only problem was that much of the money in effect came from the federal government through loans and guarantees.

To avoid a congressional probe into the company, Credit Mobilier's managers offered leading Republicans a chance to buy shares in the company at prices well below their market value. When the lawmakers sold their shares, they pocketed the difference, the equivalent of a bribe. A newspaper broke the story in late 1872 and an investigation ensued. The probe produced a few scapegoats but cleared most of the individuals involved. Nevertheless, the episode damaged the credibility of public officials.

Another embarrassing episode occurred in February 1873. At the end of a congressional session, a last-minute deal gave senators and representatives a retroactive pay increase. The public denounced the action as the "Salary Grab." The *Chicago Tribune* said that it was "nothing more nor less than an act of robbery." When Congress reconvened in December 1873, repeal of the salary increase sailed through both houses as politicians backtracked. These two incidents produced widespread calls for reducing government expenditures and rooting out corruption. As the humorist Mark Twain said, "It could probably be shown by facts and figures that there is no distinctly native American criminal class except Congress."

Twain himself captured the spirit of the times in his novel *The Gilded Age,* published in 1873. The main character, Colonel Beriah Sellers, was an engaging confidence man who embodied the faith in progress and economic growth of the postwar years, along with a healthy amount of fraud and deceit that accompanied the rapid expansion of business. In time, the title of Twain's book came to be used for the entire era between the end of Reconstruction and the start of the twentieth century. Beneath its appealing surface, this period had significant problems. At the same time, the "Gilded Age" was a richer and more complex time than the stereotype of corrupt politicians and fraudulent businessmen that Twain portrayed.

The Panic of 1873 and Its Consequences

The sense of national crisis deepened in September 1873 when the banking house of Jay Cooke and Company failed. The bank could not pay its debts or return money to its depositors; it had to close. The disaster came because the bank could not market the bonds of the Northern Pacific Railroad in which it had invested heavily. As this important bank collapsed, others followed suit, businesses cut back on employment, and a downturn began. The problems rivaled similar panics that had occurred in 1819, 1837, and 1857; however, the Panic of 1873 was the worst of them all.

The immediate effects of the problem lasted until 1879. In fact, an extended period of economic hard times had

Table 16.1 Railroad Mileage, 1869–1876

1869:	46,844
1870:	52,922
1871:	60,301
1872:	66,171
1873:	70,268
1874:	72,385
1875:	74,096
1876:	76,808

begun that extended through the 1890s. A hallmark of the "Great Depression," as it was then called, was declining prices for agricultural products and manufactured goods. Americans faced an economy in which falling prices placed the heaviest burdens on people who were in debt or who earned their living by selling their labor. An abundance of cheap unskilled labor proved a boon for capitalists who wanted to keep costs down. For the poor, however, it meant that they had little job security and could easily be replaced if they protested against harsh working conditions. Industrialization went forward at a substantial human cost.

The panic occurred because of a speculative post–Civil War boom in railroad building. In 1869, railroad mileage stood at about 47,000 miles; four years later it had risen to 70,268 miles. The new railroad lines employed tens of thousands of workers and extended across a far larger geographical area than any previous manufacturing enterprise. When large railroads such as the Northern Pacific failed because of their overexpansion and inability to pay debts, the resulting impact rippled through society. Economic activities that were dependent on the rail lines, such as car making, steel rail production, and passenger services, also fell off. Layoffs of employees and bankruptcies for businesses followed. More than 10,000 companies failed in 1878, the worst year of the depression.

The Plight of the Unemployed

Americans who were thrown out of work during the 1870s had no system of unemployment insurance to cushion the shock of their plight. In some cities, up to a quarter of the workforce looked for jobs without success. Tramps roamed the countryside. The conventional wisdom held that natural forces had to restore prosperity; any form of political intervention would be useless and dangerous. When President Grant proposed that the national government generate jobs through public works, the secretary of the treasury responded: "It is not part of the business of government to find employment for people."

People out of a job during the mid-1870s could not afford such a philosophical attitude. Laborers in the Northeast mounted a campaign for "Work for Bread" that produced large demonstration in major cities. The marchers asked city and state governments to pay for projects to create parks and construct streets to provide work. In January 1874, a demonstration at Tompkins Square in New York City pitted a crowd of 7,000 unemployed laborers against police. Many marchers were arrested; others were injured in the melee.

Labor unrest crackled through the first half of the decade. Strikes marked 1874 and 1875. In Pennsylvania the railroads used their control of police and strikebreakers to put down the "Long Strike" of coal miners and their supporters. Twenty alleged members of a secret society called the Molly Maguires were hanged. Conservatives feared that the nation was on the verge of revolution.

Distress and Protest Among the Farmers

Discontent also flared in the farm belt. The price of wheat stood at $1.16 a bushel in 1873; it skidded to ninety-five cents a bushel a year later. The price of corn stood at sixty-four cents a bushel in 1874 but went down to forty-two cents in 1875. These changes meant substantial drops in farm income. As a result, the debts that farmers had to pay for land and equipment posed an even greater burden. Faced with the economic power of the railroads and grain merchants, the farmer was, said one newspaper, "a mere bushwhacker, confronting organized and well-equipped enemies."

The Patrons of Husbandry, also known as the Grange, led the farm protests. Created in 1867, the nonpartisan Grange focused on complaints about the high mortgages that farmers owed, the prices they paid to middlemen such as the operators of grain elevators, and the discrimination they faced at the hands of the railroads in moving their goods to market.

Regulating the Railroads

Farmers argued that the answer to the power of the railroads was in using the authority of state governments to compel the rail lines to cease working against farm interests. In practice, that meant the creation of state railroad commissions with the power to establish fair rates and prevent unfair treatment of those who shipped agricultural products. In 1870, Illinois adopted a new state constitution that instructed the legislature to pass laws establishing maximum rates for the transportation of passengers and freight. The legislature responded with the creation of the Illinois Railroad Commission and gave the new agency wide powers. Neighboring states such as Iowa, Minnesota, and Wisconsin followed suit in the next several years. Railroad companies challenged some of these laws in court, and a case testing the constitutionality of the Illinois law worked its way toward the United States Supreme Court as *Munn v. Illinois*.

The pressure for regulatory legislation even affected Congress in 1873–1874. An Iowa Republican introduced legislation in the House to establish a national railroad commission. As an anonymous spokesman for western economic interests told a reporter, "Sir, you will never make me doubt that a government which could put down that mighty Rebellion can regulate the details of a few tariffs of some railroad corporation." The bill passed in the House, but the Senate never acted upon it. Federal legislation would not be enacted until 1887.

Inflationary Solutions

The decline in consumer prices and the growing burden of debt on farmers and business-men in the South and West created pressure for laws to put more money into circulation. That would make debts easier to pay. The Treasury Department's decision to end the coinage of silver aroused particular anger among southern and western advocates of infla-tion; they called it the "Crime of 1873." Proponents of the move argued that an over-abundance of silver in the marketplace required the move to a gold standard. By coining silver into money at a price above its market levels, the government was subsidizing Amer-ican silver production and cheapening the currency. Opponents of the change responded that eastern bankers were setting financial policy to the detriment of farmers and debtors.

An effort to inject a modest amount of inflation into the economy came in 1875. A cur-rency bill cleared both houses of Congress; it provided some $64 million in additional money for the financial system. President Grant decided, after getting conservative advice to do so, to veto the bill in April 1875. Congress sustained his action. The government would not intervene in the deepening economic crisis.

Women in the 1870s

Amid the male-dominated political life that marked this period, occasional episodes reminded the nation that women were excluded from the government, elections, and most of public policy. Susan B. Anthony sought the chance to address the Liberal Republican and Republican national conventions in 1872 but was turned away. On elec-tion day she and fifteen other women registered and voted at their polling place in Rochester, New York. Anthony and the voting officials were arrested. Her trial in federal court led to a $100 fine, which she refused to pay. Rather than giving Anthony a reason for appealing the case to a higher court, authorities did not collect the fine against her.

Another champion of women's rights was Victoria Claflin Woodhull. A faith healer and spiritualist from Ohio, she and her sister Tennessee Claflin came to New York, where, in 1870, Victoria announced her candidacy for president of the United States. She published a weekly newspaper that endorsed the right of women to practice free love outside of marriage. In 1872, she denounced one of the nation's leading ministers, Henry Ward Beecher, for having had an affair with a member of his congregation. The revelation led to one of the most sensational public trials of the nineteenth century. The proceedings ended in a hung jury and the Claflin sisters had to flee to England to escape public outrage. Woodhull's experience and social disgrace demonstrated the perils that faced women who defied the strict social conventions of the post–Civil War era.

Overcoming Barriers to Equality

For women from the middle and upper classes, the 1870s brought expanding educational opportunities. The number of women graduating from high school stood at nearly 9,000 in 1870, compared with 7,000 men. Aware of these trends, state universities and private colleges opened their doors to women students in growing numbers. By 1872, nearly one hundred institutions of higher learning admitted women. This process continued despite the fears of male academics. Edward Clarke, a retired Harvard medical professor, warned in 1873 that when women expended their "limited energy" on higher education, they put their "female apparatus" at risk.

Cornell University began accepting women applicants in 1875, and one of its first female graduates was M. Cary Thomas who received her B.A. in 1877. Five years later, she earned a Ph.D at a German university. By the 1890s, she had become the president of Bryn Mawr, a woman's college outside Philadelphia. Like other women in male-dominated institutions, she endured rudeness and indifference from her male colleagues. She later recalled that "it is a fiery ordeal to educate a lady by coeducation."

Obtaining a degree was not a guarantee of access to professions that males controlled. Myra Bradwell tried to become a lawyer in Illinois, but the state bar association rejected her application. She sued in federal court, and in 1873, the U.S. Supreme Court ruled that the law did not grant her the right to be admitted to the bar. One justice said that "the paramount destiny and mission of woman are to fulfill the noble and benign offices of wife and mother." That decision gave the Illinois legislature the authority to deny women the chance to practice law. In 1870, there were only five female lawyers in the nation.

The Supreme Court also rebuffed efforts to secure woman suffrage through the courts. Virginia Minor, president of the Woman Suffrage Association in Missouri, tried to vote during the 1872 election, but the registrar of voters turned her away. She sued on the grounds that the action denied her rights as a citizen. In the case of *Minor v. Happersett* (1875), the Supreme Court ruled unanimously that suffrage was not one of the rights of citizenship because "sex has never been made one of the elements of citizenship in the United States." To achieve the right to vote, women would have to amend the Constitution or obtain the right of suffrage from the states, a process that took another four decades to complete.

The Rise of Voluntary Associations

Blocked off from politics, women carved out a public space of their own through voluntary associations. Black churchwomen established missionary societies to work both in the United States and abroad. Clubs and literary societies sprang up among white women as well. In New York City, women created Sorosis, a club for women only, after the New York Press Club barred women from membership. In 1873, delegates from local Sorosis clubs formed the Association for the Advancement of Women. The New England Woman's Club, located in Boston, had local laws changed during the early 1870s to allow women to serve on the School Committee. Later the club founded the Women's Education Association to expand opportunities for their sex in schools and colleges. During the two decades that followed, the women's club movement established strong roots in all parts of the nation.

Despite being turned away at the polls, women made their presence felt in an unexpected way in 1873. Protests against the sale and use of alcohol erupted among women

The War Against Drink

The Granger Collection, New York

The temperance crusades of the 1870s against alcohol and its evils brought women into politics in an era when they could not even vote in most of the nation. This cartoon links the campaign of the Woman's Christian Temperance Union (WCTU) to the chivalry of the Middle Ages as the mounted women, armored in a righteous cause, destroy whisky, gin, brandy, and rum. The connection of reform with religion and patriotism gave the antialcohol crusade a powerful claim on middle-class sentiments. For those groups whose religious creed did not bar the use of liquor, the WCTU was an intrusive force seeking to interfere with personal rights. This cartoon thus reveals how long what are now called "social issues" have affected the nation's politics and how they grow out of cultural and economic divisions within American society. In fact, controlling the effects of alcohol has been one of the most persistent sources of social contention in the nation's history.

in New York, Ohio, and Michigan. Women marched in the streets to demand that saloons and liquor dealers close down. They urged drunkards to reform. Middle-class women prayed in front of bars and smashed barrels of liquor to emphasize their determination. Men joined the temperance movement too, but it was the fervor of women that gave the antialcohol crusade new energy. "The women are in desperate earnest," said a Missourian who witnessed one of these campaigns.

The Woman's Christian Temperance Union

As their protest successes grew, women sought to make their antialcohol campaign more than transitory. In August 1874, a group of women in the temperance ranks met at Lake Chautauqua, New York, where they set a national meeting that developed into the Woman's Christian Temperance Union (WCTU). Over the next five years, temperance leagues and local branches of the WCTU worked against intoxicating drink. By the end of the 1870s, a thousand unions had been formed, with an estimated 26,000 members. In 1879, Frances Willard became president of the WCTU, and she took the organization beyond its original goal of temperance and into broader areas of social reform such as woman suffrage and the treatment of children.

Women at Work

The 1870s also brought greater economic opportunities for women in sales and clerical jobs. The typewriter appeared in the early part of the decade. Young, college-educated women provided skilled labor to operate the new machines. E. Remington and Sons, which produced the typewriter, said in 1875 that "no invention has opened for women so broad and easy an avenue to profitable and suitable employment as the 'Type-Writer.'" By 1880, women accounted for 40 percent of the stenographers and typists in the country. These developments laid the foundation for growth in the numbers of female office workers during the rest of the nineteenth century.

The most typical experience of American women was toil. Black women in the South labored in the fields alongside their husbands who were tenant farmers or share-croppers. They did "double duty, a man's share in the field and a woman's part at home." In the growing cities, women worked in textile factories or became domestic servants. Many urban women took in borders; their routine equaled that of a small hotel.

Middle-class women with domestic servants had some assistance, but they still did an impressive amount of work. Preparing food, washing laundry, keeping the house warm, and disposing of waste all demanded hand labor. Mary Mathews, a widowed teacher in the 1870s, "got up early every Monday morning and got my clothes all washed and boiled and in the rising water; and then commenced my school at nine." Other days of the week passed in the same fashion for her and other women.

To assist women in performing these tasks, manuals about housework became popular, along with private cooking schools and college courses in home economics. Catherine Beecher collaborated with her famous sister, Harriet Beecher Stowe, in writing *The American Woman's Home* (1869). In this work, they argued "that family labor and care tend, not only to good health, but to the *Highest culture of the mind.*" Women, they continued, were "ministers of the family state." In the new coeducational colleges and universities, home economics programs offered instructions in operating kitchens and dining rooms efficiently. Cooking schools appeared in large cities with a separate class for "plain cooks" and a "Ladies Class" for affluent women who sought to link "the elegancies of artistic cookery with those economic interests which it is the duty of every woman to study."

The ease with which divorces could be obtained in many states produced a movement to tighten the conditions under which marriages could be dissolved. Laws to limit the sale of birth control devices and restrict abortions reflected the same trend. The New York Society for the Suppression of Vice was formed in 1872 under the leadership of Anthony Comstock. It lobbied successfully for a national law barring obscene information, including information about birth control and abortion, from the mails. Thus, while women had made some gains after the Civil War, they remained second-class citizens within the masculine political order of the Gilded Age.

Politics in the Gilded Age

After the presidential election of 1872, the North's already weakened commitment to Reconstruction ebbed still more. The Panic of 1873 distracted attention from the rights of black Americans. The Grant administration backed away from southern politics, and the Justice Department prosecuted fewer individuals for violations of the Enforcement Act against the Klan and pardoned some of those who had earlier been convicted of terrorist activity.

Northern support for Reconstruction waned because of charges that the experiment in multiracial government was a failure. Liberal Republicans and northern Democrats spread racist propaganda to block the aspirations of southern blacks. The editor of *The Nation* said that black residents of South Carolina had an "average of intelligence but slightly above the level of animals." Northerners found it easier to believe that the South would be better off when whites were dominant. Black Americans should be left "to the kind feeling of the white race of the South."

A damaging setback to the economic hopes of African Americans came in 1874 with the failure of the Freedmen's Savings and Trust Company in Washington, D.C. Since its founding in 1865, the bank had managed the deposits of thousands of former slaves. It was supposed to provide lessons in thrift for its depositors. However, its manager sought larger returns by investing in speculative railroad projects. The Panic of 1873 caused huge losses, and the bank failed a year later. A few customers received a portion of their savings; most lost all their money.

The Stigma of Corruption

Corruption among southern Republican governments became a favorite theme of critics of Reconstruction. There were some genuine instances of wrongdoing, but these actions were far from widespread or typical. Moreover, the white governments that took over after Reconstruction also displayed lax political ethics and committed more serious misdeeds than their predecessors had. Nevertheless, the corruption issue gave the opponents of black political participation a perfect weapon, which they used to the full. Of course, it would not have mattered if Reconstruction governments had lacked any moral flaws. Any government that represented a biracial community was unacceptable to white southerners.

Although participation of African Americans in southern politics increased dramatically during Reconstruction, their role in the region's public life never approached that of whites. Sixteen blacks served in Congress during the period, most only briefly, and several were unseated by white opponents. Many more held offices in the state legislatures, but even there, their numbers were comparatively modest. In 1868, for example, the George legislature had 216 members, of whom only thirty-two were black. In only one state, South Carolina, did blacks ever hold a majority in the legislature, and they did so in only one house. One black man, P. B. S. Pinchback, served as governor of Louisiana for a little more than a month. Six African Americans held the office of lieutenant governor in the states of Louisiana, Mississippi, and South Carolina.

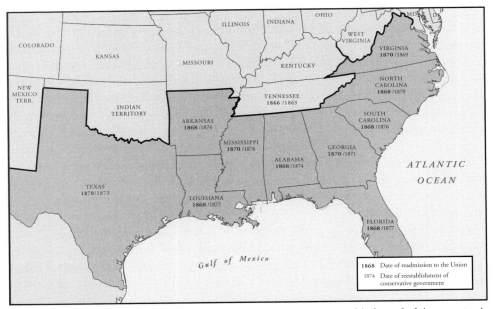

Map 16.2 Reconstruction in the South This map shows the times at which the states of the former Confederacy reentered the Union and then saw the Democrats regain political control. Note how quickly this process occurred for most of the southern states. The relative brevity of Reconstruction is one of the keys to why more sweeping racial change did not take place.

Two blacks served in the United States Senate. Hiram Revels became the first African American to enter the Senate. His term began in 1870 but lasted for only one year. From 1875 to 1881, Blanche K. Bruce represented Mississippi for a full term. Thus, by the 1870s, blacks had made their presence felt in politics, but the decline of Reconstruction made that trend a short-lived one.

The Resurgence of the Democrats

The return of the Democrats as a political force further weakened support for Reconstruction. Hard economic times arising from the Panic of 1873 worked against the Republicans. Discontented farmers wanted the government to inflate the currency and raise prices on their crops. Factory workers clamored for more jobs to become available. In this setting, the fate of African Americans in the South became a secondary concern. Angry voters turned to the Democrats in the 1874 congressional races. The party used the issue of Republican corruption to regain control of the House of Representatives for the first time in sixteen years. The Democrats added seventy-seven seats in the House and also added ten seats in the Senate in what one happy party member called a "Tidal Wave."

In the South, the revitalized Democrats "redeemed," as they called it, several states from Republican dominance. They began with Texas in 1873, then won back Arkansas the next year, and elected most of the South's members in the U.S. House of Representatives.

Louisiana saw the emergence of the White League, which was determined that "the niggers shall not rule over us." In September, open fighting erupted in New Orleans between armed Republicans and more than 3,000 White League partisans. President Grant sent in federal troops to restore calm. In Alabama, the Democrats also relied on violence and murder to oust the Republicans. Some blacks who attempted to vote in that state's Barbour County election were shot; seven were killed and nearly seventy wounded. In view of the wide support for the Democratic party among southern whites, honest elections would probably have produced similar results for that party at the polls; but intimidation and violence were key elements in the victories that the Democrats secured in the South in 1874.

The Democrats intended to use their control of the House of Representatives to roll back Reconstruction and also prevent any further expansion of black rights. During the lame-duck congressional session of 1874–1875, Republicans, who were soon to lose power, enacted a pathbreaking civil rights law that gave black citizens the right to sue in federal courts when they confronted discrimination in public accommodations such as a hotel or restaurant. The law involved a further expansion of national power; it remained to be seen how federal courts would rule when black plaintiffs sued to enforce their rights under the new civil rights statute.

Early in 1875, the Grant administration used troops to prevent occupation of the Louisiana state capital and illegal seizure of the state government by the Democrats in the midst of an election dispute. The action drew widespread protests from many northern Democrats and a growing number of Republicans who said that the white South should handle its own affairs. Meanwhile, the Democrats used more violence to overturn Republican rule in Mississippi. The state's governor, Adelbert Ames, stated that he was "fighting for the Negro, and to the whole country a white man is better than a 'Nigger.' " Without a national consensus behind civil rights and Reconstruction, the fate of black Americans lay in the hands of white southerners who were determined to keep African Americans in economic, political, and cultural subjection.

Why Reconstruction Failed

Reconstruction failed to change American race relations because it challenged long-standing racist arrangements in both the North and South. The Civil War had called these traditions into question. In the years after the fighting ended, African Americans had acted to expand their political role and become more than passive recipients of white oppression or largesse. Then the Panic of 1873, the scandals of the Grant presidency, and waning interest in black rights led white Americans to back away from an expansion of racial justice.

To help the freed slaves overcome the effects of slavery and racial bias would have involved an expansion of national government power to an extent far beyond what Americans believed was justified during the nineteenth century. Better to keep government small, argued whites, than to improve the lot of the former slaves in the South. As a result, black Americans experienced segregation and deepening oppression. The political gains of the Reconstruction era, especially the Fourteenth and Fifteenth Amendments, remained unfulfilled promises.

The End of Native American Resistance

While the United States was in the process of abandoning its Civil War commitments to African Americans, the long struggle of Native Americans to resist white encroachment also ended. Indian efforts to push back the wave of white settlers failed, and after 1876, Native Americans lacked the power to determine their own destiny.

During the 1870s, easterners and new immigrants surged westward to the prairies. The census reported over 2,660,000 farms in 1870 and just over 4 million ten years later. The newcomers competed with the Indians for space and resources. The amount of land devoted to wheat cultivation, for example, rose from nearly 21 million acres at the beginning of the decade to 62,545,000 in 1880.

The cattle industry exerted further pressure on the Indians in the late 1860s. Texans returning from the Civil War drove their herds north to markets in Kansas. These cattle and others in western territories such as Wyoming, the Dakotas, and Colorado occupied space on the prairies where Indians had traditionally pursued their nomadic hunting culture.

Annihilation of the Buffalo Herds

The systematic destruction of the buffalo herds dealt the most devastating blow to the Indians. In the societies of the Plains tribes, the meat of the bison supplied food, while the hides provided shelter and clothes. Removal of these resources was calamitous, but the cultural impact was even more ruinous. Buffalo represented the continuity of nature and the renewal of life cycles. Destruction of the buffalo ended the Indians' capacity to resist white incursions. As one Crow warrior observed after the herds had gone, "Nothing happened after that. We just lived. There were no more war parties, no capturing horses from the Piegan and the Sioux, no buffalo to hunt. There is nothing more to tell."

The decline of the buffalo herds began during the 1860s when drought, disease, and erosion shrank the animals' habitat. Then an expanding eastern market for buffalo robes and such products as pemmican (dried buffalo meat, berries, and fat) spurred the intensive hunting of buffalo. As railroads penetrated the West, hunters could transport their products to customers with relative ease. The result was virtual extermination of the buffalo. More than 5 million buffalo were slaughtered during the early 1870s. Along the Arkansas River, a British traveler reported, "there was a continual line of putrescent carcasses, so that the air was rendered pestilential and offensive to the last degree." By the end of the nineteenth century, only a few buffalo remained alive.

A Last Stand for Custer and the Indians

During the mid-1870s, Native American tribes mounted a last, futile effort to stem the tide that was overwhelming their way of life. The renewed strife in the West took place in spite of President Grant's peace policy. The original appointees of the president either resigned or left because of political attacks. Meanwhile, the church's influence over the operation of Indian policy receded as corruption and politics again shaped the treatment of Native Americans. The tribes that held on to their nomadic way of life confronted ever-increasing numbers of settlers and a hostile military.

Slaughter of the Buffalo

The manner in which the opening of the West after the Civil War is depicted in textbooks has changed in dramatic ways during the last two decades. More attention is now given to the impact on the environment and on the nomadic lifestyle of the Native American residents of the Great Plains arising from the disappearance of the buffalo herds. The critical role that these animals played in sustaining the Indian way of life meant that the task of white settlers became much less dangerous when the buffalo were gone. Pictures such as this one of 40,000 hides pulled up outside Dodge City, Kansas, convey a dramatic sense of the extermination of these animals. Of course, no text can impart the odor of that many hides.

The individuals in the image are small compared to the mass of hides, but their presence reveals how the trade in buffalo had become a key aspect of the western economy. When the buffalo were gone, as happened within a few years, residents moved on to another boom and bust cycle, whether it was in cattle ranching or farming. The picture serves as an evocation of a vanished time and place, but also says something permanent about the nature of the West.

Kansas State Historical Society

Fighting broke out on the southern plains when Comanches and Kiowas attacked wagon trains. A conflict ensued between soldiers and Cheyenne, Kiowas, and Comanches that became known as the Red River War. The army did not prevail on the battlefield. Instead, Indian resistance collapsed because of a lack of food and supplies.

In the North, the discovery of gold in the Black Hills of Dakota increased pressure on the Sioux to give up the area for white development. The Indians refused, and the government sent soldiers to protect the miners. The Indian leaders, Crazy Horse and Sitting Bull, rallied their followers to stop the army. Near what the Indians called the Greasy Grass (known to whites as the Little Big Horn), Colonel George Armstrong Custer led a force of 600 men. With a third of his detachment, he attacked more than 2,000 Sioux warriors. The result was the annihilation of Custer and his force on June 25, 1876, in a battle that became legendary as "Custer's Last Stand." The Indian victory shocked the nation, but it was only a momentary success. The army pursued the Indians during the months that followed, and by the end of the Grant administration, the only Indians who were able to fight actively against the army were the Apaches in the Southwest. The bad treatment that the Apaches received from the government led to sporadic clashes during the 1880s, and the army prevailed by the end of the decade.

One more tragic encounter, the Battle of Wounded Knee, lay ahead for the Plains Indians in 1890. For the most part, however, the Grant presidency brought an end to the centuries of white-Indian warfare that had marked the history of the West in the United States.

The Election of 1876

Several themes of late-nineteenth century life intersected as the 1876 presidential election neared. The centennial of the Declaration of Independence offered citizens an opportunity to reflect on the nation's progress and the social issues that remained unresolved. The race question confronted leaders and citizens even as the passions and commitments of Reconstruction faded. The contest for the White House seemed unusually important since it would shape the direction of the country for several decades.

The Continuing Shadow of Scandal

Toward the end of Grant's second term, political corruption continued to cast a shadow over the administration. Within the Treasury Department, the Whiskey Ring was exposed. Officials involved took kickbacks from liquor interests in return for not collecting federal excise taxes on whiskey. President Grant appointed a new secretary of the treasury, wBenjamin H. Bristow, and told him: "Let no guilty man escape if it can be avoided." The administration also faced queries concerning the secretary of war, W. W. Belknap. For some time, Belknap's wife had been receiving cash gifts from a man who sold supplies to the army. When these ties were revealed, Belknap faced impeachment by a congressional committee. He resigned abruptly and Grant accepted his hasty departure. Critics of the president argued that the trail of scandal had reached close to the White House. Few doubted Grant's personal honesty, but politicians recognized that he had not always exercised wise judgment in his cabinet selections.

Marking the Centennial

As the nation's one hundredth birthday neared, the Centennial International Exhibition to be held in Philadelphia attracted public fascination. In May of 1876, some 285 acres of fairgrounds held several hundred buildings crammed with exhibits, specimens, and artifacts from thirty-seven nations. The doors opened on May 10 for 200,000 spectators, including both houses of Congress, who heard a welcoming address by President Grant. The throng poured into the building to see what had been assembled as evidence of the advance of civilization in the United States. One of the stellar attractions was the huge Corliss steam engine. Standing forty feel tall, it weighed 700 tons. Equally alluring was the "harmonic telegraph" of Alexander Graham Bell, as the telephone was then called.

Amid the technological marvels, the complexity of American life in the 1870s slipped away. African Americans had almost no recognition. Native American cultures were depicted as "curiosities" consisting of totem poles, tepees, and trinkets. The Women's Pavilion stressed the joys of homemaking. That exhibit evoked a protest from Elizabeth Cady Stanton and Susan B. Anthony. On July 4, 1876, they read a "Women's Declaration of Independence" that contrasted their aspirations with the traditional attitudes toward women expressed at the fair.

Nearly 10 million Americans came to the fair during its run, which ended on November 10. They learned to eat bananas, and hot popcorn became a fad among city dwellers. The fair lost money, but at the same time contributed to a growing sense of national pride and confidence.

The Race for the White House

A key test of the nation's institutions occurred during the disputed election of 1876. The closest result in history produced a quarrel that threatened to renew hostilities between North and South. As the process commenced, the Democrats felt optimism about their chances to regain power for the first time since 1860. Most of the southern states would vote for the Democratic nominee; difficult economic times in the East and Middle West made voters sympathetic to the party out of power.

From the Collections of the Library of Congress

In the dramatic 1876 election, the Democrats put forward "Honest Sam Tilden," who lost to Rutherford B. Hayes in the disputed contest.

For its candidate, the party selected Samuel J. Tilden, the governor of New York. An opponent of the Tweed Ring, he was regarded as a reformer. A corporate lawyer, he believed in the gold standard, small government, and restraints on spending. The platform spoke of a "revival of Jeffersonian democracy" and called for "high standards of official morality." Since Tilden was not in good health, the custom that presidential candidates did not campaign during that era worked to his advantage.

Among Republicans, there was some talk of a third term for President Grant, but the scandals of his presidency made him a liability. The front-runner for the nomination was James G. Blaine, a former speaker of the House of Representatives. With the nomination seemingly in his grasp, Blaine came under fire for financial dealings with an Arkansas railroad while he was in the House. Despite his vigorous response to the charges, Republicans were wary of selecting him to run against Tilden.

At the national convention, Blaine took an early lead. As the balloting continued, his candidacy lost momentum. Instead, the Republicans selected Governor Rutherford B. Hayes of Ohio. Hayes had the virtues of a good military record in the Civil War and a spotless record in public office. In the campaign, the Democrats stressed Republican corruption and Tilden's honesty. In response, the Republicans relied on Reconstruction and war memories, as they had in 1868 and 1872. This rhetoric became known as "waving the bloody shirt,"

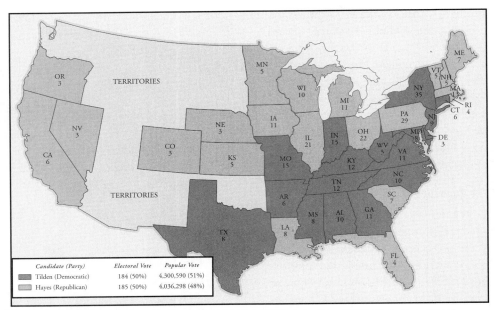

Map 16.3 The Election of 1876 The presidential election of 1876 between Samuel J. Tilden for the Democrats and Rutherford B. Hayes for the Republicans turned on the votes of Florida, Louisiana, and South Carolina to produce the narrow one-vote victory in the electoral college for Hayes.

View an animated version of this map or related maps at http://history.wadsworth.com/passages2e.

in memory of a Republican speaker who had held up a bloodstained Union tunic and urged voters to remember the sacrifices of the Men in Blue. As one Republican put it, "Soldiers, every scar you have on your heroic bodies was given to you by a Democrat." Hayes saw the wisdom of this strategy: "It leads people away from hard times, which is our deadliest foe."

When the election results rolled in, it seemed at first that Tilden had won. With most of the South in his column, the Democrat had carried New York, Connecticut, and New Jersey. The electoral vote totals indicated that Tilden had won 184 votes, one short of the 185 he needed to become president. Hayes, on the other hand, had 165 electoral votes. Three southern states, Louisiana, Florida, and South Carolina, plus a disputed elector in Oregon, were still in doubt. If they all went for Hayes, he might be in the White House.

Republican operatives moved to contest the outcome in the three undecided states. Telegrams to party members asked for evidence that African American voters had been intimidated. Honest returns from these states, Republicans argued, would show that Hayes had carried each one. The Republicans believed, moreover, that they had the advantage. In the three states that they were contesting, the Republicans could rely on federal troops to safeguard state governments that were loyal to their cause. Otherwise, Democrats could simply occupy the state capitals and count the election returns their way.

The Constitution did not specify how a contested presidential election was to be resolved. With each of the states in question submitting two sets of election returns, the

House of Representatives had the responsibility for electing a president if no one won a majority in the electoral college. At the same time, the Senate had the constitutional duty to tabulate the electoral vote. With Republicans in control of the Senate and with Democrats in control of the House, neither party could proceed without the support of the other.

To resolve the crisis, Congress created an electoral commission of fifteen members, ten from the Supreme Court. As originally conceived, the panel was to have seven Republicans, seven Democrats, and a politically independent Supreme Court justice named David Davis. Then Davis was elected to the U.S. Senate by the Illinois legislature with Democratic votes in a move to defeat a Republican incumbent. That tactic won a Senate place for the Democrat but injured Tilden's chances of prevailing in the election controversy. Davis resigned from the commission, and another member of the Supreme Court, this time a Republican, took his place. In a series of 8–7 votes along straight party lines, the electoral commission accepted the Republican returns from Louisiana, Florida, and South Carolina, and allocated the single disputed Oregon electoral vote to Hayes as well. The ruling declared that Hayes had received 185 electoral votes and Tilden 184.

Who had really been elected president in 1876? Tilden had a margin of 250,000 popular votes over Hayes and had carried sixteen states. Hayes had won eighteen states in addition to the three contested southern states. In Louisiana, Florida, and South Carolina, Tilden had received a majority of the white vote, but black Republican voters had been intimidated and terrorized to such an extent that an honest count was in doubt. Essentially the election had ended in a tie. Resolving the issue of which man would be president became an issue for the two political parties to decide.

Despite the decision of the electoral commission, the Democratic House still had to declare Hayes the winner. With the March 4, 1877, inauguration date approaching, the Democrats postponed tallying the electoral vote in an effort either to make Tilden president after March 4 or to extract concessions from the Republicans. To prevent a crisis, negotiations began among leaders from both sides to put Hayes in the White House in return for Republican agreement to end Reconstruction. The discussions were complex. They involved a variety of issues such as railroad subsidies for the South. The underlying issue was Reconstruction. If Hayes became president, the South wanted assurances that Republican rule would not be maintained through federal military intervention. After much discussion, an unwritten understanding along these lines led Congress to decide on March 2, 1877, that Rutherford B. Hayes had been elected as president of the United States.

Conclusion

The events that led to Hayes becoming president had great historical significance. Although the new president did not withdraw federal troops from the South, neither did he use them to keep Republican governments in power. Nor did Hayes attempt to enforce Reconstruction in the courts. Whites regained control of the South's political institutions, while black southerners remained second-class citizens with limited political and economic rights.

Several powerful historical forces produced that sad result. Pervasive racism in both the North and the South labeled African Americans as unfit for self-government. Pursuing Reconstruction into the 1880s would have involved giving to the national government more power over the lives of individual Americans than would have been tolerated in that era. Weary of Reconstruction and its moral claims, the generation of white Americans who had fought the Civil War turned their attention to other national problems. In so doing, they condemned black citizens to continued segregation and oppression.

The era of the Civil War and Reconstruction did have a positive legacy. Slavery was abolished and the Union preserved. Black Americans had demonstrated that they could fight and die for their country, help make its laws, and function as full citizens when given an honest chance to do so. The Fourteenth and Fifteenth Amendments at least contained the promise of the further expansion of the rights of black Americans in the future. But for the moment the nation had missed a historical opportunity to created a more equitable, multiracial society.

RECOMMENDED READINGS

Edwards, Laura F. *Gendered Strife and Confusion: The Political Culture of Reconstruction* (1997). Looks at the the role of women after the Civil War.

Foner, Eric. *Reconstruction: America's Unfinished Revolution, 1863–1877* (1988). An excellent treatment of the whole period, especially the decline of Reconstruction.

Perman, Michael. *Emancipation and Reconstruction, 1862–1879*, 2d ed. (2003). A good brief account of the issues and problems of Reconstruction.

Richardson, Heather Cox. *The Death of Reconstruction: Race, Labor, and Politics in the Post-Civil War North, 1865–1901* (2001). Considers how changing attitudes toward African Americans and labor undercut Reconstruction.

Simpson, Brooks D. *The Reconstruction Presidents* (1998). A treatment of Reconstruction from the perspective of the chief executives.

Smith, Jean Edward. *Grant* (2001). A full-scale, sympathetic biography of the general and president.

Summers, Mark Wahlgren. *The Era of Good Stealings* (1993). Uses the corruption issue of the 1870s to produce a political history of the decade.

Wang, Xi. *The Trial of Democracy: Black Suffrage and Northern Republicans, 1860–1910* (1997). Discusses how voting issues shaped the adoption and then the abandonment of Reconstruction.

Additional resources, exercises, and Internet links related to this chapter are available on the American Passages Web site: http://history.wadsworth.com/ayerscompact2/

Appendices

The Declaration of Independence
The Unanimous Declaration of the Thirteen United States of America

When in the Course of human events it becomes necessary for one people to dissolve the political bands which have connected them with another, and to assume among the Powers of the earth, the separate and equal station to which the Laws of Nature and of Nature's God entitle them, a decent respect to the opinions of mankind requires that they should declare the causes which impel them to the separation.

We hold these truths to be self-evident, that all men are created equal, that they are endowed by their Creator with certain unalienable Rights, that among these are Life, Liberty and the pursuit of Happiness. That to secure these rights, Governments are instituted among Men, deriving their just Powers from the consent of the governed. That whenever any Form of Government becomes destructive of these ends, it is the Right of the People to alter or to abolish it, and to institute new Government, laying its foundation on such principles and organizing its Powers in such form, as to them shall seem most likely to effect their Safety and Happiness. Prudence, indeed, will dictate that Governments long established should not be changed for light and transient causes; and accordingly all experience hath shewn, that mankind are more disposed to suffer, while evils are sufferable, than to right themselves by abolishing the forms to which they are accustomed. But when a long train of abuses and usurpations, pursuing invariably the same Object evinces a design to reduce them under absolute Despotism, it is their right, it is their duty, to throw off such Government, and to provide new Guards for their future security. Such has been the patient sufferance of these Colonies; and such is now the necessity which constrains them to alter their former Systems of Government. The history of the present King of Great Britain is a history of repeated injuries and usurpations, all having in direct object the establishment of an absolute Tyranny over these States. To prove this, let Facts be submitted to a candid world.

He has refused his Assent to Laws, the most wholesome and necessary for the public good.

Text is reprinted from the facsimile of the engrossed copy in the National Archives. The original spelling, capitalization, and punctuation have been retained. Paragraphing has been added.

He has forbidden his Governors to pass Laws of immediate and pressing importance, unless suspended in their operation till his Assent should be obtained; and when so suspended, he has utterly neglected to attend to them.

He has refused to pass other Laws for the accommodation of large districts of people, unless those people would relinquish the right of Representation in the Legislature, a right inestimable to them and formidable to tyrants only.

He has called together legislative bodies at places unusual, uncomfortable, and distant from the depository of their Public Records, for the sole Purpose of fatiguing them into compliance with his measures.

He has dissolved Representative Houses repeatedly, for opposing with manly firmness his invasions on the rights of the People.

He has refused for a long time, after such dissolutions, to cause others to be elected; whereby the Legislative Powers, incapable of Annihilation, have returned to the People at large for their exercise; the State remaining in the mean time exposed to all the dangers of invasion from without, and convulsions within.

He has endeavoured to prevent the Population of these States; for that purpose obstructing the Laws for Naturalization of Foreigners; refusing to pass others to encourage their migrations hither, and raising the conditions of new Appropriations of Lands.

He has obstructed the Administration of Justice, by refusing his Assent to Laws for establishing Judiciary Powers.

He has made Judges dependent on his Will alone, for the tenure of their offices, and the amount and payment of their salaries.

He has erected a multitude of New Offices, and sent hither swarms of Officers to harass our People, and eat out their substance.

He has kept among us, in times of peace, Standing Armies without the Consent of our legislatures.

He has affected to render the Military independent of and superior to the Civil Power.

He has combined with others to subject us to a jurisdiction foreign to our constitution, and unacknowledged by our laws; giving his Assent to their Acts of pretended Legislation:

For Quartering large bodies of armed troops among us:

For protecting them, by a mock Trial, from Punishment for any Murders which they should commit on the Inhabitants of these States:

For cutting off our Trade with all parts of the world:

For imposing Taxes on us without our Consent:

For depriving us in many cases, of the benefits of Trial by Jury:

For transporting us beyond Seas to be tried for pretended offences:

For abolishing the free System of English Laws in a neighbouring Province, establishing therein an Arbitrary government, and enlarging its Boundaries so as to render it at once an example and fit instrument for introducing the same absolute rule into these Colonies:

For taking away our Charters, abolishing our most valuable Laws, and altering fundamentally the Forms of our Governments:

For suspending our own Legislatures, and declaring themselves invested with Power to legislate for us in all cases whatsoever.

He has abdicated Government here, by declaring us out of his Protection, and waging War against us.

He has plundered our seas, ravaged our Coasts, burnt our towns, and destroyed the lives of our people.

He is at this time transporting large Armies of foreign Mercenaries to compleat the works of death, desolation and tyranny, already begun with circumstances of Cruelty and perfidy scarcely paralleled in the most barbarous ages, and totally unworthy the Head of a civilized nation.

He has constrained our fellow Citizens taken Captive on the high Seas to bear Arms against their Country, to become the executioners of their friends and Brethren, or to fall themselves by their Hands.

He has excited domestic insurrections amongst us, and has endeavoured to bring on the inhabitants of our frontiers, the merciless Indian Savages, whose known rule of warfare, is an undistinguished destruction of all ages, sexes and conditions.

In every stage of these Oppressions We have Petitioned for Redress in the most humble terms: Our repeated Petitions have been answered only by repeated injury. A Prince, whose character is thus marked by every act which may define a Tyrant, is unfit to be the ruler of a free People.

Nor have We been wanting in attentions to our British brethren. We have warned them from time to time of attempts by their legislature to extend an unwarrantable jurisdiction over us. We have reminded them of the circumstances of our emigration and settlement here. We have appealed to their native justice and magnanimity, and we have conjured them by the ties of our common kindred to disavow thee usurpations, which, would inevitably interrupt our connections and correspondence. They too have been deaf to the voice of justice and of consanguinity. We must, therefore, acquiesce in the necessity, which denounces our Separation, and hold them, as we hold the rest of mankind, Enemies in War, in Peace Friends.

WE, THEREFORE, the Representatives of the UNITED STATES OF AMERICA, in General Congress, Assembled, appealing to the Supreme Judge of the world for the rectitude of our intentions, do, in the Name, and by Authority of the good People of these Colonies, solemnly publish and declare, That these United Colonies are, and of Right ought to be FREE AND INDEPENDENT STATES; that they are Absolved from all Allegiance to the British Crown, and that all political connection between them and the State of Great Britain, is and ought to be totally dissolved; and that, as Free and Independent States, they have full Power to levy War, conclude Peace, contract Alliances, establish Commerce, and to do all other Acts and Things which Independent States may of right do. And for the support of this Declaration, with a firm reliance on the protection of divine Providence, we mutually pledge to each other our Lives, our Fortunes and our sacred Honor.

The Constitution of the United States of America

We the People of the United States, in Order to form a more perfect Union, establish Justice, insure domestic Tranquility, provide for the common defence, promote the general Welfare, and secure the Blessings of Liberty to ourselves and our Posterity, do ordain and establish this Constitution for the United States of America.

Article I.

Section 1. All legislative Powers herein granted shall be vested in a Congress of the United States, which shall consist of a Senate and House of Representatives.

Section 2. The House of Representatives shall be composed of Members chosen every second Year by the People of the several States, and the Electors in each State shall have the Qualifications requisite for Electors of the most numerous Branch of the State Legislature.

No Person shall be a Representative who shall not have attained to the Age of twenty five Years, and been seven Years a Citizen of the United States, and who shall not, when elected, be an Inhabitant of that State in which he shall be chosen.

Representatives and direct Taxes[1] shall be apportioned among the several States which may be included within this Union, according to their respective Numbers, which shall be determined by adding to the whole Number of free Persons, including those bound to Service for a Term of Years, and excluding Indians not taxed, three fifths of all other Persons.[2] The actual Enumeration shall be made within three Years after the first Meeting of the Congress of the United States, and within every subsequent Term of ten Years, in such Manner as they shall by Law direct. The Number of Representatives shall not exceed one for every thirty Thousand, but each State shall have at Least one Representative; and until such enumeration shall be made, the State of New Hampshire shall be entitled to chuse three; Massachusetts eight; Rhode Island and Providence Plantations one; Connecticut five; New York six; New Jersey four; Pennsylvania eight; Delaware one; Maryland six; Virginia ten; North Carolina five; South Carolina five; and Georgia three.

When vacancies happen in the Representation from any State, the Executive Authority thereof shall issue Writs of Election to fill such Vacancies.

The House of Representatives shall chuse their Speaker and other Officers; and shall have the sole Power of Impeachment.

Section 3. The Senate of the United States shall be composed of two Senators from each State, chosen by the Legislature thereof, for six Years; and each Senator shall have one Vote.[3]

Text is from the engrossed copy in the National Archives. Original spelling, capitalization, and punctuation have been retained.

[1]Modified by the Sixteenth Amendment.

[2]Replaced by the Fourteenth Amendment.

[3]Superseded by the Seventeenth Amendment.

Immediately after they shall be assembled in Consequence of the first Election, they shall be divided as equally as may be into three Classes. The Seats of the Senators of the first Class shall be vacated at the Expiration of the second Year, of the second Class at the Expiration of the fourth Year, and of the third Class at the Expiration of the sixth Year, so that one third may be chosen every second Year; and if Vacancies happen by Resignation, or otherwise, during the Recess of the Legislature of any State, the Executive thereof may make temporary Appointments until the next Meeting of the Legislature, which shall then fill such Vacancies.[4]

No Person shall be a Senator who shall not have attained to the Age of thirty Years, and been nine Years a Citizen of the United States, and who shall not, when elected, be an Inhabitant of that State for which he shall be chosen.

The Vice President of the United States shall be President of the Senate, but shall have no Vote, unless they be equally divided.

The Senate shall chuse their other Officers, and also a President pro tempore, in the Absence of the Vice President, or when he shall exercise the Office of President of the United States.

The Senate shall have the sole Power to try all Impeachments. When sitting for that Purpose, they shall be on Oath or Affirmation. When the President of the United States is tried, the Chief Justice shall preside: And no Person shall be convicted without the Concurrence of two thirds of the Members present.

Judgment in Cases of Impeachment shall not extend further than to removal from Office, and disqualification to hold and enjoy any Office of honor, Trust or Profit under the United States: but the Party convicted shall nevertheless be liable and subject to Indictment, Trial, Judgment and Punishment, according to Law.

Section 4. The Times, Places and Manner of holding Elections for Senators and Representatives, shall be prescribed in each State by the Legislature thereof, but the Congress may at any time by Law make or alter such Regulation, except as to the Places of chusing Senators.

The Congress shall assemble at least once in every Year, and such Meeting shall be on the first Monday in December, unless they shall by Law appoint a different Day.[5]

Section 5. Each House shall be the Judge of the Elections, Returns and Qualifications of its own Members, and a Majority of each shall constitute a Quorum to do Business; but a smaller Number may adjourn from day to day, and may be authorized to compel the Attendance of absent Members, in such Manner, and under such Penalties as each House may provide.

Each House may determine the Rules of its Proceedings, punish its Members for disorderly Behaviour, and, with the Concurrence of two thirds, expel a Member.

Each House shall keep a Journal of its Proceedings, and from time to time publish the same, excepting such Parts as may in their Judgment require Secrecy; and the Yeas and Nays

[4]Modified by the Seventeenth Amendment.

[5]Superseded by the Twentieth Amendment.

of the Members of either House on any question shall, at the Desire of one fifth of those Present, be entered on the Journal.

Neither House, during the Session of Congress, shall, without the Consent of the other, adjourn for more than three days, nor to any other Place than that in which the two Houses shall be sitting.

Section 6. The Senators and Representatives shall receive a Compensation for their Services, to be ascertained by Law, and paid out of the Treasury of the United States. They shall in all Cases, except Treason, Felony and Breach of the Peace, be privileged from Arrest during their Attendance at the Session of their respective Houses, and in going to and returning from the same; and for any Speech or Debate in either House, they shall not be questioned in any other Place.

No Senator or Representative shall, during the Time for which he was elected, be appointed to any civil Office under the Authority of the United States, which shall have been created, or the Emoluments whereof shall have been encreased during such time; and no Person holding any Office under the United States, shall be a Member of either House during his Continuance in Office.

Section 7. All Bills for raising Revenue shall originate in the House of Representatives; but the Senate may propose or concur with Amendments as on other Bills.

Every Bill which shall have passed the House of Representatives and the Senate shall, before it become a Law, be presented to the President of the United States; If he approve he shall sign it, but if not he shall return it, with his Objections to that House in which it shall have originated, who shall enter the Objections at large on their Journal, and proceed to reconsider it. If after such Reconsideration two thirds of that House shall agree to pass the Bill, it shall be sent, together with the Objections, to the other House, by which it shall likewise be reconsidered, and if approved by two thirds of that House, it shall become a Law. But in all such Cases the Votes of both Houses shall be determined by yeas and Nays, and the Names of the Persons voting for and against the Bill shall be entered on the Journal of each House respectively. If any Bill shall not be returned by the President within ten Days (Sundays excepted) after it shall have been presented to him, the Same shall be a Law, in like Manner as if he had signed it, unless the Congress by their Adjournment prevent its Return, in which Case it shall not be a Law.

Every Order, Resolution, or Vote to which the Concurrence of the Senate and House of Representatives may be necessary (except on a question of Adjournment) shall be presented to the President of the United States; and before the Same shall take Effect, shall be approved by him, or being disapproved by him shall be repassed by two thirds of the Senate and House of Representatives, according to the Rules and Limitations prescribed in the Case of a Bill.

Section 8. The Congress shall have power To lay and collect Taxes, Duties, Imposts and Excises, to pay the Debts and provide for the common Defence and general Welfare of the United States; but all Duties, Imposts and Excises shall be uniform throughout the United States;

To borrow Money on the credit of the United States;

To regulate Commerce with foreign Nations, and among the several States, and with the Indian Tribes;

To establish an uniform Rule of Naturalization, and uniform Laws on the subject of Bankruptcies throughout the United States;

To coin Money, regulate the Value thereof, and of foreign Coin, and fix the Standard of Weights and Measures;

To provide for the Punishment of counterfeiting the Securities and current Coin of the United States;

To establish Post Offices and post Roads;

To promote the Progress of Science and useful Arts, by securing for limited Times to Authors and Inventors the exclusive Right to their respective Writings and Discoveries;

To constitute Tribunals inferior to the supreme Court;

To define and punish Piracies and Felonies committed on the high Seas, and Offences against the Law of Nations;

To declare War, grant Letters of Marque and Reprisal, and make Rules concerning Captures on Land and Water;

To raise and support Armies, but no Appropriation of Money to that Use shall be for a longer Term than two Years;

To provide and maintain a Navy;

To make Rules for the Government and Regulation of the land and naval Forces;

To provide for calling forth the Militia to execute the Laws of the Union, suppress Insurrections and repel Invasions;

To provide for organizing, arming, and disciplining, the Militia, and for governing such Part of them as may be employed in the Service of the United States, reserving to the States respectively, the Appointment of the Officers, and the Authority of training the Militia according to the discipline prescribed by Congress;

To exercise exclusive Legislation in all Cases whatsoever, over such District (not exceeding ten Miles square) as may, by Cession of particular States, and the Acceptance of Congress, become the Seat of the Government of the United States, and to exercise like Authority over all Places purchased by the Consent of the Legislature of the State in which the Same shall be, for the Erection of Forts, Magazines, Arsenals, dock-Yards, and other needful Buildings;—And

To make all Laws which shall be necessary and proper for carrying into Execution the foregoing Powers, and all other Powers vested by this Constitution in the Government of the United States, or in any Department or Officer thereof.

Section 9. The Migration or Importation of such Persons as any of the States now existing shall think proper to admit, shall not be prohibited by the Congress prior to the Year one thousand eight hundred and eight, but a Tax or duty may be imposed on such Importation, not exceeding ten dollars for each Person.

The Privilege of the Writ of Habeas Corpus shall not be suspended, unless when in Cases of Rebellion or Invasion the public Safety may require it.

No Bill of Attainder or ex post facto Law shall be passed.

No Capitation, or other direct, Tax shall be laid, unless in Proportion to the Census or Enumeration herein before directed to be taken.

No Tax or Duty shall be laid on Articles exported from any State.

No Preference shall be given by any Regulation of Commerce or Revenue to the Ports of one State over those of another: nor shall Vessels bound to, or from, one State, be obliged to enter, clear, or pay Duties in another.

No Money shall be drawn from the Treasury, but in Consequence of Appropriations made by Law, and a regular Statement and Account of the Receipts and Expenditures of all public Money shall be published from time to time.

No Title of Nobility shall be granted by the United States: And no Person holding any Office of Profit or Trust under them, shall, without the Consent of the Congress, accept of any present, Emolument, Office, or Title, of any kind whatever, from any King, Prince, or foreign State.

Section 10. No State shall enter into any Treaty, Alliance, or Confederation; grant Letters of Marque and Reprisal; coin Money; emit Bills of Credit; make any Thing but gold and silver Coin a Tender in Payment of Debts; pass any Bill of Attainder, ex post facto Law, or Law impairing the Obligation of Contracts, or grant any Title of Nobility.

No State shall, without the Consent of the Congress, lay any Imposts or Duties on Imports or Exports, except what may be absolutely necessary for executing its inspection Laws: and the net Produce of all Duties and Imposts, laid by any State on Imports or Exports, shall be for the Use of the Treasury of the United States; and all such Laws shall be subject to the Revision and Controul of the Congress.

No State shall, without the Consent of Congress, lay any Duty of Tonnage, keep Troops, or Ships of War in time of Peace, enter into any Agreement or Compact with another State, or with a foreign Power, or engage in War, unless actually invaded, or in such imminent Danger as will not admit of delay.

Article II.

Section 1. The executive Power shall be vested in a President of the United States of America. He shall hold his Office during the Term of four Years, and, together with the Vice President, chosen for the same Term, be elected, as follows:

Each State shall appoint, in such Manner as the Legislature thereof may direct, a Number of Electors, equal to the whole Number of Senators and Representatives to which the State may be entitled in the Congress: but no Senator or Representative, or Person holding an Office of Trust or Profit under the United States, shall be appointed an Elector.

The Electors shall meet in their respective States, and vote by Ballot for two Persons, of whom one at least shall not be an Inhabitant of the same State with themselves. And they shall make a List of all the Persons voted for, and of the Number of Votes for each; which List they shall sign and certify, and transmit sealed to the Seat of the Government of the United States, directed to the President of the Senate. The President of the

Senate shall, in the Presence of the Senate and House of Representatives, open all the Certificates, and the Votes shall then be counted. The Person having the greatest Number of Votes shall be the President, if such Number be a Majority of the whole Number of Electors appointed; and if there be more than one who have such Majority, and have an equal Number of Votes, then the House of Representatives shall immediately chuse by Ballot one of them for President; and if no Person have a Majority, then from the five highest on the List the said House shall in like Manner chuse the President. But in chusing the President, the Votes shall be taken by States, the Representation from each State having one Vote; A quorum for this Purpose shall consist of a Member or Members from two thirds of the States, and a Majority of all the States shall be necessary to a Choice. In every Case, after the Choice of the President, the Person having the greatest Number of Votes of the Electors shall be the Vice President. But if there should remain two or more who have equal Votes, the Senate shall chuse from them by Ballot the Vice President.[6]

The Congress may determine the Time of chusing the Electors, and the Day on which they shall give their Votes; which Day shall be the same throughout the United States.

No Person except a natural born Citizen, or a Citizen of the United States, at the time of the Adoption of this Constitution, shall be eligible to the Office of President, neither shall any Person be eligible to that Office who shall not have attained to the Age of thirty five Years, and been fourteen Years a Resident within the United States.

In Case of the Removal of the President from Office, or of his Death, Resignation, or Inability to discharge the Powers and Duties of the said Office, the Same shall devolve on the Vice President, and the Congress may by Law provide for the Case of Removal, Death, Resignation or Inability, both of the President and Vice President, declaring what Officer shall then act as President, and such Officer shall act accordingly, until the Disability be removed, or a President shall be elected.[7]

The President shall, at stated Times, receive for his Services, a Compensation, which shall neither be encreased nor diminished during the Period for which he shall have been elected, and he shall not receive within that Period any other Emolument from the United States, or any of them.

Before he enter on the Execution of his Office, he shall take the following Oath or Affirmation:—"I do solemnly swear (or affirm) that I will faithfully execute the Office of President of the United States, and will to the best of my Ability, preserve, protect and defend the Constitution of the United States."

Section 2. The President shall be Commander in Chief of the Army and Navy of the United States, and of the Militia of the several States, when called into the actual Service of the United States; he may require the Opinion, in writing, of the principal Officer in each of the executive Departments, upon any Subject relating to the Duties of their respec-

[6]Superseded by the Twelfth Amendment.
[7]Modified by the Twenty-fifth Amendment.

tive Offices, and he shall have Power to grant Reprieves and Pardons for Offences against the United States, except in Cases of Impeachment.

He shall have Power, by and with the Advice and Consent of the Senate, to make Treaties, provided two thirds of the Senators present concur; and he shall nominate, and by and with the Advice and Consent of the Senate, shall appoint Ambassadors, other public Ministers and Consuls, Judges of the supreme Court, and all other Officers of the United States, whose Appointments are not herein otherwise provided for, and which shall be established by Law; but the Congress may by Law vest the Appointment of such inferior Officers, as they think proper, in the President alone, in the Courts of Law, or in the Heads of Departments.

The President shall have Power to fill up all Vacancies that may happen during the Recess of the Senate, by granting Commissions which shall expire at the End of their next Session.

Section 3. He shall from time to time give the Congress Information of the State of the Union, and recommend to their Consideration such Measures as he shall judge necessary and expedient; he may, on extraordinary Occasions, convene both Houses, or either of them, and in Case of Disagreement between them, with Respect to the Time of Adjournment, he may adjourn them to such Time as he shall think proper; he shall receive Ambassadors and other public Ministers; he shall take Care that the Laws be faithfully executed, and shall Commission all the Officers of the United States.

Section 4. The President, Vice President and all civil Officers of the United States, shall be removed from Office on Impeachment for, and Conviction of, Treason, Bribery, or other high Crimes and Misdemeanors.

Article III.

Section 1. The judicial Power of the United States, shall be vested in one supreme Court, and in such inferior Courts as the Congress may from time to time ordain and establish. The Judges, both of the supreme and inferior Courts, shall hold their Offices during good Behaviour, and shall, at stated Times, receive for their Services, a Compensation, which shall not be diminished during their Continuance in Office.

Section 2. The judicial Power shall extend to all Cases, in Law and Equity, arising under this Constitution, the Laws of the United States, and Treaties made, or which shall be made, under their Authority;—to all Cases affecting Ambassadors, other public Ministers and Consuls;—to all Cases of admiralty and maritime Jurisdiction;—to Controversies to which the United States shall be a Party;—to Controversies between two or more States;—between a State and Citizens of another State;[8]—between Citizens of different States,—between Citizens of the same State claiming Lands under Grants of different States, and between a State, or the Citizens thereof, and foreign States, Citizens or Subjects.

---

[8]Modified by the Eleventh Amendment.

In all Cases affecting Ambassadors, other public Ministers and Consuls, and those in which a State shall be Party, the supreme Court shall have original Jurisdiction. In all the other Cases before mentioned, the supreme Court shall have appellate Jurisdiction, both as to Law and Fact, with such Exceptions, and under such Regulations as the Congress shall make.

The Trial of all Crimes, except in Cases of Impeachment, shall be by Jury; and such Trial shall be held in the State where the said Crimes shall have been committed; but when not committed within any State, the Trial shall be at such Place or Places as the Congress may by Law have directed.

Section 3. Treason against the United States, shall consist only in levying War against them, or in adhering to their Enemies, giving them Aid and Comfort. No Person shall be convicted of Treason unless on the Testimony of two Witnesses to the same overt Act, or on Confession in open Court.

The Congress shall have Power to declare the Punishment of Treason, but no Attainder of Treason shall work Corruption of Blood, or Forfeiture except during the Life of the Person attainted.

Article IV.

Section 1. Full Faith and Credit shall be given in each State to the public Acts, Records, and judicial Proceedings of every other State. And the Congress may by general Laws prescribe the Manner in which such Acts, Records and Proceedings shall be proved, and the Effect thereof.

Section 2. The Citizens of each State shall be entitled to all Privileges and Immunities of Citizens in the several States.

A Person charged in any State with Treason, Felony, or other Crime, who shall flee from Justice, and be found in another State, shall on Demand of the executive Authority of the State from which he fled, be delivered up, to be removed to the State having Jurisdiction of the Crime.

No Person held to Service or Labour in one State, under the Laws thereof, escaping into another, shall, in Consequence of any Law or Regulation therein, be discharged from such Service or Labour, but shall be delivered up on Claim of the Party to whom such Service or Labour may be due.

Section 3. New States may be admitted by the Congress into this Union; but no new State shall be formed or erected within the Jurisdiction of any other State, nor any State be formed by the Junction of two or more States, or Parts of States, without the Consent of the Legislatures of the States concerned as well as of the Congress.

The Congress shall have Power to dispose of and make all needful Rules and Regulations respecting the Territory or other Property belonging to the United States; and nothing in this Constitution shall be so construed as to Prejudice any Claims of the United States, or of any particular State.

Section 4. The United States shall guarantee to every State in this Union a Republican Form of Government, and shall protect each of them against Invasion; and on Application of the Legislature, or of the Executive (when the Legislature cannot be convened) against domestic Violence.

Article V.

The Congress, whenever two thirds of both Houses shall deem it necessary, shall propose Amendments to this Constitution, or, on the Application of the Legislatures of two thirds of the several States, shall call a Convention for proposing Amendments, which, in either Case, shall be valid to all Intents and Purposes, as Part of this Constitution, when ratified by the Legislatures of three fourths of the several States, or by Conventions in three fourths thereof, as the one or the other Mode of Ratification may be proposed by the Congress; Provided that no Amendment which may be made prior to the Year One thousand eight hundred and eight shall in any Manner affect the first and fourth Clauses in the Ninth Section of the first Article; and that no State, without its Consent, shall be deprived of its equal Suffrage in the Senate.

Article VI.

All Debts contracted and Engagements entered into, before the Adoption of this Constitution, shall be as valid against the United States under this Constitution, as under the Confederation.

This Constitution, and the Laws of the United States which shall be made in Pursuance thereof; and all Treaties made, or which shall be made, under the Authority of the United States, shall be the supreme Law of the Land; and the Judges in every State shall be bound thereby, any Thing in the Constitution or Laws of any State to the Contrary notwithstanding.

The Senators and Representatives before mentioned, and the Members of the several State Legislatures, and all executive and judicial Officers, both of the United States and of the several States, shall be bound by Oath or Affirmation, to support this Constitution; but no religious Test shall ever be required as a Qualification to any Office or public Trust under the United States.

Article VII.

The Ratification of the Conventions of nine States, shall be sufficient for the Establishment of this Constitution between the States so ratifying the Same.

Done in Convention by the Unanimous Consent of the States present the Seventeenth Day of September in the Year of our Lord one thousand seven hundred and Eighty seven and of the Independence of the United States of America the Twelfth. In witness whereof We have hereunto subscribed our Names,

Articles in Addition to, and Amendment of, the Constitution of the United States of America, Proposed by Congress, and Ratified by the Legislatures of the Several States, Pursuant to the Fifth Article of the Original Constitution.

Amendment I[9]

Congress shall make no law respecting an establishment of religion, or prohibiting the free exercise there-of; or abridging the freedom of speech, or of the press; or the right of the people peaceably to assemble, and to petition the Government for a redress of grievances.

Amendment II

A well regulated Militia, being necessary to the security of a free State, the right of the people to keep and bear Arms shall not be infringed.

Amendment III

No Soldier shall, in time of peace, be quartered in any house, without the consent of the Owner, nor in time of war, but in a manner to be prescribed by law.

Amendment IV

The right of the people to be secure in their persons, houses, papers, and effects, against unreasonable searches and seizures, shall not be violated, and no Warrants shall issue, but upon probable cause, supported by Oath or affirmation, and particularly describing the place to be searched, and the persons or things to be seized.

Amendment V

No person shall be held to answer for a capital or otherwise infamous crime, unless on a presentment or indictment of a Grand Jury, except in cases arising in the land or naval forces, or in the Militia, when in actual service in time of War or public danger; nor shall any person be subject for the same offence to be twice put in jeopardy of life or limb; nor shall be compelled in any criminal case to be a witness against himself, nor be deprived of life, liberty, or property, without due process of law; nor shall private property be taken for public use, without just compensation.

Amendment VI

In all criminal prosecutions, the accused shall enjoy the right to a speedy and public trial, by an impartial jury of the State and district wherein the crime shall have been committed, which district shall have been previously ascertained by law, and to be informed of the nature and cause of the accusation; to be confronted with the witnesses against him; to have compulsory process for obtaining witnesses in his favor, and to have the Assistance of Counsel for his defence.

---

[9]The first ten amendments were passed by Congress September 25, 1789. They were ratified by three-fourths of the states December 15, 1791.

Amendment VII

In suits at common law, where the value in controversy shall exceed twenty dollars, the right of trial by jury shall be preserved, and no fact tried by a jury, shall be otherwise reexamined in any Court of the United States, than according to the rules of the common law.

Amendment VIII

Excessive bail shall not be required, nor excessive fines imposed, nor cruel and unusual punishments inflicted.

Amendment IX

The enumeration in the Constitution, of certain rights, shall not be construed to deny or disparage others retained by the people.

Amendment X

The powers not delegated to the United States by the Constitution; nor prohibited by it to the States, are reserved to the States respectively, or to the people.

Amendment XI[10]

The Judicial power of the United States shall not be construed to extend to any suit in law or equity, commenced or prosecuted against one of the United States by Citizens of another State, or by Citizens or Subjects of any Foreign State.

Amendment XII[11]

The Electors shall meet in their respective States and vote by ballot for President and Vice-President, one of whom, at least, shall not be an inhabitant of the same State with themselves; they shall name in their ballots the person voted for as President, and in distinct ballots the person voted for as Vice-President, and they shall make distinct lists of all persons voted for as President, and of all persons voted for as Vice-President, and of the number of votes for each, which lists they shall sign and certify, and transmit sealed to the seat of the government of the United States, directed to the President of the Senate;—The President of the Senate shall, in the presence of the Senate and House of Representatives, open all the certificates and the votes shall then be counted;—The person having the greatest number of votes for President, shall be the President, if such number be a majority of the whole number of Electors appointed; and if no person have such majority, then from the persons having the highest numbers not exceeding three on the list of those voted for as President, the House of Representatives shall choose immediately, by ballot, the President. But in choosing the President, the votes shall be taken by states, the representation from each state having one vote; a quorum for this purpose shall consist of a member or members from two-thirds of the states,

[10]Passed March 4, 1794. Ratified January 23, 1795.
[11]Passed December 9, 1803. Ratified June 15, 1804.

and a majority of all the states shall be necessary to a choice. And if the House of Representatives shall not choose a President whenever the right of choice shall devolve upon them, before the fourth day of March next following, then the Vice-President shall act as President, as in the case of the death or other constitutional disability of the President.—The person having the greatest number of votes as Vice-President, shall be the Vice-President, if such number be a majority of the whole number of Electors appointed, and if no person have a majority, then from the two highest numbers on the list, the Senate shall choose the Vice-President; a quorum for the purpose shall consist of two-thirds of the whole number of Senators, and a majority of the whole number shall be necessary to a choice. But no person constitutionally ineligible to the office of President shall be eligible to that of Vice-President of the United States.

Amendment XIII[12]

Section 1. Neither slavery nor involuntary servitude, except as a punishment for crime whereof the party shall have been duly convicted, shall exist within the United States, or any place subject to their jurisdiction.

Section 2. Congress shall have power to enforce this article by appropriate legislation.

Amendment XIV[13]

Section 1. All persons born or naturalized in the United States, and subject to the jurisdiction thereof, are citizens of the United States and of the State wherein they reside. No State shall make or enforce any law which shall abridge the privileges or immunities of citizens of the United States; nor shall any State deprive any person of life, liberty, or property, without due process of law; nor deny to any person within its jurisdiction the equal protection of the laws.

Section 2. Representatives shall be apportioned among the several States according to their respective numbers, counting the whole number of persons in each State, excluding Indians not taxed. But when the right to vote at any election for the choice of electors for President and Vice-President of the United States, Representatives in Congress, the Executive and Judicial officers of a State, or the members of the Legislature thereof, is denied to any of the male inhabitants of such State, being twenty-one years of age, and citizens of the United States, or in any way abridged, except for participation in rebellion, or other crime, the basis of representation therein shall be reduced in the proportion which the number of such male citizens shall bear to the whole number of male citizens twenty-one years of age in such State.

Section 3. No person shall be a Senator or Representative in Congress, or elector of President and Vice-President, or hold any office, civil or military, under the United States, or under any State, who, having previously taken an oath, as a member of Congress, or as an officer of the United States, or as a member of any State legislature, or as an executive or judi-

---

[12]Passed January 31, 1865. Ratified December 6, 1865.
[13]Passed June 13, 1866. Ratified July 9, 1868.

cial officer of any State, to support the Constitution of the United States, shall have engaged in insurrection or rebellion against the same, or given aid or comfort to the enemies thereof. But Congress may by a vote of two-thirds of each House, remove such disability.

Section 4. The validity of the public debt of the United States, authorized by law, including debts incurred for payment of pensions and bounties for services in suppressing insurrection or rebellion, shall not be questioned. But neither the United States nor any State shall assume or pay any debt or obligation incurred in aid of insurrection or rebellion against the United States, or any claim for the loss or emancipation of any slave; but all such debts, obligations, and claims shall be held illegal and void.

Section 5. The Congress shall have the power to enforce, by appropriate legislation, the provisions of this article.

Amendment XV[14]

Section 1. The right of citizens of the United States to vote shall not be denied or abridged by the United States or by any State on account of race, color, or previous conditions of servitude—

Section 2. The Congress shall have power to enforce this article by appropriate legislation.

Amendment XVI

The Congress shall have power to lay and collect taxes on incomes, from whatever source derived, without apportionment among the several States, and without regard to any census or enumeration.

Amendment XVII[15]

The Senate of the United States shall be composed of two Senators from each State, elected by the people thereof, for six years; and each Senator shall have one vote. The electors in each State shall have the qualifications requisite for electors of the most numerous branch of the State legislatures.

When vacancies happen in the representation of any State in the Senate, the executive authority of such State shall issue writs of election to fill such vacancies: **Provided,** That the legislature of any State may empower the executive thereof to make temporary appointments until the people fill the vacancies by election as the legislature may direct.

This amendment shall not be so construed as to affect the election or term of any Senator chosen before it becomes valid as part of the Constitution.

---

[14]Passed February 26, 1869. Ratified February 2, 1870.
[15]Passed May 13, 1912. Ratified April 8, 1913.

Amendment XVIII[16]

Section 1. After one year from the ratification of this article the manufacture, sale, or transportation of intoxicating liquors within, the importation thereof into, or the exportation thereof from the United States and all territory subject to the jurisdiction thereof for beverage purposes is hereby prohibited.

Section 2. The Congress and the several States shall have concurrent power to enforce this article by appropriate legislation.

Section 3. This article shall be inoperative unless it shall have been ratified as an amendment to the Constitution by the legislatures of the several States, as provided in the Constitution, within seven years from the date of the submission hereof to the States by the Congress.

Amendment XIX[17]

The right of citizens of the United States to vote shall not be denied or abridged by the United States or by any State on account of sex.

Congress shall have power to enforce this article by appropriate legislation.

Amendment XX[18]

Section 1. The terms of the President and Vice-President shall end at noon on the 20th day of January, and the terms of Senators and Representatives at noon on the 3d day of January, of the years in which such terms would have ended if this article had not been ratified; and the terms of their successors shall then begin.

Section 2. The Congress shall assemble at least once in every year, and such meeting shall begin at noon on the 3d day of January, unless they shall by law appoint a different day.

Section 3. If, at the time fixed for the beginning of the term of the President, the President elect shall have died, the Vice-President elect shall become President. If a President shall not have been chosen before the time fixed for the beginning of his term, or if the President elect shall have failed to qualify, then the Vice-President elect shall act as President until a President shall have qualified; and the Congress may by law provide for the case wherein neither a President elect nor a Vice-President elect shall have qualified, declaring who shall then act as President, or the manner in which one who is to act shall be selected, and such person shall act accordingly until a President or Vice-President shall have qualified.

Section 4. The Congress may by law provide for the case of the death of any of the persons from whom the House of Representatives may choose a President whenever the right of choice shall have devolved upon them, and for the case of the death of any of the per-

---

[16]Passed December 18, 1917. Ratified January 16, 1919.

[17]Passed June 4, 1919. Ratified August 18, 1920.

[18]Passed March 2, 1932. Ratified January 23, 1933.

sons from whom the Senate may choose a Vice-President whenever the right of choice shall have devolved upon them.

Section 5. Sections 1 and 2 shall take effect on the 15th day of October following the ratification of this article.

Section 6. This article shall be inoperative unless it shall have been ratified as an amendment to the Constitution by the legislatures of three-fourths of the several States within seven years from the date of its submission.

Amendment XXI[19]

Section 1. The eighteenth article of amendment to the Constitution of the United States is hereby repealed.

Section 2. The transportation or importation into any State, Territory, or possession of the United States for delivery or use therein of intoxicating liquors, in violation of the laws thereof, is hereby prohibited.

Section 3. This article shall be inoperative unless it shall have been ratified as an amendment to the Constitution by conventions in the several States, as provided in the Constitution, within seven years from the date of the submission hereof to the States by the Congress.

Amendment XXII[20]

No person shall be elected to the office of the President more than twice, and no person who has held the office of President, or acted as President, for more than two years of a term to which some other person was elected President shall be elected to the office of the President more than once.

But this Article shall not apply to any person holding the office of President when this Article was proposed by the Congress, and shall not prevent any person who may be holding the office of President, or acting as President, during the term within which this Article becomes operative from holding the office of President or acting as President during the remainder of such term.

Amendment XXIII[21]

Section 1. The District constituting the seat of Government of the United States shall appoint in such manner as the Congress may direct:

A number of electors of President and Vice President equal to the whole number of Senators and Representatives in Congress to which the District would be entitled if it were a State, but in no event more than the least populous State; they shall be in addition to those appointed by the States, but they shall be considered, for the purposes of the election of

[19]Passed February 20, 1933. Ratified December 5, 1933.
[20]Passed March 12, 1947. Ratified March 1, 1951.
[21]Passed June 16, 1960. Ratified April 3, 1961.

President and Vice President, to be electors appointed by the State; and they shall meet in the District and perform such duties as provided by the twelfth article of amendment.

Section 2. The Congress shall have power to enforce this article by appropriate legislation.

Amendment XXIV[22]

Section 1. The right of citizens of the United States to vote in any primary or other election for President or Vice President, or for Senator or Representative in Congress, shall not be denied or abridged by the United States or any State by reason of failure to pay any poll tax or other tax.

Section 2. The Congress shall have power to enforce this article by appropriate legislation.

Amendment XXV[23]

Section 1. In case of the removal of the President from office or of his death or resignation, the Vice President shall become President.

Section 2. Whenever there is a vacancy in the office of the Vice-President, the President shall nominate a Vice President who shall take office upon confirmation by a majority vote of both Houses of Congress.

Section 3. Whenever the President transmits to the President pro tempore of the Senate and the Speaker of the House of Representatives his written declaration that he is unable to discharge the powers and duties of his office, and until he transmits them a written declaration to the contrary, such powers and duties shall be discharged by the Vice President as Acting President.

Section 4. Whenever the Vice President and a majority of either the principal officers of the executive department or of such other body as Congress may by law provide, transmit to the President pro tempore of the Senate and the Speaker of the House of Representatives their written declaration that the President is unable to discharge the powers and duties of his office, the Vice President shall immediately assume the powers and duties of the office of Acting President

Thereafter, when the President transmits to the President pro tempore of the Senate and the Speaker of the House of Representatives his written declaration that no inability exists, he shall resume the powers and duties of his office unless the Vice President and a majority of either the principal officers of the executive department or of such other body as Congress may by law provide, transmit within four days to the President pro tempore of the Senate and the Speaker of the House of Representatives their written declaration that the President is unable to discharge the powers and duties of his office. Thereupon Congress shall decide the issue, assembling within forty-eight hours for that purpose if not in

[22]Passed August 27, 1962. Ratified January 23, 1964.
[23]Passed July 6, 1965. Ratified February 11, 1967.

session. If the Congress, within twenty-one days after receipt of the latter written declaration, or, if Congress is not in session, within twenty-one days after Congress is required to assemble, determines by two-thirds vote of both Houses that the President is unable to discharge the powers and duties of his office, the Vice-President shall continue to discharge the same as Acting President; otherwise, the President shall resume the powers and duties of his office.

Amendment XXVI[24]

Section 1. The right of citizens of the United States, who are eighteen years of age or older, to vote shall not be denied or abridged by the United States or by any State on account of age.

Section 2. The Congress shall have power to enforce this article by appropriate legislation.

Amendment XXVII[25]

No law, varying the compensation for the service of the Senators and Representatives, shall take effect, until an election of Representatives shall have intervened.

---

[24]Passed March 23, 1971. Ratified July 5, 1971.
[25]Passed September 25, 1789. Ratified May 7, 1992.

Index

5/09